9/02

Gloria Steinem

Gloria Steinem

Her Passions,

Politics, and Mystique

SYDNEY LADENSOHN STERN

A Birch Lane Press Book
Published by Carol Publishing Group

To feminists everywhere

A Birch Lane Press Book
Published by Carol Publishing Group
Birch Lane Press is a registered trademark of Carol Communications, Inc.

Editorial, sales and distribution, and rights and permissions inquiries should be addressed
to Carol Publishing Group, 120 Enterprise Avenue, Secaucus, N.J. 07094

In Canada: Canadian Manda Group, One Atlantic Avenue, Suite 105, Toronto,
Ontario M6K 3E7

Carol Publishing Group books may be purchased in bulk at special discounts for sales
promotion, fund-raising, or educational purposes. Special editions can be created to
specifications. For details, contact: Special Sales Department, Carol Publishing Group,
120 Enterprise Avenue, Secaucus, N.J. 07094.

Manufactured in the United States of America
10 9 8 7 6 5 4 3 2 1

Library of Congress Cataloging-in-Publication Data

Stern, Sydney Ladensohn.
    Gloria Steinem : her passions, politics, and mystique / Sydney
Ladensohn Stern.
        p.   cm.
    "A Birch Lane Press book."
    Includes bibliographical references and index.
    ISBN 1-55972-409-9
    1. Steinem, Gloria.   2. Feminists—United States—Biography.
3. Feminism—United States.   I. Title.
HQ1413.S675S74   1997
305.42′092—dc21
[B]   97-19663
                                                                          CIP

Contents

Acknowledgments

In the fall of 1994 I wrote to Gloria Steinem to explain that I had a contract to write a biography of her and to ask if I might interview her. I was asked to send a copy of the book's proposal. Subsequently, one of Gloria's assistants informed me that Gloria would talk to me, though she did not want to be interviewed until Carolyn Heilbrun, whom she had asked to write her biography, had published her book.

During the next eleven months, I visited library collections of documents on women's history, read the Gloria Steinem Papers at Smith College's Sophia Smith Collection, visited some of the places Gloria had lived, and interviewed over two hundred friends, relatives, colleagues, former lovers, feminist activitists, and people outside her circle. Gloria's assistants kindly sent me materials, supplied me with telephone numbers and suggestions as to which people were important in Gloria's life and work, and faxed me her schedule, enabling me to attend as many of her public appearances as possible.

At that time, Gloria suffered from trigeminal neuralgia, a facial nerve inflammation made more painful by talking. She began most appearances by telling her audience of her condition and explaining that if she couldn't finish, her friend and colleague Amy Richards would take over. But she invariably delivered her entire speech and stayed to answer questions until every person who wanted to talk with her had done so.

Gloria's generosity to her public was impressive. So was the public's reaction to Gloria. When she was introduced, she usually received a standing ovation. Women of every age, race, and class would rise to pay tribute to the woman who symbolized for them the enormous achievements of the women's movement. As I observed these women in their infinite variety, it always seemed to me that they were also applauding their own hopes and dreams—the expanded possibilities of their own lives—and I always found the tribute indescribably touching.

In August 1995, Gloria and I began the first of fifteen three- to four-hour interviews. Gloria agreed to the interviews on the condition that she be given a copy of the manuscript to check for the accuracy of facts and quotes. I cannot thank her enough for her many contributions. Her review of the manuscript should not be construed as her approval of the book or indicate her agreement with its contents. My characterizations of Gloria Steinem—and of the people and events in her life—are mine alone. They are based on my research and my interviews.

With apologies to anyone I have accidentally omitted, I offer a heartfelt thank you for their help to Sidney Abbott, George Abrams, Bella Abzug, Rebecca Adamson, Dolores Alexander, Lucy Lindstrom Allard, Jacqueline McCartney Alvord, Sam Antupit, Maria Astaire, Deirdre Bair, George Barris, Melinda Bass, Rosalyn Baxandall, Nikki Beare, Leonard Bebchick, Leslie Bennetts, Robert Benton, Barbara Zevon Berlin, Carole Roberts Berning, Porter Bibb, Caroline Bird, Cathleen Black, Janet Bode, Lillian Barnes Borton, Ruth Bower, Peter Braestrup, Susan Braudy, Brenda Brimmer, Esther (E. M.) Broner, Rachel White Brown, Rita Mae Brown, Susan Brownmiller, Zbigniew Brzezinski, Alice Bunker, Julie Burton, Patricia Carbine, Carrie Carmichael, Margaret Harrison Case, Jacqui Ceballos, Sey Chassler, Phyllis Chesler, Neal and Mary Jane Austin Choate, Blair Chotzinoff, Ellie Bush Chucker, Cindy Cisler, Bob Clampitt, Harry Cogan, Marcia Cohen, Tom Collins, Bob Cuniff, Evelyn Cunningham, Jane MacKenzie Davidson, Blanche Miklosek DeBarr, Ada Deer, Anselma Dell'Olio, Susan Dickler, Wilson Dizard, Margaret Dorsey, Ronald Duncan, Andrea Dworkin, Joanne Edgar, Ronnie Eldridge, Nora Ephron, Jean Faust, Brenda Feigen, Ronnie Feit, Clay Felker, Tom Fiedler, Marc Fisher, Muriel Fox, Barney Frank, Jo Freeman, Marilyn French, Theresa Funiciello, John Kenneth Galbraith, Jane Galvin-Lewis, Curtis Gans, Sharon Stokes Garrison, Cornelia Stewart Gill, Marcia Gillespie, Milton Glaser, Kristen Golden, Deena Goldstone, Denise Gooch, Katharine Graham, Clive Gray, Anne (Cookie) Chotzinoff Grossman and Herbert Grossman, Elinor Guggenheimer, Tom Guinzburg, Carol Hanisch, Cyanne Hanson, Betty Harris, T. George Harris, Seena Harris-Parker, Rosilyn Heller, Dorothy O. Helly, Aileen Hernández, Louise Heskett, George Hirsch, Sandra Hochman, Koryne Horbal, Jackie Burton Hubbard, Dolores Huerta, Dorothy Pitman Hughes, Devaki and Lakshmi Jain, Diana James, Carol Jenkins, Joyce Johnson, Rafer Johnson, Andrea

Johnston, Jennifer Josephy, Jean Joyce, Robert Kaiser, Wendy Kaminer, Martha and Tom Keehn, Florynce Kennedy, Linda Tilden Kerr, Peggy Kerry, Kristina Kiehl, Robert Kiley, Carole Klein, Ted Klein, Lucy Komisar, Marlene Krauss, Betsy McQuat Lameyer, Phyllis Langer, Martha Weinman Lear, Phil Leder, Dixie Auxter Leeds, Judy Lerner, Bob Levine, Suzanne Braun Levine, Leonard Levitt, Lillian Menne Litz, Harriet Lyons, Ali MacGraw, David MacIsaac, Frank Mankiewicz, Wilma Mankiller, Elaine Markson, Laura Stevenson Maslon, George McGovern, Martha McKay, Tom Meehan, Carol Merry-Shapiro, Cord Meyer, Maxine Coleman Mills, Susan Mitchell, Carla Morganstern, Meredith Chase Morley, Marion Moses, Debbie Nathan, Barbara Nessim, Sheila Nevins, Eleanor Holmes Norton, Jane O'Reilly, Phyllis Blake Ozimek, Karen Paget, Susanne Steinem Patch, Alan Patricof, Mary Peacock, Irene Peslikis, Walter Pincus, Letty Cottin Pogrebin, Katha Pollitt, Stan Pottinger, Colette Price, Peggey Puglisi, Beth Rashbaum, Jeri Rasmussen, Denise Rathbun, Henry Raymont, Jane Jones Reid, Amy Richards, Julia Robinson, Ray Robinson, Ruby Rohrlich, A. M. Rosenthal, Phyllis Fewster Rosser, Catherine Samuels, Marlene Sanders, Willian Sarnoff, Julia Scott, Richard Seaver, Arnaldo Segarra, David Shaber, Dennis Shaul, Paul Sigmund, Patsy Goodwin Sladden, Margaret Sloan-Hunter, Caron Smith, Liz Smith, Anne Frederick Starbird, Florence Steinem, Judith Stillinger, John Stoltenberg, David Swanson, Betty Rose Tamallanca, Arthur Tarlow, Eugene Theroux, Frank Thomas, Marlo Thomas, Sheila Tobias, Patricia Trainor, Mary Jean Tully, Gus Tyler, Edith Van Horn, Ruth Whitney, Ellen Willis, Marie Wilson, Irwin Winkler, Henry Wolf, Susan Wood, Sue Bolander Zedecker, Mort Zuckerman, and six anonymous sources.

Most of the time, writing is a lonely enterprise; completing this book seemed to require the help of at least a small village. The Toledo-Lucas County Public Library, University of Toledo Archives, Dwight D. Eisenhower Library, Arthur and Elizabeth Schlesinger Collection on the History of Women in America at Radcliffe College, and Barnard College's Center for Research on Women were valuable resources. The archivists at the Sophia Smith Collection and College Archives at Smith College were knowledgeable, thorough, and very patient. The Scarsdale Public Library reference librarians extended themselves so generously that they became true partners; this is their book, too.

My research assistant, Barrie Koegel, combined energy and enthusiasm with intelligence and judgment. My son Toby saved me hours of copying and filing, and provided in-house computer support. My son

Ken gave me five hours of research for Mother's Day, each of which yielded important material. Dolores Field arranged for my Clarklake interviews, showed me the area, researched the toboggan accident, and kept me posted on local developments. Ernest Ruffner of Washington, D.C., sent me his Western High School yearbook and suggested which of Gloria's high school friends I should contact. Judith Wheeler detailed her memories of Smith College. Nina Finkelstein lent me ten years of *Ms.* bound volumes for the duration of the project.

Marcia Cohen, who wrote *The Sisterhood,* a joint biography of Betty Friedan, Germaine Greer, Kate Millett, and Gloria Steinem, shared with me her interview transcripts, notes, and clippings. Mary Perot Nichols, who at one time had planned to write a biography of Gloria herself, gave me the material she had assembled, as well as many leads and contacts. Mary died suddenly while I was working on the book, and I regret that she could not read the results of an effort to which she contributed so much. Judith Hennessee, who is writing a biography of Betty Friedan, provided valuable professional advice and personal support. Dolores Eyler, Lesley Koegel, and Sue Neale took the time to read and comment on the manuscript. My agent, Mike Cohn, again conceived of a book project that became a labor of love.

My editor, Hillel Black, has been wonderful. He excels at all things editorial, but I especially appreciated his ability to heap on the praise while persuading me to pare away that which needed to go. It was a joy to work with production chief and veteran editor Donald J. Davidson. As a midwesterner and a member of Gloria's age cohort, he brought to the manuscript valuable perspective and gave it a rigorous reading. Copy editors Kathy Casey and Margaret Wolf were not only precise and knowledgeable, they were creative in solving problems.

As I researched Gloria's difficult early years, I became even more grateful to my parents Jean and Ken Ladensohn for giving me such a loving, secure childhood. My most constant supporter is my husband, Jon Stern. Once again, he good-naturedly put up with a book's near total occupation of my mind, my time, and much of our house.

August 1997

In general, quotations from interviews are conveyed in the present tense. Exceptions and quotes from other sources are cited in the notes. Any errors in the book are the author's alone.

Gloria Steinem

The last speaker alluded to this movement as being that of a few disappointed women. . . . In education, in marriage, in religion, in everything, disapointment is the lot of women. It shall be the business of my life to deepen this disappointment in every woman's heart until she bows down to it no longer.

—Lucy Stone, 1855
National Woman's Rights Convention
Cincinnati, Ohio

Prologue

New York
December 13, 1995
6 P.M.

The women hurry up the steps, eager to escape the cold and join the festivities inside. Tonight is the Veteran Feminists of America dinner honoring Gloria Steinem. The enormous dining room of Manhattan's Seventh Regiment Armory is sure to be filled to capacity—Gloria always attracts a crowd.

The armory reeks of militarism and masculinity. It is difficult to imagine a more incongruous setting for a feminist reunion. The wood-paneled lobby is filled with regimental banners and suits of armor, and the veteran feminists pass through quickly on their way to the elevator. Upstairs, stuffed moose with Santa hats on their antlers gaze morosely at the female invaders.

Oblivious to the melancholy moose, hundreds of women greet each other, hugging and kissing and talking as fast as they can. Kate Millett is here—and Bella Abzug and Flo Kennedy and Marlo Thomas. So are Susan Brownmiller, Phyllis Chesler, Marilyn French, and Barbara Seaman.

There are others, less famous but still important: Gloria's old roommate from the 1960s, and her best friend from college; many of the original *Ms.* staff; a group of women from Dallas, here to honor Gloria for helping them start a credit union in the 1970s; Gloria's assistants, past and present. A mother and daughter from New Jersey are dressed in matching plaid skirts. They are here because Gloria helped the mother regain custody of her daughter—her pediatrician father was sexually abusing her, but the judge refused to help until Gloria became involved. There are even a few men.

Finally Gloria arrives. Her progress through the crowded room is slow, as she turns her complete attention to every woman who rushes to greet her. Many seem to tell her long, involved stories, and Gloria listens intently to each.

Eventually she makes her way to Bella Abzug, whose back problems have forced her to use a cane. Marlo Thomas joins them, and Kate Millett, too, leaning on a tripod. As soon as they begin to talk, guests encircle them, pulling out cameras to photograph the historic group.

Tonight should have been an evening to relax among old friends and share memories with the many who came to honor her, and Gloria had hoped to enjoy the occasion. She is almost sixty-two years old, and she is tired. She has been working in the movement week after week, month after month, for more than twenty-five years.

However, even tonight there seems to be no respite. She has spent the hour before she left home arguing on the telephone with Dale Lang, the owner of *Ms.* magazine. After all these years, just when the magazine finally is profitable, Dale is on the brink of bankruptcy. It looks as if he may take *Ms.* down with him. Gloria has been searching for investors to buy him out, but he knows how much *Ms.* means to her, so he asks what Gloria considers an outrageous price and counts on her desperation to get it for him.

Tonight she is among loving friends who want to tell her how much she means to them, but she is depleted by the struggle to save *Ms.* yet again. Several who know her well sense her distress and ask what is wrong. To the others, she seems her usual self—calm, confident, kindly.

At dinner, friends and colleagues pay tribute to Gloria and recall their memories of her at work and at play. As each speaker finishes, Gloria gives her a hug and a few words of thanks. When the accolades are finished, it is her turn. "I keep wondering if I'm dead yet," she says. Then she addresses the crowd for about forty-five minutes, speaking warmly and humorously of every woman who spoke during the evening.

Gloria Steinem has been hiding her feelings all her life—she always felt she had to. She was described as "the nonthreatening one," "the pretty one," the one "not like all those other angry feminists."

How little they knew. Gloria was not like those other angry feminists; she was angrier. She could hardly be considered nonthreatening, as she was the deadliest weapon the women's movement possessed. That she was "the pretty one" was undeniable; how fortunate that turned out to be, in a world so attuned to appearances.

Gloria's reserve is part of her personality, and it has served her well for many years. In response to comments about her apparent lack of passion, she answers politely that her inside and her outside are different; it is just that she is a well-socialized female, a 1950s person.

The passion should be unmistakable to anyone who takes the trouble to think about it. What else could have fueled Gloria Steinem for the past quarter century? It has always been there. Her interlocutors need only look beyond the manner of her words to the manner of her deeds. Passion is the story of Gloria Steinem's life.

1

Ruth, Leo, and the Girls

"Men must acquire more of the qualities of women and women must acquire more of some of the qualities of men."

—Pauline Steinem, 1904

"We've learned to raise our daughters like our sons. Now we need to start raising our sons like our daughters."

—Gloria Steinem, 1994

When Gloria Steinem became a feminist, she already had women's rights in her blood. Her grandmother Steinem was one of the most prominent suffragists in the state of Ohio.

Gloria's paternal grandmother, Pauline Perlmutter, was born on August 4, 1863, in Radziewo, Poland. Pauline's father is thought to have been a cantor who wanted to compose operas. This displeased the Jewish orthodoxy, and he moved the family to Munich while Pauline was still a child. Her parents had no interest in offering their daughters a higher education, but Pauline was so insistent that they eventually relented, allowing her to attend the State Normal School of Bavaria.

Pauline was twenty-one in 1884, when Joseph Steinem, thirty-three, appeared at her house. Joseph, who was born in Olmhausen, Würtemberg, Germany, had spent the past fifteen years in the United States, seeking his fortune. He had returned to Germany to find a wife. Joseph arrived with the notion of marrying the oldest Perlmutter daughter, but when Pauline passed through the room where he was waiting, he fell in love at first sight and married her instead.

The couple lived in Munich until 1887, when they departed for the United States with their first son, Edgar. They settled in Toledo, Ohio, where Joseph so prospered in the real-estate business that his family, which eventually included three more sons, Jesse, Clarence, and Leo, was able to return to Germany for periodic visits. Joseph's success secured the Steinems' position in the community, but Pauline's prominence eventually surpassed her husband's.

Soon after she arrived, Pauline became a citizen, learned to speak English without an accent, and became active in community affairs. The first organization she joined was the Hebrew Ladies' Benevolent Society, a group of Jewish women who helped the poor of the community, whatever their religion. She soon became the organization's secretary, a post she held for fourteen years. From then on, she was a leader in virtually every organization she joined. Toledo's first female elected official—she was elected to the Toledo Board of Education in 1904—she later became so active nationally in education issues and women's suffrage that she was listed in *Who's Who in America* from 1910 until 1925.

Although always active in Toledo's Jewish community, Pauline also involved herself in the theosophical movement. Founded in 1875 in New York by an exotic, penniless Russian aristocrat, Madame Helena Petrovna Blavatsky, theosophy combined lofty humanitarian and internationalist ideals with Eastern and Western religious concepts such as reincarnation, psychic phenomena, spiritualism, and occultism. Theosophy's leaders included charlatans and credulous enthusiasts alike, and among its prominent followers were George Bernard Shaw, Oscar Wilde, W. B. Yeats, Thomas Edison, Mohandas K. Gandhi, Jawaharlal Nehru, and Frank Lloyd Wright.

As one skeptical historian noted, the movement's psychic and occult activities appealed to "the neurotic, the hysterical, the destructive, and the downright mad." However, theosophical ideology also offered a spiritual and philosophical framework to intellectually inclined women like Pauline, who naturally became a leader of the Theosophical Society in Toledo. She was one of many suffragists who found in theosophy a congenial, egalitarian belief system that was absent in patriarchal religions. In a 1914 essay Pauline wrote for the *Toledo Blade,* entitled

"Why I Am a Suffragist," she explained, "I believe in woman suffrage because I believe that the perfect equality of men and women is founded on Divine Wisdom. . . . Theosophy teaches first of all the brotherhood of man without distinction of race, creed, color or sex." Men and women, she wrote, were "differentiated only by the outer garments, the bodies they temporarily wear."

When Ohio revised its constitution in 1911, Pauline led a year-long struggle for passage of the state suffrage amendment, which ultimately failed. She testified over the years before the Ohio legislature on suffrage and educational issues, spoke to the U.S. Senate committee on women's suffrage, and traveled to Europe for various international women's meetings.

Although Pauline was an ardent suffragist, it is not clear that she was an equally ardent feminist. Not all suffragists supported women's full equality. On one hand, as 1909 chair of the education committee of the National American Woman Suffrage Association (the national body to which the Ohio Woman's Suffrage Association belonged), Pauline became involved in the organization's attempt to get more women into the history books. She surveyed four hundred school districts and twenty-six textbook publishers and, finding women other than Martha Washington and Betsy Ross noticeably absent, concluded that "the masculine point of view which has dominated civilization" had conquered the educational world as well, conveying to U.S. schoolchildren the impression "that this world has been made by men and for men."

On the other hand, during a debate about coguardianship of children at an annual meeting of the Ohio Woman's Suffrage Association the following year, Pauline remarked, "We want the man to be the head of the house." She was quickly rebuked by a nationally known feminist, who told her, "You have no right to say that if you are speaking for this association."

Pauline retired from public life after 1921 and lived quietly with Joseph until he died in December 1929, after an illness of six days. The newspapers noted that he had been preparing Christmas gifts for his tenants and attributed his death to pneumonia. Steinem family legend blames the previous October's stock market crash: Joseph supposedly contracted pneumonia from too many trips through the snow to check on his declining investments, and from a spirit broken by losing so much of what he had worked so hard to create.

Despite his losses, Joseph left a substantial estate, with real-estate properties alone generating more than five hundred dollars a month.

Pauline stayed out of public life, but when the Nazis rose to power in the 1930s, she used much of her money to get relatives out of Germany. According to another family legend, transporting each German relative to Israel cost Pauline five hundred dollars, and after helping as many as she could to escape, Pauline died in 1940 of a broken heart. However, true to her theosophical principles until the end, she told Gloria's older sister, Sue, that Hitler was "an evil someone who had not evolved at all" in his reincarnations.

In the spring of 1919, Pauline and Joseph's fourth son, Leo, was a popular campus leader at the University of Toledo. Leo was affable, witty, and intelligent, like his three older brothers. Just short of six feet tall, bespectacled, with thick, curly hair and a prominent widow's peak, he spent more time hatching schemes for school dances and organizations than studying, and he tended to be somewhat of an operator.

When he met his future wife, Ruth Nuneviller, Leo was founding a school newspaper, the *Universi-Teaser,* which he and a friend financed with their own money. The two roamed the halls hawking it for a nickel a copy, and by the fall of 1920, they had university backing, a room, a faculty advisor, and a new name, the *Teaser*.

Ruth and Leo later told their daughters they had met when Leo posted a note on the school bulletin board asking Ruth Nuneviller to report to the *Universi-Teaser* editor—he had seen her on campus and thought she looked interesting. Ruth duly reported, and within the first weeks of publication became the paper's literary editor.

A year younger than Leo, auburn-haired Ruth Nuneviller had transferred after two years at Oberlin College in the fall of 1918 because her family could no longer afford to send her there. Like Leo, Ruth had a quiet father and a strong mother. Joseph Nuneviller was a railroad engineer, and Gloria and her sister Sue grew up hearing how their grandfather, never knowing when he might be called to rush off to drive a train, always ate his dessert before his meal. It seemed perfectly logical to the sweets-loving girls.

Unlike Pauline Steinem, Ruth's mother was domineering. Her parents, who had emigrated from Germany, named her Mary Catherine, but she called herself Marie. Her father, John Ochs, had been shipwrecked off the coast of New Jersey in 1854 and lashed himself to the ship's mast to survive. Her mother, Louise Josephine Lins, entered the country more conventionally. The second of six children, Marie Ochs grew up in Kenton, Ohio, and, like Pauline Perlmutter Steinem, attended a normal school or a teachers' college. After teaching, she worked at the Hardin County courthouse until she married Joseph and moved to Toledo. Ruth was born in 1898; her younger sister Janey followed in 1900.

Money was in short supply in their working-class family, and Marie's ambitions were middle class. She pushed Ruth and Janey to excel in school and earned extra money by writing sermons for a Presbyterian minister. She economized by making all the girls' clothes herself. When the girls were young, she used the family railroad pass to take them to New York.

Marie was intelligent but insensitive. Instead of tapering off gradually when she was ready to stop nursing Ruth, she simply handed her over to an aunt until Ruth was weaned. When the girls were quite young, she often left them alone without telling them where she was going or when she would be back. That terrified Ruth, and for the rest of her life she feared being alone. She also spent years convinced she had an irregular heartbeat or a heart murmur, though she did not. (She did develop a heart problem in her seventies.)

After Ruth transferred to the University of Toledo, she lived at home and worked as a part-time bookkeeper to help the family make ends meet. She earned her bachelor's degree in mathematics in 1920 but remained at the university for another three years, teaching math for a year and acquiring a master's degree in American literature. What she most enjoyed was working on the school publications, and she continued on the staffs throughout graduate school. As *Universi-Teaser* literary editor, she published some of her own contributions, including a P. G. Wodehouse–Lewis Carrollesque mystery, "The Tragedy Among the Waterpipes," about a chef who had died in the act of making a strawberry shortcake.

In the fall of 1919 she took over as editor in chief, and the following year she wrote the *Teaser*'s humor column, "Answers by Miss Anne Circe," previously written by Leo. The mysterious Circe answered questions supposedly sent in by readers:

Q: "Do you think it's right to swear before a girl?—Heard Itdone."

A: "Not if the girl wants to swear first."

Q: "We understand that Bandolene [sic] is derived from the Latin. Is it masculine or feminine?—Univ. Student (not Charles Beard)"

A: "Bandoline is the masculine form. The feminine of it is trans-lated "hair net." It isn't derived from Latin anyway. It's a hybrid coming from cement and glue."

Q: "Doesn't Leo ever have any accidents driving so recklessly through traffic?"
A: "Yes, occasionally he gets home safely."

Leo, still writing for the paper, had transferred his enthusiasm to founding a student literary society, where he was unanimously elected president. The *Teaser* reported: "Mr. Steinem was most instrumental in bringing about the organization of such a society and it is thought he will prove a most effective leader of the organization. . . . The spirit is great and the members mean business. And don't forget, folks, many a famous debater had his beginnings in such an organization. Social functions will also play an important part in the program."

Their backgrounds differed, but Ruth and Leo shared the same sense of humor, though Leo was the more devoted punster. They both liked poker, bridge, and chess. Their religious differences seem not to have concerned them. Although his family was prominent in the Jewish community, Leo was never interested in religion itself. As an adult, he neither practiced nor sought to introduce his daughters to Judaism. He was intelligent but not intellectual. Ruth was interested in politics, literature, and ideas. After her marriage, she became a devoted adherent of theosophy, exposed to it by Leo's mother.

Ruth and Leo also had fundamentally different temperaments. Underneath Ruth's fun-loving, playful exterior lay a serious person with a great fear of financial insecurity. Leo's devil-may-care exterior reflected a carefree interior. He lacked neither energy nor ambition, and he always wanted to make it big—his daughters recall tears welling up in his eyes when he talked about people with money—but he wanted to do it through ideas and adventure. For Leo, life was for living, money for spending, and slow, steady progress was boring. As the youngest son in a wealthy family, he was spoiled. When one of his schemes went awry and lost money, Leo would receive a stern lecture from his father, who would then rescue him. As his daughter Sue says, "Having a rich father didn't do much for his character."

By the summer of 1921, Ruth, twenty-three, and Leo, twenty-four, had known each other two years. Halfway back from a summer outing at Clarklake, Michigan, Leo suddenly stopped the car and asked Ruth to marry him. Immediately. Ruth told him he was crazy.

"Oh, come on," he urged. "It'll only take a minute."

Surprising even herself, Ruth agreed. They found a justice of the peace and were married that day. Ruth insisted they keep the marriage a secret, so they returned to their respective parents' homes and merely announced themselves engaged. A few months later, despite the disapproval of both families, they had a more formal marriage ceremony at Ruth's home on Woodville Road. Not until years later, when Janey came across their first marriage certificate, did Ruth confess their elopement to her sister, though Ruth's daughters long ago had heard and cherished the romantic story.

Later the extra ceremony seemed to come in handy. When Gloria became famous and was described as the child of divorced parents, which still seemed shameful to Ruth, she would insist that she and Leo were still married. Perhaps Ruth, as a former calculus teacher, reasoned that two marriages minus one divorce equaled one marriage.

Joseph Steinem bought the young couple a lot and paid for them to build the house of their dreams in suburban Toledo. Leo tried a number of jobs, among them working as a photographer for advertising agencies. Ruth began writing a gossip column under the name Duncan MacKenzie for a Toledo tabloid, *KWK,* and eventually worked for both the *Toledo News-Bee* and the *Toledo Blade.* The year she was promoted to club editor at the *Blade* she also became pregnant.

Susanne was born on February 19, 1925. The couple sent out traditional announcements with Susanne's tiny engraved calling card affixed to theirs with a pink ribbon. Ruth left her job, and the three of them rented a cottage for the summer on Clark Lake in Michigan, about sixty miles from Toledo. (The name of the lake and the community on its banks are spelled variously Clarklake, and sometimes Clark's Lake. Gloria uses the Clarklake spelling.)

That summer, Leo thought he saw the opportunity of a lifetime. There were very few houses around the lake, and he decided he would develop the east end of the lake, where there were almost none. With his father's help, Leo and Ruth bought thirty acres. By 1926 they had constructed the first cottage. After Leo had sand hauled from the back of his property and spread on the bank of the lake to make the swimming area more appealing, he named his domain Ocean Beach. The following year he built a family home, roomy enough to accommodate the relatives who soon made summer visits.

Unlike their original lake cottage, whose cabinlike wood harmonized with most of the others on the lake, the Steinems' new summer home was Mediterranean-style. Perhaps Leo's cream-colored, two-story stucco house reminded him of Florida and California, his preferred destinations in the winter months. The house had arched openings, and on the side facing the lake was an upstairs balcony that the family sometimes used as a sleeping porch during the summer.

In 1928 Leo, thirty-one, completed a 99-by-130-foot dance pavilion at the end of a narrow, 100-foot pier. Offering dancing "over the water, under the stars," Ocean Beach Pier opened on Decoration (Memorial) Day, 1928. As Leo explained to the *Toledo Blade,* "more than half of the dance floor will be in the open, without walls or roof, enclosed only by a railing." Strings of colored lights surrounded the dance floor, and its terrazzo tiles resembled a large black-and-white checkerboard with a red border.

Sue recalls, "One summer my father arranged for a chess champion named Palmi to play chess with an opponent on a traditional board while people in bathing suits acted as chess pieces on the checkerboard floor; an attendant moved them about to correspond with the progress of the game on the sidelines. I was one of the pawns."

The primary attraction was dancing. Ocean Beach Pier opened just in time for the Big Band era. As he had in college, Leo booked the bands himself, which he enjoyed doing because he liked being in show business. Over the years, all the big names stopped at Ocean Beach, as their band buses toured the Midwest: Harry James, Guy Lombardo, Duke Ellington, Count Basie, the Dorsey brothers, Rudy Vallee, Ozzie Nelson and his singer Harriet Hilliard, Gene Krupa, Joe Venuti, the Andrews Sisters. One dancing couple with the Harry James band especially thrilled the crowd: they wore roller skates, and the man spun the woman around by her hair—which he gripped in his teeth. A cottage was built to house the visiting musicians.

The Steinems spent winters in Toledo. In 1926, Ruth had returned to work at the *Toledo Blade.* Although she resented Marie's constant criticism (which included telling Ruth what was wrong with Leo), she asked her mother to take care of one-and-a-half-year-old Sue. Marie agreed, and Pauline helped out as well.

In the late 1920s Ruth and Leo sold their Toledo house and moved into the ground floor of Pauline and Joseph's two-story duplex. The sale and move may have been for economic reasons, or Leo may have wanted to raise cash so he could go in with his father on a real-estate deal, as he sometimes did. Perhaps Ruth wanted to be closer to her work. In any case, Ruth was very fond of her mother-in-law.

Much later, Ruth talked with her daughters about those years. She had been concerned about leaving Sue. At one point she became so attracted to another man at work that she considered leaving Leo. Another time, she became so enamored of her work that she and a woman friend talked about moving together to New York to pursue their respective careers. The friend went and became very successful, and Ruth sometimes talked of their plans wistfully but with resignation.

Her difficulties were unusual, but not unique. In the May 1929 issue of *Harper's Magazine,* writer Lillian Symes, who had managed to work outside the home, wrote an article entitled "Still a Man's Game: Reflections of a Slightly Tired Feminist." First she distanced herself from the predecessors who had earned her the right to vote, explaining that *she* was not one of those "flat-heeled, unpowdered" women. Then she reversed herself, ruefully mocking the smug assumptions of her peers and herself: "Political freedom and the right to enter the professions and arts had been almost gained by a braver, grimmer, and more fanatical generation of feminists behind us. These were women who had had to make the famous choice between 'marriage and a career.' We were determined to have both, to try for everything life would offer of love, happiness, and freedom—just like men."

As always, personal fulfillment was an admirable goal for a woman so long as it did not interfere with the needs of the family. Ruth may or may not have been a feminist, but she probably aspired at least to the marital ideal in the 1920s, the "companionate marriage." Replacing the patriarchal, emotionally barren Victorian marriage, companionate marriage promised "a specialized site for emotional intimacy, personal and sexual expression, and nurture among husband, wife, and a small number of children."

Ruth later hinted to her daughters that her sex life had been disappointing, but she had never considered that reason enough to leave her marriage. A couple of years after Sue's birth, Ruth became pregnant again, but she only realized she had been pregnant when she had a miscarriage. Although Ruth bled profusely and nearly died, Marie insisted on calling in her chiropractor instead of Ruth's doctor. Then the chiropractor treated Ruth so inadequately that she needed an unusually long time to recuperate.

In the summer of 1929 Leo added a wooden toboggan run next to the pier so that swimmers could slide down it into the water. On July 7, a seventeen-year-old boy from nearby Jackson failed to lock the toboggan in place at the top of the slide. When he pushed off, the sled left the slide and fell into a safety net, but the boy fell into the water and broke his neck. He died the next day. Ruth was at the pier when it happened, and she became so upset by the tragedy that, to calm her, their friend and physician, Kenneth Howard, gave Ruth a sedative. It was a combination of chloral hydrate and potassium bromide that in large quantities was also known as knockout drops or a Mickey Finn.

Ruth continued to brood about the accident—not only the horror of the experience, but its possible consequences. Although an inquest held shortly after the event cleared both the Steinems and the manufacturer, Ruth worried that the parents would sue. They did, for $20,000. Nothing came of the suit, but the increased worrying took its toll, and Ruth began to take more frequent doses of what they came to call "Dr. Howard's medicine."

In October 1929 the stock market collapsed, and in December Leo's father died. Two months later Ruth's father died in his sleep. The crash did not affect Ruth and Leo directly, but their fathers' deaths, one on the heels of the other and both unexpected, shocked Ruth, who was already in a vulnerable state. Ruth became increasingly dependent on Dr. Howard's medicine. Sue remembers once seeing her mother so desperate that she drank vanilla extract.

In 1930, Ruth, thirty-two, suffered what her family called a nervous breakdown. She would cling to Leo and would become so keyed up that she could spend four or five days without sleeping. Finally she entered a sanitorium in Toledo. Sue had started kindergarten at four and a half, so, though she was anxious about her mother, she also had a life of her own at school. Leo and Sue were allowed to visit Ruth, and afterward Leo would take Sue out for milkshakes to console her (and himself). Ruth later said Sue had changed during that period from a slender little girl to a chubby little girl who spent many years afterward in a battle to control her weight. Heredity may have been as much the culprit as the milkshakes, however; by that time, Leo, who had been slender in college, was growing progressively stouter himself.

Ruth came home after several months. Leo soon suggested that they move to Clarklake year-round, an idea that did not appeal to Ruth. Giving up work had been bad enough, but leaving Toledo would also mean leaving her friends and relatives. Furthermore, Clarklake would be lonely; it was a vacation community, and very few people lived at the lake year-round. However, the Depression was making money even tighter, and moving to the lake would help them economize, so she agreed.

In 1931 Ruth became pregnant again. Late in her pregnancy she contracted the flu, and on January 24, 1932, she gave birth in Toledo to a stillborn baby boy. Already debilitated by grief and stress, Ruth sank into depression. Some of her relatives speculated that losing a boy, whom they assumed would have been especially valued by her husband's Jewish family, might have exacerbated her condition.

When they returned to Clarklake, Ruth continued to dose herself regularly with "Dr. Howard's medicine," but she remained coherent and usually helped Leo run the dance-pier business. Ruth and Leo were easygoing parents and Sue loved to take care of animals, so they always had pets. There usually was a collie, and a bunny every Easter. Once Sue raised a pair of baby chicks into an enormous rooster and hen. When Sue (then Susie) yearned for a pet lamb, a local farmer gave her a runt that was not expected to live. She fed the lamb with a bottle, and "Betty Jane" slept in a bed made from an old piano box. Every night Sue and Ruth would sit at the window and watch Leo chase the lamb around the yard until Betty Jane sank down in exhaustion. Then the rotund Leo could pick up the lamb and put her to bed for the night.

Sue was about eight when she and her parents were in nearby Brooklyn, Michigan (population 749), and she spied a little girl bundled up in a snowsuit. Sue thought the little girl was just adorable. She turned to her mother. "That's what I want," she commanded. "I want a little sister."

"Well, pray for one, and maybe you'll get her," Ruth responded. So Sue, whose charges in addition to the live animals included her stuffed monkey, Red Riley, and her dolls, Anne and Gloria, prayed for what she now wanted most in the world. Late in 1933 Ruth and Leo told Sue she was going to get her wish.

Ruth courageously stayed off Dr. Howard's medicine for the duration of her pregnancy, and they waited in Toledo for the baby's birth. In the evening of March 25, 1934, Ruth, thirty-four, and Leo, thirty-six, took Sue to a double-feature movie, but they saw only one film. Ruth decided it was time to go to the hospital. They dropped Sue at her grandmother's house, and as soon as her parents left, Sue fell on her knees and started praying again. Ruth's pregnancy had convinced Sue of the efficacy of prayer, and she had an emergency request. A schoolmate had informed her that mothers sometimes died in childbirth, so Sue spent the rest of the evening begging God to spare her mother.

Ruth was spared and Sue got the sibling she requested. Even more exciting, Ruth and Leo allowed Sue to name her sister, because they couldn't agree on a name. It was a difficult decision. Which doll should she name the baby after, Anne or Gloria? Sue finally settled on Gloria, and Ruth and Leo added Marie to honor Ruth's mother. (Years later the adult Gloria Steinem met Gloria Swanson, and the actress assured her, "You're named after me, dahling. They all were.")

Unlike Sue's traditional birth announcement, Gloria's was suitable for the daughter of an impresario:

Sunday, March 25, 1934, 10 P.M.
RUTH AND LEO STEINEM
of Ocean Beach, Clark Lake, Michigan
PRESENT
GLORIA MARIE STEINEM
8 1/2 Pound Blues Singer
WORLD PREMIERE APPEARANCE
Dr. Kenneth Howard, Master of Ceremonies
Benefit Women's and Children's Hospital, Toledo, Ohio

By 1934 the country was mired in the Depression; the FBI shot Public Enemy Number One, gangster John Dillinger; Cole Porter published "Anything Goes"; Adolf Hitler and Benito Mussolini were on the rise. Gloria's birth cohort included the Dionne quintuplets in Canada and Sophia Loren in Italy. In Winsted, Connecticut, Mr. and Mrs. Nader rejoiced at the birth of little Ralph.

When Leo had suggested living year-round at Clarklake, he had not really intended to stay there twelve months a year. He hated cold weather, and he reasoned that if he were fortunate enough to have a seasonal business, there was no reason to endure it. So as soon as the three moved to Clarklake, he began taking the family away during the coldest winter months. Almost every winter they closed up the house, piled into the car and a little silver trailer, and worked their way west to California, or south to Florida. Then, after spending a few months in the warmer climate, they would work their way back, always by the first of April, to get the pier ready for Memorial Day weekend.

The trips were part business, part pleasure, because they bought and sold antiques along the way. The antiques business began one summer when Ruth and Leo went to a local auction to bid on furnishings for the cottages on their property. Included in the lot with a desired item were a number of other things they didn't want, and Leo resold them at a profit. Once he saw the possibilities, he decided he was also in the antiques business. Selling antiques provided a welcome supplement to their summer income. Their investment wasn't huge—mostly, they bought and sold antique jewelry and small glass and china objects. Between trips they continued buying at auction and selling from their house or garage. Leo did most of the trading, but Gloria suspects her mother, who studied books on antiques, had a better eye.

The family's itinerant life suited the free-spirited Leo perfectly. He took pride in the fact that he never wore a hat, and he liked to tell his daughters, "Never work for one boss." His wife and daughters paid the price for his wanderlust. Their winter journeys kept Sue and Gloria from regular schooling and isolated Ruth from her family and friends even more than the Clarklake location had.

2

Life on the Lake

The three-bedroom, Mediterranean-style stucco house at Clarklake's east end was home for the first ten years of Gloria's life. Her room, though eventually as cluttered as the rest of the house, originally had been beautiful. Its walls and ceiling were sky blue; Ruth had painted silver stars on the ceiling, and on the walls, tulips that looked as if they grew out of the green baseboards.

Ruth and Leo were imaginative, but their house lacked a few amenities—such as proper heating (since it had been built only as a summer cottage) and a bath or shower. Heat for the entire house was provided, inadequately, by a fireplace and a woodstove. Preserving these shortcomings when they lived there year-round was not an oversight. It was typical of Leo's peculiar pragmatism. He decided that if the house were too comfortable, Ruth might refuse to go away during the winter. As a result, during the summer everyone had to take a bar of soap down to the lake to wash. Once it was too cold to use the lake, they bathed the old-fashioned way, with kettles of water heated on the stove and poured into a metal tub.

When winter approached, the unheated bedrooms upstairs became so cold that they all spent most of their time downstairs, which was heated, though Leo's indolence-induced ingenuity extended even to his method of fueling the fire. No wood chopping or log splitting for Leo.

He just stuck one end of a long log into the fireplace. When it burned down, he kicked the log farther into the fire.

Sometimes the downstairs population swelled to include the dogs. The collies were always having puppies, and during the cold months Gloria would put newspapers on the kitchen floor and bring them inside. Puppies were not allowed beyond the kitchen. On one of the few occasions when Gloria, age five, got into trouble, it was because she took them into the living room, thinking they were too cold in the kitchen. By the time her parents saw them, the puppies had urinated all over everything, so Gloria pretended they had gotten there all by themselves. Then Ruth asked, "Was this 'let's pretend' or was it 'truly, truly'?" and Gloria had to confess. " 'Truly, truly' was the magic phrase," she explains. "No matter what you'd said before, you had to tell the truth after 'truly, truly.' "

Beyond no puppies in the living room, there weren't enough rules for Gloria to get into trouble very often, and though she was high-spirited, she tried not to upset her mother. She did annoy Sue sometimes by trying to tag along, but they didn't argue much. Whenever they did, Ruth made them both recite, "We are sisters and we love each other," which was irritating, but it seemed to work. In spite of Ruth's attempt to impose sibling affection by fiat, they actually were devoted to each other.

Before Gloria learned to read, Leo would read the Sunday funny papers to her, and on their birthdays the girls were allowed to determine the menu and select their favorite cake. Occasionally they had parties—such as a Halloween party for Sue, complete with a haunted-house tour, and for Gloria, a skating party on the frozen lake with hot dogs and roasted marshmallows. At Christmas they each made long wish lists. Most of the requests were practical, but Leo got them thinking big by heading his list one year with a request for $500,000. Soon Sue was asking for Jewel-Encrusted Opera Glasses. Ruth alternated between A House With Lemon and Orange Trees in the Backyard and To Know My Next Incarnation. Gloria first wanted To Ice Skate in the Movies Like Sonja Henie, and later changed to A Texas Ranch With Palomino Horses.

By the time Gloria turned six, Ruth was becoming even more dependent on Dr. Howard's medicine, so Leo took over most of the marketing and most of what passed for cooking. Sometimes Gloria helped.

She relates, "We would bring home all kinds of foods—cold cuts, and bread, and sandwich spread, and ice cream—and would just make food when we wanted it. Maybe sometimes we sat down to dinner, but I don't remember ever sitting down at a table. I remember going to the refrigerator and getting food and coming to the living room and sitting down and eating. Sometimes my father or I would walk into the kitchen and say, 'Do you want anything?' My mother would lie on the couch in the living room on a foldout sofa bed, and we would bring her food. . . . My father was best at making fudge, but he could cook. Mostly he heated up cans of things. Franco-American spaghetti was one of my favorites."

Leo enjoyed his daughters. As he had with Sue, he would take Gloria out for milkshakes. He also created routines to perform around strangers. In one Leo would warn Gloria, "If you do that again, you won't go to heaven," and Gloria was to respond, "But I don't want to go to heaven, Daddy. I want to go with you."

When Gloria was a baby, Leo and Ruth bought a house trailer to hitch to their car during their trips to California or Florida. As they drove, they sang songs Ruth and Leo taught them from the Great War and the 1920s, like "Pack Up Your Troubles in Your Old Kit Bag (and Smile, Smile, Smile)," and "Oh, What a Pal Was Mary." Otherwise, Ruth looked at maps and the countryside, and the girls read constantly, ignoring their mother's pleas to look at the passing scenery. "I looked two hours ago," Gloria protested once. She must have looked out occasionally, however, because she later told interviewers she had learned to read partly from Burma-Shave signs along the road. A typical sequence: "He had the ring. He had the flat. She felt his chin. And that was that. Get him some Burma-Shave."

After driving all day they would look for a trailer park to hook up their trailer to an electrical line and to take showers. If they couldn't find a trailer park, they stayed in motels, but they avoided them when possible, to save money. In California they usually stayed at a trailer park in Laguna Beach, a now elegant area that was almost deserted at the time, and in Florida at Clearwater Beach, near Tampa.

Gloria, eight, found their 1942–43 winter in Florida during World War II particularly exciting. To conceal the trailer park from enemy attack, they had to follow the blackout rules: blackout curtains on all trailers' windows and no flashlights. Best of all, they heard that some German sailors, evidently bored with life aboard a U-boat off the Florida coast, had come ashore in a dinghy, held the patrons of a local bar at gunpoint, drunk a couple of beers, and then returned to their submarine.

During the summers, life at the Ocean Beach Pier resort was busy. In the evening her parents would sometimes put Gloria to bed in Leo's office where they could check on her. Otherwise Sue or other teenaged girls baby-sat. Sue was conscientious, but the others were a varied lot. Gloria's favorite was the cheater: "I had one baby-sitter whom I absolutely adored because she treated me like a grownup. She used to ask me before she went out—completely deserting me, against all instructions—'Do you think I should wear this? Or that? These earrings? Or those?' Then she would leave me alone and go roller skating with her friends at the other end of the lake. I would have died rather than tell on her."

Relatives made their way to Ocean Beach Pier every summer, and Marie, whom her granddaughters called O' Mommy (for "Old Mommy"), spent the season in a one-room house they called O' Mommy's cottage. Gloria loved her grandmother, though she was also a little afraid of her. Her face and arms sunburned from gardening, Marie would attack everything she did with ferocious energy, hoeing the garden, baking a pie, or raising baby chicks. Occasionally, when Ruth wasn't well, Marie would come over and clean the house "in a kind of disgusted way." Even to a child, Gloria recalls, "She seemed somewhat out of control. For example, she would decide to do something—like burn off the property the way you burn weeds off at the beginning of the summer—and she'd set it on fire and burn practically everything else down."

Sometimes Ruth and Leo left Gloria in O' Mommy's care when they traveled to nearby country auctions and shops to buy and sell antiques. They probably had few alternatives, but Gloria, who was developing the acute sensitivity of a child with troubled parents, could see that her grandmother infuriated Ruth and Leo. "I could tell, whether they told her or not, when they were angry at what she'd done in their absence, whether it was setting fire to the field or cleaning out their closets. I always felt she was kind of reckless. But she was also quite adventurous."

Well into her old age Marie traveled around the country, using her late husband's railroad pass. She loved to go to a racetrack in California and bet on the horses. She also loved to listen to baseball games on the radio. All that was not until years later, though—after she'd finished pushing her daughters around.

Gloria spent most Clarklake summer days on the beach. Each year Ruth bought her a red bathing suit so she could spot her easily, but as

Gloria grew older she was often out of sight, under the pier looking for pennies and nickels that had fallen into the water the night before. Berenice Burton, a local farmer's wife who helped Ruth with the cooking for the band members, was a second mother to Gloria, and her daughter Jackie became Gloria's best friend. The two girls spent much of their time at the Burtons' farm, playing on the rope swing or cutting out paper dolls.

They learned to tap-dance from the cigarette girl at the pier, and then Jackie joined Gloria, from the age of five or six, for real tap-dancing lessons in the nearby town of Jackson. Jackie, who was a year older, was impressed even then with Gloria's talent: "When we danced, we looked like I was the 'before' and she was the 'after.' "

Gloria loved dancing, and from the time she was about five until she was eight or nine, she would dance anywhere, oblivious to whether people were watching. She recalls, "I would dance on street corners so readily that my parents would pretend not to know me and say, 'Who's that?' " Then, when she was about nine, Gloria became shy and stopped dancing for several years.

That may have been the age at which Gloria became self-conscious about her family as well. The Steinems were outsiders. Her father was fat. Sometimes his clothes were soiled with food. He might fall asleep after he ate. Her mother was completely unpredictable, witty and hard working one minute and depressed or paranoid another. Sue was normal, but from the time Gloria was four, Sue was in Jackson, a town larger and more distant than Brooklyn, during the week. She lived at the YWCA so that she could attend a high school that offered a foreign language and other requirements that she needed to get into college. Anyway, Sue could not establish the family's identity. Parents did that. Gloria felt she belonged to a family that was "invisible."

To make matters worse, unlike many children with a troubled home life, she was unable to escape to the world of school. Her parents enrolled her in kindergarten and elementary school in the nearest town, Brooklyn, but because they left for California or Florida during almost every school year, Gloria never completed an entire year of school. She usually started school in the fall and attended until they left, but she never knew when that would be. They might stay in Clarklake through Christmas, or they might leave before Thanksgiving. They left when Leo decided he was too cold. When they returned, Gloria did not usually finish the school year.

They spent Gloria's entire second-grade school year in Clarklake because Sue, sixteen, afraid that she would not be prepared for college, convinced her father to let her stay in school in Jackson for her entire senior year. Gloria still stayed out of school some of the time, though, especially if Leo didn't feel like driving her. Ruth never drove—at first because Leo always preferred to, and later, because she was afraid to.

Gloria's erratic education left her with pockets of ignorance. She lacked a grounding in geography and simple mathematical skills like the times tables. She had learned to write early, at about five, imitating Sue's half printing, half writing, and when her teachers objected, she found it hard to unlearn. She also wasn't around long enough to become proficient at jacks, jumping rope, and the other schoolyard games that girls played.

On the other hand, from reading so extensively and spending most of her time among intelligent, verbal, witty adults, Gloria's vocabulary and her sense of humor were far more sophisticated than her classmates'. When she wrote a Thanksgiving poem in second grade with a refrain of "not only for the dead but for the living," her teacher humiliated her by refusing to believe she had written it herself.

Consequently, as much as she longed to be at school, her longing was laced with anxiety. She never knew whether she would be adequately prepared to do the classwork; at the same time, she feared saying something inappropriately adult. Gloria knew that to fit in she needed to act like a child, so she did her best. She became a child impersonator.

Even so, if she had been given a choice, she would have gone to school all the time. Besides, there were boys. Gloria does not recall suddenly awakening to the opposite sex at puberty. "I always remember being interested in boys," she explains. "I remember a boy in second grade who seemed both poor and kindhearted, which I found irresistible. I think his name was Roger. We exchanged valentines—I think that was the extent of it. But I remember the feeling of being attracted."

Apart from Jackie during the summer, Gloria had no regular playmates near her own age, and she knew she could bring no one back to the house. Her world at Clarklake consisted mostly of her family—and wherever she could travel in her head.

Gloria could read by the time she was four, but even before she could read, radio programs exposed her to lives beyond her own. She listened to children's programs like *Let's Pretend,* adult shows like *Mr. Keen, Tracer of Lost Persons,* and comedians like Jack Benny and Fred Allen. During the week, along with housewives across the country, she listened to soap operas. There were *The Romance of Helen Trent* and *Our Gal Sunday,* which asked the famous question, "Can this girl from a mining town in the West find happiness as the wife of a wealthy and titled Englishman?"

Gloria would imagine herself belonging to the families she heard about on the evening programs. The brother and sister living with their parents on *Meet Corliss Archer* appealed to her, except for the necessity of coming up with the rent each month, which sounded difficult. Then she listened to the adventures of Mother and Father Barbour and their grown children and grandchildren on *One Man's Family* and decided this was the family to which she would like to belong.

Listening to the radio not only taught Gloria about other lives, it allowed her to escape from her own. Once she learned to read, books became her magic carpet, transporting her to other worlds, other times. She read everything: children's books, adult books, whatever her mother left around, books Leo had acquired. He bought individuals' libraries to obtain first editions he could resell, then left the rest moldering in the garage where Gloria and Sue picked through them and read anything that interested them.

She read all of Nancy Drew and the Hardy Boys; a series called the *Whiteoaks of Jalna,* about an English family; and isolated volumes of a series on Civil War history that reviewed every battle, "tree stump by tree stump," but left her with no clear picture of the war's overall meaning. She learned about sex (sort of) from a couple of books her parents later said she shouldn't have read. One told of a pregnant high school drum majorette, and the other, *Silk Straps,* depicted a working-class flapper in the 1920s.

By far her favorite author was Louisa May Alcott. Gloria read Alcott's children's books from the time she was about six (rereading *Little Women* every year) and, later, Alcott's adult novels as well. Gloria liked to imagine the March family as her own, casting herself as Jo and placing herself in all kinds of interesting situations. Over time she also came to regard Louisa May Alcott as her imaginary friend. Besides fantasizing about what she would show Alcott if she traveled back in time for a visit—white bread (which she thought Alcott would say was like cake), cars, telephones, and ice cream (which Alcott would have recognized, but which Gloria liked to think about)—she scripted entire dialogues, imagining what she would say and what Alcott would say in return.

"She felt like a kindred spirit," Gloria recalls, "only someone who was a grown-up and therefore had lived in worlds I hadn't yet entered. So she was a guide." Alcott consciously put a number of her ideas into her books for children, as well as into her adult novels. Gloria absorbed a great deal from the books themselves, understanding at least some of Alcott's messages and responding to her values. Alcott supported women's rights (though she believed women should fulfill their domestic duties) and racial tolerance (though she was prejudiced against the Irish). Her plucky heroines were adventurous women who had to support themselves, but at the same time they helped others even less fortunate than themselves.

Alcott's adult novels also conveyed her pessimistic view of relations between men and women. Uncomfortable with romantic love, she portrayed love and marriage as dangerously obliterating. As Martha Saxon, one of her biographers, wrote, "Love for Louisa was too engulfing to be experienced. It was complete, blinding, and consuming. It held the promise of perfect blending, the end of struggle and separateness, total peace, and finally oblivion." Another biographer, Madelon Bedell, observed that in *Moods* (a love story), Alcott conveyed "a fear of the loss of independence and power for the woman who makes a marriage based on love." Even in *Little Women*, Jo March proclaimed at one point, "I don't believe I shall ever marry. I'm happy as I am, and love my liberty too well to be in any hurry to give it up for any mortal man."

Many years later, Gloria would delay and flee marriage with an aversion she could not understand, except to say that, for her, it felt like "surrender" or "a little death," because it seemed to mean following a husband's choices and giving up one's own. Gloria's perception of what her parents' marriage did to her mother had an enormous effect, but perhaps the writings of Louisa May Alcott influenced her belief in the possibility of independence as well. On the other hand, Gloria was under ten when she read Alcott's books, so she missed much of what Alcott was saying. Ultimately, it is interesting to speculate about, but impossible to measure, the influence Louisa May Alcott had on Gloria. What she remembers about Alcott is that "she was adventurous, questioning, and someone who enjoyed the company of women as well as men."

Ruth would occasionally suggest a book herself, but her primary response to Gloria's and Sue's voracious reading was to try to get them to cut down a little. "You'll ruin your eyes," she would insist. Eventually they compromised: Gloria agreed not to read while walking up and down the stairs. Ruth lost the battle against comic books. Sue and Gloria assiduously followed the exploits of Wonder Woman, Superman, Sheena of the Jungle, and Batman.

Like many other young girls, Gloria was horse crazy and devoured every horse story she could find. When she met a girl who actually had a horse of her own and was selling him, Gloria began to nag her parents until they bought Rusty for seventy-five dollars. Perhaps Ruth and Leo thought having a horse around to amuse Gloria was less trouble than driving her to school. They already had an old garage with a dirt floor on their property, so they stabled the horse there and Gloria would groom it for hours. It was also a way to keep things balanced, because they had bought Sue her own small sailboat, though after she took riding lessons at Smith College she, too, rode Rusty.

Imaginary horses populated Gloria's fantasy life as well. Besides communing with Louisa May Alcott, she spent a good deal of time narrating her life in the third person ("Then she got up. It was a cloudy day . . .") and devising endless scenarios. While driving across the country with her family, Gloria liked to imagine herself on horseback, riding alongside the car, galloping with a wonderful sense of freedom.

Gloria also came to believe she could influence her dreams. "What do I want to dream about tonight?" she would ask herself as she lay in bed. Besides Alcott, her favorite was a rescue fantasy with herself as the rescuer. She went to the aid of a black man who was about to be lynched. After driving up in a car with a shotgun and holding off the crowd until the man climbed into the trunk, she drove off, reaching safety after what she recalls as "a long and heart-pounding chase."

She also fantasized about being rescued herself from her real life. In the fantasies she would imagine all kinds of scenarios with various "real parents" who would come and take her away to a different life.

Gloria loved her parents, and she knew they loved her, but she did not feel protected by them. The principal sources of her anxiety were their precarious financial position and Ruth's unreliable mental state. Leo was frequently in debt, and he did not hide that fact from his family. He even took Gloria with him when he went to Household Finance to try to get a loan. More than once, Gloria watched the finance man refuse her father's request. At home she watched him park their car far away when he thought the finance company might come to repossess it. Most frightening, Leo sometimes employed Gloria in his stratagems. On the theory that no one would hurt a child, when bill collectors appeared at the door Leo instructed Gloria to tell them, "My father's not home."

Gloria's relationship with her father remains complicated. More than fifty years after the events, she responds to a comment that growing up at Clarklake must have been idyllic by saying that it was "scary." Then, when her description of that childhood as scary evokes sympathy and an observation that her father had been cruel to put her in such "scary" situations, she jumps to his defense. She explains that, though she knew he was frightened of the bill collector's power, he made her feel important by making her feel included in adult affairs. Gloria also says she always knew he was treating her "as well or better than he treated himself."

Leo's cavalier attitude toward money was deeply distressing to Ruth. Unlike Leo, she knew what it was to be without money, so she fretted and worried and carefully saved pennies, nickels, and dimes in jars in the closet. When Leo remortgaged the pier without telling her, she was furious. Ever optimistic, Leo lived close to the edge, always convinced he was going to strike it rich. He entered many contests, but he especially had high hopes for the toilet paper slogan he suggested: "You can bet your bottom dollar on Scott Tissue." A natural optimist, Leo also had expectations. Because his mother had a comfortable estate that would eventually be divided among her sons, he assumed he would not be destitute. Ruth was not as trusting of fate.

Intertwined with their shaky financial position was Ruth's mental and emotional condition. Many years later Ruth received an official diagnosis of "anxiety neurosis"; during Gloria's childhood, her behavior was unpredictable. Ruth could be paranoid, stuporous, hallucinatory, timid, angry—or often quite normal.

Gloria recalls her first five years as fairly comfortable, with occasional "moments of scariness" due to financial worries or her mother's mental state. The bad times were only "islands of fear and uncertainty and insecurity," not the frequent state of distress that evolved during the next ten years.

Gloria became more empathetic as she grew older. When she spent a week at Girl Scout camp at the age of nine, Ruth and Leo came for visiting day and Gloria saw them with fresh eyes. "It was very painful," she said years later. "Seeing my father, totally impatient and yelling at

my mother. And seeing this poor, frightened, thin, abstracted creature
and realizing, even as a child, that he was in some ways understandably
impatient. Because I had felt impatient with her too. And yet she was
so sad and wounded. And if he spoke sharply to her, she would jump
and try to obey."

The situation worsened when wartime gasoline rationing cut into
business in the 1940s. The pier's survival was in jeopardy, and Ruth
and Leo fought constantly, mostly about money. Gloria, usually alone
with her parents after Sue left for Smith College in 1942, would try to
smooth things over by placating her father or calming her mother. By
the time Gloria was ten, the dissension was so constant that when Ruth
told her they would be going to Massachusetts to live near Sue for a
year, Gloria was not even distressed at the prospect of leaving her
father. She looked forward to the respite from her parents' acrimony.
Besides, it sounded like an adventure.

3

Bad Times in Toledo

After all Leo's and Ruth's fighting in Clarklake, life in Amherst, Massachusetts, was a relief for Gloria. Sue had found a house for them to sublet, and she left school many weekends to join them. Although Gloria did miss her father, she enjoyed herself in Amherst. Ruth seemed better, too, keeping the house neater and behaving more normally than at any other time in Gloria's memory.

They arrived in the fall of 1944 and found themselves in a pleasant neighborhood of a beautiful New England village. Gloria played with the local children and learned to play softball for the first time. She even got in a fight with a boy—a real, physical, though (according to Gloria) rather good-natured fight—and knocked the boy down.

What she enjoyed most was going to school every day. She was in fifth grade, and the children were welcoming, so ten-year-old Gloria did not feel left out. As usual, she was keenly aware that there were gaps in her knowledge, even though she didn't know what they all were. She usually managed to cover them up by compensating for her ignorance in math, history, and geography with her wide knowledge from reading and her ability to write well.

Ruth had Gloria baptized in the Congregational Church. Although Ruth was still an enthusiastic theosophist, she was eclectic. Gloria and Ruth followed the war news closely. Ruth had instructed Gloria about the Nazis, anti-Semitism, and eventually, the concentration camps.

When President Roosevelt died in April 1945, Ruth, who always spoke of his help during the Depression with tears in her eyes, cried and hung out a flag at half mast.

Leo came to visit them once, and while he was there it began to snow. Gloria went sledding with her friends. When she brought them back to the house afterward, Ruth and Leo spread newspapers all over the kitchen floor to absorb the melting snow and made hot chocolate for all the children. It was the most wonderful day she could remember. She thought the other children must see them as a normal, happy, everyday father, mother, and daughter—just the kind of conventional family for which she yearned. She felt as if they were masquerading, but she enjoyed it just the same.

Fortunately Gloria couldn't see into the future. She had no way of knowing that the interlude in Amherst was the end of what she would later recall as the normal part of her childhood.

At the end of her fifth-grade year, in May 1945, Ruth and Gloria's sojourn in Amherst drew to a close. Sue had a job in New York for the summer before her senior year and a place to live in Manhattan. Gloria and Ruth house-sat at the home of a college friend of Ruth's in Scarsdale, a suburb outside the city. Although Sue came out most weekends and Ruth's sister, Janey, visited once, it was a miserable summer.

The old wooden house was dark, damp, and somewhat isolated. They knew no one, and they had no car. Even if they had had one, Ruth had forgotten how to drive, and she soon became too ill to go anywhere anyway. That summer she retreated into a world of her own, depressed and hallucinating. Gloria was left completely to her own devices. It was not a neighborhood where children played on the street. All she could find to do was read the books in the house and worry about where they were going next.

No one would tell her. Ruth occasionally asked if Gloria wanted to move into a house on the Great White Way, but when Gloria asked where that was, Ruth wouldn't respond. Gloria assumed it must be a place where she didn't know anyone, as Ruth and Sue kept talking about what an adventure being the "new girl" would be—because all her old clothes would be new to her schoolmates. That was scant comfort to the frightened eleven-year-old.

When summer ended, Gloria learned that they were moving back to Toledo. Years later she realized that Ruth's Great White Way must have been the highway—really a four-lane thoroughfare—that had been built right in front of the farmhouse where Ruth had grown up. Ruth was planning to move back into her childhood home.

She also planned to get a divorce. Leaving Clarklake had been a separation. In 1945, when Ruth was forty-seven and Leo was forty-eight, they agreed to divorce. They had entered the marriage as two apparently successful young people, but their union had been troubled almost from the beginning. By now Ruth had had enough. Although she was ill, Ruth somehow found the strength to strike out on her own. At the same time, she seemed to continue to hope Leo would change into a more responsible husband.

Leo could not have been happy in their marriage either, if for no other reason than Ruth's mental state. But he did not initiate the separation. He was a tenderhearted, sentimental man who loved his daughters dearly. As dissonant as their family became, the four had spent an unusual amount of time together through all their years on the road and in their relative isolation at Clarklake. When he agreed to the divorce, he apparently assumed that Gloria, eleven, was old enough to manage without him.

Ruth and Leo met in Toledo and divided their property evenly. Ocean Beach Pier was gone. When wartime rationing diminished business so much that they could no longer operate, Leo demolished it in 1944 by having it blown up—typical of Leo, he wanted it to go out in a blaze of glory. They sold most of the pier and house furnishings in an auction, but they still owned property at the lake in common.

Against her lawyer's advice, Ruth refused to seek alimony. Since Leo's financial irresponsibility was her most fundamental complaint, she may not have felt she was making much of a sacrifice, but she chose to portray her refusal as a heroic gesture of independence rather than as mere pragmatism. She probably considered herself the more sensible businessperson of the two of them, though Leo disagreed. When she leased out her portion of the lake property after they divided it, Leo told her he thought she had gotten less for it than the Indians had.

Toledo was a thriving industrial city at that point, population around 300,000. Most of the major factories, including Libbey-Owens-Ford, Sun Oil, Willys-Overland, and Champion Spark Plug, had operated at full capacity throughout the war and would continue to prosper in the postwar years. Moving back to Toledo, Ruth had to decide where to live until some of the tenants in her old house on Woodville Road moved out. Ruth's family home was in East Toledo, a working-class neighborhood, and had been divided into apartments. A small basement apartment was available on Lincoln Avenue in West Toledo, the more desirable side of town. There they would be close to her sister Janey, Janey's husband, Bob, and Ruth's mother, who lived with Janey and Bob.

While the neighborhood was pleasant, Gloria was shocked by the size and condition of the Lincoln Avenue apartment. Except for their trips in the trailer, Gloria had always lived in a house. This apartment was fashioned out of the space behind the utility room in an old house that had been converted into a boardinghouse. To reach the small room that doubled as living room and bedroom, they had to walk past an enormous furnace that heated the entire building. Beyond the living room–bedroom were a tiny kitchen and a bathroom. All Gloria could see through the windows were car tires as they rolled by in the driveway. She and Ruth stacked their possessions where they could and slept in bunk beds, because the room was too small for two beds side by side.

Gloria, eleven, started sixth grade at the Monroe Elementary School after classes had already begun, again watching the other children for cues. When she inadvertently hurt another girl's feelings with a joke, she realized that her sense of humor was too adult and, from then on, consciously refrained from making funny remarks. She also continued to censor her too-adult vocabulary.

Gloria found that one almost-complete year in Amherst had not made up for the years of interrupted schooling, so she continued to fake knowledge other children seemed to take for granted. It gave her a lost sensation that still troubles her. She observes, for example, that she is more confident spelling long words—which she attributes to her high school study of Latin—than short ones.

Gloria's school in Amherst had had a number of new students, but her Monroe classmates appeared to have been together for years. She made friends anyway, and even decided that one of them would be her boyfriend. At that point she began to find boys as a group a little intimidating: They liked throwing rock-filled snowballs at the girls, as well as at the nearby Toledo Art Museum's glass-paneled roof. Her closest friend lived with her mother in the boardinghouse upstairs, and they played together often, despite the fact that Ruth did not approve of the girl's mother. Gloria thought that might be because her friend's mother went out with various men.

One highlight of sixth grade for eleven-year-old Gloria was learning she was nearsighted and getting eyeglasses. Since both her parents and

Sue needed them as well, Gloria was pleased and felt quite grown up, though the glasses' initial effect was to make her feel shorter: The ground seemed closer when she could see it better.

In spite of friends and school, Gloria was sometimes anxious and depressed. She slept in the upper bunk, and her bed became her nest and retreat. "Why am I not happy?" she would ask herself, wondering simultaneously if she were not being a bit melodramatic. She also found that if she lay on her back and concentrated very hard, she could reduce her field of vision until it encompassed only one small square of the white plasterboard ceiling about a foot above her head. Then she would soothe herself. "This is clean," she would tell herself. "This is neat. I'm just not going to look at any other place."

As depressed as she was while she lived on Lincoln Avenue, Gloria at least could hope that their circumstances might improve. Maybe her mother would get better. Maybe they would move to a nicer place. However, the following summer one set of tenants moved out of the house on Woodville Road, and they moved there. Only the space was better. Otherwise, the broken-down former farmhouse next to the highway seemed to Gloria like the end of the line. "What I remember emotionally," Gloria said years later, "is the impact of suddenly realizing this was it. And the 'it' was quite depressing."

When the wind blew the wrong way, the entire east side of Toledo could smell the fumes from the factories. In Gloria's new, stolid, working-class neighborhood, the rows of neatly tended houses, mostly two-storied with steep roofs, sat close together on 30-by-110-foot lots. Many of the families were Polish or Hungarian, and most of the men worked at the factories or drove trucks, though a few held white-collar jobs as insurance agents or clerks. Most of the women were housewives.

By 1946, Ruth's family's former farmhouse was far more rundown than the other houses in the neighborhood that had grown up around it, and Woodville Road had constant truck traffic. On one side of Gloria's new home was Ruth's old Presbyterian church. On the other was an elderly widow, Mrs. Gildemeister. Although Ruth remembered and liked her, the neighborhood children considered her a crabby old lady because she screeched at them when they made too much noise. Across the street was Braun's, a butcher shop, and, past the church on another corner, an ice cream store.

When the downstairs tenants moved out, Ruth suggested to the Barnes family in the upstairs apartment that they move into the downstairs apartment, which was more spacious. The upstairs apartment was composed of former bedrooms, so much of the floor space was taken up by the hall, and the steeply sloped roof reduced the usable space even further. There were two bedrooms, a living room, a bathroom, and a kitchen, though the kitchen lacked a sink. The downstairs kitchen sink had disappeared, so when the Barneses changed apartments, Ruth told them to take the upstairs kitchen sink, and she never replaced it. Behind the house, so close that a child could only edge through sideways, was a garage.

Although he and Ruth were divorced, Leo came to Toledo to help her and Gloria move their piles of belongings—boxes and boxes of books and magazines, treasured furniture like a Chippendale rocker and the piano, household bric-a-brac, and a few remnants of Ruth's lusterware antiques. Ruth soon forgot what they had, and all the years they lived on Woodville Road she constantly fretted about lost objects and muttered dark accusations about who must have taken them.

Standing wide-eyed as their exotic landlady and her daughter moved in were Marilyn and Lillian Barnes. The Steinems' possessions were fascinating, but not nearly as fascinating as the Steinems themselves. Leo was large, round, and jovial and, as his name implied, had a full head of gray hair. Ruth, who seemed more reticent, was tall, angular, and very attractive. Her auburn hair was pulled tightly back on her head; her clothes were interesting and unlike any the girls had ever seen. Marilyn and Lillian didn't know that Leo and Ruth were divorced, but they had been told that Leo wasn't going to live there.

Later they would meet the older daughter, Sue, who seemed like a glamorous apparition from a distant world, but for now there was Ginger, the chow chow who looked like a lion and had a black tongue. Best of all, Gloria was just a year younger than Marilyn and a year older than Lillian. Marilyn, at thirteen, was rather standoffish, but eleven-year-old Lillian, friendly as a puppy, developed an instant crush on twelve-year-old Gloria. She wanted to imitate everything about Gloria and was soon begging her mother for a pleated skirt with a large safety pin. Gloria's parents had bought her a kilt in Amherst so she could dress like Sue and her friends at Smith.

The Barneses were very poor. Originally from southern Indiana, Benjamin had a third-grade education, and Lucille had graduated from high school. Benjamin, a sailor on a lake freighter, was gone nine months of the year, though he came home for an occasional weekend when his ship was docked nearby. Lucille hoped to better herself by enrolling in cosmetology school. They had very little money, but the family was happy. The girls taught themselves to tap dance, and the four of them played music together—Lucille on the piano, Ben on the mandolin, Marilyn on the clarinet, and Lillian on a squeaky violin. They owned a car in which they went to church and out for Sunday rides, and they played euchre and entertained friends.

The Steinems came from another, altogether unimaginable world. One day during the summer they moved in, Gloria dragged a pair of jointed wooden hobbyhorses onto the sidewalk. The horses were only a couple of feet tall, but they had been used at the Ocean Beach resort by adults, who sat on them and bounced up and down to spur them forward in races on the pier (they had casters). As Gloria tried without much success to teach Marilyn and Lillian to ride them, suddenly Ruth appeared on the sidewalk in what looked to Lillian like a chiffon evening dress. Ignoring Marilyn and Lillian, she walked over to the horses and spoke matter-of-factly to Gloria. "If you're going to do it," she said, "you've got to do it right."

She hitched the front of her skirt into her waistband, folded the back between her legs and tucked it up in front like a diaper, sat down on the horse and proceeded to ride down the street like a contender in the Kentucky Derby. Then she turned the horse around and galloped back. Her ride complete, she dismounted regally, adjusted her skirt, announced, "*That's* the way it's done," and walked haughtily back up the stairs.

Although she clearly was eccentric, Ruth seemed sane to the Barneses. She might be so quiet they didn't hear her moving around for days, or she might come outside for a friendly chat. Lucille, who knew nothing of her history, assumed Leo had deserted them. She told her daughters Ruth probably couldn't adjust to life without Leo and the busy social life they had had. The girls also overheard their mother speculate to a friend that Leo must be a "chaser," though they had no idea what a chaser was.

In fact, Ruth had become so hallucinatory on "Dr. Howard's medicine" that Gloria had talked her into consulting a physician. They went to the only doctor Ruth remembered trusting sixteen years earlier, the doctor who had run the Toledo sanatorium where she had been treated. After talking with Ruth for twenty minutes, the doctor told Gloria that her mother did belong in a hospital, and he advised her to have Ruth committed immediately to the state hospital. However, Gloria, who had read exposés of state asylums in *Life* magazine, could not imagine sending her often timid, vulnerable mother to such a terrifying place.

At twelve, Gloria resigned herself to taking care of her mother, Although she was the youngest member of her family, Gloria did not ask any of her relatives for help. They all could see Ruth's condition for themselves, so Gloria had to assume the grown-ups thought her situation was appropriate.

The most obvious relative to call upon would have been her other parent. For all his faults, Leo had never been a traditionally distant father, and he had already spent years taking care of both Sue and Gloria. However, years later, Gloria tends to echo Leo's explanation for leaving them: Leo left Ruth because Ruth wanted him to, and he left Gloria with Ruth because, as he said, "How can I travel and take care of your mother? How can I make a living?"

That her father might have a responsibility to her was not something Gloria dwelt on consciously, then or later. Whether or not she truly believed he was incapable of taking care of her and her mother, she would later recall neither anger nor grief when he departed, only relief from the tension of her parents' endless fighting. Yet Leo didn't just relinquish custody of Gloria; he left Gloria to take care of Ruth. His departure not only left his daughter without a competent caretaker; it forced an eleven-year-old girl to take on the responsibility of caring for a mentally ill and frequently incompetent adult.

To this day, however, Gloria responds to questions about her feelings about her father's departure by insisting that she had no anger, no grief. She doesn't blame him. It wasn't abandonment. Why does everyone characterize it that way? She understood it perfectly. How could he work and take care of her, and an invalid and often crazy wife—especially a wife who had left him in the first place, and from whom he was divorced?

As if to prove he had little choice, she offers examples of both his caring and his incompetence. Leo visited them every year when he came through town, sent oranges from Florida, and bought his daughters extravagant gifts when he could (he sent Gloria a mouton coat when she was in high school). When he was away, he always sent Christmas and birthday gifts, but, she explains, they were "wrapped with great care and no skill: with lots of Scotch tape stuck in all the wrong places; it always touched my heart."

Despite her protestations that she didn't blame him, Gloria does seem to communicate those more unacceptable emotions like anger, hurt, and blame. She just does it indirectly, in a way that allows her to deny them, even to herself. "I did not blame him for leaving once I was old enough to be the bringer of meals and answerer of my mother's questions," she wrote in "Ruth's Song (Because She Could Not Sing It)," a 1983 essay describing her mother and their years together in Toledo. Nowhere in that essay, though, did she indicate that the separation was mutual, nor did she include that fact when she told her friends the story of her childhood. Both readers and listeners were left with the impression that Gloria's father abandoned her and her mother.

Part of his absence, as Gloria was astute enough to recognize, was based on the fact that, for all Ruth's problems, Leo was the weaker character in some ways. He talked proudly to others of Sue's and Gloria's accomplishments, but he sometimes hesitated to visit Gloria because he was unsure how Ruth would receive him. Sometimes Ruth wouldn't let him in.

Still, he tried. Although he usually was in California or on the road, he would show up unannounced once or twice a year to visit family and friends in Toledo or Clarklake, driving a huge, late-model car—often a Cadillac—out of which he appeared to be living. He was quite fat by then, and his cars always listed to the passenger side when they were unoccupied and leveled when he was inside. No one could figure out how he had rigged it, because the tires looked normal. Apparently it was another invention by "Leo Steinem, Originator," as some of his stationery read.

Leo lived in the west during the winter, dealing in antiques, supposedly keeping up with his entertainment contacts, and trying his luck as a talent agent. Visiting Clarklake, he once told the Burtons he was dating the singer Kay Starr, who had sung at Ocean Beach Pier. Jackie found it hard to imagine the tall, rotund Leo with the diminutive singer. After Sue had been in the diamond business for a while, Leo decided he, too, would go into the gem business. He did some research, bought a refractometer, and took a half-business, half-pleasure trip to Brazil where he thought he could find bargain gemstones.

He did not find gems lying in the street in Brazil, but Leo did get married. He met a German-Jewish woman, younger than he, who had been trying to emigrate to the United States for years, and he felt so sorry for her that he married her to get her into the country. Then they divorced. That is what he told his daughters, anyway. There may have been a little more to it, because Leo also told Gloria she need not worry about having more brothers or sisters because he had had a vasectomy.

Gloria never met the woman. According to Leo, after he discovered he would be financially responsible for her because she had entered the United States as his wife, she had returned to Latin America and then returned to the United States on a routine quota. In the 1960s the second Mrs. Steinem called Gloria several times in New York, announcing herself as "your stepmother" and inquiring of Leo's whereabouts. Leo asked Gloria not to disclose his address. Gloria was curious about the woman, but her "stepmother" never asked to meet her. In any case, Ruth would have considered Gloria's meeting her a betrayal.

After Leo, Gloria's next closest relative was her grandmother. When Ruth and Gloria first moved to Woodville Road, Marie occasionally came over and cleaned their apartment, but she and Ruth argued so much that, after a while, Marie stopped coming.

Ruth's sister Janey tried to help in her own way, buying some of Gloria's clothes, as she had Sue's. Janey is recalled by Sue and a cousin of Gloria's with great affection as "somewhat schoolteacherish" but "a lovely person." Gloria recalls her less sympathetically. By the time Ruth and Gloria returned to Toledo, Janey, who enjoyed bridge and a good martini, had taken her mother in to live with her and her husband, Bob Brand. The reason for Gloria's animus is obvious: "I think both my grandmother and my aunt really viewed my mother's illness as willful—'She is just willfully refusing to pull herself together.' And I think Janey was socially ashamed of my mother. And was rather alarmed when my mother turned up on Thanksgiving in her house. Sometimes she would send us a basket of food, but I think she didn't always want my mother to come. There were some class feelings there, too. I remember my Aunt Janey was always living a kind of voyeuristic life. She'd always read the social columns about people who lived in Grosse Pointe and read *Vogue,* even though she was just a high school English teacher and she didn't have that much money. But she aspired to that and she wanted me to aspire to that, too. So to have a crazy older sister living on the wrong side of town in a place with rats was not part of the plan."

Janey also fought with Ruth, who one day told her to "get the hell out" of her house and not come back. Janey called Gloria afterward and said, "Call me if you need me, but I'm not coming back."

Probably the one relative who did not disappoint Gloria was Sue. When she graduated from Smith in 1946, Sue, twenty-one, took a job with the supplier for Kay Associated jewelry stores. Based in Washington, D.C., she traveled around the country conducting educational programs on diamonds. The company had envisioned "a dignified advertising man around forty-five," she explained in a *Toledo Blade* article, "Just Out of School, Local Girl Is Diamond Expert," but they hired Sue instead, on the basis of her college geology courses and summer jobs with Georg Jensen jewelers in New York.

Sue telephoned Ruth and Gloria regularly and returned every Christmas. As her annual visit approached, Gloria would count the days. Gloria was very proud of her gemologist sister and, besides, Ruth seemed genuinely to improve during Sue's visits. As Ruth's condition continued to deteriorate, Janey called Sue, urging her to do something, but it was difficult to know what to do. Sue had Gloria visit her in Washington in the summer and even looked for places where the three of them could live. However, Ruth refused to move.

Leo's oldest brother, Ed, the Steinem family eccentric, provided the most useful assistance to Ruth and Gloria. The Barneses originally thought Ed was a ragpicker because he always appeared in the same greasy black pants and dirty black overalls, but Ed actually was an engineer. He had left his middle-class first wife and children, married a working-class woman, had three more children, and worked as a licensed electrician and handyman. Despite his eccentricities, he was known and respected by Toledo's Jewish community for his brilliance and his goodness. However, his mother had left his inheritance in trust when she died, because she had feared he would give it all away.

In the fall of 1946 Gloria entered seventh grade. There she met Carole Roberts, a tiny classmate who soon became her best friend. The first time Carole came to Gloria's house, Gloria led her through a sea of boxes and piles of clothes. "You'll have to excuse the way things are," she explained with dignity. "We've just moved."

Carole, who had lived in the same house since she was two, did not recall moving and had never visited anyone else who had, so she assumed the mess in Gloria's house was how houses looked when people had just moved. As the weeks grew to months, and the months to years, and nothing changed, Carole accepted the mess unquestioningly. No one else she knew lived with piles of papers, clothes, books, and even garbage everywhere, but on the other hand, she didn't know anyone else who had moved. So Carole, in the accepting way of children, figured this must be the way a house looked when people came to a new place.

When Gloria wasn't sleeping at Carole's, Carole slept at Gloria's. Gloria's dog scared her more than Ruth did, but she got used to both.

With Ruth, she never knew what would happen. Ruth might come in and offer Carole cookies, or she might not appear at all. Once, when Carole telephoned and asked if Gloria was home, Ruth said, "I don't know. I'll go look for her." Returning to the telephone, Ruth said, "Well, I've looked everywhere. I've looked in the oven. I've looked in the teapot. I've looked in her bedroom. And she's not here." Carole wasn't even surprised. That was the way Gloria's mother talked.

Gloria often felt "big and galumphing" next to the petite Carole, but they remained best friends all through school. They took dancing lessons together, and when they went to Cyd Charisse movies, they imagined themselves dancing on-screen. When Ballet Theater came to town they fantasized about running away to join the company. They had to abandon that idea when they realized they lacked the bus fare to get out of town.

For the most part Gloria loyally refrained from complaining about her mother, but Carole knew her secrets. She knew that whatever they ate at Gloria's—usually bologna sandwiches—would be prepared by Gloria. She knew the routine for washing dishes because sometimes she helped. Gloria waited until there were none left to use, and then, because there was no kitchen sink, the girls would carry them into the bathroom, dump them in the bathtub, wash them, and without bothering to rinse them, carry them back into the kitchen. Carole knew about the dog: that Ginger was rarely taken out but rather was let into the vestibule to defecate and then, after a week or so, Gloria or her mother would shovel the shit into a garbage can. Carole even endured the rats.

Ruth was the indirect cause of the rat invasion. The second year she and Gloria lived in the house, Ruth decided to convert the garage into an apartment and rent it to a veterinarian. However, when Ed examined the garage, he told Ruth it couldn't be converted because it lacked a foundation. Since the building was useless and the roof already had collapsed partially, Ruth decided to have it torn down completely.

The garage, which was demolished during the dead of winter, was full of trash and junk and debris from the lake. Unfortunately, it also was full of rats. When the rats found themselves homeless, they sought shelter elsewhere. Descending on the house like a biblical plague, they started in the basement and soon overran both apartments. Commonly called sewer rats, they were so large they killed three of the Barneses' kittens.

Gloria was bitten one night, and her mother summoned the courage to take her to the hospital. Another time the Barneses' Scottish terrier, Sandy Mac, the only resident who actually enjoyed the invasion, chased a rat into Lillian's lap. Finally Ben Barnes came home, sent the Barneses' pets to the neighbors', and spread rat poison all over the basement. A terrible stench invaded the entire house as the rats began to die. Some of them crawled upstairs; others littered the yard outside. Marilyn and Lillian came upon dead rats so often that they began a nightly ritual of checking for dead and dying rodents before they went to sleep.

Upstairs Gloria set rat traps, giant mousetraps that snapped shut on their victims with a resounding "pop." Thirteen-year-old Gloria had to throw the rats out herself. She also used cages. She recalls, "I think I put this out of my mind, but I believe it was from those little cages that I got the idea of having a cage myself. Because I so desperately wanted something safe to sleep in." Everyone in the house was terrified. Even fifty years later, both Lillian and Gloria shift uncomfortably as they recall the experience.

Loyally, Carole continued to spend the night with Gloria, though the two girls would huddle in the same bed for safety. Then, when they were sophomores, a meter reader who happened to be a friend of Carole's parents entered the apartment. Appalled by the filth and deterioration, he warned Ruth that if she didn't get the place cleaned up he would report her to the board of health. He immediately described the house to Carole's parents in such damning detail that they forbade Carole to stay there. Eventually the health department condemned the furnace in the basement and sealed it, so there was no heat. Gloria and her mother slept together at night for warmth. To keep the pipes from freezing, Uncle Ed sometimes broke the seal on the furnace and started it up illegally.

After Carole no longer spent the night, Gloria continued to stay at the Robertses' house, and nothing was said. By then Gloria had become an expert in denial. As she wrote later, "I was just passing through, a guest in the house; perhaps this wasn't my mother at all. . . . Certainly I didn't mourn the wasted life of this woman. . . . I worried only about the times when she got worse."

Gloria did something constructive, too. She sought outside her family what most people found within: security, identity, affection. She found immersing herself in activities allowed her to distance herself both physically and mentally from her mother's frightening unpredictability. As she often explains, "At home it felt dangerous. I felt safer outside."

Outside not only was a haven, it offered opportunity as well. Away from her family, Gloria could accomplish things, be someone, make herself "visible" in spite of what she regarded as her family's invisibility. Furthermore, Gloria found that making herself useful gave her a sense of belonging.

Denying what she couldn't handle and throwing herself into activities worked so well they became a way of life. Just as she avoided unbearable thoughts and feelings in her internal world, Gloria monitored her behavior in order to assure herself a place in the external world. "I've always relied on the kindness of strangers," she quotes *A Streetcar Named Desire* protagonist Blanche DuBois, half jokingly. However, seeking security in a world of strangers is no joke; it is a precarious undertaking. The outside world is not a family where one is assured a place, whatever one's shortcomings. The kindness of strangers has to be earned, and even when earned, it can never be taken for granted.

Watching for cues, Gloria made it her business to fit in, in order to deserve the affection and respect she sought. She had been controlling her reactions all her life anyway—trying not to upset Ruth, faking what she didn't know in school, muting responses she suspected might be too adult, and, once the teenage years arrived, trying to act feminine. Spontaneity was reserved for moments of high emotion and safety with friends. As time went on and Gloria's world expanded, self-presentation would become less about merely fitting in and being useful and more about projecting a public persona; her audience would grow from a community of friends to a world of strangers. Whatever her circumstances, her hunger for respect and affection would remain.

All that lay in the future. In Toledo Gloria was pretty, witty, smart, and well liked. When her mother embarrassed her, she remained impassive. When she felt trapped in Toledo and neglected by her family, she kept her resentment to herself. Although Gloria was only an adolescent, she maintained a calm, midwestern demeanor. That way no one could suspect the terrifying depth of her feelings.

4

Gloria Takes Control

At Carole's parties in junior high, Gloria learned to play Spin the Bottle. By high school, Carole, who always had a boyfriend herself, decided Gloria needed one too, so she chose a supermarket checkout clerk she knew. He had already graduated from high school, but since Gloria looked old for her age, he was only the first of many older boyfriends.

When they started at Waite High School in 1948, Gloria and Carole befriended three girls—Sue Bolander, Dixie Auxter, and Prudy Simonds—from another junior high. Dixie was dramatic, Prudy was extroverted, Sue was quiet, Gloria was humorous, and Carole was the peacemaker. They became so close that they decided to form a sorority. Although they later joined a high school literary society that was really a school-sanctioned sorority itself, the five wanted something more exclusive. Besides, sororities were illegal, and that was part of the appeal.

They named their sorority Chi Alpha Tau (CAT) and set up rules requiring members to have good grades and belong to clubs, which they all already did. They considered themselves an elite group and consciously excluded others. "We were snobs," Carole recalls. "I think we were terribly cruel to some people." Dixie says, "We were little shits."

Eventually their exclusivity provoked so much resentment that they decided to let in a few more members. They needed more members anyway, because by the time they were sophomores they had decided that when they were seniors, they wanted to rule the school. That meant Chi Alpha Tau had to include the president of all three literary societies, the president of the art club, the chairman of the senior prom, and the vice president of the National Honor Society (the president was always a boy).

Gloria liked being involved, though even school-based activities could be risky. When the Periclean Literary Society held mother-daughter events, Gloria conscientiously invited Ruth but hoped she wouldn't come. Often, Ruth did come, so each occasion was excruciating. Gloria never knew what Ruth would do. The other mothers dressed in Sunday clothes, white gloves, and pearls. Ruth might dress similarly—or she might wear an old housedress. Her hair might be combed, or it might not. Whatever Ruth did, Gloria remained impassive, treating her mother calmly and with respect.

Most of the time school and extracurricular activities provided genuine escape. In junior high Gloria had joined a Girl Scout troop run by the school's gruff but kindly art teacher, and she so basked in the teacher's attention that she remained active through her freshman year in high school. Throwing herself into scouting as she did everything else, Gloria earned as many merit badges as she could, from Hostess and Interior Design to Typography and Western Hemisphere.

Although money was tight, Janey bought clothes for her, and Gloria usually worked part-time. When her earnings were combined with the income from the Clarklake properties, she was able to afford a few extras. She began dancing lessons at a tap-dance studio, then switched to tap and ballet at the Daryl Jervis Dance Studios. After a few years she came to think of it as "faking ballet," so she switched again. She found a studio that taught genuine classical ballet, and by her junior year Gloria was dancing in junior concerts with the Toledo Orchestra.

When another high school offered students from all over the city the opportunity to work in a radio studio, Gloria did that, too, learning to cue records and talk from scripts. Eventually she used her record-cuing skill to get an after-school job at a local radio station.

She also joined a traveling troupe called the Christian Convalescent Entertainment Society, which put on shows at nursing homes, supermarket openings, and Elks Club meetings. The man who organized the troupe worked as a magician. In addition to dancing, Gloria sometimes worked as his assistant. She earned ten dollars for an evening's work—when the troupe was paid. Toward the end of the season the magician began holding back everyone's wages and eventually absconded with whatever was left in the till.

Many of her friends had after-school jobs, and in high school Gloria worked at David's, a clothing shop in downtown Toledo. For a year or two Carole worked there, too, after school on Mondays until it closed at night, and all day Saturdays.

The girls' primary allegiance was to their illegal sorority. They took turns as officers and kept careful minutes of the meetings, which were held at all the members' houses except Gloria's. They smoked forbidden cigarettes, tried on each others' clothes and discussed all kinds of weighty subjects, from the question of women in the military to bra sizes (which they duly recorded in the minutes).

At one meeting Gloria, whom they all considered more sophisticated, told them about cashmere—what it was and why it was desirable. She had learned about it as a salesgirl, and she was so convincing that, one Christmas, Dixie spent twenty-five dollars of the money she had saved from working as a thirty-five-cents-an-hour salesclerk and bought her sister a sweater "mostly because I wanted it and it wasn't really nice to spend that kind of money on yourself." Sue, who worked almost every afternoon in a law office, also used her earnings to buy herself a cashmere sweater set.

Gloria knew all kinds of things. Using what she had learned from her gemologist sister, Gloria taught her friends about carats, another subject with which they had little experience, and she instructed those interested in the finer points of theosophy. She and Dixie had what Dixie recalls as "arrogantly erudite" discussions about religion, and Gloria loaned Dixie—who until then only had been familiar with Lutheranism and Catholicism—books to supplement their talks. When Dixie questioned some of the concepts, she says, Gloria informed her loftily, "The reason you have doubts is because you're just not ready."

They all dressed alike—sweaters, skirts, bobby socks, and brown penny loafers. Gloria always fit in, and her clothes were a cut above what the rest of the girls had seen, because of the clothes Janey gave her. In addition, she bought sweaters with her earnings and learned to sew straight skirts. Dixie, whose mother sewed beautifully and made many of her clothes, remembers learning about the desirability of Pendleton skirts from Gloria.

Her friends all understood that Gloria came from a different background. They knew her sister had gone to Smith College, which no Waite High School graduate had ever attended, and various friends recall that her father was a photographer, in show business, and an antiques dealer (as he indeed was, at one time or another). When they later heard that Gloria went to Smith, they were not surprised.

They also knew there was something wrong with her mother. The consensus seemed to be that Mrs. Steinem was brilliant but in some way not well, and that Gloria had to take care of her. Most gave it little thought, and Gloria did not invite questions. The few who called Gloria at home and talked with Ruth soon understood that Mrs. Steinem must either have mental problems or be an addict of some sort, because a conversation with her could be quite bizarre. If, in Gloria's absence, someone in the sorority asked why they never met at her house, Carole would give them a look that would silence them. She was very protective.

Only Carole, who spent a lot of time at Gloria's house, and Prudy, in whom Gloria confided, could imagine how alienated Gloria sometimes must have felt. Gloria clowned around and went to the pajama parties like everyone else, but when she went home it was not to a parent but to a responsibility. Gloria talked to Prudy about the time her mother wouldn't let her go to school because the Nazis were after her, since her father was a Jew; or how, when her mother thought someone was coming after them, Gloria had hidden Ruth under the stairs, then walked around the block, come back, and told her that everything was all right. Such confidences were rare, and though Gloria later wrote of yelling impatiently at her mother, none of her friends ever heard her raise her voice.

If most of her friends were relatively oblivious to her situation, their mothers were not. All welcomed Gloria as often as she wanted to spend the night and tried to help by adding her clothes to their laundry when she was there. "Gloria has no one to wash her underwear for her," one mother commented. "Poor Gloria," Dixie's mother remarked occasionally, giving Dixie a little frisson. Dixie considered Gloria a peer, and a relatively sophisticated one, so she couldn't understand her mother's pity.

Despite her mother's unpredictability, Gloria once risked bringing a date home. After Gloria and Carole had been necking with their boyfriends on the couch, Ruth appeared. They had disgraced her, she repeated several times. Finally Gloria protested, "Mother, we haven't done anything to be ashamed of."

Ruth drew herself up and announced with mock seriousness, "Well, what you might be ashamed of is not what I might be ashamed of," and marched out of the room. She had waited to rebuke them until after the boys had left, though.

In the fall of her sophomore year Gloria started dating Ronnie Duncan, a boy who had graduated from high school. Although she was only fifteen, Gloria was tall, curvaceous, and looked older. Her friends described Ronnie as a "hunk." He seemed the ideal boyfriend, at six feet, one inch, 170 pounds, with black, curly hair and brown eyes. Gregarious and a terrific dancer, he had a good job in the Libbey-Owens-Ford factory, drove a new Ford convertible, and played semi-professional football. Unlike many of her friends and their boyfriends, Gloria and Ron never talked about getting married. Some of the better students expected to go to college, though nowhere as exalted as Smith. Gloria, one of the top students in the class, would have been in that category. Ron certainly thought of Gloria as "deep," but they never talked much about the future. They just had fun.

At one point Gloria bought him an identification bracelet. Ron was distressed. He calculated that it must have cost her about thirty dollars, and he knew how impoverished Gloria and her mother were. Gloria made light of it, joking to Ron's mother, "We always knew when we had money, because then we'd put milk into the tomato soup. When we didn't have money, we'd fill it with water."

The two or three times Ron went to her apartment he was appalled at its condition. Meeting Leo and Sue, and even some of Gloria's Toledo relatives, he became confused and then indignant at the contrast. "It was a goddam crime to leave her there—a child—alone with her mother," he believes. At the time he said nothing; he felt it wasn't his place.

Ron witnessed one of Gloria's earliest attempts to improve her life when he drove her to the tryouts for the *Ted Mack Amateur Hour,* a television program that showcased amateur performers on national television. In later years, Gloria would explain that, in her determination to make something of herself, her original idea was that she would "tap-dance my way out of Toledo." A Toledo hometown heroine and Waite graduate, singer Teresa Brewer, had gotten her start through an appearance on the *Ted Mack Amateur Hour,* so Gloria hoped to emulate her. Unfortunately, her tap dancing failed to win her a spot on the show.

She also entered the Miss Capehart TV Contest, a beauty and talent contest cosponsored by the local radio and television station, where Gloria worked cuing records, and the Capehart-Farnsworth Corporation, a manufacturer of televisions and radios. Contestants, who had to be eighteen and single, competed at the local level for the opportunity to go to the national contest in Florida. Gloria, who turned seventeen during the contest, performed a Spanish dance with castanets, an Oriental number with finger cymbals, and an ordinary tap dance. As runner-up Gloria received a rhinestone-and-ruby necklace and earrings set. The nineteen-year-old winner had gotten a divorce to make herself eligible.

Gloria recalls, "It was all very tacky, several levels below Miss America—which I never would have dreamed of entering—and the contest director was a fast-talking, funny guy from New York who scared us all. It wasn't a terrible experience, but it wasn't good either."

Ruth's mental state was erratic. She taught Gloria to love Dorothy Parker's poetry and even passed down a few motherly superstitions. She told Gloria to never eat anything with a meringue topping, because if the baker sneezed near it, it would absorb the germs, and for years Gloria didn't. During one of her better periods, Ruth and Gloria joined a theater group that performed biblical dramas. Ruth stood behind the scenes rattling a metal sheet to provide the thunder, while Gloria performed with the group. Gloria suspects they were invited mostly to black churches because the spectacle of a group of white people with tea towels on their heads, making fools of themselves, was too good to pass up.

Besides her performances, her jobs at David's and elsewhere, checking up on her mother, and school-related activities, Gloria had to squeeze in school itself. One of her favorite teachers was Miss Fawn Berger, who taught both Latin and French. Since Miss Berger had snowy white hair and had taught Ruth as well, Gloria assumed she was extremely old. She was also very pretty, and her fluttery, silly, absentminded charm reminded her students of the actress Billie Burke. They never knew what she would do next. She recited Latin verses and used only purple ink to write on their papers in a spidery script. She once sent Gloria to the lunchroom for a dish of vanilla ice cream just so she could pour purple ink over it and show the class how beautiful it looked.

No matter how much Gloria escaped, Ruth always awaited her at home. On her quiet bad days Ruth would lie on the couch and hallucinate. At other times she descended into her own world, muttering and talking about conspiracies. People at the lake had stolen their property. Where was that table? Who took it? To Gloria it seemed as if there were whole wars going on inside Ruth's head. It occurred to Gloria that if her mother had to live in an imaginary world, it might at least have been tolerable if it were a happy one. However, Ruth's world was fully of threats and persecution. Lying on the couch, she would writhe and feint, dodging imaginary terrors. Sometimes she would talk about how terrible Gloria's father was. When she was really angry at Gloria, she would tell her daughter she was just like Leo.

When Gloria left the apartment, she never knew what Ruth would do. One night Lucille Barnes looked up from her dressing table by the front window to see Ruth painting the window black. When she screamed, her husband came running and asked Ruth what she was doing. "I'm painting this window to cover up that brazen hussy," she told him. "She's parading around half-dressed." Lucille was fully clothed.

Another night Ruth threw a bowling ball down the stairs. Five minutes after Ben took it back upstairs the Barneses heard a terrible crash and ran back to the door. This time Ruth had thrown herself down the stairs. She wasn't hurt—she was just muttering for a while. By then the Barnes girls were terrified of her.

She terrified Gloria, too. Sometimes Ruth panicked about Gloria's whereabouts and called the police. Once Gloria arrived home from school and found Ruth's clothes all over the yard. Ruth had thrown them out the window. Another time Ruth ran out into the snow wearing only her nightgown.

Nighttimes could be difficult as well. Ruth might start banging on the piano in the middle of the night, and Gloria, when she was there, would have to get up and try to settle her mother down with her medicine. Lucille Barnes became so distressed that she had a heart attack in her early thirties.

Then the Barneses' Scottie dog, Sandy Mac, was poisoned.

As Lillian Barnes (Borton) recalls, she and her sister, Marilyn, found their Scottie dead in the yard. They took him to the veterinarian, who told them Sandy Mac had been poisoned with strychnine. Lucille and the girls were still crying when Ruth appeared. "Why are you digging a hole in my yard?" she demanded.

"Sandy Mac died," the girls tearfully informed her.

"Yes, strychnine has a way of doing that," Ruth said. "It has a way of killing them."

The girls gasped. No one but they, their mother, and the vet knew how Sandy Mac had died.

Gloria and Sue consider the idea that their mother would poison a dog impossible to believe. Gloria says her mother loved animals and would never have harmed a living thing. However, she may have claimed knowledge to frighten people she had come to think of as evil. The dog could have eaten rat poison.

As soon as they could, the Barnes family moved. Carole Roberts's older brother and his wife rented the apartment downstairs for a couple of months and then moved on. Another young couple stayed for a while, frightening Gloria and her mother, who could hear the husband beating the wife.

Gloria tried escaping into religion. One Christmas someone gave her a white leather Bible, and she began reading it regularly, while simultaneously thinking what a virtuous person she must be. Although she retained her interest in theosophy, she was searching for something more formal, and somehow she became attracted to a fundamentalist Presbyterian church on the other side of town. For about a year Gloria, thirteen or fourteen, rose early on Sunday morning and took two different streetcars to attend services. She liked the way members of the congregation would offer their talents to God, which might mean playing the saxophone or the accordion or singing.

Once she began attending the church, her interest was held by a long, lanky Bible school teacher, the owner of a chicken-feed factory. Gloria was fascinated by the enormous man, whose hands were so large they made the Bible look quite small when he held it. She remembers thinking at the time, "Religion can make men gentle," and continues, "That seems to be echoed in the experience of other women. I think that's part of the appeal of religion: that you feel that male violence or the male world is so much to deal with, that the only thing that can calm it or tame it is God and patriarchal religion and its rules. I think that was my intense experiencing of that."

That is her 1990s interpretation. The attraction may have been simpler. Gloria was not just a generic female, exposed to boys throwing rock-filled snowballs. She was virtually alone in the world, lacking not only a father or a mother, but any protector at all. It is hardly surprising that she sought relief from her anxieties in a loving group that had all the answers, led by a gentle man with big hands.

However nomadic her life had been before she and Ruth lived in Toledo, it had included an underpinning of stability. If the bill collector was often at the door in Clarklake, it was still the door to a house her family owned, on lakefront property, with a going business, and when times were good, luxuries like the horse, the sailboat, a tennis court next door, and a Smith education for her sister. They had not gone on the road in a trailer because they were too poor to do anything else. It was a useful way of economizing, but that was what Leo preferred.

When she moved to Toledo at the age of eleven, all that vanished. For the next six years Gloria and her mother lived in poverty and squalor, on the periphery of a community several rungs below their former circumstances. It seemed to Gloria that no one really cared. Certainly no one rescued them. She felt alone in the world, and she was. The girl who had fancied herself a plucky heroine à la Jo March was an existential woman by the age of seventeen. She was on her own, and if she wanted to make something of her life, she would have to do it herself.

For many years after they left Toledo, when Gloria would allow herself to think of those years at all, she would visualize them in black and white. Mostly, she blocked them out, or rather she blocked out the grief and anger. She told and retold the story of the little girl taking care of her crazy mother; she simply told it from a distance, as if it had happened to someone else.

It is the fairy-tale quality of the story that makes it so compelling, both to Gloria and to her audiences. Gloria told it repeatedly, both because she recognized a good story when she found it and because she understood that those terrible years in Toledo were the key to who she was. She was saying—no matter how much she distanced herself from the feelings it evoked—"Know me. This is what happened to me. This is who I am."

Her story resonated with her audiences because it adhered so closely to the archetypal narrative of fairy tales: innocent happiness, adversity, happiness with knowledge (childhood, adolescence, adulthood). In fairy tales, the mother often dies, thrusting the child out of an idyllic childhood and into a period of hardship and suffering, often imposed on her by an evil stepmother or wicked witch. Eventually the heroine overcomes or is rescued from her cruel fate and lives happily ever after.

Gloria's story was a perfect fit. Ruth, the good mother, "died" (mentally), and Gloria, the heroine, was imprisoned by the "bad" (sick) mother in a rat-filled house for many years. She was virtuous and did her duty, and eventually she was rescued.

Ironically, Gloria was rescued, not through her own hard work, but through a stroke of good luck. Gloria did not win a beauty contest or tap-dance her way out of Toledo. Ruth had tried to sell the lot behind her house for years. Then the church next door suddenly offered her $8,000 for both the lot and the house, in order to tear it down and build an annex to the church.

The family assembled in Toledo to decide what Ruth and Gloria should do. Sue wanted Leo to take Ruth for a year, while she would take Gloria to Washington, D.C., with her. Gloria could spend her senior year at the high school half a block from Sue's house and then go on to college. Gloria, who regarded herself as mature and independent, considered Sue a foolish dreamer. "He'll never do it," she argued. "They're divorced."

Sue was determined, so before Gloria went to her job at David's, they met for breakfast at the Purple Cow, a small restaurant with incongruously cheerful plaques on the wall bearing verses like "I never saw a purple cow, I never hope to see one . . ." Sue quickly made her pitch: Leo could take Ruth for a year and Gloria could have a year off, one year of freedom to have fun in high school.

"No," Leo said immediately. "We're divorced. And besides, I can't work if I'm taking care of her."

Sue tried to persuade him, and when he continued to resist, she stalked out of the restaurant. Gloria and Leo gazed at each other sadly. The question of what they were going to do was still unresolved, but Gloria had to get to work.

As they rode away in Leo's car, Gloria sat quietly, feeling neither surprised nor deeply distressed. It was as she had predicted to Sue. Her parents had been divorced for six years. He had married and divorced again. Ruth was not his responsibility.

Then as Gloria got out of the car, she began to cry. Leo was astonished, and so was Gloria. She never cried. Somewhere inside, she had allowed herself the beginnings of hope. Self-centered as he was, Leo was kind and sentimental, and he loved her. Stumblingly, he began a retreat. Okay. He would take Ruth. All right. All right, but only for a year, and at the end of that year the girls got her back. Okay. We're synchronizing our watches. One year.

That was that. Ruth would set aside the $8,000 to send Gloria to college, but in the meantime she would go with Leo to California. The fact that she would be traveling with a man not her husband did not bother her, because in between the times she disparaged Leo to Gloria, she insisted they weren't really divorced. Sometimes she said she didn't believe in divorce. Sometimes she said that she wasn't divorced because they had been married twice. Sometimes she said if you have children with a man, you can never really be divorced. Sometimes she said there had never been a divorce in the family. So though it might not be enjoyable, traveling with Leo would not be immoral.

Gloria and Sue packed up the house, packed up Gloria's things, and headed toward Georgetown. She left Toledo behind and, for many years, didn't look back.

5

Abloom in Georgetown

Carole promised to store Gloria's dance costumes until Gloria could send for them. She waited and waited, but word never came.

Like Dorothy leaving black-and-white Kansas for Technicolor Oz, Gloria entered another world. The nightmare was over. Suddenly Gloria was a carefree teenager. Or rather, she was thrust into the role of one, and at the age of seventeen and a half, it was a role she was delighted to fulfill.

She loved living with Sue, too. With a rented town house in Georgetown, an interesting job, compatible roommates, and men to go out with when she was in town, Sue, twenty-six, enjoyed her life. She traveled across the country, took correspondence courses to become a certified gemologist, and even had a local television show, *Gem Session*. A couple of years before Gloria arrived, she had been featured in *Glamour* magazine as "a ranking authority on precious stones" and had been photographed adorned in—and surrounded by—precious gems.

Bringing Gloria to Georgetown complicated her life, but Sue didn't hesitate. Aunt Janey, who had been more attuned to Gloria's situation than Gloria had realized, had reported back to Sue. Even though Sue's previous attempts to get them to move to Washington had failed, by Gloria's junior year Janey insisted that Ruth had become too much of a burden for a young girl, and that Sue had to do something. If Leo hadn't taken Ruth, Sue didn't know what they would have done.

Now she had another problem. Sue's two roommates, especially Ellen Stern, were not enthusiastic about her plan. A seventeen-year-old roommate, no matter how well behaved, was distinctly unwelcome. They were career women, and they did not want to have their activities constrained by a high schooler.

Fortunately, Sue had a bargaining chip. She had a chow chow named Ching that Ellen couldn't stand, so Virginia Rhine, the third roommate, acted as negotiator. Would Ellen let Gloria come live with them if Sue got rid of Ching? Slightly less grudgingly than Leo, Ellen assented.

So Ching left and Gloria arrived. Ching, or Prince Su Shou Lung, returned to his breeder, an admiral whom he so impressed with his lordly bearing that he was enlisted as mascot on the aircraft carrier *Valley Forge.* He served honorably for years, often attired in his specially designed uniform.

Replacing him, Gloria moved into 3408 Reservoir Road, a Georgetown bachelor-girl townhouse, where she shared a bedroom with Sue. Exhilarated at her escape, Gloria was still apprehensive about starting a new school. She was also well aware that Ellen and Ginny regarded her presence as a distinct comedown.

To cheer her up, Sue sometimes took Gloria to a nearby hotel that allowed nonresidents to swim in its pool for a dollar. Gloria began going on her own, and one day she accepted a date with a junior naval officer she met there. She brought him back to the house, and while she changed to go out, her date, who was about thirty, chatted with Ellen and Ginny and their friends, who had just gotten in from work. After that, the two treated her as a peer. Gloria understood the women's feelings, and she could never decide if she'd brought the officer back on purpose. Somehow the fact that she went out with a thirty-year-old man made all the difference.

Georgetown was the nicest place in which Gloria had lived. The population included very affluent people, young professionals, and both black and white families of much more modest means. Georgetown was older than the city of Washington itself. It originally was developed in the eighteenth century as a seaport that oceangoing ships could reach by sailing up the Potomac.

Years later, to the considerable embarrassment of relatives and the annoyance of friends from her first seventeen years, Gloria would tell interviewers that Washington was where she first had learned that people ate regular meals at a table rather than standing in front of the refrigerator. Sometimes she would attribute that revelation to Smith

College rather than Washington. By that time she had moved into increasingly exalted circles and had learned to ingratiate herself quickly by making herself interesting.

By now Gloria was an expert in starting over. Western High School was her sixth school and fifth school community. It was also several levels above anything she had experienced. The only high school in Georgetown, Western was so well regarded academically that it attracted tuition-paying students from the nearby suburbs. Many of the wealthier Georgetown students went to boarding schools or private day schools, but the rest attended Western. There were also diplomats' and Congressmembers' children, some of whom arrived in limousines; military brats, including a fair number of generals' and admirals' offspring; and some students whose families were too poor to send them to college. Most of the students expected to attend college, though their diverse financial circumstances would influence their choices. With the exception of a few Asian students, the diversity did not extend to race. In 1951 Washington schools were still segregated. Waite High School, in Toledo, had been integrated, and it took Gloria a day to figure out what seemed odd—that there were no black students at Western.

Although Washington, D.C., was quite southern in atmosphere, Western was more sophisticated than the typical southern high school, partly because of the army youngsters and diplomats' children. After living all over the world, they tended to take the usual high school obsessions like football less seriously. Many of the students came from relatively privileged backgrounds, but the transiency of the District of Columbia population in general accustomed Western students to frequent newcomers. As a result Gloria found herself in a high school that was unusually welcoming to new students.

Even so, she made an astonishing impact in one year. As they were at Waite, sororities and fraternities were illegal at Western, but they were tolerated by the faculty. It was unusual to rush a senior girl, but the socially powerful Western girls were so captivated by Gloria's appearance, wit, and air of authority that all the best sororities vied for her. Within the hierarchy of good, better, best (discrimination being the point) Zeta Beta Psi was considered the best, and Gloria became a Zeta.

Part of Zeta's appeal to Gloria was probably the membership of Mellicent Rupp. Mellicent herself had only been at Western a year, but she was already the star of the class. Gloria thought Mellicent's military parents were unusually strict, but their regulations did not prevent Mellicent from becoming president of practically every organization she joined and the queen of many of the balls. She was beautiful, kind, fun to be with, and brilliant, winning a third place in the National Science Fair and graduating as valedictorian in a senior class that did not lack good students.

Beside benefiting from the label, a Zeta could hang out with the Zetas in the mornings, eat lunch at the Zeta table when she wished, and attend the regular Friday night meetings. Before she actually became a Zeta, Gloria and the other pledges had to endure Hell Week, which included various forms of high school hazing. She had endured it in her literary society at Waite, but Gloria found herself a little frightened and somewhat resentful. Watching her, at least one of her sorority sisters, Cornelia Stewart, sympathized. As the only senior pledge, and one who was older (seventeen and a half) than most of the seniors, Gloria seemed to Cornelia quite womanly in contrast to the other girls. Cornelia thought making Gloria wear a burlap bag and participate in silly rituals seemed demeaning to someone who seemed so mature.

Soon Gloria, too, was attending semiformal dances complete with high heels, taffeta dresses, and corsages; going on hayrides and to pool parties; wading in public fountains at the risk of getting arrested; staying up at slumber parties; and talking about how to keep up the sorority image. With the unerring antennae of youth, Gloria and her friends realized that twenty-six-year-old Sue, who was conscientiously attending PTA meetings and trying to function as a sensible caretaker, would be a perfect slumber party chaperone. The girls immersed themselves and the entire kitchen in a whipped-cream fight before Sue understood that she had lost control.

To her schoolmates, Gloria seemed older and more self-possessed, and the fact that she lived with her sister instead of her parents added to the aura. A sophomore from down the street, Cyanne Hanson, who became one of the earliest of the devotees Gloria always managed to attract, recalls her "commanding presence."

Cyanne comments, "Gloria had a social conscience before there was a word for it. She would talk about issues like poverty and race when the rest of us were talking about boys and college. I remember thinking, These are such big problems. Why does she even bother to think about them? She would look at problems and think about how they could be remedied. Early on, I learned to watch my p's and q's with Gloria, because she had such an incisive mind. Gloria wasn't a person I'd have chattered on with."

What Gloria noticed about Cyanne was that she, too, wasn't living with her parents; she lived in a small apartment with her aunt and also seemed to feel like an outsider. Lack of family and outsider status were things Gloria always noticed.

Gloria wore harlequin glasses, like her sister's, and seemed unusually poised. Her figure was stylishly curvaceous, her nails were elegantly long even then. Gloria's voice was lower than most girls'—one classmate recalls that most of the girls sounded like "chirpy birds." Her clothes were as nice as anyone else's, and she talked about going to Smith College, which was beyond many students' financial ability. As a result, they all assumed she came from a privileged family, and Gloria said nothing to indicate otherwise. Several schoolmates thought her parents were in the foreign service.

The maturity her classmates sensed in Gloria was hard-earned, but it wasn't just because she had been taking care of her mother for the past six years. She also had shared the briefer adolescence of her blue-collar Toledo classmates. Because most of her Waite classmates would be marrying or going to work in factories or offices after graduation, they were moving toward an adulthood that began at eighteen. That gave them a different perspective from that of teenagers preparing for at least four more years of school, usually courtesy of their parents.

Gloria had been on her own for so long that she took her self-sufficiency for granted. However, no matter how confident she appeared on the outside, Gloria was a jumble of inner contradictions. She had confidence in her street smarts, but at the same time she feared exposing the countless gaps in her knowledge, both social and academic. She also thought she had never seen so many happy, carefree people in her life. Released from the burden of caring for her mother, she longed to be one of them.

She was celebrating her freedom, and her joy enlivened her. As one of her friends recalls, "It was no small thing to walk into Western and do what she did. There was plenty of competition from people who did and have continued to do well. But it didn't make her hide behind a door. She was right out there."

Although there was nothing she needed to escape, Gloria threw herself into activities as a way of belonging. By the end of March, Gloria had been elected vice president of the student council, vice president of the senior class (only boys could be president and treasurer, and only girls could be vice president and secretary), secretary of the French club, and representative to the school yearbook. She also joined the archery club and Y-Teens. When the students replaced the faculty members on Student Day, Gloria was chosen to stand in for the assistant principal. Many of the organizations elected queens and princesses for their balls, and Gloria usually was one of them.

The student body voted her one of ten candidates for the Miss Western competition sponsored by the school newspaper, the *Western Breeze,* whose contestants were selected on the basis of "personality, popularity, and pulchritude."

The *Breeze* wrote that Gloria had "an engaging grin, a sparkling wit, and a genius for getting things done." In a *Breeze* interview—the first of the thousands she would give—she told the reporter that she had traveled extensively and had entered school for the first time in sixth grade, having been tutored previously by her mother, a former teacher.

During her senior year, Gloria seemed to realize that she could go beyond concealing unpleasantness from her audiences to make herself acceptable; she also could use her background proactively to make an impression. By selective use of facts and a little dramatizing, she could turn some of the negative experiences and embarrassing conditions of her life into assets. She had indeed been tutored by her mother, but she had also gone to school before sixth grade. To friends who commiserated that she must be sad that her parents were away, she tried to assume a properly sorrowful expression as she agreed that she was; actually, she was ecstatic at her freedom, but she never would have betrayed her parents by saying so.

Western was filled with pretty girls, but Gloria started going steady with the boy who was considered the school heartthrob, Ernie Ruffner. Like her Waite boyfriend Ron Duncan, Ernie was tall, dark, and handsome. The son of a general, Ernie was also one of the more worldly members of the class. As one of their classmates recalls, "I'm sure a lot of the boys wanted to go out with Gloria, but they were too intimidated. Ernie was more mature because he was an army brat."

Ernie wasn't intimated, but he remembers Gloria as a force. "People were in awe of her—she was a thinker and expressed herself well. She was serious but still had a sense of humor. I remember she had strong beliefs and feelings and was very strong-willed. She was very respected. She fit in with those of us who thought of ourselves as sophisticated."

Gloria wasn't one of the top students, but she sought and won many of the school offices they often filled. She even ran against Ernie for second-semester student council vice president—on a ticket with

Mellicent as president—and defeated him, though Ernie was very well liked and had been around for three years. Her victory did not dampen their relationship, nor did cochairing a drama club event. "Gloria had very strong opinions," Ernie recalls, "and we couldn't agree on things. So we split the decisions down the middle."

Naturally Gloria was interested in Ernie's parents. As she says, "With all my boyfriends, I was always looking for a family." Both Major General Ruffner and Mrs. Ruffner, who was the daughter of a general herself, were kind, but Gloria was completely intimidated. She watched her forks and spoons as carefully as her conversation when she ate at their house and recalls feeling embarrassed because she didn't know the difference between a lobster and a crab.

She also was learning about both the possibilities and the limitations of social mobility. When Ernie, who wanted to attend West Point and become a career officer, talked about army life, he once mentioned (or joked) that a career officer needed to marry a woman with money. The army provided everything else—social rank, servants—all kinds of perquisites, except money. So you had to marry it, he said. Gloria, who possessed far less of that particular commodity than Ernie could imagine, felt as if he'd driven a stake into her seventeen-year-old heart.

In later life Gloria would tell reporters that Smith College took a chance on her based on her strong English Scholastic Aptitude Test scores and her "legacy" status through Sue, even though her high school grades were poor because of her lack of formal education. That explanation gives too much credit to Smith and one SAT score, and too little to Gloria's determination and hard work.

She did have academic gaps, especially in math, but at Waite she had managed to compensate enough to receive academic recognition every year and election to the National Honor Society as a junior. When she left Waite she had enough credits to graduate but not enough to enter a college like Smith. At Western she enrolled in a college preparatory schedule so rigorous it included physics, a subject taken only by Western's top students and one that seems almost unimaginable for such a mathematically deprived student. She passed, but only with the help of Mellicent and three students who shared her work table. Gloria, again with only the school's most serious students, even entered an exhibit in the National Science Fair, though she also remembers that as a group effort.

The gaps were apparent in her lopsided College Board scores. Gloria managed a 640 out of 800 on her verbal SAT and a 675 on her English achievement test. She scored 443 on her French achievement test, and her social studies achievement score of 494 and mathematics SAT of 484 were only slightly higher. Considering the fact that 500 was the average and that achievement tests measured what students retained from what they had been taught, her scores were far better than might be expected from a student who essentially skipped most of the first four grades, never sat through times tables or learned other basic concepts in elementary school arithmetic, never colored maps or learned geography in any systematic way. They were even more admirable triumphs of compensation at the time when she took the tests; the pool of students taking Scholastic Aptitude Tests in 1951–52 was a narrower, more privileged stratum than in later years, and many benefited from taking them twice.

Both the guidance counselor, Miss Marion Magruder, and the vice principal, Miss Irene Rice, took an interest in Gloria. After consulting with Sue, Gloria applied to Stanford, Cornell, and Smith, but by the time she met with Miss Magruder she had decided that Smith was where she most wanted to go. The counselor evaluated Gloria's situation sympathetically but honestly. Gloria's grades at Western were not high, and her College Board scores were weak. The fact that no one had ever gone to Smith from Waite was a problem, too—though Gloria had excellent grades from Waite, Smith had no way of evaluating them. On the other hand, Smith strove for some geographic and economic diversity, so coming from an unknown, working-class high school could be seen as a positive. Miss Magruder knew her recommendation would count for a great deal with Smith. "So if you're really sure you want to go to Smith and you promise to work really hard," the counselor explained, she would do her best to get Gloria in. She and Miss Rice combined their efforts, and Smith admitted Gloria, who excitedly told people she planned to major in political science.

As the year wound to an end, Gloria continued to stand out. She won a part in the spring play, *Stardust*. Their senior class chose Gloria as Prettiest Girl and Ernie as Most Handsome Boy. As class vice president she was one of the leaders in planning the class's end-of-the-year activities. She and Bob Barash, the Drama Club's colorful president, cochaired the graduating seniors' class night committee and awarded themselves leading parts in the evening's program, which they based on the theme of a trip to Mars. The two liked to leave school and repair to the nearby Peacock restaurant for planning sessions, where

Bob impressed the suppposedly sophisticated Gloria by washing down his lunch with a couple of martinis.

At last, on June 12, 1952, the class graduated. Only the class president's name appeared as many times on the program as Gloria's, as she was both a class officer and class night committee member. Diplomas were handed out by Albert Steinem, a member of the District of Columbia Board of Education and a second or third cousin of Leo. Gloria had never met him, but her relative's prominence added to her aura of privilege, and Ruth and Leo, still in California, were not there to dispel the illusion.

The caption beside Gloria's yearbook photograph summed up the Gloria her classmates knew: " 'Glo' . . . hit Western with a bang . . . gal of many talents . . . smart and stylish . . . humorous and alluring . . . enjoys dancing and cooking . . . a sure success at Smith . . ."

6

Miss Steinem Goes to Smith

During the summer of 1952 Gloria's confidence began to ebb. Volunteering in Adlai Stevenson's presidential campaign that summer, she met a couple of Smith freshmen who so intimidated her that she began to worry that she wouldn't fit in. Sue tried to reassure her, though her innate honesty somewhat undermined her attempt. Sue had had a classmate whose father was a junk dealer, but, yes, there also had been a girl in her class whose kitchen was so large she had learned to roller-skate in it. At least she omitted her freshman roommate's comment—that she was relieved to meet Sue because, "with a name like Steinem we were afraid you might be a Jew."

Gloria also worried about leaving her mother. Soon after graduation, Leo had arrived with Ruth, returning her to her daughters like an overdue library book. Sue had rented a house for the three of them and changed jobs so she could stay in Washington instead of traveling. Even so, Gloria feared Sue would not be able to manage both Ruth and her job. Although Sue was nine years older, Gloria considered herself more competent in dealing with Ruth, whose worst spells Sue had not witnessed, and who was not doing well.

Even Gloria's departure was fraught with tension. Sue and Gloria missed the train to Northampton, Massachusetts, and when they returned to the apartment to wait for the next one, they found Ruth practically unconscious after having taken a huge dose of Dr. Howard's medicine. Both were upset, Sue because she wasn't used to seeing Ruth in such a state, and Gloria because it confirmed her worries about leaving her mother. Still determined to get Gloria to Smith on time, Sue and Gloria left later that day and checked on their mother as often as they could en route, by telephone.

At Smith, Sue checked Gloria into her old dormitory, Laura Scales, bought her bedspread and curtains, and tried to leave her in a confident state. The freshman handbook had informed incoming students of a formidable array of rules and suggestions. Bermuda shorts were standard attire—"two inches above the knee is the upper limit"; blue jeans, plaid shirts, and knee-length socks were popular, according to the handbook, though "skirts and sweaters are usually worn for dinner." An August issue of the school newspaper added cheerful suggestions "intended to tell you how to dress and look like a typical Smithie." "Wardrobe Includes Jeans to Cashmeres" advised incoming freshmen to bring a polo coat for those cold football games and "at least half a dozen of [your father's] shirts—monogrammed, button-downs, or even those with frayed collars-and-cuffs."

Gloria took part in a ritual common to students at many of the Ivy League and Seven Sisters schools during the forties, fifties, and sixties. Like other future leaders of America, including George Bush, Jane Fonda, and Hillary Rodham, she posed nude for several of the infamous "posture photos," photographs actually used for a secret anthropological research project that wasn't phased out until years later.

Opened in 1875, Smith College sat in the middle of Northampton (population 25,000), next to the town library and town hall. The buildings were scattered across the tree-filled campus in a hodgepodge of styles: Victorian brick Gothic, neoclassical clapboard, red-brick modern, wooden cottages. Down the street was a quadrangle of Federal-style dormitories, including Laura Scales. The overall effect was idiosyncratic and charming. Most of the thirty-five houses, as the dormitories were called, housed fifty to seventy students representing all four classes. Most of the 2,100 students lived in the same house all four years.

Gloria loved it from the start. She loved the beauty of New England as well as the serenity and stimulation of academic life. She loved curling up in a big chair in the library. She loved the library's open stacks with 381,390 volumes, which meant research often turned into pleasurable browsing. She luxuriated in the privilege of eating three meals a day prepared by someone else. She treasured the camaraderie of friends and sometimes danced up and down the halls for the sheer joy of it.

Smith took her farther up the social ladder. At the time, the so-called Seven Sisters—Wellesley, Barnard, Vassar, Mount Holyoke, Radcliffe, Smith, and Bryn Mawr—were the most prestigious women's colleges in the country, the counterparts of the all-male Ivy League schools. A Seven Sisters graduate was presumed to be bright, probably affluent, and frequently well connected. Not all the students were wealthy, but most were at least comfortably well off. Many had attended boarding schools, and some brought their own horses.

If it did nothing else, a Seven Sisters school conferred the aura of eastern Establishment, female version, upon its graduates. Although the colleges naturally expected to provide more than just a label, they were conflicted about their goals, and always had been. When they were founded, the women's colleges had been revolutionary in their attempt to educate women the way men were being educated, but both their nineteenth-century creators and their twentieth-century administrators understood the conflicts an education could create.

They wanted to turn out educated women who would utilize their educations. At the same time they wanted their graduates to be exemplars of "womanhood"—loving wives and mothers—not the defeminized, bluestocking spinsters so despised by society. However, the intellectual assertiveness prized in students sometimes endangered the development of that sweet passivity so desirable in wives, so it probably was no accident that Bryn Mawr's first president was frequently misquoted with such hostility. "Only our failures marry," she is said to have sniffed, when what she actually said was "Our failures only marry."

The semiweekly Smith newspaper, the *Sophian,* reflected those concerns. In the fall of 1952, Gloria's freshman year, the editors ran an editorial supporting single-sex education, stating

> We've heard too often the platitudes that "it is a man's world," that women should not be "ivory-towered" into an unnatural environment for four years. It is, however, this "unnatural environment" which develops the mental resources of women. We cannot sit back, let the men monopolize class discussions and run campus organizations. The woman's college alone compels the female student to realize her potentialities.

Evidently, even in that sheltered, "unnatural environment," the Smith students seemed to need encouraging, as the *Sophian* also ran pieces urging the students to overcome their fear of speaking up, particularly when outside speakers appeared. "Don't students ask questions?"

James Reston inquired at the end of a speech, when no one had dared. One editorial even suggested that the group inviting a speaker should plant a couple of its members in the audience to ask prepared questions afterward, to break the ice.

Gloria later wrote, "My college years were full of uncertainties and the personal conservatism that comes from trying to win approval and fit into the proper grown-up and womanly role, whether that means finding a well-to-do man to be supported by or a male radical to support." After she became a feminist, she would disparage Smith for not preparing its students for the world, saying she hadn't learned a thing there. At the time she loved the atmosphere and the customs like chapel, the weekly meeting. The college president or dean officiated, speakers sometimes were presented, and announcements were made to the entire student body, many of them still wearing their pajamas under their coats.

As a freshman Gloria took English, theater, government, French, geology, and gym. She found French "a total trauma" and geology "almost as much of one." The courses were far too advanced for her, and she managed only D's in French and C's in geology. Aside from the grade, geology turned out to be one of her most valuable courses, though not in the way Smith intended. As she explained at Smith's 1995 commencement, her geology field trip provided Gloria with what she calls her first political lesson.

"I took geology because I thought it was the least scientific of the sciences. On a field trip, while everyone else was off looking at the cutoff meander curves of the Connecticut River, I was paying no attention whatsoever. Instead, I had found a giant, GIANT turtle that had climbed out of the river, crawled up a dirt road, and was in the mud on the embankment of another road, seemingly about to crawl up on it and get squashed by a car. So, being a good codependent with the world, I tugged and pushed and pulled until I managed to carry this huge, heavy, angry snapping turtle off the embankment and down the road.

"I was just putting it back into the river when my geology professor arrived and said, 'You know, that turtle probably spent a month crawling up to that dirt road to lay its eggs in the mud by the side of the road, and you just put it back in the river.' Well, I felt terrible. But in later years, I realized that this was the most important political lesson I learned, one that cautioned me about the authoritarian impulse of both left and right. Always ask the turtle."

By her sophomore year Gloria found her academic footing, and she made the dean's list for the rest of her time at Smith. There was only one course she couldn't master. More difficult even than French was physical education. Two years of P.E. were required. Despite her stamina, natural grace, and years of dancing, there was not one sport in which Gloria performed adequately. Her gym teachers sent her from tennis to golf, but to no avail. Her only athletic feat of competency was passing junior lifesaving, which proved quite useful, for she worked as a lifeguard for two college summers in Washington.

During her freshman year, government was the only class in which Gloria felt confident. She was pleased to discover that she could read philosophers such as Plato and Aristotle and understand them completely. Gloria's classmates found her very bright—also fascinating and rather exotic. She had an hourglass figure and long legs, arms, fingers, and toes. She maintained her long fingernails carefully and told her friends they were good protection (presumably for fending off overly amorous dates). She moved like a dancer. She wore eye makeup when most Smith students didn't (a holdover from Toledo) and taught classmates how to extend their eyes at the edges. She had interesting costume jewelry. She told them her father had not been allowed by her mother to swear and so had named their dog Dammit. She displayed prominently a photograph of her gemologist sister surrounded by gems. She told cosmeticized and funny stories of Toledo.

Gloria could be relied upon for late-night conversation. She was a good listener, and because she liked to solve other people's problems, she was always holding court in her room. Her friends liked word games, and if someone threw out a word, within minutes Gloria could concoct a one-act play. From the beginning she befriended professors and met them for tea or dinner.

Even her study habits were intriguing. She was nocturnal and a persistent procrastinator. Most students spent weeks conscientiously taking notes for their research papers, but Gloria would work furiously at the last minute, spreading her books all over the floor and writing the paper in a night or two, directly out of the books—and obtaining high marks. Although she would later tell some people that no one ever encouraged her to write at Smith, a writing instructor told her during her sophomore year that she wrote so easily and so well, she should do something about it. "What do you mean 'easily'?" Gloria complained, and was both gratified and chagrined by his response. "If you're so paranoid that you notice the word 'easily' and not the word 'well,' that just shows you're a real writer," he told her.

By the time the students had lived together for three or four years, each class in each house was like a family. Having 10:15 P.M. curfews, they were in the dorm much of the time, and most days they ate all three meals together, walking the several blocks even for lunch. At night they took shifts on telephone duty, dusting in preparation for weekly inspection, and setting or clearing the tables where they ate family-style. On Sundays there was breakfast upstairs in the morning and a "gracious living" tea in the afternoon, with coffee served from a samovar. They coped with the honor code that required them to turn in anyone they saw cheating by keeping their eyes down during exams so they couldn't see one another. Gloria's freshman-year housemother was so easygoing that her only rule was, if you go to visit someone at Yale in New Haven, do not stay at the Taft Hotel.

They went to movies like *Picnic* and *Sabrina* together, played bridge, and knitted constantly. As it had been at Western, knitting argyle socks was a fad, particularly because it showed one had a boyfriend to knit for. The mania even extended to the classroom, where some students knitted during lectures. One government professor found the habit so irritating he yelled, "Why don't you talk? You people are so silent! And stop doing all that silly needlepoint!" Gloria was an experienced knitter who taught friends in both high school and college to knit.

Gloria's class in her dormitory, who eventually named themselves the Twelve Foolish Virgins, spanned the usual Smith range, with backgrounds varying from affluent boarding school to middle-class public schools. A few, like Gloria, had families who had scraped and scrimped to send them to Smith. In her freshman year Gloria became especially friendly with Phyllis Fewster, who came from a religious Baptist family in Rochester, New York, and was very intimidated by Smith, and Nancy Howard, who belonged to a relatively affluent Jewish family in the suburbs of New York City and left after her freshman year to get married.

Four of them, including Gloria, formed the Back Rub Club to give each other backrubs—Jane MacKenzie, a boarding-school graduate whose father had invented Janie's Spot Cleaner; Patsy Goodwin, a wonderful writer whose grandfather had invented the Check Protectograph, an automatic check-writer; and Judy Wheeler, who was bright and witty. Gloria's unremitting cheerfulness once drove Judy to drag her by the leg down the hall, exhorting, "Why don't you ever get angry? Get angry! Get angry!"

For the less privileged, the atmosphere could be oppressive. One of their housemates was always flinging her polo coat on the floor, exposing the lining made from her mother's old mink coat. Older students teased Phyllis about her Rochester accent and even satirized the way she talked in a Christmas play. During their sophomore year, Cornelia Stewart, a younger friend of Gloria's from Western, came to Smith, and though Gloria and her friends were kind to her, Cornelia found many of the students patronizing and intimidating. She felt more comfortable visiting her cousin, a minister's daughter who lived in Lawrence House, a separate scholarship students' dorm where students did all the housework in exchange for lower fees. When one of the older Laura Scales students asked, "What are you trying to do, wear out all your old clothes?" she so unnerved Cornelia—who had brought the nicest clothes she had—that she fled Smith after one semester.

As in Toledo and Washington, Gloria had diverse friends while at Smith. Her father always said never work for just one boss, and she followed the spirit of his advice, maintaining a wide circle of connections with teachers and students from other schools, as well as with different groups at Smith. She didn't want to miss anything.

Gloria watched her schoolmates carefully, always trying to understand and get it right, but she also was conflicted. She conformed up to a point and then no further. She always looked a little different, and she preferred it that way: a little more makeup, and jeans instead of Bermuda shorts. She thought her legs looked fat in Bermuda shorts, and besides, she thought the shorts were ugly. Even so, her Smith friends took up a collection and bought her a pair.

Gloria wanted to fit in and she had dreams. She seemed drawn to money, self-assurance, and knowledge, though she was put off by arrogance. She was pleased to be able to teach her friend Nancy Howard to iron, but she also enjoyed the idea of exchanging ironing lessons for help in French from someone who had learned from a French nanny. Afraid to take a music appreciation course because the other students seemed so knowledgeable, she subscribed to a record-of-the-month club to try for a quick classical music education.

Gloria had a kind of code. As she phrased it to herself, she didn't want to be like the wives of the factory owners. In reality, some of the students at Smith had surpassed the wives of the Toledo factory owners long ago, but this was the conflict she calls her "class problem." She seems to have bargained with herself to maintain a sort of class loyalty: She could rise in the world, but Toledo still would be in her heart—

which didn't necessarily mean her Toledo-ness had to show, or even
that she had to love it. She just wanted to stay loyal.

The atmosphere at Smith changed dramatically when men appeared
on weekends. As freshmen, Gloria and Phyllis went to their Saturday
morning government class wearing jeans over their pajamas, with their
hair in curlers, though they were embarrassed when their classmate
brought her boyfriend, Adlai Stevenson III (son of the presidential candidate and eventually a senator himself), to the class. Gloria went out
with a number of men during her freshman year, but she also continued
to date Ernie Ruffner. His parents took her with them to West Point for
Plebe Christmas, a celebration that lasted about a week.

However politically passive the 1950s are reputed to have been,
many students were involved and aware. Senator Joseph McCarthy
began proclaiming in February 1950 that the State Department was
riddled with Communists, and McCarthyism reached Smith's campus in
the fall of Gloria's freshman year. In September 1952, a former Communist Party member testified before the Senate that there were more
than 1,500 card-carrying Communists in American colleges, and she
included Smith with Harvard, Columbia, Vassar, and Wellesley in her
list of schools having three or more Communist staff members.

In February 1953, the National Student Association (NSA) held a
regional conference at Smith, and Allard Lowenstein, the NSA's former
president, a recent chairman of Students for Stevenson, and an avowed
anti-Communist, asserted that the present investigations were "worse
dragons than the evils they are trying to cure." Opposing Lowenstein
and speaking in support of loyalty oaths was Brent Bozell, brother-in-
law of William Buckley, who believed Communists and their sympathizers should not be free to teach at colleges.

Also that month, the Smith faculty assembled a joint committee with
Smith's board of trustees to answer McCarthy's attacks against educators and scholars. Their response evidently inflamed other members of
the Buckley family, because a year later, in February 1954, on stationery headed "Committee for Discrimination in Giving, Hartford,
Connecticut," Mrs. Aloise Buckley Heath, class of 1941, sent a letter to
3,200 Smith alumnae, accusing five faculty members by name and several others left unnamed of belonging to Communist or Communist-
front organizations. Alarmed that "young minds" might be influenced
in "a direction contrary to the philosophical principles in which most
of us believe," the committee, whose other members remained anonymous (if they existed at all—no others ever identified themselves by

name), urged the alumnae to stop contributing to Smith until the administration explained its education policy to their satisfaction.

Smith's president, Benjamin F. Wright, a constitutional scholar, was furious, as were many of the students. The news media picked up the story, and in a heartening gesture, many donors doubled their usual contributions. Of the first six hundred responses to the letter, only two were interested in further information, and the rest were incensed. The episode was a firsthand lesson for the students, who were stunned to see such esteemed professors as visiting professor of government Vera Micheles Dean and Melville scholar Newton Arvin cited by name by accusers too cowardly to use their own. President Wright read the letter in Chapel and discussed the damage that could be wrought by character assassination and false accusations. There was some dissent within the Smith community—most conspicuously from senior Maureen Buckley.

Gloria was as angry as everyone else, and attempted one small strike against McCarthyism. She was standing by the elevator of the House office building, in Washington, D.C., where she had gone to do research for a school project, when Senator McCarthy approached the group. As he began to shake hands with everyone within reach, Gloria turned her back and refused to shake hands. McCarthy didn't notice the slight, but she was pleased she had done it. Later she would credit McCarthy's inquisition for her growing interest in Marxism.

A memorable figure at Smith in the 1950s was the poet Sylvia Plath, one of the most admired students on campus during Gloria's freshman year. She was a brilliant, beautiful, well-liked junior, an honors English major who not only had won elections and academic prizes at Smith, but also had published short stories in *Seventeen* and *Mademoiselle*. (The latter also made her a guest editor.) By the time Gloria and her class returned for their sophomore year, Plath was at McLean Hospital in Belmont, Massachusetts, undergoing psychotherapy and, later, shock treatments. Furthermore, her schoolmates all knew she had hidden under her porch and tried to commit suicide in August; the newspapers had been full of stories of her disappearance. Plath eventually returned to Smith to finish her degree and graduated in 1955, a year late. She won five more academic prizes and graduated summa cum laude, Phi Beta Kappa. Everyone thought her very brave.

7

Junior Year in Switzerland

When Gloria realized that she could take her junior year abroad for the same $1,800 that living at Smith for a year cost, she seized the opportunity, assuming it would be her only chance to travel to Europe. In March she learned that she was one of fifty-two sophomores accepted to go to Geneva.

The summer before she left was a busy one. Besides preparing to be away for almost a year, she was maid of honor when Sue, twenty-nine, married patent attorney Robert Patch. Leo came east for the wedding, and Ruth was doing fairly well. In the fall of Gloria's freshman year the family had decided that Ruth would benefit from institutional care. Sue visited a number of places and chose Sheppard and Enoch Pratt Hospital, a prestigious psychiatric hospital in Baltimore, Maryland.

Ruth remained there for less than a year, and Gloria visited her every weekend during the summer. They sold one of the houses on Ruth's Clarklake property to pay for her stay, and Janey and her husband, Bob, contributed as well. When she left Sheppard and Pratt, Ruth lived with Sue briefly. Then, a few months before Sue married, Ruth rented an apartment in northwest Washington. She also worked in a hotel gift shop, partly to make herself eligible for social security.

During the summer of 1954 Gloria worked as a lifeguard at a public swimming pool in an all-black neighborhood. Although the pool was not legally segregated, Gloria was the only white person on her shift, and she loved the experience. As she recalls, "The people I worked with knew I was self-conscious but what was wonderful was they just waited until it went away. Black people are much more skilled at understanding white people than vice versa—you know, like women understand men much better than vice versa. The powerless always understand the powerful better. They have to.

"Gradually they would include me in their activities. If it was raining and there were no kids in the pool, we would put blankets down in the locker room floor and play bid whist, a southern form of bridge. Or the little kids would teach me to do bones—on your body, you make this rhythm while you recite a rhyme.

"I remember once we were all leaving in a group and there was a white kid in the black neighborhood, a poor-white-trash kid who was very shocked to see a white girl. He said something like, 'What's this white girl doing with all these niggers?'

"One of the other lifeguards, who was a student in some college, went over to him and grabbed him by the shirt, and the poor kid was absolutely shaking with fear. Then he said, 'You see that girl? She's just one big recessive gene walking around.'

"Now the kid didn't know what recessive meant, but it made us all laugh, and it helped me get over that terrible self-consciousness."

Gloria's entire family was excited about her trip to Europe, and Ruth, Sue, and Bob traveled to New York in September to see her off on the *Queen Elizabeth*. The students were chaperoned by a Smith history professor, Elisabeth Koffka, who accompanied them on shipboard and spent the year with them in Geneva.

The ocean liner was luxurious. Gloria's classmates recall the pleasure of having the stewards draw their baths—even in steerage—and serve them hot consommé at eleven in the morning. Gloria, who tends to minimize her association with privilege, recalls that they were packed three or four to a room. All the students devoted a great deal of energy to sneaking into first class to crash the dances or use facilities like the squash courts. Gloria remembers one night when they all sneaked into first class as usual, only to find that many from first class had gone to the third-class dance, convinced that it would be more fun.

The students spent six weeks in Paris, living with French families and attending intensive classes taught by a birdlike Frenchwoman whom they nicknamed Mademoiselle Oiseau. They memorized portions of *Madame Bovary* (which some can still recite today) and walked all over Paris learning about the museums, cathedrals, architecture, culture—all in French.

Mme. Koffka was joined in France by Mme. Claire Davinroy, who took care of the more practical arrangements. The group went on to Geneva, where the students occupied almost all the rooms of the five-story Hotel de Russie on Lake Lucerne. Some had balconies overlooking the lake. There were telephones in the rooms, and maids to make the beds. The Smith group had a private dining room where they ate together nightly and gathered to talk and sing.

Mme. Koffka and Mme. Davinroy, who lived there as well, fascinated the students. Mme. Koffka was Prussian—large, rather elegant, distant, and serious. Neither friendly nor unfriendly, she was considered a brilliant professor and taught the entire group a course in her subject, German history. As a European, she probably considered the regulations "protecting" a group of twenty-year-old women silly, and for the most part she left the students alone. Mme. Davinroy was warmer and more involved in their day-to-day lives. She was a veteran of the Resistance, and her husband had been killed by the Nazis. She had written about the war in a book called *The White Rabbit,* but in 1954 the events were still too fresh for her to discuss easily.

During her first semester in Geneva, Gloria was one of the students chosen at random to live with a family. Because her host family lived on the other side of the lake, Gloria had to ride a streetcar to and from the university every day. Her geographical distance and her continuing lack of proficiency in French combined to make her feel isolated and lonely. She consoled herself chiefly with Swiss chocolate and ice cream. Although she remembers gaining weight, everyone else remembers admiring her figure.

During spring vacation Gloria went to Italy with one of the women in the program, and the student's parents. She returned with a new hairstyle, cut to imitate a style she had seen in Italy. Bangs and wispy side tendrils surrounded her face, while the back half of her hair hung long and straight. Everyone who knew her then remembers it, and no one liked it except Gloria, who thought she looked quite Italian.

Gloria moved in with other Smith students for the second semester. Installed at the Hotel de Russie, Gloria attracted scores of men, many of whom were much more attracted to her than she was to them. Her classmates recall her agonizing about how to extricate herself without hurting their feelings. Besides the quantity of men she attracted, her classmates remember that she was, as Barbara Zevon Berlin puts it, "socially precocious—there were such strong social mores, but she didn't believe in any of that and would just do what she wanted. Like sleeping with men, which most of us weren't doing in those days. You knew the people who were, but most people weren't. She went out with a lot of people in Geneva, everyone including a medical student who later married one of the people in our group and the bellhop in the hotel. She wasn't discriminating, and it struck me as very bizarre, because she was so brilliant and attractive and had such a wonderful sense of humor. For example, people who had asked me out whom I wouldn't be seen dead with, she would go with. She was adventurous in that way—she was a democrat with a little 'd.' "

Gloria was too worried about pregnancy and too naive about contraception to have a full-fledged affair while she was in Europe, but she did have a somewhat advanced attitude toward sex for 1955. She had lost her virginity during the summer of 1953 with "a wonderful person who I was very attracted to—fortunately he was more knowledgeable about how not to get pregnant than I was." She doesn't remember being obsessed about virginity, anyway. "The moral stricture in the 1950s in my memory was not so much about having sex as it was about getting pregnant and being seen as promiscuous. There was a difference between behavior and social perception that was pretty pervasive in the 1950s."

She was reprimanded once, when she was caught allowing the hotel bellhop into her room. Barbie believed she was reaching out for the attention and affection of which she had been so deprived. Barbie was in a position to know. Of all the Smith friends to whom Gloria related bits and pieces of her Toledo years, Barbie Zevon was one of the few to whom she seems to have confided the truth about how painful the experience had been.

Barbie had broken her leg skiing and had to spend several months in the hospital. Visiting Barbie, Gloria told her all: her mother's mental illness, and even of reading Dickens while keeping an eye on her mother, who had the habit of running out into the street without her clothes. Then she swore Barbie to secrecy.

After Ruth died in 1981 and Gloria published an account of those experiences, Barbie, who had kept her promise to tell no one, was one of the few friends not from Toledo who was not shocked. She remembered what Gloria had told her, and was only surprised by how closely

Gloria's essay "Ruth's Song" adhered to the story she had told almost thirty years previously.

Although she never directly expressed anger at her father, Gloria was honest about the pain of those years. She told Barbie that because her father and sister were gone, she was left to deal with her mentally ill mother. Barbie, who came from a warm, sheltered background, was shocked, because Gloria seemed to be such a happy, outgoing person.

Why Gloria chose to confide in Barbie is a mystery; Gloria doesn't even remember doing it. Maybe it was the shipboard-romance effect— they were far away from home, far away from Smith, isolated, even, from the others in Geneva. Barbie, alone in the hospital, may have seemed a safe confidante. Gloria was lonelier in Geneva than she had been at Smith, and with all her dates she didn't really have a boyfriend to provide her with sustained companionship.

The most meaningful relationship she formed with a man in Geneva probably was with Harish Kapur, the young Indian section leader for one of her courses. The course was taught by Jacques Freymond, a famous and charismatic professor who was known for thinking very little of the young women students. Many who were in Geneva recall that Freymond pronounced Gloria's paper on the Indian Communist Party the best he had seen by an undergraduate and that he offered to have it published if she made certain alterations. Gloria believes it was Harish who suggested publication.

Writing the paper helped disillusion Gloria about Marxism, or at least about Indian Communists. Marx's theories had attracted her during her freshman government course, because they at least addressed the issue of poverty. Although Gloria continued to support anti-Communist liberals like Adlai Stevenson, the McCarthy persecutions in the United States inclined her toward greater sympathy for the Communists. Researching the actions of the Indian Communist Party, she saw concrete examples of ways in which Marxism in theory and Marxism in practice might not be the same.

Throughout her years at Smith, Gloria patched together money as best she could. Ruth's $8,000 dwindled quickly, so while she was abroad, Gloria applied to Smith for scholarship money. When Gloria was told Smith did not have enough money to grant her any, she wrote to her mother resentfully that there were three girls, even within the small group in Geneva, who had been given some scholarship aid— and two of them had plenty of cashmere sweaters, but "not two brain cells to rub together and make a fire." At the end of the summer Smith reversed the decision and gave her the money.

Her academic year in Europe concluded, Gloria wanted to stay overseas as long as possible, so she found a summer program at Oxford University on politics and literature in twentieth-century England. Catering to Americans, it was probably conceived as a way of getting dollars into the British economy, and Gloria had saved enough money so that, with a contribution from her father, she was able to pay for the course. Along with about thirty students, she heard lectures by an assortment of politicians and authors like Labour Party leader Richard Crossman and novelist Joyce Cary. At the end of the summer she joined a girlfriend for a week of cycling in Scotland. They hadn't anticipated the difficulty of bicycling the steep terrain of the Highlands, but they enjoyed themselves just the same.

Finally it was time to go home. Believing she would never visit Europe again, Gloria went around Oxford and London, seeing everything for the last time and melodramatically saying goodbye to every place—even the streets and the trees. She sailed on the *Ile de France* and went home for a brief visit with her family, who hadn't seen her for nearly a year. Sue was enjoying married life. Ruth still was living in her own apartment. Leo was in California. After that, Gloria dragged out her vacation a little longer by visiting her boyfriend Peter Clarke, a Wesleyan student (and Korean War veteran) at his family's cottage on Cape Cod. Then, after visiting Washington once more, Gloria returned to Smith.

8

The Terror of Marriage

During her senior year, Gloria and several of her friends got to know the new theater instructor, David Shaber, a twenty-seven-year-old Ohioan and graduate of Yale Drama School. David developed a crush on Gloria, who went out with him a few times before turning him into a friend.

To Dave there was no question that Gloria would become famous; the only question was in what way. He describes her as a "superior example of the species" (Smith women) and recognized in Gloria "a kind of hustling quality which I share—the ability to make something out of nothing." The two swapped Ohio stories and David recalls Gloria describing Toledo as a large, open grave and characterizing her mother as a tragic, heroic figure who couldn't fight her way through her problems.

Not much older than the seniors, Dave was fascinated by the Smith students and what he considered the college's hothouse atmosphere. He explains, "They were all poets: all super-sensitive, very expressive, very intelligent, very talented, endlessly hung up, young women . . . No one at Smith would talk about chemistry when she could talk about metaphor. It was life without benefit of biology. Twenty-four hundred girls, none of whom ever went to the bathroom."

Gloria was glad to get back to Smith. She faced a heavy workload because she had chosen to "honor" in government. Honoring was more onerous than merely majoring in a subject: It required departmental permission and theoretically, demanded more independent work, fewer classes, a long honors thesis, and a heavier but less structured workload. In practice, requirements varied among the department. In return for their effort, honors students enjoyed prestige and were given priority in enrolling in courses.

By then Gloria, elected to Phi Beta Kappa during her junior year, was one of the top students. Gloria says that when her name was announced, there was surprised laughter—she believes that she was primarily regarded as a dancer in Smith's Rally Day shows. For her honors thesis, which she called "Humanist and Ideologue," she compared George Orwell and Arthur Koestler as men with parallel careers but very different psyches.

In the fall, Nancy Howard Garfinkle, the friend who had married after her freshman year, invited Gloria to a weekend at her family's home in Westchester County, north of New York City. Nancy and her husband, Sam, had invited Sam's closest boyhood friend, Blair Chotzinoff, and they thought Blair and Gloria might enjoy each other.

By the first night, "I'd fallen," recalls Blair. "I'd never met anybody like her. She was fascinating because, first of all, she was very attractive and very sexy and so damn smart that I was being very careful what I said. She was a little less allowing of people making fools of themselves in those days than she is now. She would jump on some statement if she didn't agree with it. And she was very much into the whole academia/Smith bit. . . . the authors they were reading, the philosophy they were reading."

Gloria was attracted to Blair. "I remember Sam and Nancy sort of plotting, throwing us together. He was very funny and terribly handsome. He had dark hair, dark skin, and greenish eyes. He looked like a Mogul prince with a skinny nose."

When Monday arrived, Blair decided to impress Gloria. "I'm not going to drive you to the train," he told her. "I'm going to fly you back to Northampton." He rented a tiny four-passenger plane and off they went. "About halfway back to Smith, I had this wild idea. It just struck me that it would be so funny. Up till then I hadn't laid a hand on her, hadn't kissed her. Nothing. But flying along at six thousand feet I put my hand on her knee." Blair looked at her inquiringly.

Gloria looked back at Blair. Then she looked at the ground far below. Then she looked at him again and shrugged her shoulders.

The two of them broke up laughing. "We laughed all the way back to Northampton." Blair says. "It was such a preposterous idea. What was she going to do? Get out and walk?"

Gloria was not as amused as Blair imagined. She was too worried about surviving. The dashboard of the ancient airplane he had rented had holes where instruments should have been, and Blair, who smoked the entire time, kept flicking cigarette ashes into the holes. Gloria was afraid he would blow up the plane.

Blair's attraction for Gloria is easy to understand. He was unlike anyone she had ever met. He was older—twenty-eight to her twenty-one—and at once worldly and rebellious. A wonderful raconteur, he was adventurous and led a glamorous life.

Besides, he came from a fascinating family, and Gloria was always attracted to families. The nephew of the world-renowned violinist Jascha Heifetz, Blair lived with his family for many years in his grandmother's brownstone on West Eighty-fifth Street in New York. Upstairs lived Blair's "crazy grandfather," who rented an apartment from his estranged wife and departed every summer to pursue moneymaking schemes such as the construction of factories in Portugal that would manufacture toothpicks and can sardines.

The Heifetz family had left Russia just before the Russian Revolution, when Jascha was only seventeen, but already famous. While Jascha's mother managed his career, the rest of the family traveled around the world in his entourage. Blair's mother, Pauline, and her sister, Elsa, were so beautiful that they had appeared in a Broadway musical.

Eventually the entourage included Blair's father, Samuel Chotzinoff. A gifted pianist and music teacher who grew up on the Lower East Side of New York, Chotzie had accompanied another Russian prodigy, violinist Efrem Zimbalist, before he became Heifetz's accompanist. By the time Gloria met Blair, he lived with his parents in a small apartment across the street from Carnegie Hall. Chotzie was music director of the National Broadcasting Company (NBC) and a well-known music critic. As members of the music world's highest circles, the Chotzinoffs were close to people like the wealthy Dorothy Schiff, who owned the *New York Post*, and whose daughter Chotzie had taught to play the piano.

When Blair was young, the household had included a maid, a cook, a handyman, and a nurse to care for Blair and his sister, Anne, who was always called Cookie. There was private school in the winter and camp in the summer. Blair was a talented violinist, though he refused to practice as much as his parents expected.

Not practicing was the least of his problems. His parents took him out of private school and sent him to public school, reasoning that if he wasn't going to work, they might as well not pay. It still took him five years, plus two years of summer school, to graduate, partly because of his penchant for part-time jobs. He worked on the docks as a stevedore, in a mattress factory, on a banana truck in Queens ("until I found a tarantula"), and as a runner on Wall Street. When he finally graduated from the private Rhodes School, he took great pleasure in telling people he was a Rhodes scholar.

The second world war was calling. At seventeen, Blair signed up for the Army Air Corps reserves because he wanted to fly fighter planes. After a few months as a copy boy at the *New York Post,* he was called into service and thought he was going to be a pilot. By then it was 1945 and the war was winding down. When he realized that he wasn't going to get into the fighting, he reverted to his old patterns. In his few months in the Army Air Corps Blair went AWOL several times; got himself court-martialed; gambled away thousands of dollars and a gold medal given him by Toscanini; broke into his commanding officer's office to recover a letter he needed to show that Army Air Corps men could be discharged if they chose; won thousands of dollars, then spent it by treating his friends to a five-day drunken spree in San Francisco.

Discharged in November 1945, he went back to his old job as copy boy at the *Post,* worked his way up to leg man to gossip columnist Earl Wilson, and eventually had his own restaurant column. He worked at the *Post* for about nine years, visiting restaurants and clubs and running around with show business people. At one point he began spending so much time with Walter Winchell that the *Post*'s editors, who wanted to run an exposé on Winchell because the powerful columnist was allied with Senator McCarthy (and because he was writing terrible things about Dorothy Schiff), talked Blair into wiring himself to "get the goods on Winchell." He succeeded, but then felt he had betrayed a friendship, so he destroyed the tapes instead of handing them over.

Blair had been serious about a woman only once before, when he had fallen in love with Toscanini's granddaughter. As he recalls, he mostly dated "showgirls, strippers, society gals, whoever crossed my path. My mother and father used to say to me, 'You know, we know so many nice girls. Why do you have to go out with showgirls?' But it was obvious why: they were gorgeous and they were available and we could all do each other some good. There was no falsity in that."

Then he met Gloria. Gloria found Blair's parents exotic and intimidating. The family played games constantly, fast and furious charades, word games, musical games, and Gloria felt, somewhat accurately, that her entire social future lay in her ability to compete successfully. Fortunately, she could keep up with the word games, and though she was lost in the musical games, she didn't feel inadequate, since no ordinary person could expect to keep up with the Chotzinoffs.

The Chotzinoffs were not wealthy, but as members of the international musical community, they socialized with a wide range of world-renowned people. Through them Gloria met wealthy music lovers like the Harrimans, as well as Isaiah Berlin and a then little-known conductor-composer named Leonard Bernstein. Gloria was clearly an improvement over the starlets and strippers, but Blair's parents were not as taken with her as their son was. They considered her an upstart, somewhat of a social climber (which she was) and a gold digger (which she was not).

Pauline ridiculed Gloria's hairstyle to Cookie, who liked Gloria very much. Chotzie was not much more enthusiastic about Gloria. He was used to deference, and Gloria's willingness to argue startled him. However, he asked her to give him tap-dancing lessons, and Gloria did her best.

Blair and Gloria spent every possible weekend together, either in New York or in Northampton. Flying for the Air National Guard about three days a week while looking for another job, Blair had very little money, and Gloria had almost none, but somehow they managed to do things like treating themselves to steak and martini dinners in a charming Northampton inn. To save money, Gloria sometimes put Blair up at David Shaber's, which Blair thought was rather insensitive, since the drama instructor would get into bed at night and moan about how in love he was with Gloria.

Around March or April, Gloria, twenty-two, agreed to marry Blair—who had wanted to marry her after knowing her five minutes. He gave her a large diamond ring to which (naturally, since it came from Blair) there was a story attached. Soon after World War I, Pauline's father had acquired a few diamonds with the vague intention of giving them to his future sons-in-law to give to his daughters as engagement rings. When Blair's father had become engaged to Pauline, her father called him in, handed him a diamond, and said in a heavy Russian accent, "Chotzie, I had hoped for something better. But here." The sentiment was repeated unto the second generation.

Within a few weeks of agreeing to be married, Gloria called Blair tearfully. She couldn't go through with it. Blair immediately drove to Northampton, where they shared several hours of "tears and remonstrations and various agonies" that ended with their becoming reengaged. Blair never doubted Gloria's feelings for him, but he had seen from the beginning that she had "reservations" about the whole idea of marriage and children. Whether intentionally cruel or merely insensitive, Blair's father made things worse by telling Gloria, "I can't wait for you guys to get married. I'm going to give you a set of Revereware for a wedding present and then you can make my favorite beef stew."

Gloria didn't just have reservations. She was terrified. She says, "I remember being in Blair's parents' apartment and feeling totally bleak, thinking, This is the only way I can ever change my life and now I've done it. And that's it."

Gloria adds, "I didn't articulate it, but I felt it. Well, I felt two things. One was that marriage was the only way a woman could change her life. Therefore once you chose the man you were going to marry, it was the last choice you made. After that you had to follow his work and his friends and his life, and ultimately, your children's lives. And if you really believe that, as we did in the 1950s, at many class levels, it becomes a little death. Because it's the last choice you can make."

Even happy marriages seemed annihilating: "The woman was still cooking and cleaning and giving up her identity and having no life of her own." It seemed like entrapment, and Gloria was an expert in entrapment. She believed her mother had been trapped by her marriage and her children. Gloria had felt trapped into taking care of her mother for six years. Only her father had seemed free. As a result, Gloria's feelings were the opposite of those experienced by many of her peers, who sought security through committed relationships. In Gloria's experience, commitment meant losing the ability to control one's own life. Avoiding commitment made Gloria feel more secure.

At war with her aversion to marriage was her attraction to Blair. "I loved him and cared about him and had discovered sex with him and I didn't want to leave. And I felt I had no life of my own. So I was just totally confused." In addition, college was ending. Gloria mused, If I don't attach myself to Blair's life, what will happen? Maybe I'll end up back in Toledo in the same circumstances. Or maybe I'll have to move in with my mother in Washington.

After she became engaged, her Smith friends held a shower for her. Gloria felt unreal in the role of fiancée. She says, "I just kept thinking they were talking about somebody else. I remember, literally, someone saying congratulations to me and I turned around to see who she was talking to. I couldn't imagine who she meant. They gave me a shower with coffee spoons, and it felt like a hallucination. It just felt as if someone else must be doing this. Not me."

Gloria did articulate her fears to David Shaber. Agonizing about committing herself to one man forever, she described marriage to him not so much in terms of giving up her own identity as in finding the right identity through the right man. "You have to take your identity from the man, and I don't know who I'll pick because I don't know who I am," she told him more than once.

The intensity of her sexual relationship with Blair magnified the conflict. Fear of entrapment fought with the joy of sex. Gloria was not completely inexperienced when they began their relationship, though, as she told reporters years later, once she became sexually active in college, in between encounters she "sort of 'revirginized' myself; I talked myself into the idea that I was still a virgin, or should pretend to be." Her relationship with Blair, though, was beyond anything she had experienced.

"I was in love with him," she recalls. "He was a kind, good, sensual person, and I was amazingly lucky to have this wonderful person as my first real sexual experience. I was a little prudish because I hadn't lived around men. I remember that he would get up out of bed and walk across the room nude, and I would think, This is totally amazing that there's a nude man walking around the room. I'd never seen that before. But I don't think I was inhibited, because I hadn't had many forces in my life to make me that way. I just had the absence of knowledge, which is different."

In 1950s fashion, Gloria went to get a diaphragm and told the doctor she was getting married long before she and Blair were engaged. That was the only way most doctors would prescribe one.

Between schoolwork and the agonies of romance, Gloria cast about for work. She talked in a vague way with a placement counselor about going to law school, but the advisor discouraged her, explaining that even with a law degree, as a woman she would be doing law research rather than law. She wrote several book reviews for the *Sophian* and began to think she might be able to try for some kind of writing job. She interviewed with *Time* magazine, which hired women to be researchers but not writers, but she decided she was not interested.

When Gloria applied to advertising giants J. Walter Thompson and Ogilvy & Mather, at one office she was asked to take a copywriting aptitude test. The test determined phrasemaking ability by giving drawings for which to create blurbs, and the copywriter who read Gloria's efforts commented presciently: "If this candidate could make up her mind to move merchandise instead of mountains, she'd make a good copywriter."

Throughout the spring, Gloria found no job that appealed to her. The engagement continued of its own momentum. Ruth liked Blair very much, though she remarked to Gloria one day, "It's probably a good idea if you get married right out of college, because once you get a taste of being independent, you'll never want to get married."

Blair liked Ruth, too. He explains, "We were two kind of naked souls who trusted each other, and from that grew affection. And she was the only one in that family who made me feel that she really liked me, cared about me, wasn't measuring me by accomplishments, or wasn't so protective of Gloria that she didn't want to let her into the hands of this terrible person who was going to ruin her life. Which I ran into a lot. There were a lot of people very protective of her."

Blair met some of Gloria's family at her graduation. Cookie, who accompanied her brother for moral support, was shocked at Leo's girth and general appearance. Gloria, filled with conflicting emotions—sad to leave Smith, apprehensive about finding work, frightened of marrying Blair, anxious and self-conscious about her friends' impressions of her family—hardly had time to worry about her family's reactions to Blair.

She could have predicted them, anyway. Sue was less than enthusiastic, and her aunt, Janey, "wanted me to get married and live in Grosse Pointe, and nothing could have been further from Grosse Pointe, at every level, than Blair. He rode around on a motorcycle, he was a pilot, he didn't quite have a job, he hadn't gone to college. Among my aunt's worst nightmares." Perhaps that was part of his appeal.

Leo wasn't particularly judgmental, especially since he did not share Gloria's sense of the enormity of the step she was contemplating. "With my father it was, okay, if I wanted to do that, fine. If I didn't want to do that, also fine. It really didn't matter." Now that he was a gem expert, Leo did have an opinion about her diamond, though. "It's yellow, you know," he told her. Then he showed her how to use an indelible pencil to make it look bluer, and therefore more valuable.

Leaving Smith, the most wonderful place she had ever lived, was painful. Voted class historian, Gloria compiled a history that recalled events and places and contemplated the eternal question of "matrimony vs. career." For the *Alumnae Quarterly* she wrote:

> We have decided to name the senior disease "Lasttimeitis" in honor of its most prevalent symptom. If we had a penny for every time we've said with sad finality such things as, "This is my last Rally Day," or "I'm filling out my last Smith course card," we could all become life members of the Alumnae Association without batting a checkbook.

Smith graduations are tradition-filled occasions. In the Ivy Day parade, alumnae walk with their classes, followed by the seniors wearing white dresses and carrying long-stemmed roses. The previous year's commencement speaker, presidential aspirant Adlai Stevenson, had told the class of 1955 that women, especially educated women, had "a unique opportunity to influence us, man and boy. . . . far from the vocation of marriage and motherhood leading you away from the great issues of our day, it brings you back to their very center" with "an infinitely deeper and more intimate reponsibility than that borne by the majority of those who hit the headlines." The poet Archibald MacLeish offered the class of 1956 a less condescending exhortation, encouraging them to embrace change and reject the rigid ethos of the cold war.

Gloria knew her life had to change, but, adrift and confused, she packed up and returned to Washington for the summer. She lived with her mother and visited Blair periodically in New York, where they looked at apartments and Gloria searched for a job. Her generation, MacLeish had said at Smith, "needs room to turn around in, needs the breath of possibility, the chance of choice."

Gloria felt she had chosen and was in love with a wonderful man. So why wasn't she happy?

9

An Abortion Alone

As it turned out, Gloria, twenty-two, wasn't quite through with Smith, though she did not know it when she left. She spent the summer of 1956 volunteering in Adlai Stevenson's presidential campaign against President Eisenhower, lifeguarding, hunting for a job, and, in desultory fashion, preparing to get married. Answering a newspaper ad, she also got a job writing lyrics for a team of songwriters at the Old New Orleans nightclub and created "sort of Gershwiny" songs like "Louisville Lou," a "kind of semiparody of the 'St. Louis Blues.'"

Ruth was not doing well and soon would return to Sheppard and Pratt for another few months, so Gloria kept her emotional turmoil to herself. When Blair confided to his parents that Gloria was vacillating, they alternated between nagging him about getting a proper job and belittling Gloria. "She doesn't want to marry you because you're not rich," they told him smugly.

Blair was confused, because he knew Gloria loved him. "In those days I was not able to make the distinction between her loving or not loving, and these other things that she did or didn't want to do. To me it was all in one package. It was everything. If you loved somebody, you didn't think about not-this or not-that." He even had advocates. A kindly radiologist friend of his father who lived in Washington and the playwright S. N. Behrman both offered to intercede on his behalf.

Gloria finally acted, though she couldn't bring herself to do it directly. In the late summer she went to New York and spent one last night with Blair. In the morning, while he was still asleep, she crept out, leaving the engagement ring on the bedside table. Underneath it was a note saying that she just couldn't go through with the marriage.

Blair was devastated. He wrote Gloria several times in the next few weeks, but she never wrote back.

Gloria had decided she was going to India. Fleeing to the other side of the earth to avoid getting married was a little extreme, but Gloria felt too susceptible to Blair's magnetism. Besides, she had felt drawn to India, ever since she had sat on the floor coloring and listening at Theosophical Society meetings with her mother and grandmother. The possibility of a fellowship seemed like fate.

Smith students had been interested in India for years, and several student organizations had initiated a variety of cultural exchange programs, with varying degrees of success, including lectures, juniors going abroad, and student pen pals. A few months before Gloria's graduation, the International Relations Organization's Asian Scholarship Fund had finally raised enough money to award two $1,000 scholarships to send two graduating seniors to study in India. The scholarships were named after Chester Bowles to honor the former ambassador to India (1951–1953). According to Margaret Harrison (Case), one of the students who worked on the project, that was partly because "the dean of the college was an old battleaxe who stipulated that Smith's name not be attached." Most of the faculty were equally tepid about the enterprise, but the students' enthusiasm had moved it along.

Chester Bowles was gratified by the honor. His wife had a Smith master's degree, his niece (Smith '55) had visited him during his tour as ambassador, and a daughter was entering Smith in the fall. He liked the idea of students serving as goodwill ambassadors, and he had spoken at Smith in 1954 to help the International Relations Organization (IRO) raise money, even before they named the scholarships for him.

The students also managed to have Eleanor Roosevelt speak, which added $1,300 to the $800 they had saved from Chester Bowles's lecture. Although raising $2,000 took a group of dedicated students several years of painstaking fund-raising, the arrangements were haphazard, to say the least. IRO officers calculated that a Bowles scholar would need $2,000 to $2,500 to live on, but when they lacked that amount, they decided to send two students anyway and trust them to figure out how to raise the rest of the money. They never determined where the Chester Bowles scholars, or fellows, as they sometimes began calling them, were actually to go in India, or what they were to do once they got there.

By October 1956, after they already had awarded the scholarships, the committee was still discussing what the "responsibilities of the girls" should be vis-à-vis Smith. Should they write articles for the school newspaper? Should they send reports to the college president or the committee? If so, how often? Should they have definite projects in mind before they went? Produce tangible results?

Gloria had always been interested in the project. When the committee had announced its "Smith in Asia" scholarships during her junior year, she had cabled her interest from Geneva. Once they decided to offer the scholarships as an interim year between junior and senior years, Gloria had withdrawn her application. She tried unsuccessfully for a Fulbright scholarship after she returned for her senior year, but when the India scholarships were changed to postgraduate stints, she was not interested and did not reapply. By then she assumed she was getting married.

During the summer Gloria saw Chester Bowles fellow Kayla Achter in Washington and learned that the other woman had backed out. There, Gloria thought, was the perfect solution—work, adventure, and escape, all in one package. In August 1956 she wrote to John Chapman, the Smith professor in charge, explaining that she was no longer engaged. She had seen it coming, she wrote, because while others might be ready for marriage, she realized she was not. She was "not the stuff of which 'career girls' are made," she explained. However, she did not expect to marry for another few years, because she was "not yet the person that a man I would want to marry would want to marry."

Gloria went on to assure Chapman that her application was neither a dramatic reaction to the demise of her engagement nor a superior alternative to lackluster employment prospects. Rather, it was the result of her longtime interest in India. In reality, those were exactly her reasons—or at least two-thirds of them—but Gloria did have an affinity for India and a history of activities to prove it.

Besides taking Indian dancing, Gloria wrote, she had considered Vera Micheles Dean's course on modern India one of her favorite courses (true); had received an A+ on her long paper in Geneva, which had been written on the Indian Communist Party and had been recommended for publication by an Indian expert at the Institute (true); had worked on India during a special project at Oxford (doubtful); and, upon hearing of the scholarship while in Geneva, had written to several people at Smith of her interest (also true). Gloria had also been exposed to Indian philosophy and religion all her life through Ruth's interest in theosophy, but fearing that the faculty might consider theosophy too weird, she left that out.

She needn't have worried. Both faculty and student committee members were delighted that she was interested. As Margaret Harrison Case recalls, "Kayla was wildly brilliant but quite erratic, so it was to everyone's great relief when Gloria broke her engagement and said she'd like to go. Gloria was considered a golden girl."

Good-hearted and intermittently hardworking, but extremely unreliable, Kayla Achter was beautiful, with "Elizabeth Taylor coloring" of blue eyes and black hair. She had dropped in and out of college, wrote brilliantly but not necessarily on schedule, wore the same black skirt for months on end, and avoided Smith's physical education requirement for so long that she tried to make up all four semesters in the last half of her senior year. She had been involved with the International Relations Organization since its founding, and was its president her senior year, so, despite their reservations about her eccentricities, the scholarship committee found it difficult to deny her the award.

Both Kayla and Gloria must have thought awarding the scholarship to Gloria a foregone conclusion. A month after Gloria wrote to Smith, but two weeks before the committee met to consider her application, Kayla also wrote to them.

> About Gloria, you know her, she is bright, delightful, observant, and I think a wonderful person to send there and to depend upon at her return. She has even fewer plans then [sic] I, and together we've laughed at our collective ignorance and tried to compile something useful from what we know. We have been reading, and reading, and reading, Santha Rama Rau, Rostow, post reports, Bowles, and even the state dept's reccomended [sic] lists, and articles in a UNESCO Fundamental Education seies [sic]. What this has pointed out is that we know nothing about India, that collecting general information on a variety of subjects and atmosphere from books is not any sort of real preperation [sic], that a culture can't be conned, that a year there may not even serve as a humble beginning, so we smile and go about our business here and I at least hope for good sense and good health and lasting improvement in

each for the next year.

Because the lowest round-trip airfare alone was $1,200, both women had to find ways to supplement the stipend. Kayla managed to interest the head of Bergdorf-Goodman's public relations department in paying her to conduct a poll "on tastes in clothes translated into 'Indian women's terms.'" That way the store could "be a scoop ahead of the scoop hungry public relations world, do a public service, and be able to publicize, with dignity, 'in India they wear . . . and . . . in America. . . .'"

Perhaps this was not quite what Chester Bowles had envisioned for his community ambassadors, but Kayla was full of schemes. She also urged the committee to approach people who frequently helped students, like renowned Washington hostess and diplomat Perle Mesta, and suggested, "Gloria might contact these people for you in Washington, she's excellent at such matters . . . and has an appointment of this sort allready [sic] for next week." (Kayla's second letter was written several days before the committee met with Gloria about the scholarship.)

Kayla had a backup source of funds: her parents. Gloria had to be more enterprising. She contacted magazines about writing articles, but they offered very little. After she finally secured airfare in exchange for a publicity piece for TWA, the arrangement fell through. Gloria was so upset, someone in TWA's publicity department took pity on her and convinced someone else in TWA's education department to finance her way over. With one way paid for, Gloria went to London to await her visa, fearing that if she stayed in the states, the siren song of Blair would be irresistible.

When Gloria arrived in London at the beginning of December, she found that obtaining a student visa to India was more than a formality. Days stretched into weeks as she haunted the High Commissioner's office at the Indian embassy, and still there was no word. Although she was staying with Jane Bird Nissen, a Smith friend who had married an Englishman, she lacked the money to remain an indeterminate time in London, so she cast about for a job. Without working papers the best she could do was waitressing in an espresso bar. The work was not onerous, the other employees were students from all over the world, and the place was in a pleasant neighborhood, so it would do until her visa came through.

About a month after she arrived, Gloria began to suspect she might be pregnant. On her way to London she had stopped in New York and, unable to resist, had picked up with Blair where they had left off.

However, while living with her mother during the summer, she had worried that Ruth would find her diaphragm, so she had thrown it away. Now she panicked.

She couldn't bring herself to tell anyone, so her first instinct was to look for the solution in a book. Maybe horseback riding would cause a miscarriage. She went to the library, and it took very little research for her to realize there was no way out. No matter how depressed she had been as a child, she had always considered herself a survivor. Now, for the only time in her life, she considered suicide.

She was trapped. She hadn't wanted to get married, so she certainly didn't want to have a child. She had only been free of responsibility for her mother for five years. Was she about to begin again, this time for eighteen or twenty years?

Then she thought about abortions. She didn't know much about them—just that "you didn't *necessarily* die" from them. And that they were illegal. Maybe she could get one in France, she conjectured. After all, Paris was the sin capital of the world. Then she learned that abortions were illegal there, too. She went to a kindly old doctor near the Nissens' house (she found his name in the telephone book) and told him her story—or what she thought should be her story. "I told him a long story about how this man didn't want to marry me. Because I thought I couldn't admit that I was the one who didn't want to get married."

The doctor mentioned nothing about abortion and Gloria was afraid to ask. He gave her a medication that would bring on her period if she weren't pregnant, but when she took it, nothing happened. Numbly, Gloria continued in her routine: work, the Indian embassy, parties, friends. Meanwhile she grew more desperate. Her usual resourcefulness deserted her. She knew nowhere to go, no one to ask.

Just before it was too late, she found the solution at a cocktail party, of all places. She overheard an obnoxious American playwright complaining that two of the actresses in his play had gotten pregnant and that he had had to help them to get abortions. Gloria willed herself to look casual. "Where?" she asked. "In France?"

"No," he said sneeringly. "It's much tougher to get one in France. You're in London." He explained that it wasn't easy, but it could be done in England if the woman found two doctors to agree that the abortion was necessary for her physical and mental health.

Gloria returned to her doctor's office the next day. When she asked about the procedure, he agreed to sign the form and send her to another doctor who would give her an abortion.

The other doctor was an elegant Harley Street gynecologist who wore a tweed suit and smoked cigarettes in a holder. Unlike Gloria's elderly physician, she was unsympathetic, and rather contemptuous of Gloria's situation. What ignorance to get pregnant. What carelessness to wait so long to do something about it. Gloria had gotten pregnant in November; now it was early January and almost too late. However, the gynecologist offered to prescribe a contraceptive and asked about Gloria's plans for the future. When Gloria explained she was bound for India, the doctor commented flippantly, "I don't suppose you'll get pregnant there."

What the doctor lacked in pleasing bedside manner, she made up in efficiency, performing the abortion with anaesthetic, cleanly and competently. Gloria stayed in bed for a few days and then returned to work.

Almost twenty-three, Gloria felt alive again, released from the terror that her life would not be her own. She assumed she should feel guilty, but she couldn't. She was too relieved. She also felt it was the first time she had really taken responsibility for her own life, by acting, not just going along with circumstance.

With the abortion behind her, her luck changed as well. As she wrote to the scholarship committee on January 27, her visa finally came through. It had not been easy. She had spent two hours in the High Commissioner's office persuading the consul that he should admit her though she lacked the proper documents to show she had someone to serve as her Indian sponsor. By then she had regained her ability to relish and convey her experiences, writing that when the kindly consul gave her advice about India, she felt "coarse and jejune and ridiculously Western."

En route to India, she stopped in Geneva to see Harish Kapur and then in Greece to see the Acropolis. She went with two people she had met in her hotel, and when they stayed too long on the mountain, they had to make their way down in the dark. They communicated as best they could in French, which was the first language of none of them.

Every stop between London and New Delhi was suspenseful. The airlines weighed both the baggage and the passenger, so, to save money, Gloria kept sneaking around the corner after she had been weighed, to strap things on, load up her pockets, and put on extra layers of clothes.

In Greece she boarded a flight to India. She was on her way at last.

10

Passage to India

Gloria landed in Bombay and fell in love with India the moment she arrived. Years later she would say that she felt strangely at home there. Her sense of relaxation is not surprising. She had felt like an outsider her entire life. In Clarklake her family was different, and she rarely went to school; in Amherst she imitated the other children and pretended to have a normal family; in Toledo she came from a higher social class than her neighbors, but was poorer and concealed a crazy mother; in Georgetown she jumped several social classes and began actively to dramatize her past; at Smith she continued to learn from those around her, while gazing anxiously ahead, wondering where she would fit into the world after college.

Gloria had been observing the natives of every new society she entered, trying to understand their customs and learn their language in order to fit in. She had fit in, magnificently, but it always had required effort.

Nor had she ever wanted to fit in completely. Gloria was a product of both parents: the idealistic, intellectually inquiring Ruth, who nevertheless craved middle-class respectability and financial stability, and the adventurous, pleasure-loving Leo, who dreamed of worldly success but dreaded the idea of a humdrum life. Their conflict lived on in Gloria, who was drawn both toward and away from the groups she observed. Yearning for connection, she wanted to belong, yet at the same time, her sense of herself as an outsider was the most familiar part of her identity, and she clung to it. As long as she conformed outwardly, she could find companionship and some security through her affiliation, while secretly assuring herself she wasn't really part of the group.

In India, for the first time in her life, she entered a society in which there was no preconceived role for her to decipher. Gloria was so obviously an outsider that there was no question of blending in. Other than assuming an appropriately modest feminine demeanor, she was free just to react. India, land of the caste system, released Gloria from the American class system: Whatever her money worries, the poverty she witnessed in India rendered all the gradations within the United States meaningless. Alone and unaffiliated, Gloria felt free to plunge in among the myriad people of India. Like a character in an E. M. Forster novel, she need "only connect."

Gloria's plane landed near midnight and she knew no one in Bombay. The TWA traffic manager took pity on her and brought her home to his family for a few days. They took her to a Europeans-only country club she found appalling, and to a Parsee boy's confirmation party where she found herself conversing about theosophy with a diamond-covered banker's wife and listening to an Irishwoman complaining about curry powder, all accompanied by songs from *Oklahoma*.

Gloria used the last section of her airplane ticket to fly to Delhi. A few days later Jean Joyce looked up from her desk at the Ford Foundation office in New Delhi and beheld a beautiful but bedraggled young white woman. Jean, who had accompanied Chester Bowles to India, had lost her job when President Eisenhower replaced Bowles with a new ambassador. Loving the country, she had stayed on as head of cultural activities at the Ford Foundation.

Gloria introduced herself and asked if Jean had heard anything about Kayla Achter. Jean had not. "Where are you staying?" she asked.

Gloria looked at her and said nothing. "Come stay with me, then," she offered, and Gloria did, for several days. Because the Ford Foundation was often involved in scholarly exchange programs, Jean was used to dealing with young people, and she sized Gloria up quickly. "She was very bright and very resourceful—she had to find her way through a lot of academic and bureaucratic hurdles because nothing had been set up for her, no place to live, no academic program. She was also very interested in blending properly into the environment."

The same could not be said of Kayla, who appeared a couple of days later. Jean found her not only distinctly unreliable, but also in "a very nubile state." Gloria behaved appropriately, but Kayla was a disaster. Warmhearted and friendly, Kayla had no interest in moderating her behavior to fit her milieu. She would stare openly at young men who approached her—hesitantly at first, and then brazenly. When Jean took her to a local fair, Kayla practically caused a riot, requiring the two women to flee, "with men chasing us and pinching her fanny and about to pinch mine," Jean recalls.

Like Gloria, Kayla adopted native dress, but unlike Gloria's modest saris, she chose the *salwar-kameez,* a costume of pants, a long tunic, and a bit of chiffon draped over the bosom. However, "Kayla was careless about the chiffon piece, and she had big cantaloupe-sized bosoms. I hadn't noticed whether she was casting her eyes about or not, but the men got the message, and pretty soon we were encircled by a group of guys."

Kayla got into other scrapes as well, and Jean heard about young maharajahs making scenes in hotel lobbies. During their sojourn in India, both Kayla and Gloria visited Jean frequently. Once Gloria and Walter Friedenberg, her lover for much of the time she was in India and for a few years afterward, accompanied Jean and her nephew on a trip to Kashmir. Walter, whom she met through friends in Delhi, was a foreign correspondent. At the time he was working as a stringer for the *Chicago Daily News.*

Gloria and Kayla eventually moved into Miranda House, which was the more liberal of the University of Delhi's two women's colleges—women were allowed to leave the college in groups of fewer than four, and they could stay out as late as eight in the evening. There they lived among two hundred Indian undergraduate and graduate students who watched them constantly and deluged them with endless questions.

Gloria wrote in a dispatch to the scholarship committee that they sat talking far into the night, answering questions about every conceivable subject: "the Christians' conception of God, the intricacies of Western lingerie, the dating system, Rock and Roll, how much milk the average American cow gives, our favorite American authors and, the one question that always recurs in any group, why did the U.S. arm Pakistan against India."

When they asked her to sing American songs, Gloria wrote, she gave them a ballet lesson instead and "a sort of quasi-sociological lecture on the progression of tap dancing from its original, loose-limbed Negro shuffle through sand dancing and soft shoe to its present Gene Kelly-ish combination with ballet," adding that next time Smith should send emissaries who could sing.

She grew accustomed to being stared at everywhere she went, which in India was not considered rude. Gloria and Kayla were besieged with invitations for coffee, lunch, and dinner, each occasion hours long. Once they learned refusing would not be offensive, they were able to choose more discriminatingly and attended a number of weddings where they learned Indian customs such as how to eat with their hands off plantain-leaf plates, how to properly *namasthé* (bow with praying hands), and how to wear saris.

Being linked with Kayla was a constant trial to Gloria, who was as conscientious as Kayla was irresponsible. When they finally began pursuing separate activities, Gloria concealed her relief from the committee, writing only that they would no longer be "ambassadorial Bobbsey Twins."

India was at a particularly interesting point in its history. Led by Mohandas K. Gandhi, the country had finally wrenched its independence from the British in 1947, and the bloody religious war that followed had led to the nation's partition into predominantly Hindu India and predominantly Muslim Pakistan. Gandhi was assassinated in 1948, and by the time Gloria arrived in 1957, India, like other nations emerging from colonialism, was fraught with struggle. The various political parties and movements competed both violently and nonviolently to determine who would lead and what method of economic development should be pursued.

Eager to meet a wide variety of people, Gloria befriended, among others, some Gandhians who became her lifelong friends and *New York Times* correspondent A. M. Rosenthal, a young reporter on his first foreign assignment, who considered Gloria a wonderful representative of the United States. Rosenthal also recalls her as one of the few westerners who managed to look good in a sari. "It requires a different style of walking," he explains.

She went out with Harish Kapur, who had returned from Geneva to see his family after being abroad six years, and arranged for him to lecture to some of her friends who were political science graduate students. Afterward she wrote that the students found him to be "the best lecturer and leader of discussion they had ever heard. . . ." Gloria added, "I shall probably be remembered in future only as 'that American girl who brought Jagdish.' " (She changed Harish's name in her dispatch because she had included a detailed discussion of his personal life.)

Gloria was full of ideas for cross-cultural exchanges, some of which she undertook herself. Others required Smith's participation. She sent detailed instructions for conducting a book drive to stock the Miranda House library, adding, "as you can see, there are unlimited possibilities for anyone with a fixit, Mary Worth type instinct!"

Because of her paper on the history of the Communist Party in India, Gloria already had a point of view about Indian politics, which was anti-Communist (because the Communist Party had followed Soviet instructions to support the British instead of the independence movement), and pro-Gandhian (because he had created an independence movement that was nonviolent and democratic). It was with great interest, therefore, that she encountered her first Soviet Communists. Early in their sojourn, she and Kayla took a sightseeing bus trip and met, in addition to the Indian students, a group of Russian "students" whose average age was over thirty. One of the women, Gloria wrote to Smith, "needed only a babushka over her circlet of heavy braids to look like the photos with the inscription: 'And the women of Russia dig in the rubble to help their men in constructing this brave new . . .' " Once Gloria realized that the Russian woman could speak English and understand French, the two talked for several hours, though Gloria never managed to make her companion understand the concept of a student project that had no government connection.

On the return trip Kayla and Gloria waged their own small battle in the cold war. Asked to sing something, they sang an East African folk song. Then the Russians responded with a song from the revolution. Back and forth it went, with Gloria and Kayla singing camp songs and trying to keep from being drowned out.

Gloria wrote also of a phenomenon for which she and Kayla thought they had coined a term: culture shock. Like all visitors to India, she found the poverty overwhelming. She noted,

> The Five Year Plans that looked so brave and inspiring in books lose some of their stature when I see the price of suffering and deprivation the masses pay for them. . . . when I see Delhi's huge Aśoka Hotel which averages thirty guests a week and was built and is now maintained for prestige . . . and then count the number of village well projects that are being abandoned for lack of concrete, I can't help but wonder a little. But as yet, I know not whereof I speak: I only sense and feel these things. . . .

How will I ever, *ever* become accustomed to the bundle of dirty rags on the sidewalk which often as not turns out to be a little boy . . . or the leper who stretches out his fingerless hands to beg; or the sweeper-woman who trails a wandering cow that she may catch its dung and form it into patties of fuel. . . . And beneath all sounds, however gay or distracting or sensible, there is always a silence, the deafening, patient silence of the millions who have never had full bellies.

In May 1957 the school term ended, and for a couple of weeks Gloria took a room for eighty cents a day with an Anglo-Indian family in New Delhi. She explored Delhi (New Delhi was the newly built business portion of the city). Gloria made a number of new contacts, including "a 125-year-old swami" and Indira Gandhi, who was heading a youth organization and serving as the official hostess for her father, Prime Minister Jawaharlal Nehru. They talked of Indira's three years in prison, of her visit to the United States, of her two sons, and of how Gloria's short time in India might best be used. Gloria was surprised to find the thirty-nine-year-old Indira "shy to uncertainty, gentle, a little whimsical and infinitely more lovely than [her] pictures," adding, "I felt her incapable of being 'social' in any way that meant a façade, however innocent, and that in spite of our relative ages and positions, I should do my best to put her at her ease."

She spent ten days in May at a Radical Humanist study camp in the foothills of the Himalayas with about forty Indian men and the widow of the Radical Humanists' founder, M. N. Roy. In his teens Roy had fled India when British authorities sought to arrest him for pro-independence activities. In the 1920s he made his way to Mexico and there laid the foundations for the Mexican Communist Party as a representative of the Comintern, then organized and directed the Indian Communist movement from abroad for nine years. After a break with the Soviet Union over its colonialist policy in 1929, he returned to India in 1930, whereupon the British sent him to prison. Supporting the Allies during World War II estranged him from Gandhi's followers (who maintained neutrality), and after independence he formed first a political party and subsequently the Radical Humanist movement.

M. N. Roy's widow, Ellen Roy, with whom Gloria shared a room and sometimes even a bed, was the daughter of a U.S.-diplomat father and a German mother. She had met Roy in Germany when she worked with Communists there against Hitler. Most of the other Radical Humanists were former Communists as well, and Gloria was startled at first to hear them affectionately greeting each other as "comrade," then grew to enjoy using the term herself. For ten days, eight hours a day, they sat on the floor of a gracious old house they had rented and discussed India's future.

In addition to extensively analyzing Indian politics and providing short profiles of several participants, in a dispatch to the scholarship committee, Gloria described her own contribution. A Yugoslavian press attaché at the retreat had been invited to address the Radical Humanists on the subject of Yugoslavia and its worker cooperatives. He had described his country in such glowing terms that, Gloria wrote,

> had I not known better, I would have left for the Dalmation coast immediately. But looking around, I became worried. Too many of the politically less mature were believing him. . . . I needled a little but not convincingly, so that night I did a little reading and the next day— I'm about to brag, so prepare yourself—nailed him to the wall with a few questions about Djilas, what he thought could be bettered in the election system, the control of mass media, and even trapped him into contradicting Tito about the relationship of Hungary and the Suez. The tide turned and people began to realize that the very fact he dared not utter a critical word bore silent testimony to the sort of regime in which he lived. This little battle was watched with much interest by all and, afterward, I found myself congratulated and wholly accepted as if I had passed my trial by fire. Perhaps that's dramatizing a little . . . but I felt gratified at carrying on a definitely unclassroom type debate and having made a point that swayed opinions instead of academic averages.

Evidently Gloria enjoyed swaying a crowd.

Meanwhile, back at Smith, the Chester Bowles Scholarship Committee was in trouble. Maggie Harrison, the third Bowles scholar, was to go to India in the fall of 1957, but two years and three scholars into the program, the committee was $700 in debt and still unsure of the scholarship's purpose or the duties of its recipients. In July Chester Bowles had written to the committee expressing his concern and had enclosed portions of a letter he had received from Jean Joyce, in which she had written,

> I'm worried about this "Chester Bowles Fellowship" being set up the way it is by Smith. The truth is they haven't "set it up" at all. The girls— both of whom are very nice—are attached in a desultory fashion to Miranda House, without having to study anything in particular. It can't

be the girls' fault—it must be Smith's—(and I'm worried that it looks rather unorganized for something carrying the great Bowles name here.)

Not surprisingly, Barbara Jean Stokes, the committee chairperson, was offended, but she did concede in a letter to Smith's president, Dr. Benjamin Wright, that "perhaps our hopes have been too idealistic." She suggested that the program spend the coming academic year in a state of "animated suspension" until they could learn more about India and repay the $700 loan to the Student Bank. After 1957 the Chester Bowles fellowship ceased to exist.

Oblivious to the dispute, Gloria brimmed with tales of her adventures. She traveled considerable distances by bus and rail to spend several days walking through caste riots in Ramnad, visit the theosophical headquarters in Madras, and investigate the activities of a newly elected Indian (as opposed to Soviet) Communist government in Kerala, India's southwesternmost state. When she went into the countryside, she reported proudly back to Smith that she had interviewed the owners of ten plantations. They were so remote that it was as if she had talked to "ten Tibetan lamas." She also "donned my homespun sari to stay with the workers and union people."

Gloria would later write that experiencing the caste riots in Ramnad was one of the experiences "that divide our lives into 'before' and 'after.' " She had gone to visit an ashram (retreat) run by Vinoba Bhave, a follower of Gandhi who was trying to carry out land reform by walking from village to village to convince local landlords to contribute land to the landless poor. When she arrived, Gloria found that Bhave and his followers had gone to Ramnad, a nearby rural area, because riots had broken out between castes. They were walking in small groups from village to village, trying to stop the riots.

Gloria had not been aware of the riots, because the government had cordoned off the area and imposed a press blackout in an effort to contain the violence. Bhave's groups had entered anyway, and a U.S. Protestant missionary whom Gloria met at the ashram invited her to join his group. He wanted a woman in each group, because otherwise they would have no one to go into the women's quarters, invite them to participate, and demonstrate that women were welcome, too.

Gloria, who had already helped the Radical Humanists with their publications, welcomed the opportunity to work with Indians even more directly. She joined the group. In her 1994 book, *Moving Beyond Words,* Gloria recounted the experience:

Each day, we set off along paths shaded by palms and sheltered by banyan trees, cut across plowed fields, and waded into streams to cool off and let our homespun clothes dry on us as we walked. In the villages, families shared their food and sleeping mats with us, women taught me how to wash my sari and wash and oil my hair. . . . I found there was a freedom in having no possessions but a sari, a cup, and a comb, and, even in the midst of turmoil, a peacefulness in focusing only on the moment at hand. I remember this as the first time in my life when I was living completely in the present.

After Ramnad and the Kerala adventures, Gloria traveled back up the west coast and stayed in a YWCA hostel in Bombay, where she fought the bedbugs and explored the city as long as her money held out. Then she borrowed more and stayed on, meeting people whose names she had been given and continually seeking ways to earn enough money to pay for her passage back to the United States.

An Indian executive with the J. Walter Thompson advertising agency hired her to write an article on the Ajanta and Ellora caves from a Western tourist's point of view. He used her account to promote Air India International's domestic subsidiary—but Gloria had to travel crammed into a third-class railcar with a group of chained-together Indian convicts. He also introduced her to a Muslim film company owner interested in exporting sandals. For him, Gloria helped design the sandals and then wrote promotional material for them. Back in Delhi, she secured a three-month assignment that would pay enough to get her home: a guidebook about India that would encourage Western tourists to fly all over the country on Air India's domestic subsidiary instead of seeing only the usual triangle of Delhi, the Taj Mahal, and Jaipur.

She wrote cheerfully and humorously to the Smith committee about her successful ventures, omitting the many that failed. Several of her failed ideas for securing return passage had involved some kind of shepherding: conducting a group of students on a ship; working as the attendant on a flight taking Muslims to Mecca ("someone told me I would spend the entire flight handling vomit bags because the passengers had never been on an airplane before"); and accompanying a planeload of rhesus monkeys destined for experiments in the United States. (The plane was flown by ace pilot Chuck Yeager, who had broken the sound barrier in 1947.)

Finally, after a year and a half in India, she had enough money to go home. Gloria traveled east to see just a little more on her way. She took a train to Rangoon, Burma, stopping for a time in Calcutta, which she adored. She even audited classes at Calcutta University. "Calcutta is a wonderful city." she explains. "It's where Satyajit Ray, the film-maker, is from, and wherever two or three people are gathered together, suddenly there's a literary magazine. I'd say it's the France of India, except that it's much more whimsical and open than France." (A dislike of the cultural egotism of France is one of Gloria's admitted biases. The other is rich people—at least those who strike "the Toledo in me"—though some of her best friends . . .)

Arriving in Rangoon, she checked into a hotel on the main square. Upon awakening in the morning she saw a tank in the middle of the square. There had been a revolution during the night, but it was peaceful enough so that she stayed on, visiting Indian relatives of friends she had made in Calcutta.

Waiting in the Rangoon airport for a plane to Hong Kong, she began chatting with an elegant Chinese woman from Hong Kong and Burma, who turned out to be a Vassar graduate seeing her husband off. Gloria and the husband, Y. H. Kwong, talked together all the way to Hong Kong. An interesting man of culture, Kwong seemed to be involved in everything from electronics to construction. When Gloria eventually asked him what he had built, he said, "the Burma Road."

He invited her to stay at his family's apartment, but she insisted on going to the YWCA as she had planned. A few days and many bed-bugs later she thought better of it. Kwong asked her to dinner with some of his family, and after that she moved into the apartment, where he taught her to use an egg cup and cut a grapefruit half into sections. He also took her along when he entertained a group of Burmese officials he was about to accompany to Tokyo for discussions of war reparations.

Gloria went to Tokyo as well, but she flew on a cargo plane piloted by a U.S. flyer who had flown with the Flying Tigers and then stayed on after World War II. The pilot invited her into the cockpit, where he was eating pineapple and dripping syrup all over the instrument panel, and encouraged her to talk to the ground-control crew on his radio, just to give them a surprise.

In Tokyo, Kwong took her along with the Burmese ministers to elegant nightclubs and teahouses where they were served by geishas. She went on to Kyoto by herself.

By July 1958 it was time to leave Asia. Gloria, twenty-four, had been abroad since November 1956. She sailed on the *President Cleveland* ocean liner, in steerage with several hundred Chinese immigrants and a

U.S. fundamentalist Christian family. They tried to convert her, inquiring in broad southern accents, "Why have you forsaken the faith of your fathers?"

"I had a choice. Either I learned Chinese or I got converted or I talked to the crew," Gloria explains. Not only did the crew speak English, they sneaked her above decks during the day so she could mingle with the more privileged passengers. Among them were Rear Admiral and Mrs. Quiggle, and when Admiral Quiggle disappeared en route, the tragedy was the talk of the ship—especially since one of the ship's officers had overheard the admiral tell his wife, "You'd be better off a widow."

When they docked, the captain forbade the crew to speak to the press about the incident, but Gloria had received no such instructions, so she tried to be helpful. She answered reporters' questions and was shocked to find herself quoted from Washington to Tokyo.

Leo met Gloria in San Francisco, with not quite enough money to get them back east, so the two of them worked their way across the country by car. They stopped to play the slot machines in Las Vegas because Leo thought Gloria was lucky, and she earned them about fifty dollars in gas money. Like the father and daughter in the movie *Paper Moon,* Leo sold antique jewelry while Gloria acted as his shill. In small towns where he suspected the pickings were lean, Gloria would put on some of the jewelry. The jewelers were supposed to believe they were getting a bargain by buying Gloria's own things.

When they stopped in Toledo, Gloria was interviewed by the *Toledo Times.* She told the reporter she was moving to New York, where she hoped to get a job in television news.

11

Fighting the Communists

When Gloria returned from India in 1958, she was filled with idealism and ready to save the world. She also burned to tell everyone all she had learned, but, to her dismay, no one was interested. "If I brought up India, an island of polite silence would appear in the conversation—and then the talk would flow right on around it," she later recalled.

Her listeners' apathy was a disappointment, but her reception in New York was worse. India had been open to an enthusiastic foreign visitor. New York was full of intelligent, attractive young graduates of Seven Sisters colleges with a desire for interesting and socially meaningful work, and many had better contacts than Gloria. After hobnobbing with people like Chester Bowles in the United States and Indira Gandhi in India and declining the opportunity to help archive M. N. Roy's material, Gloria was unprepared for the transition from distinguished foreign visitor to anonymous nobody. She expected to work for someone like Eric Sevareid, whose book *Not So Wild a Dream* she admired, or barring that, at least for a magazine like the *Saturday Review*.

Even with a résumé that included "Documentary and TV film clip scripts for Chotzinoff–Genser Productions," she could find nothing appealing. In addition to her discouragement, she felt pressured, because job hunting was expensive. After she felt she had exhausted the hospitality of a college friend on whose living-room floor she was sleeping, she answered a newspaper ad. She spent the next few weeks sharing an apartment on West Fifty-seventh Street with a group of young women she now speculates must have been "semihookers"— they "had a pay phone in the kitchen, no visible means of support, and went out every night."

Someone had noticed her talent, however, and he eventually gave her a chance to help the developing world. In India, Gloria had met Clive Gray, past international vice president of the National Student Association (NSA). He was in India for eighteen months, ostensibly to research a dissertation on Indian higher education at Delhi University and to promote NSA ties with student organizations in South and Southeast Asia. Unbeknownst to Gloria, Clive also was working as a contract agent for the Central Intelligence Agency, identifying likely foreign student leaders and developing useful relationships with them. He met Gloria and Kayla when his case officer at the U.S. embassy suggested he look up the two Smith graduates as possible sources for contacts within the student community.

Kayla had been active in NSA at Smith, but Clive found her "extremely neurotic." Gloria, on the other hand, so impressed Clive with her perceptions of India and Indian students that he included her on a list of candidates he gave to the CIA for a new operation the agency was planning in connection with the upcoming international youth festival in Vienna in summer 1959.

Clive's association with the CIA had grown out of his year as NSA international vice president. Students from between two and three hundred colleges and universities belonged to the NSA, whose activities included a travel bureau; representing students at UNESCO and other national and international organizations; lobbying on student-related issues; and an annual National Student Congress at which positions were developed and resolutions were passed on national and international issues of interest to students, from lowering the voting age to supporting desegregation.

The NSA actually began as a student-generated response to the cold war. At the end of World War II, many international organizations were formed to transcend national boundaries, but they quickly became instruments in the cold war. In some cases they were created for that purpose in the first place.

When the International Union of Students (IUS) held its first World Student Congress in Prague, Czechoslovakia, in 1946, twenty-five U.S.

students paid their own way to attend. Interested in promoting student exchanges and in other nonideological issues, these students were shocked by the party-line rhetoric of the Soviet representatives and by their ability to manipulate the organization. On their way home they decided they needed a national organization to represent United States students at future international gatherings. By 1947 they had organized the National Student Association.

As the Soviets' control of the IUS became more overt—the IUS's first Soviet vice president, Aleksandr Shelepin, became chief of the KGB in 1958, for example—the NSA students participating in international organizations became increasingly frustrated. Finally, in 1950, the student groups of the non-Communist West formed an alternative organization, the International Student Conference (ISC).

When the two international groups began competing for the affiliation of young people from the third-world nations emerging from colonialism, the Soviets had several advantages. First, because the Western nations were the former colonial powers, the Soviets could quite plausibly depict themselves as anticolonialist opponents of the third world nations' former oppressors. Second, the idealism of Marxism was more appealing than the selfishness of capitalism. Third, the Western students were undisciplined, individualistic, uncoordinated amateurs with no financial backing other than NSA dues. The Communists were well-disciplined, well-financed professional employees of the state.

Then the Central Intelligence Agency became involved. The NSA's liberal positions on domestic issues and its brief contact with the IUS, a Communist organization, ruled out any chance of attracting private sources of funding on the scale needed to counteract the IUS. However, the CIA was willing to help.

At that time the CIA was considered a glamorous Ivy League enclave (Yale was a prime feeder) and a haven for liberal internationalists. While domestic anticommunism reached massive proportions, opponents of overseas Soviet-exported communism ranged from right-wing attackers all the way across the spectrum of the left, from liberals to social democrats and socialists. Although a number of liberal anti-Communists worked for the CIA, even they were not immune to McCarthyist attacks.

One was Cord Meyer. In 1947 he had cofounded the United World Federalists, an organization that advocated a united world government to promote world peace. In 1953 he was charged by the FBI on the basis of such shadowy accusations about his opinions, associates, and probable Communist Party membership as, "An individual in contact with you in 1948 is reported to have said that he had concluded, on the basis of that contact, that you must be in the Communist Party." Meyer was suspended from the CIA without pay and took several months to clear himself. CIA director Allen Dulles stood by him and, in the following year, appointed Meyer chief of the International Operations Division, which oversaw the CIA's activities assisting the non-Communist left, including international student, labor, and cultural groups.

Accounts vary about exactly when some NSA officers began working with the CIA, but by 1951 the agency was providing financial support for the NSA's international activities. Over time—and probably inevitably, given the relative resources of the two organizations—the CIA involvement grew so extensive that the CIA funded most of the NSA's international activities, underwrote the budget of the International Student Conference (ISC), and recruited former NSA leaders as contract agents in the ISC secretariat. Only the international activities were funded—mainly through a New York-based conduit, the Foundation for Youth and Student Affairs.

Most students active with the NSA, even those interested in international activities, were unaware of its link to the CIA. NSA officers were elected annually, and only two or three of them—usually only the president and international vice president—were told about the CIA funding (in CIA terminology, they were made "witting"). Starting in the early 1950s, several of the "witting" NSA officers continued their involvement beyond their one-year NSA terms. Some became full CIA employees, though nominally working for a different U.S. agency. Others served as contract agents in the field. Contract agents were independent operators under contract with the CIA, as Clive Gray had been in India.

According to agency sources, when each group of new officers was told about the NSA–CIA relationship, they were offered the choice of continuing it or not. Invariably, they continued—they wouldn't have to raise the funds themselves (the alternative) and many were flattered by their introduction to realpolitik. Furthermore, the people who made them "witting" were usually people they already knew and respected, because they tended to be past NSA officers now working for the agency.

Once "witting," the officers were given a short course in spycraft. As Leonard Bebchick, a past NSA international vice president who later worked with Gloria, recalls, "I received one day of training. I learned how to destroy documents: burn them in an ashtray, stir up the ashes, and flush them down the toilet." If he had important conversations, he was to go into the bathroom and run the water (bugging equipment in those days could be defeated by the sound of running water). The agency also taught him how to tell if he was being followed and warned him always to unscrew a lightbulb to check for wiretaps.

Clive recommended Gloria for an operation in which American young people would be encouraged to go, and in some cases would be sent, to an international youth festival. Every two years the IUS, along with another international organization, the World Federation of Democratic Youth (WFDY), held a "World Festival of Youth and Students for Peace and Friendship," an enormous propaganda exercise attended by young people from all over the world. Cultural exhibits, performances, and workshops were offered; resolutions were passed; friendships were formed; candidates for scholarships were identified. The festivals were always held in a Soviet-bloc country.

While she was in India, Gloria had considered attending the 1957 event in Moscow. However, she wanted to go with Indian friends, and the Indian government made it difficult for Indian citizens to attend. Approximately 150 American students attended the Moscow festival, and though the State Department had actively discouraged attendance, twenty-five or thirty NSA student activists and their friends had some contact with the CIA before they went. Besides receiving financial assistance to travel, they were briefed on what to expect and who to call if they were harassed. They were also given information about issues—what was not known in the Soviet Union about such events as the Hungarian Revolution, for example, or what had happened to some Soviet writers whose work was no longer being published.

When they arrived, they found Soviet citizens and students, as well as young people from all over the world, so thirsty for information that some of them spent most of their time in Moscow talking to anyone who approached them. Among the U.S. young people was George Abrams, just out of law school, who had gone to the festival after hearing about it from an NSA friend. George regarded the experience as such an extraordinary opportunity for two-way communication that he was determined to interest more young people in attending the next one.

"All you had to be was open," he recalls. "There was no heavy pressure from the CIA. You were turning students loose in an arena in which they'd be very effective . . . they would be catalysts. It was natural and uncontrolled, with no direction to what you said and did. The students were just able to convey what they felt."

Then the Soviets decided to hold their 1959 festival in Vienna, though it would be riskier, because Austria was a genuine democracy. Not only would the Communist delegates be exposed to the non-Communist delegates, they would be exposed to a free press and citizens who could say what they chose. This meant that the Soviets could send only the most reliable delegates. Besides the delegates, they would have to send extra monitors to police them and to protect the third world delegates from undue Western influence. Even so, they considered it worth the risk and extra expense, because holding the festival in a neutral country would make the gathering seem more genuinely international and less like Soviet propaganda.

The CIA student-watchers were ecstatic. The conference's neutral site would offer unprecedented opportunities to counter the Soviets' propaganda. The Soviet-bloc locations had hampered their efforts at previous festivals, though the agency's operatives had done their best. Their previous festival-disrupting activities, financed by unwitting U.S. taxpayers, had included setting off stink bombs and sending out glossy invitations to nonexistent receptions at Communist-bloc embassies. (Eventually the opposition retaliated: At the 1962 festival in Helsinki, Finland, a hotel housing many American students was stink-bombed.)

Zbigniew Brzezinski (who later became President Jimmy Carter's national security advisor) learned of the festival's location while a Harvard graduate student, and he recalls the delight of the students interested in going: "We essentially strategized on making the case for the democratic perspective. . . . how to evoke memories of the Hungarian Revolution and how to identify ourselves with the Algerian Revolution. We wanted to show we were for self-determination and not for colonialism or imperialism, and that the communists did not have a monopoly on the national liberation struggle."

Inside the CIA, the youth affairs group planned to back an organization to recruit young people to attend. Like all the Austrian student organizations except the Austrian Communists, the NSA was officially boycotting the festival to avoid participating in a Soviet propaganda exercise. NSA students were free to attend as individuals, however, and for the first time the U.S. State Department, while discouraging students from attending as representatives of official organizations, did not discourage them from going as individuals. The CIA group wanted an organization that would do for many what they had done for a few:

seek out young people to go and brief them enough to enable them to participate effectively in both formal meetings and informal discussions. The point was to counter Soviet propaganda by talking about the United States realistically with third world students.

Most of the official American delegates to past festivals had been members of the Communist Party and Communist sympathizers. This time the CIA hoped their organization could get some of their own people into the delegation, because the official delegations passed resolutions on behalf of their countries. It wouldn't be easy, since the Communists controlled the credentials. (Most young people attended the festivals without belonging to delegations, as Gloria would have done had she traveled to the 1957 Moscow festival.)

When Clive Gray contacted Gloria, he told her some ex-NSA people were setting up an organization to send more non-Communist young people to the festival and asked if she was interested in working for it. Gloria did not want to be in Cambridge, Massachusetts, where the organization was to be headquartered, but she considered the offer because she hadn't found anything else—at least the job would be something meaningful. Before she went to Cambridge to be interviewed, she met an ex-NSA president, Harry Lunn, in New York. Although he told her he worked for the Defense Department, Harry was actually a CIA case officer working on the youth festival operation.

Once Harry approved, Gloria was sent to meet Len Bebchick and Paul Sigmund, both ex-NSA international vice presidents, and George Abrams, who was practicing law in Boston and working with them. While getting his Ph.D. in government at Harvard, Paul was teaching and serving as the resident tutor in Winthrop House, which allowed him to recruit students he thought could contribute to the festival. Len had finished law school and was working for the Civil Aeronautics Board while waiting to go into the active army reserves. He was bored, so when the CIA contacted him and asked if he wanted to run the festival organization, he accepted.

George, Len, and Paul liked Gloria and offered her the job of co-executive director of the Independent Service for Information on the Vienna Youth Festival (ISI). Gloria would help recruit students, but her primary responsibility was public relations. She was to deal with the media, get press coverage on the festival and the U.S. delegates, and help write publications about the festival before and afterward.

Gloria had a couple of concerns. Attending the Vienna festival presented obvious political risks, and she wasn't sure she would be comfortable encouraging people to go. McCarthy had self-destructed in 1954, but McCarthyism and anti-Communist sentiment were far from dead. She rightly suspected that Americans attending a Soviet festival would automatically have FBI dossiers opened. As she also correctly suspected, a record of attendance at a Communist youth festival could be enough to bar a government job or do other harm.

Gloria did not realize it, but there was also the possibility of physical danger. The Communists played rough. The Soviets' concept of "youth" stretched well up to the age of forty, and their concept of "student" was equally elastic. KGB agents would be everywhere, monitoring not only the Soviet delegates and their activities, but the delegates of both its captive allies and its first-world competitors.

Gloria's other concern was financial. How were they going to raise money to send students to a Communist festival? No corporation or foundation would touch it. At that point the men told Gloria that the CIA would fund the ISI through foundations, so money would not be a problem. Although the CIA would maintain files vouching for the people they funded or encouraged to attend, Gloria knew no one could guarantee that attending a Communist youth festival would not cause future problems. She was glad to learn the government was supporting an activity she considered important, however, so she took the job as co-executive director of the ISI.

Len, who had already worked with the CIA as NSA vice president, found working for the ISI to be a completely different experience.

"The festival operation was a brainstorm of the agency. When I made contact with Gloria, I knew that the agency knew of her and she was okay. I don't think I would have hired anyone, or agreed to hire anyone, unless I knew it was okay. This was an agency operation. I was an employee of the agency. For the first time, I was getting paid by the agency. I was reporting to the agency. This was quite different from being an officer in the NSA. Fundamentally different. And it was a new role for me. I had a boss.

"When I was an NSA officer, my boss was the National Student Congress, which set policy for the NSA. I had a case officer, but he wasn't running me. He was my liaison, my point of contact. With the Independent Service, in effect it was their operation. Not that I didn't use my judgment. I was hired to use my judgment. But it was a different relationship."

Paul Sigmund and George Abrams saw the operation in less dramatic terms. Paul had known about the connection and had run a seminar at the CIA's request even before he had become NSA international vice president. He viewed the NSA and the CIA as symbiotic and considered the ISI merely an extension of the previous arrangement. George believes the U.S. student participation at the Vienna Festival would have happened with or without CIA assistance.

Gloria, who had no previous knowledge of the NSA's connection to the CIA, saw the ISI as a front for the NSA rather than for the CIA. The NSA, as a member of the non-Communist ISC international student organization, was officially boycotting the IUS-sponsored festival, so the ISI would help U.S. students to attend.

Gloria worked mostly with Len and Paul in Cambridge, though she spent a fair amount of time with Harry Lunn. Harry developed an enormous crush on Gloria, who regarded him as a friend, and Len watched the proceedings from his "ringside seat." Recalling that Harry was only one of many who fell in love with Gloria, Len also notes, "A characteristic of Gloria's that I observed was that she was very open and engaging, but there came a point when you hit a brick wall. I noted it at the time. There was a part of her that was absolutely walled off and you couldn't penetrate it."

Harry may have been smitten from the beginning. How else to explain the fact that Gloria was given a slightly higher salary than Len? Len thought he had been clever to get the equivalent of his Civil Aeronautics Board annual salary of $5,000, but Gloria was paid $100 a week, plus a $5 a day supplement for living expenses "because Cambridge rents were so expensive."

Despite the opportunity to meet people like socialist Michael Harrington and political scientist Daniel Ellsberg, Gloria was unhappy in Cambridge. Living in a basement apartment that brought back memories of the basement apartment in Toledo, she was lonely. She was also disappointed that she had not found the kind of job she wanted and feared that she might be on the road back to Ohio.

Furthermore, she was in, but not of, the Harvard community—in a rather peripheral, second-class position. Although Gloria clung to a vision of herself as an outsider, it was a complicated outsiderness. She felt like an outsider, and at some level she wanted it that way. However, though Gloria felt like an outsider in her heart, she was usually an insider as far as others were concerned. In that way she combined the benefits of being an insider with the psychic gratification of distancing herself defensively.

Part of her discomfort at Harvard was that she really was on the outside. As usual, though, she threw herself into her work and did a superb job, encouraging students to go to the festival, writing pamphlets, and dreaming up schemes to publicize the festival. Publicity was important, not just to let students know about the event, but to protect those who went. The ISI wanted to make the general public aware that students who attended a Communist youth festival were not all Communists, but rather covered the entire political spectrum.

One scheme actually drew coverage from the *New York Times*. Gloria and Len dressed up as third world festival delegates, "Mohini, an Indian girl, and Kofi, a Ghanaian." They peppered an American delegate, University of Wisconsin senior Gary Weissman, with questions like "Why does your government denounce the Soviet suppression of the Hungarian revolt when it has itself sent troops to Lebanon and interfered in Guatemala?" A suggested answer for the U.S. student was to concede that Mohini and Kofi had a point on Lebanon, but to note that the Lebanese government had asked for troops. (The response to the Guatemalan portion of the question was not recorded in the *Times*. In fact, the CIA had assisted in a coup to overthrow a democratically elected president, who then was replaced by a military junta, but Len and Gloria would not have been given such information.)

Gloria also persuaded CBS to produce a documentary on the festival, but three weeks before the festival CBS canceled it because it was deemed not newsworthy. Frantic, Gloria wrote to C. D. Jackson, a Time–Life vice president. Gloria didn't like C. D. Jackson. When she visited him, he kept her waiting for hours. She recalls, "He was blustery, a name-dropper always talking about how he wrote speeches for Eisenhower. An asshole—no, a king-sized asshole." However, he was very powerful and helped her in a number of ways, from getting free photographs for pamphlets to raising money from American Express. Gloria thought he was especially important because he could encourage *Time* to cover the festival.

C. D. Jackson was a leading figure in the history of the cold war, serving as Eisenhower's chief of psychological warfare during World War II and much of his presidency. Among other things, Jackson helped establish Radio Free Europe and Radio Liberty, which beamed U.S.-backed, CIA-financed radio broadcasts into the Communist bloc. When he left government service to return to Time–Life, he continued his involvement and kept in close contact with high-level CIA officials.

When Gloria asked for help with CBS, Jackson wrote to CBS's president, Frank Stanton, who was also on the board of Radio Free Europe and was another of the most powerful men in the country. Explaining that he had been "unobtrusively quite active" in "acting as a clearing house" for some of ISI's problems, Jackson asked Stanton to help, explaining, "The Vienna Youth Festival itself is an extremely important event in the Great Game. This is the first time commies have held one of these shindigs on our side of the iron curtain."

In response, Stanton invited Gloria to his office. He assured her that while CBS did not plan a full hour-long documentary, the network would assign its best documentary cameraman and one of its top correspondents, and, if possible, it would create a half-hour special. Jackson reported triumphantly to Cord Meyer, head of the CIA division that ran the festival efforts, "Gloria Steinem asked me to help out on this, and Frank Stanton came through handsomely." According to Gloria, "Of course, this was more blustering by Stanton. What his letter really said was that the hour documentary had been canceled and would remain so."

Jackson assisted in other ways as well. Gloria sent him a letter asking for help financing four delegates too prominent to include on the ISI chartered plane. Three were members of ISI, but the ISI thought they should travel independently. They were Zbigniew Brzezinski, a Polish diplomat's son, who was knowledgeable about Soviet and East European communism and worked as a teacher at Harvard and researcher at the Harvard Russian Research Center; Julius Várallyay, a Hungarian refugee who would be valuable in coordinating "counter-Festival activities" and contacting Asian and African delegations; and Tom Garrity, a young lawyer and experienced in-fighter who had worked with the NSA and student groups "when the Communist attempts to infiltrate youth groups [were at their] post-war peak." The fourth was socialist leader Michael Harrington, who was "far too identifiable to participate in the Festival officially."

Jackson found the money, but Michael Harrington withdrew his name. In spite of the ISI's interest in sending a politically heterogeneous group (Catholic anti-Communists, socialists, liberals) and encouraging all participants to say whatever they wanted, someone slipped up with Harrington. As he later wrote, he had been concerned about accepting the offer of plane fare: "Was it permissible for a socialist to accept a subsidy from an outfit being patronized by the State Department? (Had I dreamed that the CIA was involved, there would have been no issue.)" After engaging in a long debate that included as an argument the fact that in 1917 Lenin had accepted the Kaiser's largesse in order to get back to Russia, the National Committee of the Young People's Socialist League decided that "I would tell the front group that I would accept an airline ticket from them only if I could go on my own, completely independent of their organization, and with the explicit understanding that I would attack American capitalism and foreign policy as vigorously as Communism. That did it. The offer of help was withdrawn forthwith and I paid my own way, having nothing to do with what turned out to be the CIA's dirty games."

At one point Jackson wrote to ask Gloria about the U.S. Festival Committee, the young people officially credentialed by the Soviets to send delegates and run the U.S. delegation during the festival. Gloria responded, "The most tactful thing one can say . . . is that its publications are indistinguishable from those of the Festival organizers." Her letter described the backgrounds of some of the leaders, but asked Jackson not to use any of the material for publication without discussing it with her first. Jackson, who was in close contact with Cord Meyer and CIA director Allen Dulles, undoubtedly could have gotten the information from the CIA (which probably was Gloria's source), but for whatever reason, he preferred to ask Gloria.

Jackson was helping the CIA with more festival-related activities than Gloria knew. He worked with Radio Free Europe strategist Sam Walker to arrange for the translation, printing, and distribution to festival delegates of a number of works critical of communism, such as *Dr. Zhivago*. He also facilitated financial and technical assistance to an Austrian newspaper editor, so that he could publish newspapers during the festival to counter the official festival daily newspaper. The official newspaper was printed by the Soviets in advance of the festival and shipped to Vienna.

The festival began during the last week in July. It was a mixture of youthful high spirits, high-minded idealism, Russian thuggery, and hopeless bumbling. A movie version might have been called *Mission Impossible Meets Animal House* or *Campus Commie-Fighters Con Communists*. Walter Pincus, who later became an eminent journalist, working chiefly at the *Washington Post*, recalls the event as "a college weekend with Russians." The Americans, though patriotic and idealistic, were also out for a good time. Many of the Russians and their allies were humorless, heavy-handed, and prone to beating up people, though their seriousness was understandable under the circumstances—

the penalties facing Russians who failed their missions were far more severe than an FBI dossier.

Tens of thousands of young people poured into Vienna for ten days of fireworks, parades, ballet, opera, workshops, and discussion groups. The festival was an enormous undertaking. The previous event, held in Moscow, had cost an estimated $100 million. Housed in hotels, dormitories, and even riverboats, the delegates were assigned accommodations by the festival committee according to their importance to the undertaking.

The Soviets had to manage their own people as well. The Leningrad Ballet, for example, not only had to be fed and housed in Vienna, but every member of the company had to be guarded at all times to prevent contact with outsiders with dangerous ideas. Many performers were even transported in buses with windows covered, so they couldn't look out. The Chinese were so sequestered that the restaurant where they took their meals barred everyone, Austrians as well as other delegates; even the waiters were not allowed to speak to them. Burly guards checked credentials at all entrances to the festival (though the Americans found secret routes in and out) and tried to prevent photographs if they thought the shot might seem unfavorable—such as photos of themselves manhandling delegates.

Festival organizers also had to contend with unhappy hosts. With CIA assistance, the Austrians took busloads of delegates to the Hungarian border to show them the watchtowers and barbed wire fences that had been erected to keep the Hungarians from escaping from their supposedly happy Communist country into decadent, neutral Austria.

When the ISI directors arrived in Vienna, offices had been prepared for them. Across the street from Len's, the Soviets had a camera recording everyone going in and out of the office, and they were obvious as they followed Len wherever he went. When the Austrians then put a tail on Len's Soviet tail, he felt like a real spy.

Len never got to visit the festival ground anyway, because, as he says, he was "mission control." The ISI people were given public telephone locations from which to call whenever they knew anything. Len tried to coordinate the "intelligence" and issue instructions. Every morning the ISI leaders gathered to decide the day's plans. Zbigniew Brzezinski recalls, "We would have strategizing sessions in the little hotel where some of us stayed. I remember Gloria lying in bed in a sort of frilly robe while the rest of us sat around the bed strategizing. I thought it was kind of an amusing and slightly eccentric scene."

Besides inserting themselves into meetings and discussions, the ISI-recruited students acted as agents provocateurs, which was dangerous, but part of the fun. Zbigniew walked through the Russian encampment—each country had an area—and bumped into Russians on purpose so he could say, "Out of my way, Russian pig!" in Russian with a Polish accent, just to stir up dissension between the Russians and the Poles.

On the last day of the festival, Zbigniew, a student of his, and Walter Pincus crawled across the rooftops of eight- and ten-story buildings. When they reached a building facing a downtown Vienna square where the festival's closing ceremonies were to be held that evening, they concealed themselves and lay for hours, waiting for nightfall. Once the evening program began in the well-lit square, they unfurled an Algerian and a Hungarian flag, each with its center cut out to symbolize the revolutions, and a banner they had made out of sheets that read "Peace and Freedom" in German. When the Communists realized what was happening, they doused the lights in the square and sent security men into the building. In total darkness, the three dashed across a board they had left between theirs and an adjacent building, lifted their plank, hurried down the next-door building's stairs, and joined the crowd in the square.

Even getting into the meetings was difficult, since the Communists controlled admission, location, timing, and technology. When the ISI students tried to attend the U.S. delegation meetings, the Soviets offered swimming parties in the Danube and other distractions. When that failed to distract them all, they challenged delegates' credentials. When the ISI people finally tried holding meetings out of doors, they were drowned out by Scottish bagpipers who suddenly came marching by.

Gloria ran a press bureau and handled the media, writing press releases, and finding delegates for reporters to interview, since the press was not welcome inside the festival. To help determine the day's approach, she was provided with a daily report on what appeared in the U.S. press. Most reporters relied on the bureau's daily press release, which allowed the coverage to be manipulated to an extent that amazed Len. Only the *New York Times*'s Polish correspondent, Gloria's friend from India, Abe Rosenthal, seemed to do his own legwork. "Rosenthal did his own reporting, and it pissed us off no end," Len recalls, "but he was the exception. Most of the press had no discipline at all."

Sam Walker wrote to C. D. Jackson, "Gloria is all you said she was, and then some. She is operating on sixteen synchronized cylinders and has charmed the natives, including Molden [a newspaper owner help-ing the operation], without beads. Her Independent Information Center is small but effective; largely thanks to female intuition, she has set up an International News Bureau which has at least a 50-percent chance of being *the* place to go for the other side of the story, *with* each of the Austrian groups operating under the assumption that they are running it. To be sure, she has able help, and guidance, but a good deal of credit goes to her and the immediate organization which planned her role. I think you will be pleased with this (i.e. friends) aspect of things all the way up and down the line."

Published in five languages, the daily festival newspapers were very popular because they covered real events, in contrast to the Commu-nists' preprinted newspapers. As a result, the Communists did every-thing they could to prevent the printing and distribution of the competing dailies, including arson at the printer and beating up the people who tried to distribute them.

Gloria assisted wherever she could. Sam Walker wrote to C. D. Jack-son again, commenting, "Gloria's group continues to do yeoman ser-vice, distributing books etc. to the point where the cry has gone up 'Never before have so many Young Republications distributed so much Socialist literature with such zeal!' "

By the end of the festival most of the ISI participants believed they had succeeded in their efforts. They had provoked the Soviets into betraying their totalitarian nature to their target audience of developing nations' potential leaders. George Abrams recalls, "The youth festivals were massive propaganda, and by challenging them, we had enormous impact on public relations. As a result, the Russians didn't get what they wanted." Many regarded the Vienna festival as a good first step and were determined that the next festival operation would be bigger and better.

12

Launched Into Social Orbit

After the festival Len went into the army, returning occasionally to help Gloria and Paul Sigmund compile a report on the festival for publication. Through Walter Friedenberg, who visited her in Cambridge, Gloria met Walter's college roommate, Harold Hayes, an *Esquire* editor. Hayes was at Harvard for a year on a Nieman fellowship, a program for journalists. Although Gloria was put off by the controlling way Harold treated his wife, Susan, they became friends, and Gloria met a number of magazine people through the couple. She was especially impressed by *Esquire*'s assistant art director, Robert Benton.

By early 1960 Gloria had finished working on the report and moved to New York, determined this time to find work as a writer. She found an apartment in a brownstone on West Eighty-first Street, across from the Museum of Natural History. Her first real apartment had large windows that let in the sunshine, and she cherished it, furnishing it mostly from secondhand shops and auction houses. She bought a tea cart and painted it red, telling her friends she had always wanted a little red wagon, and a pair of tattered brocade imitation-medieval chairs that were so large the sitters' feet dangled. Ruth came to visit and sewed curtains for the windows.

Harold Hayes introduced her to Harvey Kurtzman, the cartoonist and editor who pioneered antiwar horror comic books in the middle of the cold war and then in 1952 created *Mad* magazine. Kurtzman hired her to help him put out a new, humorous magazine called *Help!* She was paid for only two days a week, but she worked more because, except for a layout artist, they produced the entire magazine themselves. Among her editorial duties were writing humorous captions, setting up photo shoots, and persuading famous people to appear on the magazine's cover and in *fumetti* (comic strips made with real photographs).

Gloria also began hanging around the *Esquire* offices, helping on projects, especially with Robert Benton. At that time *Esquire* was becoming one of the liveliest, most exciting magazines around. It published work by James Baldwin, Gay Talese, and Norman Mailer, and featured examples of what later would be called the New Journalism— stories that used the techniques of literature, such as narrative, scenes, and dialogue, to tell factual stories. Although he was an art director, Robert Benton had begun to work with David Newman, the fiction editor's assistant, producing clever, irreverent pieces, full of charts, artwork, and mock sociology. With his college roommate Harvey Schmidt (who later wrote *The Fantasticks*), Benton already had produced *The In and Out Book,* and now Benton and Newman and others were determining what was in or out, cool or uncool, in the pages of *Esquire.*

After writing several uncredited pieces, Gloria had her first tiny byline (it really was in tiny type) in a four-page spread, "Sophisticated Fun & Games," in the July 1961 issue. In the September *Esquire* she wrote captions for a fashion spread ("If you're out with a very New York kind of girl—career, debutante or possibly Sarah Lawrence . . .") and recipes for bachelors to serve their dates. Her "10-Minute Gourmet" relied mostly on canned food, while the "15-Minute Gourmet" included canned, frozen, slice-and-bake, a jar of béarnaise sauce, and a fresh steak.

Gloria and Robert Benton began dating. Gloria describes their relationship as the first time she really had been in love, demoting the relationship with Blair—an attraction so compelling she took herself off to India at least partly to escape it—to "infatuation. . . . That is, Blair was a kind, sexual, sensual, funny person, but we didn't share interests, so there was an awful lot of both of us that was left out of the picture. But with Benton [as she calls him], we were totally in this relationship."

Benton was about Gloria's height and was the same age (twenty-six in 1960), twinkly-eyed, with a warm smile. Gloria says she was in her "one black skirt, one brown men's sweater period," but everyone else (male) recalls her as looking spectacular. The two spent a great deal of time with Benton's boss at *Esquire,* Milton Glaser, and his wife, Shirley. The latter thought the pair complemented each other perfectly: Benton quiet and "teddybearish," and Gloria so verbal and confident. The four often were joined by art director (and later, photographer) Henry Wolf and his current lover. Courtly and talented, Henry dated women so young that, though he was older than she, Gloria always teased him that she was too old for him.

Through Henry, Gloria met an artist named Barbara Nessim, and when Gloria's landlord announced he was raising her rent beyond her means (from $150 to $180 a month), Gloria asked Barbara if she could move in with her. Six years younger than Gloria, Barbara was living in a tiny studio apartment ten blocks away, but she was looking for a roommate and was agreeable as long as they were compatible. "Two things," she told Gloria. "I'm not the neatest person in the world, and I like to stay up late working." Both suited Gloria perfectly. Soon afterward, Gloria found them a larger studio above a French restaurant on West Fifty-sixth Street, off Fifth Avenue in a block filled with restaurants and offices. There the two of them lived, in a 25-by-20-foot, $125-a-month studio with a tiny galley kitchen and a bathroom, for the next six years.

On the surface, the two women seemed completely different. Gloria was a tall, willowy, serene Seven Sisters graduate with an elegant accent and midwestern reserve, a witty "wiseguy," but always serious about politics. Barbara was voluble and effervescent, with a strong Bronx accent and a total lack of interest in politics. At Pratt Institute, where she had studied fine art, she had had trouble fitting in.

"At Pratt," she recalls, "the fine artists were expected to starve and suffer, and they were all interested in getting to Europe. I couldn't have cared less about Europe. I was happy living in New York and eager to start my career as an illustrator. I was very much from the Bronx [she had been chosen Miss Sephardic of Mosholu Parkway], and I tried to bring dancing and fun to college. The fine artists were too depressed, so I decided I must be a commercial artist. I was interested in supporting myself." She was so apolitical that when Gloria wanted to talk about India, Barbara only wanted to hear about the saris.

In fact, in many ways they were similar. Both were kind, generous women, serious about their work and eager for success, but ready to go dancing and have fun; both expected to marry, only "someday—not yet," whenever that would be. Over the years, each was gone much of the time, staying overnight or for a weekend with various lovers, but always returning to their own place. They spent many hours, day and night, working together in the same room with never an argument.

Because of the magazine, Gloria and Benton could go to free screenings, so they liked to meet after work, see a movie, and then go for a hamburger and talk about what they had seen. They loved the same movies, the same books. If they didn't love them equally, "at least," says Benton, "we could bring each other into our interests and passions." The exception was politics, which interested Benton hardly at all.

It was an important relationship for both. Besides encouraging Gloria to write, Benton taught her a "sense of place." He was "totally himself, and this person had come to New York on a Continental bus from Waxahachie, Texas." Benton was the first person to ask her about Toledo "in a way that made me feel I could or should talk about it without trying to be amusing. He would say, 'Tell me a Toledo story.'"

In other words, Benton showed her that she need not reinvent herself to fit her current milieu. She could just be the sum of all her experiences. Gloria understood the concept in theory, but in practice she was too insecure to emulate him. She might let down her guard within the confines of their relationship, but certainly not to the world in general. Gloria negotiated her passage through the world by depending on the kindness of strangers, and she had been doing it for too long and too successfully to abandon her caution.

Gloria helped Benton as well. During their time together she convinced him he was more than just an art director, no matter how talented, and no matter how visual his thinking. "I can only speak for myself," he muses, "but I was a very different person at the end of that relationship than I was at the beginning." An avid reader, Benton had taken one creative writing course in college, which he had flunked, but Gloria encouraged him. "She believed in quirky ideas. When you're friends with someone, then you say all the quirky stuff you think. And when you find someone who really listens to you and encourages that, it is terrific." In retrospect, Benton sees Gloria as the first in a progression of people who helped him become the writer and director who created *Bonnie and Clyde, Kramer vs. Kramer,* and *Places in the Heart.* Benton remains an admirer: "She was always a star. From the time she was five years old, she was a star in some way. . . . She's also a wiseguy. She cannot resist being an irreverent wiseguy, and it's deeply appealing." He also recalls the importance to Gloria of "her political world—her sense of politics was always there."

They socialized with a number of Benton's Texas friends from the "Texas Mafia," including writers Liz Smith and Harvey Schmidt and actor Tom Jones. Sometimes the group would arise early or stay up all night, don white clothes, and go to Central Park to play croquet, retiring afterward to the Plaza Hotel, where the losers paid for brunch. Checking their croquet set in the cloakroom, they felt terribly sophisticated and glamorous and pleased with themselves. (In what appears to be one of her characteristic attempts to counteract the impression that she might actually have been an insider, Gloria explains, "Now this was a Sears and Roebuck croquet set, because in Texas and Ohio you don't know about English croquet. So we weren't sophisticated enough to know this was the totally wrong kind of croquet set and croquet philosophy.")

Deeply in love, by 1962 Gloria and Benton were talking of marrying. It seemed the obvious next step to Benton, who says, "I think I was planning on getting married more than she was." However, the qualms Gloria had experienced during her engagement to Blair reappeared, so they decided to take things step by step. They decided they would get a marriage license and wait to see how they felt. Then Benton would buy a new suit and Gloria would buy a dress and see how they felt.

Gloria felt terrible. She was not twenty-eight years old and she adored Benton, so what was her problem? "I really cared about Benton," she says, "so I kept thinking there was something wrong with me that I didn't want to get married." Marriage seemed so annihilating. "Then, you couldn't really remain yourself in a free way, as you can now. It's not easy now, but it's possible. Then, it just didn't seem possible," she muses, more than thirty years later. "It wasn't just compromising—I can deal with compromising. It was giving up your entire professional life, your name, your identity. It wasn't just compromises. It was surrender."

She was so distressed, she visited a psychiatrist, hoping he would help her with her fears. She spent most of the sessions crying. When the psychiatrist, who had been recommended by Harvey Kurtzman's friend Milt Kamen, said anything, Gloria found his comments wildly inappropriate. Now she recalls him as outrageous. "In the middle of my telling him some emotional story, he would ask me how much I was paid a word. Then when I went to a group session he ran, he just sadistically beat up on people."

Finally Gloria decided for herself that she just couldn't marry Benton. When she told him she didn't want to get married, their affair ended. Benton recalls, "It just became clear that we should have stayed friends and nothing more. Unfortunately, once you've crossed one kind of line, you can't say, 'Hey, whoa, we've made a mistake. Let's go back to being friends.' It doesn't work that way."

In retrospect, Gloria wonders if their shared sense of all or nothing—that they had to do everything together or not do it at all—was part of the problem. She had not gone south for a sit-in during the civil rights movement because it was not a passion Benton shared, and she regretted it. "A gift for holding loosely is the key to holding at all," she later wrote, "and neither [of us] yet possessed this understanding."

Meanwhile, another youth festival was imminent. Because of plans to continue working on future festivals, the name of the Independent Service for Information on the Vienna Festival had been changed to Independent Research Service (IRS) in late 1959, when the organization's official headquarters traveled to New York with Gloria. She had provided the IRS with a mailing address in New York and had dealt with whatever desultory correspondence arrived in the interim between festivals.

By late 1961, Gloria was securing an increasing stream of writing assignments, so she did not have time to serve as a full-time co-executive director. She told Paul Sigmund and the others that she would volunteer when she could and would work with the press during the festival itself. The 1962 festival was to be held in Helsinki, Finland, and Gloria found the IRS a new headquarters in a two-room office in an East Thirty-seventh Street townhouse. Rhodes scholar and incoming NSA president Dennis Shaul became the new full-time director, and Gloria found people to work on a group of festival newspapers similar to the ones produced in Vienna.

Among those who recall being recruited by Gloria is *Washington Post* managing editor Robert Kaiser. The Yale sophomore met Gloria when he attended the IRS festival-orientation meeting she ran in Cambridge. Along with other Yale students and a number of Harvard *Crimson* staffers, he planned to write for the newspapers in Helsinki.

Another editor who says Gloria recruited him is Henry Raymont, who was United Press's Latin American diplomatic correspondent, based in

Washington. As acting United Press Havana, Cuba, bureau chief during the 1961 Bay of Pigs invasion, he had been arrested and falsely accused of working for the CIA. He was saved from being shot only after twenty-seven countries appealed to Fidel Castro on his behalf. Given that history, Henry considers involving him in a CIA-front operation to be "unconscionable—it jeopardized my career by giving ex post facto credibility to the Cubans' unfounded charges."

When he met Gloria, he was at Harvard as a Nieman fellow. He recalls, "Gloria represented herself as a delegate or recruiter for the NSA. It was my understanding that the NSA was paying my way to Helsinki, so I accepted and asked United Press to extend my stay at Harvard. I remember Gloria and Paul Sigmund had a meeting and told us that it was a group of people interested in keeping the Communists from dominating the festival, rather than just anti-Communists going. The journalists they recruited were totally professional. I remember one of my meetings with Gloria in New York. After we had tea at Schrafft's and she told me the story of her life, I would have voted for her as senator. It was a great performance."

Still at Harvard, Paul Sigmund again recruited a number of people, including graduate student Sheila Tobias. Sheila worked in the New York office for several months before the festival and then went to the festival as editor for one of the newspapers. A 1957 Radcliffe graduate, Sheila was puzzled by some of the anomalies in the operation—the secretary who lived in the townhouse and acted more like the boss, for example—but when she confronted Paul, who was sometimes in the New York office, he was evasive.

Gloria was in and out of the office, too, and the two women became friendly. Sheila recalls Gloria as "an interesting bundle of contradictions"—her good looks, queenlike manner, and long fingernails contrasted with her obvious intelligence and the fact that she wore the glasses she needed instead of squinting, which was more usual in those days. "I'd call her a good-looking nerd," Sheila says with a laugh.

Gloria enlisted the volunteer services of *Esquire*'s features editor, Clay Felker, and Sam Antupit, the art director for *Show*, another magazine from which Gloria had begun to get writing assignments. After creating a poster for the festival, Sam became so interested that he decided to go to the festival, too. They were going to produce English-, French-, and Spanish-language newspapers, each with a separate editor. Sam, who was told the enterprise was being underwritten by Danish businessmen who didn't want Helsinki to go under to the Soviets, would be art director for all three.

Before they left for Helsinki, Gloria took Clay to visit Gus Tyler, who as political director of the International Ladies Garment Workers' Union was used to dealing with Communists. Gus gave them a crash course in tactics: "I told them, in great detail, how to line up delegates; how to get them out for a vote; how to find out what the opponents were doing. For example, you used meeters and greeters: you got your people to befriend and act as guides to people. And I taught them how to use rumormongers to start rumors. And how to use plants to find out what the opposition was doing. And how to organize voting in committees. Because the Communists always outlast everyone else—they wait for people to fall asleep. So I told them to have people take turns sleeping and have all the room numbers ready, so they could call their people when a vote came up. And how to use the loudspeaker system to multiply cheers. And how to have a 'prominent candidate': you make a prominent candidate by saying there's a call for you from the White House several times, until it gets heard."

Gloria and Clay spent most of their time putting out the newspapers and dealing with the press. Former and current CBS Moscow bureau chiefs Daniel Schorr and Marvin Kalb were there, and it was some of Kalb's questions that led Sam Antupit to suspect the government might be involved.

The IRS's Helsinki festival operation was better run than the ISI's had been in Vienna, but there were always complications. Gloria had asked Clay to edit the English-language newspaper and Henry Raymont the Spanish edition. She had found a Togolese writer to run the French edition. Ted Whittemore, unbeknownst to the others a CIA employee, served as managing editor for all three. Then the Togolese editor decided to spend his time in Helsinki socializing instead of working, so Gloria promoted Bob Kaiser, who knew a little French, to take his place.

Bob roomed with David Swanson, a Harvard student who served as photographer for all three newspapers. David received a call every morning from the embassy telling him where to shoot. Festival destinations could be hazardous for photographers, and David was chased a couple of times by "KGB people with gold teeth." Fortunately he was on the Harvard track team.

When Sam wanted to photograph the meetings, Gloria gave him a telephone number to call and said, "There's a man in Denmark. If you call him, he'll send over some Polaroid cameras." Sam recalls, "We gave Polaroid cameras to these Harvard kids and they went in and took pictures of all the proceedings. David Swanson was just fearless— like Jimmy Olson in *Superman*. He was a bespectacled Harvard youth, innocence personified."

Once in Helsinki, Clay was impressed by the skills of Gloria, whom he knew at that point only as a young writer with whom he had worked at *Esquire*. An East German ship housing delegates was anchored outside their newspaper offices, and every day they watched the East Germans march in military ranks to the festival. Just as the festival was ending, the Soviets committed a horrendous public-relations gaffe by exploding the largest nuclear bomb to date, and Gloria took advantage of the opportunity. When delegates staged a demonstration in front of the ship with signs reading "Stop the Bomb," and "No Testing East or West," Clay recalls, they "so infuriated one of the festival organizers that he seized one of the banners and ripped it up." Having foreseen that something like that might happen, Gloria had alerted a UPI photographer, and a photograph was run all over the world. Clay notes, "It was an enormous defeat for the Soviets."

Clay explains admiringly, "Gloria has incredible political savvy and a seemingly effortless ability to organize and get people to do what she wants them to do." It was those "remarkable political instincts," he adds, that led him to make her a political reporter years later.*

Of all the associates, friends, and lovers Gloria met in the early 1960s, none had as much influence on her career as Clay Felker. Clay had been fascinated from the beginning by the "striking young woman" hanging around the *Esquire* office trying to get work, so when he heard she was a Smith graduate, he saw his chance. As he later announced often and in public, "I thought anyone with legs like that must be a writer." About a year before she impressed him in Helsinki, he had conjured up an assignment for her. The birth-control pill seemed to be revolutionizing sexual behavior, so he suggested that Gloria write a piece about its effects on young women and use Smith as a base for her research.

It was her first major feature assignment, and Gloria was thrilled. Always an enthusiastic researcher, she amassed piles of material and labored painstakingly to shape it into a typical *Esquire* article, serious but witty. Her first effort was so pedantic that Clay couldn't resist

---

*Gloria disagreed with some of this account. See the notes for some of the details.

telling her, "Congratulations. You've managed to make sex dull." Then he had her rewrite it until she turned out a publishable piece.

It is clear from the result of their combined effort, "The Moral Disarmament of Betty Coed" (September 1962), that Clay's forte was ideas, not line editing. Gloria took interesting research, a touch of humor, and some protofeminist ideas, and mangled them with garbled syntax. Sample: "Constant fear was hardly the condition prior to the pill in this country, but removing the last remnants of fear of social consequences seems sure to speed American women, especially single women, toward the view that their sex practices are none of society's business."

After she became a famous feminist, Gloria's last paragraph was frequently cited as evidence of her prescience:

> The real danger of the contraceptive revolution may be the acceleration of woman's role-change without any corresponding change of man's attitude toward her role. As one psychiatrist said in a paraphrase of Margaret Mead's verdict on the education of women, "The main trouble with sexually liberating women is that there aren't enough sexually liberated men to go around."

What those sentences also demonstrated was her ability to identify and convey the important points of an issue—an attribute that would prove infinitely more valuable. Although convoluted sentences would remain a problem, her writing improved over time. Her perspicacity was already apparent.

When Gloria and Benton broke up, they were still bound together by a contract with Viking Press to write an anthology called *The Pleasure Book*. They planned to combine already-published writing with original pieces and illustrations. Together, they had already created a number of clever, smart-alecky pieces for *Esquire,* and Gloria had begun to write them for *Show.* Typical of their collaboration was "The Student Prince, Or How to Seize Power Though an Undergraduate" (September 1962), which advised college students how to create an interesting persona by faking it. A typical ploy was "Rent a very good painting for your room. When you have to send it back, say the artist was having a show." Poor students working their way through school were advised to eschew academic jobs or waiting tables at sorority houses in favor of driving a beer truck at night or selling their blood.

After the breakup, Benton suggested that she work on the book with Sam Antupit, and Viking agreed to the change. Therefore, in 1963, at the age of twenty-nine, Gloria published her first book. Because most of the material seemed to be about the beach, she and Sam changed its name to *The Beach Book*. Gloria wrote some chapters herself (and forgot to sign them), including several about role playing (a specialty of hers) and an essay called "White Skin as a Status Symbol" ("If you . . . cannot tan at all, the only recourse is to make white skin seem desirable"). She combined those with an eclectic collection of material all somehow connected to the beach—"Noah and the Flood" from the Bible, Amy Vanderbilt's advice on swimming-pool etiquette, D-Day photographs, Renoir's *The Bathers,* songs like "I Am the Monarch of the Sea," and Edward Albee's play *The Sandbox*.

She organized a section of "Things to Read While Lying on Your Front" into a seven-days' supply of articles of increasing length, "scientifically planned to occupy the time you should spend in the sun." Then, to toast the reader's other side, she offered suggestions for "Things to Think About While Lying on Your Back," such as:

> THE THIRD DAY: Who should play you when they make a movie of your life.

> THE FOURTH DAY: Okay, so here you are and there's the earth and the sun and the universe and a lot more universes . . . and then what?

> THE FIFTH DAY: How did they lay the Atlantic cable and is it all right. Who should play your friends in the movie of your life.

The cover was foil-lined to double as a reflector, which provoked an indignant letter from the American Cancer Society. Sam supplied clever graphics, and Gloria talked a new friend, Harvard economist John Kenneth Galbraith, into writing the book's introduction.

By the time *The Beach Book* was published, Gloria was involved with Viking publisher Tom Guinzburg. They had met through Benton and began going out in late summer 1962, when the book was already in progress. Gloria recalls that Tom, concerned about dating a writer his company was publishing, asked her to meet with her editor, Catherine Carver, in the Schrafft's downstairs from Viking's offices.

Besides Gloria, Viking Press, which Tom's father, Harold Guinzburg, had founded in 1925, had published such authors as John Steinbeck, Graham Greene, Rebecca West, and Saul Bellow. When Harold died unexpectedly in 1960, Tom took over the firm at the age of thirty-four.

Soon after his father's premature death, Tom's marriage ended. The following January, he left his wife, the actress Rita Gam, and two children.

Not only was Tom well connected, he was polished and charming. He was eight years older than Gloria, and full of stories of the *Paris Review*, where he had worked in the early 1950s, and of his adventures in Mexico with his college roommate, William Buckley. Tom was completely smitten. "I remember I borrowed a house on the beach in Amagansett and Gloria was to come out for the weekend. She had to go to a wedding in New Jersey, so we decided she would take a little plane out. The plane landed in a potato field in East Hampton, and when she got off that plane in some red dress she'd worn for the wedding, it was the most romantic thing that had ever happened to me."

Tom impressed Gloria, too. "I think I remember the first time we went out. I was in our studio apartment on West Fifty-sixth Street and he was divorced and living in his mother's house on the river somewhere. He said, 'Leave your house and walk east on Fifty-sixth on the south side of the street, and I'll walk west on Fifty-sixth and we'll meet somewhere along the way.' I thought it was very romantic, walking in this breezy summer New York night."

Tom had grown up among the privileged "WASPy Jewish" families like the Sulzbergers, who owned the *New York Times,* and the Knopfs, who founded Alfred A. Knopf. He introduced Gloria into exalted New York intellectual and show-business circles. His closest friends at that time were songwriters Betty Comden and Adolph Green. The Chotzinoffs, who were slightly lower on the scale, saw Gloria and Tom together at parties and reported to Blair that their suspicions had been confirmed. "You see," they needled him, "now she's hooked a real one." Blair, who knew Gloria better, insisted she wouldn't marry Tom either.

Tom gave Gloria wonderful gifts—a hard-to-find Cartier watch from Paris and a trip to Italy to meet his sister—and Gloria gave him a custom-made red blazer that lasted about thirty years. As Gloria began to discern distinctions among the wealthy, she realized that, compared to many of the very rich people he knew, Tom did not consider himself rich at all.

Aware of Gloria's ambition, Tom was insecure enough to feel threatened. He comments, "We were both moving into heavy territory, but she actually had more confidence about that territory than I did and I think one of the reasons why we didn't stay together longer was because she had a clearer sense of where she was going and more confidence about how to get there. Not so much on a feminist level. Really more on her writing, and her coming into focus with people who *were* the writers, thinkers, and talkers of that period."

He adds, "Not that we were exactly competitive, but I think I understood that she was able to ingratiate herself with some of the people she was meeting in ways that I was either unwilling or unable to do— I was more cautious about it. I was in publishing, and I couldn't be as open or didn't feel as easy with them. Gloria has always been very good with older people. Ken Galbraith, for example. And Steinbeck adored her. I was publishing him and he was later best man at my second wedding. Arthur Miller liked her. They all liked her. How could you not like her?"

Gloria's ability to move gracefully in any company was a primary survival tactic, and it continues to be one of her most salient characteristics. It is one she does not like to discuss, however. References to her skill at social code-breaking and her ability to fit in with any group are invariably deflected with analysis of women and class.

She says, for example, "Well, I think that's what makes you a journalist. The ability to become, to enter into a different life, is kind of what a journalist needs. And it's something that women are especially trained to do, because we're supposed to fit into society. To acquire the persona of our husbands or our—the men we're with, even for the evening. So it's a journalistic skill that our socialization gives us.

"And class, I must say, gives you a terrific ability to learn quickly. You know, that desperate feeling of not knowing what's right, or what fork or what social mores. And you—it's amazing how fast you can learn because you're scared—so you absorb this knowledge very quickly. It's a great lesson in the power of socialization, actually. Because if in even one social situation you can certainly learn, oh, you're supposed to do this, oh, you're supposed to do that . . ."

Up to a certain point, Tom relished the role of Pygmalion, taking Gloria "from one stage of her emergence to another . . . moving her into the orbit I was in." According to Gloria, one of Tom's suggestions to facilitate her journey into the haut monde was that as she approached thirty, she subtract the five years from her age she had shaved to apply to the Playboy Club. He was married to an actress, Gloria notes, and "knew how cruel the world could be about women's ages." Sometimes Gloria adds that she also may have begun lying about her age because Sue's children thought Sue—and thus Gloria—were two years younger than they really were.

Tom says his first wife habitually subtracted a year from her age, and that he undoubtedly told Gloria a story about the problem that caused when he gave a psychic the wrong age, prior to a reading. Sue says she did not volunteer her age to her children, but did not lie about it.

As much as Tom enjoyed helping her, when Gloria contacted James Baldwin on her own, Tom resented it. He says, "It was as though she had a much clearer sense of how to capitalize on an opportunity for her next developmental stage. . . . She would say 'I interviewed so-and-so,' and I'd be amazed and think, 'But she met that person in the context of our having had dinner with him as a couple—entertaining the writer in my publisher's role—and then she slipped around me.' "

Recalling his feelings years later, he laughs, and adds, "That may not be as much a judgment of Gloria as it is about my own fears of 'How dare you? You're my girlfriend.' The traditional male, macho kind of attitude."

Tom Guinzburg is generous. It would have taken a more confident man than he was at that point to avoid wondering if he were being loved for himself or for what he could do for Gloria. He seems to have made his peace since then, and he considers it a tribute to Gloria that she has retained the affection and esteem of almost all her previous lovers.

He also comments, "Any ignorant person who makes a claim that Gloria was anything less than a full-blooded, passionate woman just doesn't know her. She is able in an extraordinary way to convey her feelings, and she's very earthy. It's not the kind of quality you associate with someone from a modest Midwest background. I've known a lot of midwesterners one way or another, and she's much more expressive."

Tom never doubted Gloria was special, and in a paroxysm of devotion he once conceived the ultimate gift. Reuben's Delicatessen featured sandwiches named for famous people, like Jack Benny and Bob Hope. "What could I do to get you to name a sandwich for my friend Gloria Steinem?" he once asked the owner. "But she's not famous" was the objection.

"She's not now," her lover replied staunchly, "but she will be. Wait and see."

13

"A Bunny's Tale"

Before she became involved with Tom, Gloria had an affair with Paul Desmond, Dave Brubeck's saxophonist. Paul lived a block away from Gloria, and they had met at the Sixth Avenue Delicatessen, a hangout for the many show-business people who lived in the neighborhood. Paul would call Gloria to walk around the Museum of Modern Art with him after he had taken mescaline, and Gloria tried it, too. She reacted "like the classic person who said, 'Nothing's happening' and then suddenly realized that I hadn't listened to anything anyone had said, and that for fifteen minutes I'd been totally into the painting or whatever."

When her jaw hurt afterward and she didn't sleep for the next two days, Gloria's adventures in drug experimentation ended. The only exception was marijuana, which she tried several times with friends, but she found it gave her "a sense of impending doom." Although she smoked cigarettes or thin cigars for a few years, she didn't inhale (as she said in 1971). Nor did she have much interest in alcohol—she says "It made me sick in college and it makes me sleepy now, and anyway, I'd rather have my sugar in ice cream." In short, she was and is relatively abstemious.

Paul was a voracious reader who planned to write a book about his experiences and call it *How Many of You Are There in the Quartet?* He was quite witty. When pianist Marian McPartland once asked him about the succession of models he dated, he responded, "They'll go out for a while with a cat who's scuffling, but they always seem to end up marrying some manufacturer from the Bronx. This is the way the world ends, not with a whim, but with a banker."

In 1962, Leo died in a California hospital, from complications following an automobile accident. Neither of his daughters was notified until he had been in the hospital several weeks, and he died unexpectedly while Gloria was on her way to see him. Sue, who was too far along in a pregnancy to fly, had to page Gloria in the Chicago airport during her changeover to tell her of their father's death.

In the early 1960s, Gloria's career began to progress. In addition to her work at *Help!* and *Esquire,* Gloria started to get assignments from *Show* magazine. Slick, elegant, and politely daring, *Show* was the property of Huntington Hartford, the eccentric heir to the A&P supermarket fortune. Hartford spent so lavishly that he attracted a talented group of editors who hoped to use his money to create an outstanding arts and culture magazine. At the same time, according to art director Sam Antupit, the staff regarded Hartford as "a whiny little spoiled rich boy" with a secret desire to compete with *Playboy,* and they considered it their duty to conceal their real activities from him as much as possible.

From the moment she arrived in New York, Gloria also attracted publicity. In 1960 a WNS syndicate article headlined "Pretty Girl Genius Helps Edit 'Help!' For Tired Minds," had described her as the "willowy beauty, 34-24-34 . . . Phi Beta Kappa graduate of Smith College," who at the age of twenty-six "is a national magazine editor and a specialist in international politics."

In 1963, the year *The Beach Book* appeared (and Betty Friedan published *The Feminine Mystique*), Gloria also had a two-part article in *Show* that made her a name both in the publishing world and with the public. A Playboy Club had just opened in New York, and during a discussion at a *Show* editorial meeting about how they might cover it, Gloria jokingly suggested that they hire Lillian Ross, a *New Yorker* writer known for her fly-on-the-wall pieces, to infiltrate the club by posing as a Playboy Bunny. Hiring Ross was impossible, but the concept was a terrific idea—and there was someone in the room who might just be able to pull it off. Everyone looked at Gloria.

Gloria was apprehensive about the assignment, but she agreed to write about interviewing to be a Bunny and expected the matter to go no further. She was over the age limit of twenty-four, and besides, New York State required identification for anyone who served liquor. However, using the name Marie Ochs (she had saved O'Mommy's Social Security card out of sentiment), she was hired as a Playboy Bunny. During her month at the so-called glamorous job, Gloria lost more than ten pounds, nearly ruined her feet, endured propositions, and fended off worse. She also talked to the other Bunnies, asked her employers as many questions as she dared, and scribbled notes about everything, from the Bunny Bible (officially, the Playboy Club Bunny Manual) to the coatcheck assistant's technique for concealing tips. The result was a two-part exposé of the Playboy Club's systematic exploitation of their Bunnies.

Gloria described the categories of customers and their hierarchy of privileges; the demerit system that assessed Bunnies for minor infractions of unreasonable rules; the private investigators hired to monitor Bunnies for unsatisfactory costumes or even demeanor. ("When a show is on, check to see if the Bunnies are reacting to the performers. When a comic is on, they are supposed to laugh.")

There were also the false promises of $200–$300-a-week pay (for one week's work Gloria took home less than $40); the costumes so tight many Bunnies experienced numbness in their legs (Gloria's was made two inches smaller than each of her measurements except the bust, which was made larger so it could be stuffed); and, of course, the Bunnies' humiliating powerlessness. Descending a spiral staircase in her costume during lunchtime, Gloria realized she was on display to the gazers on the street. "One of the room directors was waiting for me at the bottom. 'Go back up and come down again,' he said, gesturing toward the crowds in the street. 'Give the boys a treat.' Disobeying a room director was an automatic fifteen demerits, according to the Bunny Bible. I searched for an excuse."

She had entered the assignment lightheartedly, and she regaled Barbara Nessim and Tom Guinzburg with stories that made them laugh. "You wouldn't believe how cheap people are," she told Tom indignantly. "[RCA chairman] Bobby Sarnoff stiffed me at the coatcheck." The experience was chilling, though, and she conveyed it powerfully in her article.

Introducing the piece, *Show* noted that Gloria combined "the hidden qualities of a Phi Beta Kappa, *magna cum laude* graduate of Smith College with the more obvious ones of an ex-dancer and beauty queen." For years afterward Gloria would insist that the piece had been a mistake. She said that after "A Bunny's Tale" she was offered assignments such as going undercover as a prostitute and could no longer get the serious assignments that had begun to come her way. (When I protested during an interview, "That piece put you on the map," Gloria quipped, "Well, it was the wrong map.")

In fact, Gloria was not in great demand as a writer of major articles, so she really had no promising career as a serious journalist for "A Bunny's Tale" to derail. She did not have many clips, and those she had were not very good. The few politically oriented pieces she had written—such as a two-page account of the Helsinki festival for *Show* and a piece on the U.S. establishment with a friend, Jean vanden Heuvel—read like college papers and lacked the liveliness and confident analysis of her India dispatches. Her humor, wit, and discerning eye were her strengths, and her light pieces were often enriched by at least an undercurrent of seriousness. Even so, Gloria believed the Bunny exposé impeded her progress. For example, after "A Bunny's Tale" appeared, *Show* withdrew her assignment to write an exposé on the conservative bias of the U.S. Information Agency and offered her more frivolous topics instead. However, the change may have resulted less from sexism than from the editors' response to the superiority of "A Bunny's Tale" over Gloria's other articles.

On the other hand, her complaint is not baseless. There is no doubt that the publishing world was as sexist as any other industry. Male writers without much experience were given many more opportunities than female writers without much experience, and female writers certainly were less likely to get serious assignments than were male writers. What "A Bunny's Tale" undeniably did for Gloria was garner attention—and that attention was based, as the *Show* introduction indicated, on the luster of the package.

Gloria usually portrays her first seven years of freelancing as a lengthy period of frustration caused by sexist male editors who refused to take her seriously. On the other hand, when she is charged with getting assignments through sex appeal, she protests that she couldn't have—because "all" of her editors were women. This is an example of Gloria's remarkable ability to have her cake and eat it, too. In fact, female *Glamour* editors made ample use of her sex appeal and male editors at *Ladies' Home Journal* and the *New York Times Magazine* gave her respectable, if traditional, assignments, though the celebrity profiles and fashion articles were not the ones she would have preferred.

What is not revisionist history is Gloria's memory of frustration. She was resentful long before she developed a feminist consciousness, and she said so at every opportunity. Even without the assignments she would have chosen, though, she was a successful freelance writer. She was made a contributing editor of *Glamour* "to bring some chic and smarts," according to Ruth Whitney, who later became *Glamour's* editor in chief. Whitney also recalls with amusement that Gloria and *Glamour's* features editor, Marilyn Mercer, a journalist formerly with the *New York Herald Tribune*, had a "twinsome routine" that worked with Whitney's predecessor. "Marilyn would promote some outrageous story they knew she'd never produce. Then Gloria would come in with a slightly moderated version and get the assignment. The first meeting I was editor I accepted the first suggestion and told them the jig was up." They were actually relieved, and pleased to work with Whitney, who included far more serious material in the magazine.

Beginning in 1963, Gloria's work appeared often in *Glamour*. Syntax remained a problem, but because she used her own voice, her pieces were funny and appealing. In keeping with one of her favorite activities, she often gave advice. Her particular area of expertise was life as a single woman (or "single girl"), and she wrote *Glamour* versions of *Esquire* pieces, such as "How a Single Girl Spends Her Money" and "How to Put Up With/Put Down a Difficult Man," full of quizzes, hypothetical situations, and tongue-in-check solutions.

In "How to Put Up With/Put Down a Difficult Man," she defined a difficult man: "(a) less interested in you than you are in him, (b) too interested in you and you'd like to get rid of him, (c) prevented by some ridiculous preconceived notion of his own from realizing your true worth, (d) has one characteristic so irritating that you can't figure out whether you're interested or not." That, she explained, took care of everybody.

She also offered case histories of difficult men such as Serge, who is Socially Involved: "He majored in political science . . . gets paid for writing pamphlets for a small labor union, and doesn't get paid for writing articles in a smaller literary quarterly. He also does not wash." Serge criticizes his lover for her white-collar job, high heels, and high salary, and makes her pay for half of everything when they're out, but freeloads at her apartment and hates to be reminded that he went to Yale and is very rich.

One of Gloria's suggestions for civilizing Serge was "Give a party to which you invite the most chic and successful of his Yale friends as well as his parents. When the inevitable arguments come up, leap to his defense with sentences like 'It's not a small labor union, it has forty-two members.'" To put him down, Gloria counseled, "Write an article on difficult men and put him in it."

Her identity as a single woman secured assignments in other publications as well. Asked to review *Sex and the Office,* the sequel to Helen Gurley Brown's *Sex and the Single Girl,* for the *New York Herald Tribune's Book Week,* she panned it. The *New York Times Magazine* assigned her an article to be run with Malcolm Bradbury's "American Girls Are Rude," and Gloria produced "Visiting Englishmen Are No Roses."

A preoccupation with identities during the mid-1960s—"How to Find Your Type (And, If Necessary, Change It)," for example—enabled Gloria to play with one of her favorite themes: deception. References to deception, role playing, and mystery filled her articles, and she told one interviewer she liked deceptive men. "Deception is neuter," she began in "Secrets of Deception." "Like money, it may be used for good purposes or bad." Gloria even explained how to deceive an elevator: push all the buttons above one's destination so the elevator would think it was full and leave immediately.

Gloria's pieces were also full of references to spies and spying, Mata Hari, James Bond, and espionage. In *Glamour,* September 1964, she wrote "So You Want to Be a Spy," a humorous piece that spoofed typical career advice articles. Discussing the requirements of the job, she noted, "It's easy to see that a good spy must contain the qualities of actress, linguist, psychologist, sneak-thief, cat burglar, and commanding officer."

She wrote about herself as well—one of her most enduring topics, and one of her most interesting. For a person who shunned introspection (she liked to say "the examined life is not worth living"), she made some astute observations. "I had learned most of what I knew about human behavior from novels," she explained at thirty, in an August 1964 *Glamour* piece, "College and What I Learned There." She attributed her inability to express anger to her lack of knowledge that one could lose one's temper and still maintain a relationship. "I took care never to show any anger at all. For [her college friends], my terrible even-temperedness must have been a little like having a plastic classmate, and it was only when one of them asked me kindly *why* I never got angry that I began to realize how nonsensical it was." In fact, she still does not express anger easily.

If in some ways she remained opaque to herself, Gloria's powers of observation eventually gained her assignments from the *New York Times Magazine, Ladies' Home Journal,* and *Glamour* to write profiles on celebrities and literary figures—Jackie Kennedy, Julie Andrews, Barbra Streisand, Margot Fonteyn, Michael Caine, Truman Capote, James Baldwin, Saul Bellow. The profiles usually featured her human composites, a device she had favored since college, when she had told a friend she wanted a future husband with the mind of a poet and the body of a truck driver. She called Rudi Gernreich "an infinitely elegant Beatle," dubbed Truman Capote a "teenage marzipan Peter Lorre," and explained that after President Kennedy's death some civil rights leaders had envisioned Jackie's role as "a kind of good-looking Eleanor Roosevelt who would lead Negro children into school, and give fireside mother-to-mother talks on integration."

Gloria was also a natural arbiter of cool, explaining in a number of pieces what was In or Out in behavior, cultural choices, and men. After Susan Sontag wrote a much-talked-about essay for the *Partisan Review* on the phenomenon of camp in 1964, *Life* paid Gloria $3,000 to write a piece on pop culture and illustrated it with drawings and photographs of Gloria herself.

Gloria continued to try to get articles published on more serious subjects. She went to Virginia to interview students and families about an integration battle that had shut down much of a local school system, but was unable to interest any magazines in the story. Sometimes she produced a piece with more substance than the assigning editor intended. In 1964 she wrote " 'Crazy Legs'; or, the Biography of a Fashion," for the *New York Times Magazine,* a piece about textured stockings that she still calls the low point of her career. Although the topic was undeniably frivolous, Gloria researched it creatively and produced a creditable article.

Eventually, she began to secure better assignments, and by 1965 she was respected enough to be asked to write about being a writer for *Harper's* November issue. Among the joys she listed were: "I can call myself a writer"; "I get paid for learning"; "I can advocate change, or say, 'Oh, come off it,' to society"; and finally, "Writing is the only thing that seems worthwhile."

She was being written about by others as well. To queries about herself from Mel Shestack, who was writing an article on her for *Writer's Digest*, Gloria responded, "Strange things happen to people who make their living with their outsides instead of their insides, especially girls. . . . I've never been married or analyzed. I feel like a buffalo nickel, and like feeling like a buffalo nickel. I'm afraid of people who are efficient and always on time and have never eaten out of a can."

14

Some Enchanted Lovers:
Ted Sorensen, Mike Nichols,
and Herb Sargent

In the fall of 1963 Gloria began an affair with Theodore Sorensen, then President John F. Kennedy's chief speechwriter. She was also involved with Tom Guinzburg, but he was resigned to sharing her. As Tom explains, "Gloria was *always* seeing someone else. Jealousy and Gloria do not go together."

Like many across the country, Gloria was entranced with everything about the Kennedys—their youth, their style, their energy, their apparent liberalism—and she wanted to be a part of it. She was especially excited about the Peace Corps, which she imagined would offer others the kind of experiences she had had in India. She recalls, "It was a huge uplift when Kennedy was elected. Those three years were full of excitement and fresh start and a sense of purpose. For the first time in my life I could imagine that something I, or anyone else I knew, wrote might be read in the White House, and I felt connected instead of ashamed of the government."

As special counsel to the president, Ted Sorensen was President Kennedy's closest aide. He had worked for Kennedy for ten years and was considered the most brilliant among a stellar group. He helped draft all of Kennedy's important speeches, including the famous inaugural address that proclaimed, "Ask not what your country can do for you—ask what you can do for your country." He also functioned as legal advisor and political strategist.

Although part of her lovers' appeal to Gloria usually was their work or position in the world, that was almost the total basis of her attraction to Ted Sorensen (though he was also quite handsome). She met him at a gathering with her friend and coauthor, Jean vanden Heuvel, and to Gloria, Ted represented the world of the Kennedys. What she must have imagined they would have in common was that he was political beyond any man she had been with, and possessed a formidable intellect. As they got to know each other, she found that they had another bond as well. Ted's mother, originally an ardent feminist and pacifist, had become depressed while Ted was still a boy. Gloria and he traded stories of their childhoods with incapacitated mothers and felt they understood each other.

Gloria loved to visit Sorensen at his White House office, but as the short-lived relationship progressed, they seemed to have less in common. Later Gloria would reflect, "We were misfits from the beginning. I think he was just fascinated with me because I was something outside his very tight, restricted work habits and upbringing. He had been married very young and had three sons and had been divorced. Sometimes if you marry young, you're sort of not part of the world and then suddenly you come out in the world, blinking in the bright light. So while I can't speak for him, that's what I think happened to him and was his attraction to me."

Ted, who was six years older than Gloria, had been married since his graduation from the University of Nebraska in 1949. A biographical sketch described his "frugality, abstemiousness, and Puritanism," noting that while he indulged in an occasional sherry, he avoided tobacco and coffee. Gloria was almost infinitely adaptable, but this was too much, even for her. "If I said 'shit' or 'damn' he would get really upset. If I smoked a cigarette—and I never really smoked because I didn't inhale—but if I would smoke a cigarette after dinner or something, he would get very quiet or very upset—as if it were immoral for women to smoke."

The Beach Book appeared in November 1963, complete with frivolous Kennedy references and a photograph of President Kennedy on the beach. Then Kennedy was assassinated on November 22, and Gloria and Ted comforted each other in telephone conversations over the next few weeks. Their misalliance ended shortly afterward, and Gloria entered into an affair with Mike Nichols just as he was becoming the hottest director in New York.

Mike, who was born in Berlin in 1931 as Michael Igor Peschowsky, left Germany with his family in the late 1930s and settled in New York, where his father took the name of Nichols. In 1950, he enrolled at the University of Chicago as a premed student. After participating in student productions, he left college to study acting with Lee Strasberg at the Actors Studio in New York. He returned to Chicago and, with Elaine May, was among the founders of an improvisational group later named Second City.

In 1957 Nichols and May moved to New York to perform satirical sketches they had written. Soon they were performing in nightclubs all over the country, appearing on television programs such as the *Jack Paar Program* and *Omnibus,* and making records. Their sketches depicting the anxieties of everyday situations—a couple on their first date, a pushy mother and her son—were so popular that in 1960 they took *An Evening With Mike Nichols and Elaine May* to Broadway.

After the show ran a year, Nichols and May amicably split up and Mike began directing. He won a 1963 Tony Award for his first Broadway assignment, Neil Simon's *Barefoot in the Park,* starring Robert Redford and Elizabeth Ashley. In 1964 he directed two more hits, *The Knack* and Murray Schisgal's *Luv,* for which he won a second Tony. When Gloria began seeing him, *Barefoot in the Park* was running and he was beginning rehearsals for *Luv.* By 1966, with three Tony winners still running on Broadway, Mike had a hit three-act musical, *The Apple Tree,* starring Barbara Harris, had directed his first film, *Who's Afraid of Virginia Woolf?,* and was preparing to direct *The Graduate.*

Gloria sat in on meetings with Charles Webb, author of the novel *The Graduate,* and when the producers of *Who's Afraid of Virginia Woolf?* could not find a film location for the faculty house, she kept trying to help. "I know exactly where they would have lived, exactly the right yard and campus and surroundings," she insisted. No one would listen, because "nobody pays attention to the girlfriend of the director." Eventually they did, and as she had told them, Smith College was perfect. Gloria later heard that some Smith alumnae feared moviegoers would think the events actually took place at Smith.

Gloria's role as "the girlfriend" rankled. She had lost the sense of purpose she had found in India, was writing on subjects for which she had no passion, and felt "invisible" in the eyes of the world. Mike was enormously successful, both critically and financially, and Gloria could not stand the idea that she might be viewed—or worse yet, become— a hanger-on.

Meeting "the second, third, fourth, or fifth wife of the accomplished man," Gloria feared she was seeing herself. "I remember the wife of one composer—she was young enough to be his granddaughter and had nothing whatsoever to do with his work—who used to say, 'Well, *we're* working on the last song in the second act,' or . . . '*we're* not sure that it's really going as it should.' " The thought that she might be lumped in with these women, even in "the eyes of people who didn't know you, or headwaiters, or whatever"—was unbearable.

In those days, the status acquired by becoming a star's lover or wife was regarded as a natural goal for a woman. However, while Gloria didn't mind taking advantage of helpful connections, borrowed status wasn't good enough. She might lack self-esteem, but Gloria did not lack ambition. She wanted status of her own, and she wanted it based on accomplishments of her own. In retrospect, one of the aphorisms she made famous, "We are becoming the men we wanted to marry," seems to capture perfectly the difference before and after the women's movement.

Gloria was in the "before" stage at that point, but even then she coveted the male prerogative of doing, acting, achieving. Females were valued for their beauty, ability to please, and supportiveness. She didn't mind reaping the benefits for fulfilling that role as admirably as she did. However, ambition for the other part—the doing part—was not only uncommon in a woman, it was considered unfeminine and even not very nice. Slinky, sexy Gloria, who perfectly fulfilled the feminine ideal, would later describe herself during this period as "outwardly conforming while secretly rebelling." "Secretly resenting" was more like it.

In addition to her preoccupation with the way she was perceived, in private she was dealing with the familiar pressure to get married. Gloria was around thirty when she began the affair with Nichols, and she still expected to marry and have children. However, she recalls that when he was "on the phone arranging to have dinner with friends or making plans for four of us to go someplace for the weekend, and he would, with all goodwill, turn to me and say, 'You see, when we're married you can do this'—meaning the social arrangements—my heart would just plummet. I would get so depressed."

As usual, she tried to talk herself into it. At her ten-year Smith reunion in 1966, Gloria, who had begun to see writer Herb Sargent in addition to Mike, discussed the relative merits of the two men as husband material. If she married Mike Nichols, Gloria speculated to an old friend, he would be very entertaining, but she didn't know if he would be a good father. On the other hand, she thought Herb Sargent would be a wonderful father, but she wasn't sure he would keep her interest. As it turned out, Mike Nichols, who already had one daughter, went on to have more children (and another three wives, the last being Diane Sawyer) and seemed to be a fine father, and Gloria fell deeply in love with Herb Sargent and stayed with him for the next several years.

Herb Sargent's profile was as low as Mike Nichols's was high. Herb is very quiet, though when he speaks, he can be very funny. He is tall and handsome, and Gloria describes him as "sexy, very sexy and very sensuous, with a shock of gray hair that is now white."

In 1964 Herb hired Gloria to write for television. Producer Leland Hayward (who was married to Pamela Churchill between her marriages to Randolph Churchill and Averell Harriman) had bought the U.S. rights to a popular British program of satirical sketches, *That Was the Week That Was*, or *TW3*, and Herb was producer and head writer. Gloria wrote for the show's second season (1964–1965), along with Buck Henry and Alan Alda, who acted in it as well. David Frost, who had starred in the British original, commuted back and forth to appear in the U.S. version.

Everyone worked together, but Gloria's particular responsibility was the "Surrealism in Everyday Life" segment. As the program was based on events from the previous week and broadcast before a live audience, the writers had a week, at most, to create each show. Most skits were written even closer to show time. It was fun but stressful and there was little room for error.

Leland Hayward added to the tension. Hawkish on the Vietnam War, in contrast to his writers, most of whom were dovish, he was always objecting indignantly to their political humor and issuing impossible orders, such as that they balance every antiwar joke with a prowar joke. Ignoring him as much as possible, the writers enjoyed themselves immensely and were all sorry when the program ended after two seasons.

Herb wrote for a number of television programs, such as the *Tonight* show and many specials, but he always loved live television. When *Saturday Night Live* began in 1975, he was hired as head writer and script consultant and stayed with the program until 1995.

Ruth, who had lived with Sue and her husband, Bob, since 1964, was particularly fond of Herb, and the pair once took her with them on vacation to Curaçáo. For Gloria's thirty-first birthday, in 1965, Herb gave her a six-month option on Elie Wiesel's book *Town Beyond the Wall*. Gloria had been touched by the story, of a young man so traumatized by Nazi imprisonment that he could not speak, who was healed through the kindness of others. She hoped to turn it into a play. Although she was unable to carry it off, "the fact that Herb had enough confidence in my ideas and writing made a big difference in my life. . . . I had been assigned by the *Ladies' Home Journal* an article on lovelorn columns . . . and Herb's present gave me the courage to quit doing it, even after months of research." Clearly, Herb perceived and was able to give Gloria what she craved above all else—respect and professional encouragement.

Herb was quiet, but they were very much part of the scene, hanging out in places like Elaine's. This eponymous Upper East Side restaurant-bar was famous in the 1960s both for its celebrity clientele and for the snobbishly cruel treatment its owner, Elaine Kaufman, meted out to some less-favored customers.

Jane O'Reilly, whom Gloria helped to become a writer, recalls that Gloria befriended her while she was seeing Herb. Gloria often took Jane—or whomever she had under her wing at the moment—along with her, and Jane was dazzled. She says, "Herb was very, very, very funny. . . . He was writing another script, and Gloria always took an intense interest in the work of whoever she was going out with. Some chunk of Gloria is a courtesan. . . . One time I was with them in Elaine's, which was certainly not too hard, that's where they were mostly. . . . I was a young mother from Washington, completely uninteresting, but Gloria brought me along. . . . It was snowing, snowing, snowing, and we looked out the window and I was imagining walking back to Gloria's. Then Herb ordered a limousine and I thought this was the absolute height. . . .

"I was deeply, deeply jealous of Gloria. Well, not really jealous, but I thought Herb was just marvelous. He was my favorite. I have no idea what he was like as a person. Quiet. He was slightly scary to me. But then, everybody's husband or boyfriend is scary to me."

In 1966 when Truman Capote, basking in the success of his "nonfiction novel" *In Cold Blood,* decided to give the party of the decade—or maybe of the century—Gloria was on the guest list that the *Washington Post* called "Who's Who of the World." The favored five hundred included Charles Addams, Jackie Kennedy, Marlene Dietrich, Bennett and Phyllis Cerf, Alice Roosevelt Longworth, Stephen

Sondheim, Governor Nelson and Happy Rockefeller, David Webb, Thornton Wilder, Frank Sinatra and Mia Farrow, and some Kansas friends from *In Cold Blood*.

Inspired by Cecil Beaton's Ascot scene in *My Fair Lady*, Capote called his party the Black and White Ball and ordered his guests to wear masks and costumes of only black and white. He held it at the Plaza Hotel because it had "the only really beautiful ballroom left in the United States." The guest of honor was Katharine Graham, though she says, "I was just the excuse—it was Truman's party."

Capote labored long and lovingly over the list, enjoying an exquisite sense of power as he added a maharajah here, subtracted a president there. Only those he invited would be allowed to attend, and no one could bring a date. Capote had not considered Herb sufficiently important to invite, but he eventually capitulated. According to Gloria, who wrote an article on the affair for *Vogue*, "The only thing I really enjoyed about the Black and White Ball was that I forced Truman to take the guy I was going with. Truman, being Truman, said he was only inviting the people he wanted and they couldn't bring significant others because he didn't have enough room. Herb was not categorized by Truman as someone he would invite—whatever that meant. But I said to him, 'I'm not going unless you invite him, too, because that would be disloyal.'" Truman, she says, understood loyalty.

Within her first seven years in New York, Gloria's professional accomplishments included a year as a television screenwriter, a coffee-table book, a growing body of amusing, creditable articles, and a reputation for quirky originality. She wasn't writing the serious pieces she still wanted to write, but she was progressing. Meanwhile, Gloria was becoming far better known as a personality than many more established and prolific writers were. She was a celebrity.

Gloria's talent for self-promotion, all the more effective in its subtlety, impressed and amused some observers. Her Western High School English teacher still chuckles at the memory of Gloria in her senior play: "She had a very small part, but when she was supposed to be in the center, she advanced very graciously up center and made the most of her two lines in a way that didn't hurt the play."

In the wake of the publication of both *The Beach Book.* and "A Bunny's Tale," the attention increased. When Nora Ephron interviewed her for a January 1964 article in the *New York Post*, Gloria told her that writing "A Bunny's Tale" had produced two unfortunate results.

Pauline Perlmutter Steinem, Gloria's suffragist grandmother.
(Toledo-Lucas County Public Library)

Gloria's parents, Ruth Nuneviller and Leo Steinem, at the University
of Toledo. (University of Toledo Archives)

Getting served at Ken Wah Lo's nightclub is the goal of underage Toledo patrons. After boyfriend Ron Duncan, Gloria, best friend Carole Roberts, and Carole's boyfriend, Chuck Berning, are photographed with beer bottles, Carole hides the picture from her parents for years. (Courtesy Carole Roberts Berning)

Gloria among friends from Laura Scales, her dormitory at Smith College. (Courtesy Judith Wheeler)

Gloria finds the perfect gift for Blair Chotzinoff, her senior year boyfriend and eventual fiancé. (Courtesy Judith Wheeler)

Gloria goes undercover to write "A Bunny's Tale," a 1963 *Show* magazine exposé on the Playboy Club's treatment of Bunny employees. (Corbis-Bettmann)

After "A Bunny's Tale" appears, New York's State Liquor Authority subpoenas Gloria to testify about the Playboy Club. (Corbis-Bettmann)

In an Estevez chinchilla-ringed dress reportedly inspired by Lady Macbeth, Gloria dances with television writer Herb Sargent at a 1966 benefit for free performances of Shakespeare in Central Park. When CIA funding for National Student Association activities is exposed the following year, the *Washington Post* accompanies its news story with a photo of Gloria in this dress. (Corbis-Bettmann)

Another friend of Gloria's in the 1960s, Tony Award–winning director Mike Nichols. (Corbis-Bettmann)

Clay Felker assigned Gloria her first major magazine article at *Esquire* and made her a political columnist at *New York* magazine. (Corbis-Bettmann)

Gloria met former Olympic decathlon gold medal winner Rafer Johnson at the 1968 Democratic Convention in Chicago. (AP/Wide World Photos)

Writers Jimmy Breslin and Norman Mailer announce their candidacy for City Council president and mayor of New York in 1969. (Corbis-Bettmann)

Gloria with Cesar Chavez, founder of the United Farm Workers. (Bettye Lane)

Gloria with other keynote speakers at the National Women's Political Caucus founding conference in 1971. From left are Betty Smith of the Wisconsin Republican Party, Dorothy Haener of the United Automobile Workers Union, and Fannie Lou Hamer, Mississippi civil rights leader. (Corbis-Bettmann)

Gloria nominates Frances (Sissy) Farenthold for vice president of the United States at the 1972 Democratic Convention in Miami Beach. (Corbis-Bettmann)

Gloria develops a lifelong political alliance and close personal friendship with Representative Bella Abzug. Shown here with Dr. Benjamin Spock and Jesse Jackson at a February 1972 press conference to announce the Children's March for Survival the following month. (Corbis-Bettmann)

Gloria and Bella applaud Senator George McGovern after he addresses the women's caucus at the 1972 Democratic Convention. (Corbis-Bettmann)

Bella even wears a hat to go rowing with Gloria in Central Park for an anti-inflation demonstration. They are reminding the public that rising prices leave Americans "up the creek." (Corbis-Bettmann)

One was that *Playboy* sued her for libel, ostensibly for remarks characterized in a newspaper article after publication but, Gloria believed, really more to harass her. The other was that she became known as "the girl who exposed the Playboy Bunnies."

"There are people who know me only for having done the Bunny piece," Gloria said. "I am constantly being referred to as an ex-Bunny, and that's a high price to pay." As Ephron explained, Gloria was really a "freelance political activist and writer, with a string of magazine articles and, more recently, a book, to her credit." Although she had attended the historic March on Washington in August 1963, when Martin Luther King Jr. gave his "I Have a Dream" speech, at that point Gloria's claim to political activism was based primarily on her past work in India, volunteering in political campaigns, and her association with the Independent Research Service, which, she told Ephron, she had cofounded and then transferred to New York. "Most of the Americans who had gone to the Festival were either in sympathy with it or rather naive," she commented. "We were in favor of presenting a diversity of views, because that seemed the best way of countering the Communist monolith."

Gloria added that she really wanted to write fiction. "I used to delay writing by being a big political activist. Now I delay writing fiction by writing nonfiction."

The topic to which she considered herself unfairly consigned by editors was "women"—beauty, fashion, homemaking, and other subjects about which she was presumed to know, by virtue of having been born female. In Gloria's opinion, "women" required research: "I'd never read anything about women, so I went out and read sociology. That situation has been forced upon me—as a magazine writer, you develop what are regarded rightly or wrongly as your specialties." Even if Gloria had to bone up on women to cover these topics, there was a level to which she would not descend. "I still don't write about fashion. Fashion is like extra-sensory perception—it's a worthy field for research, but like ESP, the people in it discredit the field."

"A Bunny's Tale" was a genuinely admired piece of journalism, but there is no question that the attention Gloria attracted was based on the total package. As Gloria later put it, "She walks, she talks, a pretty girl who can write." She was correct that the assumption was patronizing, but, in fact, she *was* unusual. Most women were not attractive enough to land a job as a Playboy Bunny, and the population of women who could write a powerful magazine feature on the experience was even smaller. The fact that Gloria had attributes in both areas, plus the cachet of a Seven Sisters, Phi Beta Kappa, magna cum laude degree, was what made her newsworthy.

Gloria hoped to become a successful writer, and it was obvious what attracted attention. She could choose to play the game by promoting that interesting package—a pretty girl who could write—or she could refuse. She did not refuse, and she became a personality. She might have made it as a writer anyway, or she might not have—not everyone who can write gets work. There never was any question, though, that she had looks, charm, credentials, and contacts; that she used them; and that having them and using them boosted her career.

In truth, Gloria would have been foolish not to take advantage of any attribute she possessed. People capitalize on their advantages all the time, be it money, family connections, old school ties, charm, or good looks, and successful people tend to be those who seize the opportunities that come their way. Long-term achievement generally depends on long-term performance anyway, so the importance of those initial advantages tends to diminish over time. Gloria might have obtained an assignment to interview James Baldwin by meeting him through Tom Guinzburg, but if she hadn't produced an interesting article, she wouldn't have gotten another assignment. However, she never lost her defensiveness about the role her appearance played in her career.

In later years, when she would insist to interviewers that she wished she weren't pretty, or that she wished she were old, or even that her looks had been a hindrance, she sounded unconvincing to many. Her looks were a natural attribute, and she had cultivated them. That was the way the world worked. If she had been able to say, more accurately, that she wished she had made it as a writer without her looks, everyone would have understood. To say that, though, would have required acknowledging the role her appearance had played. That evidently was too difficult and became even more so in later years, once she came to represent a movement dedicated to the idea that women be evaluated on their performance rather than their appearance.

In February 1964 Gloria appeared in a six-page spread in *Glamour,* "A Girl—Signed Herself." The piece described her style, her clothes preferences, her favorite accessories, her cosmetics, and, oh yes, her work. Calling her "one of the bold spirits," *Glamour* explained,

"Gloria Steinem signs her own looks—as well as her checks. Dark glasses, straight-slung 'mustachioed' hair, trench coat, pale orange Fu Manchu nails, a long exposure of beautiful legs on thin-heeled shoes . . . all Steinem markings." After noting that Gloria would like to be "Audrey Hepburn in the CIA . . . with bosoms," *Glamour* explained that the Gloria Steinem look included kohl-rimmed eyes (from her India sojourn); "skirts shorter than almost anyone's"; dark glasses; small scarves; alligator, satin, or snakeskin pumps; and—though she admitted, "I can't resist pressing my nose against Buccellati's window every time I pass it"—antique jewelry.

During the 1960s Gloria was written about in *Vogue, Harper's Bazaar, Women's Wear Daily,* and *Ladies' Home Journal,* as well as *Time* and *Newsweek* and various newspapers. The longest feature, a syndicated September 1965 *Newsday* story by staff writer Harvey Aronson, was headed "The World's Most Beautiful Byline." By then her lovers were as much a part of the story as her intriguing background, which at this point included the Smith Phi Beta Kappa and a family she portrayed as slightly rakish but not poor.

Aronson juxtaposed the fact that Gloria would earn $30,000 that year (an astonishing sum for a freelancer when 1964 median income was $5,900 for men and $3,700 for women, but that included her television income) with a description of her five-foot-seven, 120-pound figure and her "wide, long-lashed brown eyes that focus on the interviewer and make him think that he never had a better steak nor saw a prettier tablecloth. . . ."

Ask if being a pretty girl had helped her career, Gloria said, "It helps in a short run, but not in the long run. In the short run? Well, people remember you, it's at least as good as being a Negro. In the long run? Well, it hinders your being taken seriously. Editors tend to assign you to stories on women." When asked if she tried to charm the men she interviewed, Gloria replied, "I try to charm everybody—man, woman, and dog."

After describing her political identity (evolved from Orwellian socialist to liberal Democrat—"you have to be effective as well as liberal") and her apartment, Aronson reported that Gloria, "who wants to write fiction, likes 'deceptive' people, gets a couple of marriage proposals a year and concedes that she has never accepted any because she has probably never met anyone she really loved that much or that way," might indeed be "the world's most beautiful byline."

In 1965 *Newsweek* profiled her in a full-page article entitled "News Girl." To be covered in *Newsweek* was incredible publicity for a free-lance writer with five years' experience. Even better, the piece took her seriously as a writer, including none of her showgirlish protestations about the serious work she really wanted to be doing instead of what she actually was doing.

The story also earned Gloria the irksome sobriquet "the thinking man's Jean Shrimpton." Ironically, the man who coined the phrase was one of her most fervent admirers, twenty-six-year-old Georgetown law student Eugene Theroux (brother of novelist Paul). In a letter to *Newsweek*'s editor, Gene linked the *Newsweek* article on Gloria to that issue's cover story on supermodel Jean Shrimpton by describing Gloria as "our foundress, Gloria Steinem, the thinking man's Cover Girl Shrimpton." Newly recruited by the CIA as executive director and sole employee of the Independent Research Service, Gene had met Gloria at an NSA Congress. When he became IRS director, he was informed that she, along with fellow IRS predecessors Dennis Shaul and Paul Sigmund, would be on his board of directors.

"I think it's fair to say that I wrote the letter mainly to get Gloria's attention," explains Gene, who confesses he was in "complete awe of her." "Gloria was involved as a board member of the IRS about the time that *The Avengers* [first aired in the United States in March 1966] was a popular television serial. . . . Diana Rigg played a lithe, glamorous, wisecracking, pistol-packing international spy. . . . I always felt that fact far surpassed fiction in our 'witting' work—Gloria was a real-life secret agent, infinitely more fascinating in real life than Diane Rigg's character."

That was hyperbole—Gloria was hardly a secret agent, and Dennis Shaul recalls their "board meetings" as a few informal occasions that were "mostly dinner," because it was so tough to get together. He also remembers them as delightful because they were all such witty people. "Paul was the most serious, but he had a great laugh, and Gloria knew everybody under the sun." The board was "a curious arrangement because we had so little guidance from the agency." As for the meetings, "We spent an inordinate amount of time trying to protect our own integrity to make certain that we were not perceived as attached to the agency. We wanted to be seen by the public as above the fray and not identified with any faction of cold warrioring. We wanted an alliance with all the groups who were interested, including those who would have found the whole agency connection repugnant." Gene

Theroux later described Dennis and Gloria as "two of the most remarkable, bright, witty, and able people I have ever met."*

That was behind the scenes. Ex-*New York Times* reporter Marylin Bender summed up Gloria's place in society in her 1967 book *The Beautiful People.* Diana Vreeland, editor of *Vogue,* had coined the term to describe that 1960s phenomenon, the combined worlds of fashion, socialites, and what would later be called the glitterati: "We mean people who are beautiful to look at. It's been taken up to mean people who are rich. We mean the charmers but there is no harm to be rich." Bender described Gloria's position.

> Miss Steinem swings with the new society despite the fact that she is what used to be called whistle-bait. (As a rule, overt sexiness and fashion leadership are incompatible.) She also earns her own living, has a Phi Beta Kappa key and has evidenced more than casual interest in politics and civil rights. But then, after all, the New Frontier made intellectualism fashionable. Miss Steinem is one of several working girls with whom the leisured classes mingle in the new society.

Although Gloria would recall herself as "outwardly conforming but secretly rebelling," her interior rebellion was not clear-cut. Part of her struggle was with herself—what she calls her "class problem" (or her "emotional identification with [my] Toledo experience"). While she was outwardly conforming enough to secure a desirable place in society, and secretly rebelling against the very society she was penetrating, she was also enjoying herself, at least sometimes, even while disapproving of her own enjoyment. Clinging to an outsider-bohemian-nonbourgeois self-image, she didn't mind acting the opposite part—just so she could continue to believe it was only acting. The struggle began at Smith and continues to this day. Asked if she really hated being a Beautiful Person–celebrity as much as she insists she did, she pauses and then replies, "Well, I didn't hate it completely. But I hated it a lot."

Gloria's friends remember differently. They remember her enjoyment of clothes and furs and gifts and being invited to the right places. However, Gloria, who is infinitely tolerant of other women's shortcomings, draws a censorious gray veil over this more frivolous earlier self.

In 1967, Mary Ann Madden, whom Gloria had gotten to know when Mary Ann had worked as Mike Nichols's assistant, told her about an apartment available in her building. After six years in their

---

*Gloria disputes the existence of this board, however informal. See the notes.

shared studio, Barbara Nessim and Gloria moved into the parlor floor of a beautiful, if slightly shabby, nineteenth-century brownstone on a tree-lined street off Park Avenue.

Their new neighborhood, situated in a section of the Upper East Side of Manhattan called Lenox Hill, was more residential and considerably more elegant than the one they were leaving, and their new space—two large rooms, kitchen, and bath—seemed palatial by comparison. They set about fixing up what Clay Felker later called the Tri-Delt House: Between the parade of young women always staying there and the men coming and going all the time, their apartment reminded him of a sorority house.

Among the visitors were Ali MacGraw, who brought along her Scottie when she came to escape "a melodramatic love affair" and stayed for a few weeks, and Jane O'Reilly, who arrived to escape her suburban marriage. Jane says that she stayed so long Barbara eventually told her it was time to move on—and that Gloria would never have said a thing. Barbara's and Gloria's mothers visited, too, and before each occasion, just as they had on West Fifty-sixth Street, thirty-four-year-old Gloria and twenty-eight-year-old Barbara would prepare by carefully hiding their contraceptives.

15

Becoming a Political Operative

The year 1968 was one of the most tumultuous in U.S. history, singular even for the dramatic 1960s. In January, the Vietcong and
North Vietnamese initiated the brutal Tet offensive. Beginning with an
invasion of the U.S. embassy in Saigon, they attacked all major cities,
provincial capitals, and large American bases. The force of the attacks
stunned the public, and the offensive's effectiveness irreparably damaged the Johnson administration's credibility. "What the hell is going
on?" CBS anchor Walter Cronkite asked. "I thought we were winning
the war."

The resulting escalation of the war and the widened credibility gap
further intensified antiwar efforts. Running as an opponent of the
war, Wisconsin Senator Eugene McCarthy had declared his candidacy
for president on November 30, 1967, and unexpectedly defeated President Johnson in the New Hampshire Democratic primary in March
1968. New York Senator Robert Kennedy threw his hat into the ring
two days after McCarthy won the primary. On April 1, two
weeks after Kennedy's entry into the race, President Johnson went
on national television and announced that he would not run for
reelection.

On March 10 Cesar Chavez broke a twenty-five-day fast he had
undertaken to dramatize the migrant farmworkers' plight and to deter
them from violence.

On April 4 Dr. Martin Luther King Jr. was assassinated. The nation was stunned, and the following week was filled with riots in cities all across the country.

On April 18 students rioted at Columbia University in New York City.

On June 5 Robert Kennedy was assassinated.

At the end of August the Democrats held their presidential nominating convention in Chicago. Gloria went both as a campaigner and as a journalist. She had finally achieved her longed-for goal. She was a political writer.

During 1967, Gloria had helped Clay Felker start *New York* magazine. The two had remained close since their *Esquire* days. Shortly after Clay left *Esquire* in 1962, he became unemployed. Without saying anything to Clay, Gloria prevailed upon Tom Guinzburg to give him a job at Viking. A year later Clay became editor of the *New York Herald Tribune*'s Sunday supplement magazine, which was called *New York*.

Clay built the *Herald Tribune*'s *New York* into a lively and compelling publication that, along with *Esquire,* became one of the centers of New Journalism. James Baldwin, Gay Talese, Terry Southern, and Norman Mailer were among *Esquire*'s most prominent practitioners, but there was considerable overlap between the two publications. The *Herald Tribune*'s *New York* stars included Jimmy Breslin, Tom Wolfe, and Gail Sheehy, though Tom Wolfe's initial effort, "There Goes [Varoom! Varoom!] That Kandy-Kolored Tangerine Flake Streamline Baby," was written for *Esquire. New York* was so successful that after the *Herald Tribune* merged with two other New York newspapers in 1966, Clay was also put in charge of the *World Journal Tribune*'s Sunday literary supplement, *Book Week.*

In 1967, after only ten months, the merged newspaper folded. Clay, along with writer Jimmy Breslin and designer Milton Glaser, decided to start an independent magazine version of the Sunday supplement. Clay bought the name *New York* from the expiring newspaper for $6,575, worked on prototypes with Glaser, and set out to wine and dine investors. Much as Broadway producers bring along an actor or two for glamour, Clay brought along writers he liked, including the urbane, gentlemanly Yale Ph.D. Tom Wolfe, the Brooklyn-born, Runyanesque Jimmy Breslin, and Gloria. Gloria always called their performances tap-dancing for rich people, and she was very good at it.

After working for about a year to raise $1.1 million from a group of investors eventually led by financier Armand Erpf, Clay and a few professionals from the old *New York,* including movie critic Judith Crist, music critic Alan Rich, and promotion director Ruth Bower, moved into the top floor of the East Thirty-second Street brownstone that housed Milt's Push Pin Studios. Clay hired George Hirsch, the thirty-three-year-old assistant publisher of *Life International,* to be publisher.

The staff often held meetings at Gloria's apartment, and she loved working on the start-up, contributing section ideas and titles and finding the right people to make the right contributions. Gloria thought of the concept as well as the title for "The Passionate Shopper," one of the magazine's most popular and enduring sections. She also suggested hiring Stephen Sondheim to construct crossword puzzles, which he did, carefully explaining in the initial issue how to solve British-style cryptic puzzles.

The premier issue of *New York* was uneven, cluttered, and full of a year's worth of ideas, which prompted a *Newsweek* writer to remark that *New York* "hasn't yet been able to decide what it wants to be—the new *New Yorker,* a hip *Cue,* or the graduate-school *Harvard Lampoon.*" Within a few weeks, totally unprepared for the rhythm of a weekly, they made even more mistakes. Their most controversial was a profile of Andy Warhol's superstar Viva, which featured nude photographs by Diane Arbus. Rather than seeming glamorous, Viva appeared anemic in the photographs, which showed her unshaven armpits. The text depicted her as pathetic and in thrall to Warhol, and the piece provoked such an outcry that the magazine lost a number of advertisers. Some stayed away for a year; others never came back. The episode taught the editors, as Milton Glaser explains, that they could run nude pictures, but not naked ones.

Eventually *New York* found its voice and its look, and while it was not the first of the modern city magazines—*Los Angeles* was launched in 1960—*New York* magazine's impact was enormous and inspired many imitators. The magazine didn't pay more than a few hundred dollars for an article, but it was the hot book of the magazine world, and everyone wanted to write for it.

Like many of their original misfires, Gloria's story for the premier issue was less than promising. Actually, "Ho Chi Minh in New York" was bizarre. Antiwar sentiment may have been tearing the country apart, but Ho Chi Minh was the leader of enemy forces who were killing U.S. soldiers. Gloria, however, had learned in India that many Asians regarded Ho as a revolutionary "George Washington of Asia," so she set out to "humanize" him in her article. She wanted readers to know he had visited New York as a young man and was a great admirer of American democracy. She says the piece she wrote was cut by probably two-thirds, so it is impossible to determine whether the original version could have worked. What remained was a mélange of facts and conjecture that read like parody. Even more amusing was her attempt to contact Ho. When she called the Western Union office to send a fact-checking telegram to "Ho Chi Minh, President's Palace, Hanoi," the U.S. operator asked her for a street address. Gloria explained that it probably was not necessary. She sent two telegrams, but received no reply.

New York changed Gloria's life. She finally had a forum to write about political subjects, and as a political writer for the hottest magazine in town, she had an enormous audience and comparable clout. Part of the magazine's mystique stemmed from its writers, who were personalities in their own right. Tom Wolfe dressed like a dandy, complete with white suits and spats. When Jimmy Breslin, heavy, sweaty, smoking, and swearing, and Gloria, lion-maned and miniskirted, arrived at City Hall for a press conference, the other reporters stepped back reflexively, opening a path for them. They were stars.

In addition to writing feature stories, Gloria began sharing a political column, "The City Politic," whose title she also conceived, with Peter Maas. A column is a journalistic plum. Publications generally run articles whose subjects its editors believe merit coverage. In allocating space to a specific writer, the editors are signaling that the writer, not the topic, is worth the space; that is, whatever that writer covers will be worth reading about, simply because that writer presented it. Even if *New York* was an experiment, the position of political columnist—especially in a city full of writers—conferred enormous prestige.

In the late 1960s, just before Gloria became a columnist, she became increasingly active politically. She had never stopped caring about politics, but while the three major social justice movements of the 1960s (civil rights, antiwar, and women's liberation) had been unfolding, Gloria had been in New York, trying to find satisfying work and be taken seriously as a Keynesian liberal while posing for photographers and giving lifestyle interviews. As she reflects, "I'm afraid the idealism with which I came back from India had been kind of squashed out of me. I think I was mostly trying to earn a living."

The civil-rights movement began in the 1950s, but in the 1960s it took on a more youthful cast, beginning in February 1960, when four black college students in Greensboro, North Carolina, sat down in the whites-only section of the Woolworth's lunch counter and refused to leave. The sit-in movement exploded from that point, and the Student Nonviolent Coordinating Committee was formed a few months later. The SNCC community organizers became known as the shock troops of the movement, taking over the Freedom Rides soon after they were initiated in the summer of 1961. The rides were demonstrations in which mixed-race groups traveled on interstate buses through the South, trying to integrate the bus-station facilities as well as lunch counters, restrooms, and drinking fountains. The SNCC demonstrators were beaten, jailed, and even murdered.

Gloria was supportive but never went. "I was very drawn to the sit-ins. I wanted to go on one of the buses that was going to the South, but at the time I was seeing Benton, and while he wasn't consciously being restricting, he asked me not to go because it would be such an important experience that if we didn't have it together it would push us apart. . . . So I didn't go, and I've regretted it."

The second of the major movements of the 1960s was the peace movement. In 1967 Gloria went to Washington to demonstrate against the war with the Women's Strike for Peace, and there she met Bella Abzug for the first time. She also helped organize demonstrations in New York. In 1968 she joined a group of writers and editors who pledged to withhold the portion of their taxes that would have gone to finance the Vietnam War and began working for antiwar presidential candidate Sen. Eugene McCarthy. For the most part, however, Gloria was a supporter rather than a participant in the political cataclysms of the 1960s. In 1968 her political and professional lives began to converge, and sometimes she chronicled her own political activities in her articles and columns.

The first issue of *New York* magazine was just hitting the stands when Martin Luther King Jr. was assassinated on April 4. When riots broke out in cities all over the country, Clay called Gloria. "What are you doing in your apartment?" he asked. "You call yourself a reporter? Get up to Harlem and interview people and see what they're saying." Gloria and a young black writer, Lloyd Weaver, followed Mayor John Lindsay for several days after the assassination and wrote a piece attributing New York's lack of riots at least in part to Lindsay's willingness to go into the black community and show that he cared.

Because 1968 was a presidential election year, Gloria began to write about national electoral politics immediately. She also supported three different Democratic presidential candidates. She had begun by working for McCarthy, writing campaign literature, raising money, and

helping organize rallies. Then she decided to switch to Sen. Robert
Kennedy. Before she could help with his campaign, Kennedy was assassinated on June 5. After that, she traveled with the McCarthy campaign as a reporter for a few days. Then she described her experiences
in an August 5 *New York* cover story, "Trying to Love Eugene," that
effectively damned McCarthy with faint praise.

Gloria wrote that she had been dismayed from the beginning by
McCarthy's coldness, intellectuality, and downright dullness as a candidate. However, when Kennedy had become a candidate after
McCarthy defeated Johnson in the New Hampshire primary, she hadn't
known whether to switch. The antiwar Democrats were bitterly divided
between the two candidates. Kennedy seemed opportunistic to
McCarthy supporters but electable to his own, whereas McCarthy, she
wrote, "had been something between a decent man and the Only Game
in Town before his victory." Shuttling back and forth between friends
in the two camps, Gloria had found herself so torn that she was
relieved when Cesar Chavez asked her to go to California to help with
the grapepickers' strike. There, she explained in her article, Chavez had
talked her into switching her allegiance to Kennedy. Some of the growers were important Democratic contributors, and Kennedy had been
the only candidate who went to California and supported the strike.
Right after her article appeared, Gloria switched to Sen. George
McGovern.

Gloria had first met McGovern in 1965, at Logan Airport in Boston.
She was going to Kitty and Ken Galbraith's Vermont farm for the first
time, and she was to drive up with Senator McGovern. She had met
John Kenneth Galbraith a few years earlier, at the Long Island summer
house of mutual friends, and the eminent economist had been so taken
with Gloria that he had asked her to keep track of an article he had
written for *Esquire* after he returned to India as ambassador. Later he
agreed to write the introduction to *The Beach Book*.

By the end of the three-hour drive to Newfane, Vermont, George
McGovern and Gloria were fast friends. Gloria was impressed by his
lack of pretention, his kindness, his humorous stories about Galbraith,
his frankness despite the fact that she was a journalist, and his politics,
especially his early opposition to the Vietnam War. Once at the farm,
McGovern recalls, he saw that Gloria was highly regarded both by the
Galbraiths and by their guests, who included Arthur Schlesinger Jr. and
his wife, and other Harvard and Kennedy-administration luminaries.
By the end of the weekend, McGovern shared their opinion of her.

Three years later, on a summer night in 1968, Gloria appeared on an all-night radio talk show to promote "Trying to Love Eugene." As the hour grew late, she began to say what she really thought: "McCarthy hates people, especially the kids. He calls them 'ski bums' and tells them to get lost. He continually reminds them '*I'm* the cause.' He is very remote and seems inordinately lazy." Warming to her subject, she speculated, "Probably George McGovern is the real Eugene McCarthy."

Within days, Gloria began receiving calls and telegrams from former Kennedy supporters. In a final attempt to stop Vice President Hubert Humphrey and nominate a candidate who would reverse Johnson's policy on Vietnam, they wanted to run another candidate. They hoped, at the very least, to prevent Humphrey from winning on the first ballot at the Democratic Convention in August and to draft Senator McGovern. They wanted to know whether Gloria would join them.

Just before McGovern declared his candidacy, one of his daughters, nineteen-year-old Terry, was arrested in South Dakota for marijuana possession.* Although she had had some problems, the arrest seemed to be politically motivated, and the family reconsidered whether he should seek the presidency. McGovern decided to go ahead, so with very little money and only a few weeks until the convention, the small group launched a campaign. Gloria wrote pamphlets, talked to delegates, and raised funds.

She also had buttons printed saying "George McGovern: He's the *Real* McCarthy." McGovern found the motto somewhat embarrassing, even though he understood that it telegraphed his authentic antiwar credentials, and the buttons were not used for fear of offending the real, real McCarthy. Gloria arranged luncheons with the top editors of the *New York Times* and *Time* magazine. Such meetings were ordinarily routine for presidential candidates, but McGovern was not taken very seriously. McGovern was impressed with Gloria's connections. "She knew them all, and they knew her. It was comparatively easy for her to do," he explains. Before she let him appear in the media, Gloria performed emergency surgery on his wardrobe. From then on, Senator McGovern considered her one of his fashion consultants.

---

*When McGovern received the Democratic nomination four years later, in 1972, Terry, who was the middle of his five children, campaigned for her father with a group that included Gloria as well as Arthur Schlesinger Jr. They traveled around the country in a van organized by Liz Carpenter, called the Grasshopper Special. Terry's substance-abuse problems persisted through the years, and she died tragically in 1994, leaving two children. To assuage his own pain and in hopes that he could help others, her father wrote *Terry: My Daughter's Life and Death Struggle With Alcoholism,* which was published in 1996.

He recalls, "I was from South Dakota and my socks weren't long enough to cover my hairy legs, so she ran over to Saks Fifth Avenue and bought me some over-the-calf hose. It was the first time I'd worn them and I've been wearing them ever since. She also gave me other wardrobe tips. She gave me ideas on suit styles and shirts and socks— nothing that wouldn't occur to a normal, sophisticated person. She sharpened me up."

Gloria was not the only one who thought he needed sartorial first aid. According to McGovern's press secretary and campaign manager, Frank Mankiewicz, "There was a lot of comment about McGovern's clothes. He had electric blue suits. I conspired with Eleanor [McGovern] about it."

To Gloria's annoyance, however, news of her sharpening him up— rather than her speechwriting or fund-raising activities—appeared in print. Four years later, at the 1972 Democratic National Convention, she complained to McGovern's biographer, *Time* writer Robert Sam Anson, "You said in that article that I give him advice about socks and shirts. I don't talk to him about things like that. He listens to men about clothes." Gloria still complains about what journalists mention when they write about her, even though as a journalist herself she knows that the colorful or amusing detail is the one they will choose— as she does herself. On the other hand, she has a point when she asks, "Is Frank Mankiewicz remembered for this kind of advice or for press advice?"

Gloria had also become self-conscious at the press luncheons, because the editors were so ill at ease with her and another woman present. They made "endless 'lady' jokes," apologized for swearing, and laughed about whether to offer the women cigars and ale. Gloria smoked half a cigar, drank the ale, concealed both her irritation and her surprise at the "low intellectual quality" of their questions, and extricated McGovern in time to take him to a farmworkers' demonstration. Later she said, "I don't think I'm cut out for this job."

She was certainly cut out for fund-raising. When she had offered to help, McGovern quipped, "Come with a bunch of money." To his amazement, Gloria arrived with a $10,000 check from a first-generation immigrant in Chicago. She went to Chicago as part of the McGovern group and later reported for *New York* on her experiences at the convention. Once the Chicago police attacked demonstrators and turned the convention into a nightmare of violence and bloodshed, George McGovern's candidacy turned out to be a comparatively minor sideshow. McGovern himself witnessed one conversion. A conservative

Washington physician told him angrily that "those hippies should get out of politics." Then they watched out the window as the police beat up people in the streets and, according to McGovern, the physician "became an antiwar liberal in about four hours."

During the last few days of McGovern's eighteen-day candidacy, Gloria worked practically around the clock. Frank Mankiewicz, who had been Kennedy's press secretary, recalls that his room was their unofficial McGovern headquarters and that he and Gloria both slept there intermittently. He recalls Gloria joking, "You're the only politician I can imagine who could share a room and spend the whole night working." Gloria recalls she was impressed that Frank would call his wife to discuss political tactics.

Laura Stevenson, a twenty-two-year-old who answered Gloria's correspondence and worked as her assistant for a few hours a week, also went to the convention. Gloria stayed with her, too. Laura recalls, "About five of us shared a room, which didn't matter because we were working most of the time. When we weren't, we'd all crash for a few hours. But I remember being impressed because Gloria would go into the bathroom and do the complete Ernest Lazslo routine [a multi-step, multi-cream skin cleansing process] before she lay down."

What most people remember about the 1968 convention is the brutality of the Chicago police, under orders from Chicago's mayor, Richard Daley, but Gloria took away some treasured memories as well. Years later, she wrote about a debate among Senators McGovern, Humphrey, and McCarthy before the California delegation. Humphrey defended the administration's Vietnam policy and was too cheerful; McCarthy was cold; McGovern was wonderful—angry about Vietnam and charitable toward the mistakes of others, including Humphrey. Gloria wrote in *Ms.*, "The room was jammed, and the debate was being televised nationwide. It was one of those electric moments when you know a person or an idea is being born. Magically, McGovern had become a presidential candidate."

McGovern's candidacy did not stop Humphrey, so after it ended, Gloria tried to help elsewhere at the convention. "When all else failed and there seemed nothing else to do, I handed out farmworker and welfare-rights literature. I was distributing literature on the floor when the Daley guards shoved me aside and broke my glasses," she recalls.

McGovern was also up for reelection as a senator, so after the convention he had to return to South Dakota to campaign. Gloria offered to help again, and arrived with more money. She also brought, as instructed, two long skirts and "a properly terrible sweater" to blend in. She made some radio and television appearances and tried to inspire the local women. "Most people from out of state really don't help you that much in a senatorial campaign," McGovern muses, "but when Gloria came back with hard cash, she lifted morale. And though she wasn't much into the women's movement, she talked to people about some women's concerns like job discrimination."

McGovern worried that South Dakota's residents might be angry at him for running for president, but they seemed to like the way he had handled it. He won reelection by the largest margin in his career. In December Gloria collected her first political favor, asking McGovern to speak at a benefit for Cesar Chavez and the United Farm Workers.

In July 1969, McGovern called Gloria to invite her to a meeting to discuss his candidacy for the 1972 race. Sen. Abraham Ribicoff of Connecticut was leading the effort, and this time it was serious.

Before the meeting took place, Gloria joined McGovern and the Galbraiths in August at their annual Vermont gathering. Although the group spent the entire weekend talking about McGovern's candidacy, McGovern took Gloria aside at one point and apologized to her. She wasn't going to be invited to the strategy meeting after all. Ribicoff had crossed her name off the list and said, "No broads."

As Gloria later wrote, "According to McGovern, he then explained to Ribicoff that I had been his advance 'man,' helped to write speeches, raised money, and so on. Ribicoff listened patiently to all of it, and then repeated, 'No broads.'"

16

New Left Woman

Community organizers Cesar Chavez and Dolores Huerta founded the United Farm Workers Organizing Committee in 1966. Both dedicated their lives to La Causa—unionizing farmworkers. Migrant laborers endured some of the most inhumane working conditions in the country: ten- or twelve-hour workdays, six- or seven-day workweeks, abysmally low wages, crumbling shanties if housing was even provided, exposure to toxic pesticides, and frequently no toilets or clean drinking water in the fields.

Unionizing was a formidable task because the growers were not bound by the laws protecting other workers, and they had access to a virtually limitless pool of Mexican immigrants so poor they were willing to work under any conditions. Chavez and Huerta decided that the best strategy to empower the farmworkers was to mobilize public opinion on behalf of their cause, and they succeeded. By the late 1960s La Causa had become a civil-rights issue, involving young people, antipoverty organizations, clergy and religious groups, political leaders, unions, and minority organizations.

Cesar Chavez was stocky, sad-eyed, soft-spoken, self-educated, brilliant, and extremely charismatic. A devout Roman Catholic, Chavez managed to make his organizing a religious cause as well as a civil-rights mission. After using nonviolent protests modeled after Gandhi's, Chavez sent organizers to various cities to live on five dollars a week to publicize the cause and to encourage local boycotts of table grapes (most wine-grape growers by then had negotiated union contracts). In early 1968 Chavez went on a twenty-five-day fast to dramatize the cause and to dissuade workers from resorting to violence. He broke his fast at an ecumenical Mass attended by four thousand supporters, including Sen. Robert Kennedy.

Gloria, thirty-four, became involved in La Causa in April 1968, when she received a telephone call from Marion Moses, a thirty-two-year-old nurse who worked closely with Chavez. Chavez had sent Marion to raise funds in New York after she ran a very successful boy-cott in Toronto. Marion had managed to book Chavez for interviews with *Time* and *Life* and was soon to get him on the *Today* show, but she had made little progress in raising money. Everyone she contacted was sympathetic, but no one offered concrete help—until she called Gloria. Then, she recalls, "This wonderful voice said, 'Of course I'd like to help.' I met her at the Russian Tea Room, where she took me to lunch—a treat since all the organizers had to live on five dollars a week—and we talked and she said, 'You need to do this, you need that, we have to let people really know.' Afterward I walked around the streets of New York and looked at the tall buildings and thought, I've finally found the person who understands and is willing to help."

Gloria had media contacts and ideas for generating publicity. Most important, she provided assistance in raising money. In addition, Marion recalls, "Gloria recognized needs I didn't even realize I had—like a nice place to live." At the time, Marion was living dormitory-style in space loaned to the farmworkers in the Brooklyn Seafarers' Union building. The room was clean and the food was good, but she slept in a bunk bed and shared a bathroom with the other women who were there to organize the boycott. Dolores Huerta was there sometimes.

Gloria installed Marion in her sleeping loft in June and proceeded to take care of her. According to Marion, "You did not get a refrigerator full of food at Gloria's—though she loved ice cream and cake—but when I was sick, Gloria even got me chicken soup." Marion also appre-ciated being included in Gloria's social life, though at one point she said, "You know, Gloria, my last name is not She-works-for-Cesar-Chavez."

She has vivid memories of those days: "I have one picture that Jill Krementz took of me with Gloria and Lauren Bacall—and when I saw Lauren Bacall years later, she said, 'I haven't had a grape in years.' And

I remember running across George McGovern calling her from the pay phone on the corner to see if it was all right to come up.

"Gloria always looked great in her miniskirts, and she had God knows how many pairs of shoes and lovely, lovely clothes. In those miniskirt days, stockings were a big expense, so I had to wear mine with runs. For Christmas, Gloria gave me several pairs of stockings, which was very thoughtful. Once when she wasn't going to a party I wore something of hers and she loaned me her fur coat. It was a full-length mink coat. It was the only time in my life I've worn a mink coat, and I must say I looked pretty good.

"I went to one party with her at the Dakota [a famous New York apartment building that was home to Lauren Bacall and John Lennon and Yoko Ono] where I've never seen so many famous people in my life. It was after Bobby Kennedy was killed, and Richard Goodwin was trying to get Bobby's people to swing over to Johnson. Philip Roth was sitting with his legs crossed, staring at everyone. Claude Brown was there and Myrna Loy. And the next day the *New York Times* said the four hundred most interesting people in New York were there, and I thought, you mean 399."

Gloria met Cesar Chavez when he came to New York for a week of media appearances in May 1968. After he left, she and Marion began to plan a big benefit at Carnegie Hall. In the meantime Gloria also started working with Dolores Huerta. She took Dolores to dinner with A&P heir Huntington Hartford (owner of by-then-defunct *Show* magazine), and the two women were so persuasive that Hartford joined their picket line at the A&P supermarkets although he declined to carry a sign. The sign reading "Huntington Hartford Gets Rich on Scab Grapes" was diplomatically whisked out of sight when he arrived to march.

The event at Carnegie Hall had five cochairs, including Gloria. Marion enlisted socialite-philanthropist Marietta Tree, whom she knew through Paul Schrade, a UAW friend injured when Robert Kennedy was shot; Ann Israel, who directed General Motors heir Stewart Mott's foundation; and socialite Amanda Burden, a Beautiful People leader Marion knew through Amanda's husband, Carter Burden, a Robert Kennedy aide. Gloria asked actress Phyllis Newman. She also wrote the event's script, which was read by Lauren Bacall, Anne Jackson, Eli Wallach, and Robert Ryan, and enlisted Herb Sargent to run the show itself.

Marion returned to California in December 1968, but Gloria continued to work for La Causa. In 1969 she helped get Chavez on the cover of *Time* and wrote an article on him for *Look*.

In May 1969 Cesar Chavez and Dolores Huerta asked Gloria for help again. Chavez and Huerta were planning a hundred-mile march from UFW headquarters in Delano, California, to Calexico, on the Mexican border, where the farmworkers would try to persuade the Mexican workers not to break the U.S. workers' strike. The point was to demonstrate that the poor in one country should not be used against the poor of another country. Whatever the outcome, publicizing La Causa was their primary purpose, and Dolores asked Gloria to help. They were not getting the press coverage they needed.

As they were hours from the nearest airport and marching in the summer heat, Gloria was not surprised. She flew to California immediately. Working out of a series of hot (about 110 degrees) unair-conditioned motel rooms, she spent hours on the telephone convincing celebrities and journalists to come to the border. Once political leaders such as Ted Kennedy, Walter Mondale, and Martin Luther King Jr.'s successor as head of the Southern Christian Leadership Council, Ralph Abernathy, joined the marchers, they helped draw media coverage.

In June Gloria supervised an enormous United Farm Workers fund-raising party at the elegant Southampton estate owned by the father of Andrew Stein, who then was a Manhattan representative in the New York State Assembly. The contrast between the grapepickers and the wealthy partygoers aroused the satirical instincts of *New York Times* women's news editor Charlotte Curtis, who reported that the wife of the farmworkers' union vice president "had never before seen uniformed waitresses pass hors d'oeuvres on silver trays" and didn't know if she was allowed to eat them. "I thought maybe it was only for the millionaire guests," Curtis reported her saying. Marion Moses says the woman was more sophisticated than that, and that the joke was on Curtis.

Curtis's response pained Gloria, who nevertheless wrote philosophically in her August 24, 1970, "City Politic" column (after Curtis had written similarly of a feminist event), "The only solution to having reporters perceive, and write ironically about, the drinking-champagne-for-starving-children endemic to such parties is not to invite the press at all. I, for one, would respect anyone who kept me out. Fund-raising is necessary, but it's an indecent activity, and should be carried on in private."

She was not as philosophical about Tom Wolfe's far more savage twenty-thousand word piece "Radical Chic: That Party at Lenny's" in *New York* (June 8, 1970). Describing Leonard and Felicia Bernstein's party to raise funds for the Black Panthers, Wolfe depicted the event as part of a trend in which wealthy liberals attempted to associate themselves with radicals and their causes—preferably "exotic" radicals like Latino grape workers or Black Panthers. Wolfe's account devastated future fund-raising efforts, infuriating Gloria, who was nothing if not a chic radical. Except for Gloria and a few others, the chic turned their attention to other causes.

Although from 1969 onward her energies shifted toward women's issues, Gloria remained close to Marion Moses and Dolores Huerta and continued to help the farmworkers whenever she could. Gloria and Dolores met with the Black Panthers and with the Young Lords, to broaden the UFW's base, but Dolores also recalls Gloria's behind-the-scenes kindnesses. Besides Marion and Dolores, a group of Filipino farmworkers were living in Brooklyn to work on the boycott. The workers were middle-aged, and none of them had families, because antimiscegenation laws allowed the California growers to threaten them with deportation if they married white women. They sometimes cooked Filipino dishes for one another in Gloria's kitchen, and when Gloria learned that one of them was having a birthday, she took the entire group downtown for a Chinese banquet. "It was probably the greatest night of his life," Dolores says. "And when he went back to California, Gloria continued to communicate with him. Every once in a while he'd tell me he got a postcard from Gloria."

After resisting feminism herself, Dolores eventually was won over, and she credits Gloria. Her conversion probably was encouraged by the hours she spent at the *Ms.* magazine offices after 1972. *Ms.* staffers sometimes helped her with union work, making telephone calls, lending her lists, and even going out to the farmworkers' picket lines during their lunch hours. Dolores, who opposed abortion, eventually had eleven children by two husbands and a lover. Neither her children's fathers nor her mother was pleased with her decision to have so many children, but she attributes her fecundity to a desire to replenish her race—"my genetic response to genocide," as she calls it. She credits Gloria with persuading her that reproductive freedom really meant supporting free, individual choice for all women.

Although Ribicoff had put a "No Girls" sign on McGovern's 1972 campaign in 1969, Gloria remained active in Democratic Party politics. In November 1969 she was appointed to the Democratic Policy Council, along with John Kenneth Galbraith; Averell Harriman; the mayors of San Francisco, Philadelphia, and St. Louis; sociologist Daniel Bell; Cyrus Vance; labor leader Walter Reuther; Oregon Senator Wayne

Morse; United Artists president Arthur Krim; Betty Furness; and
Marian Wright Edelman.

Organized in response to the tragedy of the 1968 convention and
chaired by Hubert Humphrey, the council was the Democratic Party's
attempt at bringing together its disparate elements. Gloria was flattered,
but she never confused council membership with real power in the party.
"It just meant we were regarded as dissidents who needed to be talked
to or included and who wouldn't throw a bomb," she explains.

She did her best to be a dissident, even though she was terrified of
speaking to the group: "You know how you keep anticipating the
moment you have to speak and your heart is pounding and your mouth
goes dry?" Gloria used inventive tactics. She brought women leaders
from the National Welfare Rights Organization into the room before
the council met, so that when the members arrived, they would have to
throw the welfare mothers out or listen to them. They chose to listen
and later helped defeat Nixon's Family Assistance Plan, which would
have drastically lowered welfare benefits.

Early in 1970 the council called for "a firm and unequivocal commitment" from President Nixon to withdraw U.S. forces from Vietnam
within the next eighteen months. They hoped that by demanding a
deadline for withdrawal, they would be able to position the Democrats
as the antiwar party in time for the 1970 congressional elections. Gloria,
whom the *New York Times*'s account called "an antiwar leader who
writes for *New York* magazine," fought a losing battle to get the council to make a stronger statement. She wanted its statement to accuse the
Nixon administration of following a policy "to obscure the importance
of the war, to mislead the American people on the true cost, tragedy
and purposelessness of our continued presence in Vietnam."

Apart from the Policy Council, Gloria also joined Galbraith and a
number of others to form a group to promote the 1970 congressional
elections as a referendum on the war. Calling itself Referendum '70,
the group included veterans of the campaigns of all the 1968 Democratic candidates: Richard Goodwin of Harvard, who had advised both
John and Robert Kennedy and had worked for McCarthy; Andrew
Young, who was vice president of the Southern Christian Leadership
Conference; and Gloria, who hosted one or two of the meetings at her
apartment. The members planned to find the most liberal candidates
and offer to help them with staff training, research on issues, and campaign advice. Gloria thought their efforts seemed to make a difference
in the 1970 congressional elections.

In 1969, Gloria also became involved in New York City politics through the quixotic campaign of novelist Norman Mailer for mayor and Jimmy Breslin for city council president. It was an escapade intended, as Gloria wrote in her column at the time, to promote "a little truth-telling and iconoclastic thinking about the city that our 'serious' politicians can't or won't do." By those criteria, they succeeded.

The idea of Norman Mailer for mayor was hatched jointly by Noel Parmentel, a conservative contributor to William Buckley's *National Review,* and Jack Newfield, a left-leaning *Village Voice* political writer. Mailer originally called his backers the Hitler-Stalin pact, and later, "a hip coalition of the left and right." Not long after the two had talked, Newfield, Peter Maas, Jimmy Breslin, and Gloria were bemoaning the dismal prospects for the upcoming Democratic mayoral primary. Then they began to consider the possibility of Norman Mailer.

As Gloria later wrote in *Running Against the Machine,* a group portrait of the campaign:

> We sat for a minute, savoring the beautiful absurdity of it. Four-times married, famous peace marcher, defender of the young, braver of any available lion's den, confessed wife-stabber at one low point of his life, best writer and probably best political or any kind of mind in America at several high points; he might just be the big excessive visionary who could turn this big excessive city on its ear.

They knew from the start he couldn't win, but the point was to plant ideas, as McCarthy's, Robert Kennedy's, and McGovern's campaigns had done on a national basis. As Gloria recalls, they could plant them even more effectively because, unlike the senators, "Mailer was not a politician and needn't worry about making enemies—to put it mildly." At that time New York elected its city council presidents, and Newfield suggested Jimmy Breslin as the perfect running mate. The group loved it. Gloria described the ticket:

> Mailer, the wild-eyed Jewish, Harvard-bred, intellectual-activist; combined with Breslin, the tough, street-bred, would-be Irish cop—a perfect coalition for New York. As we all knew and as his readers probably suspected, Jimmy secretly reads books. . . . But his ideas, at least as radical and humane as Mailer's, were couched in unphony, shit-free street language that Queens and Red Hook could take to heart.

Norman Mailer required a little courting, and Gloria volunteered. She had known him since her *Esquire* days and had even gone out with him once. On an evening in 1963 they had gone to dinner, and when they reached Gloria's building, Norman had stopped her. "How much money do you have?" he had asked.

She had pulled out her wallet. About twenty dollars. "I have the same," he had said. "If we pool it, we could get a hotel room."

Gloria, twenty-nine, had declined, but she found the offer both touching and tactful. Many years later he told her that night had been his fortieth birthday.

To encourage Mailer to enter the 1969 race, Gloria met with him twice. Their respective accounts of the process are characteristic both of the protagonists and of their prose.

Norman wrote (in *The Prisoner of Sex*):

> Sitting at lunch one day in the Algonquin with the wise, responsible, and never unattractive manifestation of women's rights embodied in the political reporter of *New York* magazine, sitting at lunch when Gloria Steinem first asked him to run for mayor (and so slipped the terminal worm of political ambition into his plate) he should have had a clue, for in response to his protestations third time around that he would certainly not run, she had smiled and said, "Well, at least I won't have to explain you to my friends at Women's Lib."
>
> "What could they have against me?"
>
> "You might try reading your books some day."
>
> In an interview he had once said, "Women, at their worst, are low sloppy beasts." He made reference to this now, and added, "I thought the next question would be, 'What are women at their best?' but the question never came." Enormously fond of his stratagems, he gave a Presidential smile to Gloria Steinem and added, "I would have replied that women at their best are goddesses."
>
> "That's exactly what's wrong with your attitude."

Gloria wrote (in *Running Against the Machine*):

> I get further off on the wrong foot by trying to explain why women's political groups won't support him. His mystical resistance to birth control and to repeal of the abortion laws seems unrealistic, especially to poor women. He thinks about that for a while. Legal abortion, he decides, is preferable to birth control. "At least that way women *know* they're murderers."
>
> I silently write off the women's groups and wonder if the whole thing is worth it. Imagining Mailer storming through New York like an excommunicated Old Testament prophet, and Breslin's black-Irish rages against Establishment injustice, I decide again that it is.

Besides Gloria, Jimmy Breslin, and Peter Maas, the group that gathered in Mailer's book-lined Brooklyn living room to discuss the idea included Yippie Jerry Rubin; militant Black Panthers' attorney Florynce Kennedy, who wore a shark's tooth around her neck and habitually paid her bills during meetings; political activist, eventual city council member, and later, wife of Jimmy Breslin, Ronnie Eldridge; *Village Voice* city editor Mary Perot Nichols; radical feminist and *New Yorker* rock critic Ellen Willis; and former light-heavyweight boxing champion José "Cheque" Torres.

The group decided a ticket of Mailer for mayor and Breslin for city council president needed a comptroller who could balance the ticket (whatever that meant), and someone suggested Flo Kennedy. Flo passed the hot potato by suggesting Gloria. Gloria didn't want it either, but agreed to "run" until they found a replacement. They never did, and ultimately the pair ran without a comptroller candidate.

Before the next meeting, a few details had to be attended to, such as whether four-times-married Mailer, who had been convicted of stabbing his second wife, Adele, was eligible to run. The answer was yes, and a group began meeting at Gloria's to hammer out the platform. Foremost was Mailer's proposal that New York City secede to become the fifty-first state. According to one of the campaign managers, *Village Voice* writer Joe Flaherty, "It was an idea he had acquired from Clay Felker, . . . who (I presumed) got it from Pete Hamill, . . . who may have lifted it from the late William Randolph Hearst, . . . who in all likelihood latched onto it from Fernando Wood, a New York City mayor who proposed it in 1861—all of which buoys the Hemingway literary canon that good writers never plagiarize, they steal."

At that time New York City residents sent about $14 billion in taxes to Washington and Albany annually and only got back $3 billion in funds. As an autonomous city-state New York would be able to decentralize much of the power back to its neighborhoods. That way, as Mailer figured it, Harlem could declare a day to honor Malcolm X if its residents so chose, while Staten Island could celebrate John Birch Day. There could be "compulsory free love in those neighborhoods that vote for it, and compulsory attendance at church on Sunday in those that vote for that." Mailer thought this enabled him to declare with complete veracity that, "I am running to the left and to the right of every man in the race," and he told a Columbia University audience that his left-right axis extended from "free Huey Newton to end fluoridation."

Another Mailer-Breslin proposal was a monthly "Sweet Sunday," during which all mechanical fuel-dependent transportation and equipment, including elevators, would cease operation, offering citizens pure air for a day. Mailer later had to make an exception for generators in hospitals when he was accused of prescribing genocide for the infirm. Other planks included a monorail around Manhattan and legalized gambling at Coney Island.

Six weeks into the campaign, Mailer won the Pulitzer Prize for *The Armies of the Night*. That prompted Jimmy Breslin to decide he was a drag on the ticket, and he tried to quit. Mailer had to talk him out of it.

Gloria found the campaign a headquarters at Columbus Circle, the same shabby room where she had worked for McCarthy with other antiwar writers. She also began raising funds from donors and finding celebrities to appear at fund-raising events. After a while, Norman Mailer wanted more from Gloria, though. He wanted to sleep with her. Although she didn't really want to, she eventually consented. When their attempt was unsuccessful, Gloria, a perennial optimist, managed to find the positive. She says their encounter provided a valuable learning experience: "It taught me that if you go to bed with a man that you don't want to go to bed with, you jinx him as much as you. And I never did it again. It was a real lesson. The thing was, he was so focused on it, you know, it mattered so much to him. And he's so vulnerable, in a weird way. And we were working together all the time, and I think some part of me thought it would make the tension go away."

They parted on good terms. It was at that point in the campaign that Cesar Chavez and Dolores Huerta called to ask for Gloria's help on the Calexico march. Gloria recalled, "Norman and I had dinner at one of those Aegean fish places, and I explained that I thought it was more important for me to be an outside organizer and press contact for the California farmworkers' march to the Mexican border. It was a fine, amicable conversation, and then I sort of just drifted away."

By May 1969, Gloria's love life was overcrowded anyway. She remained involved with Herb Sargent, who still wanted to marry her, but she was seeing other men as well. In 1968 she had written a feature story on professional-football-player-turned-movie-actor Jim Brown and later had a brief affair with him. In New York in 1968–69 she became involved with Arnaldo Segarra, an aide to Mayor Lindsay. A handsome veteran of the War on Poverty, Arnaldo worked with the Puerto Rican Young Lords, the Black Panthers, and other community groups. He remembers meeting Gloria at a play about Malcolm X in Spanish Harlem. "She walked in and we sort of looked at each other and I said to myself, 'Goddam, that woman's fine.' The next day she seduced me."

When he called *New York* magazine, the receptionist told him, "She said if you called to put you through." They went to lunch, and their affair began that day. Arnaldo, an experienced community organizer, was impressed with Gloria's ability to communicate with anyone, from the "shoeshine guy on 126th and Lenox Avenue to the chairman of the board of a major corporation." Furthermore, "At one point I was very threatened. At her apartment there could be Warren Beatty [on the telephone] and George McGovern and then here's little old me, Lindsay's assistant. It throws you off balance. But she was so cool—she handed me my ego.

"She also got rid of a lot of my macho. In her special way, without being threatening, she showed me there's another way of dealing with women. Not that I ever beat up women or anything, but I give her a lot of credit."

While Gloria was seeing Herb and Arnaldo and others in New York, she had a new lover on the West Coast. Amid the carnage at the Chicago Democratic convention, Gloria found a friend in California delegate Rafer Johnson. They worked together to get an antiwar film about Robert Kennedy screened at the convention. The celebrated 1960 Olympic decathlon gold medalist comments on their first meeting, "I think the first day I saw this woman I thought a great deal of her. You had to be transfixed by the way this woman looked."

Gloria says of Rafer, "You know how sometimes very big, strong men are gentle, because they can afford to be gentle? He's like that. He's very tall, very elegant, not in the sense of how he dresses, but in his body. He looks attenuated, long and sinewy, and quite tall—I would say six-foot-three or six-four. Very ebony—not ebony, not quite that dark but very beautiful skin. You know, that kind of clear, dark skin, almost translucent. He's just a very kind person with a depth of wisdom that gives him a calm center. He also describes political issues in exactly the way they are experienced. Watching him with people— whether in sports or in politics—you know that he's helping each person to be a little better than they were before."

Rafer was still grieving for Robert Kennedy. He had been standing next to Kennedy when he was shot, and had grabbed the gun away from the assassin, Sirhan Sirhan. With Los Angeles Rams football star Roosevelt Grier, Rafer had restrained Sirhan and protected him from the crowd. After the funeral he had gone into seclusion, but soon afterward Kennedy's sister Eunice Shriver asked him to help with the Special Olympics. He now credits that involvement with healing his grief—since 1968 Rafer has devoted so much time to volunteering for the games that many assume he was an employee. In fact, he worked for fifteen years as a Continental Telephone vice president for public and community affairs.

Rafer became famous as an Olympic medalist but, like Gloria, he had always been a leader. He was born in Texas in 1935. His family later was among the first black families to settle in Kingsburg, California, where Rafer starred in football, basketball, baseball, and track and was elected president of both the junior and senior high school student bodies. After becoming interested in the decathlon as a junior, he placed third in the National AAU championships as a senior. At UCLA he was president of the student body, the first black to pledge a predominantly Jewish fraternity, and a campus leader for Youth for Christ, a national nondenominational religious movement. When he went to the Olympics in 1960, he was chosen to carry the American flag during the opening ceremonies.

Shortly after he became an NBC sports reporter—a job he loved—Rafer became close to Robert Kennedy, actively supporting him in his run for president. Then NBC suddenly dropped him, explaining that because he was so closely associated with Kennedy, and was on the air every night, Kennedy rivals might ask for equal time. Rafer considered the firing a politically motivated action against Kennedy, so when the network invited him back after the assassination, he refused to return.

During the three years they saw each other, Gloria became more and more famous as a feminist, but Rafer recalls the diversity of the demands on her time: "Feminists would call her, writer friends would call with you-name-it, Black Panthers would call, George McGovern's office would call her. She was open to helping anyone with a sound cause." Both continued to see other people, though Rafer saw fewer as time went on. He was in love with her, and while they never discussed it, he thought about the possibility of marriage.

He remembers, "That woman was an absolute joy to be with—my kind of person in how open she was in listening and almost proactive in terms of her involvement with other people. So marriage was going through my head, although we never talked about it. What I ended up thinking—without any conversation with Gloria, but it got to a point within me—was that Gloria was someone I easily could have married. So if we'd had that conversation and gotten anywhere close to yes, that would have been it. But I thought an interracial marriage would have hindered her wherever she was going to go—that it would have affected that whole process. That was only in my head, but it was one kind of red flag.

"The other was the East Coast–West Coast split. I was grounded in southern California; she was grounded in New York. Therefore there were two obstacles to me, but I didn't discuss them with her. I loved her and I believe she loved me. But because there were these other factors, I didn't pursue the question of marriage."

Gloria was uninterested in marriage, but their racial difference was not a problem. The year 1968 not only was a watershed in national politics, it was a watershed year for Gloria politically and professionally, and her personal life reflected it. Until then, most of her lovers had been involved with writing, publishing, or television and, except for a colleague in India, they had been white. Starting in 1968, the year she became a political columnist, they tended to be more political— Rafer and Arnaldo were activists. Arnaldo was Puerto Rican. Jim Brown and Rafer were African American, as was Frank Thomas, the man with whom she became involved in 1971. This reflected a new stage in Gloria's life.

From 1968 on, Gloria's political activity expanded and intensified. From affiliations with predominantly white, middle-class groups such as Women Strike for Peace, Writers and Editors Against the War, and the Democratic Party, she began to work with and write about more diverse and more radical groups, such as the National Welfare Rights Organization, the Black Panthers, the Young Lords, and the United Farm Workers.

Until the 1960s, the political left could have been defined as a combination of the Old Left—the Communist Party U.S.A. and its splinter groups—and the non-Communist left, which covered everyone else, from socialists to liberals. Gloria was—and is—part of the non-Communist left. Other than her primary political identity as a feminist, she describes herself politically today by saying that the male politician who best represents her views is the late Michael Harrington. (Harrington became famous when his book about poverty, *The Other America,* was published in 1962, and he later founded the Democratic Socialists of America, to which Gloria belongs. Democratic Socialists believe that more of society's institutions should be socialized, but that the socializing should occur organically and democratically, from the bottom up.)

The New Left movement of the 1960s represented both a political and a generational change. Shaped by events such as the 1956 Hungarian Revolution, young people of the 1950s left, such as Gloria, liberal Allard Lowenstein, and socialist Michael Harrington, opposed overseas Communist regimes because of their totalitarianism. They had lived through the terrors of McCarthyism, but they distinguished domestic anti-Communism, which they abhorred, from their opposition to Soviet imperialism.

Young people of the 1960s also witnessed McCarthyism at home, but their perceptions of the cold war were more influenced by U.S. actions abroad, like the Bay of Pigs fiasco in 1961 and, most important, the Vietnam War. To them, anti-Communism seemed less disinterestedly noble and more the province of reactionaries—or just an excuse for U.S. imperialism.

Furthermore, the New Left's diminished anti-Communism was accompanied by an increasing antipathy toward liberals. As young people joined the antipoverty, civil-rights, free speech, and antiwar movements, they found themselves frustrated with the limitations of the democratic system. They were especially disappointed when liberals repeatedly failed to deliver on their promises. On a number of occasions the Kennedy administration failed to uphold federal laws protecting blacks in the South, for example, and many liberal politicians continued to support the Vietnam War. As a result, liberals began to seem indistinguishable from the rest of the establishment. Increasingly radicalized, young activists became convinced that the only way to achieve their goals was to work outside the system. Frustrated black activists came to believe that their only hope lay in political separatism and self-help—Black Power—rather than working with white sympathizers.

Without sacrificing her belief that wherever possible one should work for change from within as well as without, Gloria gravitated toward New Left groups. Some, like the United Farm Workers, attracted some establishment support, but most did not, and for those Gloria was a valuable supporter. She not only worked with some of them directly, she covered them sympathetically in her column. By focusing on their community projects instead of the violent rhetoric of some—which was what the media usually covered—Gloria publicized their positive contributions.

That involvement spilled over into her love life. Gloria clearly had her pick of men. Even many who were not among her lovers—Clay Felker, for example—were widely assumed to be in love with her. So it is fair to say that she had a wide range of choices.

Her lovers had been attractive, lovable men who adored and were kind to her, but they were also men with positions in the world to which she aspired. In each relationship, Gloria, at least in part, had been trying on an identity. Therefore, their individual attractions notwithstanding, the fact that Gloria chose one black or Latino lover after another for the next seven years appeared to be, to some extent, an act of self-definition.

Her romantic relationships with black men coincided with her New Left period, but her exposure to racial difference and acceptance went back to her childhood. Gloria had been raised in a family associated with musicians, one of the few truly integrated worlds in the United States, and she saw her parents treat black and white musicians equally. Whatever their race, Leo housed them in the band cottage and Ruth cooked for them. Gloria was also influenced by Louisa May Alcott, an ardent abolitionist who, Gloria recalls, wrote in her Civil War stories about "working as a maid or a tutor and sitting in the kitchen with the black cook. It was clear that she was not comfortable, but it was also clear that she was trying to be comfortable."

Gloria's first important experience with regard to race was working as the only white person at a Washington swimming pool. The second was her exposure to India, with its endless variety and intermingling of races. She says that when she returned to the United States she felt "snow blind" among a sea of white faces. She vowed to herself that she would not live such a segregated life, or "let a racist society" choose her friends for her, but in the early 1960s she drifted away from her resolve. Frustrated with her inability to use her Indian experience to the degree she had hoped, she concentrated on building her career and establishing a place for herself in New York.

When she became involved in a more integrated world through politics, it felt good, a gratifying fulfillment of her long-standing desire. The men were a part of that. Her attraction was both emotional and intellectual. They were individuals, but part of their individual characters was formed by their experiences because of their race. "It isn't race that makes a difference, but society's treatment of race," she explains. "They're not 'black men.' They're men who are—it's part of their humanity. Having that sense of being an outsider. It connects with being a woman in a big way. It connects with my class experience but also with our female experience of being outside the structure.

"So men, certainly not all, but many men who are black or who have some other ethnic experience or whatever, or sometimes who are Jewish, depending on their experience of being Jewish, share a view of what needs to be changed and could be changed and how important it is for people to be unique individuals and not study only European history and present God as white and all the myriad ways in which we've been living in a pretty narrow paradigm. They feel that too. So it's a great bond."

The political battles of the late 1960s were intense emotional experiences. Days of hope alternated with days of rage, and meanwhile more people died every day in Vietnam. Gloria's advantages as an insider did not preclude feelings of powerlessness—everyone who opposed the war felt that way. She shared, as well, the frustrations of the poor and minority groups with whom she worked. That kind of intensity is a bond, so her description of those relationships as strengthened by a shared "sense of being an outsider" is understandable, even though in many respects she was not an outsider. The quality of her empathy and the passion for justice it prompted were to drive Gloria in the years to come.

At the same time Gloria was also the most self-conscious of women. When, in 1995, a reporter for *Mother Jones* asked her about the role of men in her life, she volunteered, "I suppose if you look at the men in my life, they're disproportionately men of color, and I think for obvious reasons, because they identify more with the women's struggle."

17

A Feminist Is Born

While Gloria wrote her "City Politic" column and political feature stories for *New York,* she continued to cover the lifestyles of the rich and famous from the pop-sociological stance the New Journalism had made fashionable. However, as she had since her 1962 *Esquire* piece "The Moral Disarmament of Betty Coed," she tended to focus on the relationships among sex, gender roles, and social expectations.

In "Notes on the New Marriage," (*New York,* July 8, 1968), an article about the New York City phenomenon of wealthy, intelligent women marrying homosexual men, she wrote:

Blurring of sex lines, especially public ones, is forever being condemned by mass magazines and other proponents of the Conventional Wisdom; perhaps wrongly. For one thing, strictly polarized roles are a mark of authoritarian societies with very little individual or sub-group freedom. For another, growing up with an impossibly omnipotent male image to fulfill is one reason that boys take refuge in homosexuality. This much-feared "neuterization" of society may even help the planet to survive. Anthropologist Geoffrey Gorer discovered that the few peaceful human tribes were those in which sex differences were at a minimum: boys weren't taught that manhood depended on aggression (or military skills or short hair), and girls weren't taught that womanhood depended on submissiveness (or working at home instead of in the fields). . . .

Unfortunately, psychologists don't seem to talk to anthropologists very much: the former are rooted to the norms of this society and this time (or Freud's work-oriented, male-chauvinist society and 19th Century time), and are therefore much more worried by changing roles. Based on Western history, they believe roles should flow more from biological function, i.e., dominant, food-hunting men and passive, gestating women. Anthropologists believe role determination is more societal.

Gloria now says she deeply regrets that article because she hadn't understood "the political and human problems that would motivate such marriages in the first place: the penalties for being a strong, creative woman without a male escort or for being a gay man who wasn't married." She was clearly moving toward that understanding, however.

In August 1968, she reviewed Caroline Bird's *Born Female: The High Cost of Keeping Women Down* for the *New York Times Book Review,* writing enthusiastically, "*Born Female* is enough to convince anyone literate, from male chauvinist to female Uncle Tom, that the superstition and restrictive prejudices on which our system of work is built are depriving the country of nearly half its talent."

Using the term "sexism" for probably the first time in a popular work, *Born Female* explored both sexism's obvious costs to society and its hidden costs to men's and women's psyches. In her review of the book, Gloria cited examples that she still uses to show audiences how popular beliefs keep women down—women have more manual dexterity, but only for factory work, not for brain surgery; or women are more moral, rather than just less tainted by power. Adding her trademark composite, she noted, "Caroline Bird is something of a Malcolm X for women, but Malcolm X just before he died, when he had developed beyond anti-white feelings."

In "Women and Power," Gloria responded to a statement by Jacqueline Kennedy that there were two kinds of women: "those who want power in the world and those who want power in bed." Recalling the article years later, without having reread it, Gloria made a point of saying that the story was Clay's idea. She wouldn't have written it otherwise, she explained, because that had not been her experience.

Her disavowal is not new. For years Gloria would insist that she didn't choose her lovers because they could help her. On the other hand, at times she would say exactly that. She told Liz Smith in *Vogue*, June 1971, "I was into the success, the 'important' right man for all the wrong reasons," and she told Joan Barthel for a March 1984 *Cos-*

mopolitan profile, "I used to seek out rich and famous men. Not to the extent of going out with somebody I didn't like, but it used to matter to me."

Her attempt to distance herself from the article is the it-wasn't-my-idea excuse she employs when she has to own up to something she can't explain away: she didn't go on a Freedom Ride because Benton didn't want her to; she got the idea of lying about her age from Tom Guinzburg and her sister; she wrote about women seeking advantages through men because Clay assigned it.

In fact, if Gloria were not so defensive about her image—or if she had had more faith in her earlier self—she might have realized she was disowning something she should have been proud of. "Women and Power" was a powerful feminist statement that women who sought power in the bedroom often did so because they were denied power in the world. Furthermore, they were even deprived of understanding their plight (as feminists later put it, they weren't conscious of their oppression). Gloria wrote about "the sexual segregationist argument that women aren't interested in power at all; that something in their genes makes them prefer to be ordered about." Actually, that "turns out to be no more fundamentally true than all the other past myths: that women enjoyed sex less than men, for instance, or that Negroes were dependent creatures who didn't want power either."

She also made it clear that she had no problem with the idea of women wanting and valuing power, though she could see some who did. "Power may be a dirty word, especially among New Left-through-Hippies who fear that it must be manipulative and bad. . . ." She closed:

> Perhaps if women had more encouragement, more opportunity to gain power on their own, there would be less of the bitterness and hypocrisy that comes from using men for subversive ends. If society stopped telling girls that men would have to give them their total identity on a silver platter, wives wouldn't be so resentful when it didn't happen. And ambitious women could relax, and look for pleasure instead of power in bed.
>
> Men ought to encourage the idea. It might take a load off all of us.

In December 1968, Gloria participated in a television panel that included Jean Faust, the national legislative chairperson of the National Organization for Women (NOW). Faust took notes on the event to report on the discussion to her New York NOW chapter:

This was a very interesting experience; everyone started out very hostile to me. They were expecting an aggressive, screaming battle-axe. But after we had taped one show, they became very friendly. Suddenly, everyone was taking the "feminist point of view"—all I could do was agree. So, I escalated and said, men, if necessary, should follow their wives to new jobs. That set up some waves! At the last show, Aline Saarinen, the moderator, made a beautiful speech which could easily have been written by any of us—it was that feminist. Gloria Steinem, especially, was just great. She talked about the Negro parallel. She said that, as a writer, she was expected to write about women or makeup or other "feminine" subjects.

Faust, who also had been New York NOW's first president, was so impressed that, after the taping, she asked Gloria out for coffee and tried to talk her into joining NOW. Gloria demurred. She sympathized with the goals of feminism, she explained, but she preferred to be a humanist rather than narrowing her focus to "feminist."

"I'd prefer to be a humanist, too," said Faust, who considered herself one anyway, "but I also feel there has to be an interim period in which specific areas of discrimination against women need to be addressed." Gloria was adamant, but Faust added another comment to her notes. Gloria, she wrote, "is a feminist, but calls herself a 'humanist.'" Faust knew it was only a matter of time.

A month later Faust tried again. A group of women were planning a demonstration and she wondered if Gloria would join them. On February 12, 1969, they planned to attempt to integrate the Plaza Hotel's Oak Room, which barred women at lunchtime. *Feminine Mystique* author and NOW president Betty Friedan, public relations executive Muriel Fox, *Newsday* reporter Dolores Alexander, and others had alerted the press, so they expected to attract a lot of media attention.

Gloria had been humiliated at that very hotel, only a couple of weeks before. Waiting in the Plaza's lobby to meet an actor she had an appointment to interview, she had been told by the assistant manager to move along. When she explained that she was a writer meeting her subject for tea at the hotel's Palm Court, he overrode her protests, repeating, "Unescorted ladies are not allowed," as he escorted her right out the door.

Although she agreed to cover the demonstration for possible inclusion in her "City Politic" column, Gloria refused to join it. Not only did she not consider herself a feminist, but this was not a group with which she wanted to align herself. She had read *The Feminine Mystique* but considered it important mostly for white middle-class suburban women. She valued women friends, and in spite of her own frustrating failure to get the assignments she wanted, she had always gone out of her way to help other women professionally. But she had no interest in being identified with a group of middle-class white women protesting for women's rights at the Oak Room of the Plaza Hotel.

A couple of weeks after observing the demonstration she was reluctant to join, Gloria found herself back at the hotel for another interview. On her way to the elevator she saw the assistant manager who had evicted her before. She gave in to a sudden impulse to linger. The man again told her to leave, but this time Gloria refused, telling him the Plaza was a public place and she had every right to be there. Besides, she asked, why weren't unescorted men banished—they might be male prostitutes, mightn't they? It was well known that hotel staff members supplied call girls, she told him. Maybe he was just worried about losing a commission?

When the startled manager backed down, Gloria experienced an unexpected surge of well-being. The difference between the two occasions, as she explained in her 1992 book *Revolution From Within,* was that seeing the women stand up for their rights had increased her own self-esteem. "It had been raised almost against my will—by contagion."

The following month she attended an event held by another feminist group. Thinking it might yield material for her column, she went downtown to a speakout on the issue of abortion. The flyer read:

Redstockings, of the
Women's Liberation Movement
presents
Abortion
Women Tell It Like It Is
137 West 4th St.   8:30 p.m.
Contribution $2   March 21
Also: a preview of
The New Feminist Theatre
Washington Square Methodist Church

The standing-room-only crowd filled the sanctuary so completely that Gloria perched on a windowsill at the rear of the room.

The evening began with a playlet simulating an abortion hearing in which a pregnant male legislator had to appear before an all-woman panel to beg for permission to obtain an abortion. Then the Redstockings, distinguishable because they were the only ones actually wearing red stockings, arranged themselves behind a long table on the stage. The first speaker described the bravery of the women who were about to discuss their abortions in public. Some of the women who had wanted to testify, she explained, had feared that publicly acknowledging that they had broken the law or had had an abortion might cost them their jobs or provoke reprisals or police harassment.

The speaker noted that there were about a million illegal abortions a year in the United States. However, though an estimated one in four women had had one, abortions were not something women discussed openly. The New York State legislature had just held hearings about changing its abortion law, but the Redstockings had been prevented from testifying. The legislators refused to allow the Redstockings to speak because they only wanted testimony from fourteen "experts": clergymen, physicians, lawyers, and one woman—a nun.

That rejection prompted the meeting Gloria attended. The Redstockings had decided to conduct their own public hearings, to present testimony from "the real experts": women who had actually had an abortion, or who had tried unsuccessfully to get an abortion, or who might in the future want an abortion—the only people, in fact, who were actually covered by the law. The Redstockings intended to provide the public with the opportunity to understand how the law worked in the real world.

One by one, the women told their stories. Gloria listened intently. Their experiences were heartbreaking, enraging, and sometimes even funny.

"I thought I knew a lot about birth control, but I got pregnant because my boyfriend told me that when he came the second time, the sperms wouldn't be potent."

"I went to eleven hospitals before one would give me an abortion. The doctors at the tenth offered me a deal: I could have an abortion if I agreed to be sterilized. I was twenty."

"You get into a car at 54th Street and Lexington Avenue and you're blindfolded and taken someplace, you don't know where. You're not given an anaesthetic. The instruments aren't even sterilized. You can get an infection. You can wind up never able to have children. You can die."

"He told me not to use birth control. When I got pregnant, he said, 'Oh, god, I'll have to sell some of my stock.' When I asked him to go to Puerto Rico with me, he said, 'That's silly. All kinds of women do it every day. I don't have time. I have to go to class.' After I got back, he called me and said, 'Hey, did you get the birth control yet?' "

The Redstockings had more in mind than catharsis, and they related the women's stories to the role of women in society. "I went to those hearings a few weeks ago," said one, "and some judge in his sixties or seventies—this is the expert on abortion—got up and said he had a great reform. His reform was that after a woman had paid her debt to society and had had four children, then if she got pregnant with her fifth, guess what? She could have an abortion. This is the way women are thought of."

The Redstockings pointed out that women's roles—wife, mother, helpmate—all required women to subordinate their own desires for the good of others. So if "good" women by definition put others first, then women who paid attention to their own needs must be "bad." From that perspective, the laws on abortion made perfect sense. Women who tried to get abortions were selfish and needed to be deterred; making abortions almost impossible to obtain certainly was an effective deterrent. Should a woman persevere in her selfishness and actually get an abortion, then even if the abortion were legal, the experience should be made as painful, humiliating, and dangerous as possible. That way if the woman couldn't be deterred, at least she would be punished.

Near the end of the evening, one of the Redstockings was even more explicit. She didn't use the phrase "the personal is political" (which was coined about this time by a woman who worked closely with this group) but she explained the concept: "People have asked me, 'What does abortion have to do with the women's liberation movement?'

"Well, we're women up here who have had an abortion. And when each of us had an abortion, we didn't think, 'Look what's being done to women.' We experienced it as, 'Oh, what a horrible misfortune has happened to me. How will I possibly get out of this horrible situation that has happened to me?'

"What became apparent tonight is that being pregnant and having to have an abortion and having to go through these kinds of experiences is that it isn't just a horrible thing that happened to Ros, and a horrible situation that happened to Ann, and a horrible thing that happened to Helen. It's a horrible situation that is happening to many, many women in this country. It's one of the ways that women are victims in this country.

"And women's liberation women have got to get together to organize to change it and overthrow it. And that, I believe, is the best connection I can make."

As Gloria sat, quietly taking notes, her eyes filled with tears. Sharing with everyone in the room the laughter, sorrow, rage, exhilaration, she was overcome.

Gloria had come to the meeting as a detached observer; she was not prepared for such strong feelings. Now the memories of her pregnancy came flooding back: the feeling of entrapment; the terror; the hopelessness; a desperation so intense she had been willing to risk her life to escape it.

She was also well aware of discrimination against women. She had experienced it, resented it, complained about it, and even written about it. However, that night the Redstockings made connections that put everything together for Gloria in a new way. By providing a political framework, they gave her a context for her experiences.

That framework acted as a lens. When Gloria looked through that lens at her life, she was astonished at the clarity with which she saw. Years later she could still recall the power of her epiphany: "Suddenly, I was no longer learning intellectually what was wrong. I knew."

18

The Birth of NOW

Gloria went home from the meeting in an exalted state and began reading everything she could find about feminism.

That feminist realization, as Gloria later called it—seeing oneself for the first time not only as an individual confronting problems but also as a member of an oppressed group—was an overwhelming experience for every woman who went through it. It was enraging, but it was also exhilarating. Women said to themselves, and then to each other, "I'm not alone" or "There isn't something wrong with me" or "I'm not crazy." Most empowering was the realization, "That means it doesn't have to be this way."

The revelation had an even more powerful effect on Gloria. Over the years it would become clear that Gloria's specific attributes and abilities were of enormous value to the movement, but it was also true that the ideology of feminism addressed perfectly Gloria's own emotional and psychological makeup. The girl whose childhood idol, Louisa May Alcott, had communicated the idea that love and marriage was the road to self-annihilation grew into a woman who considered marriage "surrender." The girl who watched her responsible mother's broken spirit immobilize her grew into a woman who did not want to have a child. The girl whose irresponsible father left her so he could roam the world in pursuit of his dreams grew into a woman who protected her autonomy above all else.

Feminism provided Gloria with an ideology that so comprehensively explained her life to her that it would not be an exaggeration to say she became a feminist fundamentalist. Everything could be explained and judged within that belief system.

Feminism rationalized Gloria's Manichaean view of the world, in which women were vulnerable and men were free. In a sense, seeing gender used as a caste system is exactly what the feminist realization was. However, as time went on, most people saw those categories as less fixed and more complex. Class, race, or individual circumstances might be more important, depending on the circumstances, and Gloria's understanding of class and race exceeded most people's. Even so, she never lost her visceral reaction. She responded instinctively to women in need as if they could be her mother—only this time Gloria might actually be able to save her.

It would take almost twenty years and a great deal of turmoil for Gloria to credit the degree to which some problems were individual rather than social. Sometimes the personal was not political; sometimes it was just personal. Leftists, by definition, incline toward sociological or political explanations, but Gloria's rejection of the psychological was extreme, even for a leftist. As it turned out, even that limitation of Gloria's benefited the movement. Her usual assumption that a woman's problem was political or social only added fuel to her determination to bring about the changes necessary to effect a political or social solution.

In short, Gloria was no ordinary convert. Inside the ambitious writer with designer clothes and long legs and short skirts and powerful friends and desirable lovers and radical-chic causes and a clever wit and an imperturbable calm lay the heart and soul of a zealot. Not only was hers an unlikely exterior for a missionary, but because she was so used to hiding her feelings, she didn't sound like one, either. As she describes herself, "People have to be on LSD to figure out if I'm angry."

Because of that exterior, no one could tell that as far as Gloria was concerned, she had just been given the word, and she longed to spread it. That very combination—the Trojan-horse exterior and the fire-in-the-belly interior—made Gloria Steinem invaluable to the cause that became her life's work. When Gloria found feminism, a historic exchange occurred: The movement offered Gloria an ideology and a raison d'être, and Gloria Steinem offered the movement what she would later call her "talents and demons."

By 1969 the women's movement had caught fire. The most trans-formative movement of the second half of the twentieth century is often

called the second wave of feminism, to distinguish it from the first feminist movement in the United States. Led for many years by Elizabeth
Cady Stanton and Susan B. Anthony, the first wave began among abolitionist women in the mid-nineteenth century and faded after activists
finally won the vote for women in 1920. Suffragists disappeared from
history into a footnote about ridiculous women in funny clothes who
were "given" the vote.

The second wave of feminism developed from two separate groups
of predominantly middle-class women, most of whom were white. One
group emerged from the ranks of young radical activists; the other was
made up of housewives and women in the workplace. Betty Friedan's
Feminine Mystique, an instant best-seller when it appeared in 1963,
awoke many women to their situation. Observing that modern American women had been trapped by a "problem that has no name,"
Friedan named it "the feminine mystique." The problem, she explained,
was that woman was defined only as "husband's wife, children's
mother, server of physical needs of husband, children, home," and
never as a person "defining herself by her own actions in society."

Step by step, Friedan's book awakened women to their oppression
by describing the various ways women were kept in their place. Corporations needing women as consumers reinforced the idea that housework was important and required a great array of products; government
wanted women out of the workplace so there would be enough jobs
for (white) men; Freudian psychological theory was used to convince
women who wanted achievement that their aspirations were inappropriately masculine and due to penis envy; educators encouraged girls to
prepare for a subordinate role in society; media, particularly women's
magazines, reinforced the message that true femininity meant passivity,
altruism, nurturance, and a childlike dependency.

Millions of women who read *The Feminine Mystique* underwent a
powerful feminist realization. As Friedan traveled across the country
to promote her book (referring frequently to her husband and three
children, as instructed by her publisher), she was overwhelmed by the
response.

American women were ready for Friedan's message. With fewer children due to contraception advances, improved education, and an
expanding economy, middle-class and working-class women were entering the workforce in unprecedented numbers (poor women had always
worked outside the home). Once there—and most were working for
economic reasons—they experienced the pervasive discrimination that

suppressed both wages and opportunities for women of all races, as well as for nonwhite men, and maintained them as a reserve or under-paid labor force. Women were denied jobs for which they were quali-fied because "no woman could do that job" or because the quota for women was filled. They were passed over for promotion because women weren't promoted any higher. They trained boss after boss, while doing all his work. They endured sexual harassment, though they had no name for it. They received lower pay than men for doing the same job.

Then the climate of the 1960s arrived, with its spirit of activism cre-ated by the civil-rights movement. The ferment prompted women to examine their own lives and question the status quo, instead of just accepting the injustices they encountered.

That climate of rebellion, the discrepancy between the women's rising expectations and their frustrating reality, and a jolt into con-sciousness from *The Feminine Mystique* were the tinder. The spark was inadvertently supplied by the federal government. In 1961 President Kennedy appointed a Commission on the Status of Women, and two years later the commission issued its report. Although Friedan's book, which also appeared in 1963, had envisioned working outside the home as the solution to women's problems, the commission's report cata-logued the "pervasive limitations" women encountered once they were in the workplace.

The issues raised by the report were troubling, but the government had no compelling interest in addressing them. In a response intended to bury the issues, two new federal organizations were established: the Interdepartmental Committee on the Status of Women and the Citi-zens Advisory Council on the Status of Women. At the same time, state governors began appointing state versions of the presidential commis-sion to study laws and other impediments to women's equality.

Beginning in 1964, the council and the committee began holding an annual national conference in Washington for representatives of the state commissions, thus gathering many of the most politically active women from all over the country in one place. Meeting to discuss a range of issues affecting women, the delegates shared problems and solutions, developed networks, and became more determined than ever to act on their issues.

Congress also passed the Civil Rights Act of 1964. Included in that historic act was Title VII, which prohibited employment discrimination on the basis of race, creed, national origin—and sex. Just as bringing together hundreds of activist women yielded unintended consequences, Title VII's prohibition of sex discrimination happened by inadvertence. It was proposed almost at the last minute, not by a supporter of women's equality, but by an opponent of the civil-rights bill, eighty-one-year-old House Rules Committee Chairman Howard W. Smith of Virginia, who hoped the inclusion of sex would kill the entire bill. The strategy looked promising, since the House broke into laughter when he introduced the preposterous amendment.

However, led by Representative Martha Griffiths, all but one of the women in Congress went to work, as did several women's organizations. With the support of a number of southern congressmen—all but one of whom opposed the civil rights act itself and supported the amendment as an effort to kill it—the amendment to include sex as a protected category passed. Then the Civil Rights Act itself passed. Although it became law, there was little administrative or congressional support to enforce the sex-discrimination provision. It was viewed as an accident and an embarrassment—and at some level, of course, a threat.

To enforce Title VII's provisions, the act created the Equal Employment Opportunity Commission, which began operating in 1965. One-third of the complaints that began streaming into the EEOC were filed by women, but since the majority of the commissioners were uninterested in enforcing the prohibition against sex discrimination, nothing happened. Two of the five commissioners, Richard Graham and Aileen Hernández, the only woman and one of two African Americans, were supportive, and Hernández later described her experience: "Commission meetings produced a sea of male faces, nearly all of which reflected attitudes that ranged from boredom to virulent hostility whenever the issue of sex discrimination was raised. The message came through clearly that the Commission's priority was race discrimination—and apparently only as it related to Black *men*."

In September 1965 the EEOC, pressured into issuing its first ruling on sex discrimination, determined 3–2 that sex-segregated classified advertising was permissible. In November the agency upheld the legality of protective state labor laws, even though their effect was largely to keep women out of many categories of high-paying jobs by such means as limiting their hours or barring them from occupations that required lifting loads heavier than thirty-five pounds.

In June 1966 women from the state commissions gathered for the third annual Conference on the Status of Women. The conferences were always tightly controlled by Women's Bureau and Labor Department

officials, who were determined to prevent any criticism or action that
might embarrass the administration. However, many of the women
attending in 1966, including some who worked for the federal government, were furious at the EEOC's failure to enforce the law. Catherine
East, who was executive secretary of both the council and the commission, saw to it that state commission delegates received copies of
an angry speech by Representative Griffiths on the EEOC's failures,
and even its hostility, to women's rights.

A number of those inside and outside government were already
thinking about starting an organization to exert pressure on behalf of
women's rights, and the idea floating around was "an NAACP for
women" (the National Association for the Advancement of Colored
People was the sixty-year-old organization that had led battles for racial
equality, such as the *Brown* v. *Board of Education* suit to integrate
public schools). Commissioners Graham and Hernández had privately
supported the idea among some advocates they knew.

During the last night of the conference, some of the dissidents met in
the hotel room of Betty Friedan, who was attending the conference as
an observer. Friedan had already been in contact with Dr. Pauli Murray,
an African-American professor at Yale Law School who had been
speaking and writing about the EEOC's failure to enforce the law. Also
in the group were Dorothy Haener of the United Auto Workers (in
spite of the fact that unions generally supported protective legislation);
Wisconsin State Commission chief Kay Clarenbach; and Mary East-
wood, who had to be particularly discreet because she was a Justice
Department lawyer. The group talked for hours about starting an organization and finally decided to continue their conversation during the
next day's closing session. Meanwhile they agreed that Clarenbach
would make one last try to work within the system. She would propose
that the conference pass resolutions demanding that the EEOC enforce
the law against sex discrimination and that President Johnson reap-
point Graham, whose commission was expiring.

As the plotters expected, the conference officials rejected Clarenbach's attempt, telling the group they had no authority to pass resolutions. With that, the women began organizing in earnest. During the
final luncheon, about fifteen of them gathered around a couple of
tables and, right under the noses of the conference officials, created the
National Organization for Women (NOW). Betty Friedan thought of
the name, with its stirring acronym. She scrawled it on a napkin and
passed it around to the women. Before they left to catch their planes,

twenty-eight women gathered in a nearby conference room and con-tributed $5 apiece to fund the birth of the new organization for women.

At the end of October they returned to Washington, held an orga-nizing conference, and presented themselves to the press. Declaring their mission to be bringing women into "full participation in the main-stream of American society," they defined their goals as equal legal rights, equal opportunities in education and employment, and increased women's participation in the political system. They elected Betty Friedan president, Kay Clarenbach chairperson of the board, and, sub-ject to her agreement, Aileen Hernández as executive vice president. (Hernández would eventually become NOW's first and only African-American president.)

Although they were professional women and housewives, many of the women who joined NOW were quite radical. Over the years a number of them took greater, not smaller, risks than the younger women of the New Left—the other group developing the second wave. The older, more established women had more to lose. They put their jobs, their community positions, and, in some cases, their marriages in jeopardy. They pursued and won many of the legal and judicial battles, and like their younger New Left sisters, they went into the streets and demonstrated, enduring ridicule and vilification when they did so.

NOW activists were media oriented and media savvy. One of the ear-liest members was Muriel Fox, the highest-ranking woman in the public relations industry, whose press releases created an impression of great numbers where few existed. NOW women created events to draw maxi-mum publicity with minimum participants. In New York they demon-strated for a year, sometimes in costumes, to convince the *New York Times* to desegregate its want ads. When they called for a boycott of Col-gate Palmolive to protest its protective labor regulations, a group picket-ing the company's Park Avenue headquarters held a "flush-in," where they poured Ajax down a toilet sculpted by NOW member Kate Millett.

Around the same time NOW formed in the late 1960s, many young women active in the civil-rights and New Left movements were becom-ing disillusioned with their treatment by men in the movement. Move-ment men competed among themselves to do the thinking, writing, and speaking, while movement women were expected to provide typing, cleaning, cooking, and sex for the men. Eventually the women, like their abolitionist-women predecessors, began to notice the parallels between their own condition and that of the people they were trying to help. If they were engaged in the struggle to gain equal rights for people suffering from discrimination based on their skin color, why were they categorized on the basis of their gender?

When they voiced their concerns to movement men, they were met first with ridicule and then with hostility. In response, the women began to talk to one another. Then a number of them began to gather in groups, specifically to discuss their feelings and experiences. These "rap groups" eventually became "consciousness-raising" sessions. Out of their never-before-shared experiences came the women's realization that their personal experiences were due, not to their individual situations, as they had assumed, but to a systemic sexual caste system, perpetuated by the capitalistic system and the patriarchal family. Whether the primary oppressor was capitalism or men was the subject of endless debate, as was the question of why men oppressed women. Was it nature or nurture?

Some radical women began breaking away from their various organizations entirely; others attempted to work from within. Some joined NOW. The older, professional women provided one source of the movement, and the radical young women another, but there was always overlap. The groups worked together on projects, and a number of women joined both NOW and radical groups. Radical women formed small groups all over the country. At one time or another, the groups in New York City included New York Radical Women, WITCH (Women's International Terrorist Conspiracy from Hell), Redstockings, and Radical Feminists, each with slightly different agendas and rules. In a conflict over leadership styles, one of NOW's presidents, an elegant, charismatic woman named Ti-Grace Atkinson, broke away and organized a group called The Feminists, who stipulated, among other things, that no more than a third of the members could be married or living with men.

The younger women organized their groups differently from the NOW women. NOW organized traditionally and concentrated on legal battles and raising awareness of the issues. The radical women believed in from-the-bottom-up, participatory democracy. As members of New Left groups, they acted. Participant and chronicler Todd Gitlin recalled, "You put your body on the line. . . . The New Left's first raison d'être was to take actions which testified not only to the existence of injustice but to the imperative—and possibility—of fighting it."

By 1967 and 1968, the radical women hoped to build a national movement. In 1967 the young black activists had essentially pushed whites out of the civil-rights movement, telling them thanks, but blacks had to fight their own oppression. That experience provided a powerful model for the women who were wavering about whether to leave the other New Left struggles to which they also were dedicated, such as antiwar, civil-rights, and antipoverty work.

The radical women held several national meetings, and their experience with New Left men continued to push them toward breaking off to form separate women's groups. When some women tried to present a women's caucus report at a 1967 New Left conference in Chicago (National Conference on New Politics), the women were refused the opportunity to speak. A few rushed to the platform. The chairman turned them away, saying to Shulamith Firestone as he patted her on the head, "Cool down, little girl, we have more important things to talk about than women's problems." He had the wrong little girl.

Consciousness was rising all over the country. In early 1968, an SDS organizer speaking at the University of Washington explained that some of the SDS college students had established a closer relationship with the working-class youth with whom they worked by spending some of their leisure time "balling a chick together." That did much to enhance the political consciousness of the poor white youth, the SDS speaker explained.

"And what did it do for the consciousness of the chick?" asked a woman in the audience. After that speech, some of the women present formed Seattle's first feminist group.

In January 1969 women from several groups planned to hold a feminist demonstration as part of the New Left counter-inaugural protest during Richard Nixon's inauguration. The protest was run by the National Mobilization Committee to End the War in Vietnam (MOBE), which agreed to allocate one speech during the rally to a women's group. Two women—Marilyn Webb, from a Washington, D.C., group, and Shulamith Firestone, the "little girl" from the Chicago conference who was now a member of the New York Radical Women—decided to share the time slot. However, when they began to speak, the radical men heckled them and began chanting, "Take it off!" and "Take her off the stage and fuck her!"

As Ellen Willis, another New York Radical Woman, observes drily, "It was a radicalizing experience." On the way back from Washington, Firestone and Willis, who would emerge as two of the movement's most brilliant theorists, decided to form the Redstockings (they modified the term *bluestockings* with *red*, for revolution). They wanted a militant, action-oriented group, and they handpicked as members a number of women who also became important theorists, such as Kathie Sarachild, a major creator of consciousness-raising, and Patricia Mainardi, an art historian who would write the influential article "The Politics of Housework."

While the older women's groups, most prominently NOW, worked for legislation, provided amicus curiae briefs in court cases, and changed institutions from within, the radical women provided feminist theory. There was never one radical feminist theory; there were evolving and competing analyses. (Ideological battles continue in the present over issues like pornography, and they are just as intense.) All radicals agreed, however, on some overarching principles. Unlike NOW, whose expressed goal was integrating women into the mainstream of society, the radicals sought to change society itself. They saw that society's patriarchal caste system was built upon, taught through, and reinforced by every institution within that society—family, school, religion, workplace, media.

About a month after they organized, the Redstockings held their March 1969 abortion speakout, carefully orchestrating the evening to make clear to the audience the political implications of the testifiers' personal experiences. Gloria was certainly their most famous convert (a success not without irony, as all parties would later note), and she still praises Shulamith Firestone's 1970 book *The Dialectic of Sex:* "Aside from her assumption that biology and birth are restrictions to be overcome—rather than a monopoly that can help achieve balance—this book was more insightful than almost any other."

Energized as she was by her discovery that she was an oppressed person, too, (although hardly to the degree of her Black Panther and Young Lords friends), Gloria did not join an existing group. She assumed she would contribute by writing and working with a variety of groups. Her first article as a conscious feminist was an April 7, 1969, "City Politic" column, "After Black Power, Women's Liberation." She defined the movement's two major groups—the activists centered on NOW and the radical groups with whom her sympathies clearly lay—and described the speakout she had attended.

"After Black Power" captures Gloria as a brand-new feminist. Although she eventually became more sympathetic, for many years

Gloria wrote in a contemptuous fashion about middle-class married women. She explained, for example, that the punishment for deviating from a woman's traditional role of serving could be severe, even if subtle: "Being called 'unfeminine,' 'a bad mother' or 'a castrating woman,' to name a traditional few." However, when she depicted some of those traditional women, she described them rather unkindly as "women, who have been able to remain children, and to benefit from work they did not and could not do."

Defining the benefits of the women's movement to men, she noted that guilt and alimony might be eliminated and that women might become less boring and less bitchy: "No more tyrants with all human ambition confined to the home," she wrote. "No more 'Jewish mothers' transferring ambition to children."

What makes the harsh tone so startling is that Gloria was unfailingly kind to individual women. The idea of affiliating with a women's rights group was still unthinkable, but Gloria didn't need feminism to teach her to be sisterly; she had always loved helping women, both personally and professionally.

If "After Black Power" exhibits an attitude Gloria would later outgrow, it also makes clear Gloria's immediate understanding that poor women and women of color, two overlapping but not identical groups, had to be made to feel the movement was theirs, too. Noting that poor women were already organized to work on welfare rights and other issues of concern, she suggested, "A lot of middle-class and radical-intellectual women are already working with the poor on common problems, but viewing them as social. If the 'consciousness-raising' programs of the WLM work, they'll see them as rallying points for women *qua* women. And that might forge the final revolutionary link."

The welfare-rights movement declined, but Gloria never lost her focus on inclusivity. Her commitment has been so unwavering that at least some of the diversity the women's movement has achieved over the years, in terms of race and class, has to be attributed to the personal tenacity and the determined leadership of Gloria Steinem.

19

On the Road With Glo-ball

When Gloria published "After Black Power, Women's Liberation," she felt she had undergone a cataclysmic change. Her readers saw only the latest in a long line of articles on the plight of women in society. Like Jean Faust, many of them viewed Gloria as a feminist already.

Gloria had been crusading for women's rights even before the March 1969 abortion speakout. A month earlier she had interviewed Dorothy Pitman, a woman who had started a childcare center in an abandoned storefront on New York's Upper West Side. During Gloria's visit, Bob Gangi, a radical social worker who worked with Dorothy, mentioned that he didn't want his future wife to work after they were married. Dorothy reacted just as she did with the children in the center: "I stopped what I was talking about and dealt with him." Gloria chimed in to help show Bob the error of his ways. She tried to connect an understanding of the sexual caste system to Bob's radicalism, and by the time they were finished, they had made their first convert. Gloria later received a note from Bob's fiancée saying, Thank you, now I can marry him.

A couple of months later Gloria called Dorothy. She had been invited to give a speech about women's rights at New York University and she wanted Dorothy to speak with her. The fact that Dorothy was African American would be helpful in discussing the parallels between society's treatment of women of all races and black men and women on the basis of race—not to mention demonstrating that feminism was not only for white women. However, that was not the only reason Gloria called. Gloria called Dorothy because public speaking terrified her. She was comfortable speaking to small groups, but not large ones. Clay Felker had pushed her into television appearances to promote *New York* magazine, and she had hated that, too.

Now she was motivated, but even her missionary fervor could not ameliorate her paralyzing fear. The only way Gloria could imagine surviving the ordeal was to bring along a friend. Besides, Gloria and Dorothy had succeeded with one person—why not try for more?

She chose well. By the time Gloria met her, Dorothy Pitman of Lumpkin, Georgia, was a comfortable public speaker with several years of church speeches, neighborhood organizing, and civil-rights experience behind her. In New York she had worked as a saleswoman, housecleaner, and nightclub singer, sometimes combining the jobs in unusual ways. When she worked as a housecleaner for impresario Warner LeRoy Jr., her voice so impressed him that he encouraged her to sing for prominent guests. As a saleswoman, she told her boss she wanted to buy one of the blouses in the store. He offered her a deal. "I'll give it to you for free if you give me a blow job," he proposed. Not long out of Lumpkin, Dorothy had no idea what a blow job was. Figuring he must mean that he wanted his house vacuumed, she vacuumed and cleaned and then asked for the blouse in exchange for her "blow job." The man was so startled that he gave her the blouse.

Dorothy had created the childcare center because she needed it herself. She sang at night, but she also needed time off in the daytime to sleep and rehearse. When she went to apply for childcare services for her daughter Delethia, she was told to go on welfare or pretend her husband beat her. What kind of a system makes me lie about who I am? she wondered. And what kind of system would that be to raise my children in?

She sent Delethia back to Georgia but missed her so much that she brought her daughter back. When her second daughter, Patrice, named for Patrice Lumumba, was an infant, she formed what grew into the West Eightieth Street Day Care Center, a multiethnic cooperative arrangement that also provided job training for neighborhood teenagers and mothers trying to get off welfare. In a *New York* "City Politic" column about the center, Gloria described Dorothy as "a beautiful black female Saul Alinsky . . . [with] a natural gift for organizing."

Not long after their speech at NYU, a speakers' bureau asked Gloria if she would be interested in talking on other college campuses. Gloria agreed, as long as her friend Dorothy could go, too, and soon the two were flying all over the country. Dorothy was terrified of flying, so Gloria held Dorothy's hand during takeoffs and landings and Dorothy did what she could to boost Gloria's confidence for the speeches. In all her years of speaking, Gloria never completely conquered her stage fright, and even today she experiences an occasional bout.

Although Gloria was the main attraction, she always spoke first, believing she would be an anticlimax after her partner's stirring oratory. Her partner would talk about her own experience as a black woman and then discuss her area of special interest or expertise—Dorothy tended to talk about nonsexist childcare—after Gloria had offered a basic Feminism 101 presentation of the issues. She quickly became known for her aphorisms:

> "The actress Lee Grant told me she'd been married to a Marxist and a fascist, and neither put out the garbage."

> "What happens to men is politics. What happens to women is culture."

> "I'll know progress has been made when young men on campuses get up and ask as much as young women do, 'How can I combine a career and family?'"

> "The technical definition of women's work, as we all know, is shit work."

> "If women could sleep their way to power, there'd be a whole lot more women in power right now."

> "If we're here today and there's no trouble tomorrow, we haven't done our job."

When they called for questions after they spoke, Gloria and the other speaker usually found that questions about women's roles were directed toward Gloria and questions about race went to her African-American partner. Gloria and Dorothy decided that even if their questioners did not consider Gloria qualified to talk about racism, they at least ought to realize that the black women were women, too, so they developed a routine. They would let the questions go on for a while and then they would stop and point out to their audiences what they were doing.

They would stay as long as anyone had questions. Over the months and years, they heard hundreds of stories—of incest, domestic violence, date rape, sexual harassment by professors—all before many of these acts had names. As Gloria would later say, "They were just called 'life.' " Gloria split her speaker's fees down the middle. Even as her fee began to rise from $1,500, to $2,000, $5,000, $7,500, she always gave her partner half.

In 1972, in a rare appearance before a predominantly male audience, the two addressed 4,100 Annapolis cadets and 2,000 other people, including naval officers and their wives, at the then all-male naval academy. Dorothy and Gloria appeared as part of a lecture series that included Brig. Gen. Daniel "Chappie" James, the deputy assistant secretary of defense, and Dallas Cowboy quarterback (and academy alumnus) Roger Staubach. "Women have been much too docile and for much too long, but I think that era is about to end," Gloria told them. When a few women at the back of the auditorium applauded, she added, "I see that here you have all the problems of a ghetto."

As she proceeded and met with occasional jeers and whistles, she joked, "I don't think I've been in a place where the frustration level was this high since I was in the Senate dining room."

When the pair answered questions, most were hostile. Gloria gave it right back. Asked if some women didn't prefer being subjugated, she said, "I believe there are female masochists and I believe there are male masochists. I believe there are men who like passive roles, who like to be given orders, because look at all of you out there. I wouldn't take it if I were you." Afterward, she admitted to a *Washington Post* reporter that the experience had been grueling.

By 1970 Dorothy was beginning to find traveling with her new baby, Angela (named for Angela Davis), too difficult, so Florynce Kennedy began taking her place. Flo, who has written three books, *Abortion Rap* with Diane Schulder, *Color Me Flo: My Hard Life and Good Times,* and with William Pepper, *Sex Discrimination in Employment: An Analysis and Guide for Practitioner and Student,* is gallant, loving, acerbic, combative, and extremely funny. She believes her major contribution to Gloria's speaking career was to teach her (by example) to be a little more outrageous. As she told Gloria's subsequent speaking partners, "I want to be so outrageous and kick 'em in the ass so hard that by the time you kids come in, it'll be light stuff, and you can do anything you want and they'll be glad to have you."

There could be no better teacher. One of Flo's many ideas was a pee-in at Harvard Yard, to protest pay toilets in general, and the lack of toilets available to women students at Harvard in particular. "If God meant women to have pay toilets, we would be made with exact change," one poster read. Flo led the crowd in chanting, "To pee or not to pee, that is the question . . . pee on Harvard Yard."

The second of five daughters, Flo was born in 1916 in Kansas City, Missouri. She described her family as "pooristocrats" of the black community. Her father was a Pullman porter and later owned a taxi service. They lived in a predominantly white ("poor white trash") neighborhood, and the Ku Klux Klan once came to threaten the family. Flo's father stood on the porch with a gun and said, "Now the first foot that hits the step belongs to the man I shoot. And then after that, you can decide who is going to shoot *me*." They left and did not return.

In 1942 Flo followed her married sister to New York and enrolled at the age of twenty-eight as a prelaw student at Columbia University's night school. When the A-average student attempted to combine her last undergraduate year with her first year of law school, the Columbia Law School initially rejected her application because she was a woman. After Flo wrote the dean that some of her more cynical friends thought the real reason was race, she visited the dean and used what she came to deem the "testicular" approach. "If you have admitted any white man with lower grades than mine, then I want to get in too," she told him. Fearing a discrimination suit, the dean yielded. Flo graduated from Columbia Law School in 1951.

After law school Flo went into private practice. Although she eventually represented the estates of singer Billie Holiday and jazz saxophonist Charlie Parker, her interest in practicing law declined as her activism increased. Her political work during the 1960s included electoral politics with New York's Reform Democrats, Black Power conferences, a media workshop on racism in media and advertising, and speeches against the Vietnam War.

She joined the group of New York women who were founding the National Organization for Women, but when Ti-Grace Atkinson broke away in 1968 to form the group eventually called The Feminists, Flo went along. In 1971 she formed the Feminist Party, and its first important action was to support Shirley Chisholm for president in 1972.

Gloria marveled at Flo's genius at maximizing the drama and humor in any subject, including herself. When asked if she and Gloria were lesbians, Flo would look at her male interlocutor and ask, "Are you my alternative?"

When criticized for wearing her mink coat while meeting with Australian aboriginals: "To me it's a part of the phoney baloney to wear ragged clothes to go talk to poor people. I should imagine they'd think—it was certainly true when I was poor—'Who would wear raggedy clothes if they don't have to?' "

On tactics: "When you think you are going to lose, you might as well lose partly biting and not sucking."

On sports: "I call it 'jockocracy'—and it's fascinating to note the preoccupations of our society with balls. Tennis balls, footballs, basketballs—there shouldn't be a season without some balls to focus on."

On herself: "I'm just a loud-mouthed middle-aged colored lady with a fused spine and three feet of intestines missing, and a lot of people think I'm crazy. Maybe you do too, but I never stop to wonder why I'm not like other people. The mystery to me is why more people aren't like me."

Flo began substituting for Dorothy in 1970, and in 1971 she brought Margaret Sloan to Gloria's attention. A civil-rights activist in Chicago, Margaret met Flo when they served together on the "people's jury" of a mock trial of state's attorney Edward W. Hanrahan. It was staged by the Chicago Black Panthers to protest the exoneration of the Chicago police in the deaths of Panther leader Fred Hampton and Mark Clark, another Panther member. They had been shot in their beds during a police raid that was ostensibly a search for illegal weapons.

Flo decided to introduce Margaret to Gloria, whom she had nicknamed "Glo-ball." Flo had a busy schedule of writing, lecturing, and organizing, and intermittent health problems, so Gloria needed yet another speaking partner. In 1971 Gloria was also involved in starting *Ms.* magazine. Margaret, who had worked, among other things, as a taxi driver, was interested in writing, but she was reluctant to leave Chicago. Besides starting a black women's support group, she had recently come out as a lesbian and at that point was happily living with her two-year-old daughter and her lover. However, by the end of 1971 Gloria had persuaded Margaret to write for *Ms.* and become Gloria's new speaking partner. Margaret liked to say that Gloria and her partners traveled in pairs, like nuns; Flo had called Gloria and herself Little Eva and Topsy.

Margaret also was a willing bodyguard. She and Gloria were sometimes met with hostility, but occasionally the problem was an excess of affection. Gloria turns no one away, which leaves her friends and colleagues to play the heavy, extricating her from hecklers, hangers-on, and even, on one occasion, "a little cheerleader girl" who just wanted to come back to their room and brush Gloria's hair.

Their speaking engagements were rarely limited to a single speech; they were marathons packing in as many events as possible. In one day there might be a luncheon, a tea, a press conference, what Margaret called a "$25 to touch your hand" cocktail party before or after a dinner, and even sometimes a late-night event for a group that couldn't afford to pay to hear them. Then, after her partners collapsed in exhaustion, Gloria would stay up for hours, talking and strategizing with women they invited back to their hotel room.

Gloria always tried to learn in advance what the groups' issues were, so she could address them in her speeches and help with suggestions if she had ideas. Many of her suggestions required further assistance from her ("You need a lawyer/social worker/talk with someone I know. Give me your number and address and I'll get in touch with you"), and she always returned to the *Ms.* offices with a wad of little scraps of paper, which she would follow up herself and dole out to various people in the office. Her assistant joked that *Ms.* existed to take care of Gloria's little pieces of paper.

Gloria eventually added another speaking partner. She met Jane Galvin-Lewis in Washington, where Jane was working as a lobbyist and program representative for the National Council of Negro Women, a coalition of black women's organizations founded by Mary McLeod Bethune and run by Dorothy Height. Gloria and Jane both were at an unusual press conference Congresswomen Shirley Chisholm and Bella Abzug had called to introduce a childcare bill. Unlike most such conferences, it was run almost like a congressional hearing, with spokespeople getting up and testifying. When Jane heard a speaker begin, "Just because we have vaginas . . ." she whipped her head around to see who would say such a thing and beheld a very attractive woman in a blue and white minidress with "not at all the kind of face that would say that."

She and Gloria became friendly, but Jane moved to Africa shortly afterward with her diplomat husband. When she returned, Jane worked as deputy director at the Women's Action Alliance, an organization Gloria and her friend Brenda Feigen Fasteau founded in 1970. Since Jane had been speaking professionally for years, she also began to fill in for the other partners.

Jane, who moonlights as a comedian, was impressed by Gloria's wit: "Two things gave Gloria her voice. One was the look she established. The other was that she was absolutely, positively blessed with the English language. You'd have to get up early in the morning—well, you might as well not even go to bed—to beat her on rejoinders. She was a dream for the press. When she was doing a lot of media, there was no one better."

Almost every friend of Gloria's mentions the importance of her looks as a factor in her appeal to audiences and the media, and they usually preface the remark with something like, "I know Gloria doesn't like to hear this, but . . ." It is hardly surprising that Gloria does not want to hear her contribution put in terms of her appearance after working so long and so hard. In a November 1970 interview, the reporter mentioned that Gloria was chic.

> "———chic!" she snaps, removing her blue-tinted prescription aviator goggles and setting her unchic feet flat on the floquati carpet in her study. "I hate that! God, I HATE that! Anyone who doesn't have terminal acne or isn't over 50 is automatically chic, right? I mean no woman can possibly have done anything by herself, right? It implies she must have something else going for her—money, a rich husband, wealthy ancestors."

Since her looks are an undeniable part of her appeal, the comments have continued, but over time Gloria has developed a repertoire of responses to the inevitable questions about her appearance or its relationship to her position as a movement leader. While some are less than completely true, literal truth is not the point.

Her favorite is "Nobody ever talks about Ralph Nader's looks [or asks about his romances or marital status], so why are you asking about mine?" Another favorite—often in response to observations about her miniskirts—is "Women should wear whatever they fucking well please."

Neither response really addresses the question of the relationship between Gloria's looks and her stature as a feminist leader. In public life, though, as Gloria realized long ago, answering the question is optional. And though her rejoinders fail to answer the question, they succeed in raising consciousness—which is why Gloria is answering questions in the first place. Comparing herself to Ralph Nader is somewhat misleading: Not all feminists are asked about their appearance, and Gloria's looks really *are* more worthy of comment than Ralph Nader's. However, her point that women's looks and personal lives generally are more closely scrutinized than men's is valid. As for her second rejoinder, women *should* wear whatever they fucking well please. So, as Gloria points out by implication, if she wants to wear short skirts and show off her legs, that doesn't mean she isn't a feminist.

Her third rejoinder could be called the "If only you knew—my looks are really a disadvantage" response. It is usually phrased, "Editors used to say, 'I want a writer, not a pretty girl.' " Actually, one *Life* magazine editor said that—once. Furthermore, while there is no doubt that women suffered from discrimination in journalism, just as they did in every other field, there is also no doubt that if Gloria's gender was a disadvantage, her looks were a decided advantage.

The least believable of her top four is "I wasn't considered all that great-looking until I became a feminist" or "People must mean I'm pretty *for a feminist,*" implying that her interlocutor has made a stereotypically derogatory assumption about what feminists look like. This statement is a bit of a whopper, no matter how distorted Gloria's self-image may be. She was voted "Prettiest Girl" in her senior class—and she was quite confident of her ability to attract a large number of aspiring lovers—so it is difficult to believe she is not more aware that others have considered her pretty.

Gloria finesses that problem by forgetting inconvenient facts, a manifestation of what her friends call "history according to Gloria." (The first time we talked, I told Gloria I had been researching her one year at Western High School and was impressed that her schoolmates admired her enough to elect her, a new girl, to student council and class office as well as to vote her a "princess" of the various balls. She explained that the princess election was just a joke—that the dance was called the Okefenokee Swamp. Despite the nonsequitur, and not yet familiar with the concept of "history according to Gloria," I tried to remind her of the other dances. She just repeated that it was a joke.)

Soon after Gloria began speaking to large audiences, there came occasions when she just couldn't bring along a friend for security. In October 1969 she went to Washington to address the Women's National Democratic Club. It was her first major speech and, unaccompanied by Dorothy, she was, as she later told a *Washington Post* reporter, in a catatonic state.

Clay Felker had been asked to introduce her. When he saw her legs shaking, he became so unnerved that he said, "Gloria is the best thing that has happened to women's rights since the exploding corset." Trying to extricate himself, he added, "I love Gloria—I want to marry her."

Afterward, Gloria was feted at a party hosted by Washington socialite Barbara Howar. Among the guests were senators George McGovern and Jacob Javits, and President Nixon's foreign policy advisor, Henry Kissinger. After *Washington Post* reporter Sally Quinn pulled Kissinger over to be photographed with Gloria and McGovern, Quinn teased him, "You really are a swinger underneath it all, aren't you?"

"I'm really a secret swinger," he responded. "If I didn't tell people I was a secret swinger, they'd think something was wrong with me."

When the photograph of Gloria and Kissinger (McGovern was cropped out) appeared the next day with Kissinger's quote, his reputation as a secret swinger was born, and for the next few years he basked in it, dating a number of starlets and movie stars. Gloria received clippings from as far away as Yugoslavia that assumed they were a couple.

In 1971 President Nixon happened to see a newspaper photograph in which Gloria appeared with other founders of the National Women's Political Caucus. When he asked who she was, Secretary of State William Rogers joked, "That's one of Henry's old girlfriends."

Hearing of the remark, Gloria responded in the style made memorable by witnesses testifying at sessions of the Communist-hunting House Un-American Activities Committee: "I am not now and never have been a girlfriend of Henry Kissinger." The *New York Times* reported that "the attractive author retorted in a written statement" and ran the item under the headline "No Girl Friend, She."

In fact, they had gone out a few times. According to Gloria, she met Kissinger when he called to compliment her on an article after the death of Robert Kennedy, whom he described as his hero. After talking about who might work for the newly elected Nixon, an act Kissinger described as "the collaborationist's problem," Gloria suggested he write an article with that title for *New York*. He called her back to say he could not write the article because, to his surprise, he had been asked to leave Harvard and work for Nixon. Gloria describes the extent of their social engagements as "two argumentative dinners."

The gentleman recalled it differently. In "The Making of a Sex Symbol" (*McCall's*, November 1972), Nora Ephron reported that Kissinger was "quite hurt by Miss Steinem's attempts to slough him off as a mere acquaintance" (she did so in her "City Politic" column as well), and "insists that he has had dinner with her seven or eight times." He had responded to her HUAC-style statement in the style of Civil War general George Sherman. "Gloria Steinem is not now and never has been my girlfriend, but I am not discouraged," he told the audience at a Washington Press Club dinner. "After all, she did not say that if nominated, she would not accept or if elected, she would not serve."

Gloria countered Kissinger's Shermanesque pronouncement with one of her own: "If elected I will not serve. I don't want to be a candidate. If nominated I will not run."

Gloria may have had the last word in public, but stamping out false impressions was an endless task. When *Time* ran a photo of the two and referred to Gloria as a "Gucci liberal," Gloria fired off a letter to editor Henry Grunwald. "Okay, who's the bastard who called me a Gucci liberal?" she began, and proceeded to inform him she had never bought a thing at Gucci.

Describing the incident, she recalls with amused indignation, "And you know what that bastard did? He sent me a Gucci purse! And it wasn't even returnable."

20

Marching for Women's Rights

In 1970 the national media discovered the women's movement. Until then the movement had been covered occasionally. Now the trickle of articles became a flood.

It was not that activists had not tried to draw press coverage all along. NOW had always publicized its actions, and in 1968 the radicals attracted their first major publicity with a demonstration at the Miss America pageant. About two hundred women carried posters, sang, chanted, crowned a live sheep as Miss America, mock-auctioned off a Miss America dummy, and threw dishcloths, steno pads, false eyelashes, girdles, copies of *Playboy, Cosmopolitan,* and *Vogue,* and bras into a Freedom Trash Can.

That occasion is also noteworthy because it seems to have prompted the media obsession with brassieres. The demonstrators only threw them in the trash can, but after that, "bra burner" became synonymous with feminist. Draft-card burning was popular among antiwar protesters, so perhaps the media assumed feminists had to burn something, too.

In March 1970, forty-six *Newsweek* researchers filed a complaint with the EEOC, charging systematic discrimination against women in both hiring and promotion. Like *Time, Newsweek* employed men as writers and women as researchers. The researchers were paid lower salaries and had no hope of promotion. In May, New York's attorney general filed a similar complaint against Time Inc. on behalf of one hundred *Time, Life, Fortune,* and *Sports Illustrated* women employees. Noting that the late Henry Luce had characterized his research staff as "a modern female priesthood, the veritable vestal virgins whom levitous writers cajole in vain and managing editors learn humbly to appease," the Time Inc. women alleged that it was indeed a rare virgin who was promoted from Delphi to Olympus.

On Wednesday, March 18, 1970, about two hundred women invaded the *Ladies' Home Journal* offices. Led by Susan Brownmiller, Ti-Grace Atkinson, and Shulamith Firestone, women from groups including NOW, Redstockings, and New York Radical Feminists occupied the offices of the second largest women's magazine for eleven hours. They demanded from editor in chief John Mack Carter that the *Journal* stop publishing articles that were "irrelevant, unstimulating and demeaning to the women of America" and proposed instead that *Ladies' Home Journal* allow them to publish a special issue with articles about abortion, balancing work with childcare, and women's liberation. Eventually the editors agreed to publish a supplement, which appeared in the August issue.

In 1970 all the national magazines ran major feature stories on the movement, including *Saturday Review* (February 21), *U.S. News & World Report* (April 13), and *Esquire* (July). *Newsweek* (March 23) and *Time* (August 31) ran cover stories. In spite of its gladiatorial cover line, "Women Against Men—A Special Issue," *Atlantic*'s March issue was generally favorable. The Catholic magazine *America* ran a sympathetic overview that described media hostility and quoted an editor's directive, "Get the bra-burning and karate up front." The *New York Times Magazine* ran "Sisterhood Is Powerful," by Susan Brownmiller, on March 15.

The climax of the year was the Women's Strike for Equality on August 26, 1970, the fiftieth anniversary of the ratification of the women's suffrage amendment. The strike grew from a proposal Betty Friedan sprang on an unsuspecting Chicago audience at NOW's fourth annual conference. Betty Armistead, a NOW member in Florida, had reminded her that the nineteenth amendment's fiftieth anniversary was approaching and had suggested that NOW observe the occasion with a strike.

At the end of her two-hour address, Betty dropped the bombshell. Calling for a twenty-four-hour general strike—"an instant revolution against sexual oppression"—she proposed that women put down their typewriters, notebooks, trays, and cleaning supplies, and leave their jobs or homes. "When it begins to get dark, instead of cooking dinner or making love," she expanded, "we will assemble and we will carry candles alight in every city to converge the visible power of women."

Betty's suggestion took the NOW board completely by surprise, and they hated the idea. It went forward anyway, and NOW chapters all over the country participated. The first meeting to plan the strike in New York was held in mid-June, drawing women's groups from all over the city: Redstockings, Radical Lesbians, WITCH, Women's Strike for Peace, the YWCA, the National Welfare Rights Organization, and the National Coalition of American Nuns, as well as volunteers who came in off the street. The Socialist Workers Party tried to take over the event. They failed, but its members ended up doing much of the organizing work.

Other organizations, evidently formed by women who wanted to remain sex objects, sprang up to oppose the strike. These included MOM (Men Our Masters) and the Pussy Cat League, Inc., whose slogan was Purr, Baby, Purr.

Gloria was asked to join the strike coordinating committee and appeared at an East Hampton fund-raising cocktail party held in the summer house of wealthy art collectors Ethel and Robert Scull. Although the party made money, the event became a public relations disaster when a series of mishaps were reported in meticulous detail by *New York Times* women's section editor Charlotte Curtis. Curtis had already ridiculed the farm worker's party the previous summer, but the strike event offered her even better material.

Representative Patsy Mink disappeared when it was her turn to speak, so Gloria took Mink's place. Then *Village Voice* writer Jill Johnston jumped into the swimming pool and, after swimming some laps, stripped off her shirt and floated around on her back, barebreasted. When Betty Friedan's low-cut, girlish dress, weighed down by a political button, slipped so far that her breast almost popped out, the *Times* photographer was there to capture the moment. Curtis even deadpanned a typical society-page description of the attendees' attire, informing her readers who at the party had worn bras and who had not.

The strike committee planned a day of events all over the city, culminating in the march down Fifth Avenue at 5:30 P.M. and a rally at Bryant Park that Gloria would emcee. Many of the organizers worried that they would hold a march and no one would come. Instead, thousands and thousands of women—and some men—massed in midtown

Manhattan. The marchers had been granted only half of Fifth Avenue, but they filled it all. As the *Times* reported, there were

> limping octogenarians, braless teenagers, Black Panther women, telephone operators, waitresses, Westchester matrons, fashion models, Puerto Rican factory workers, nurses in uniform, young mothers carrying babies on their backs. . . . marching because they wanted equality with men—and, they said, because they wanted men to think of them as human beings, not just sex objects.

Hecklers and supporters stood on the sidelines. One man wore a brassiere and carried a sign that read "If you don't wear one, I will."

Marching at the head of the parade behind Betty and other leaders, Gloria carried a picture of the recently revealed massacre of women and children in My Lai, Vietnam, with the words "Q: . . . and children? A: . . . and children. The Masculine Mystique."

Gloria emceed so successfully that emceeing later became yet another role for which she was in constant demand.

As the movement became increasingly visible nationally, so did Gloria. She shared a column in *Look* magazine with poet Sandra Hochman and writer Betty Rollin, and in January 1970 she wrote "Why We Need a Woman President in 1976." Using the accessible language, analogies, and vivid images with which she would tirelessly disseminate her Feminist 101 overview for the next quarter century, Gloria explained:

The overt barriers to employment: ". . . the production assistant who trained each new young producer, watching him get the credit and the cash for a television series that she had created."

The loss to society of wasted talent: "There are Golda Meirs in both parties, but their function is limited to winning elections for men."

The backlash: "Women trying to step out of their nineteenth-century roles will be punished with ridicule, just as Negroes who refused to act like Negroes were greeted with violence and fear."

In May 1970 Gloria testified before a Senate subcommittee on the Equal Rights Amendment, which declared, "Equality of rights under the law shall not be denied or abridged by the United States or by any State on account of sex." In remarks picked up in newspapers all over the country, she disabused the senators of myths concerning both women's alleged biological inferiority and their supposed already-equal treatment. She also assured them that penis envy was fast disappearing. In June she spoke at Vassar's commencement to a graduating class attired in peace signs and colored armbands, and the *Washington Post* excerpted her address. Edith Van Horn of the United Auto Workers also sent out thousands of copies of the address to union members.

Time's cover story on the women's movement appeared the week of the August 26 Equality Day March with *Sexual Politics* author Kate Millett on the cover. *Time* dubbed Millett "the Mao Tse-tung of Women's Liberation," though, the editors admitted, the appellation was "the sort of description she and her sisters despise, for the movement rejects the notion of leaders and heroines as creations of the media— and mimicry of the ways that men use to organize their world."

Besides Millett, Gloria was the individual most prominently featured. The magazine ran her photograph and assigned her a two-page essay, "What It Would Be Like If Women Win." Described as "not only a critical observer but a concerned advocate of the feminist revolt," Gloria enjoyed the plum assignment, though she learned afterward she had been paid less for the essay than male writers customarily received.

By 1970 the so-called gay/straight split—conflicts over the role of lesbians in the movement—was becoming a major issue among feminist activists. In 1967 a mischievous, young, aspiring writer named Rita Mae Brown had joined NOW and embarked on a one-woman mission to make the straight women understand both the discrimination faced by lesbians and the point that the issue affected them as well. At one meeting attended by a group of suburban women interested in starting a NOW chapter, Brown sat on the floor in a demure white blouse and black pleated skirt and addressed the group. "Well, as your local neighborhood lesbian . . ." There goes Long Island, one of the others thought resignedly.

Brown subsequently left NOW (or was pushed out, depending on who tells the story), but the momentum had begun, and lesbian feminists began forcing the issue at feminist gatherings. Until that point, lesbians had been as closeted within the movement—often from each other as well—as they were in society at large. The original groups of feminists, in both the radical and NOW branches, were not only predominantly white, middle-class, college-educated women, they were also predominantly heterosexist (assuming and privileging heterosexuality). However, acrimonious as the gay/straight split became, it was a family fight.

Then, in December 1970, *Time* attacked the movement by lesbian-baiting. After Kate Millett acknowledged at a public meeting in 1970

that she was bisexual, *Time* used Millett's admission as an excuse to
backtrack on its positive portrayal of the movement. Placed in the
Behavior section of its December 14 issue (as if the article were a scientific examination of inexplicable behavior), "Women's Lib: A Second
Look" simply strung together comments from other magazines' negative articles about the movement. The purpose of the article obviously
was to allow *Time* to print its scoop about Millett's sexuality while
retracting its approval of the movement:

> Kate Millett herself contributed to the growing skepticism about the
> movement by acknowledging at a recent meeting that she is bisexual.
> The disclosure is bound to discredit her as a spokeswoman for her
> cause, cast further doubt on her theories, and reinforce the views of
> those skeptics who routinely dismiss all liberationists as lesbians.

Accompanying the article was a caricature of Millett that had run in
Esquire. Captioned " 'Esquire's' feminist, a splenetic frenzy of hatred,"
the drawing depicted a heavyset woman with Millett's hair and glasses,
her skirt hiked unflatteringly up a pair of heavy legs, holding aloft the
media's favorite movement symbol, a bra. Unfortunately for the editors, Millett's face is beautiful, so the caricaturist was unable to render
her as too-ugly-to-get-a-man, the usual characterization of those angry,
hairy-legged women's libbers.

Betty Friedan wanted the lesbian issue buried. Calling it a lavender
menace, she insisted for a while that there was a lesbian plot to take
over NOW. There was a plot, but it was a joke, hatched by Rita Mae
Brown and Anselma Dell'Olio, a heterosexual actress and playwright
whose abortion playlet Gloria had seen at the Redstockings' abortion
speakout, and another straight NOW member. Later Betty pushed the
NOW board into firing NOW's executive director, Dolores Alexander,
on the grounds that Dolores was insubordinate. When the executive
committee resisted, she threatened, among other things, to call the press
and say that Dolores was part of a lesbian plot to take over NOW. At
the time, Dolores was a heterosexual divorcée who had left her
$10,000-a-year job as a *Newsday* reporter to work for $5,000 a year
as NOW's first full-time employee.

A few years later Dolores Alexander did become a lesbian. Years
after that, Betty apologized publicly for firing Dolores, but then she
spoiled the effect by making excuses for herself: When Dolores brought
her news of the lesbian plot, Friedan explained, she had fired the mes-

senger. NOW members say lesbianism was an excuse; they say Dolores was fired because she stood up to Betty too much.

In 1970 Betty supported lesbians' right to their own sexuality in private, but she wanted them to remain in the closet, fearing an open alignment of feminism with lesbianism would scare away women with its stigma and divert movement resources from other issues. Other feminist activists believed the *Time* article required a response, so about thirty women gathered at Dolores's apartment to strategize.

They decided on a "Kate Is Great" press conference to support her and express solidarity with lesbians. Surrounded by about fifty supporters, Kate Millett read a statement explicitly linking the goals of the women's liberation and homosexual rights movements. Both sought "a society free from defining and categorizing people by virtue of gender and/or sexual preference. 'Lesbian' is a label used as a psychic weapon to keep women locked into their male-defined 'feminine role.' The essence of that role is that a woman is defined in terms of her relationship to men."

Other prominent feminists participated, including Susan Brownmiller, Flo Kennedy, who called for a "girlcott" of products advertised in *Time,* and Ti-Grace Atkinson, as well as openly lesbian feminists such as Ruth Simpson, president of Daughters of Bilitis (the oldest lesbian organization in the United States), and Barbara Love, who was active in the gay rights movement. Congresswoman-elect Bella Abzug, author Caroline Bird, and NOW president Aileen Hernández sent supportive statements. Hernández denounced the use of lesbianism against the women's movement as "sexual McCarthyism." Betty Friedan was "out of town."

After Kate Millett herself, Gloria was the most noticeable person at the press conference. Her presence proclaimed that man-pleasing feminists could be friends of lesbians, too. She sat next to Kate, conspicuously held her hand throughout the press conference, and appeared in many of the photographs, including the Associated Press picture published in the *New York Times.* Kate never forgot. Years later she would say, "Gloria has beautiful political instincts. She always takes the ethical position, and it's from the heart."

During those years Gloria was evolving on the issue of homosexuality. By 1971 she was telling audiences that lesbianism was an important issue because it could be used as a bludgeon to beat women into conformity. When she was asked, Gloria refused to deny that she was a lesbian, for just that reason. In the 1990s, when public opinion presumably had become more enlightened, she responded in an interview:

I've never had a sexual relationship with a woman. I'm the last non-lesbian, non-bi-sexual person in the Western world, I think. Mono-sexual. It sounds so boring. I don't know how to explain it except I'm sure it's socialisation. I really believe that we are all bi-sexual and probably we're socialised one way or the other. It's wonderful now to see young women and some young men too who really do fall in love with the person, not the sex.

Even as Gloria placed more articles on feminism in 1970, she remained a high-profile personality. Now, in addition to her interesting career, smashing looks, powerful friends, and New Left allegiances, the mix included feminism. In the February *Harper's Bazaar*, Eugenia Sheppard saluted her and wealthy socialite Gloria Guinness ("You can never be too rich or too thin") and wealthy socialite–collage artist Gloria Vanderbilt. To the smart set and its aspirants, Sheppard proclaimed nonwealthy socialite Gloria Steinem to be a feminist role model:

> Not because her name appears consistently in the gossip column linked to some celebrity or other, but because she is a great American girl. She dresses neither like a model nor a square. When she goes to a party she may wear a long red evening dress she found in a thrift shop or a short leather sheath decorated with gold medallions that she picked up somewhere on one of her trips. In the daytime she looks in the groove with short skirts, long hair and tinted glasses. Women like her as much as men do. She has an open mind for causes and, in the course of one week, may take in a Black Panther benefit and a meeting of the Women's Liberation Movement. She is consistently a good writer, informative, direct and amusing. She never grinds her own personal axes in print and she is not out to kill.

For all her protestations that even if she spent time with the rich and famous, she didn't really like it, Gloria reinforced her celebrity image by writing about her recently redecorated apartment for the July 1970 *House & Garden*. It was the first of several articles and interviews on her apartment to appear over the years, always with the same message: Gloria Steinem had finally, reluctantly, decided it was all right to grow up and allow herself to decorate her apartment nicely.

In her 1970 article she described a year-long quest for the perfect apartment and the decorating assistance of Beautiful People socialite-"actress"-decorator "Baby Jane" Holzer. Glamour on a shoestring was her theme: "a junkyard yielded fragments of somebody's old front porch, which made the perfect sleeping balcony." Then "an out-of-work art director" hung it for her. Secondhand couches and poster-sized photographs of Robert Kennedy, Che Guevara, and actress Jeanne Moreau, surrounded by Indian fabrics to remind her of India, completed the effect.

Her apartment would undergo a couple of ill-fated attempts at decorator-assisted metamorphosis over the years, but the look was clearly Gloria's, because all incarnations are similar: crowded, eclectic, full of candles, sensuous colors and fabrics, curving lines. Entering Gloria's apartment, which one writer called "seragliesque," can be a startling experience, because Gloria's taste in clothes is so different from her taste in surroundings. While usually figure-revealing and occasionally dramatic, her clothes are spare and simple, never fussy. Only her jewelry—curving, serpentine rings and dangling earrings—hints at the voluptuous environment she creates for herself at home.

21

Esquire's Cruel Attack

In the March 8, 1970, *New York Times Book Review,* Marylin Bender surveyed "Books to Liberate Women." Expected within the year were books by Kate Millett, "a Barnard philosophy instructor;" Robin Morgan, "poet and women's lib leader who is an editor for Grove Press;" Shulamith Firestone, "the 25-year-old organizer of the Stanton-Anthony Brigade and an underground writer who has hitherto supported herself by waitressing, portrait painting on sidewalks, and nude modeling; and Letty Pogrebin, "the resourceful public-relations director of Bernard Geis" (whose view of the movement at that point was "I say yes economically and legally, but I don't want it romantically and I don't want my children in a kibbutz."); and Juliet Mitchell, "an English feminist scholar whose essay, 'The Longest Revolution,' appears in at least the footnotes of nearly every radical analysis of the cause."

Then there was Gloria: "Gloria Steinem, whom many consider the quintessential liberated brainy beauty, is preparing a collection of women's liberation readings for *New York* magazine's sortie into book publishing." The contrast could not have been plainer. Millett, Morgan, Firestone, Pogebrin, and Mitchell were what they did. Gloria was what she was.

The fundamental point of the women's movement was to move women beyond the sphere of being and into the realm of doing, as men did. In contrast to her descriptions of the other feminist writers,

Bender's reference to Gloria epitomized Gloria's initial role in the women's movement. It was a role she did not choose, and it was one she would struggle to transcend for more than a quarter century.

In a sense, Gloria became the women's movement's woman: the movement exerted enormous pressure on Gloria to fulfill the "being" role. It was ironic. Gloria, who had always tried to make herself useful as a way of belonging (as well as for the sheer pleasure of helping others), was widely perceived to be most valuable to the movement as a personality who could be counted on to draw attendance or press coverage or to raise money for an event or an organization. From the moment she realized she was a feminist, Gloria never stopped doing actual work for the movement. Yet her identity as a role model ("the quintessential liberated brainy beauty") and her subsequent renown as a symbol always seemed to eclipse her deeds.

When she began speaking on college campuses in 1969 and writing as much on the subject of women's equality as she could, Gloria became somewhat associated with the issue of women's rights. However, *New York* magazine was directed at a New York–area readership, and her college speeches were relatively isolated affairs. In 1970—just when the national media began the inevitable search for individuals to personify the movement—Gloria began to participate in more national forums. She testified before the U.S. Senate, spoke at Vassar's commencement, appeared on the Dick Cavett and David Frost shows, and published articles on women's liberation in *Look, Time,* and *McCall's.* That was enough to attract the attention of the national media, and reporters began to gravitate toward Gloria.

There were several reasons for her appeal. One was a lack of alternatives. Betty Friedan was the only figure nationally recognized for her association with the movement, but the forty-nine-year-old divorced mother of three was not the press's idea of a role model. Among the radical feminists in New York City, where the national media operated, Robin Morgan and Ti-Grace Atkinson were relatively prominent and articulate spokeswomen, but the radical groups were fragmented, and radicals were ideologically opposed to spokespeople, leaders, and, worst of all, "stars."

An absence of competition was not the only reason the media were drawn to Gloria. She already seemed like an archetypal heroine—prettier, smarter, wittier, and thinner than the average woman. She had work she loved, an apparently endless supply of desirable lovers, an exciting, interesting life—and, of course, she was photogenic.

Gloria herself had always been self-conscious about her face. She combed her hair to conceal as much of what she considered her "chip-munk cheeks" (or "moonface" or "pudding face") as she could, even to the extent of hooking the earpieces of her glasses over her hair. Despite Gloria's view of herself, the camera loved her wide face, and her aviator glasses and leonine hair so captivated the public that by 1972 *Life* ran a two-page spread entitled, "Gloria in Excelsis: It's the Steinem Look." Featuring photographs of women in aviator glasses and "long straight hair, with a part like a scar in the middle," *Life* challenged readers to "pick out the real Ms. Steinem from the other young women on these pages."

Gloria's verbal skills completed the package. Quick with a retort, she could frame a witty response economically and often humorously (Betty Friedan tended to go on and on), a talent which made her invaluable to the media when reporters needed a quick quote from a feminist.

Gloria was also good copy because she instinctively made herself interesting—her star quality was a natural extension of her long prac-tice at self-presentation. She had been performing all her life, after all, and not just in tap shoes, so the perennial outsider knew quite a bit about ingratiating herself with an audience.

By 1971 the media had coalesced around Gloria as their symbol. *Vogue, Redbook,* and *Esquire* ran long profiles on her, and *McCall's* and *Newsweek* put her on their covers.

Gloria's old friend Liz Smith chronicled Gloria's life in the June 1971 *Vogue* as a story of personal transformation, divided into chapters like "Depression's Child Yearns to Be Rockette" and "Bright Butterfly Breaks Chrysalis—Turns Social Professional Sex-Star Success." Once Gloria saw the light and became a feminist, Smith explained, she exuded "that faint nimbus of sexy fanaticism thrown off by those who are righteous in dedication and devotion."

Smith described the old Gloria as "a Pop Culture star up with Tom Wolfe and Baby Jane Holzer," and Gloria obligingly recalled the bad old days:

> At the time I guess, like most women, I was sort of shopping for the right husband. I went out with Tom Guinzburg (the book publisher) because I liked his family so much and longed to be part of something like it. I fell for the glamour and for the idea of marrying accomplish-ment rather than doing it myself. I was brainwashed as a woman. I was into the success, the "important" right man for all the wrong reasons.

It happened, too, with Mike Nichols—it was my fault that I let it go on and then fall apart, because I was in it for the wrong reasons. . . . Many people go through a social-butterfly stage; you have that party thing going for you. You wonder if by not going out you may be missing something. Now I really don't care.

By contrast, Smith found the new Gloria to be an awesome creature:

When I asked what size dress she wears, she said, "You'd never ask a man his suit size." When I asked what brand of cigarette she smokes, she said, "Pall Mall—because of the red package." This let me know that she's no movie star willing to be treated like a second-class citizen and that too many silly interview questions have already been asked of too many women. But she added, "I don't inhale."

Newsweek's August cover story pointed out Gloria's value as a feminist symbol: "What gets nearly everyone about Steinem as Liberationist is that she Didn't Have To." In other words, Gloria, "a Winner and a Beautiful Person, too," refuted the common assumption "that those who reject woman's traditional role must be losers who cannot play the game according to conventional rules and so seek to change the game."

Newsweek also praised Gloria's "quick tongue" and suggested that she might become a political candidate. "The truth seems to be that Steinem is a good deal better speaker, formally or informally, than she is a writer—and this despite the fact that audiences and/or cameras panic her . . ." As an example, the magazine reported that when Gloria so angered actor Hans Conried on a talk show that he growled, "If you were a man, I'd punch you in the mouth for saying that," she responded, "Why don't you? At least you'd be taking a woman seriously for once."

Gloria's close friend, writer Jane O'Reilly, had tried to convey to the *Newsweek* reporter Gloria's behind-the-scenes efforts as a sort of glamorous big sister to the world:

Gloria is the kind of friend who sees one's best potential and acts upon it . . . I was the dull, young housewife who used to come in and see [Gloria and Barbara Nessim]. I envied them so much and the glamorous life I thought they were leading. I remember Gloria had the most elegant underwear and the most beautiful nightgowns and the two of them would get up late like theater people . . . I had a bad marriage and she told me that you either do something about it or shut up about it. So four years ago, I packed up and moved to New York to try to be a writer and Gloria helped me in every possible way. She lent me money, got me jobs, put me up at her apartment. She salvaged me off the scrapheap of humanity and since then I've discovered there are dozens of other people she has salvaged off the scrapheap. She has an intense idealism that is completely real. She is occasionally naive about people's motives but her motives are pure.

Betty Friedan also was interviewed. Assisting in her usurpation as best-known American feminist could hardly have been pleasant for Friedan, who enjoyed her prominence and believed she deserved it—she had, after all, written the book. She did her best to remain positive, however, lauding Gloria's decision to remain single as a courageous choice. "When she got out of Smith in the '50s it was very difficult for a woman to strike out on an independent course, and she did. She rebelled against the feminine mystique without an ideology."

When it came to contemplating the idea of Gloria as a leader, she seemed torn. First she said that Gloria needed to get over an "anti-elitism hang-up," noting that it was "far worse to say you're standing back when you're actually pulling strings." Not that Gloria was necessarily doing that, she hastened to add, but Gloria should "take the responsibility to go along with the fame." Then she described Gloria as always "the princess among the grape pickers," whereas the women's movement was about "us—equals—women among ourselves."

Both *Redbook* and *McCall's* profiled Gloria specifically because their editors wanted to present the women's movement in a positive light. *Redbook*'s editor Sey Chassler, who was one of the few men on NOW's board of directors, recalls, "We were looking for a way to introduce the whole subject to our readers. Gloria was coming on very strong, and since we wanted to present a real person versus what they were reading in the daily press, we thought using Gloria was a sound way of talking about the renaissance of the women's movement, rather than talking about hairy legs."

In naming Gloria their 1972 Woman of the Year, the *McCall's* editors called her the "most effective spokeswoman and symbol" of the women's movement. She bridged the gap between militants and "the thoughtful, dedicated women who understand that woman's status *must* change," they explained. "She is, in short, a transitional figure, proof that change is not so frightening after all, and that it has to come—for the good of women and men alike."

For Gloria 1971 was a transitional year. Until then, her public persona was an extension of her personal and professional self—conventionally appealing, smart, funny, socially conscious, and politically committed. In 1971 she came to understand that she had a new kind of public. She had gone out to deliver a message on behalf of a cause, but somewhere along the way she had become the message. As Jane O'Reilly recalls, "It made her nervous and anguished and upset. She felt tremendous responsibility for what she said. Because she wasn't just famous because she was famous, she was famous for standing for something and still being beautiful and intelligent and funny. She was always in an odd position. She didn't hate it—part of her life is being famous—but I don't know if she still anguishes as she did. Years ago she used to call when she was upset about something that had been in the papers."

In the early to middle 1960s Gloria had presented herself as Holly Golightly with brains—a charming but intelligent "Keynesian liberal"; serious about her writing; politically involved in directing a small foundation. She portrayed her background as early show business and late Smith Phi Bete, and her parents as charmingly feckless. During her New Left period in the late 1960s, Gloria began stressing the working-class part of her background. The emphasis shifted from show business and the resort to the house trailer, the rats, and the poverty of the Toledo years.

Talking about the bad times felt more honest anyway, though Gloria, with the flair of an instinctive storyteller, dramatized her history in such broad terms that, as the years went by, she managed to leave the denizens of all her former communities, from Clarklake to Smith, sputtering at the unfairness of it all. For *Newsweek* Gloria described "the industrial slums" where she and her mother went after her parents' divorce:

> East Toledo is "Joe" country, the kind of place where they beat up the first available black on Saturday night. They considered us nuts on two counts: we read books and we were poorer than they were. The girls all got married before they graduated because they were pregnant. I had one girl friend like that who had four children too fast. Her teeth fell out. Now she sits at home and her husband beats her from time to time.

Her Toledo friends were startled to learn they had lived in a slum. Gloria's house had been dilapidated, but their working-class neighborhood had been generally well kept. Julia Robinson, the one Toledo friend Gloria still sees, says charitably, "I understand—Gloria was just trying to make a point." Gloria often mentioned her "tiny friend" whose too-close-together children drained the calcium out of her teeth. Carole Roberts (Berning) was terribly hurt by this because the characterization seemed so close. She had married young, but she had not been pregnant; her first two children were born close together because they were twins; she lost some teeth from bad dental work, not pregnancy-related calcium loss; she went to college once she was able to afford it; and her husband decidedly did not beat her. Gloria heard from several people who thought she meant them or others they knew, though when she was asked, she explained that her description had been a composite.

As she became more prominent as a feminist, Gloria continued to emphasize her supposed working-class background and her Toledo neighborhood. The subtle changes may not even have been conscious on Gloria's part—the nature of her reinventions was shaped by her changing perception of herself.

As it turned out, Gloria's interpretation of herself and the meaning of her life would be an important contributor to her development from spokeswoman to leader. Her feminist consciousness fueled her passion, but that alone would not have been sufficient—feminist consciousness fueled the passion of many. Gloria was unique not in the intensity of her beliefs but in her talent for communicating them.

In *Leading Minds: An Anatomy of Leadership*, Howard Gardner described the key to leadership as the creation and embodiment of an effective story. Preferring "story" and "narrative" to "theme" or "message," Gardner explained,

> I want to call attention to the fact that leaders present a *dynamic* perspective to their followers: not just a headline or snapshot, but a drama that unfolds over time, in which they—leader and followers—are the principal characters or heroes. Together they have embarked on a journey in pursuit of certain goals, and along the way and into the future, they can expect to encounter certain obstacles or resistances that must be overcome. Leaders and audiences traffic in many stories, but the most basic story has to do with issues of *identity*.

Even without embellishments, the story of Gloria's life resonated with some of the culture's most powerful narratives. One of Gloria's

gifts was her ability to turn personal dramas—her own and others'—
into political lessons. She fashioned such effective feminist moral-
ity tales that she ultimately became the movement's most effective
proselytizer.

The most obvious narrative Gloria's life evoked was the American
Dream. By characterizing herself as poor or working class and eliminating muddying details like the Clarklake resort and affluent grand-
parents, Gloria simplified the story into the familiar format of triumph
over deprivation—and sexism. Ironically, reducing her biography to a
simple rags-to-riches saga omitted some of the elements that made the
story of her years in Toledo even more shocking—the descent from relative comfort into relative poverty, the loss of her father and, in a sense,
the loss of her mother.

Gloria's years in Toledo also bore a startling resemblance to the por-
trayals of adolescence found in fairy tales such as Snow White, Cin-
derella, and Sleeping Beauty. Gloria used the rats to convey the
nightmarish quality of her adolescent years, though, as with the American Dream, her real experience was worse than her narrative. Once
Ruth died and Gloria felt free to tell the truth about her mother as
well as about the rats, her story acquired a perfect feminist moral as
well. Gloria's evil stepmother figure was not really evil; she had been
driven into mental illness by a patriarchal society.

Finally, as Liz Smith had conveyed, Gloria's story could be interpreted as a conversion narrative, complete with a personal transformation after she "got religion." The worse the sinner, the more
dramatic the story of her conversion, and for a time Gloria cooper-
ated, contrasting the bad old Beautiful People Gloria with the good
new Feminist Gloria.

However, Gloria did not not exist in a vacuum. As Gardner noted,
the interaction between leader and audience is dynamic. While Gloria
was sending messages, she also was receiving them. As early as 1971,
Gloria suffered attacks as well as praise, and the criticism hurt. She
sometimes felt, as she sighed at one point, "as if I were holding a balloon. I'm down here. I'm a person who picks up her own laundry and
watches the Late Show. But people are looking at that balloon and
shooting arrows at that balloon, which is where they think I am. It's
very difficult to be a public person."

To the limited extent Gloria could influence her characterization by
the media, she began to offer them less of a target. Over the years, the

strong, determined heroine of her early stories sometimes seemed to recede, giving way to a one-dimensional, relatively passive victim of sexism.

Esquire's article on Gloria—the other major magazine story to appear in 1971—certainly contributed to Gloria's desire to lower her profile. Just as *McCall's* and *Redbook* used Gloria as a constructive role model to convey the ideas of the movement to their female readers, *Esquire*'s October story "SHE," by Leonard Levitt, dissected this "enigmatic *femme fatale*" for its male readers:

> No man who seeks to know how the wind blows can afford to ignore Gloria, the intellectuals' pinup, but no man can claim her undivided attention. And no man can ever know just where she stands. . . . she discards movements—and the leaders of movements—as once she laid aside the rolled athletic socks with which, she reported, she stuffed her bosoms during the Bunny days. Most recently this woman, who advanced in public favor by appealing to powerful men, has moved to the front ranks of women's liberation, appealing now to women who do not like powerful men.

Her friends were outraged by this, and Gloria was devastated. Walter Pincus recalls that several of her ex-lovers, finding themselves together at a party shortly after "SHE" appeared, gathered in a corner to ask each other what they could do to help Gloria. The answer was nothing. Before the piece was published, Gloria had lawyers send *Esquire* a threatening letter, and she would later insist that "SHE" was "character assassination," found by lawyers to be "defamatory and knowingly inaccurate enough to be actionable."

But despite the sneering tone and some minor factual errors, Levitt had captured something real about Gloria. She was ambitious. She did use men. She did reinvent herself. However, if *Esquire* found the enigmatic Gloria worth examining, the assumptions underlying *Esquire*'s article are worth examining, too.

Levitt portrayed Gloria as a puzzling and threatening phenomenon, a woman who used traditional feminine means to achieve traditional masculine ends. Most likely, the underlying question was not What did this woman want? but rather What chance were men going to have if other women wanted it, too?

Gloria had shared *Esquire*'s assumption that her ambition was unwomanly and should not be admitted. Self-sacrifice, not self-promotion, was expected of women, so though neither she nor *Esquire*'s editors necessarily articulated it to themselves at that point, Gloria understood that expectation as well as, if not better than, the men. That was what she meant when she later described herself as outwardly conforming while secretly rebelling against her prescribed role.

In addition to the crime of ambition, Gloria was charged with using men, both professionally and socially: " 'Gloria chooses her men very deliberately,' says [her old *Help!* boss, Harvey] Kurtzman. 'To all outward appearances it seems that she is climbing. She wanted to get into publishing and she went with a publisher. She wanted to get into politics and she went with politicians. She has this social-climbing sex appeal.' "

Kurtzman also said, "While Gloria always seems to regard herself as the political fighter, the good thinker, and the good writer, her real talent, whether she knows it or not, is a social ability. Much of her success had to do with her effect on men."

That evaluation was reinforced by quotations from a number of Gloria's admirers, including Ken Galbraith. That Gloria's prominence exceeded that of many superior writers was undeniable. So was the fact that her personal qualities enhanced her career as well as her social life. However, the same could be said of many men. Furthermore, since men already enjoyed the privilege of being taken seriously simply because they were men, it was hardly fair to condemn Gloria for playing by their rules and turning the disadvantage of her sex into an advantage. If contacts with powerful people aided her career, it is not surprising that they were men—most people with power were men.

The emphasis on her sex appeal was overstated anyway—sex appeal could only take her so far. Galbraith admired her looks but respected her political instincts. Clay Felker, the man who most helped her career, admitted he had been in love with her, but he had hardly assigned Gloria *New York*'s political column and many cover stories because of her legs. On the contrary, Clay always credits Gloria with helping with every aspect of *New York,* from naming sections to rewriting the magazine's subscription solicitations.

Besides, as she herself often pointed out, Gloria had received some of her best assignments from women editors. And if her panache was one of the reasons female *Glamour* editors hired her as a contributing editor, it was not the reason *Seventeen* editor Ray Robinson hired her away from *Glamour* in 1970. (She had a $5,000-a-year contract to consult for *Seventeen,* but lost it after the first year. When *Seventeen* owner Walter Annenberg heard Gloria was defense fund treasurer for Communist Angela Davis, he ordered Robinson to let her contract expire. Gloria proudly called the experience "my first political firing.")

However genuine she knew her achievements to be, Gloria was miserable anyway. Making matters worse, *Esquire* demolished her character as well as disparaging her achievements. She was portrayed as an opportunist masquerading as an idealist, rather than an idealist trying to pretend she wasn't also opportunistic: "[W]as Gloria ever conscious that she was using her charm to further her personal ambition? Kurtzman doubts it. 'She seems to be an opportunist,' he says, 'but I'm sure that Gloria sees herself as an idealist. And in one sense she is. She believes in things and she is motivated by her beliefs. After all, she's not collecting real estate.' "

Taking Gloria's ambition and opportunism for the whole of Gloria was cruel. There was nothing wrong with ambition anyway, but to dismiss Gloria's idealism and political commitment as inconsequential was to deny Gloria her core—as well as the part of herself she valued most. To regard Gloria's political commitment as a mere route to self-advancement was to mistake ends for means.

To demonstrate Gloria's metamorphosis, Levitt noted that her shift from publishing to politics was accompanied by a new cast of friends:

> Today the girl who used to be seen with Bob & Tom & Herb & Mike & Ted & Ken & Gene & George is more likely to be seen with Rafer & Angela & Jim & Dorothy. That is, Rafer Johnson, the Olympic decathlon gold medalist; Angela Davis, the woman accused of supplying the guns used to kill a San Rafael judge; Jim Brown, the retired football superstar who now works in the movies; and Dorothy Pitman Hughes, the women's-rights crusader (who recently named her baby daughter Angela in a ceremony held at Gloria's). All of the above are black; two are women. Gloria says that being born black and being born female make one the victim of similar prejudices, adding that women are "a bridge between black and white, the latest of a series of steps in the civil-rights march." Friends say women's liberation is her first real love.

Accompanying the article was a three-page comic strip that ridiculed Gloria's transformations. "Superwoman" chronicled the exploits of Super Gloria as she transformed herself from Lithesome Lolita at Smith

College to Fearless Agent of the Free World, fighting Communism in Helsinki ("Take *that* #@&*! You rabid, raunchy, radical Red!"). The magic word CHAZOB (CH for the political instincts of Shirley Chisholm, A for the chutzpah of Bella Abzug, Z for the staying power of Zsa Zsa, O for the adaptability of Jackie Onassis, B for the verbal finesse of Jimmy Breslin) transformed her from a belligerent Bunny into a femme fatale, then a pretty politician, and finally, "I am Superwoman. Protector of the weak, the meek, the ugly . . . the ugly? The plump, the short, the piano legged. . . . Up against the wall Male Chauvinist Pigs! Our Black Brothers are our sisters."

Levitt's attribution of insincerity to Gloria was aided considerably by her own propensity to reinvent herself and rewrite history because she was too insecure to trust her audiences to accept her as she was, contradictions and all. Her tendency to present herself as "seamless" was, and continues to be, her most self-defeating characteristic. It was not the ardor with which Gloria threw herself into her incarnation of the moment that gave her an air of inauthenticity; it was the way she insisted on depicting it. The ardor was real, but the concept of evolution seemed to be unacceptable.

When her past contradicted her present, she rewrote the past. When her actions contradicted her words, she would redefine the actions. She sought attention but said she hated it. She would insist that she had not really been part of the rich and famous crowd, just "accidentally" associated with it through the men with whom she had been involved. Or she would explain that she had spent time with them because she had been assigned to write about them. Or she would distance herself from some who had been kind to her by ridiculing or disparaging them. She devoted a great deal of time and attention to her appearance but insisted, "I've never worn a designer dress or spent more than ten minutes getting dressed."

The *Esquire* article was the cruelest attack, but by 1971 Gloria was well aware that men were not the only ones who objected to accomplished women. Many feminists resented and attacked women who emerged as leaders, not only because of an ideological objection to elitism, but out of personal jealousy—or both. Not all radical feminists objected, and the NOW and nonradical women were not as opposed to the concept of leaders. Many were ecstatic to see the press respond so positively to a feminist. They were grateful to have Gloria as an advocate and thought she conducted herself admirably.

Between the antielitism of radical feminists and the antipathy against ambitious women of the culture at large, the taboo against personal ambition was clear. Gloria was in a delicate position. Like the radicals, she, too, believed in communal effort. At the same time, she understood that the media attention she attracted offered her an unparalleled opportunity to advance the ideas of the movement.

The media treated her more positively than they had hitherto treated any advocate of the radical feminists' agenda, and Gloria was an extremely effective communicator. Her presence was frequently described as nonthreatening, a fortuitous misnomer, as what Gloria advocated was extremely threatening if one happened to be in power. Her good manners and sympathetic demeanor were disarming, and she knew not only how to make herself interesting, but also how to frame a response to her interlocutors that aimed over their heads to the greater watching, listening, or reading audiences.

Gloria persisted, but she understood quickly that resentment and jealousy were the price of fame. Unable to resist justifying herself, she responded to charges of opportunism by insisting that she was uninterested in power and that her personal ambition applied *only* to her desire to be a good writer or to do good. She refused to concede that she derived any ego gratification from her role as a leader or that ambition played any part in her renown. Instead, she portrayed herself as a reluctant leader, a characterization she continues to the present.

Like many of Gloria's descriptions of herself, that is not entirely inaccurate, but it is too simple. The pressure on women to deny ambition was great and remains so. Selflessness is still idealized in women. Even today, female politicians have far greater difficulty than men expressing personal pleasure in their own achievements, for example. They tend to describe their rewards solely in terms of serving others rather than acknowledging both factors.

Gloria did and does want to be a writer. Furthermore, much of the work of a public figure is so tedious, boring, and draining that only the idea that one is helping others makes it palatable. However, wanting to be a writer hardly precludes other ambitions—or the enjoyment of other achievements, or the gratification derived from the recognition, or the affection that accompanies these accomplishments.

During the 1970s Gloria would develop from a celebrity feminist and role model into a spokeswoman, and from a spokeswoman into a genuine leader. She would continue to yearn to return to writing, because she loved it and because she desired recognition as a writer. It was what she wanted to do as well as to be. She would never quite seem to appreciate the uniqueness of her contributions. Writing came so hard to her, while being a leader came so easily. In the way of human nature, she overvalued what she sought and undervalued what she possessed.

22

Battle of the Titans

On July 10, 1971, Bella Abzug, Shirley Chisholm, Betty Friedan, and Gloria Steinem addressed over three hundred women at the founding conference of the National Women's Political Caucus (NWPC) in Washington, D.C. At that time, there were one female U.S. senator and twelve U.S. representatives, no female Supreme Court justices or state governors. Women filled only 1.6 percent of the top jobs in government, Bella Abzug pointed out, noting that was "more like a pinprick than a breakthrough." The group assembled in the Statler Hilton was determined to change that.

Betty Friedan had begun speaking publicly about a "national women's political caucus" the previous January. Soon afterward she formed a steering committee to organize it and enlisted Rona (Ronnie) Feit, a young Manhattan housewife, to coordinate a founding conference. Betty wanted the caucus organized in time to affect the 1972 national party conventions.

Meanwhile, Bella Abzug, who had been sworn in as a New York congresswoman in January, was also interested in building a national women's political movement. Once she learned of Friedan's plans, Ronnie Feit recalls, "It was a battle of the titans for ownership."

Ronnie felt caught between the Betty people and the Bella people. Although Betty had hired her, Ronnie tried to utilize all of the various women's groups. It was not easy: "Betty was very nervous about Bella.

She seemed to have her own political ambitions [Betty was considering running for the Senate], so she didn't want to be preempted."

The titans also differed in their conception of the group's membership. Betty wanted a broad-based, mainstream organization that utilized already-active political women and established women's organizations, and she was determined that it be bipartisan and racially diverse. Racial diversity was a priority of Bella's as well, but she envisioned a coalition of politically like-minded women. After a May 22, 1971, meeting in New York, Bella wrote:

> Gloria Steinem, [Brooklyn Congresswoman] Shirley Chisholm and I have this major difference of opinion with Betty as to what the nature of a women's political movement should be. She seems to think we should support women for political office no matter what their views, and we don't. I feel our obligation is to build a real political movement of *women for social change.* . . . [Abzug's italics]

After another meeting five days later, the issue was still unresolved:

> [I]t's nice to say that by 1976 we're going to have two hundred women in Congress, but do we want the kind of women who are going to vote for missiles and Vietnam wars? Or do we want the kind of women who are going to put our tax money into housing and health and child-care centers and abortion clinics and things like that?
>
> It's a crucial point, and the differences between Betty and me have to be handled delicately.

Bella had never been known for her delicate touch, but she did not shrink from the job:

> Power fights, unfortunately, are inevitable. . . . My role, as I see it, since I am the only woman who's ever successfully run for national office on an essentially women's rights–social change program, is to help give the entire movement the kind of guidance and perspective that nobody else is qualified to do. . . . It can be tedious, but if we mean business we have to be on top of everything.

At first Ronnie Feit considered Bella too exclusive. She recalls: "When Liz Carpenter was interested, Bella was almost antagonistic toward her because she was allied with the Johnsons [Carpenter had been Lady Bird Johnson's press secretary]. She pulled in [Hawaii Congresswoman] Patsy Mink, but including Liz seemed to go against her gut. . . . but I watched Bella grow and see that even Republican women could be dealt with. You could see a gradual lowering of her distrust."

Bella and Patsy Mink made their congressional offices available for NWPC planning meetings, and Ronnie followed up with mailings. On June 9, 1971, a group including Bella, Betty, Gloria, Patsy Mink, National Welfare Rights Organization vice president Beulah Sanders, and the United Auto Workers' Edith Van Horn met to plan the initiating conference. One month later, more than three hundred women from twenty-six states converged on Washington. Gloria described their variety in a "City Politic" column: "union women . . . employers' wives, young collectivists . . . parliamentarians." *Newsweek* quoted a twenty-year-old saying, "If I get called 'gal' one more time I'm going to scream."

Gloria was considered one of the leaders. She had worked on Bella's 1970 congressional campaign, but their NWPC work that summer cemented a political alliance, and a close personal friendship, that deepened over the years. In fact, Gloria usually tries to steer credit for the NWPC's origins to Bella, not Betty, by explaining, "People said to me it wasn't serious; that because [Betty] was involved it wouldn't happen. But then after Bella and Patsy Mink and Shirley Chisholm got involved, there was a conviction that it was a different 'it.' "

At the founding conference, Gloria's low-key style belied her fighting words:

> Some people have asked, are we a woman's party? Are we a third or fourth or fifth party? We are not a woman's party, at least not yet. We have not given up the existing political machinery to the male elitists, because we see that there are empty clubhouses and a turned off electorate and a great poverty of ideas. We believe that we can humanize and renew that machinery so it will respond to people's needs. We do want to take our rightful position in this country. And our rightful position means fifty percent of every elected and appointed body that exists. We happen to be fifty-three percent. But we'll give them the three percent—for the moment.

For all the dissension on individual issues, the conference was exhilarating. Conferees broke up into individual workshops and caucuses to thrash out their ideas. Should they support candidates just because they were women? Should there be certain bottom-line issues? If there were to be bottom-line issues, what should they be? What were candidate criteria to be? Should the NWPC endorse candidates at all? What if a male candidate were good on the issues? Betty continued to insist they should welcome almost all women; Bella wanted to set criteria based on a set of issue positions.

One of Gloria's major contributions was drafting the statement of purpose. Between the June planning meeting and the July conference, Gloria worked on the statement with a group that assembled in New York. Several women, including UAW leader Edith Van Horn from Detroit, flew in for meetings. The group contributed to one anothers' airfares so that representatives from welfare and working-class groups could afford to attend. Joanne Edgar, who had become Gloria's assistant, was very involved. At the July conference, Letty Cottin Pogrebin, who had helped Betty Friedan and Ronnie Feit organize the conference beforehand, worked with Gloria for the first time on the final draft. Then it was adopted by the larger group.

Although it was written by committee, the NWPC statement of purpose is a powerful, angry document. According to Gloria, "We tried to make it concise and inspiring. Or at least, compared to organizationalese, somewhat inspiring." It *is* inspiring, and Gloria's comment is about as close as she gets to saying she is proud of something she has written or helped to write.

The statement of purpose was a call to arms, reaching out to, among others,

> every woman whose abilities have been wasted by second-class, subservient, underpaid, or powerless positions to which female human beings are consigned.
>
> To every woman who sits at home with little control over her own life, much less the powerful institutions of this country, wondering if there isn't more to life than this. . . .
>
> To every woman who has experienced the ridicule or hostility reserved by this country—and often its political leaders—for women who dare to express the hopes and ambitions that are natural to every human being.

A few of the conference's speakers had to be unceremoniously squeezed into a half-hour break from the official meeting. Among them were former senator Eugene McCarthy and pediatrician-antiwar activist Dr. Benjamin Spock. When they were allowed to speak, McCarthy endured jeers of "sexist" and "silver-haired smoothie," and Dr. Spock fared worse. In 1970, Spock had published *Decent and Indecent,* in which he had written that, as women belonged in the home, at least during child-rearing years, it would be fairer to gear female education to make them "feel proud of, and fascinated by, the creativity of child rearing."

Spock apologized to his NWPC audience and assured the group he had revised the book's paperback edition. The audience continued to hiss and boo, however, and as he wrote later that year, "Gloria Steinem said sternly she hoped I understood that I was considered a symbol of repression, like Freud and other male supremacists." In response, according to *Newsweek,* "Spock bowed his head humbly."

Dr. Spock must have had dined out on that story for twenty-five years. In a 1996, *New Yorker* profile he recalled that as soon as his speech ended, Gloria Steinem "stood up and thundered in the tones of Jehovah, 'Dr. Spock, I hope you realize you have been a major oppressor of women in the same category as Sigmund Freud!' "

Gloria says, "I was trying to explain to him why everyone was so upset, but I probably made matters worse." That sounds more likely, since Gloria does not thunder. However, Bella Abzug, who sat next to Gloria during the incident but has probably heard her friend Spock's recounting more than once, recalls a very stern Gloria pointing her finger at Spock and reprimanding him severely.

In addition to the struggles over issues, the power struggle among the leaders was obvious to anyone who cared to watch. Nikki Beare, president of the Dade County, Florida, NOW chapter, had been invited by Betty but found herself acting as mediator. She recalls: "Bella wanted to be the leader. Betty wanted to be at least the titular head. Shirley Chisholm thought she could be the first person running for president as a black. . . . Brenda [Feigen] Fasteau and a couple of the other young women had their own agendas, too. Gloria was with them, but I never remember Gloria with a personal agenda. . . . She wasn't as high in visibility at that time, but she was so focused that you had to admire her and agree . . . she was wonderful at placating different factions and saying let's look for an alternative choice."

Others recall the contrast as well—Betty ordering people around, proclaiming her own importance, and trying to preserve her position as *the* feminist leader while Gloria ran copy machines, stood in line to get people coffee, explicitly encouraged other leaders to take the originators' places, and never openly thrust herself into the limelight. Ronnie Feit recalls the way they seemed to her: "Betty had a clearer sense of political groundedness. She cares about issues and is a big thinker. I didn't think of Gloria in the same league. She's a good consensus builder, but was defending an ideologically narrower viewpoint—political correctness—and she seemed insecure about how much she was willing to stand up and say what she really stood for. . . . She was a careful operator.

"Betty was a sloppy operator. She had raw energy and showed her flaws. Gloria was much more image-conscious. Bella is conscious of her image, but she's sensitive, too, and has been hurt plenty by people. At steering committee meetings when Bella was under fire, she'd cry. I saw tears well up several times in her eyes. But sometimes she would come in so tired, and by the end of the meeting she would be completely rejuvenated, rosy cheeks and all. It was remarkable to see.

"Gloria had a mother-daughter relationship with Bella. It gradually became clear that Gloria was dependent emotionally and checked in with her."

In the end, the ideological battle was something of a draw. Bella and Gloria prevailed in defining the issues by which candidates would be evaluated. However, enough women shared Betty's desire for broad political inclusivity to force a compromise. After accepting by acclamation a resolution disavowing racism, the conference eventually decided that any other position statement it adopted would be considered a "guideline." Ultimately adopted were positions supporting the Equal Rights Amendment; abortion- and contraception-law repeal; withdrawal from Vietnam and a rejection of physical violence as a means of solving conflict; an adequate income for all Americans; and fair treatment for working women. However, these were to be guidelines only. Local groups would be allowed to decide for themselves whether they wanted to use them as criteria for evaluating candidates.

All factions agreed on what the NWPC itself should do: develop chapters throughout the country; encourage women to run for office; help train them to be candidates; assist with their campaigns; compile lists of qualified women to help elected officials appoint more women to various positions. They would also rate male and female candidates on a number of feminist concerns—their positions on issues, of course, but also on the number and relative importance of women on their staffs.

After the convention Gloria helped various groups all over the country raise funds and organize into local NWPC chapters—and that was in addition to her already-full schedule of speechmaking, writing, campaigning, and trying to start a magazine. Apart from her appeal for the media, it soon became evident that Gloria was a talented organizer. She was especially useful in situations where the participants cared passionately and interacted with rancor. Endowed with empathy, a soothing personality, and the capacity to grasp an issue's important points, she was an effective listener. Because she could understand and articulate the various participants' concerns—sometimes better than the participants themselves could—she was good at framing compromises.

Because her organizing work took place largely behind the scenes and was by nature ephemeral, it left no more record than the memories of the participants (and in the existence of organizations and institutions that evolved). For that reason, organizing would be Gloria's least known, most underrated contribution to the movement. However, the quality of her organizing work was of incalculable value. Gloria was astute politically; she had media skills, so she could see the picture from the outside in; she was kind; she didn't need credit and enjoyed helping others help themselves; she had stamina; she was inspiring.

The quantity of Gloria's organizing work was remarkable as well. She believed in grassroots political work, and though it was unglamorous and often required enormous effort to produce minuscule results, she did it—day after day, week after week, year after year.

In February 1972 the NWPC held a Women's Education for Delegate Selection meeting to plan strategies for getting more women delegates sent to the Democratic and Republican presidential nominating conventions in Miami that summer. Caucus strategists hoped to create a women's caucus at each convention that would attract not only delegates connected to the NWPC, but as many women delegates as possible. The goal was to create a women's power bloc so that they could negotiate with the candidates about their concerns.

Gloria managed the unusual feat of endorsing George McGovern in February and becoming a Shirley Chisholm delegate in March. At a Manchester, New Hampshire, rally in February for the state's March 7 primary, she declared McGovern to be "the best white male candidate" running for president, adding "he's not a prisoner of the masculine mystique. He can admit mistakes . . . relate to people who aren't powerful . . . has the full range of human choices open to him—not just the things that a 'real man' is supposed to do." The *New York Times* characterized Gloria's endorsement as "praising him with faint damns" and accompanied the article with a photograph of a miniskirted Gloria perched on the arm of McGovern's chair, a pose that a number of feminists still recall as "that awful picture of Gloria looking sexy next to McGovern."

Not surprisingly, Gloria was criticized for working simultaneously for two competing candidates. The candidates complained, too.

McGovern had to spend more money in New York to explain that a vote for Steinem was not a vote for McGovern. Gloria ascribes Chisholm's criticism to the fact that "she tended to demand total loyalty, even in states where she wasn't running." Gloria's explanation—"What were the women who lived in states where Shirley Chisholm was not a candidate supposed to do?"—makes sense only if one assumes women voters without a Steinem-endorsed candidate were disenfranchised. With that logic, Gloria's decision was understandable. One candidate represented the causes Gloria embraced with her whole being (antiracism as well as feminism) and shared her positions on issues. The other was a kindly friend and an honorable, longtime political ally for whom she had respect and affection. Perhaps more to the point, George McGovern was certainly the more likely nominee.

Despite her defection in New York and other states where Chisholm was on the ballot, Gloria was highly valued by McGovern associates, especially campaign director Frank Mankiewicz. He recalls Gloria's role in persuading the New Democratic Coalition (of New York's Reform Democrats) to endorse McGovern instead of McCarthy in 1972: "Gloria must have known all the delegates, and she was very helpful—it was absolutely mad. There were women's movement delegates, gay delegates, regulars, reformers, Village Independent delegates, some McCarthy delegates, a blind delegation, the welfare people. They all had something to say. At one point I said to Pat Moynihan, 'Every little meaning has a movement all its own.' Gloria was just plain ward-heeling that day, buttonholing delegates. God knows what promises she was making on behalf of McGovern, but we got the sixty percent we needed."

Gloria ran as a Chisholm delegate in the New York primary, but before the primary she and four others, including Flo Kennedy and Brenda Feigen Fasteau, held a press conference to announce that, if elected, they would not necessarily support the candidate nominated by the convention. They lost anyway. At the same time, Gloria campaigned and raised money for Chisholm and even wrote her only major television speech. She campaigned for McGovern as well.

Betty Friedan also ran as a Chisholm delegate and lost. She attended the convention anyway, with press credentials from *McCall's* and as an organizer of the National Women's Political Caucus.

By then Betty and Gloria were viewed as rivals. The 1972 Democratic-primary season offers almost laboratorylike conditions in which to compare the two as political operators. What the results prove is that life is indeed unfair. Both espoused virtually the same general politics, and both ran as delegates for the most ideologically correct candidate. Gloria somehow managed to pull off the unusual feat of simultaneously operating in the inner circle of two competing campaigns while retaining the trust, friendship, and respect of both candidates and their staffs almost until the end.

By contrast, though Betty followed an internally consistent path, her insensitive blundering rendered her candidacy a complete disaster. If Chisholm was trying to ameliorate the black community's distrust of feminists, she should have told Betty thanks, but stay home. The Saturday before the primary, a press release from Chisholm headquarters announced that Betty was coming to Harlem to campaign as part of a "Traveling Watermelon Feast." As one local writer exclaimed, "Yes, Betty Friedan was coming to Harlem, band and all and to distribute watermelon to the natives." When confronted, Betty reportedly insisted she had "checked it out with some of her Black sisters and they thought it was a great idea."

Gloria's decision to support two competing candidates illustrates not only her unusual ability to succeed at having her cake and eating it, too, but also her politics. Michael Harrington, the political figure with whom she most identifies, liked to say, "I want to be on the left wing of the possible." That could define Gloria as well. Her ultimate goals are radical, but, as was true for Harrington, she considers incremental measures to be fine if they help people in the here and now. She is too pragmatic to wait for heaven or the revolution. So for Gloria, the champion cake-haver-and-eater, the competition between McGovern and Chisholm was not the same either/or conundrum it was for everyone else. It was both-and.

During Democratic platform-committee hearings a few weeks before the convention, Gloria, Betty, and about a dozen NWPC members met with McGovern at his house to discuss women's issues. With his campaign advisor on women's issues, actress Shirley MacLaine, McGovern agreed to consider an abortion plank in the platform—abortion would not be legalized on a national basis until the *Roe* v. *Wade* Supreme Court decision the following January. Gloria had written the plank: "The Democratic Party opposes government interference in the reproductive and sexual freedom of the individual American citizen." However, the next day, the women heard nothing.

In a *New York Times Magazine* article the following year, MacLaine described Gloria's subsequent attempts to get abortion included and MacLaine's role as McGovern protector:

At the hotel I found Gloria lobbying the platform-drafting committee—namely Bella Abzug, who deserves credit for the language of most of what is progressive in the platform.

"Gloria, Bella, you realize the language puts McGovern in the position of defying states' rights where sex laws are concerned, so that some imaginative, clever journalist can do research on sex laws and conclude that George McGovern is for sodomy in the streets? . . ."

Gloria's hand flew to her mouth. "Shhh," she said. "No one will think of that—we want this language regardless."

"You mean you want McGovern to run on a platform that makes it okay to ---- a goat in the street?"

"It might do him good." . . .

The next morning Gloria and Betty Friedan gave a press conference [with about a dozen other NWPC women]. They attacked McGovern as ". . . not at all in touch with the concerns of women."

At 2:30 A.M. the morning of the second day in Washington, I found Gloria had successfully lobbied the platform committee's task force on abortion . . . and her language had been included at the bottom of one page of a series of proposals to the drafting committee. . . .

I rushed to the front desk of the hotel and picked up a pair of scissors: then I collected the stack of proposals and . . . cut off the bottoms . . .

Gloria described the women's meeting with McGovern in an account for the October *Ms.* that appeared a couple of months after the event but before the general election. She seemed to be trying to report on McGovern's preconvention waffling on abortion without repelling her readers so much they would refuse to vote for him: "Not having the gut instinct on this issue that he does on the war or the economy, he did something out of character: he backed down. First he said it was a question for the states to decide; then implied the opposite by personally criticizing the New York law as too liberal." Gloria added that she had suggested without success that McGovern use the phrase "reproductive freedom."

She also wrote about Betty Friedan at that meeting. By October 1972 Betty had stepped up her public attacks on Gloria. Nora Ephron described the developing feud in her November *Esquire* column:

It is probably too easy to go on about the two of them this way: Betty as Wicked Witch of the West, Gloria as Ozma, Glinda, Dorothy, take your pick. To talk this way ignores the subtleties, right? Gloria is not, after all, disinterested in power. And yes, she manages to remain above the feud, but that is partly because, unlike Betty, she has friends who will fight dirty for her. Still, it is hard to come out anywhere but squarely on her side. Betty Friedan, in her thoroughly irrational hatred of Gloria, has ceased caring whether or not the effects of that hatred are good or bad for the women's movement.

On the few occasions when Gloria actually allowed herself to respond—as opposed to letting her friends "do her kneecapping for her" (as another observer describes it)—she was always more subtle. In her *Ms.* article on the election she allowed herself to take a tiny, retaliatory swipe when she described an exchange between Betty and the McGovern campaign that did not help the women's cause:

> Betty Friedan, overstating in her own frenetic style, told [McGovern] he had to have "more women visible in the campaign, because right now they just aren't there." McGovern responded quickly that her statement was "sheer nonsense—you just don't know what you're talking about." And indeed, Jean Westwood was in the room, as were several other top women from the McGovern staff.
>
> One of them came to Betty's rescue by noting that, even though they were in the campaign, women weren't always listened to. McGovern himself was open, she explained, in what by now had become a truism of the campaign, but taking women's issues and women campaign aides seriously hadn't been impressed on the staff.

Poor, misguided Betty, so blundering she managed to offend even the mild-mannered George McGovern. How fortunate that one of his "top women" was able to "rescue" her by using the some-of-my-best-friends defense to damn the candidate. When that exchange took place McGovern was still a potential good guy. He just kept forgetting to tell his staff to take women's issues (and the women on the campaign) seriously.

A couple of weeks before the Miami conventions, the NWPC Democratic Task Force further antagonized Betty when they elected Gloria to be their spokeswoman at the Democratic convention. Betty had gone to the meeting and campaigned for the position, but the group chose Gloria. That meant that during the convention Gloria, who had both press and NWPC credentials, would have several duties.

She would represent the women's caucus at the morning round table of the various caucuses, serve as NWPC coordinator, and help lead the daily women's caucus meetings. She would also speak to the press, though never alone: When the NWPC was to be represented at press conferences, the women always presented a diverse group. Bella was chosen as floor leader for the NWPC delegates.

The NWPC headquarters were at the Betsy Ross Hotel. To interest women delegates in participating, NWPC staffers contacted at least one woman in every state's delegation and issued a continuous stream of press releases. In *The Making of the President, 1972,* Theodore White described the scene at the Betsy Ross: "One might be amused by the high-octave span of women's voices gathered together, or the rooms with the unmade beds, half-unpacked suitcases, yogurt cartons, chests covered with blue jeans and bras—but only briefly." (Gloria notes that Betty Friedan stayed at one of the large Miami Beach hotels where most of the media people stayed. Betty stayed at the Fontainebleau because *McCall's,* which furnished her convention credentials, had booked her there.)

The convention's composition was radically different from that of 1968. There were five thousand delegates and alternates and about thirty-five thousand others. In 1968 women had been about 13 percent of the delegates; in 1972 they were almost 40 percent. Day-care facilities were available for the first time.

Gloria described the convention scene amusingly in her October 1972 *Ms.* article: "If you let Barnum & Bailey interpret a play by Stendhal . . ." She did not find the Democratic convention amusing, however.

The National Women's Political Caucus led daily women's caucus meetings, open to all women who wanted to attend. At the meetings, candidates spoke, complicated issues and parliamentary procedures were explained, and the group planned strategy. Just before the convention, the group voted to challenge the South Carolina delegation, because only 28 percent of its delegates were women. When one woman worried that South Carolina might simply add male delegates' wives, Gloria reassured her. "We've all been through this, and we've all been subverted. We think we can subvert these women as well."

McGovern appeared at the women's caucus meeting the following day, and to enthusiastic applause, he promised his "full and unequivocal support" for the women's South Carolina delegation challenge. Not everyone was pleased with McGovern's performance, however. Flo Kennedy thought NWPC women were too easy on McGovern when he evaded a query about abortion. "Honey, if you'll fuck for a dime, you can't complain because somebody else is getting a fur coat," she observed.

Once the convention began, the women issued their South Carolina delegation challenge. Like all such challenges to the seating of a delegation, the entire convention had to vote on it, state by state. During the roll call, something went wrong. Votes that had been promised suddenly began to evaporate. As soon as Gloria realized McGovern's campaign managers were involved, she went to Frank Mankiewicz and asked why the women suddenly had lost twenty votes in Wisconsin.

"I guess there's a lot of chauvinistic sentiment in Wisconsin," he said. Gloria laughed through clenched teeth and said, "Come on, don't be silly. What's going on?"

The women had been sold out. In the middle of the voting, the McGovern operatives began instructing their delegates to reverse course and vote against the challenge, though previously they had been instructed to support it if they chose. The reversal had nothing to do with South Carolina or feminism. It was a parliamentary maneuver relating to complex voting rules. McGovern's floor managers decided the South Carolina challenge had to be defeated. Otherwise, the winner-take-all, unit rule in the California delegation could be challenged, McGovern would lose delegates, and his nomination would be jeopardized.

Observing the reversal in voting patterns, the television commentators, apparently oblivious to the fact that the fate of the nomination was affected, used the occasion to joke about women. Walter Cronkite observed that "the ladies" were angry. When Theodore White noted that he wouldn't mind being represented by a woman, Eric Sevareid joked, "If you are going to carry it all the way, who's going to represent the left-handed Lithuanians?"

At one point CBS correspondent Mike Wallace approached Gloria on the convention floor. "There was some emergency," she later recalled, "and he turned to me and said something sexual. I forget what it was, but it was slightly obscene." Thinking quickly, Gloria said, "Your headset is on." It wasn't, but Gloria savored his discomfort. "For a moment he thought what he had said to me had gone out over the air."

When Frank Mankiewicz explained the parliamentary problem to Gloria, he assumed she sympathized with his political priorities and agreed with the campaign's assessment of the risk. To the contrary,

Gloria believed South Carolina had not needed to be sacrificed. Then that challenge turned out to be only the beginning. Worse was to come.

The following evening the women introduced their reproductive freedom plank. They already knew it would lose. As Gloria wrote in *Ms.*, "There was enormous pressure to withdraw the minority plank from those who were legitimately against the issue, from those who were for it but thought it could be used to defeat the Democratic candidate, and from those who were for it but feared that a bad defeat would set back the fight to repeal these laws through the courts."

However, the NWPC had voted to submit it, and the women were in no mood to compromise after the South Carolina defeat. The floor fight was the most emotional moment of the convention. As Nora Ephron wrote, "Female members of the press lobbied for the plank. Male delegates left their seats to allow women alternatives to vote." Three women delegates spoke in favor of the plank. Then the McGovern operatives sent first Shirley MacLaine and then a male right-to-life delegate, who said, "Next thing you know they'll be murdering old people."

Since McGovern's staff had explicitly promised the women they would not send in an antiabortion speaker, the betrayal was complete. Gloria told Ephron, "Because of that pledge we didn't mention butchering women on kitchen tables in our speeches." She was so furious she started crying.

"You promised us you would not take the low road, you bastards," she told McGovern's campaign manager, Gary Hart.

The next day Gloria was still beside herself. Nora Ephron met her in the lobby of McGovern's hotel, where Gloria began to cry again. Ephron was nonplussed:

> I begin babbling—all the pressures on you, no private life, no sleep, no wonder you're upset. "It's not that," says Gloria. "It's just that they won't take us seriously." She wipes at her cheeks with her hand, and begins crying again. "And I'm just tired of being screwed, and being screwed by my friends. By George McGovern, whom I raised half the money for in his first campaign, wrote his speeches. I can see him. I can get in to see him. That's easy. But what would be the point? He just doesn't understand. We went to see him at one point about abortion, and the question of welfare came up. 'Why are you concerned about welfare?' he said. He didn't understand it was a women's issue." She paused. "They just won't take us seriously. We're just walking wombs."

The NWPC women enjoyed at least a token revenge. Once Shirley Chisholm declined to run for vice president, they joined in nominating the first female vice-presidential candidate, Frances "Sissy" Farenthold, who had surprised all the politicos by coming in second in the Texas gubernatorial primary. Unaware that the caucus had been waiting for Chisholm to decide, Frank Mankiewicz suspected that the NWPC timed its press conference to draw people away from McGovern's announcement that Missouri Senator Thomas Eagleton would be his running mate:

"I remember Gloria bustling around sponsoring another candidate for vice president. I thought they were hurting us and I thought it was very divisive and unfortunate, and it raised a lot of questions because obviously it suggested that McGovern had no feeling for the—what we used to call the women's issues.

"But I could hardly object, considering what happened to Tom Eagleton [who was later driven to withdraw as a candidate when the press uncovered the fact that he had been treated for depression and received electroshock treatments]. That was a tough omen. That's when I realized that for Gloria, and I guess it's true of some others, too, her cause seemed more important than our candidate."

Frank Mankiewicz had it exactly. Gloria's cause was more important than their candidate.

That night Gloria put on a dress and, along with Texas delegate David Lopez, Mississippi civil-rights leader Fannie Lou Hamer, and New Yorker Allard Lowenstein (who had led the Dump Johnson movement before the previous election), she addressed the convention to place the name of Sissy Farenthold in nomination. Farenthold placed second, defeating an Alaskan candidate who had been campaigning for months. It was an exciting, historic moment, even though the delegates eventually became so punchy that CBS newsman Roger Mudd, Yippie leader Jerry Rubin, and Martha Mitchell (the wife of Nixon's attorney general) all received votes as well.

Gloria would treasure memories of that nomination for years afterward. The women organizing Sissy Farenthold's campaign in a ladies' room. Fannie Lou Hamer's moving nominating speech. The way women delegates surrounded Willie Brown on the convention floor to prevent him from giving the signal to vote for Eagleton.

Finally, it was time to relax. Visiting the women's caucus at their hotel, Nora Ephron found them sitting out by the pool. "They were all wearing the uniform that the whole women's group had worn," she recalls, "It was kind of a Gloria Steinem uniform, jeans and a T-shirt, that looked great on Gloria Steinem. Then Gloria walked out to the pool in a bathing suit, and it was as if a creature from another world had landed. She was so beautiful—in a very nice way. She sort of radiated radiance. And I thought, 'She's like Ozma. Ozma of Oz.'"

23

Ozma and the Wicked Witch

The situation was endlessly clichéd. Oedipus (or Electra); the evil stepmother and Snow White; the scene in *All About Eve* when the swarm of reporters deserts the aging film star, Margot Channing, to dash over to Eve, the young actress on the way up. As Nora Ephron wrote in *Esquire*:

> Betty's lips tighten as she hears the inevitable introduction coming: "Betty Friedan, the mother of us all." That does it. "I'm getting sick and tired of this mother-of-us-all thing," she says. She is absolutely right, of course: in the women's movement, to be called the mother of anything is rarely a compliment. And what it means in this context, make no mistake, is that Betty, having in fact given birth, ought to cut the cord. Bug off. Shut up. At the very least, retire gracefully to the role of senior citizen, professor emeritus. Betty Friedan has no intention of doing anything of the kind. It's her baby, damnit. Her movement. Is she supposed to sit still and let a beautiful thin lady run off with it?

One woman's name had been synonymous with the women's movement: Betty Friedan. Now there was Gloria, radical in her thinking and both radical and Establishment in her contacts. Because the medium of her glamour contradicted the subversiveness of her message so effectively, the media often covered her positively instead of ridiculing her or lesbian-baiting, as journalists often did to other radical feminists. Gloria was a radical in liberal's clothing.

There is little doubt that Betty used her ideological differences with Gloria to rationalize her personal jealousy. However, to attribute her animus solely to personal feelings is to underestimate Betty. She was also a leader in a political movement. She had promoted attractive feminists, and she understood very well the value of attaching pretty faces to the idea of strong women. However, she had genuine political differences with Gloria. Betty Friedan was fighting for her ideology as well as her ego.

Betty was a reformer. She desired enormous social change, but she hoped that women's equality could be achieved with less upheaval than ultimately proved to be the case. The backlash Betty feared was inevitable, no matter how the calls for change were phrased, but Betty kept trying to counter the radicals' angry rhetoric. She would object, for example, to their characterization of women as an oppressed class. Liberals preferred to talk of discrimination.

Radicals believed that the problem went far beyond laws and employment practices: it was oppression. That oppression went deeper than the capitalist system—built on the unpaid labor of women in the household—down into the traditional patriarchal family structure. Although Betty objected to much of the radicals' rhetoric, she was ultimately unable to refute their concept of women as a class. Actually, she had helped prove it in *The Feminine Mystique*.

Even if Betty's animus toward Gloria was inevitable, the rivalry was unfortunate. They shared the goal of equality for women, and their strengths and weaknesses complemented each other.

Unlike Gloria, Betty grew up in an intact family. Like Gloria, she came from the Midwest, felt like an outsider among her peers, and found refuge in the world of books. Betty's sense of exclusion began when she was rejected by the sororities in her Peoria, Illinois, high school because she was Jewish. While Gloria adapted by blending in with her environment, Betty set out to prove to everyone that she was "the best." She started a literary magazine with a couple of the boys and graduated as one of the class valedictorians.

Fourteen years before Gloria did, Betty went east to Smith, where her classmates and professors considered her brilliant. (Besides having educated Betty and Gloria, Smith can boast the American translator of Simone de Beauvoir's *Second Sex*, zoology professor H. M. Parshley.)

Betty was editor in chief of the school newspaper, a junior Phi Beta Kappa, and graduated summa cum laude in psychology.

While studying for her Ph.D. at Berkeley, Betty gave up her fellowship ("I was that girl with all A's and I wanted boys worse than anything") and moved to New York City's Greenwich Village, where she worked for a news service and labor newspapers. She married and continued to work until after the birth of her second child. Then she freelanced, writing four or five articles a year, mostly for women's magazines. By the time *The Feminine Mystique* made Betty famous in 1963, she was the unhappily married mother of three, living in a Victorian house in the suburbs.

While Gloria could rely on beauty and charm as well as brains, whatever Betty achieved, she owed to her intelligence. Both were insecure, but while Betty worried about being physically appealing enough to attract men, Gloria never knew whether she was being valued for her exterior or her interior. She longed for the latter, but dared not let the former lapse.

Their personalities and temperaments were completely—fascinatingly—opposite. Both were hungry for approbation, but where Gloria was controlled, Betty was overtly needy. Gloria was subtle; Betty was direct, often brutally so. Gloria avoided conflict and was never directly unkind; Betty could be rude and abusive. Gloria had a horror of bragging; Betty's writing was so full of the self-congratulatory "I" that some of her descriptions of historic moments in the women's movement read as if she had been the only one in the room. On more than one occasion she compared herself to Joan of Arc.

In short, Betty was socially uncontrolled. She would express her feelings, no matter how horrible, and worry about the effect later. On the other hand, Betty could be very sensitive to the public's perception of the movement—too sensitive, perhaps. In her concern for the sensibilities of mainstream women, Betty could become too worried about angering men or too fearful that identifying with out-groups like lesbians would turn mainstream women away. She was right—fear of being perceived as lesbians and fear of rejection by men did turn many women off. (Hence the common disclaimer "I'm not a feminist, but . . .").

However, that was where leadership came in, and Gloria provided it. It was the controlled, unfailingly gracious Gloria who nevertheless liked to say, "This is a revolution, not a PR movement." On the other hand, while Gloria was better at thinking beyond the white, middle-class mainstream, she could get carried away with political correctness and too caught up in identity politics. She had a tendency to respond to women and their problems indiscriminately and to assume that they were oppressed, or victims, or deserving, simply because they were women.

Their differences complemented each other's shortcomings in other ways. Although Betty was unwilling or unable to control her behavior, she was psychologically sophisticated—knowledgeable from her academic background, and comfortable with the complexities and ambiguities underlying human behavior. In contrast, Gloria, who controlled her behavior as carefully as she did her weight, was psychologically unsophisticated. While she was insightful about others' behavior and understood how to behave to her own advantage, she understood very little about herself, and she was simplistic about psychology in general. Avoiding self-knowledge was a necessary defense for much of her life, but it nevertheless produced in this complex woman a core of naïveté that many close to her believe she has never lost.

Betty was more understanding of the importance of marriage and parenthood to most women. One didn't have to be white, middle-class, heterosexual, or even female to want a mate, and most people of both sexes seemed to want children. In Betty's desires, she was far more typical than Gloria, who, while she wanted a loving relationship with a man, didn't really want a mate.

Gloria often has been described as incapable of intimacy, but what Gloria feared was not intimacy, it was losing her autonomy. She wanted a man in her life, but to her, marriage was an undesirable fallback position, not a goal. Gloria enjoyed many intimate relationships over the years, but they were relationships that did not threaten her autonomy—lovers, longtime friendships, and short-term but intense friendships. As a result, Gloria's freely chosen, untraditional relationships provided a positive alternative model to women who did not want—or did not have available—marriage, with its presumption of a lifelong, for-better-or-worse commitment, or parenthood.

As for children, Gloria often said she had lived her life backward—she didn't need to have children because she had already experienced being a mother by taking care of her mother. That was a rather limited conception of parenthood. Gloria had experienced the bondage of motherhood with none of the joys that make the sacrifices meaningful—and often render them selfish rather than selfless pleasures. Gloria eventually would experience exactly that kind of relationship, when she nurtured the feminist movement, *Ms.* magazine, and the thousands of women she helped to help themselves. However, that understanding lay in the future.

In contrast to Betty's continual attention to the power of conventional familial bonds, Gloria and a number of other feminist leaders who were childless and single in the early 1970s underestimated the importance women's families had for them. Radical feminists saw the nuclear family as the training ground and socializing institution for patriarchy, and therefore the institution most in need of change. Betty understood that this very analysis was one of the reasons radical feminism was so threatening to so many women: Patriarchal training ground or not, most women wanted a nuclear family. Alterations were welcome; elimination was not.

To the degree that Gloria subtly or not-so-subtly denigrated childcare and volunteering, in favor of paid work ("How many opera singers are singing lullabies, how many Golda Meirs are running the PTA?" she would ask), she contributed to the impression that the women's movement was antihousewife. Gloria would say, "With homemakers having the highest rate of alcoholism, chemical dependency and depression, the most dangerous place for a woman is in her home." And "Children suffer from too much mother and not enough father." And "The women's movement is not the cause of divorce. Marriage is."

Over time, Betty's and Gloria's positions converged. Gloria continued to believe that the patriarchal nuclear family was "a five- or ten-thousand-year-old experiment that we should just declare a failure," but as radical feminism and its openly antifamily impetus lost steam in the mid-1970s, she came to include the two-parent heterosexual family as one option among a number of possible choices that included single-parent families and communal arrangements. Betty's rhetoric eventually gravitated to the same pluralistic ground.

In the beginning of the 1970s, when Gloria was becoming more prominent, Betty did most of the sniping by far, but Gloria appeared to take a potshot now and then. A 1970, *New York Times Magazine* article, "Mother Superior to Women's Lib," portrayed Betty as heroic but obnoxious, and described her as "the albatross [the radical feminists] would like to shed." The article quoted several feminists, including writer Sally Kempton, who condemned Betty for reformism, elitism, wearing sexy clothes, and projecting a star image, and insisted she "is not the movement mother; that is Simone de Beauvoir."

Described as "the writer, who worked with Betty on the Aug. 26 strike," Gloria was quoted as well: "She found that love between unequals can never succeed and she has undertaken the immense job of bringing up the status of women so that love can succeed. Hopefully, so that her own emotional needs as a woman can eventually be fulfilled." Gloria frequently used the "love among equals" line in her own speeches to assure audiences that men were going to benefit from women's equality, too, but the reference to Betty's own emotional needs seemed gratuitous. Betty had not been attacking her yet, at least not in print, and in fact Gloria had meant no offense.

Then Gloria's star began to outshine Betty's. When Gloria was invited to speak at Smith's 1971 graduation ceremonies, her selection by the students of their joint alma mater hurt Betty: She had never been asked. Once Gloria appeared on the covers of *Newsweek, New Woman,* and *McCall's,* Betty became increasingly derogatory. In a February 1972 speech at Trinity College in Hartford, Connecticut, she said that Gloria had "never been a part of the organized" women's liberation movement. She added, "The media tried to make her a celebrity, but no one should mistake her for a leader." In the question-and-answer period after the speech she accused Gloria of "ripping off the movement for profit."

Gloria had tried to lower her profile after the Ocotober 1971 *Esquire* piece, but she was so stung she answered the charge. "The truth is that [working in the women's movement] continues to cost me money and every penny is worth it," she told the press.

Betty was forced to retreat. Explaining that there was "no feud between Gloria and me," she said the "ripping off the movement" statement had been "misquoted and out of context." Betty never provided the redeeming context, nor did she learn her lesson. She continued to dismay her friends as well as Gloria's by attacking Gloria.

In May 1972 Gloria addressed the thirtieth annual convention of the League of Women Voters. One of the issues facing the organization was whether to admit men, and Gloria agreed with the exclusionary position. "I can't understand why you need the validation of a man. The truth is we are not ready. We cannot integrate with men on an equal basis until we are equal," she told the group, adding, "If you admit men, let them do the typing, run the child-care centers, and donate money."

Her feisty speech drew several standing ovations. In discussing abortion she described "ancient white men and state legislatures . . . legislating the reproductive freedoms of women." Observing that 80 percent of the welfare rolls consisted of women and children, and that one-third of all women live in poverty, compared to 10 percent of the male population, she used one of her favorite lines to warn the middle-class audience, "Most of you in this room are only one man away from welfare yourself." Warming to her subject, she estimated that a husband would have to pay between $9,000 and $14,000 a year for the 99.6 hours of work a week provided by the average housewife and added, "And that's not including part-time prostitution privileges."

In her August 1972 *McCall's* column, "Beyond Women's Liberation," Betty came out swinging. She even held a press conference to publicize the fact that she had called Gloria, Bella, and all those who shared their ideas "female chauvinist boors." She used Gloria's quip about part-time prostitution to accuse her of equating marriage with prostitution, alleging Gloria had meant that "no woman would ever want to go to bed with a man if she didn't need to sell her body for bread or a mink coat."

If Betty's attack was prompted by her refusal to go quietly into the night, she also feared the movement was at a crossroads. The column's subhead summarized her contention: "The founder of the women's movement [*sic,* but it was her column] attacks the extremists of her own sex and warns that 'female chauvinist boors' are inviting a back-lash—from both men and women—which could destroy everything that has been so painfully won." Although the notion that eliminating angry rhetoric would prevent a backlash was wishful thinking, Betty had a point: "the assumption that women have any moral or spiritual superiority as a *class*" was "male chauvinism in reverse; it is female sexism." Furthermore, her misgivings that feminists in ensuing years would become diverted from their quest for equal rights into a path of separatism, polarity, and compensatory thinking were accurate to a certain extent.

On the other hand, while Betty was not wrong to object to a "female chauvinism that makes a woman apologize for loving her husband or children" the idea of encouraging female pride was not so terrible. And if Gloria's one-liners were chauvinistic, her explanations usually made clear her belief that women's supposedly superior virtues were acquired through conditioning or by adjustment to their circumstances, not innate to an alleged "female" nature.

In her column's silliest assertion, Betty used a male friend's reaction to an article Gloria had written for *Ms.* to prove that Gloria's inflammatory rhetoric was harmful. "Sisterhood," one of Gloria's most moving essays, was her introductory essay to *Ms.*'s first issue. In it she had chronicled her journey from pride at making it in a man's world, to "feminist revelation," to joy and pride at being among women. Incredibly, Betty seemed to believe she was making a case against Gloria by describing her male friend's reaction: "In a tone of cold, measured outrage I find positively startling (previously he has identified completely with the women's movement), he says: 'I think we have had just about enough of this.'" The essay that so outraged Betty's friend concluded with these inflammatory sentiments:

> For myself, I can now admit anger, and use it constructively. . . .
>
> I have met brave women who are exploring the outer edge of human possibility, with no history to guide them, and with a courage to make themselves vulnerable that I find moving beyond the words to express it. . . .
>
> I can sometimes deal with men as equals and therefore can afford to like them for the first time. . . .
>
> I no longer feel strange by myself, or with a group of women in public. I feel just fine.
>
> I am continually moved to discover I have sisters.
>
> I am beginning, just beginning, to find out who I am.

Betty may have thought she was objecting to Gloria's message, but it certainly seemed to most people that Betty's real target was the messenger.

There were many such slurs over the years, but Gloria rarely responded publicly. When she did, she was usually indirect or restricted herself to relatively obscure forums. That was her nature anyway, and she didn't want to fuel the media characterization of debates between women as cat fights. In the January 1974 *Lesbian Tide*, for example, she discussed the phenomenon of "horizontal hostility"—the attacks by movement women against each other:

> It's a little easier for me. It's harder on women whose total identity comes from the movement. Somehow if you've had a profession before [Ms. Steinem was an established journalist before entering the Movement] it's not quite so hard. But a woman who has never been able to be herself, to accomplish or to aspire, gets into the Movement and for the first time, she can. So one of two things happen. If she's like an old-style Betty Friedan person, she may go power-crazy because it's the first time in her life she's had a chance to express herself. Or if it's a younger

or out-of-the-male-left kind of person, then the version is, "I've been shit all my life so everyone else is going to be shit, too. No last names, no credit, communal everything." Somehow between these two extremes, we have to find a way of separating those things that can be done collectively from those which have to be done individually. You can't write poetry or edit communally.

On the rare occasions when Gloria lets slip a little hostility, she'll say that hers and Betty's times in the movement didn't overlap—which would be news to Betty and everyone else; or refer to Betty's "one book" in a tone that suggests that, after all, Betty's contribution was limited to her first book; or describe *The Feminine Mystique* as pertaining only to white, middle-class, suburban women, a group whose experience had no relevance for Gloria or for many others; or say that Betty doesn't like women; or suggest that no one took the National Women's Political Caucus seriously until Bella got involved; or use the explanation she gave the *Lesbian Tide* reporter: that, unlike herself, Betty relied on the movement for her identity.

Although they would cooperate and appear together over the years, Betty sometimes spoke to Gloria, and sometimes she didn't. In New York, at least, Bella Abzug and Gloria became one political center and Betty another.

24

Ms.: A Magazine for Female Human Beings

Ms. is a magazine for female human beings. Unlike traditional women's publications, it does not identify us by role—as wives, mothers, lovers or even as workers and professionals. It assumes that women are full human beings who are both complex and individual. . . . *Ms.* will help us seize control of our own lives and humanize the values around us.

Ms., A Statement of Purpose

Steinem promises to "refuse ads that are insulting," and has already ruled out vaginal deodorant promotions because she considers them "physically harmful." But ads for bras, which the movement supposedly regards as symbolic shackles, will be accepted.

Time, December 20, 1971

I give *Ms.* five months, tops.

Harry Reasoner, ABC News

Brenda Feigen Fasteau first met Gloria Steinem when Gloria testified at the May 1970 congressional Equal Rights Amendment hearings at Brenda's request. Right afterward, Brenda went to work at a large New

York law firm and the two became friends. One November day six months later, Brenda walked out of the firm and straight over to Gloria's. Although she had been NOW's legislative vice president, Brenda wanted to form a separate organization to help women at a local level, and she wanted Gloria to help.

Gloria agreed. In the year and a half she had been traveling and speaking, she had seen how much information women needed. They began planning the Women's Action Alliance, an organization they envisioned as particularly oriented toward women who were not in organizations, but who needed help dealing with a number of problems in their daily lives. They planned to start with a clearinghouse and information-referral service for local action projects all over the country. From there they would expand to offer those projects educational and technical assistance. Eventually they hoped to develop projects and publish materials themselves, such as information packets on how to start a consciousness-raising group or a nonsexist childcare center.

Gloria and Brenda contacted funding sources, put together a prestigious board that included John Kenneth Galbraith, Bella Abzug, and Shirley Chisholm, and began visiting foundations to get grant money. Most had no category specifically for women, but eventually they received some contributions. They began developing, in-house, an early-childhood education project on nonsexist childcare that included bibliographies, a curriculum guide for teachers, and even games and other materials.

Gloria and Brenda thought about raising money through a newsletter, but they found that the only newsletters that were making money offered stock tips. Brenda thought in grander terms anyway. "You're already too well known to just do a newsletter," she told Gloria. "We should do a magazine."

"We'll never get advertising," Gloria objected. Brenda thought otherwise, and a couple of businesswomen she consulted agreed that advertisers would support such a magazine.

Brenda was the first to suggest that Gloria start a glossy feminist magazine, but the idea was already in the air. Clay Felker had considered doing it himself. Gloria, who always says Clay's idea of a feminist solution was to run an article about importing more women from Jamaica to be maids so U.S. women could go out and get jobs, discouraged him. Clay eventually abandoned the idea, but he still thought a feminist magazine should be started. He regarded Gloria as the ideal person to develop it.

There were other contenders. Writers Susan Brownmiller, Nora Ephron, and Sally Kempton wanted to launch a magazine they would call *Jane*, but they could not attract investors. Another group actually began publishing *New Woman* in July 1971, but *New Woman*'s only credible association with feminism was Caroline Bird, who wrote several pieces for it and advised the editors. Other than that, *New Woman*'s editors seemed somewhat confused about the concept of women's liberation: Their first issue featured a well-endowed, bare-breasted woman doing business from her bed. "It was a feminist publication for five minutes," *Ms.* publisher Pat Carbine later joked.

Radical feminists had been publishing news and ideas since 1968, when Jo Freeman started *Voice of the Women's Liberation Movement* in Chicago. By 1971 there were more than one hundred feminist journals and newspapers, but they had small circulations and many were only mimeographed.

Gloria remained unconvinced that a magazine should be launched. Even if it were, she was not at all sure she wanted to launch it herself. She finally was getting the writing assignments she had sought for years. Besides, freelancing suited her. As she always told people, she found security in insecurity and dreaded the idea of knowing what she would be doing the following year.

However, in January and February 1971, Gloria and Brenda invited a number of New York women to two meetings, one at each of their apartments, to discuss whether there really was a need for such a magazine. Writers, editors, and activists crowded in and talked for hours of their frustration. The prospect of publishing their ideas and reporting on the concepts and activities of the movement, uncensored and unfiltered through biased, trivializing, hostile editors, was exhilarating.

Finding writers obviously was not going to be a problem, but finding backers was. Kennedy aide Richard Goodwin suggested to Brenda that Elizabeth Forsling Harris might be able to help them. An intelligent and charming ex-journalist and public relations executive, Betty Harris was well connected politically. After working in magazines and television in New York, she spent sixteen years in Dallas, Texas, where she got to know then-Senator Lyndon Johnson and Speaker of the House Sam Rayburn. She later worked closely with R. Sargent Shriver, as the highest-ranking woman in the Peace Corps. When she became interested in founding a women's magazine "that was really about women, not fifteen ways to make hamburgers," she went to California to work with the publisher of *Psychology Today*, publishing a non-glossy periodical called *Majority Report*.

Betty seemed to be qualified for the job, but when Brenda and Betty began to discuss Betty's role as the magazine's publisher, they disagreed so much that Gloria interceded. Until then she had not spent much time with Betty, but she suggested that Brenda concentrate on the alliance and she would work with Betty and the magazine.

That was fine with Brenda. She worked full-time on the alliance until February 1972, when she left to run the American Civil Liberties Union's Women's Rights Project with Ruth Bader Ginsburg. Gloria was left with what would become a beloved albatross—apparently for the rest of her life.

As soon as Gloria began to believe she really might be starting a magazine, she met with Patricia Carbine, the new editor of *McCall's* and highest ranking woman in magazine publishing. The two had known each other professionally for several years through *Look* magazine.

Gloria's Playboy Bunny piece "was the first zap, as far as I was concerned, of Gloria as a journalist," Pat recalls. In 1963, Pat had been *Look*'s managing editor, which was unusual for a journalist in her thirties, much less for a woman. There were no others at a general interest magazine. Although *Look* was more welcoming to women than many other magazines, Pat recalls, "Would-be journalists who were female went into the steno pool and would-be journalists who were male would start at a more elevated level."

Pat had been more fortunate. She had edited her high school and college newspapers and had always wanted to be a journalist. Fresh out of college in 1953, she obtained an interview at *Look*. When she appeared in white gloves and a veil, she so impressed promotion staff member Gene Shalit that he told the personnel department she should be hired because she was "one of a dying breed." The research director hired her as a researcher. Six years later the editor shocked Pat by elevating her to assistant managing editor. The promotion would have been a meteoric rise, even for a man in his twenties, and Pat insisted that the editor explain why she, as opposed to the other possible candidates, had been chosen.

Then she had to adjust to her new status: "What was on my mind was offsetting or resisting the temptation to believe that being in the room with the 'grown-ups' meant that you were the exceptional woman. It's hard to resist that, and it was an ongoing process. I think you go through stages. The first is, what am I doing here? The second is, can I do it? The third was I'll prove I can do it to make this gutsy editor appear as if he made a gutsy and intelligent move. Then one discovers that you bring quite a lot to the table—that your ideas are very often as good, if not better. And from there, it's a very short step to, why aren't there more of us in the room? Especially because this is a magazine talking to what we called a dual audience."

Pat became managing editor in 1966 and executive editor in 1969, which made her the highest-ranking woman at a general-interest magazine. Although by then she was not the only female magazine executive, the concept of women in high places still seemed so strange that when *Look's* editor died, the owner, Gardner Cowles, refused to consider promoting Pat to take his place. Cowles had offered her the editorship of *Family Circle* years before, but, he told her, he didn't think the world was ready for a woman editor to run *Look* magazine.

Also dismayed at the conservative path the business side of the magazine seemed to be taking, Pat left in 1970 ("as a protest and in a way I felt would be least hurtful to *Look*") to become the editorial director of *McCall's* magazine, a position that made her the highest-ranking woman in magazine publishing.

Pat recalls Gloria's arrival at the *Look* offices to discuss writing a column: "I liked her very much. She was extremely smart and funny and she undid the guys with the combination of—I don't know in what order, but the elements were the hair, the smile, and the leather miniskirt. We all came up from the dining room and were on the editorial floor, and you know there's someone special when the gents all poke their noses out of their offices to get a look at 'the visitor with the great legs.' As good legs go, she's got 'em. And they were very visible with that miniskirt. But predictably, it was her mind and her insights that we discussed with admiration after she left."

Pat stuck her neck out for Gloria, both at *Look* and *McCall's*. *Look's* advertising managers were trying to kill an article on Cesar Chavez, because they worried they would lose advertisers if they ran a favorable story about the labor organizer. After much negotiating, Gloria suggested she write the interview as a dialogue, using only Chavez's words. They finally agreed, and Gloria did not find out until years later that they had capitulated not because of her idea, but because Pat had threatened to quit if they didn't. "It was just like Pat to threaten," she says. "And also just like her not to tell me."

Pat also had to fight to get Gloria named *McCall's* 1972 Woman of the Year. After the magazine's editors had chosen Gloria—and seven million covers with Gloria's picture had been printed—Pat's superiors balked. "No way," they said, when they saw the cover. "She can't be *McCall's* Woman of the Year."

They ordered Pat to scrap all seven million and start all over. "What's your idea, then?" Pat asked. "Who did you have in mind?"

"How about Pat Nixon?" someone suggested.

"Then you'll have to scrap me, too," Pat told them. They backed down.

Pat was an obvious star, and Gloria knew that if she started a feminist magazine, Pat should be its editor in chief. Although she was at the top of her profession, Pat was intrigued. "The idea of starting out fresh with a totally clean slate—or a totally clean roll of paper—was very, very, very appealing," she says. She did not know if she would leave her position with all its perquisites and stock options and opportunities, but from the beginning she cared enough about the idea to spend many evenings with Gloria, in a bar close to their apartments, talking about everything from circulation and advertising to ideas for stories and sections.

In the meantime, Betty Harris was not finding backers. Finally she and Gloria decided to accept Clay Felker's offer to try out the concept as a special section in *New York* magazine and then publish a sample issue.

New York put out a double issue at the end of the year, and since Clay also wanted practice in producing a "one-shot" (a magazine devoted to a single subject), he had offered to test the feminist magazine by wrapping a 44-page section into *New York* magazine itself. From the material that would be prepared for a sample issue, Clay would choose about 30 pages for the insert, and *New York*'s advertising sales staff would sell ads to run in both publications. Clay also supplied *New York* magazine production staff for the entire 130-page sample issue and underwrote the $125,000 out-of-pocket expense. In return, he planned to keep the advertising revenues and half the proceeds, if there were any, from the newsstand sales of the 300,000-copy sample issue.

With the participation of many of the women at *New York* magazine, Gloria, Betty Harris, and a few others began organizing. The original group consisted of Gloria, Betty Harris, Joanne Edgar, Nina Finkelstein, Mary Peacock, and Letty Cottin Pogrebin.

After working together at the National Women's Political Caucus, Gloria had invited Letty to come to help organize the magazine. Letty, thirty-two, had graduated from Brandeis University at the age of nineteen and worked as a publicist and vice president overseeing a staff of four for publisher Bernard Geis. She had already written a book, *How to Make It in a Man's World,* and was extremely efficient.

Joanne Edgar was Gloria's personal assistant. A gentle, soft-spoken Southerner, Joanne had left her job at Facts on File in 1971 to work in the Mississippi gubernatorial campaign of Charles Evers, the brother of slain civil-rights leader Medgar Evers. Then civil-rights activist and Democratic Policy Council member Patt Derian sent Joanne to help Gloria work on some hearings the Democratic Party was planning on women and employment. It never held the hearings, but when Gloria began working on the National Women's Political Caucus, Joanne joined her. Once the caucus was formed, Joanne returned to New York as Gloria's administrative assistant, doing research, typing her letters, and coordinating her speaking engagements.

Mary Peacock, a magazine veteran, had worked at *Harper's Bazaar* and had just founded a counterculture fashion magazine called *Rags.* She accepted Gloria's invitation to work on the trial issue when Gloria agreed to let her edit the sections she wanted. Letty brought in Nina Finkelstein, a Scribner's editor who could both edit and utilize her publishing contacts with book editors and agents.

Although everyone worked on every piece in the initial issue, its editorial sensibility was Gloria's. "You can see me in the first issue, I think," she allows—an unusual admission from Gloria, who likes to describe everything connected with the magazine as a group process. "That I edited essentially by myself, and you can see that. You can see the female Krishna on the cover and the articles, but after that I never again edited an issue."

The insert issue set a *New York* newsstand sales record, and the entire preview issue went on sale the last week in January 1972. Because they feared it might sit on the newsstands a long time, they dated it "Spring 1972." Gloria went to San Francisco to promote the magazine and found none on the newsstands. She called Clay, upset because the copies were late, but when Clay checked, he learned that the magazine had sold out. Nationwide, all 300,000 copies had been bought in eight days. They had a hit.

It took another month for Gloria to talk Pat into leaving *McCall's.* No matter how much enthusiasm *Ms.* had generated, giving up

McCall's was an enormous risk. Pat's financial sacrifice would be immediate, and even if they were able to get financing—which they still lacked—they had no idea when or if *Ms.* would become profitable. Although 26,000 readers had responded to the trial issue with subscription requests and checks, that was not enough to start a magazine, much less to continue operating.

It was also clear by then that Betty Harris had to be replaced. There had been conflicts from the beginning. Not only had Betty not raised the needed money, but she had interfered and argued with everyone. Pat was already a silent third partner with Gloria and Betty in the magazine's holding company, Majority Enterprises, Inc. Once Pat and Gloria saw that the partnership was not going to work, they began negotiating to buy Betty out. The discussions eventually became so protracted and acrimonious that at one point Gloria and Pat told Betty to take the magazine herself if she could do so. When Betty was unable to find a backer, Gloria and Pat finally bought out her interest in the company by giving her the $20,000 proceeds from the spring 1972 issue.

That left them with even less money for a start-up, and still no major backing. They did have $20,000 from Katharine Graham, the owner and publisher of *Newsweek* and the *Washington Post*. Gloria had first met Graham in 1969, several months after Gloria became a feminist. Filled with missionary fervor, Gloria had asked if she could talk with her about the women's movement. "No, no, that's not for me," responded the most powerful woman in publishing, who felt a little overwhelmed.

"If you understood it, it would make your life better," Gloria persisted, but still Graham demurred.

Eventually Gloria wore her down. As Graham wrote in her 1997 autobiography,

> I recall her encouraging me to throw off some of the myths associated with my old-style thinking. She said, "That's General Motors passing through our womb—you know, it goes from our fathers to our sons. But there is this kind of authentic self in there that is a guide if it's not too squelched and if we're not too scared to listen to it." I was pretty certain that whatever authentic self I may have had had been pretty well squelched, but Gloria kept telling me that if I came to understand what the women's movement was all about it would make my life much better.

When Betty, Pat, and Gloria came to see her, Graham was torn. She regarded the project as a worthy endeavor and hated to turn them away, but she was reluctant to invest. Clay Felker suggested that she give them a small amount, so instead of the requested one million dollars, Katharine Graham contributed $20,000 of her own money. They were grateful and believed it enhanced their credibility—not to mention, giving them walking-around money. They needed it.

Finally, in May, through Letty Pogrebin's contact with Warner Communications executive Kenneth Rosen, Warner agreed to give *Ms.* one million dollars in exchange for 25 percent of the preferred equity. It was Warner's first minority position and a tiny investment for the corporate giant, but it was a nice public relations gesture. For *Ms.,* it was a godsend. When Betty Harris learned of the Warner investment, she became convinced that she had been cheated out of her share of *Ms.*'s equity. In 1975, she sued Gloria, Pat, and the magazine, but the suit was dismissed when she failed to follow up.

After the preview issue succeeded, Gloria and Pat began to expand the staff in anticipation of launching a monthly magazine. They had assumed that Pat would run the editorial side, but with Betty gone, Pat functioned as both editor in chief and publisher, and most of her time was taken by the business side. There was no indication of Pat's position in the magazine, however. In an attempt to avoid traditional, supposedly masculine hierarchies, and in keeping with the idea that everyone's ideas counted equally, *Ms.* eschewed titles and listed staff members alphabetically on the masthead, under general headings such as Editing, Publishing, and Advertising.

In reality, some employees were more equal than others. Pat was indeed the publisher, and she and Gloria had final editorial authority—they were also the owners, after all. Gloria later recalled, "I remember we sat around a table in a Chinese restaurant and fixed each others' salaries. We decided that the top should be no more than three times the lowest. I said I needed $15,000, so they gave me $20,000 so I could give away $5,000."

Pat brought in two *McCall's* associates, copy editor Cathy O'Haire and production chief Rita Waterman, and by the September 1972 issue, she had an advertising sales staff of four. Through Betty Harris's friendship with Bill Moyers, Moyers's friend, financier Jim Marshall, and Marshall's accountant, Arthur Tarlow, had become involved in advising the magazine. Even after Betty left, Arthur continued to work at *Ms.* as consultant and accountant for the next fifteen years, cherishing his position as *Ms.*'s "token man."

The editorial side expanded as well, to include, among others, Mary Thom, who had worked with Joanne Edgar at Facts on File; Margaret

Sloan, Gloria's frequent speaking partner; and Harriet Lyons, a *Fan* magazine veteran, who was hilarious, as well as a talented editor. She had met Dorothy Pitman Hughes when she used her childcare center. Knowing that Gloria's penchant for inclusivity bordered on parody, Dorothy sent Harriet to Gloria with the message, "I'm sorry she isn't black or on welfare, but she could help you." Letty brought in Suzanne Braun Levine, besides Pat and Mary Peacock, the only one who had actually run a magazine (*Sexual Behavior*). Suzanne was managing editor, although, to maintain the fiction of equality, she was never given the title.

Gloria and Pat envisioned their new monthly as a general-interest magazine, comparable more to *Newsweek* and *Time* than to other women's magazines—it would cover world and national news and culture, albeit from a feminist perspective. Although neither Gloria nor Pat was particularly motivated to make a lot of money (fortunately), they intended to make *Ms.* a commercially successful venture that would attract advertisers. At the same time, they envisioned the magazine as a movement vehicle. The two purposes were at loggerheads from the beginning.

They wanted to serve the movement editorially by disseminating feminist ideas to the greater public and by providing a forum for women's voices. They also planned to serve the movement financially by contributing at least 10 percent of the magazine's profits to feminist causes. Gloria liked to say she hoped *Ms.* would be a "portable friend," but it became much more. *Ms.* became the dominant voice of feminist ideas and information to the world.

The communication went both ways. From the beginning, *Ms.*'s readers felt an intense sense of ownership. They considered themselves part of a community and deluged the magazine with their poetry, fiction, articles, and letters. About 500 unsolicited manuscripts arrived each week, plus 400 submissions to the "No Comment" section, which displayed offensive ads sent in by readers. The "Letters to the Editors" column, always a popular magazine section, was overwhelmed. The 7 million readers of *McCall's* usually sent in 200–400 letters per monthly issue. *Ms.* received between 200 and 1,000 letters a week during its first year, from a much smaller readership. Subscriptions rose during the first year from 145,000 to 200,000, plus almost 200,000 newsstand sales, which, with multiple readers per copy, translated into about 1.5 million readers.

Readers wrote *Ms.* about everything, in or out of the magazine. They responded to the articles; they responded to the other readers' letters;

they sent in their own life stories. They complained about or praised individual advertisements—one reader found an ad in *Ms.* so offensive, she sent it to the magazine's "No Comment" section.

Feminist activists were vociferous as well. Feeling the same sense of ownership, they complained that *Ms.* was too radical, too male-bashing, not radical enough, too conservative, too politically correct, too elitist, too white-middle-class. Letty Pogrebin recalls, "We were visited by every possible interest group. A housewives' rights group came when we'd just finished meeting with a lesbians' group. The lesbians thought the magazine didn't have enough about lesbians. The housewives complained that there was too much about lesbian lifestyles."

Writers complained that their work was watered down and too heavily edited to conform to a *Ms.* style and a *Ms.* party line. The problem was too many good intentions. As Mary Peacock recalls: "The reason *Ms.* wasn't as vital as it could have been is that we were afraid of saying something bad. Everything had to put women in a good light instead of letting doubting and confused voices be heard. Although Gloria tried to have a big-tent policy, in that sense, the big tent didn't work. . . . In *Ms.* women's voices were being heard in a fresh way for the first time, but in my opinion, as time went by and it became more established, that's when they should have blown it out a little and let some wilder points of view in."

Ex-Redstocking Ellen Willis worked as a part-time contributing editor for a few years. In addition to her background as a political activist and theorist, Ellen was an experienced journalist and rock-music critic for the *New Yorker*. To Ellen, "There were two different kinds of editorial problems. One was that there was very much a disregard for, and even contempt for, writers and writing. It was a very editor-driven magazine. They did not really have any interest in the writers' individual voice.

"The second is that it was very what would now be called politically correct. Trying to get a view in there that was unorthodox or quote, irresponsible, unquote, was not impossible, but it was difficult and involved fights, yelling and screaming fights. I was a yeller and screamer, and I think I got my way sometimes just because most of the people there hated yelling and screaming, hated confrontation. Things tended to be done sort of by quiet manipulation. I would win fights, but it was very exhausting always having to make them."

Gloria defends the editors: "Writers treated us so differently from other magazines, it wasn't funny. We felt like battered editors. They would give us manuscripts that were illegible that they would never have given to anybody else. They would object to the smallest changes . . ."

Many of the changes didn't seem so small to the writers. Susan Braudy, who worked as a staff writer and editor, edited *Ms.*'s high-selling but controversial issue on men. She recalls, "In the beginning, it was fresh and exploring new territory. Then it became like cant. One time Robin Morgan [who came to work at *Ms.*] inserted a paragraph about child pornography into a movie review I wrote. That was the beginning of the end for me."

Patricia Mainardi, another ex-Redstocking and an art critic, was appalled by her experience: "I always assumed *Ms.* never paid much so people tossed off their articles for them. Then my piece came back with the barbarous *Ms.* style. Jerky sentences, non sequiturs, *Ms.* words. They would use a bullshit word instead of a strong word. I had the word 'loved.' They changed it to 'had a fondness for.' . . . [W]hen the article came out [December 1973] they had changed the title. I had 'Quilts, the Great American Art.' They changed it to 'Quilts, a Great American Art.' My whole thesis is that quilts are *the* American art form, undervalued as jazz was once undervalued in music. . . . As a critic I have the right to say quilts are the great American art."

Gloria recalls the same incident: "There was a woman who wrote a piece called 'Quilts, the Great American Art.' And we changed it to 'Quilts, a Great American Art,' out of deference to five hundred Native American nations and a few other things. She never forgave us. For changing 'the' to 'a.' "

Gloria also recalls *Ms.*'s nontraditional sources of material: "It was very helpful that I traveled, because it was important to us—two things: one, that we not only use New York writers and, two, that we not only use writers. So we often used tape recordings and diaries and letters. That's why it was so labor intensive to edit the magazine."

Suzanne Levine remembers it differently: "If Gloria really stopped to think about it, I can't think of a single piece by a nonwriter that ever ended up in the magazine. Well, there must have been two or three."

Besides examining every aspect of the world through the fresh lens of a feminist perspective, the editors tried to run the magazine as democratically as possible. Other publications had experimented with equally egalitarian goals, but the process at *Ms.* was probably the most heavy-handed. In the beginning the editors passed around every article for everyone else's comments, but soon even the most idealistic realized the process was too cumbersome. Their idea of a solution was to reduce the number of extra editors per article to three. That meant the editor in charge of an article chose three other editors and those three edited it as well. Actually, each piece was edited by five editors, since managing editor Suzanne Levine also saw everything. Although Suzanne had the authority to decide which articles went in which issue, she did not have veto power: If three editors wanted an article published, she had to include it at some point.

Then there was the determination that they should be their own secretaries—an idea they later realized was elitist. For a long time, as Letty Pogrebin recalls, "We all did our own shitwork. And let me say there was a huge amount of shitwork, and there was nobody to help you. At times we found ourselves trapped in our own theory. We were very idealistic and thought everyone should be valued for what she brought to the table and tried to find each woman's particular strength. But when too many weak links slowed down the publishing process or made things difficult for the rest of us, there were some painful confrontations having to do with what Jo Freeman called the tyranny of structurelessness [*Ms.*, July 1973]."

Mary Peacock, who was one of the few experienced magazine professionals on the staff, remembers, "I viewed myself as a magazine editor, not as a feminist whose day job was magazine editing, though I was delighted to work at *Ms.* The alphabetical masthead was a silly idea, because the magazine was not a commune. We had meetings and the people with no experience would sometimes complain afterward that their ideas always lost out to other people's. But of course the professionals would prevail. Anyway, experimenting wasn't horrible."

Reflecting the group's fear that the first issue might represent their only chance to get the word out, the preview issue was packed. In one of several classic articles, Barbaralee Diamonstein discussed the inhumanity and danger of the prevailing abortion laws. With it, *Ms.* ran a two-page spread entitled, "We have had abortions," followed by the names of fifty-three prominent women, who were not only revealing an extremely personal secret; they were confessing to an illegal act. They included singer Judy Collins, tennis star Billie Jean King, poet Ann Sexton, and many writers, including Anaïs Nin, Nora Ephron, Lillian Hellman, and Barbara Tuchman. Gloria signed it as well, and told Ruth and Sue about her abortion just before the ad appeared. Ruth was hurt because Gloria hadn't told her years before and, Gloria says, because

Gloria was admitting she had had sex before. She accused Gloria of pretending and told her daughter, "Every starlet says that."

They assigned *New York* contributing editor Jane O'Reilly to write about housewives, because she had been one, and she produced another classic of 1970s popular feminist history, "The Housewife's Moment of Truth." She used the word *click* to portray those moments when women's consciousness was raised, as in, "In New York last fall, my neighbors—named Jones—had a couple named Smith over for dinner. Mr. Smith kept telling his wife to get up and help Mrs. Jones. Click! Click! Two women radicalized at once."

Issues of marriage and children were well covered. Besides "I Want a Wife," by Judy Syfers, which was the most reprinted and anthologized article in the issue, they included "How to Write Your Own Marriage Contract," by Susan Edmiston, "Down With Sexist Upbringing," by Letty Pogrebin; "Child Care Centers: Who, How, and Where," by Linda Franke and Dorothy Pitman Hughes; and "Boys and Girls, Girls and Boys: A Story for Free Children," by Eve Merriam. Letty, assigned to write on children's issues because she had twin daughters, became so interested in the subject that she devoted the next seven years to writing a nonsexist child-rearing guide.

Working women were addressed in "Heaven Won't Protect the Working Girl," by Louise Bernikow, which discussed sex discrimination (the concept of sexual harassment did not yet exist); "The Black Family and Feminism: A Conversation With Eleanor Holmes Norton," by Celestine Ware; and "My Mother, the Dentist" by Nicholas von Hoffman.

They approached politics from several angles. In "Rating the Candidates, Feminists Vote the Rascals In or Out," Brenda Feigen Fasteau and Bonnie Lobel evaluated eleven political leaders in terms of Taking Women Seriously, Making Waves, and two dimensions of Machismo Factor ("personal rejection of the traditional 'masculine' role," and "opposition to militarism and violence"). *Ms.* also ran "Welfare Is a Woman's Issue," by Johnnie Tillmon, who had organized the first welfare-rights organization, and "Daniel Ellsberg Talks About Women and War."

The issue addressed concerns the radical feminists were exploring—psychological and biological issues, sexuality, the internalization of oppression. They ran "Men's Cycles (They Have Them Too, You Know)" by Dr. Estelle Ramey; "Why Women Fear Success," by Vivian Gornick; and "The Sexual Revolution Wasn't Our War," in which feminist actress Anselma Dell'Olio wrote on vaginal orgasms. (Gloria had called Anselma and said, "Write that thing you say.") Anne Koedt, author of the famous "Myth of the Vaginal Orgasm," wrote about being a lesbian in "Can Women Love Women?" because, as Gloria said, "People said we shouldn't write about lesbians in the first issue, so naturally we had to."

As a magazine devoted to a movement that was political in every sense, *Ms.*'s politics were important. In the beginning, there was Gloria. The others on the original staff considered themselves feminists, but none of them had Gloria's political experiences—electoral, radical, non-Communist left, New Left. When Ellen Willis, bona fide radical, joined the staff, sparks began to fly. Ellen, whom Gloria describes as pugnacious, recalls: "I think that Gloria—who I liked personally and got along with until I left at the end—invented a certain kind of politics that was a logical outgrowth of what was going on in the women's movement. . . . I think the difference between Gloria Steinem and Betty Friedan was analogous to the difference between Gene McCarthy, Robert Kennedy, and the New Politics–type of liberals versus liberals like Hubert Humphrey . . .

"That is, Gloria's was a kind of liberal adaptation or assimilation of radical feminist ideas, which traditional liberals like Betty Friedan were just rejecting—they were saying this is about economics. . . .

"Gloria certainly made a big contribution to getting certain kinds of ideas into the mainstream. She was sort of a liberal, New Politics feminist. She's not a radical, and I deeply disagree with her about any number of things. But, in America, radical ideas tend to assimilate into liberalism, and I don't think it's fair to demonize her."

Robin Morgan, another leading radical activist, also became a *Ms.* contributing editor, but by the mid-1970s radical feminists were diverging, and she and Ellen Willis were going in different directions. As Letty Pogrebin sees it, "There were real philosophical differences. With Ellen Willis, and between Ellen and Robin Morgan, whereas Robin and Gloria bonded. When Robin joined us, it was a seismic moment for the magazine, because Robin had been one of the key thinkers of radical feminism, and it was important to have her voice on our pages." (Robin strongly influenced Gloria's feminist politics.)

The 1970s were years of incredible discovery. Gloria still said the problems that had new names were what women used to just call "life": unequal pay for equal or equivalent work, sexual harassment and all kinds of other workplace inequities; rape, date rape, marital rape; the connection between pornography and violence against women; wife battering; the prevalence of incest; illegal abortion and, once abortion became legal, barriers to obtaining one.

Ms. covered it all—and good news, too. It retrieved women's history by running stories about the lives of real women of the past, both achievers and ordinary women. Every issue included fiction and poetry by women, and reviews of works by and about women—stories, poetry, books, plays, music, visual art, crafts. They published some of the earliest work by Alice Walker, Andrea Dworkin, and Mary Gordon, widened the reading audiences for Doris Lessing, Margaret Drabble, and Margaret Atwood, and included work by such diverse authors as Virginia Woolf, Margaret Fuller, and Anaïs Nin.

Politics were at the core: feminist political theory, general electoral politics, women candidates, and the implications for women of every issue. *Ms.*'s coverage of economic issues and the workplace included stories of labor organizing as well as entrepreneurial and corporate successes. The magazine explored women's health issues like the dangers of breast implants and alternatives to radical mastectomy. Nonsexist childrearing was a frequent topic, as were marriage and alternative living arrangements. Lesbians were portrayed positively, both in terms of lesbian issues and just as individuals who happened to be lesbians.

In their desire to be democratic, positive, and inclusive, the editors committed excesses—editing to the point of homogenization, inclusivity to the point of silliness, positivity sometimes to the point of distortion, cliquishness to the point of favoritism, self-promotion to the point of exaggeration (there seemed to be a *Ms.* view of feminist history). Their contributions far outstripped their faults, though, and *Ms.* became the voice for the second wave of feminism.

25

They Looked at Us Like
We Were Martians

At *Ms.* they always had more editorial material than they knew what
to do with, but they never had enough money. They earned a profit
for the first time in 1974, and lost money most of the time thereafter.

In their original discussions, Gloria and Pat actually considered
accepting no advertisements and letting subscriptions and newsstand
copies support the magazine. They wanted to be taken seriously, however, and they believed that, without advertising, the magazine would
seem too much like a movement vehicle and not sufficiently mainstream. Besides, Pat says, they thought "much could be done through
influencing advertising."

"Much" was certainly what they attempted—they created such a
high-minded and difficult-to-fulfill advertising policy that they seemed
motivated by a death wish. First, they priced their advertising space
completely out of scale to other women's magazines. Magazines typically set their advertising-space rates on a cost-per-thousand-readers
(CPM) basis. When *Ms.* was launched in 1972, women's magazines
typically charged advertisers a little over two dollars per thousand readers. By contrast, magazines not catering to women charged far more—
the going rate for male readers was a little over eleven dollars per
thousand.

Pat and Gloria made *Ms.* the first magazine to segment the women's market. They decided to reinforce the point that women were worth as much as men by charging advertisers the going rate they paid to attract men. It seemed perfectly logical to them. Since *Ms.* resembled a newsweekly more than a traditional women's magazine, they assumed they would attract a readership demographically and psychographically similar to the newsweeklies' (psychographics provide attitudinal profiles based on socioeconomic and geographic profiles). They modeled their rates after *Psychology Today* because they envisioned a similar readership and told advertisers they expected them to pay the same rates they were willing to pay for the same type of male reader.

Their decision was based on practicality as well as principle and wishful thinking. They knew from the beginning that their magazine would never attract the circulation in the millions of a typical "Seven Sisters" magazine like *McCall's, Ladies' Home Journal,* or *Redbook.* Theirs was predominantly text, and such magazines' circulation usually ran up to 500,000. Mostly-illustration magazines' circulation typically ran much higher. For example, with *McCall's* paid circulation of seven million (plus pass-along readers) the typical women's rate of two dollars per thousand would generate enough revenue to be profitable. At *Ms.*'s expected circulation—a few hundred thousand—it would not.

The media buyers were not impressed with their logic, and they certainly did not care about their economics. "They'd say, Why should we buy from you? We can get them cheaper. . . . I got hooted at with such regularity," Pat recalls. After all, women were women, regardless of psychographics. As she liked to say, advertisers thought women could be bought "by the ton."

Gloria and Pat also planned to change the world by attracting advertisers who did not traditionally market to women, another goal based on both principle and practicality. The traditional advertisers to women were manufacturers of food, household products, and cosmetics, industries dominated by packaged-goods giants like Procter & Gamble, Kellogg's, Kimberly-Clark, Nabisco, and Revlon, who bought media in terms of volume. They were not going to be interested in the kind of circulation *Ms.* would offer, so Gloria and Pat knew they initially would have to look elsewhere. Pat considered them Phase II.

Making a virtue of necessity, they turned to the automobile, liquor, and electronics industries, which they believed should be advertising to women anyway. When at *Look,* Pat had spent a lot of time in Detroit, and she was determined to get automotive advertising for *Ms.* Auto-

3

2

mobile advertisements in women's magazines were not completely unknown—a couple even had run in *Glamour*—but they were extremely rare. Manufacturers believed men bought the cars, women chose the upholstery color.

Gloria and Pat also planned to reject advertisements they considered demeaning to women. Since advertising agencies generally created their ads in campaigns—one series of advertisements that ran everywhere during a given time period—that meant *Ms.*'s policy could add yet another barrier. Even if they managed to convince a media buyer and his client (they were usually men or groups of men) to take not one but three chances—(1) go into a new, unproven magazine, (2) spend more than five times the going rate for female readers, and (3) sell to women, which they did rarely, if ever, then they might have to ask them to adapt an ad just for *Ms.* If that happened, they knew they would be taunted with "So you think we're going to make a special ad just for *Ms.*?" They tried as much as possible to avoid that trap by soliciting ads from companies they thought might be more receptive to their goals. It wasn't easy.

Making a hard sell even harder were two other complications. One was that the ad salesmen were going to be women. Like automobile advertising to women, ad saleswomen were not totally unknown (*New York* had some), but they were so rare that Pat finally decided to create them by hiring women out of advertising agency media-buying departments. Pat explains, "I figured there was a pool of talent sitting in media departments listening to guys pitching every day. So their experience came from listening."

The last barrier to ad sales was the magazine's content. Much of it far surpassed unprecedented; it was downright threatening. Part of the problem was what would not be there—the "complementary copy" advertisers in women's magazines expected and often demanded, but which *Ms.* was unwilling to provide. Cosmetics companies wanted articles on makeup; apparel manufacturers wanted fashion spreads; food companies expected recipes.

The other part was what *would* be there. Much of what *Ms.* did include was controversial; it created what the trade called a "hostile editorial environment." *Ms.* was putting in battered women. Lesbians. Abortion. Black women and white women together. Old women on the cover. Genital mutilation. Angry women on page after page.

Even more important, the ideas *Ms.* espoused threatened the very privileges of those to whom they were trying to sell. Pat recalls: "I used to refer to our sales folks as agents of change, educators. They were not selling a commodity. They were selling a world change, a life change, a culture change to the major decision makers. And the decision makers were mostly men, and they didn't welcome the implications of the change. They were going home at night and hearing from their wives, 'I'm going to look for work that pays me,' and in the office, they were hearing, 'I'm not going to get your coffee.' We were perceived as the folks making their personal and office lives more uncomfortable."

The fact that *Ms.* had trouble attracting advertisers is not surprising. That it got any at all seems a miracle. Amazingly, it did—slowly, painstakingly, at great expense in hours, dollars, effort, and humiliation. Even when they could interest the agencies' media department, the agency people would ask the *Ms.* salespeople to talk to the client directly, which meant they had to sell every account twice. Gloria recalls, "I used to go out to Chicago or to Los Angeles, places where we had one lone salesperson, and it used to bring tears to my eyes, because I'd see them getting up in the morning and trying to look nice and putting on a nice suit when they would rather put on jeans. And taking heavy cases of issues and photographs and whatever presentation they had. And renting a car and taking a map and going into literally unknown territory to go see some advertiser. And having to do everything twice. . . . To see these young women going off in the morning so bravely . . . well, it was incredibly touching."

They endured every response, from ridicule to derision to outright hostility. Ad saleswoman Seena Harris-Parker recalls, "I went on a sales call at a well-known agency. The guy admitted me to his office and then said, 'I wouldn't buy a page in your lesbian rag if you paid me. I just wanted to see what a lesbian looked like. You don't look like a lesbian.' I couldn't think of a thing to say. It was all a baptism by fire. In that case Pat called the president of the agency."

When they finally succeeded in making a sale, their challenges were only beginning. If they actually landed an advertising schedule, the ad saleswomen were the ones who had to tell the agencies when their ads were unacceptable. Seena recalls: "I broke my back to get Bulova at Doyle, Dane and I finally got the business. Then they called me to come over and see their brand-new ad campaign directed at women. The first ad was two kids looking forlorn on the school steps, and the headline said, 'If Mommy had worn a Bulova . . .' The second ad showed a woman standing in the rain, drenched, and said, 'If Harry had worn a Bulova, the evening would have turned out . . .'" Like she was left. So

I looked at these ads and knew we couldn't take them. And I wondered, how could they do this?"

Then there were the times when they sold the space, got an acceptable ad, and then the magazine's articles attacked the advertisers' products. Tension between editorial and advertising is a fact of life in serious magazines (as opposed to those that make no pretense about trading editorial coverage for advertising purchases), but the combat conditions under which the *Ms.* ad saleswomen operated made the setbacks even more heartbreaking. Seena again: "I landed fifteen pages of Elizabeth Arden and fifteen pages of Clairol, all in one year, so I went to Greece on vacation. When I came back, Pat was waiting for me. We had the Gazette [for late-breaking news items], and Pat said to me, 'You're not going to like this.' And I said, 'What?' The issue had gone to bed and on the front page of the Gazette was 'Is hair coloring dangerous to your health?' She said, 'They're going to pull the business.' And I said, 'You're right. They're going to pull the business.' And she said, 'You're going to have to get it back.' And I said, 'Over my dead body. No way I'll do it, Pat. I'm as good as my next trick. And I can't do it. I can't go to those people after I promised them that freedom of the press did not mean soliciting for hair-color and hair-care products for ten months, getting the biggest schedule this magazine has ever seen, and just laughing in their face at Bristol-Myers Clairol.' And that's the day I picked up the phone and called other magazines for jobs. I left."

Pat was in the middle. As their accountant, Arthur Tarlow, recalls, "Pat understood the principles, but Pat had to meet the printing bill. The burden of the magazine was on Pat."

Pat, like Gloria, is reserved: "I didn't fret out loud or mutter on a very regular basis. I believed my role was to enable folks to perform and not burden them with the downside—which on any given day ranged from predictable potholes to canyons you could fall into."

Gloria appreciated her position: "Pat was wonderful. She never asked us to change things. The most she would do was say, 'Maybe you could take "shit" out of the caption and put it in the body of the work.' She was so honorable. She took stuff that she never told us about."

The ad saleswomen who survived the ordeal considered the experience unparalleled training and became stars in the profession. The most prominent is Cathleen (Cathie) Black, whom Pat hired from *New York* to be advertising manager. She left *Ms.* in 1976 to become publisher of *New York.* She eventually became publisher of *USA Today,* left Gannett to be president of the American Newspaper Publishers Association, and in 1995 was named president of Hearst Magazines. In 1996 Valerie Salembier, who had been her successor as *Ms.* advertising director, became publisher of *Esquire,* one of the Hearst magazines, after serving as publisher of *TV Guide* and *Family Circle.*

Cathie considers working as *Ms.*'s first advertising manager the most challenging job of her career, because she had to confront such an "openly hostile, defensive, male-dominated environment." When Pat first took her to Detroit, they had to share a room. "You can have your own room when you sell an ad," Pat told her.

"They looked at us like we were Martians." Cathie recalls of Detroit. "I'm a very upbeat personality, but it was very tough on the ego. They would not take us—or the magazine—seriously. New York wasn't much better. Once I had an appointment at an ad agency to talk about the magazine. There were two men, one an old duffer, the other, a younger guy. While I was going through my pitch, point by point, the older guy was looking around the room and taking calls. Then he threw the book aside and cleared his throat and acted as if he were going to spit on the magazine. I said, 'It looks as if Mr. B. is not interested. Goodbye. I'll call another time.' I went to the publisher's office and we called the president of the agency, who said, 'Was it in the afternoon? Mr. B has a drinking problem.'"

While problems with advertisers limited *Ms.*'s revenues, skyrocketing operating costs forced up expenses. Writers were paid very little, a necessity the editors rationalized by convincing themselves that at least *Ms.* treated writers better than other magazines did. The staff members took salaries of $10,000–$20,000 a year—the married ones had the benefit of two incomes and the others scraped by out of dedication. Gloria often did not draw her salary, and over the years she contributed her speaking fees and other earnings to the magazine. Pat occasionally sold her own stock to meet the payroll.

In *Ms.*'s first year alone, the price of paper rose 20 percent, ink rose 40 percent, and postage climbed 60 percent. Promotion was expensive but essential. The editors were always trying other ventures that they hoped could make money, promote *Ms.,* and reach a wider audience with their message—all at once.

Pat and Gloria hired Ronnie Eldridge, a veteran politician (she had been a top aide to Robert Kennedy) to supervise special projects. In *Ms.*'s first three years, the magazine sponsored the Ms. Mile, featured at a track meet in Madison Square Garden, and the Celebration of

Women Composers, a concert of compositions by women, performed at Lincoln Center and conducted by Sarah Caldwell. It was the New York Philharmonic's first concert conducted entirely by a woman. They also coproduced a series of magazine-format television programs, *Woman Alive!* some of which Gloria narrated. Segments included a story on Crystal Lee Jordan, the labor organizer upon whose life the later movie *Norma Rae* was based, and a couple discussing their egalitarian marriage.

They published books like *The Ms. Guide to a Woman's Health* and *The First Ms. Reader,* an anthology. They even established a market-research firm, Ms. Marketing Inc. Nothing made enough money. Their most successful project was conceived by actress Marlo Thomas. *Free to Be . . . You and Me* was a hit record of nonsexist songs and skits for children, performed by various actors and singers. *Free to Be . . .* was so popular that it was turned into a book and an Emmy Award–winning television program, but the proceeds went to the Ms. Foundation for Women, which was established in 1972.

Whether *Ms.* functioned as a movement vehicle or a commercial product, Gloria was the product spokesperson. Advertisers and their clients often would insist on a visit from Gloria and no one else. Sometimes they were curious. Sometimes they were hostile. Sometimes they turned out to have no intention of buying space. Gloria remembers being invited to an advertising agency "to talk in general about the women's movement. They had brought together perhaps twenty of the ad executives in one room. I was speaking, holding a small mike they'd given me, and about two-thirds of the way through, a man was so enraged that he got up out of his chair and took the mike away from me. And he went on about athletics.

"Gradually I realized that the point of this was that since men were better at athletics, and men were stronger and men had more upper body strength and men had more endurance, they would always do better in business.

"This had not happened to me so often at that point, so I really didn't know what to do. But this elderly secretary got so upset that she stood up, voice shaking. Now this woman was not at all comfortable speaking in public or in front of her bosses, but she was so enraged that she got up and said, literally quaking, 'You get here at ten in the morning. I get here at eight. You go out for three hours of lunch. I am here working. I write your reports. You put your name on them. And I go home and I have my family to take care of.' And she was shaking.

"Needless to say, I was worried that she not lose her job. So I called back later to find out what had happened, and it worked out all right. Because someone had had the sense to reprimand him. He didn't lose his job, but they reprimanded him and moved her to work for someone else."

Ms. also used Gloria to generate publicity. If she were in a city to campaign for a prochoice candidate or speak at a college campus or raise funds for a battered women's shelter (or in the 1980s and 1990s, to promote her books), *Ms.*'s promotion department would book her onto every television, radio, and newspaper they could find, while the advertising department might ask her to see an advertiser or speak at a Rotary Club.

The effect of all this was that in promoting itself, *Ms.* promoted Gloria beyond all other feminist leaders. Nationally known activists like Betty Friedan, Kate Millett, Susan Brownmiller, and Phyllis Chesler, originally prominent because they had written important books, lacked the visibility and institutional support that a monthly magazine provided. Congresswomen such as Bella Abzug, Shirley Chisholm, Geraldine Ferraro, and Pat Schroeder were also active feminists with national platforms, but the representative nature of their work diluted their identification with the women's movement.

When the media focused on Gloria to personify the movement in 1971, she took advantage of the exposure to promote the movement's ideas—at least when she was able to keep the subject on the issues and off her legs or her lovers. However, once *Ms.* began publishing, Gloria was actively and systematically promoted, month after month, year after year. *Ms.* used other editors and writers when they could. Pat, who was an excellent speaker, had a high profile in the advertising and corporate worlds. Gloria was the charismatic figure, though. Understanding her value to the magazine, she never said no when they needed her.

While she continued to talk wistfully of leaving to get back to writing full-time, Gloria also kept organizing. The number of organizations that relied on her only increased over time. She continued to help the National Women's Political Caucus when she could, and remained so involved in the Women's Action Alliance that when some people had to be fired, they asked her to do that, too. Mary Peacock watched, and remembers, "Gloria was a combination of working journalist and champion of ideas. The poor woman had so much to do, so many responsibilities. Like any ideological movement, there was fussing and feuding, and Gloria was the one who could get it done. She was expected to trot around and make every television appearance and get all the money for the magazine.

"It makes me furious when anyone tries to depict her as spotlight hogging. I'm not saying she had to be dragged kicking and screaming to the TV studio—she was good at it and obviously must have enjoyed it in some way. But she worked like a dog.

"She was always very graceful and calm and nice. She had no temperament. She really worked to raise money for everyone's feminist causes. They'd all come begging to Gloria because she could do it, and they didn't mind exploiting it."

As Gloria told *Redbook* in 1976, "I confess—maybe I shouldn't confess it—I have a sort of pleasurable fantasy that the economy will kill the magazine. Then not only would we all be free, but we'd get a lot of sympathy because it wasn't our fault." Missing the days of less responsibility and more freedom, she also fantasized that a fire would destroy the magazine. Whatever the cause, *Ms.* couldn't be allowed to fail itself—that would reflect on the movement.

Still preoccupied in the late 1970s with finding ways to keep *Ms.* going, Gloria approached the Ford Foundation for a grant. The grant officer explained that if *Ms.* were a tax-exempt operation and could match it with funds from other contributors, Ford would give it about $250,000. At that point, Pat and Gloria began to consider converting *Ms.* into a foundation. Besides enabling them to solicit grants from foundations, nonprofit status would save *Ms.* about $600,000 a year. A few magazines like *National Geographic, Smithsonian,* and *Mother Jones* were already owned by foundations, but *Ms.* would be the first magazine the Internal Revenue Service allowed to change from for-profit status to nonprofit.

They were approved. In 1979 *Ms.* magazine became the public information arm of the Ms. Foundation for Education and Communication, itself a subsidiary of the Ms. Foundation for Women. Pat, Gloria, and Warner Communications donated their holdings to the new subsidiary. The only new constraint its status imposed was a prohibition on endorsing political candidates, but *Ms.* still was free to write about both candidates and issues.

At the end of the 1970s *Ms.* faced yet another challenge. Right-wing fundamentalist and conservative groups, energized by the abortion and Equal Rights Amendment fights and gearing up to nominate Ronald Reagan for president, were going after mainstream institutions in an attempt to influence a number of social issues. Church-backed groups attacked school curricula and textbooks, and the American Library Association reported more incidents of censoring library books in 1979 than in any of the previous twenty-five years.

The first attempt to get *Ms.* banned from a high school library occurred in Nashua, New Hampshire, in 1978, and the local court reinstated the magazine. In 1980 Baptist and Mormon groups in Contra Costa, California, a town outside San Francisco, organized a seven-hundred-member coalition to force the school board to ban *Ms.* from the high school. "*Ms.* would be rated 'X' if it was a movie," one of the leaders said. The mother whose indignation had sparked the conflict observed that *Ms.* made students "experts in sex. They know a homosexual from a heterosexual. And they can tell a bisexual from a lesbian!"

After a fiery session, the school board's three men outvoted its two women to force a "compromise": *Ms.* could remain in the library, but high school students were forbidden to check it out without permission from both a parent and their teacher. The *San Francisco Examiner* characterized the meeting as "reminiscent equally of the Scopes trial and *Invasion of the Body Snatchers*," and reported the results as a semivictory: "An angry crowd of Bible-thumping Contra Costans tarred and feathered *Ms.* magazine, but they couldn't drive the controversial woman's monthly out of town."

Back at the magazine, Gloria suggested that *Ms.* include a section based on her *That Was the Week That Was* segment, "Surrealism in Everyday Life." The title could have defined life around the *Ms.* offices themselves. As the years passed, the offices expanded from one tiny room at 370 Lexington Avenue to the entire fifteenth floor, to larger space on West Fortieth Street in Times Square in 1981. The art room was always cheerful and clean, and the rest of the space was always a mess—piles of papers everywhere, dust, and crowds of people coming in and out. Various children accompanied their mothers and played in a tot lot in the corner. Feminists, writers, feminist-writers, aspiring writers, and other assorted hangers-on would visit and even attend editorial meetings, which were open to visiting feminists, the entire staff, and outside authorities on various subjects.

Suzanne Levine recalls the working conditions: "The first day, I came to work in a pink skirt and pink silk blouse—a kind of lady-going-to-work outfit. And then I realized there were no chairs, there were no desks, and everything was dusty."

Nina Finkelstein loved it: "The first five years were absolute heaven. I have never been so happy in my entire life. It changed my life. It changed my family. It changed my husband. It changed my kids."

Phyllis Langer, promotion assistant, received an education: "I was twenty-nine, naive, and pregnant, and I shared an office with Margaret Sloan and another woman who were both lesbians. My mother said, 'Are you sure you're safe?' It was hysterical. They would wiggle their fingers at me and go, 'woo woo woo' so I'd have a 'lavender baby.' Margaret was wild. We had so much fun going out together—the whole staff would go to a restaurant or a club together. When I had Alix I brought her to work. She was the *Ms.* baby and they put her on the cover."

Harriet Lyons recalls the intensity: "We did incredibly, wonderfully nutty things. . . . It was constant laughing. We could make fun of ourselves, but publicly we were awfully earnest and awfully heady and on the barricades. Pat Carbine was the oldest person and she had just turned forty."

Gloria was in and out of the office. She often worked at night when she was in town. Everyone recalls her propensity to steal food left in or on the desks, and Pat says they always knew it was Gloria when the food "thief" left money in the drawer. Phyllis Langer kept snacks for her baby Alix. "Sometimes I'd find a little note," she recalls. " 'Dear Alix, I took your cookies because I was starving, but I promise to replace them.' "

Besides stealing food, publicizing the magazine, selling advertising, writing articles, suggesting story ideas, and sometimes even editing, Gloria performed other tasks. There were personnel matters to be managed, for example. As Suzanne Levine recalls, "Gloria was the one the interns always went to when they felt slighted. She'd have meetings with them and meetings with the staff—and the interns were always feeling slighted. Because of the mixed message: 'We value you, but please copy this.' She spent endless hours on that kind of personnel problem—hurt feelings."

Gloria did in-house consciousness-raising, too. Arthur Tarlow, who is very short, recalls, "Gloria did two things for me. One, she wouldn't tolerate my small-man jokes. If I made one, she'd turn around and point her long finger at me and say, 'You stop that shit.' Two, she got me to go out with my daughter and spend more time with her. I'll always be grateful."

She often gave speeches to mostly male groups, such as Rotary Clubs. Seena Harris-Parker recalls the suspense on those occasions: "Gloria could be wonderful in speeches. It was very funny. She would either be wonderful, or she would rip men to shreds. And you never knew which she was going to do. Pat would have to be the one to say, 'Thank you, Gloria, but now I think everybody needs to get back to the office.' "

Suzanne remembers Gloria as a boss: "I don't remember the names of Gloria's secretaries, but there was one after another. They'd come in injured birds, and would be transformed into voracious egos, suddenly offended at being asked to type. It was, 'Why should I be a lackey to this celebrity when I have all this to do, and I'm writing poetry, and I'm an activist?' I just remember a series of people who Gloria would pick to be her secretary for no particular professional reason, who would then become enormous problems."

Publicist-to-the-stars Lois Smith shared the *Ms.* offices for a while, and Susan Braudy once found herself standing next to Raquel Welch putting on mascara in the ladies' room. The lone *Ms.* male, Arthur Tarlow, recalls, "I always knew when Robert Redford was there. All the feminists were running up and down the hall." Actually, the feminists tried so hard not to make Redford feel self-conscious that he later said he thought they hadn't liked him.

Arthur loved being part of the magazine. He says, "When we played *Esquire* in softball in Central Park, I was six months out of a heart attack, but *Esquire* wouldn't let me have a runner. They said, 'If you're too sick to run, you're too sick to play.'

"The *Ms.* women got so angry. *Esquire*'s pitcher was the main culprit, and when my ball hit him in the thigh, one of the *Ms.* team said, 'You missed.'

"I said, 'If he'd been any kind of man, I wouldn't have.' Later he apologized for being such a jerk."

As a combination commercial enterprise and movement hangout, the *Ms.* offices also attracted more than their share of crazy people. As their favored target, Gloria sometimes received a call at home from her colleagues, instructing her to come to work through the rear entrance. One man sat quietly in the reception area for several days until one day he simply took off all his clothes. Another was so worried about Martians that *Ms.*'s receptionist made him a helmet out of tin foil, and that evidently satisfied his need to ward off the aliens.

Some strange people managed to break through anyway and latch on to Gloria, who is known among her friends as an easy make: If she is *la belle dame sans merci* with men, she is Mother Teresa with women. Her friends tend to describe her with some variation of "Gloria is a terrible judge of people." Letty Pogrebin makes a finer distinction: "She's a good judge of men, but a terrible judge of women. People take advantage of her. If someone wants to be her friend, she lets them. . . . You practically have to kill someone for Gloria not to like you."

Even Gloria concurs that she is a "much better judge of men's characters than of women, because, well, I think the reason is obvious." She explains, "In my experience the balance of power between men and women is different. I'm more cautious with men. And because with women, it's so easy to see or imagine what happened to them to make them this way."

Given Gloria's propensity to suffer fools enthusiastically, there was no way she was going to resist some of the more determined, or even the obnoxious. In fact, Gloria says the fact that one of them was "such an unattractive person" probably made her redouble her efforts to be kind to her, because "you thought, no one's going to help her with her problems precisely because she is so unattractive."

With the magazine's permanently precarious financial position, the staff's sense of mission, and a sense that they were under constant siege from antifeminists and critical feminists alike, working at *Ms.* was an intense experience. At one point psychologist Phyllis Chesler decided that since Gloria had become so famous so quickly, Phyllis would form a consciousness-raising group to help her. "It's difficult for others to tell you to your face what they think—there's always an agenda. It's like being at the court of a ruling monarch. People say, 'I love you and I agree with you,' and behind your back, 'Fuck that bitch.' "

Phyllis assembled some of the *Ms.* and Alliance employees, along with Marlo Thomas, Judy Collins, and writer Jill Johnston, and they began meeting. Phyllis was impressed by Marlo's and Judy's ability to look within themselves and deal with challenges, but ultimately Phyllis thought the C-R group did not work to help Gloria in the way she had hoped. The *Ms.* employees could not speak their minds, and, it seemed to Phyllis, neither could Gloria: "How could Gloria speak and talk about her vulnerabilities and terrors or even say, 'Let's just have fun and forget all this' when she had all this responsibility?" As far as Gloria was concerned, the group helped tremendously, because it showed her that her friends cared.

Gloria describes the atmosphere at *Ms.* as similar to a political campaign headquarters. *Ms.* was clearly far more than a job to Gloria.

Although she avoided parenthood precisely because she did not want to replicate the experience of taking care of her mother, she re-created it anyway, with *Ms.* The magazine was like a sick child who never became healthy enough to survive on its own, and Gloria never gave up trying to save it. Like a child, *Ms.* was a labor of love for Gloria as well. For many years, *Ms.* was her pride and joy. It was her family.

26

The Redstockings, Gloria, and the CIA

In 1967 a New Left magazine called *Ramparts* revealed that the CIA had funneled funds to the National Student Association (NSA). Two paragraphs in the eleven-page story described the Independent Research Service (IRS) as one of the CIA's beneficiaries.

The national media picked up the story on February 15, and Gene Theroux, the IRS's director (and only employee), immediately called Gloria. She was in Washington, too, picketing the Pentagon in a Women's Strike for Peace demonstration with twenty-five hundred other women.

As the media probe of the IRS expanded, Gloria handled many of the press queries, though Gene—and Dennis Shaul, who was, like Gloria, an ex-IRS codirector and board member—were interviewed as well. About a week after his name appeared in the Washington newspapers, Gene received a letter of encouragement and a twenty-five-dollar check from a woman named Ruth Steinem. When he told Gloria about the strange coincidence, she laughed and said, "Good heavens, that's my mother."

When the media frenzy began, IRS cofounder George Abrams called Gloria to ask if she was comfortable answering reporters. "I'm fine," he recalls her telling him. "I'll take the heat on this." She appeared on Walter

Cronkite's evening news program and patiently explained the youth festivals' origin as Soviet propaganda. She also described the kinds of activities the IRS had undertaken, such as helping young people to attend,
financing a news bureau, cultural exhibits, jazz bands, and jazz clubs.

Gloria was open about the CIA link. She explained to the *New York
Times* that other governments funded some of their student delegates
and activities. However, American students' funding had come from
the CIA because in the McCarthyite 1950s, neither private industry
nor any branch of the government had dared to fund anything relating
to a Communist youth festival. "Far from being shocked by this
involvement," she explained to the *New York Times* reporter, "I was
happy to find some liberals in government in those days who were far-
sighted and cared enough to get Americans of all political views to the
festival." She added that the "CIA's big mistake was not supplanting
itself with private funds fast enough."

Robert Kaiser reported in the *Washington Post*, "Miss Steinem said
yesterday that she had worked extensively with CIA agents in this
country and at the two Youth Festivals" but that the CIA had never
tried to alter their policies nor asked her to report on other Americans
or assess foreign nationals. The CIA "wanted to do what we wanted to
do—present a healthy, diverse view of the United States."

In another interview with the *Post* in December, she told Nancy L.
Ross, "In my experience the Agency was completely different from its
image; it was liberal, nonviolent and honorable. I found the CIA my
best journalistic training because the one instruction one receives from
them is to be accurate, whereas publications tell you to find an angle."*

However, by 1967 young people's attitudes had changed. The Vietnam War and the federal government's dismal civil-rights record had
already alienated young (and not so young) people from the government itself, and the cold war had lost its imperative, especially in light
of Vietnam. Many considered the CIA even more repugnant than the
rest of the government, particularly as revelations of some of its other
activities began to leak out.

Partly in response to the shift in attitudes, the NSA–CIA relationship
had deteriorated. The NSA people with whom Gloria had worked had

---

*Gloria wanted the following sentence added: "At the time, the conflating of the CIA
with the NSA—like other organizations of the non-Communist left that CIA-funded foundations had supported—seemed harmless, but this would only add to future confusion." Readers may judge for themselves whether her statements to the press seem to be describing the
NSA rather than the CIA.

felt fortunate to be assisted by the CIA. For many of them, liberalism and international anti-Communism were linked. Furthermore, among Gloria's peers, the NSA people and the CIA people with whom they worked not only shared the same cold war goals, they were often the same people.

In the mid-1960s, the NSA students were ten years younger than their CIA contacts, many of whom were still from Gloria's generation. Then some of the CIA people became increasingly heavyhanded with the NSA people. As a result many of the NSA young people who were told of the relationship (made 'witting') felt, not empowered, but tricked into the association and imprisoned by the arrangement. Because they had been made to swear a secrecy oath before they were told, they feared that if they tried to extricate themselves or the NSA, they would be prosecuted under the National Security Act.

Finally, one of the NSA officers refused to cooperate and went to the press, and that led to the *Ramparts* story. As a result of the exposé, the CIA and the NSA severed their relationship. For Gloria, that seemed to be the end of the issue. She assumed that if the festivals continued, the IRS would continue on its own, just as the NSA had done.

Eight years later, on May 9, 1975, a small reconstituted group of Redstockings, some of them from the original group, called a press conference at a convention held by the liberal and radical journalists' magazine *More*. There they issued a sixteen-page tabloid-style press release headlined "Redstockings Discloses Gloria Steinem's CIA Cover-up." The release explained that the Redstockings had "uncovered" information showing that Gloria Steinem had "a ten-year association with the CIA stretching from 1959 to 1969 which she has misrepresented and covered up." The alleged cover-up was said to be part of a conspiracy in which Gloria was the CIA's secret weapon to sabotage the women's movement. As they saw it,

1. Gloria Steinem had a long-running and undisclosed association with the CIA.
2. "[O]ne major CIA strategy is to create or support 'parallel' organizations which provide an alternative to radicalism."
3. The women's movement had been popular, radical, and successful until *Ms.* "substituted itself for the movement, blocking knowledge of the authentic activists and ideas" and replaced them with "watered-down" voices and ideas.

The implication was clear. Just as Lenin had been sealed in a railroad car in 1917 and injected into Russia like a poison virus, Gloria had been sent into the women's movement as the CIA's secret weapon. In this case, though, Gloria was evidently more vaccination than virus. The Redstockings hypothesized that, to the CIA, a little dose of women's-movement liberalism might seem just the cure for a bad case of women's-movement radicalism. They also offered as an alternative theory that Gloria might be acting not as an agent of the CIA, but on behalf of the rich and powerful corporate interests. Either way, the Establishment was killing the revolution through Gloria.

The Redstockings saw evidence everywhere. Under Gloria's direction, they asserted, the CIA-financed Independent Research Service had gathered names and dossiers on political activists. Now Gloria was associated with *Ms.* magazine, the Women's Action Alliance, and the National Black Feminist Organization—which also had ties to the Women's Action Alliance—and all of them were "major center[s] for collecting names and information about the movement and individuals."

The Redstockings observed that Pat Carbine, who was a *McCall's* editor when Gloria was named *McCall's* Woman of the Year, had been heard to remark on television that "the women's movement was currently in 'Phase Two,' " That meant, Pat had explained, that the "radicals had a part to play in getting things started . . . but the moderates were now in control."

They noted that Clay Felker, who had both attended the Helsinki festival with Gloria and launched Gloria as a political columnist at *New York,* had subsequently become editor of the *Village Voice.* Once there, they alleged, he had chosen not to run a previously commissioned article critical of *Ms.*

There were *Ms.*'s backers. *Ms.* shareholder Katharine Graham had been "featured on *Ms.*'s cover as 'the most powerful woman in America.' " The willingness of Warner Communications to accept a 25-percent interest when providing nearly 100 percent of the capital for *Ms.* was also deemed suspicious, as was *Ms.*'s use of Wonder Woman, a Warner comic-book property. The fact that *Ms.* put Wonder Woman on its second cover was bad enough, but what *Ms.* did with Wonder Woman's politics was even worse, according to the Redstockings: "In both her old and new forms Wonder Woman's guiding motive is 'Patriotism,' i.e., protecting the interests of the American powers-that-be." However, in *Ms.*'s 1973 version, Wonder Woman would become "more of a pacifist, a general line pushed by *Ms.* in talking about women's 'cultural superiority.' "

The possibilities were endless. Stating the obvious as if it were sinister, the Redstockings noted, "The conflict over whether *Ms.* is a commercial or a political venture has caused a lot of people confusion." The other occupants of *Ms.*'s building were scrutinized suspiciously, as was the fact that the Women's Action Alliance received grants from such powerful sources as the Carnegie Corporation and the Chase Manhattan Bank Foundation, thus linking them with the Rockefellers.

In short, Gloria was everywhere: "She has had a finger in every pie, from domestic workers' organizing to stewardesses' conventions; from women's labor conferences to simultaneous work in the McGovern and Chisholm presidential campaigns (prompting Shirley Chisholm to finally insist that Steinem decide who she was working for)."

It was Gloria's very ubiquity—which to most observers seemed evidence of her dedication and her value to the movement—that seemed so telling to the Redstockings:

> It is necessary that people with access to this much information be trustworthy and that they actually be using the information to further the interests of the movement. Gloria Steinem has a history of gathering information for the Central Intelligence Agency. She has been dishonest in the past about this and is still covering it up. She has therefore not earned the trust her present position requires.

The press release exposing Gloria Steinem, suspected feminist saboteur, was part of a chapter in *Feminist Revolution,* a book Redstockings was about to publish. The collection of essays and other material analyzed feminist theory and examined the successes and failures of the women's movement. The group explained that they were releasing the material on Steinem in advance "because of its pressing importance." Since they were accusing Gloria of being associated with the CIA since 1959 and the book was to be published in a few months, the only need so pressing that it required a release with such fanfare—and at a journalists' convention, no less—could have been the need to take advantage of the publicity value of Gloria's name.

They achieved their objective. Journalists at the convention raced to call their editors. However, once they studied the Redstockings material, they considered it a combination of old news and a silly conspiracy theory, and dropped the story. The only exceptions were a few small feminist publications that ran articles calling for Gloria to respond to the charges.

In fairness to Redstockings, suspicions of government interference in the women's movement were not groundless. The FBI had a long history of infiltrating and disrupting groups considered a threat to the status quo. By the time the Redstockings began investigating Gloria, information about an FBI program called COINTELPRO—a multi-pronged campaign combining domestic intelligence-gathering and disruption of various left groups, from the Black Panthers to the Socialist Workers Party—had begun to seep out.

Also in 1975, a commission headed by Vice President Nelson A. Rockefeller to investigate CIA domestic activities found that the CIA had spied on and provoked various leftist groups, including women's liberation groups. That venture, Operation CHAOS, was completely illegal, as, unlike the FBI, the CIA was barred by charter from operating within the United States or spying on American nationals.

In addition to the genuine existence of outside agitators, Redstockings was responding to changes within the feminist movement. During the late 1960s and early 1970s, the original radical feminist theories emphasized women's similarities to men and analyzed women's socially constructed role in society, with the goal of eliminating that role in order for women to achieve equality. Gender polarization was to be replaced with some form of androgyny.

From about 1973 on, a more woman-centered analysis came to predominate, emphasizing women's differences from men. Rather than urging women to seek androgyny, a wide variety of feminist thinkers celebrated qualities more associated with females—empathy, for example, and a lower propensity to violence—and suggested that the culture itself be changed to reflect more of the traditional feminine values. At its best this analysis offered an improvement over the original radical feminist impulse and a blueprint for change; at its worst it led back to a Victorian concept of woman as more virtuous, more moral, less rational (emotions often were praised over intellect), and more in need of protection.

Feminist Revolution was a serious, intelligent contribution to that debate and a call for a return to the original radical impulse. Although Redstockings leader Kathie Sarachild had actually written a review praising the first issue of *Ms.*, by 1975 the group was attacking the magazine. Redstockings objected both to the feminist politics of Gloria and to *Ms.*'s hegemony among feminist publications. They believed *Ms.*'s politics were displacing Redstockings beliefs not because of their merits, but because the magazine's commercial success allowed it to reach a national audience that other feminist publications could not.

Whatever their objections to *Ms.*, the attack on Gloria was vicious, even for a movement characterized by such vehement and bitter attacks that the movement had even coined a name for it: trashing. While Redstockings considered their quarrels with Gloria strictly political, Gloria considers them personal as well, citing dealings she had had with Kathie Sarachild, the leader of the attack.

At Ellen Willis's suggestion, *Ms.* had contracted with Sarachild to assemble a consciousness-raising anthology, since she and other Redstockings members had developed the concept. Then Sarachild objected to some of the *Ms.* editors' conditions. Gloria says they wanted more contributions from writers outside the New York City and more women of color. Sarachild said she wanted control over structure and content and objected to including an introduction by Gloria. According to Gloria, when Sarachild turned in the manuscript, the *Ms.* editors considered it unpublishable. Gloria was designated to tell Sarachild they did not want to publish it, but she also told Sarachild to keep the advance unless she published it elsewhere. Since the advance was never returned, Gloria conjectures that "the fact that other publishers also apparently found her anthology unpublishable may have only increased her feelings of being left on the sidelines."

Friends of each party attribute the Redstockings' attack both to genuine political differences and to genuine personal jealousy. Once Betty Friedan became involved, the personal element could hardly be missed. Betty had been muttering about Gloria's CIA connection for years, but those who worked with Betty paid her no mind, attributing it to jealousy or to her concern about outside agents disrupting the movement. They considered Gloria's previous association with the CIA irrelevant to her feminist activities.

Once Redstockings issued its press release, Betty, whose feminist politics were to the right of Gloria's, jumped in to support them—even though the Redstockings' politics were more radical than Gloria's and their rhetoric was far more antimale, also a pet complaint of Betty's. First Betty called other feminists privately to ask if they didn't think the matter should be investigated. Then she began speaking out in public.

Attending the June 1975 International Women's Year Conference in Mexico City, Betty observed, "With the Watergate revelations—how the CIA has manipulated and infiltrated, and usually under the guise of pushing, like an agent provocateur, a radical or pseudoradical in every other movement to render it ineffective—one can assume that the same thing has been happening in the women's movement." She even encouraged Ingrid Stone, a writer covering the conference for the feminist newspaper *Majority Report,* to bring copies of the Redstockings press release with her to Mexico. Gloria was there to speak at the Encounter for Third World Journalists, a three-day prelude to the conference. Stone not only distributed the release, she followed Gloria around at the conference, trying to get her to respond to it.

In July, Sagaris, an experimental feminist summer school in Lyndonville, Vermont, called the Ms. Foundation to ask for a $10,000 "emergency" grant to continue its second session. The first session's faculty had included Rita Mae Brown, Charlotte Bunch, Mary Daly, and Margo Jefferson. The endangered second session included Ti-Grace Atkinson, Jane Galvin-Lewis, Alix Kates Shulman, and Barbara Seaman. Although the foundation had already contributed its first major grant of $5,000, an amount far out of proportion to its usual $500–$2,000 contributions, the foundation issued the $10,000 check. A board member, past NOW president Aileen Hernández, was going to Sagaris as an evaluator, so the board asked her to deliver it.

Arriving to save the feminist summer school, Hernández was met, not with gratitude, but with suspicion. Some of the faculty and students so feared the possibility that *Ms.*'s contribution might be CIA-tainted that they decided to vote on whether to accept the money. After the majority voted to accept it, about twenty students and a majority of the nine-woman faculty withdrew to form an alternative program, the "August Seventh Survival Community." By the time *Majority Report*'s Stone arrived to cover the session, the group made her swear on a stack of Redstockings press releases (she had brought another 150 copies) that she was not an agent for the feminist press and would not write about what was taking place. She swore and then wrote about it anyway.

Gloria maintained a public silence from May to July. When they first heard about the issue, her friends and colleagues considered the attack so ridiculous that CIA jokes were flying around the office; they put a sign on the door, "Welcome to the CIA." Then they saw Gloria's response. Even knowing how sensitive to criticism Gloria could be, they were stunned, because her reaction seemed so out of proportion either to the nature of the criticism or the prominence of the critics.

Gloria was distraught. As painful as the *Esquire* profile had been, at least she had been able to consider the source. *Esquire*'s editor Harold Hayes had made his resentment of her quite clear. The attacks by Betty Friedan had been hurtful, too, but Betty's personal jealousy was obvious and Betty's complaints that Gloria was promoting too radical a line were, in a way, a professional compliment, since Gloria considered herself a radical.

However, the Redstockings were some of the women from a group she had respected. Furthermore, they had attacked Gloria for not being radical enough. Being called "pinko-commie," "slut," "nigger-lover," "kike" was one thing—Gloria saved some of those letters and joked that they proved she was attacking the right targets. But the Redstockings were part of her movement. As Stan Pottinger, the man with whom she was involved at the time, would observe later, "She loves to be attacked from the right. She likes that. But she can't stand having anybody to her left. The Redstockings were attacking her from the left." (In truth, Gloria doesn't love being attacked by anyone.)

By far the worst part of the accusations was that they attacked her authenticity. The Redstockings were not saying that she had slept her way to the top, as *Esquire* had implied, nor that she was using the movement for personal gain, as Betty Friedan had contended. These accusers—whose radical feminist credentials were impeccable—were saying something far worse: that she was an inauthentic feminist.

There was nothing inauthentic about Gloria's feminism. Feminism was her life. In Gloria's terms, her outside matched her inside. What she was—and what she was known as—were identical, and they were who she wanted to be. Although she had a self with which she was comfortable, feminism had not been able to provide her with the self-esteem to dismiss criticism, especially from people she respected. No matter how sincere she knew she was, no matter how much hard work she knew she had put in, she remained vulnerable to the opinions of others she valued—their esteem informed her of her own worth and their disapproval made her feel as invisible as she had as a child.

Gloria's friends and colleagues were mystified by the depth and duration of her response. Phyllis Chesler recalls her as so depressed that she moved like an old woman. Writer Rita Mae Brown says she took Gloria to lunch and was completely mystified when she burst into tears. Suzanne Levine told Gloria that Kathie Sarachild (née Amatniek) had been a year behind her at Radcliffe and that she wasn't the least surprised that this person was attacking Gloria—that she had always had to have a cause.

The support helped, but not enough. Always inclined to seek advice, she polled a wide circle of friends and acquaintances to ask what she should do. Most said, "Ignore the charges. They are ridiculous.

Answering them will just attract publicity." Except for the attention given to Betty Friedan's comments, the mainstream media and even the publications of the left ignored the story. Joanne Edgar dealt with the few inquiries by alternately describing Gloria's CIA-connected work and questioning the critics' right to use the name Redstockings since most of the original Redstockings were not involved.

She also felt betrayed by Ellen Willis. Just before the charges were made in May 1975, Ellen, who had been a part-time editor at *Ms.* for about two years, had asked to be put on the permanent payroll, and Pat Carbine had accommodated her. Then the Redstockings held their press conference, and Ellen, who had cofounded the original Redstockings but did not belong to the reconstituted group, felt caught in the middle: "I had mixed feelings about the article and was upset about the press conference, which by villainizing Steinem and implying a conspiracy, could only undercut the credibility of Redstockings' valid critique of *Ms.*'s politics and impact on the movement. But I was incensed by Steinem's response, a disdainful who-are-these-people dismissal of Sarachild, [Carol] Hanisch et al. as crazies and not real Redstockings."

Ellen recalls that she had been tired of being what she considered *Ms.*'s token radical and that she had begun to think about quitting. She was vacillating, however, so she had procrastinated, deciding to let things slide until the end of the summer.

Right after Redstockings made their charges, Gloria asked for her help and Ellen refused. She recalls, "I thought, 'You know, if it weren't for these people, you would not be where you are. So respond.'" However, when Ellen declined to help her, "Gloria compared it to a person who sees an automobile accident and doesn't want to get involved. I've always thought about that, and it bothers me. . . . In retrospect I feel I didn't handle it well. I criticized Gloria in a really public way [Ellen wrote a public letter of condemnation] and I didn't criticize them. I told the Redstockings what I thought was wrong, but I didn't criticize them publicly."

Finally Gloria decided to respond to the charges, but only in the feminist press. She knew answering them would draw coverage they had not been able to attract on their own merits, but she was being pressured to respond "in the interests of the movement." She sent an elaborately composed six-page letter to six feminist newspapers, accompanied by letters of support from prominent feminists such as Robin Morgan and Rita Mae Brown who had belonged to the original Redstockings.

Complete silence would have been preferable. Gloria could not have done a worse job on her own behalf. Her attempt to clear her name was an agglomeration of obfuscations, evasions, and name-calling. There was probably nothing she could have said that would have convinced the Redstockings she wasn't allied with the CIA (some of the accusers still suspect her), but her response—the letter and subsequent libel threats—ceded the moral high ground and left a cloud that has never entirely dissipated.

Gloria's problem was not that she had done anything wrong. It was that she never seemed to trust people to accept her as she was, contradictions and all. Infinitely tolerant of other women, she was a rigid perfectionist with herself. Old opinions may be embarrassing, or they may not. Confronted with his youth festival activities, Clay Felker responds comfortably, "I was an anti-Communist liberal then, and I'm an anti-Communist liberal now." Antiwar activist and Yale chaplain William Sloane Coffin, who had worked directly for the CIA, was unashamed of his continued friendships with old agency hands: "They look on me as a traitor, and I look on them as murderers," he explained cheerily.

Gloria lacked that kind of confidence. In 1975, just as she felt truer to her best self than she had ever felt in her life, she was being accused of being a fraud.

The fact that Gloria was falsely accused of dishonesty just when she had become her most authentic self was ironic. The fact that Gloria was unable to present her past without apology was tragic.

The Redstockings had looked at some facts, added one and one and one and one, and come up with five. According to Gloria, "Some of the ones weren't correct either." But some were.

It was certainly a fact that Gloria had helped run a CIA-front operation, and she had said so, freely and publicly, in 1967. She had believed in the goal and had done nothing dishonorable or opposed to her values at the time. She had not been hired to report on people—her job had been getting them to the festivals and generating prodemocracy propaganda. If, over the years, her attitude toward the CIA had changed with the subsequent disclosures of its activities, that was perfectly understandable. She had gone to fight international communism, not to report on other Americans' political affiliations, and neither her participation at the time, nor her changed view of it was to her discredit.

But Gloria responded as if she had something to hide. Apparently incapable of presenting her own history in a straightforward, unapologetic that-was-then, this-is-now manner. She would get only as far as explaining the cold war context before she began to use tortuous explanations that made her sound guilty of something, even if it wasn't clear what. For example, she never could (and still does not) simply present the IRS as the CIA-front organization it was. Instead she described it as an operation in which "some of the American participation was partially funded by foundations that were in turn funded by the CIA." Of course the funding was indirect. Why would the CIA have set up a separate operation if it could have issued the checks itself?

Furthermore, Gloria wrote, she had worked "with the Independent Research Service." In fact, she had worked *for* it, not *with* it: She was its codirector. "I took no orders at all from the U.S. government in any of its forms or agencies." The point wasn't whether or not they gave orders or controlled her. They didn't need to. She was neither automaton nor unwilling employee—she wanted the job, she understood its requirements, she knew she was expected to use her initiative, and in fact she was in frequent communication with Harry Lunn, one of the CIA case officers for the operation.

Gloria's entries in Marquis's *Who's Who* had provided some basis for Redstockings suspecting her of a continued relationship with the CIA. When Gloria first appeared in the 1968–69 edition of *Who's Who,* her entry had included the description, "Dir., ednl. found. Ind. Research Service, Cambridge, Mass., N.Y.C., 1959–62, now mem. bd. dirs., Washington." The 1968–69 edition went to press before the Independent Research Service's CIA connection was exposed in 1967. All subsequent editions omitted reference to the board of directors and reduced her term of employment to 1959–60, a change that Redstockings duly noted.

The truth seemed to be that Gloria had used the connection when it suited her, and when it became an embarrassment, she expunged it. For example, in a May 4, 1964, letter, Gloria wrote that in 1959 she had moved the IRS to New York where she worked both for the foundation and for *Help!* Then, after the 1962 Helsinki festival, She "dropped all but advisory work for the Service (technically, 'Executive Director') and began free-lancing full time."

In her 1975 response to her Redstockings adversaries she explained:

I was co-director through the 1959 Vienna Festival; then director through the clean-up period until the Service essentially folded in 1960. . . . When the Service re-opened before the 1962 Festival, I was no longer the director, but worked sometimes, mostly as an unpaid volunteer. . . . As for the "bd. dirs." listing in the 1968–69 *Who's Who*, I understood the Service to be an unincorporated association, and I don't believe it had a Board of Directors. Certainly I never went to a meeting of one. More important, after completing work on the 1962 Helsinki Festival, my work for the Service was over.

In an effort to demonstrate that the biographical publication had acquired the information from sources other than herself, Gloria pointed to other errors in the *Who's Who* entry, noting that it even had her age wrong. Since Gloria herself perpetuated the lie about her age until the October 1971 *Esquire* article exposed it, her effrontery in attributing that 1960s error to unreliability of *Who's Who* was truly breathtaking.

She did not state categorically that she had not supplied any particular piece of information to *Who's Who*. She had called the Marquis Company, the publisher of *Who's Who*, she explained, and learned that if the forms were not returned, the publisher might piece together an entry from published material. Therefore, "neither Marquis nor I knows which parts of what were filled out by whom."

In her six-page letter, Gloria also responded to a number of Redstockings charges about her current affiliations. Redstockings noted ominously that because the National Black Feminist Organization shared offices with the Women's Action Alliance, Gloria would have access to NBFO files. Gloria described their suspicion as "racist in the extreme to assume that a Black women's organization must somehow be under the thumb of a racially integrated organization like the [Women's Action] Alliance." Her description of the press release's "McCarthyite style" in linking the two organizations was certainly accurate (though both actually did have ties to Gloria and to each other), but the Redstockings assertion was hardly racist.

In short, apparently unable to believe she could be appreciated, trusted, loved as she was, Gloria seemed compelled to make all the details fit her image. Anything that contradicted it was a threat that had to be countered with every weapon at her disposal.

When the Redstockings contretemps began, Gloria had practically the entire feminist community in her corner. The general public was oblivious to it and would have ridiculed the entire affair if they had heard the charges. However, when Gloria responded to the pressure and replied, she made things worse, though she was clearly the injured party. Then her attempts to protect her image became increasingly heavyhanded, and she forfeited some of the original sympathy she had attracted and deserved. Most feminists forbore to criticize her anyway, out of affection, gratitude, loyalty, fear of antagonizing her or her associates, or a conviction that Redstockings deserved whatever it got.

Betty Friedan, apparently relishing the novelty of having allies in her attacks on Gloria, attacked again. When she published her second book, *It Changed My Life*, in 1976, she mentioned the CIA connection. She also implied that Bella Abzug and Gloria had used the National Women's Political Caucus for their own purposes during the 1972 Democratic Convention and insinuated that they had conspired in 1973 to wrest control of the NWPC from Betty and her supporters.

Gloria was not completely without recourse—or allies. After the attack, the *Ms.* editors asked Jo Freeman to write an article about trashing in the movement, and in 1976 they asked her to review *It Changed My Life*. As one of the early movement leaders, Freeman's feminist credentials were unimpeachable, and she suspected the editors' hidden agenda was to use her to trash Betty. However, she believed she could be fair, so she accepted the assignment.

Freeman thought *It Changed My Life* was a bad book. She wrote what she considered a balanced but critical review and sent it to three of her friends who knew Betty but were not Betty's friends. It was much too hard on Betty, all three said. Freeman sent it to *Ms.* anyway, but the editors rejected it—on the grounds that she had been much too kind to Betty.

Betty must have found the Redstockings material an irresistible opportunity to get at Gloria yet again. She told Jim Silberman, editor in chief at Random House, about *Feminist Revolution,* which Redstockings had published privately in October 1975. Silberman decided in 1976 to publish it in a trade edition.

In March 1976 the publishing house began sending out requests for permission to reprint various entries from other sources, including those in the chapter about Gloria, such as her *Who's Who* entries, excerpts from *Ms.*, and some Women's Action Alliance material. As soon as she learned that Random House was issuing the book, Gloria went on the offensive. A privately published edition was one thing; the imprint of a respected publisher was another.

Bypassing the project editor, Christine Steinmetz, as well as Silberman and the Random House legal department, Gloria talked to Random House president Robert Bernstein, whom she already knew.

At the end of the talk, she left him with a lawyer's letter claiming the material about herself was "false and defamatory" and could be grounds for a libel suit if Random House published that material without checking facts. (Proving libel against a public figure is more difficult because the standard is higher—one must prove knowledge of falsity or reckless disregard as to truth or falsity.)

She also notified others mentioned in that section, and Random House eventually received letters from the attorneys for Clay Felker, Women's Action Alliance, and Frank Thomas threatening libel suits. Warner Communications sent a complaint, and Katharine Graham sent a personal note to Bernstein.

In response, the Random House attorneys asked Gloria's attorney for the specific points Gloria considered libelous. After protracted negotiations, they received a list of 114 items, most of which, according to Redstockings documents, refer to "innuendos."

The Redstockings were able to substantiate their assertions—not that Gloria was a CIA agent, which they implied in the strongest possible manner but never said directly, but some of the facts upon which their suspicions were based. They lost the battle anyway. When the Random House edition of *Feminist Revolution* appeared, the entire section covered by the press release "Gloria Steinem and the CIA" was deleted. So was "From a Finnish Notebook," an essay by a Finnish television producer describing her experience at the 1962 Helsinki festival and a 1975 conversation with Gloria. Random House also prohibited Redstockings from using the title "Agents, Opportunists and Fools" (which originally had been for the chapter on Gloria and *Ms.*)—even for a section that had nothing to do with Gloria.

The Redstockings were allowed only two relatively meaningless concessions. They were able to salvage a couple of articles critical of *Ms.*'s editorial policies that Random House wanted removed, though even in those they had to cut some of their "libelous" contents. Random House wanted to delete the following paragraph about the effect of *Ms.* on other feminist publications: "They're the Teamsters of the women's movement. They've moved in on the women's movement the way the Teamsters moved in on the Farmworkers Union. They don't break hard ground themselves. They only go where people have been." After prolonged argument, Random House allowed Redstockings to retain the paragraph, but only if they omitted the second sentence. The affair dragged on so long that Random House did not publish even the expurgated version until 1978.

Whether the publisher was intimidated or influenced by the prominence of Gloria, Clay Felker, Katharine Graham, Warner Communications, and Frank Thomas compared to the relative obscurity of
Redstockings—or genuinely believed the facts did not justify the
charges—Gloria's counterattack succeeded. Many Redstockings suppo-
sitions about Gloria and the CIA may have been wrong, silly, or even
vicious, but Redstockings had accompanied them with what they considered supporting evidence. Readers were never given the opportunity
to decide for themselves whether or not the Redstockings had proved
their point.

In 1979 Nancy Borman, a journalist and the publisher of *Majority
Report,* wrote an article for the *Village Voice* recounting the history of
Feminist Revolution's publication, including Gloria's success in getting
the chapter about herself eliminated. When she heard about the article,
Gloria sent another lawyer's letter to the *Village Voice* putting the editors on notice that "they were at legal risk if they did not check facts."
The *Voice* lawyers checked the contents for libel and could find none.
After the article ran, a number of prominent feminists wrote letters to
the editor to protest Borman's article and to insist that the issue was
not censorship, but rather that Gloria did not deserve such coverage
because of her contributions to the movement.

Gloria never sued. Her lawyer had told her from the beginning that
proving damages would be impossible anyway, because the charges
were not credible and had not damaged her earning power or her reputation. However, as she sees it, she gained two valuable lessons:
"when not to respond (by making the mistake of answering at length
when [I] shouldn't have responded at all), and when to respond (by
asking responsible publications to check their facts in advance). The
lessons were painful, but worth it."

The lesson she apparently did not draw from the events was that
accepting her past actions for what they were and moving on from
there might have saved her a great deal of pain in the first place.

27

The Ms. Foundation:
The Cutting Edge

As the 1970s wore on, the movement took over more of Gloria's life, leaving her even less time to write. The free spirit who had never wanted to know what she would be doing the following year became enmeshed in an endless stream of organizations. The two that became an important part of her life for many years were the Ms. Foundation for Women and Voters for Choice.

Ms. people like to say that the Ms. Foundation started out as a drawer in Ronnie Eldridge's desk. When Ronnie left, the Ms. Foundation moved to a drawer in Joanne Edgar's desk. When the founders of *Ms.* formed the Ms. Foundation for Women in 1972, they expected to donate at least 10 percent of the magazine's profits to the movement. The anticipated profits failed to materialize, but the magazine gave the foundation start-up funds anyway. Then Gloria and others dutifully went out and raised money for it. She jokes that fund-raising is the world's second-oldest profession, but there must have been times when she failed to see the difference.

Among the foundation's earliest recipients were a battered women's shelter in Michigan, a gathering of all the female elected officials in California (including then-state-legislator Dianne Feinstein), and the National Black Feminist Organization in New York (created by Margaret Sloan, Jane Galvin-Lewis, Eleanor Holmes Norton, and Flo Kennedy, among others). In 1975 the Ms. Foundation acquired tax-exempt status and a full-time executive director. Until then most of the work was performed by the founding board members, Gloria, Pat Carbine, Letty Pogrebin, and Marlo Thomas.

Gloria and Marlo had been friends since the 1960s, when a producer brought them together. "I was doing *That Girl*," Marlo recalls, "and some producer had the idea that I should play Gloria as a Play-boy Bunny. We didn't like the producer, and we thoroughly intimidated the agent—he said later he had to go home and check his private parts because he'd been in the room with the two of us. We thought, What a geek, that he would say that. But I guess it was odd to have strong, independent-speaking women in those days. Neither of us particularly wanted to do the story, but we became very good friends from that time on."

Neither was a feminist at that point, but both were strong-willed and strong-minded. Innovative for its time, *That Girl* featured a young woman living on her own in New York. She had a boyfriend and no obvious plans to marry—and Marlo had to fight for her character's right to live without a roommate. Gloria was involved with Herb Sargent while Marlo was living with writer Herb Gardner, and the four sometimes socialized.

In 1969 Gloria launched Marlo as an activist when, unable to speak to a group of welfare mothers in Rhode Island, Gloria asked Marlo to take her place. "They needed an F.F." Marlo explains—a famous feminist. Although Marlo was an actress, she had grown up petted and wealthy in Beverly Hills, and the idea terrified her. "I can't possibly do that," she objected. "First of all, I'm not married. I'm not a mother. I've never been on welfare. These women will hate me. What could I possibly have in common with them?"

"They'll love you just for going," Gloria reassured her. "Just go and be yourself."

Marlo finally agreed, and she loved it. "You couldn't get any farther from me than a welfare mother," Marlo recalls, "but there I was speaking to these women, and I told them exactly that. I said, 'There's a lot of reasons about which we don't connect. I'm not a mother, I've never been on welfare. I'm a rich kid from Beverly Hills. But I care about you.' It was the beginning of my realizing that there weren't really barriers between me and other women."

Marlo is a devoted friend to Gloria. "I think our gift-giving is a metaphor for our friendship. She always gives me exquisite and wonderful political gifts—statues of goddesses, a bullfight poster with the only woman bullfighter—and I give her satin pajamas and negligees and very beautiful pieces of clothing to enjoy her womanhood. So our gifts are exquisite in different ways," she explains.

For many years afterward, their single status was another bond, but in 1980 Marlo married talk-show host Phil Donahue. Although they married secretly at the home of Marlo's parents and left the country without telling any of their friends in advance, Marlo felt somewhat traitorous about marrying without talking to Gloria about it, not to mention marrying at all.

"The night before I got married, I wrote Gloria a long letter and said that I felt in many ways I was abandoning her. We'd been so singular all of our lives. Not just single, but singular. And we'd taken such strength from each other. We were sort of the other side of one another—the blonde and brunette of what we each stood for, and we could always take solace in the fact that we each felt as the other felt about many things, like the institution of marriage. We both thought the institution of marriage was practically a plantation-type mentality.

"Gloria used to say such wonderful things, like 'I can't mate in captivity,' and I used to say, 'Marriage is like a vacuum cleaner: if you stick it to your ear, it sucks out all your talent.' We had said all these things for years and years and years, and so in many ways, we were assured and reassured by each other's presence on the planet as to who we were. We'd never been married; we weren't divorced; we weren't single mothers; we were heterosexual; men were attracted to us. So they couldn't say the usual things they say about women: 'They hate men.' 'Men don't like them.' All that other stuff.

"We had conquered so many of these things, not to mention our middle-class values. So it was very important to me to let her know that I was sorry to be abandoning her and that I hoped she wouldn't see it that way and that this might be the final test for feminist friendship: that one of us entered the institution we weren't quite sure about."

When the couple returned, Gloria gave Marlo a bridal shower and reassured her. As Marlo recalls happily, "She loved the letter—we'd been through a lot and had talked about what a bad institution it was and that the only way marriage was possible was to redesign and redefine it."

That was many years into their friendship. When Marlo went shopping in 1972 for a gift for her niece and found the toys and records dismayingly sexist, she decided to produce a record album for her. She called Gloria. "I need two things," she said. "One is someone who understands the children's market and children's publishing, and the psychology of children. The other is that I want to put the money from the record back into the women's movement."

Over a couple of lunches, Marlo, Gloria, and Letty Pogrebin—whom Gloria brought along as Ms.'s resident expert on the subject—planned the project. Then Marlo and Carole Hart, who had won an Emmy for *Sesame Street*, assembled a group that included songwriter Carole King, actors Mel Brooks and Alan Alda, and singers Harry Belafonte, Michael Jackson, and Diana Ross. The result was the classic "Free to Be . . . You and Me," a nonsexist, multiracial children's record with original songs, stories, and poems. In 1974 they followed up with an Emmy Award–winning television special, and the record sold so many copies it went gold in 1976.

When Marlo conceived the idea, Gloria and others had begun the process of forming the Ms. Foundation. The "Free to Be" royalties provided it with its first ongoing source of funding. In 1975 the Ms. Foundation hired Brenda Brimmer as its first professional director. Soon Brenda had Gloria visiting cities around the country to educate small gatherings of wealthy women about opportunities to become active philanthropically.

"Gloria was careful not to be interfering, but she was terrific—always there when I needed her," Brenda explains. It seemed to Brenda, after three and a half years of traveling with Gloria, that "Gloria had *no* private life. She was so giving—it was all the movement. I always felt bad getting in line to ask for her time because she was so busy, but there were just some things she could do better than anyone else—like reach out to wealthy women and do fund-raising and consciousness-raising at the same time."

Brenda helped expand the board of directors to include, among others, former Equal Employment Opportunity Commission member and past NOW president Aileen Hernández, and a Minnesota Democratic Party leader, Koryne Horbal. One of the myriad friends of Gloria, Koryne has spent many nights in Gloria's apartment, and she compares staying there to visiting a spa, because Gloria's refrigerator is always empty.

For many years the board included only activists, and Gloria found the board meetings stimulating: "We had the greatest meetings—even though I always think if you die and go to hell, it'll be a meeting. But these were different. No matter how difficult things were, we went around the room and said what was happening to us. I used to invite women to meetings if they were feeling depressed. One of our editors was upset because her husband had gone off with someone she knew. She and her husband were black and the someone else was white. And one of the older women there said, 'That's funny. My husband went off with a white woman too.' Suddenly, the editor turned from tears to laughter, because, she said, 'I realized that, statistically speaking, *most* men run off with white women!' "

The board decided the foundation's key program areas would be "economic justice" (employment), reproductive health and rights, safety (violence against women), and various girls' issues (such as gender stereotypes or teen pregnancy). Within those areas, they particularly wanted to take on the controversial issues. Envisioning the Ms. Foundation as the cutting edge, they hoped the foundation's contributions could add visibility and credibility to the underlying issues. In 1976 they were the first national foundation to grant awards to battered women's shelters. In 1977 they supported a project to defend lesbian mothers threatened with losing custody of their children.

The foundation also acted as a referral service for larger foundations and educated them about newer, more controversial issues and projects. Eventually some of the larger foundations began to funnel funds to the Ms. Foundation to help with projects that were too small for them or in areas where the Ms. Foundation had greater expertise.

In 1982, a couple of directors later, Julia Scott took over. The foundation staff had grown to six or seven, but the foundation still had no endowment, which meant the staff and board members had to continually raise all the money they wanted to give away. Julia, who is African American, increased the allocations of funding to women of color and attempted to diversify the board by rotating some of the members off instead of appointing them for life. Gloria and Pat were willing to rotate off, but Marlo and Letty were not, so Julia judiciously left that problem for her successor. The compromise was to grandmother the original four as founding directors and rotate everyone else, and eventually the original four went off the voting board.

In 1984 the board hired Marie Wilson. Marie had worked in academia and private industry and in the Des Moines, Iowa, city government as the first woman elected to an at-large position on the city council. Even with her varied experience, Marie found herself in culture shock working with the Ms. Foundation. Much of its culture, she believes, reflects Gloria.

First, there were the finances. Examining the financial statements when she arrived for a job interview, Marie turned to Gloria. "I think you're in a deficit position," she said.

"No, no, no, no. It's just a— It'll be corrected in December," Gloria assured her. "It's no problem. It's fine."

After Marie took the job, she learned that the foundation staff was moving upstairs to smaller offices because there was no money. What Gloria had meant was that in December they were sure to get donations. Marie reflects, "That was a fabulous experience of how the world is framed for Gloria. I mean, *of course* they were in a deficit position, but in her mind, we would raise the money soon and it would be fine. . . .

"And I think that's why we've worked well together. Because if you want to work with women, if you want to be working with visionaries and be a visionary, you can't get too bogged down in what does it mean on paper."

Although Marie likes fund-raising, she had not expected to jump in before she had even moved into an apartment. Even so, she says, "I think that's a big piece of the way Gloria has operated in the world, and I think it's very powerful—expecting, and then the thing happens. I sometimes think that when a person's life is as complicated as Gloria's, all the things around it are kind of beautifully confusing. And the great thing is, they're not confusing to her. . . . A big vision is a wonderful thing, and I'd rather be with somebody who keeps things beautifully confused or beautifully muddled because it's a good cause and because she truly believes we can get enough resources."

Just after Marie accepted the position, and before she even moved to New York, the board members asked her to go to Chicago for a fund-raiser honoring Phil Donahue. She recalls: "I'm a city council member and the vice president of the Iowa Banker Association, and I get a call from Gloria asking, 'Could you pick up some note cards that we can make into place cards?' That should have told me about this organization. The evening was at the biggest chichi home, with artwork on the walls like I've never seen in my life. And I think, what in the world? I'm going to a new job and I'm out getting these place cards? What is wrong with this picture?

"So then we meet at a board member's house, and what Gloria wants us to do is sit there and write something about a grantee on each of these place cards. So we sit around and look at the annual report and pick a grantee and write about it on these place cards. And Gloria's doing it too.

"Which is part of the whole ambience of the work. And it's also important. If I were writing a book about Gloria, I'd say what she's done is try to keep people personally connected, really personally connected to important ideas and work. And in just those ways. That's her brilliance."

Marie's first exposure to one of the Ms. Foundation's treasured board meetings was yet another shock: "Here I was, the new director, frantic about an organization that seemed not to have a whole lot of structures or resources or whatever. And I'd moved to New York, left my political office, burned my bridges. I could not go back. And I sat there for the first two hours of the meeting while all eleven of them went around the room and talked about their lives, updating each other. I guess their ritual—because they were always in the 'personal is political'—was important. But I'm heavy breathing because I'm wondering when we are going to get to the real meeting.

"I was panicked. I had a real mission—I came to do this economic development work—and I know that I have a honeymoon of about one meeting. I've brought in experts to inform them about this small, growing movement for small and micro businesses for low-income women; I've had a video made.

"Also, I was from Iowa, and if you were from Iowa, you had to be more than sophisticated. So I've got this elaborate thing planned. I'm planning to talk with them about teleconferencing, and they're spending two hours talking about their lives."

Marie eventually instituted the economic development program, which was also of great interest to Gloria. By 1992 the foundation ran a $2.3 million Collaborative Fund for Women's Economic Development. Economic development, especially micro-lending directed specifically at women, had become a worldwide movement, pioneered by Muhammad Yunus, a Bangladeshi economist, in the 1970s. His Grameen Bank lent tiny sums to women in villages to buy inventories to get started in business. He lent the money without collateral and created cells of five women who guaranteed one another's loans and supported one another with advice and encouragement. The loans might be as small as $10 or $15, but sometimes that would be all they needed to buy a duck to sell its eggs, or rags to wash and resell.

The Collaborative Fund, which involved the Ms. Foundation and twelve other donors, combined funds to be distributed to both micro-enterprises and cooperatives. A typical micro-enterprise project might help a woman to get off welfare by supplying her both with the funds needed to buy shoes that she could then sell door to door and with business training from other women business owners. Among the cooperatives receiving grants were the Home Care Associates Training Institute, an organization that trained black and Latina women in the South Bronx and Harlem to become home-health workers, and the Watermark Association of Artisans, a North Carolina crafts cooperative that marketed individual women's crafts so successfully that it secured contracts from Ralph Lauren and Esprit.

The Ms. Foundation's most visible project has been Take Our Daughters to Work Day, which began in 1992. Gloria says her major contribution to that project may have been suggesting "Our" instead of "Your" for its title, but she spends every Take Our Daughters to Work Day speaking at a number of sites, from large corporate supporters like Merrill Lynch to foundation grantees like Local 1199 of the Health and Hospital Workers Union.

Take Our Daughters to Work Day has always been controversial. Some critics on the right fault the idea for discriminating against boys, and a religious group in Arkansas even initiated a "Take Your Daughter Home" day to teach girls cooking and other domestic skills. A few men from the "Men's Action Network" even picket the Ms. Foundation's offices every year, one year handing out flyers that asked, "Who are these women and why do they hate our sons?" Some critics on the left consider it elitist. A number of less political observers consider it unkind to boys, and some corporations have experimented by including boys as well as girls.

Marie Wilson responds to critics by saying, "We'd love to see other organizations create occasions for boys. We're the Ms. Foundation for Women, and this is part of our Girls' Initiative." Foundation spokeswoman Jill Savitt would say, "Executives with glass ceilings shouldn't throw stones." Gloria usually quotes Eleanor Holmes Norton, who said, "There's no Take Our Sons to Work Day for the same reason there's no White History Month." She sometimes suggests that boys could use a "Take Our Sons Home Day" because "the parallel crisis for boys occurs between five and eight, or so, when they, too, are encouraged to fit a whole, complex self into a gender role."

Without doubt, under Marie the Ms. Foundation became an institution. She spent money in order to raise money, and her strategy worked. The budget has grown from $700,000 when she arrived in 1984 to over $6 million and the $100,000 endowment she inherited is now more than $12 million. In 1989 she initiated the Gloria Awards, or Women of Vision Awards (as Gloria calls them), which honor women for outstanding work in their local communities. The first year's award winners included some nationally prominent women, but in general the honorees seem to be selected to showcase categories of grassroots programs.

The first black-tie, celebrity-filled Gloria Awards dinner was held at the Rainbow Room in New York City and included as presenters Cybill Shepherd, Madeline Kahn, Cicely Tyson, and Alice Walker's daughter Rebecca, who is Gloria's goddaughter and protégée. Gloria became sufficiently involved in the arrangements to insist that a sculptor she had met make the statuettes to be given to the honorees.

In 1979 Gloria cofounded Voters for Choice, another organization to which she has devoted a great deal of time and effort. Gloria, Koryne Horbal, California Assemblywoman (later U.S. Congresswoman) Maxine Waters, and others on the Ms. Foundation board believed they needed a separate entity to work electorally on the abortion issue. The previous year Gloria had helped Koryne with the Democratic Labor Party's Project 13, a program to elect more prochoice Minnesota legislators. A group of Minnesota Democratic women had decided they would visit every precinct in the state and offer training and workshops on the issue of abortion. Gloria agreed to help out, and so she flew all over the state in a tiny plane.

Koryne and Gloria continued to talk afterward about how effective the right-wing political action committees had been in the 1978 election, and though they did not particularly approve of PACs, they eventually decided they had no alternative but to organize one of their own. The National Abortion Rights Action League (NARAL) existed, but it was organized state by state, and they did not consider it adequate. Planned Parenthood did not have a PAC, but at the same time that Koryne and Gloria were forming Voters for Choice some of Planned Parenthood's national board members were creating Friends of Family Planning, and later the two organizations merged.

Through Voters for Choice, the founders hoped to provide on a national basis what Project 13 had offered throughout Minnesota—

not just funds, fund-raising and other campaign assistance for political candidates, but also media and training for candidates on dealing with the issue of abortion. They planned to allocate their resources—the most valuable of which was Gloria—among the electoral races where they thought they could be most beneficial.

For the board, which they felt had to be bipartisan and include men, Gloria recruited Massachusetts Senator Edward Brooke and her current lover Stan Pottinger, both male Republicans. General Motors heir and constant contributor to liberal causes Stewart Mott, in whose Washington house they held their original meetings, sat on both the board of Voters for Choice and Planned Parenthood's Friends of Family Planning. Koryne was the first president. Gloria persuaded Kristina Kiehl, a Washington activist who had been raising money for the Ms. Foundation, to be treasurer.

For the first few years Voters for Choice gave small donations to candidates and embarked on a few grassroots projects. Koryne contacted Jeri Rasmussen, with whom she had worked before. While public affairs coordinator of Planned Parenthood of Minnesota, Rasmussen had written a pamphlet on how to deal with the issues of abortion in the political arena, and VFC used it. In 1981 VFC executive director Susan Dickler and Kristina Kiehl, now VFC president, decided to develop something more elaborate.

They assembled political consultants and pollsters to discuss the issue and hired a writer to write *Winning With Choice: A Campaign Strategy Handbook*. The first book was a ring-binder notebook with information demonstrating to candidates they need not be ambiguous on the issue of abortion and giving them information and strategies for dealing with the issue. Later they simplified it into a twenty-four-page booklet that concentrates on what to expect in dealing with the issue and how to handle it. The concept has been copied by other organizations, and the booklet is still in use by candidates and activists across the country. VFC updates it every few years.

Like the Ms. Foundation and *Ms.* magazine, Voters for Choice both promoted and traded on Gloria's star power to attract press coverage, funds, and voters. Gloria went wherever she was asked to go—fundraiser luncheons with Gloria Steinem, cocktails with Gloria Steinem, dinner with Gloria Steinem.

The fund-raisers were relatively small and oriented toward big donors, until VFC hired executive director Julie Burton in 1989. In addition to her skills as an organizer, Julie had rock-music connections, so in 1992 VFC began sponsoring concerts with performers like Pearl Jam, Neil Young, Bonnie Raitt, Rosie O'Donnell, Phish, and Rickie Lee Jones. Gloria emcees, and occasionally bestows upon the male performers the ultimate accolade, pronouncing them honorary women.

Gloria was deeply involved. "For our first ten years, I was going to board meetings and doing more of the scut work. It's only recently gotten to the point where I don't have to go and I can just be sent." Much of the work involved strategizing. "We looked at records, sent out questionnaires to get the candidates' positions on all aspects of reproductive rights, made decisions about primaries. Should we stay in congressional races only? Should we get into state races?"

During Ann Richards's successful 1990 race for the governorship of Texas, Voters for Choice helped in several ways. Gloria explains, "Ann is clearly fine on this issue and doesn't need our help in any way to speak about it. But she had a fairly conventional staff running her campaign who didn't know how to do media about this issue. So we would do independent expenditures . . . because usually the opposition is trying to muddy up the record. They know this is a majority issue, so they try to say that they are middle of the road or prochoice in some sense when they're really not. So you just need to get the information out."

VFC's national spokesperson, Cybill Shepherd, appeared many times on Richards's behalf to help raise money. In the last ten days of the campaign VFC produced and aired a prime-time television commercial featuring Annie Potts, one of the stars of the television program *Designing Women*. Also in 1990, VFC targeted state legislatures in Maryland, New York, and Oregon. To assist prochoice challengers and incumbents in the primary and general elections, Voters for Choice provided funds and VFC-produced radio commercials. At a three-day training seminar in Washington, D.C., they provided for twenty-eight candidates one-on-one sessions with national political consultants.

Before President Bill Clinton vetoed the bill regulating late-term abortions in 1996, Gloria and Julie met with his aides Betsy Myers, Harold Ickes, and later, George Stephanopoulos, to suggest a more constructive way of dealing with the issue. As Gloria explains: "We told them we hope they will consider signaling their supporters. The other side signals its supporters and ours doesn't. Clinton voted right, but he met only with the bishops, not with the prochoice people, instead of doing, in my opinion, what he could have done, which was simply say, 'I support the American College of Obstetricians and Gynecologists.'

Period. He wrote a long letter about how agonizing it was and how terrible this procedure was and so on. He doesn't need to do that. And I understand that he may feel that because he's under such pressure. But outside of Washington, it only muddies up the real issue of who decides about abortion, a woman and her physician, or Congress?"

In 1997, Voters for Choice was still fighting the battle.

28

Gloria's Little Marriages

In 1971 Gloria began seeing a new lover. A disguised account of her affair with Franklin Thomas appeared in 1992 in *Revolution From Within*:

> When we first met in the late 1960s, he was a quiet presence in a noisy group arguing about the merits of a political campaign. I remember thinking that he looked like a large friendly tree, inclining slightly toward us as he listened intently, with an occasional response when the wind of our talk rustled in his branches.

Gloria portrayed him as a doctor who had returned to work in the southern inner city where he had been born.

The analogy was apt. Franklin Thomas headed the Bedford-Stuyvesant Restoration Corporation, an urban-renewal project in the section of Brooklyn where he had been born in 1934. The youngest of six children, Frank was an outstanding student and athlete, turning down a number of athletic scholarships to enroll at Columbia, where he helped pay his tuition by waiting on tables. He was the captain and star of Columbia's basketball team and one of the Ivy League's first black varsity-team captains. He also joined the local NAACP and campaigned for the admission to Columbia of more black students and for the end of discrimination in off-campus housing.

After law school he became an assistant U.S. attorney in New York State and later was appointed New York City's deputy police commissioner for legal affairs at the age of thirty-one. In the following year, he so impressed Sen. Robert F. Kennedy that Kennedy sought him out to head an experimental development corporation formed to combat the urban decay and unemployment in Bedford-Stuyvesant, the largest black community in New York City except for Harlem.

As president of the Bedford-Stuyvesant Restoration Corporation for ten years (1967–1977) he earned a national reputation for the operation's success. The corporation attracted government, corporate, and nonprofit contributions to the community and spent $63 million dollars during his tenure, training previously unemployed workers, constructing and rehabilitating buildings, lending residents funds to start their own businesses, and attracting corporations to the area. In 1979 he became president of the Ford Foundation, the largest foundation in the world.

Gloria and Frank met when Clay Felker decided *New York* should run an article entitled "Why Isn't This Man Mayor of New York?" and told Gloria to call him. Frank, who had no interest in being mayor of New York, refused to cooperate. When they began their affair, Frank was separated and the father of four children. He was divorced the following year and, for two such prominent people, he and Gloria managed to keep a low profile. When reporters asked, Gloria said she was in a relationship, but refused to give her lover's name, and the press did not pursue it. In her 1992 book, Gloria wrote:

> We walked the hot streets that everyone else was trying to get out of, went to movies, enjoyed free concerts, and ate every possible kind of ethnic food. It felt as if we had always known each other, yet also as if we were just exploring and exploding into a new part of ourselves. Sometimes, we stayed in all weekend talking, making love, listening to the new music tapes we brought each other, watching old movies, and ordering food so we never had to go out.

As she explains, "We created a world for each other where we didn't need other people. It wasn't as if we were rejecting other people. We both had busy work lives, so when we could see each other, we generally wanted to see each other by ourselves."

Their relationship lasted more than three years, 1971–1974, and they were Gloria's first years as a nationally known feminist. Frank watched Gloria juggle her efforts to keep *Ms.* afloat with the obligation she felt to utilize her rising visibility: "The increasing focus of attention on her and her increasing involvement was exciting, although I don't think she fully appreciated the extent of the public demands. She was comfortable talking directly to groups of men and women, but the groups kept getting larger and the frequency increased. She began to more consciously take the same message in different forms to a range of different groups and so often, it was very much an unfolding experience for her. She was recognizing feminism within herself and letting her mind really range over the plurality of ways in which it would benefit society.

"The demands grew and grew, so the time available for writing became more and more compressed. The magazine start-up and financing made it a very stressful time—she always tried to be available to people who needed or wanted her attention, so she was in constant motion. I tried to encourage her to carve out some time that wasn't booked because it might lead to some great organizing, but Gloria always made time for people. To this day anyone who has a serious need or an issue will find a receptive, interested response. It's very much a part of her personality, although I don't think she recognized that was true in the seventies.

"If you'd asked her, 'Are you going on a national speaking tour?' she wouldn't have said she was. But in the process of carrying out these responsibilities and responding to the press, that's exactly what happened. Over those exhilarating couple of years, the way she ultimately began to spend her time was not a plan that she had adopted but rather was a by-product of what she'd taken on."

The thought of marriage occurred to both of them, but Frank had just come out of a marriage and already had children, so he did not push for it. Gloria, as usual, did not seek it. However, their relationship was one of the most fulfilling of her life. Their friendship endured after their affair ended, and they talk to each other frequently.

In *Revolution From Within* Gloria attributed the decline of the affair both to temperament and circumstance. Eventually the fact that they were so much alike, she explained, meant that "we each began to need someone with perspective to get us out of deep grooves in our minds." That is a typical Gloria euphemism—she infallibly depicts the decisions to terminate her relationships as mutual.

The other cause to which she attributed their breakup illuminates one of the limitations in Gloria's relationships with men. During their time together Frank went through a variety of difficulties. Gloria, portraying them in *Revolution From Within* as an illness, described her reaction. "[A]s I realized later, taking care of him pressed such a painful and familiar nerve in me after the years of caretaking for my mother that I responded to him in the same way: I was right there and responsible, but turned off emotionally—a familiar form of automatic pilot."

That statement is interesting, for Gloria has spent all her years as a feminist in caretaking relationships with individual women as well as institutions like *Ms.* magazine and the Ms. Foundation, though that is not the same as feeling responsible in the way she did for her mother. However, caretaking was not what she was willing to give men. The degree to which she was self-protective in her relations with men (and felt like an adult partner) were opposite of her defenselessness against her own empathy for women's neediness.

As Gloria ended her relationship with Frank Thomas, she was moving into another relationship. In the fall of 1974, J. Stanley Pottinger, assistant U.S. attorney general for civil rights, called Gloria at work. He didn't know her, but he wanted to involve the Justice Department in sex discrimination suits, and he needed to learn more about the issue.

The middle of three sons, Stan had grown up in Dayton, Ohio. After graduating from Harvard College and Harvard Law School, he had married his high school sweetheart (also named Gloria) and moved to San Francisco.

He had come to Washington in 1970 as a protégé of Robert Finch, President Nixon's first secretary of Health, Education, and Welfare, and had served as director of HEW's Office of Civil Rights, enforcing school desegregation. After the 1972 election he moved to the Justice Department. He spent the next four years serving under three presidents and seven attorneys general. (He started after John Mitchell resigned to run Nixon's reelection campaign in 1972. Richard Kleindienst served for sixty days. Elliot Richardson and William Ruckelshaus resigned during the so-called Saturday Night Massacre, after refusing to fire the special prosecutor who was investigating the Watergate scandal. Robert Bork held the position briefly. William Saxbe, the successor to Bork, "had the distinction of saying while serving as AG that Nixon didn't know what was going on the way a piano player in a whorehouse didn't know what was going on." Ed Levi served under President Gerald Ford. Griffin Bell was attorney general under President Jimmy Carter.)

Stan's move to the Justice Department was fortuitous. "The department was so preoccupied with Watergate at that point, I was able to do what I wanted," he recalls. "The division attorneys were fairly happy to have me. I shared many of their beliefs, and we filed more than 212 lawsuits, more than at any other time in the history of the division." Stan reopened Kent State. "Everyone said it was impossible, but Elliot Richardson and I were in synch on the matter. We set policy. They were golden days."

Members of the Ohio National Guard had killed four students and injured nine others during an antiwar demonstration at Kent State University on May 4, 1970. Until the Justice Department convened a federal grand jury in December 1973, the only governmental response had been a state grand jury's indictment of twenty-five people, mostly students, and a report criticizing the university for permissiveness.

Stan wanted to talk with lawyers, so Gloria assembled a group that included Brenda Feigen Fasteau and Ruth Bader Ginsburg, then a professor at Columbia Law School. When Stan, who was separated from his wife, heard that Gloria needed to get to Hartford, Connecticut, for a speech later that day, he slipped out of the meeting and rented a car so that he could drive her. They spent the ride talking about their mutual Ohio backgrounds and their predilection for Vernor's ginger ale, a regional specialty.

Stan stayed in Hartford for Gloria's speech and was appalled at the way she was treated at the press conference. He was used to dealing with the press as a government official. "In Washington you're fighting to humanize what is otherwise a talking-head presentation," he explains. "This was the exact opposite. She was trying to talk about policies and everyone wanted to know, 'Who are you going out with? Who are you sleeping with? Are your skirts too short? Are your heels too high?' "

Stan drove Gloria back to New York and sent her a case of Vernor's. A few months later, they began seeing each other. They spent nine years together, the longest of Gloria's "little marriages." Gloria always describes Stan as "my record."

Moving from Frank to Stan was not simple—Gloria's transitions never were. Her sexual appetite fascinated her friends; her moves from one relationship to another were complicated affairs that amused them. As the long and happily married Letty Pogrebin recalls: "She spent a lot of time in relationships. . . . and I remember the intrigue. Especially in the transition between Frank and Stan. She couldn't stand to hurt Frank, and she must have done it right, because they've remained friends, good friends. She has done something better than most of us, because there's no rancor when she walks away from these people.

"She was led around by her libido all those years. It was so complicated. These days, it seems to me she has zero libido and is quite happy
about it. . . . She's gained a lot of time now, because those relationships
were complicated and they took a lot of her attention and time. Getting
in and out of things. She'd have long talks on the phone. And she'd
leave *him*. To go find *him*. To go meet *him* . . . That kind of thing. It
was Byzantine intrigue."

To make things even more complicated, while Gloria considered herself usually monogamous, from time to time she had casual affairs, a
few of them with married men. According to Blair Chotzinoff, he and
Gloria continued to see each other intermittently during both his marriages. Gloria once had a brief affair with a news executive whose wife
later told Gloria that another woman had asked her, "What would
happen if it turned out that your husband was having an affair with
Gloria?"

Gloria recalls, "Then she said to me, meaning it from all her heart,
'It would be just another evidence of his good taste.' So maybe either
she knew, or she didn't mind. But it wasn't a bad feeling—it wasn't
like I felt we were going to hurt her."

She adds, "It's more than consenting adults. It's balance. I think the
problem comes not from affairs, but from whether or not both people
are in the same place. In other words, if both parties in a married
couple feel equally dependent and caring and vulnerable to each
other—and equally able to sometimes have a relationship with another
person, whether it's a friend or a sexual partner, it seems to work out
all right. The problem seems to come when one person behaves very
differently from the other. When the balance is very off.

"I don't think there's any magic. You know, there are many kinds of
betrayal that are worse than sexual betrayal."

With Stan in Washington, and with Gloria in New York when she
wasn't on the road—which was almost every week for most of the
years they were together—they saw each other mostly on weekends in
Washington, because Stan's two oldest children lived with him. When
Stan had gotten divorced from Gloria I, as they called his ex-wife
(Gloria II joked that Stan didn't even have to change the towels) he
and his wife shared custody of the children. Other than Tom
Guinzburg, whose children had been with them on occasional weekends, none of Gloria's previous partners had lived with their children.
She enjoyed their company, however, and children always liked Gloria,
because she never patronized them.

Sharing Stan with his children was not difficult anyway, because Stan is, as Gloria puts it, "very high energy." He was always initiating activities for the two of them and thinking of ways to be helpful to her. When an interviewer once asked her what was the most romantic thing a man had ever done for her, Gloria replied, "Ironed my blouse." That was Stan, she explains. "I was running around in the morning and was late and he ironed it. He wouldn't think of not doing it. He's a very healthy person, very positive and well balanced."

Once they took a cruise on the *Queen Elizabeth 2*. Gloria had been offered two free passages in exchange for speaking to the passengers, and Joanne Edgar urged her to go. The other speaker on the ship was a famous memory expert, Joanne told Gloria, suggesting, "If you go on this trip, it'll be a nice vacation and you can take the memory course."

That sounded like a good idea, so Gloria invited Stan. "Then," Gloria recalls, "as soon as Stan and I got on the *QE2* I made Stan go and find this man. Right away. I was so full of enthusiasm that I went right up to this man and said, 'I'm so glad to meet you and I'm going to take your course every day. I know it's going to change my life.' And he said, 'Don't you remember me? We lectured together in Philadelphia.' So I took dancing lessons or something else instead. I think."

Stan loved Gloria's sense of humor: "People who know her professionally often think she's consumed with women's issues and sees virtually everything through the prism of feminism. She does. But in a private setting she's also relaxed and more broad-based than she gets credit for. Sometimes she's just plain funny, even from the feminist viewpoint. Once we were watching *Close Encounters of the Third Kind* at the theater. When the being comes out of the spacecraft with big almond-shaped eyes and an elongated neck and a lightbulb head and long arms, and starts gathering up all the people, and the light is shining from behind, and the music is playing, and this is the moment when you actually see this foreign person, I leaned over to her and said, 'See. All hope is not lost. The superior intelligence of the universe looks like a woman.' And she said, 'With our luck that's the stewardess.'"

During the later years of their relationship the pair lived in the same city. Stan practiced law in Washington after leaving government. In December 1977 and for much of 1978, Gloria was there, too, on a fellowship at the Woodrow Wilson International Center for Scholars at the Smithsonian Institution.

Gloria had been talking for years about breaking away to get back to writing. On the other hand, she also used to complain that she had writer's block, and she knew that, to some extent, she was using the other activities to avoid the writing she wanted to do, but found diffi-cult. Sometimes she would tell friends she liked having written, but not writing. Sometimes she would blame it on her gender conditioning. As she told one reporter, "Any male writer my age I know has written at least one book. I haven't written any. I never took control of a whole year or two of my life and said, 'This is what I want to do.'"

Gloria longed to produce a serious feminist work. When she won the fellowship, which was based on her proposal to write a study of the impact of feminism on political theory, she hoped the structure at the Smithsonian would help force her to stay in one place and concentrate. It did not. During her stay, she did write several articles, most notably, "The International Crime of Genital Mutilation," with Robin Morgan, about female genital mutilation, but she did not produce a book of feminist theory.

She also failed to get more work done because she lacked the tem-perament to isolate herself. She continued to respond to her various constituencies, and because Stan lived in Washington, she spent more time with him. On top of that she left Washington frequently, because she disliked both the city and the Wilson Center, which she considered stuffy and conservative.

In 1980 Stan moved to New York City to work on financial deals. He made and lost a great deal of money during the gyrations of the real-estate market in the 1980s. Gloria's relationship with him ended in 1984, when she moved on to her next lover. A few years later, Stan embarked on a new career as a novelist.

His first book, a medical thriller, *The Fourth Procedure,* spent sev-eral weeks on the bestseller lists in 1995. During a spate of publicity for the book, Stan was annoyed to find himself covered in the same way Gloria had been—in terms of his personal life. While it was less typical for a man to receive that kind of coverage, the media interest was understandable. Like Gloria's, Stan's personal life was interesting. He tended to become involved with high-profile women, such as Kathie Lee Epstein (Gifford), Connie Chung, literary agent Lynn Nesbit, and publisher and literary agent Joni Evans.

Gloria and Stan remain close friends, so Gloria probably was amused by the appearance in Stan's book of a character named Victo-ria. In creating Victoria, Stan combined elements from real people, including feminist lawyer Catherine MacKinnon, with imaginary ones. As Stan says, "Hence the word, 'fiction'." Victoria was "a moving willow tree with a steel-trap mind. A walking contradiction, which had always been one of her attractions." Her favorite T-shirt displayed the words, "A woman needs a man like a fish needs a bicycle." Her lover in the book speculated on Victoria's attitude toward the opposite sex:

> Ah yes, he thought. Men. "The enemy." The people she loved to hate and hated to love. Maybe that was going too far, but saying she regarded them with deep ambivalence wasn't. A complicated relationship with her father, Dr. Steven Winters, was part of the equation, but most of it came from her work. Fifteen years of watching women limp into her law clinic looking for help. Fifteen years of peering into the snake pits of angry marriages, witnessing punching-bag violence, knife-wielding rage. Fifteen years of working with female victims, seeing the public in general growing tired of them, guiltily offering them the sanctuary of the courts, like modern-day leper colonies, and wishing they'd disappear. Fifteen years of battered women's anemic self-esteem transfused into her own bloodstream. She loved Jack, needed and trusted him, and there were other men whom she respected, too, once she got to know them. But at a distance, in the abstract, in their *essence,* she saw men the way weary social workers regarded welfare payments: with suspicion.

Like the character to whom she bore at least a passing resemblance, Gloria's work was emotionally draining, but her 1970s were invigorating as well as exhausting. Her speaking engagements were repetitious, but like all dedicated teachers, Gloria never lost her pleasure in helping others to see the world in a new way. Her ability to convey the fundamental message of the women's movement so simply was what made her such a powerful communicator.

In 1973, for example, Gloria addressed an American Association of Advertising Agencies Central Region annual meeting in Chicago. The audience was almost completely male—of the few women present, only two were executives.

Four years into her mission and unaware that she was just beginning her life's work, thirty-nine-year-old Gloria dutifully proceeded through her basic Feminism 101 presentation, gyneocracies, race-sex parallels, and all. Then in closing, the only revolutionary leader the American Association of Advertising Agencies ever invited told her audience, quite simply, what it was women wanted: "If you want to understand what women expect, I guess the best advice that I can offer is just to consider what you would feel like if, with all the same hopes and dreams and ambitions that you have now as individual human beings, you had been born female. And then you will understand why we are angry and what we want, individually and collectively.

"And you'll also understand that this movement is a very deep one, a very long term one, and a very inevitable one. It doesn't matter whether there's a magazine. Or books. Or whether polls are taken or not. It is the most alive and far-reaching and forceful movement in the country now, and it's not confined to this country. It is part of a whole worldwide revolution against caste, whether it's race or sex.

"We're really only asking you to move over. But it would be nice if you understood your own interest in moving over. And if you understood that really, without any doubt, revolutionary feminism is the only path to humanism. Thank you."

29

Ruth's Song

The 1980s were discouraging years for feminists. Republican Ronald Reagan was elected president in 1980, running on a conservative platform that called for a constitutional amendment banning abortion, the appointment of antichoice judges, and an explicit rejection of the Equal Rights Amendment for the first time since its introduction in 1923. In her 1996 book, *The Republican War Against Women,* Tanya Melich would describe the Republican Party's strategy of consciously pursuing antiequality policies as a way of attracting northern male voters. The approach was an adaptation of the successful Nixon-Agnew "Southern strategy" that had used racism to attract George Wallace Democrats to the Republican Party.

Feminist groups had complained about President Jimmy Carter, but Reagan was far worse. After his election, a Ku Klux Klan leader from Georgia announced that three of the state's chapters had hung up their robes because they expected the Reagan administration to do their work for them. The backlash against feminist gains, increasingly well organized and well funded during the 1970s, now had the unconcealed support of the federal administration.

The first Equal Rights Amendment had been introduced at the urging of National Women's Party founder Alice Paul, by two Kansas Republicans, one of whom was the nephew of Susan B. Anthony. The modern campaign began in 1967 when Paul, by then eighty-two, persuaded

NOW to endorse it. The contemporary version, "Equality of rights under the law shall not be denied or abridged by the United States or by any state on account of sex," passed both houses of Congress in 1972 by large majorities and went to the state legislatures for ratification.

By the end of 1974, thirty-three states had ratified it and reaching the thirty-eight states necessary for enactment seemed certain. However, within a year, a combination of conservative forces, through a concerted lobbying effort, managed not only to slow the momentum, but in some cases to reverse it. The groups included the Ku Klux Klan, the John Birch Society, conservative religious groups, organizations like Phyllis Schlafly's Stop-ERA and Eagle Forum and Jerry Falwell's Moral Majority, and some business interests, particularly the insurance industry, whose rates were differentiated by sex (women live longer, so rates they paid were higher).

In 1976, no states ratified the amendment, and attempts at recision had to be fought in five states that had already passed the amendment. In 1977 eleven newly elected Nevada legislators, after accepting pro-ERA funds and using pro-ERA supporters in their campaigns, voted to defeat the amendment, reportedly in response to pressure from highly placed Mormon officials. The strictly patriarchal Mormon Church was one of the amendment's leading opponents. Along with Christian fundamentalists, Orthodox Jews, and conservative Catholics, Mormons believed in rigidly separate roles for men and women and feared that the ERA would challenge male authority and upset the father's position in the family. Many women feared it would remove the obligation of fathers to support their children and would require women to work. The Catholic church did not take an official position, but many conservative Catholic organizations and members of the hierarchy were active opponents, in part because, like the amendment's other opponents, they also believed it would strengthen homosexual rights and the right to abortion, which those groups also opposed.

The Equal Rights Amendment issue provided some of the most frustrating political battles of Gloria's life. She later blamed the media for the amendment's defeat, saying they carried the opponents' charges without taking the trouble to investigate and report the amendment's real impact and rarely even reported the twenty-four words of the amendment itself. Furthermore, their practice of providing equal time assisted the ERA's opponents in spreading misinformation to the public. Describing Schlafly as "an artificial creation of the fairness doctrine,"

Gloria continually pointed out that the amendment said nothing about unisex bathrooms, abortion, or gay rights.

The deadline for ratification by the necessary thirty-eight states was March 22, 1979, and when it became clear that the amendment was in trouble, New York Representative Elizabeth Holtzman introduced a bill to extend the deadline. As the extension worked its way through Congress, Katharine Graham asked Gloria to speak to the *Washington Post*'s editorial board about extending the ratification deadline. Her editorial board opposed the extension. Although Gloria had become far more relaxed at speaking over the years, she was quite apprehensive on that occasion: "Speaking got easier, but there were certain kinds of audiences that could bring all the nervousness back. Like the *Washington Post* editorial board. That stands out in my mind as the worst experience I've ever had. It wasn't their doing, it was mine.

"There were two circumstances that made it the worst. One was that I had a feeling a lot depended on it. The *Washington Post* was editorially opposing the extension of the ratification deadline, and Kay had asked me to come and speak to the board. She was too democratic to just tell them what to say, so she invited me to speak to the editorial board about this question. That made me feel there was a lot depending on that, because the editorial position of the *Washington Post* counts for a lot in Washington.

"Also, they were exactly the kind of people with whom I felt least at home. They were—again, that isn't their fault, it just is my resonance—they were kind of East Coast, journalist, intellectual guys with tweed jackets and a supercilious attitude and sports metaphors. You know. Can't change the rules in the middle of the game.

"So I was incredibly nervous. And I did not persuade them, incidentally. We won the extension anyway, but they remained editorially against it."

The extended period for ratification expired on June 30, 1982, with the amendment still three states short of the necessary thirty-eight legislative approvals.

In addition to the general political setbacks of the 1980s, Gloria faced personal losses as well. Ruth died in 1981, a month before her eighty-third birthday. Only after Gloria had been in college and Ruth had received several years of good medical care had Gloria begun to see her mother as a person and not just a problem. As she later wrote in an

1983 essay describing her mother's life and their years together, "Pity takes distance and a certainty of surviving."

In 1964 Ruth had moved in with Sue, Sue's husband Bob, and their six children, and she could be very difficult. Sue recalls that her mother wanted not just to be with others physically, but in interesting conversation as well. Even so, Ruth was a wonderful grandmother to Sue's children.

In 1975, at the age of fifty, Sue finished writing a book, *Blue Mystery: The Story of the Hope Diamond,* which was published the following year by the Smithsonian Press. Also in 1975, Sue went to law school. To study, she often sat in the family's Volkswagen bus in front of the house. That way she could separate herself from her family but remain available if someone needed her. Ruth responded to Sue's efforts by telling her grandchildren what a neglectful mother they had. Sue perservered and became an attorney at the Federal Trade Commission, where her responsibilities included guides for the jewelry industry.

As Gloria's fame increased over the years, Ruth attracted publicity as well. Gloria tried to keep reporters from covering Ruth's mental-health problems, and she largely succeeded. Some of Gloria's descriptions of their poverty and class background distressed her (she would protest that she was not divorced, for example), but on balance, Ruth enjoyed the attention. In a May 2, 1972, *New York Times* article, she was quoted discussing her attempts to combine a career and motherhood:

"I'd been on the *Toledo Blade* for five or six years, and all of my friends were having babies. I was naive enough to think I could have one and still be a newspaper woman. It didn't work."

When she was at home she read the *Ladies' Home Journal* and cookbooks; at work she read H. L. Mencken and the *Smart Set;* "I had a dual personality. It actually made me sick. I left the paper to take care of the baby—that was Sue, she's nine years older than Gloria. Well, you may love the baby, but a hundred baths are a hundred baths. I went back to work." . . .

Recalling the frustrations of an active and intelligent woman trying to live a meaningful life in the twenties, Mrs. Steinem said "I was being torn apart. Finally my doctor said I wasn't cut out for it. I left the paper when Sue was five or six years old and never worked again, except to do press releases for the resort."

Ruth also liked to tell reporters that though she tried to stay in the background when she accompanied her daughter to speeches, "I do occasionally bask in reflected Gloria."

The spotlight of Gloria's fame fell on Sue, too. As the sister of a celebrity, Sue sometimes had to endure judgments from strangers. "Didn't you *know*? Why didn't you *do* something?" a writer once asked her accusingly, referring to Gloria's years in Toledo.

One mildly irritating blow came from Ruth herself. Referring to Gloria's pattern of sequential love affairs as opposed to marriage and children, Ruth remarked one day, "I think it has really been a good thing."

"Thanks a lot, Mother," joked the dutiful elder daughter. "I did everything the way you taught us, and now you say that."

Sue and Gloria are actually devoted to each other. Sue says she can't imagine what she would have done without Gloria's help with her mother during Ruth's later years. Throughout most of the years that Ruth lived in Washington, Ruth visited Gloria in New York and Gloria took her on a vacation every year. At Gloria's fiftieth birthday party, Gloria made a point of publicly thanking Sue for all she had done as a surrogate parent to Gloria.

When Ruth began to fail, Sue and Gloria moved her into a nursing home near Sue's home. Gloria frequently visited her there, and both Gloria and Sue were with her in the hospital when she died. Afterward, Gloria and Sue honored their promise to sit with her for a while, because Ruth had feared a coma might be mistaken for death.

When Ruth died, Gloria lost more than a mother. The nightmare the two had shared in Toledo was a mutual wound, but it was also a mutual bond. They had been comrades as well as mother and daughter—joint survivors.

"Ruth's Song (Because She Could Not Sing It)" appeared in *Outrageous Acts and Everyday Rebellions,* Gloria's first book since her 1963 *Beach Book.* Gloria's schedule in the 1980s was still so filled with speaking, organizing, and keeping *Ms.* afloat that she hardly had time to produce even the articles she wrote for *Ms.* However, after Gloria failed to write a book during her fellowship, Letty Pogrebin decided to make sure Gloria produced one. Gloria often said she didn't like to write, she liked to have written. In Letty's opinion, Gloria had already written enough material for a book—and by then she had produced several longer and more serious essays as a result of the fellowship. She reviewed Gloria's articles all the way back through the 1960s, copied the ones she considered the best candidates for an anthology, and sent them around to a few publishers.

"There was not a lot of interest in Gloria's first book," recalls Jennifer Josephy, who was a young editor at Holt, Rinehart and Winston at the time. "People saw it as a collection, which is a difficult publishing project, so we got it for a modest $35,000 advance. But I was very enthusiastic, and so was the publisher, Dick Seaver." Actually, at the time, $35,000 was substantial for a collection—even established authors often received five or ten thousand dollars for similar projects.

Once Letty had negotiated the advance, she stacked the articles on *Ms.*'s conference table, handed Gloria the contract to sign, and said, "There's a book here. All you have to do is write an introduction and a little commentary about each piece. It won't take very long."

Although Gloria later joked that Letty had told her a complete lie about how much time the book would take (it would not have taken Letty very long), she was pleased. Gloria agreed with most of Letty's selections, but she found herself updating, restoring cuts, and revising most of the pieces, at least a little. Also, she not only wrote an introduction about her past twelve years as an organizer, "Life Between the Lines," but composed what would be one of her most-reprinted essays, "Ruth's Song (Because She Could Not Sing It)."

Jennifer Josephy was thrilled to work with Gloria, though, like many who had come before her, she was dismayed at Gloria's work habits. "We didn't know we were getting genuine writer's block, but after Gloria handed in the clips and the commitment to write another piece about her mother, she was rewriting the galleys to make the other pieces more consistent. As far as we were concerned, they were history, and we had no problem with them the way they were."

Besides the two new pieces, the book included twenty-six of Gloria's best articles. There were five profiles of women: Marilyn Monroe, Patricia Nixon, Linda Lovelace, Jacqueline Onassis, and Alice Walker. Essays about her personal experiences included "I Was a Playboy Bunny" (previously, "A Bunny's Tale"); "Campaigning," which combined excerpts from longer pieces on her experiences with George McGovern, Eugene McCarthy, and others; and "College Reunion," an account of her twenty-fifth college reunion, in which she compared the women from her working-class Toledo high school with her privileged Smith classmates, asserting that "many of us are still overcoming the 'advantages' of our traditional educations."

A number of the essays examined the cultural manifestations of sexism. "Why Young Women Are More Conservative," for example, noted that "Women may be the one group that grows more radical with age," because young women "haven't yet experienced the life events that are most radicalizing for women." She included experiences like discrimination in the workplace; marriage, with the women's unequal share of responsibility for the home and children; and aging, "still a greater penalty for women than for men." "Men and Women Talking" prefigured the many books on the difference between women's and men's speech patterns, including Deborah Tannen's *You Just Don't Understand.*

Some of the essays, such as "The International Crime of Genital Mutilation" (coauthored with Robin Morgan), tackled feminist political issues. "If Hitler Were Alive, Whose Side Would He Be On?" critiqued the claim of antichoice activists that abortion was comparable to the Holocaust and noted the resemblance between Nazi antiabortion rhetoric and that of the contemporary ultraright. Gloria's talent for satire was displayed in a role reversal, "If Men Could Menstruate," which she wrote to demonstrate that "Whatever a 'superior' group has will be used to justify its superiority, and whatever an 'inferior' group has will be used to justify its plight." It became another of her most reprinted essays.

Outrageous Acts and Everyday Rebellions was published on September 1, 1983. The book's title was a reference to Gloria's usual closing admonition to her audiences. She calls it her organizer's deal:

> If each person in the room promises that in the twenty-four hours beginning the very next day she or he will do at least *one outrageous thing* in the cause of simple justice, then I promise I will, too. It doesn't matter whether the act is as small as saying, "Pick it up yourself" (a major step for those of us who have been our family's servants) or as large as calling a strike. The point is that, if each of us does as promised, we can be pretty sure of two results. First, the world one day later won't be quite the same. Second, we will have such a good time that we will never again get up in the morning saying, "*Will* I do anything outrageous?" but only "*What* outrageous act will I do today?"

The book generally received favorable reviews, leaped onto bestseller lists within a few weeks, and sold around 100,000 copies. As a result, when the paperback rights were sold to the New American Library, Gloria received a $220,000 advance.

Gloria's authorial voice—witty, compassionate, quirky, moving—was the book's strength. Instead of feminist theory, she offered readers feminism in everyday life. When Gloria discussed feminist theory, she usually mentioned Shulamith Firestone's *Dialectic of Sex,* an analysis with which she essentially agreed, except for Firestone's assumption that women's freedom depended on extrauterine birth. Gloria may not have wanted children herself, but she had enough imagination to know that most women regarded childbearing as more than a biological inconvenience to be supplanted as soon as possible by technology. Gloria also considered *The Dialectic of Sex* a little indirect for the average reader. As she explained to a reporter during her own book tour, "[I]t comes to the philosophy through historical references and therefore it tends to make many readers feel that in order to understand, they should know something else. I think there's a way in which you can come at something directly, as Plato did in writing *The Republic,* without ever referring to anything else, no footnotes, no nothing. Just straight. I think that would be useful."

Outrageous Acts did exactly that. Taken all together, the essays provide a feminist view of the world. Gloria's greatest talent was not for defining the forest, it was for depicting the trees. Her ability to communicate what she saw, understandably and entertainingly, was one of her most valuable and often underappreciated contributions.

Her essays were to feminist literature what her aphorisms were to feminist speeches—pithy insights, "clicks" of consciousness-raising. This happened to me: Senator Ribicoff said, "No broads." This happened to Linda Lovelace: Not only was she physically degraded, she had to pretend she liked it. These are political problems. Feminism is the solution.

One reviewer complained that Gloria considered her Playboy Club experience worthwhile in the end because it had taught her that "all women are Bunnies." The reviewer, British feminist writer Angela Carter, wrote, "This is a problematic statement: it is impossible to imagine Emma Goldman, a heroine of Steinem's, resembling a Bunny in any way. Rosa Luxembourg? Djuna Barnes? Precision of thought is the enemy of polemic but that is no reason why ideologues should eschew it."

Carter was right about Bunnies, but wrong about ideologues. Gloria was valuable to the movement precisely because she was an ideologue. Ideologues can be dangerous, but they can also be useful. There were plenty of theorists, and the movement certainly did not lack writers. However, charismatic leaders with a gift for communication were rare, and charismatic leaders with a passion for spreading the word were even rarer. While Gloria's inclination to evaluate everything in terms of its benefit or harm to women limited her intellectually, it fueled her missionary passion.

Furthermore, aphorisms may not be intellectually precise, but they convey powerful truths. They also reflect Gloria's temperament—she favors emotional truth over literal truth (except when she feels unfairly portrayed—then she can become quite literal, seizing upon the minutest of errors to pronounce an entire article "wrong."). Of course, all women weren't Bunnies. They weren't all man-junkies either.

However, phrases like "Aunt Tom" and "We are all female impersonators who tell men, 'how clever of you to know what time it is' " and "We are becoming the men we wanted to marry" are far more powerful communicators than phrases like "internalized oppression" and "class interests" and "socially constructed gender." "The Moral Majority are the people many of our ancestors came here to escape" instantly illuminates the politics of religious intolerance. Gloria enabled people to see and learn without thinking "they should know something else" first.

Gloria wrote "Ruth's Song" more quickly and easily than anything before or since, though she felt tears at the back of her throat as she wrote. The fact that "Ruth's Song" may be the most moving piece Gloria has ever written is not surprising. For Gloria, Ruth's plight was a paradigmatic female condition. Everything that is fundamental to Gloria is in that essay: Gloria's abandoning father, her mother "defeated by life," as Gloria sometimes characterized her; an indifferent or hostile world; and Gloria herself, who was as much the subject of the essay as her mother was.

The essay not only is Gloria's version of Ruth's life; it is Gloria's explanation of who Gloria is. "Ruth's Song" is a simple story, poignantly told: Gloria's mother had most of what gave her a sense of self taken away from her, and as a result she became mentally ill. Gloria's explanation for Ruth's condition was sociopolitical, and in subsequent interviews Gloria explicitly rejected suggestions that Ruth's individual psychology might have been a factor as well. Gloria considered only two facts relevant: Society was unjust to women, and Ruth suffered. In a way, Gloria was right. The degree to which Ruth suffered may have been a function of her individual psyche, but that didn't mean the conditions were not worth changing.

In "Ruth's Song," Gloria wrote of her mother's effect on her:

I know I will spend the next years figuring out what her life has left in me.

I realize that I've always been more touched by old people than by children. It's the talent and hopes locked up in a failing body that gets to me; a poignant contrast that reminds me of my mother, even when she was strong.

I've always been drawn to any story of a mother and a daughter on their own in the world. . . . Even *Gypsy* I saw over and over again. . . . I told myself that I was learning the tap-dance routines, but actually my eyes were full of tears. . . .

My father was the Jewish half of the family, yet it was my mother . . . who encouraged me to listen to a radio play about a concentration camp when I was little. "You should know that this can happen," she said. Yet she did it just enough to teach, never enough to frighten.

It was she who introduced me to books and a respect for them, to poetry that she knew by heart, and to the idea that you could never criticize someone unless you "walked miles in their shoes."

It was she who sold that Toledo house, the only home she had, with the determination that the money be used to start me in college. She gave both her daughters the encouragement to leave home for four years of independence that she herself had never had. . . .

I miss her, but perhaps no more in death than I did in life. Dying seems less sad than having lived too little. But at least we're now asking questions about all the Ruths and all our family mysteries.

If her song inspires that, I think she would be the first to say: It was worth the singing.

In "Ruth's Song," Gloria wrote lovingly of what her mother had given to her daughter, and yearningly of the person Ruth might have been. In the book's final essay, "Far From the Opposite Shore," Gloria wrote as the inspirational leader she herself had become:

In my first days of activism, I thought I would do this ("this" being feminism) for a few years and then return to my real life (what my "real life" might be, I did not know). Partly, that was a naive belief that injustice only had to be pointed out in order to be cured. Partly, it was a simple lack of courage.

But like so many others now and in movements past, I've learned that this is not just something we care about for a year or two or three. We are in it for life—and for our lives. Not even the spiral of history is needed to show the distance traveled. We have only to look back at the less complete people we ourselves used to be.

And that is the last Survival Lesson: *we look at how far we've come, and then we know—there can be no turning back.*

30

Of Bubble Baths and Birthdays

Embarked on a twenty-six city, nine-week publicity tour for *Outra-geous Acts and Everyday Rebellions*, Gloria crammed *Ms.* and movement appearances into every city she visited. *Ms.* was still losing money in 1983, and she hoped the publicity generated by the book tour might boost the magazine as well. Attracted by her combination of celebrity glamour and serious purpose, Gloria was beloved not only by the audiences but also by the publicists and escorts, to whom she was unfailingly courteous.

All went well until Gloria wrote an article for *People* magazine. Although the October 21, 1983, article offered invaluable publicity for her book, it included a two-page photograph of Gloria, forty-nine, taking a bubble bath, one leg extended out of the bubbles as she soaped it with a washcloth in a typical sexpot, movie-star pose.

The press carried the story, and many of Gloria's friends and colleagues were stunned. "I walked around the block and said, 'Oh, how could she?'" recalls Phyllis Chesler. "Then I thought to myself, oh lighten up. It's her body. It's her choice. . . . But I think it's because she's comfortable doing some of these things, that the misogynist media may find it easier to seek her out as the feminist leader—as opposed to others who are less able to please, or less eager to please."

For someone who continually complained about the attention paid to her appearance instead of her opinions, Gloria's decision to pose in a bubble bath was bizarre. Could this be the same Gloria who indignantly asked reporters if they would ask Ralph Nader the questions they asked her about her looks? Few people may have really believed her when she insisted that she wished she weren't pretty. However, most had assumed that Gloria meant it when she deplored the extent to which the media concentrated on her physical appearance and that of other women.

In that light, the bubble-bath pose was just too much. It was difficult enough to imagine a photographer asking Ralph Nader to pose in a bubble bath; it was impossible to imagine him agreeing. Gloria, characteristically rationalized her action with some kind of socially redeeming purpose that would convince her listeners that the photographed pose wasn't what it seemed.

On one talk show she explained that since "sometimes people confuse feminists with nuns," she thought, "maybe it was a good thing in the end, because after all, you know, it isn't a question of bodies. There's nothing wrong with bodies or sensuality or sexuality. The question is, who controls that, you know. I mean, is it being used against women or anything."

She also explained how innocent the whole thing had been: "Well, it maybe was not the smartest thing I ever did, but it just seemed natural because the photographer from *People* magazine was a wonderful woman traveling with me on a speaking tour. And she was doing a piece for *People*, and she said, 'All I have is pictures of you sitting and talking or signing books or whatever. I mean, don't you jog?' 'No.' 'Don't you play tennis?' 'No.' "What do you do to relax?' I said, 'I take a hot bath.' She said, 'Well, you know, if I promise that it will be as decent as any other photo,' which it was, 'can I take your photograph?' I said sure, because it seemed real."

One of Gloria's funniest responses to the incident was her reaction to a woman who called *Ms.* to ask what she was doing in such an expensive bathroom. "I explained that it was a hotel, and she said that was okay," the *soi-disant* bohemian told her talk-show host.

Ann Arbor News columnist Jane Myers captured the reaction of many when she asked, "Has Gloria 'Bubbles' Steinem's mind turned to cheese?" Observing that not a single man in America who wanted to be taken seriously would do such a thing, she noted:

Women are allowed to be sillier and funnier and more frivolous than men, which is one of the reasons that women, on the whole, are saner than men. It's also the reason they get paid less, don't get appointed to important positions, don't get elected to high national office, don't run big companies, don't sit on diplomatic councils, and, in general, have little to do with the running of the world.

It would be nice, and good for the human race, if people like the aforementioned men [including William Buckley, Walter Mondale, Dan Rather] . . . (and maybe, say, Caspar Weinberger—yes, I like that—Caspar Weinberger) *were* to take their clothes off and be photographed nude in a bubbly bathtub. . . .

But, hey, that's all theoretical, and we're dealing with the here and now, in which the men who are in control are clothed. The women who want to be in control better be clothed, too.

In 1984 Gloria turned fifty. About nine months before her birthday, a group of her friends, including Suzanne Levine, Letty Pogrebin, and Marlo Thomas, met to decide how to mark the occasion. *Ms.* had held a gala for twelve hundred people in 1982 to celebrate the magazine's tenth anniversary, but they wanted to have another party anyway.

Marlo explains, "We talked about the fact that if as large a contributor to the world as Gloria were a man, she'd have a party at the Waldorf-Astoria. And we'd always given our parties in the basement of places to keep the overhead low. So I wanted to have black-tie and at the Waldorf and charge a lot of money to make her fiftieth a real celebration as well as a fund-raiser."

Marlo spearheaded the planning for the occasion, and she and Phil Donahue were the official hosts. Gloria had been flaunting her age ever since her fortieth birthday, when someone had said to her, "You don't look forty," and she had replied, "This is what forty looks like. We've been lying so long, who would know?"

(By her sixties, announcing her age would become one of her standard lines, with unintentionally comic results. Gloria would evoke delighted laughter by joking, "At this age, remembering something right away is as good as an orgasm." Then, proclaiming that she was sixty-one or sixty-two she would explain that she was telling her age to aid age liberation. Her audiences usually would applaud enthusiastically, and Gloria would smile back, innocently pleased with herself for striking a blow on behalf of older women. Meanwhile, the women in the audiences were not necessarily applauding because Gloria was doing something terribly brave. Many of them were commenting to each other that she looked so damned good that they wished they could look that good, too, whether they were older or younger than Gloria.)

The organizers always assumed the party would be a benefit for both the Ms. Foundation and *Ms.* magazine—it never occurred to them to have a significant party without using it to raise money. Marlo thought of hiring Bette Midler for the entertainment, though Phil kept saying Gloria wouldn't like it. Marlo knew better. Gloria had interviewed Midler for *Ms.* and she was one of Gloria's favorite entertainers. Marlo made the arrangements and although her band was paid, Midler agreed to perform for free.

As it turned out, everything about the affair went perfectly, except that someone stole some of the professional videotapes of the occasion. At $250 a person, almost eight hundred guests, including journalists and corporate contributors, filled the Waldorf's grand ballroom to bursting and earned the beneficiaries a healthy sum. For once Gloria seemed to relax and enjoy the glitzy tribute without guilt—or almost without guilt. She usually responds to questions about the party by alluding to the fact that it was a fund-raiser and mentioning guests like Rosa Parks (the African-American woman whose 1955 refusal to go to the back of the bus in Montgomery, Alabama, sparked the civil-rights movement). Marlo and Phil had flown up Parks as well as Ralph Nader because they believed other important leaders should be at the event.

The guest list spanned the political, entertainment, and journalistic worlds, with a few corporate sponsors thrown in. Movies and television were represented by Shirley MacLaine, Sherry Lansing, Carol Burnett, Judy Collins, Teri Garr, Alan Alda, Alan King, Betty Buckley, Diane Sawyer, Ahmet Ertegun, Marvin Hamlisch, Margo Kidder, Bob Benton, Irwin Winkler, Lee Grant, Herb Sargent, Jane Pauley and Gary Trudeau, Frances and Norman Lear, and Tom Brokaw. Writers, editors, and magazine colleagues included Liz Smith, Rita Mae Brown, Mary Gordon, Gail Sheehy and Clay Felker, Erica Jong, Ronnie Eldridge and Jimmy Breslin, Cathie Black, Bina and Walter Bernard, and Milton Glaser. (Glaser's studio designed the silver-covered souvenir book *Gloria at Fifty*. Written by Harriet Lyons, it was filled with photographs, including her bubble-bath pose, captioned "Gloria in the tub. So, this is what fifty looks like.")

Politicians, activists, and other celebrities included Bella and Martin Abzug, Ralph Nader, Congresswoman Barbara Mikulski, F. Lee Bailey, Diane von Furstenberg, Dolores Huerta, Liz Holtzman, Donna De Varona, Mary Cunningham and William Agee, Stewart Mott, Jean Nidetch, Sally Ride, and Barbara Seaman, who told the *Washington*

On the road. Gloria tours the country with her speaking partners. Activist-childcare advocate Dorothy Pitman Hughes and Gloria demonstrate woman power. (Dan Wynn, Sophia Smith Collection, Smith College)

Activist-lawyer-writer Florynce Kennedy called Gloria "Glo-ball" and says she taught Gloria to be outrageous. (Sophia Smith Collection, Smith College)

Writer-organizer Margaret Sloan speaks at a women's rally. (Bettye Lane)

A lunch meeting at *Ms.* magazine. (Courtesy Patricia Carbine)

Ms. publisher Pat Carbine at work. (Courtesy Patricia Carbine)

Speaking at a 1977 news conference, Gloria unveils a *Ms.* cover featuring a very pregnant President Jimmy Carter. (Corbis-Bettmann)

Organizing and demonstrating in the 1970s. Gloria speaks during a 1977 Women's Equality Day rally. (Bettye Lane)

Strategizing at the 1977 New York State International Women's Year conference. (Bettye Lane)

Marching at a 1979 Women Against Pornography and Violence Against Women demonstration. (Bettye Lane)

Speaking to the crowd at a 1979 rally in support of Iranian women. (Bettye Lane)

Feminist leaders unite. Ti-Grace Atkinson, Flo Kennedy, Gloria, and Kate Millett at a 1978 matriarchy conference. (Bettye Lane)

Gloria joins writer-activists Robin Morgan and Susan Brownmiller at a 1979 antipornography rally in New York. (Bettye Lane)

Gloria and Betty Friedan add their signatures to NOW's petition supporting the Equal Rights Amendment. (Corbis-Bettmann)

Triumphs in the 1980s. Gloria and Pat Carbine celebrate *Ms.*'s tenth anniversary in 1982. (Bettye Lane)

In 1983, Gloria publicizes *Outrageous Acts and Everyday Rebellions,* and her first book as a feminist is a bestseller. (Corbis-Bettmann)

This is what fifty looks like (sometimes). Phil Donahue, Marlo Thomas, Gloria, and "my record" lawyer Stan Pottinger at Gloria's fiftieth birthday celebration at the Waldorf-Astoria Hotel in 1984. (Robin Platzer, Twin Images)

Gloria with real estate and publishing magnate Mort Zuckerman, 1986. (Robin Platzer, Twin Images)

Members of Gloria's "chosen family." Goddaughter Rebecca Walker and "sister of my heart" Alice Walker. (Corbis-Bettmann)

Longtime friend Frank Thomas. (Corbis-Bettmann)

Rebecca Adamson and Koryne Horbal at the 1995 Veteran Feminists of America dinner in Gloria's honor. (Photo by author)

At the Hollywood Women's Political Committee press conference publicizing the 1989 Washington march for abortion rights, clockwise from left: singer Judy Collins, Planned Parenthood president Faye Wattleton, Gloria, Voters for Choice president Kristina Kiehl, actresses Marlo Thomas and Glenn Close, and Feminist Majority president Eleanor Smeal. (Corbis-Bettmann)

Gloria in the 1990s.
(Robin Platzer, Twin Images)

Post that her "date," Phyllis Chesler, was "quite upset because she feels the sponsors don't include too many old feminist people . . . that there are too many show business people and rich people on the committee." (Betty Friedan was not there, but she probably was not who Chesler meant.) Alice Walker was a cochair, and Jacqueline Onassis contributed, though neither attended.

In addition to Stan Pottinger, there were at least two other Republicans, Jill Ruckelshaus and former Republican Party national chairwoman Mary Louise Smith. The latter noted upon her return to Des Moines, "I don't like New York very well, but that next morning was the first time in a long time I was wishing I could stay longer."

Phil Donahue took a microphone around the room and "interviewed" various guests, who paid tribute to Gloria. Alan Alda read fake telegrams from "Ron" Reagan, Phyllis Schlafly, Bobby Riggs, Hugh Hefner, and William Buckley. Liz Smith described Gloria as "one of the Gandhis of America." Bella Abzug said, "Gloria has been the chopped liver giving me the strength to carry on." (Gloria had been called many names in her fifty years, but that was probably the only time anyone called her chopped liver.) Marlo called her a "feminist fatale," and Ralph Nader (who received a birthday cake because he, too, turned fifty in 1984) insisted that, contrary to what Gloria always said, the press really did ask about his personal life and appearance.

The highlight of the toasts was a performance of the "Steinemites," Dorothy Pitman Hughes, Marlo, Letty, Suzanne, Bella, Flo Kennedy, Pat Carbine, and Joanne Edgar, singing songs composed by Herb Sargent for the occasion. Marlo even hired a vocal coach beforehand, and rehearsals were hilarious. In "Glow Little Gloria" to the tune of "Glow Little Glow Worm," Joanne's verse was:

> Glow little Gloria from Toledo
> You lead a movement as your credo
> And like the pushy girl mosquito
> Nothing could stifle your libido. . . .

Marlo sang:

> Here are a couple of birthday wishes
> May Jerry Falwell wash your dishes.
> May Nancy Reagan say, "I get it."
> And Phyllis Schlafly—ah, forget it.

> May Jesse Helms go back to Dixie
> And Henry Hyde become a pixie.
> We just thought we'd let you know
> Glow little Gloria glow.

Bella sang:

> Glow little Gloria, glisten, glisten
> You know how to make 'em listen
> Even though some are confused yet
> You got chutzpah you ain't used yet
> You know Bella, I may seem tough
> Compared to you I'm just a cream puff
> Glad we don't stand toe to toe
> Glow little Gloria, glow.

Gloria spoke briefly, thanking many, but especially her sister Sue for "doing so many things for me that our parents simply couldn't do, things big sisters shouldn't have to do, but who never made me feel it was a burden or other than she wanted to do." She also reminded everyone to enjoy the party, because, "As Emma Goldman said, 'If you can't dance, it's not my revolution.'"

Before everyone was invited to dance to an all-woman band, Bette Midler performed. Besides donating her performance, Midler evidently had not minded a dose of feminist frugality. Marlo kept joking that it was strange to have a feminist event in a clean place, but however elegant the affair, the organizers had been unable to forgo asking the Divine Miss M if her musicians would mind flying World Airways from California into Newark to save money. Midler agreed, but only if she flew World also—she wouldn't ask her band to do what she wouldn't.

Midler's campy act brought down the house—especially the show-stopping number "Great Big Knockers," featuring, first, enormous balloons that looked like breasts, and when they popped, breast hand-puppets. Marlo Thomas had the satisfaction of saying "I told you so" to her husband.

Newsweek devoted an entire page to the event and described Gloria, "with her signature blond-streaked mane, aviator glasses and contentedly single state" as "a dashing role model, the adventurous aunt who inspires others to follow her off the high diving board." People described her: "Tan, bony, a trifle fragile-looking, she wears a dress of periwinkle silk set off by a rhinestone serpent coiled around her upper arm. Her smooth shoulders are dusted with glitter, and her hair is—as always—perfect."

Dorothy Pitman Hughes wrote to Gloria afterward, "It was a wonderful party to make a fool of myself at. (smiles) I didn't get a chance to say much, but you know that I wish you the best of all you ever wish to have. You are nifty and cute, so for the next fifty, if I feel up to it, I may do the funky chicken."

Later that year, Gloria's friend, producer Irwin Winkler, optioned *Outrageous Acts* for a possible movie. Unaware that Gloria-fan and former Independent Research Service director Gene Theroux had already noted their resemblance, Gloria joked to Irwin that she would like to be played by actress Diana Rigg, the Emma Peel character of the popular television series *The Avengers*, though what Gloria had in mind was her role as a mystic in the movie *Hospital*.

Gloria had always been attracted to popular media, both as a consumer and as a possible producer. In 1984 she wrote a movie treatment for a live (as opposed to animated) film on Wonder Woman, and a few years later she took a weekend screenwriting course in New York. Irwin Winkler has yet to produce a movie based on *Outrageous Acts,* but in 1984 Gloria finally sold the production rights to "A Bunny's Tale" to Joan Marks, a producer who had asked several times. Gloria had enough reservations to insist on script approval, but she accepted the fact that to a certain extent the titillation of beautiful women running around in Bunny costumes was going to be part of the made-for-television movie's commercial appeal. As she acknowledged to a reporter, "You can perpetuate something merely by depicting it. I hope that some people who tune in for the wrong reasons will still get something out of it. When I speak . . . lots of people come out of curiosity. . . And that's fine as long as a more human understanding comes through at the end. I hope the same will be true of the film."

The script compressed Gloria's feminist awakening from six years to the seventeen days she worked at the Playboy Club. For the other leads, fictional characters were created. As they developed the story, the producers monitored the portions about the Playboy Club itself vigilantly. According to Gloria, the former Bunny who served as a volunteer technical advisor said she received threatening telephone calls. Because they were depicting a real corporation, they had to adhere exactly to Gloria's published material or risk a libel suit. Playboy executives had tried to participate in the creative process, but the producers had rebuffed them—and then worried about a lawsuit up to the time the program was aired.

"Our concern was really a rather crass, commercial concern," Playboy Enterprises president Christine Hefner explained. "For ABC to—in effect—end-run *Playboy* and say we're going to take advantage of the tremendous commercial appeal of *Playboy* and make a film about it but not pay you any money for it and not let you be creatively involved in it all because we're going to call it Gloria Steinem's view of *Playboy* struck us as . . . not very kosher. It's a gray area."

Besides coproducer Joan Marks, the movie's director, screenwriter, associate producer, assistant director, and assistant cameraperson all were women. Screenwriter Deena Goldstone found working with Gloria "easy and fun—she gave over material without any sense of ownership." Although Gloria made it clear that she hoped Goldstone would emphasize the political aspect of the story rather than the personal, she did not object when the screenwriter created a lover to provide a counterpoint in her personal life to what was happening to her at the Playboy Club. She understood that Goldstone had to be creative with the parts outside the Playboy Club for legal reasons.

The Gloria character was to be conflicted between her sympathy for her Bunny coworkers and the demands of her lover. During her actual work at the club, Gloria had been involved with Tom Guinzburg, but Goldstone made Gloria's lover a beginning off-Broadway writer on the verge of becoming successful.

Goldstone found constructing the Gloria character to be an unexpected challenge. Impressed by "Ruth's Song," Goldstone believed the essay provided her with important insights into Gloria, and she looked forward to filling in the blanks when they worked together. The process turned out to be more difficult than she had anticipated.

"I work from a psychological perspective, from the inside out," she explains, "but when I asked questions to help form her character, she couldn't address them. You want to see where the edges are, but I couldn't get anywhere. It seemed important to her to be intact, to be together, which gave her a seamless quality so that there wasn't any 'give.' She was more focused on outward actions—I couldn't get her to talk about her demons.

"And it wasn't that she didn't want to help: she was lovely to be with, bright and funny. And of course, she was entitled to be self-protective. Anyway, I think it was partly her Ohio background—there's a Midwest stoicism that is antipsychological. People have to say things are okay because they don't have the psychological tools, the coping mechanisms, to deal with the pain. So they deny it."

Gloria was pleased with the film, but uncomfortable at being portrayed. At the movie's screening she confessed that when she used to fantasize about a film version of her life, she had envisioned being played in the beginning by Audrey Hepburn and at the end by Margaret Rutherford. "Gloria" in the movie was played by Kirstie Alley, who then was best known as Dr. Spock's fellow Vulcan in *Star Trek II*. Alley later gained fame starring in the television series *Cheers* and the *Look Who's Talking* movies. Although Alley was awed at the prospect of playing Gloria, the costume designers equipped her with what looked like Lee Press-On Nails to duplicate Gloria's famously long talons, and she perfected a wide-eyed gaze that captured Gloria's gentle diffidence, if not her acerbic wit.

Gloria told the press her one disappointment was the title, with its pun. She preferred the less suggestive "I Was A Playboy Bunny," which she used when she included her piece in *Outrageous Acts*. On the other hand, when a young waitress in the shop where she bought her morning coffee told Gloria she had asked her boyfriend to watch the program so that he could see how hard her job was, Gloria found that reward enough.

31

The Wrong Man

Converting *Ms.* to nonprofit status in 1979 had reduced the postal costs, and increased revenues by allowing *Ms.* to solicit contributions. However, the struggle for advertisers continued, despite the fact that the demographics of *Ms.*'s readership were just what many potential advertisers wanted. By 1981, the median age of *Ms.* readers was thirty; 63 percent attended college or had completed college; 86 percent were employed full-time outside the home, nearly half in managerial or professional categories. Furthermore, psychographic measures based on questions about readers' level of activity in community groups, speaking, and writing letters to newspapers found the overwhelming majority to be activists and opinion makers, regardless of their income or education. In 1982 its circulation was 450,000. Even so, *Ms.* never could sell enough advertising pages.

In 1982 *Ms.* used its tenth anniversary to generate as much publicity as possible. Special mailings were sent to distributors, Gloria went on tour, Phil Donahue devoted an entire program to the magazine, and the *Today* show saluted it for a week. They held an anniversary party for 1,200 guests. *Ms.* published a special combination July-August issue with Gloria's photograph on the cover.

Gloria had originally refused to be on the cover, but Ruth Bower, who was consulting on the issue, believed they needed her photograph to generate the kind of newsstand sales they desired. A seasoned businesswoman, Ruth had worked at the *World Journal Tribune* with Clay Felker and had helped him found *New York*. As *New York*'s executive vice president and general manager, she had helped launch *Ms.* by overseeing the sample issue's circulation, promotion, and public relations campaigns. Shortly after *Ms.*'s tenth anniversary issue appeared, she left her job at Select Magazines to become associate publisher at *Ms.*

When Ruth continued to insist they feature Gloria, the editors finally compromised. They ran a foldout cover that included a number of women representing various occupations; Gloria's photograph was blown up larger than the rest.

Gloria's old friend, photographer Henry Wolf, shot the cover photo. He recalls the occasion with amusement: "It was a gate-fold cover. She was with all kinds of women—a policewoman, a black woman, and so on. Gloria, who had renounced brassieres and cosmetics, came to the studio with a makeup artist and eight Givenchy dresses. I said, 'Gloria, what's happened?' She said, 'Well, times change.'"

The editors tried everything to make *Ms.* profitable. When postage rates continued to rise, they reluctantly raised subscription rates. More than one hundred readers donated $1,000 or more to become *Ms.*'s Special Friends of Equality and Lifetime Subscribers. Gloria persuaded Sallie Bingham, who had received 15 percent of the proceeds of the sale of her family's Louisville, Kentucky, newspapers for $434 million, to donate $1.2 million to the magazine.

The *Ms.* staff continued to create events that combined fund-raising, publicity, and consciousness-raising. In 1983, in imitation of *Time* magazine's Man of the Year awards, *Ms.* began holding breakfasts to honor *Ms.* Women of the Year. The first was psychologist Carol Gilligan. The following year they decided to name more than one. *Time*'s Man of the Year, Peter Uberroth, joined Gloria at the New York discotheque Studio 54 for the 1984 breakfast, which honored congresswoman and defeated Democratic vice-presidential candidate Geraldine Ferraro, Olympic athlete Joan Benoit, and singer Cyndi Lauper.

In 1984 Gloria began seeing Mortimer Zuckerman. While Mort did not share Gloria's international reputation, the multimillionaire real-estate developer had a high profile in New York and Boston, and their affair was conducted before a fascinated—and in some cases, horrified—audience of friends, acquaintances, well-wishers, ill-wishers, and gossip-column devotees. Although Gloria's choice of lovers was presumably her business, the reactions to her relationship with Mort resembled the public dismay when Jacqueline Kennedy married Aristotle Onassis.

Mort, who was born in Montreal, Canada, in 1937, was the youngest of four children—the only son of Jewish immigrants. Because of his father's poor health, his parents spent the winters in Florida, leaving their children in Montreal, and Mort likes to say he raised himself. At the age of nineteen he earned honors degrees in political science and economics from McGill University, where he wrote for the college newspaper and became the first Jewish president of the campus honor society.

After accumulating law degrees from McGill and Harvard and an M.B.A. from Wharton, Mort took a $8,750 job with a traditional, Boston-Brahmin real-estate-development firm, Cabot, Cabot & Forbes. Within seven months he was chief financial officer, and in three years he became a partner. He earned $5 million in the five years he was with the firm.

In 1969 Mort left to start his own development firm, Boston Properties, with a colleague he had worked with at Cabot. When Cabot paid him half of what he believed his partnership interest was worth, he also sued his former employer. The court agreed, awarding him the full amount in what was the first of his many public, high-stakes battles. While he developed properties all over the country, he taught city and regional planning at Harvard's Graduate School of Design and at Yale. He also managed to alienate much of the Boston Establishment. After he won the contract to develop a site adjacent to the Boston Public Garden, community groups began fighting the complex because it would have cast shadows on much of the landmark. He spent seven years and $1.9 million fighting for the project before finally abandoning it in 1977.

As he accumulated his fortune, Mort searched for an opportunity to move into politics or journalism. By June 1979, when *Atlantic Monthly* editor Robert Manning approached Mort about investing in the magazine, Mort owned real estate valued at an estimated $150 million, lived in a Beacon Hill mansion, and employed a Chinese chef. Mort bought the magazine and fired Manning, who consoled himself by proclaiming to the press that his ex-boss was "a liar and a cheat." He also said, "All of his integrity would fit into the navel of a flea. And there'd be room left over for a caraway seed and his heart." Mort later became involved in lawsuits with Manning and some of the magazine's other previous shareholders.

Although he had kept a New York apartment and had spent time in East Hampton since the 1970s, Mort made New York his primary

residence in 1983. In 1985 he moved into a Fifth Avenue triplex pent-
house that cost $8.5 million—according to the *New York Times*, the
highest price ever paid for a Manhattan cooperative apartment.

Angering neighbors is an occupational hazard of developers, and
despite his social ambitions, in 1985 Mort embarked on a replay of
the Public Garden incident, alienating in one stroke a number of
extremely powerful New Yorkers—through the same offense. In partnership with Salomon Inc., Mort had won the right to develop a city-
owned site next to Central Park. The city had instructed applicants to
design as large a building as zoning would allow, but when he
announced plans for a pair of buildings, fifty-seven and seventy-two
stories high, a celebrity-filled group that included Jacqueline Kennedy
Onassis, Walter Cronkite, and Henry Kissinger organized in opposition because the buildings would cast shadows over Central Park. He
later scaled down the design.

Mort's money was in real estate, but his heart was in media. He had
been passionately interested in journalism from the time he was a
teenager, and he wanted to be an opinion maker. In 1984 he bought the
weekly *U.S. News & World Report* for $163.2 million and began
spending several days a week in Washington overseeing the magazine,
hiring and firing editors and reporters, writing editorials, and obtaining
advice from people like editors Harold Evans and Clay Felker. In 1993
he would add the *New York Daily News* to his monthly and weekly
magazines, and he refers to himself as a journalist.

Gloria had known Mort superficially during his involvement with
NBC journalist Betty Rollin, who, along with poet Sandra Hochman,
had been Gloria's cocolumnists at *Look*. In 1976 Rollin had published
a book recounting her bout with breast cancer and her subsequent mastectomy, *First, You Cry*. It had included a disguised account of her
affair with Mort so damning that Mort had sued to try to stop publication (the case was settled out of court). "David," the charming lover
in Rollin's book, was so determined to have children that even after he
heard her doctor explain that pregnancy could trigger cancer, he had
said to Rollin, "The doctor didn't say you *couldn't* have children, did
he?" According to Mort, what he told Betty Rollin was that he did not
wish to have children because she did not wish to have them.

Stan Pottinger accompanied Gloria to her fiftieth birthday party in
May 1984, but Mort was there as a guest. Gloria was in one of her
transitions, and she and Mort had been seeing each other for over a
month. Mort later said he had not liked sneaking around, and that he

had told Gloria he would not continue in a relationship that involved sneaking around. Once Stan had been eased out, Gloria and Mort became a very visible couple. On June 27, 1984, Gloria's old friend Liz Smith ran an item:

> Being seen around together—Gloria Steinem, the finest flower of the Women's Liberation Movement, and tycoon Mort Zuckerman, the magazine king. (Mort always tells the fabulous females he dates that he wants to get married and have children, but then he never does. Now he has met the perfect woman; she doesn't even WANT to get married and have children!)

On April 23, 1985, Smith reported:

> That was some gemütlich party Gloria Steinem and Mort Zuckerman tossed for themselves and a clutch of pals at the 42nd St. Automat last weekend. The best part? It wasn't given for any reason except for the fun of it. The theme was "Funky Glitz," and you had to see the multimillionaire host in his white top hat and gold-sequined tailcoat to believe it. Gloria was more formally turned out in a slinky black gown and feather boa. Warner Leroy wore his usual clothes . . . Henry Grunwald of *Time* had a chestful of medals, given him by Louise Melhado. . . . Phil Donahue wore a Chicago Cubs baseball uniform. . . . Then there was his wonderful wife, what's her name—Marlo Thomas. . . . Movie director Joel Schumacher said: "This reminds me of parties back in the '60s!" I think that's what Gloria and Mort intended . . .

Gloria told friends that Mort was the smartest man she had ever met and confessed to Bella Abzug that she was obsessed with him. They danced, went out with friends, and spent weekends at Mort's East Hampton house. Gloria took long walks on the beach with Mort's chocolate Labrador retriever, Stockman, who was named after Reagan White House budget director David Stockman. An *Atlantic* magazine journalistic coup had exposed the doubts of Stockman, the human being, about the Reagan administration's economic policies.

Gloria also watched Mort play softball in the media-star-studded softball games in Sag Harbor, another village in the Hamptons. Mort pitched and says that he was selected as the best pitcher of the group and voted by the local newspaper to be the best clutch pitcher over the last twenty-five years. He loved being part of the game, though writer Ken Auletta's comment to the *Washington Post* was typical of the level of gossip Mort attracted: "Some people say he ... cheats on the mound. He takes an extra step in front of the rubber." Auletta later said he had been joking, and Mort says that Auletta's statement was completely rebutted in a subsequent letter to the *Post* by John Leo (a *U.S. News & World Report* columnist).

Gloria long had realized she didn't want children or marriage, but Mort told everyone that he wanted to marry and was eager to have children. Over the years, however, he had repeatedly involved himself with highly intelligent, attractive, accomplished, high-profile women— including Nora Ephron, Arianna Stassinopoulos (before she married Houston oil multimillionaire Michael Huffington), and Diane von Furstenberg, not one of whom, at the time of her involvement, appeared to be both able and willing to have children. "It's sad because he *dreams* of it," Diane von Furstenberg told an interviewer, "and yet he's attracted to women who can't have children anymore."

For all the differences between the pair that Gloria's friends kept pointing out to her—and many objected quite openly to her seeing him—Gloria and Mort had similarities as well. Both were highly intelligent, witty, fun-loving as well as hardworking. Both were well connected and powerful, both were used to being the leader, and both were enormously concerned with their public images.

The difference between their respective approaches to protecting those images is instructive. Gloria was an internationally famous figure and greatly beloved. When she felt covered unfairly in the media, her friends would rise up on her behalf, and on a couple of occasions she sent a "lawyer's letter" threatening to sue for libel. She never did sue, and only occasionally would she get what she wanted, as in the case of the Redstockings book. (When *Screw* magazine received a lawyer's letter about a pornographic poster of Gloria, owner Al Goldstein sent her a small box of candy and a note saying, "Eat it.")

Mort, by contrast, was far less known than Gloria. Among those who knew him, he had a few extremely devoted friends and was otherwise frequently disparaged. However, when Mort disliked his coverage he was known among reporters for complaining vociferously to the reporters' bosses in a way that somehow got results. Two days after an August 1985 *New York Times* profile on Mort, the newspaper ran a virtually unprecedented apology—not for factual errors in the article, but for its attitude toward its subject. As the four-paragraph editor's note explained, "Through opinionated phrases and unattributed characterizations, the article established a tone that cast its subject in an unfavorable light." The note even included examples of the offenses: the article had stated that Zuckerman "had befriended people 'in an effort to win a place in their world'" and had "described Mr. Zuckerman's 'architectural taste' pejoratively."

Poor Gloria. She never got an apology like that. She says she only wants the power to empower people, not the kind of power to make other people do what she wants. But there must have been times . . .

Besides sharing a love of dancing and a mutual physical attraction that was obvious to everyone around them, Gloria and Mort had in common the fact that both wanted to change the world. Gloria encouraged Mort when he sought to buy *U.S. News & World Report* and gave him journalistic advice. She asked him to help her with *Ms.* Over time, he guaranteed some loans to the magazine and donated about four hundred thousand dollars, for a total of $1.4 million. He also talked with Gloria's lawyer and close friend, Bob Levine (Suzanne's husband) about what could be done to save the magazine. Mort envisioned setting up *Ms.* so that it could be run as a tax shelter; Bob would help with the legal work. However, according to Bob, Gloria was offended by Mort's terms.

"Mort's a businessman," Bob explains, "and the kinds of conditions he wanted were the kinds of conditions any businessperson would ask. I think Gloria expected unconditional help. And I don't think Gloria has forgiven me for thinking the conditions were quite reasonable— we finally stopped talking about it."

Mort, who also offered the help of some of his employees, wanted to look at *Ms.*'s entire operation and help with advice and counsel, and Bob suspects Gloria objected because she didn't want Mort telling her what to do with her magazine. "Whenever they needed money, Gloria went out and found it. Her response was as if *Ms.* were a charitable organization—instead of asking, as you should with a business, is this the best way for it to be run? If there was something fundamentally wrong with the business, then someone should have been examining it to make it work better." Mort's conditions also may have hurt Gloria because she herself gives so unconditionally, even to people with whom she has no relationship. For those she loves, she gives even more unstintingly.

Gloria had other reasons for resenting his help, no matter how well meant. She found it unbearable to watch Mort and the young men who worked for him condescend to Ruth Bower and Pat Carbine, who had far more magazine experience than they. Much as Gloria appreciated Mort's generosity in sending over *Atlantic Monthly* employees as advisors, she says she also knew he had lost at least $20 million on his long-established monthly in less time than *Ms.* had begun operations, grown to *Atlantic Monthly*'s size, and achieved enormous national visibility and influence—all on about ten percent of that amount. (Mort says he had spent about $15 million by then, covering losses and building up the magazine's operation and circulation.) Gloria felt she was wasting time that could have been better spent raising contributions.

According to many of those around them, Gloria and Mort talked of getting married. According to Gloria, Mort talked about it and Gloria did not correct him. Mort also talked about fathering a baby and told various friends such intimate facts as that Gloria still got her period (she was fifty when they started seeing each other), or that she was trying to get pregnant, or that she was pregnant.

Rumors about Gloria's putative pregnancy or visits to fertility specialists swirled around New York during the relationship and persisted even after it ended. Mort's best friend since Harvard Law School, writer Jeff Steingarten, and Jeff's wife, Caron Smith, a museum curator, spent a great deal of time with Gloria and Mort, and Caron recalls talk of marriage and a baby. At one point Mort told them that Gloria was pregnant and that he and she were talking about marriage. Another old friend of Mort's speculated that the reason Gloria seemed interested in having a baby was to show the world it could be done.

According to Mort, Gloria had told him that she had been pregnant and had had a miscarriage. Mort also says that Gloria was disappointed about the miscarriage. He believes she had wanted to have the baby for two reasons: because she knew he wanted it, and because she wanted to stun the world by having a child at her age.

Gloria's reaction to Mort's contention is: "He did [talk about marriage and a baby] all the time, but if he had wanted to get married and have children, he would have done it long ago."

But he talked about it?

"He always talked about it. And, in fact, before we started to go out, I was trying to think of other women to introduce him to. Because at that moment in time I still believed that he meant it." She adds, "While we were seeing each other, I also suggested that he adopt a baby on his own—there are certainly plenty of kids who need help."

Asked specifically about talk of marriage during their relationship, Gloria says she didn't believe him and adds, "In response to his jokes about prenuptial agreements, I made super-clear that I would never get legally married. I also told the many reporters who asked and the few friends who didn't know better."

People thought she was considering it, though. "The people who thought that only thought that anybody would want to marry a rich man. They're projecting their own stuff."

What about Mort's assertion that she was pregnant and had a miscarriage? Mort may have mistook what she told him, Gloria suggests. She explained to him, she says, that she had stopped using contraceptives in her forties because of gynecological problems. Her gynecologist had believed then that, for her, the likelihood that she would get pregnant was low and even if she did, having an abortion would be much less dangerous for her than the problems of contraception. According to Gloria, she explained to Mort that it was quite possible in her situation that a fertilized egg would miscarry rather than implanting, so she could be having miscarriages without being aware of them.

Even so, when Mort talked about a baby to her or to others, she did not contradict him. She was being tactful, she explains. If she had gotten pregnant, she would have had an abortion without telling him. She says: "I was at fault for not looking him in the eye and saying that I wouldn't do this even if I were twenty-two. Instead, I explained that after forty-five or so, a fertilized egg doesn't stay implanted in the womb for more than a few weeks—which is why I hadn't had to use contraception in years. The odds are a million to one against staying pregnant. He took this to mean I would if I could, and I was so surprised that I didn't reject the impossible. I thought having a child was just a fantasy on his part anyway. This is what I meant when I said that in a romance, you allow yourself to become the other person's fantasy—that's very different from love, where you feel supported for being yourself. Now that he's having a child at sixty, I've apologized to him for not believing that he really wanted to do what he hadn't done before." (Mort married in 1996, and he and his wife, National Gallery curator Marla Prather, became the parents of Abigail Zuckerman on July 7, 1997.)

No matter how many New York women insist they saw Gloria visiting fertility specialists, the idea of Gloria trying to get pregnant is rather farfetched. Gloria would later say she had not been exactly herself during her relationship with Mort, but wanting a baby—and at fifty-two, yet—would not have been just not-herself; it would have been a complete personality transplant, a possession by an alien force.

Gloria can be extraordinarily passive in going along with people, so her contention that others developed the impression she was going to marry Mort or was planning to have a baby without her active participation is at least plausible. Not one of their friends who remember the conversations about marriage and babies can say for certain that they heard Gloria herself actually say she wanted a baby. Furthermore, the phrase one of Mort's friends used to describe what she suspected was Gloria's motive for advanced-age motherhood—"she wanted to show the world it could be done"—was almost the same one Mort used.*

Gloria is rebellious enough to like doing what she has been told she cannot or should not do, but "wanting to show the world it could be done" in regard to giving birth at an unusually late age sounds nothing like Gloria. Quite the opposite. She is conscientious, sometimes to the point of earnestness, about her position as a role model. The role she models is authentic: She is a woman who believes the unconventional choices she has made are positive alternatives to the traditional women's roles of wife and mother. "Wanting to stun the world" with a baby in her fifties sounds more like Mort.

Many of Gloria's friends were appalled by Mort—his business practices, his politics, his sometimes callous treatment of her and, in other affairs, of other women. Other friends of Gloria's enjoyed him and thought Gloria should see anyone who pleased her. Gloria later wrote of the relationship that she had played down who she was and played up who he wanted her to be to make Mort fall in love with her, but Mort certainly did not notice a lack of combativeness. He relished her intelligence, but felt oppressed by her tendency to interpret everything in ideological terms. On flights back from business trips, he says, he would find himself wondering what he had done this time that he was going to be told was morally wrong. He often said to Gloria, living with a saint is a lot tougher than being one.

According to Mort, the affair became increasingly acrimonious, and they stopped seeing each other after about two and a half years. Then, after a few weeks, Mort says Gloria told him her sense of being abandoned was overwhelming, and they continued to see each other for another year and a half, although they also saw other people.

---

*Mort Zuckerman is evidently more intimidating than the CIA. Only one source who had worked for the CIA asked me to exclude his name, even from the acknowledgments, whereas three people asked for complete anonymity before they would talk about Mort. Caron Smith, whose name Mort gave me, spoke of him affectionately and unguardedly, but when I attempted to follow up, she did not return my calls.

Gloria later attributed her infatuation with Mort to her vulnerable state at that point in her life. Mort believes her vulnerability extended into the relationship itself. Gloria seemed less self-protective in that affair—there was usually something unattainable about Gloria in her relationships with men. Until Mort, she always seemed to be the one who ended the relationship.

Even the relationship's demise was public, making not only the gossip columns, but the pages of *Fortune:*

> About the only thing Zuckerman, 50, admits could be better is his personal life. . . . He split earlier this year from Gloria Steinem, 53, editor of *Ms.* magazine. "That was the real thing for a long time," says an acquaintance of Steinem's. "But they are very different people." She's big for causes; he's busy making money.

32

Marilyn Monroe:
A Feminist Morality Tale

Gloria wrote much of her next book at Mort's beach house in the summer of 1985. It was *Marilyn: Norma Jeane*, a biography of Marilyn Monroe.

Gloria had written about Marilyn previously, in *Ms.*'s August 1972 issue. Editor Harriet Lyons, whose *Fan* magazine background made her *Ms.*'s celebrity expert, had suggested that *Ms.* commemorate the tenth anniversary of Monroe's death, and the magazine had received extraordinary letters in response. So when Dick Seaver, the publisher of *Outrageous Acts and Everyday Rebellions*, called, Gloria was interested. Photographer George Barris had taken photographs of Marilyn Monroe in 1962, just before Marilyn died, and Seaver wanted to know whether Gloria wanted to write a text to accompany them.

The idea appealed to Gloria. More than forty books had been written about Marilyn Monroe since her death, but all had been written by men. Besides, *Ms.* owed money to Holt for copies of *Outrageous Acts* the magazine had used as subscription premiums, so Gloria figured writing for the money rather than begging for it would be a pleasant respite. She did not realize until the contract arrived that the publisher expected not merely long captions, but sixty thousand words (there are about two hundred words on this page).

The project seemed too fortuitous to pass up, however. Both Marilyn Monroe's persona as an actress and in her tragic life story offered Gloria a wonderful vehicle to explore the female condition.

"I think women can learn from her because she's an exaggerated version of what can happen to us," she told an Australian reporter during the book's promotional tour. "We're valued for who we are on the outside, and not for our heads and hearts. So we have a harder time with aging and with self-confidence. And I think she would be instructive to some men who may have thought that women were really enjoying our own denigration, rather than just pretending to." In other words, Gloria's story of Marilyn Monroe was a feminist parable.

The link between Gloria and Marilyn Monroe was more complicated than mere feminist biographer and subject. As Gloria explained in the introduction, Seaver had sought her help as a writer who could "help explain Marilyn as an individual and as an icon of continuing power." That Gloria was also an icon of continuing power was obvious but unstated.

Mutual iconhood was only one of the similarities between Gloria and her subject. The parallels between their lives were striking. Marilyn Monroe had a much worse childhood and eventually committed suicide, while Gloria gained strength from her childhood adversity, but both had absent fathers and mentally ill mothers, both were public figures who tried to respond with generosity to their publics, and both became icons into whom fans projected their fantasies.

As a result, exploring the life and character of Marilyn Monroe and their relationship to her childhood helped direct Gloria toward an exploration of her own life. As Gloria would subsequently write in *Revolution From Within*, we "write what we need to know." As Gloria sought to understand Marilyn Monroe, she seemed to realize there was much she did not understand about herself.

In spite of her exquisite social antennae, Gloria was extremely uninformed about psychology, and it showed in *Marilyn*. Her authority for the idea that "the child we used to be lives on inside us" was psychiatrist W. Hugh Missildine, author of *Your Inner Child of the Past*. That specific childhood experiences shape adults in predictable patterns may not have been much of a revelation to most readers, but Gloria wrote as if Missildine had figured this out by actively rejecting Freud. "It was an analysis of adult emotional problems based on his nine years as director of the Children's Mental Health Center in Columbus, Ohio.

Without the artificial language or gender-based theories of Freud," she explained, "he simply wrote what he had concluded from observation." Despite her previous lack of interest in psychological exploration, Gloria took to it enthusiastically, linking the terrors of Marilyn's childhood to the heartaches of her adulthood.

Some of the major themes of Marilyn's life were so resonant of Gloria's that at times Gloria seemed to be explaining not just Marilyn but herself—she even used many of the same words and phrases she uses to describe herself.

She wrote, "One of the consistencies of her life was this habit of attaching herself to other people's families . . ." Of Marilyn's lovers, she said, "The life-style and relatives that came with a particular man seemed to attract her more, and to survive longer, than the man himself." She conjectured of Marilyn's childhood, "Each time she came home to that apartment, she must have worried about what she would find."

Perhaps she also felt some empathy when she wrote, "Many of Marilyn Monroe's biographers would accuse her of lying about her childhood suffering, because she sometimes exaggerated facts . . ." And later, "Marilyn may have been dramatizing the deprivation of her background, as she sometimes did, as if to justify her real feelings of being deprived."

Noting how closely Marilyn fit Missildine's profile of an adult who was still suffering from childhood neglect, she quoted part of Missildine's description: "The childhood of persons who suffered from neglect usually reveals a father who somehow wasn't a father and a mother who somehow wasn't a mother. . . . In childhood such a person may have discovered that he could win . . . momentary attention and love through his achievements."

That may or may not have captured Marilyn Monroe's interior life, but it certainly echoed Gloria's descriptions of her own childhood and her way of coping by going outside to find what she couldn't find at home.

The critics were generally favorable. Diana Trilling wrote a positive review for the *New York Times,* and writer Florence King "loved" Gloria's treatment, even though, as she wrote in the *San Jose Mercury News,* "I can't stand [Gloria], chiefly because she slammed feminism's door in my face when she stated in *Ms.* that it is impossible to be both a feminist and a conservative. I am so conservative that anyone who

tried to stand to the right of me would fall of the edge of the Earth—
it's flat, you know—yet my whole life has been a feminist statement."

King approved of Gloria's treatment of Monroe as a feminist moral-
ity tale because "Monroe's vulnerability, her need to be taken seriously,
her desperate search for identity, and her frantic fear of aging were not
just the familiar problems of Hollywood sex goddesses but the univer-
sal condition of womankind."

Some of the reviewers, including Trilling, mentioned Gloria's super-
ficial understanding of psychology, and a few objected to her feminist
moralizing, but by then Gloria's message had become paramount. Years
before she herself realized it, Gloria had metamorphosed from a writer
who was politically active into a political leader who wrote to persuade. The last frivolous piece she wrote was probably a 1981 four-
paragraph piece for the *Village Voice*, "My Life with Long Nails." She
had become a skillful polemicist, and her writing, humorous or serious,
was almost always an extension of her work as a feminist leader.

By the time *Marilyn* was published in 1986, Gloria was exhausted in
every way. Looking back at those days, she says, "I don't know how to
express to you how hard it was. There's no way to tell you what it's
like to have to— The magazine, raising money for everything. . . . We
couldn't go on with the magazine. We'd been living on the edge of
bankruptcy for years, trying to keep it going. I felt responsible for
others. For the foundation, other organizations, fund-raising. I don't
know how I survived it."

It seemed as if Gloria would feel responsible for *Ms.* for the rest of
her life, and its financial condition was worse than it ever had been.
She had finished *Marilyn* and would soon embark on another exhausting book tour. Her relationship with Mort was not going well, though
it would drag on for another couple of years. She felt tired and joyless.
Everything seemed to be closing in, and she saw the world in dreary
black and white instead of in color.

In May 1986 Gloria began seeing a psychotherapist. Suzanne and
Bob Levine had suggested to Gloria that it was time to let someone
else help her.

Suzanne and Gloria had become closer over the previous couple of
years. Suzanne's brother had been diagnosed with AIDS in 1984, and in
the months before his death in 1985, Gloria had helped where she
could. In addition to making herself available to Suzanne, Gloria had
visited Suzanne's brother at the hospital because, as Suzanne explains,
"She knows how to use her power in that way. She knows if she goes

into a hospital to visit somebody, that person will get better care. Because the nurses in particular are so excited to see her and have so much feeling for her."

Suzanne and Bob recommended she talk to a man they knew. He suggested she see a woman with whom he sometimes worked, a family therapist named Kitty La Perriere. "She had a confluence of stressful events," Suzanne recalls. "First was her mother's death. That was a crisis and it brought back a lot of stuff. She'd been very attentive, and it was exhausting. Second was the pressure and sense of prostituting herself for the magazine. The advertisers took terrible advantage of her willingness to go to them. They'd parade her around as a celebrity and then not give us an ad. Then there was her writing. And the foundation. And politics. And the [Women's Action] Alliance. People and things all making demands. And thinking about selling the magazine. And what to do next. And money. She didn't make much and she gave it away."

Besides La Perriere, whom Gloria met for conventional therapeutic sessions, Gloria visited Nancy Napier, a therapist and the author of *Recreating Your Self*. She went partly out of personal curiosity and partly as research for *Revolution From Within*. As Gloria later wrote, Napier was "an experienced travel guide for journeys into the unconscious—that timeless part of our minds where events and emotions of our personal past are stored along with the wisdom of our species." By facilitating meditation or self-hypnosis, Napier enabled Gloria to travel back to find her "inner child."

Also in May, Gloria began appearing on the *Today* show. She had been on television many times, and in 1984 had hosted a Lifetime cable program, *A Conversation With . . .* On that program she had interviewed friends such as Alice Walker and John Kenneth Galbraith, as well as guests such as Walter Cronkite, Abigail Van Buren, Bianca Jagger, Andrew Young, and Sally Ride.

During the 1984 presidential campaign, Gloria had gotten to know producer Carla Morganstern, who was helping vice-presidential candidate Geraldine Ferraro with media preparation. Carla decided Gloria should do interviews for the *Today* show and proposed to *Today*'s producer that she and Gloria produce a number of taped interviews on a freelance basis. The producer agreed. Gloria's interviews with Cher, Robert Redford, and Marlo Thomas and her reports on subjects like a Minnesota childcare center and a Texas AIDS program began airing in May 1986.

Then *Today*'s producer asked if she wanted to substitute as co-anchor for a week in September during Jane Pauley's maternity leave. Coanchoring made her even more nervous because it was live rather than taped, but she agreed. She practiced dealing with the equipment and thought she sounded terrible. However, she was determined to proceed.

Gloria did something else that summer to prepare for her appearance on the *Today* show. At the age of fifty-two, she had an operation to remove excess fat from her drooping upper eyelids. She later wrote that it had taken her twenty years to overcome her bias against unnecessary surgery and walk two blocks from her apartment for what turned out to be a simple office procedure.

Since the culture's valuation of women by their appearance has been one of feminism's primary concerns, it would seem that having her eyes done would be something of a political issue—especially for a feminist leader who saw practically everything as political, used expressions like "the political equivalent of a face-lift," and, moreover, insisted that her looks got in her way. Gloria dealt with the issue in general, and her own experience in particular, in "Bodies of Knowledge," a section on body image she wrote for her 1992 book *Revolution From Within*. She suggested that in considering plastic surgery, the important point to consider was one's motivation: "Do we want to make the change out of feelings of hope or fear? a longing for self-expression or a need for other people's approval? pleasure or pressure?" The point was to choose what was "healthy and empowering—and reject the rest." She noted elsewhere in the essay that when her mother had expressed a desire to do something about her "dewlaps," Gloria had encouraged her, recognizing immediately that Ruth's interest was "clearly a sign of hope."

Although she was clearly going through one of the most depressing periods of her life, according to Gloria, her own procedure was neither age related nor intended to change her appearance. Furthermore, "it was not a big decision." Even so, she says, she probably would never have done it if she had not been going on the *Today* show. She wanted to wear contact lenses early in the morning, she explains, and once she had the operation, she could wear sleep-in lenses and stop taking diuretics.

Then, the Friday before her week on *Today*, Gloria went for her annual checkup and learned she had breast cancer. She went ahead anyway, the following Monday, coanchoring for the entire week. When it was over, one of the producers said, "Not bad."

No, Gloria thought to herself, not bad at all, considering I've just learned I have cancer.

On September 12, Gloria had gone to Dr. Penny Budhoff's Women's Medical Center in Bethpage, a Long Island town about an hour east of Manhattan. Gloria had a local gynecologist, but she began going to Dr. Budhoff's clinic for an annual checkup because of the physician's diagnostic skills, her extensive experience with woman patients, and the fact that "they do all your body parts at once."

The previous November, she had felt a tiny lump in one breast, but a mammogram had revealed nothing suspicious. Later, Dr. Budhoff had checked it with sonography, but it still did not seem to be a problem. This time, since the surgeon who spent one day a week at Dr. Budhoff's clinic happened to be there, she suggested they check it. Because it was small, she took out the entire tumor.

She "gave me a little Novocaine shot and I sat there and watched her take it out," Gloria recalls, "It was nothing. I'm grateful I watched, because it makes it much more comprehensible. Otherwise you imagine that it's some sort of terrible thing and there's really this little innocent piece of flesh."

It was not innocent. They sent it across the street to the laboratory and were shocked when the diagnosis came back malignant. All of Gloria's doctors were surprised.

Gloria remembers thinking, as she returned alone to her apartment, "How interesting. So this is how it's going to end." She contemplated the idea of dying "not tragically. Just mysteriously. It's what people must think when they're going down in a plane. And then, in the next instant, this feeling rose, as if from my toes upward. Which was, 'I've had a good life.' "

"I wouldn't say it was good or bad. But it was kind of feeling, 'Well, it's okay.' It certainly was not peace, because if you'd asked me did I want to die, certainly not. But that it was all right. And I valued that. I was really really grateful for that. Now some of that, I suspect, was that I was so exhausted and worn out and down at the time. I had come to the end of my ability to continue living the same life anyway.

"Once I was past the breast cancer and thought about it, I knew in my heart that if I had a recurrence I would be angry. So it had partly to do with the circumstances. I think I would have felt grateful for the life I'd had up to that point, but it was partly to do with the stage I was in."

Gloria investigated alternative methods of treating breast cancer, while simultaneously informing her close friends and reassuring them that everything would be fine. Her assistants, Lee Chiaramonte and Kristen Golden, had been working for her only for a couple of weeks before the diagnosis was made, and they were drawn into the crisis as well.

Lee and Kristen had been hired as an antidote to the chaos of Gloria's affairs. Gloria's office was completely overburdened. She received as many as sixty calls a day, so it was impossible to return them all. Furthermore, many of Gloria's assistants, who also worked for *Ms.* magazine, took the job because they wanted to be writers. Finally, Kristina Kiehl, who worked with Gloria at the Ms. Foundation and Voters for Choice, decided that Gloria needed an assistant whose only priority was Gloria and her activities. Kristina, whose husband is a member of the Levi Strauss family, set out to enlist some of Gloria's wealthy friends and associates to finance a second assistant for Gloria for a couple of years.

First she contacted Alida Rockefeller Dayton (now Alida Dayton Messenger), a contemporary of Kristina's who is a generous supporter of liberal causes. Sharing a taxi after their meeting, they were caught in a traffic jam. Kristina jumped out of the cab and began directing traffic. After she moved about eight cars to ease the gridlock so that their cab and an ambulance could move along, she climbed back into the cab and turned to her companion. "That's what I want to see happen in Gloria's life," she explained.

Alida and Marlo Thomas joined Kristina in contributing $10,000 to $20,000 a year to finance an assistant, at $30,000 a year plus benefits, for a couple of years. Gloria was embarrassed by the idea, but Kristina prevailed.

The first assistant Gloria hired was Lee Chiaramonte, who was working for Walter Cronkite at CBS. Joanne Edgar interviewed her first, and thought she was a good candidate. Because Lee was not sure she wanted to leave CBS, she kept throwing up roadblocks. One was asking to bring her assistant, Kristen Golden. Gloria and Joanne were determined to hire Lee, so they hired twenty-eight-year-old Kristen, too.

Before Lee and Kristen began calling to cancel engagements, Gloria said she wanted to keep her cancer out of the press. She didn't want to be asked questions before she knew the answers, nor did she want her illness known to advertisers or creditors of *Ms.* They told people Gloria had a severe inner-ear infection, which helped to explain why she couldn't fly. Meanwhile, she was exploring her options. At the same time, Gloria told about eight people the truth—and not just her close friends. As a result, when someone called, Lee and Kristen were completely confused about what to say. They were so new they had no idea who was in Gloria's inner circle, or who knew about her diagnosis, or what else the caller had been told.

Lee and Kristen were not yet familiar with Gloria's operating style. She is as free with information as she is with money, so her assistants change her telephone number every few years, because she gives it out to so many people.

For treatment, Gloria chose the Memorial Sloan-Kettering Cancer Center in New York, because she had learned that the Boston medical community tended toward less radical procedures (lumpectomies instead of mastectomies), and Sloan-Kettering's new president, Dr. Sam Hellman, had just come from Boston. However, when Dr. Hellman left her in the examining room while he talked with the surgeon, she could hear them arguing. The surgeon wanted to take out a quadrant of her breast to make sure the previous surgeon had gotten it all, and Hellman was arguing for a less radical procedure.

Even taking a quadrant was far less radical than the standard procedure in many other hospitals, but since it now seemed to Gloria that the New York surgeon lacked experience in lumpectomies, she decided to go to Beth Israel Hospital in Boston. Stan Pottinger helped her find Dr. William Silen, a surgeon who had trained Dr. Susan Love. She told Mort he need not come, because she knew how he disliked hospitals after his father's illness. He sent his corporate plane to bring her home and visited her there. Suzanne Levine went up to be with Gloria for the surgery. She says, "I don't know why I went. I thought lots of people would go up, but there weren't other people there. But if ever there was anything I could do for her, it was to do this. Although I gave her bad advice. Somebody said when you come out of anesthesia you'll be very thirsty but you shouldn't drink anything because you'll throw up. Then I heard you wouldn't necessarily throw up if you had crushed ice. So I got her crushed ice and she threw up anyway. I felt terrible."

The margins of the tumor area were clean and her lymph node sampling was negative, so Gloria returned to New York and began radiation treatment. Often accompanied by Koryne Horbal, Gloria went for early morning treatments under her grandmother's name, for privacy. The treatments just preceded her fall book tour for *Marilyn*.

Then she proceeded with her book tour. Even without the physical and emotional strain of cancer worries, Gloria's book-promotion tours are marathon endurance contests. Not only does she take on a staggering number of events each day—back-to-back print, radio, and television interviews, speeches, book signings—but Gloria puts herself out in all of them. People stand in book-signing lines for hours, and when each reaches her, Gloria patiently and interestedly talks to anyone who wants to talk to her.

Following cancer treatments with a media-filled book tour would have exhausted any ordinary person, but Gloria was urgently involved elsewhere as well. She was trying to move forward on her next two books while at the same time searching for yet another solution for *Ms*. The magazine was sinking deeper and deeper into debt.

33

Ms. Ms.

The august *New York Times* announced on June 20, 1986, that "Ms." henceforth would be used in its pages as the standard form of reference to women. Until then, executive editor Abe Rosenthal explained in a public statement, the term "had not passed sufficiently into the language to be accepted as common usage."

When contacted, Gloria told the press, "We're very pleased that the *Times* has caught up with the times." She also took a bouquet of flowers to her old friend to celebrate the occasion. They had continued to see each other socially and for a ritual lunch over the years, and Gloria had never stopped lobbying him. "Of course she was enormously influential in the decision," he says. "She was Ms. *Ms.* But I don't mean just the magazine. She was enormously influential in changing my mind."

For Rosenthal, the decision was not a frivolous one: "I knew that what was taking place was that the people who were in favor of [using] *Ms.*, on and off the staff, wanted the *Times* to use it because they felt that if we used it, it would be official. And they were right. It would have had an effect. And I was kind of stubborn about it because I was dealing with all kinds of titles, blah-blah-blah. And I just didn't want the *Times* to bow.

"I had refused to use *Ms.* for a reason that I obviously felt was a valid one at the time, which was that I didn't think the *Times* should use titles or nomenclature or whatever, in response to political pressure or political fashions, no matter how much I might like them or not. You'd be quite astonished that whether we spell Romania with a *u* or without a *u* is one hell of a big issue to Romania. . . . The whole question of what you call people was extremely important at that time."

Rosenthal was always making that kind of decision. He had to determine whether or not to use Mr. (or Mrs.) with criminals; when or whether to change from Negro to black or African American; whether to accede to some groups' insistence that the *Times* not use the word *Mafia* (his refusal to ban it earned him temporary police protection). So when the *Ms.* issue came up, "I knew I could do it or not do it. But I did not know that it would make so many people on the paper—the women—so happy. I mean, they were really delighted. Well, they had told me before, we'd had professional discussions about it, but some of them were hugging and kissing and crying. I thought, Oh, God, I should really not have withheld it this long."

The imprimatur of the *Times* was a triumph, but public victories like that were palliatives. Behind the scenes, Gloria's patient was hemorrhaging. In 1986, Gloria, together with Pat Carbine, who had lent the magazine a lot of money, decided they had to do the unthinkable. It seemed to them that the only way to save *Ms.* was to sell it.

By summer they found people who seemed to be the perfect buyers: a pair of feminists employed by a corporation with deep pockets. Sandra Yates had moved to New York from Sydney, Australia, in June to become president of Fairfax Publications (U.S.) Ltd., a subsidiary of one of Australia's largest publishers. Largely family-owned, John Fairfax Ltd. had sent Yates to New York to launch *Sassy,* a new magazine for teenage girls to be modeled after an Australian Fairfax publication, *Dolly.* As soon as she read that *Ms.* was looking for an investor, Yates was determined that Fairfax should buy it and that her colleague, Fairfax's New York bureau chief, Anne Summers, should become its new editor. Summers had written a book sometimes called the bible of Australian feminism, *Damned Whores and God's Police,* and had served for three years as head of Australia's Office of the Status of Women and chief advisor to the prime minister on women's issues.

In November 1987 the Ms. Foundation for Education and Communication sold *Ms.* for about $10 million, part cash and part the assumption of the magazine's liabilities. After everyone was repaid, the Ms. Foundation for Education and Communication was left with about $3 million. Gloria and Pat, who had made nothing when they had donated their stock in *Ms.* to the foundation, received back pay and contracts to be paid $100,000 a year for five years as consultants to the magazine. The fees were also in return for "noncompete" agreements—Gloria observed that they could get paid for *not* starting a magazine but not for starting one. The rest of the *Ms.* staff received severance bonuses, with added consideration for the three oldest employees.

After the sale, Rosenthal, who had become an op-ed columnist for the *Times*, devoted a column to Gloria, *Ms.*, and their contributions to "one of the most successful and pervading social crusades of the century":

> ... Ms. Steinem became a kind of brand-label for the movement, instantly recognizable throughout much of the world. Many of the profiles printed about her attribute her fame largely to her appearance. Nonsense; many women are attractive and chic, but they do not achieve international reputation. There must be something more; there is.
>
> I have known Ms. Steinem since my reporting days in India. . . . Many of her political opinions, the people she admires and her romanticism about the third world would normally give me instant hives.
>
> But she is wonderfully good to talk and argue with. There is an intensity and sharpness of mind, but also a civility of discourse, an ability to explain and teach, that come across in a living room or a lecture hall. That ability to differ strongly without assuming enmity has made her valuable for the feminist movement, outside as well as within. She reminds me, in those traits, of William F. Buckley, a thought I trust will test the equanimity of both.

When Yates and Summers took over in January 1988, they changed the look of *Ms.* as well as the contents, with mixed results. Yates was just beginning to court advertisers with the generous funds she expected Fairfax to provide, when her employer announced it was pulling out of the American market. After the death of the senior Fairfax and the October 1987 stock-market crash, his son Warwick Fairfax had fended off two takeover bids and borrowed heavily to take the company private. He needed funds to pay off the debts, so Fairfax put *Ms.* up for sale only months after Yates and Summers had taken over the magazine.

In those few months, Yates and Summers had become so dedicated to *Ms.* and *Sassy* that they were determined to hold on to them. They formed Matilda Publications to buy the magazines from Fairfax. *Sassy*, which premiered in March 1988, was an immediate hit, attracting a circulation of 280,000 by May. Living up to its name, it took on subjects previously untouched in teen magazines—abortion, losing one's virginity, condoms, gay teens, AIDS, kissing techniques—and attracted the attention of religious fundamentalist groups, whose boycotts prompted several big advertisers to withdraw from the magazine.

Sassy eventually won some of them back and began a slow climb to health, but not quickly enough for Matilda Publications to achieve its quarterly goals. In June 1989, its investors put Matilda Publications on the block again, and *Ms.* was sold for the third time in two years, this time to the owner of *Working Woman* and *Working Mother,* Dale Lang.

As soon as *Ms.* was officially acquired in October 1989, Lang fired *Ms.*'s advertising and circulation departments, suspended publication, and canceled both the December issue, which was ready for the printer, and the January Women of the Year issue, which was close to completion.

Gloria, who still was receiving a consulting fee, an office, and salary for her assistant, also possessed the leverage of her name and historic identification with *Ms.* When she objected to Lang's plans to have *Ms.*'s subscribers shift to *Working Mother* or *Working Woman,* he tried to placate her by offering to publish a six-times-a-year, reader-supported, low-cost, nonslick, eight-page newsletter. That seemed to her to be just a way to fulfill the subscriptions of *Ms.* subscribers who did not want to switch to *Working Woman* or *Working Mother.* Besides, she pointed out, "That's not in the spirit of *Ms.* at all. It doesn't have fiction and poetry and theory and letters."

Gloria wanted Lang to experiment with an advertisement-free, reader-supported *Ms.* for which the costs would be covered by subscribers and newsstand purchasers. Lang only agreed to allow the staff to investigate the idea after Gloria threatened to publicly encourage subscribers to ask for their money back rather than switch their subscription to one of his other publications.

Ruth Bower, now the publisher of *Ms,* ran the numbers and concluded that it should be published six times a year, not twelve, and that subscriptions had to cost a steep $40. Because they would not be running advertisements, they wouldn't need four-color printing or slick paper. "Let us take 155,000 of the old subscription names and do a mailing," Ruth and Gloria proposed. "It'll be a referendum and we'll ask the readers to vote for the return of *Ms.* The solicitation will be a ballot and the readers will have to vote with a check for a year's subscription to *Ms.*"

They estimated that 2 to 3 percent would be a strong response; they received a 19.8-percent response. When Lang saw the numbers and the money, he agreed to try their plan.

Robin Morgan became the new editor in chief. By July 1991, a year after first publication, the new *Ms.* was in the black. All 100 pages were devoted to editorial copy, and the editors were free to cover even more of the controversial subjects that had offended advertisers in the past. The first issue carried a scathing attack by Gloria on advertisers' demands and their effect on women's magazines, particularly *Ms.* Circulation settled around 150,000, which was double the magazine's estimated break-even point.

"I wish I had six magazines like *Ms.*," Lang told the *New York Times*, explaining that its profit margin was "way above the average of the industry." Though she found it difficult to get accurate figures because Lang seemed to inflate overhead to absorb profits, Gloria pressed until he allocated $50,000 to the Ms. Foundation.

Then Lang's other publications began faltering. He sold *Sassy* in 1994 and used *Ms.*'s profits to support *Working Woman* and *Working Mother*, which also were losing money by 1995. While looking for additional investors, Lang slowed and then shut off payments to *Ms.* writers. Marcia Gillespie, who had succeeded Robin Morgan as editor in chief, was so furious that she spoke publicly about her boss. "It's a nightmare from hell that we're going through," she told the *New York Observer*. Eventually she even suggested to writers that they take Lang to court, if necessary, to get their money. Gloria was equally furious. Besides treating writers poorly, Lang was "trading on our good name with the printers and other vendors." Through all its difficulties, *Ms.* had always paid in full its debts and loans. Lang conceded he was willing to sell *Ms.*, and Gloria was eager to get *Ms.* away from him and back to owners who would care about *Ms.* as a national forum rather than using it as a "cash calf" for other magazines. She began yet another search for buyers. Because the magazine was profitable and Lang knew very well how much *Ms.* meant to Gloria, she says he held out for over $3 million, a price, according to Gloria, two to three times its appraised value.

Finally, when he was on the verge of bankruptcy, Lang sold the trio of magazines to thirty-nine-year-old Jay MacDonald, in May 1996. MacDonald, a former advertising salesman for *Fortune* and *U.S. News & World Report* and former publisher of *Inc.*, was convinced that women living on their own constituted an enormous, underserved market.

MacDonald, who had no money of his own to buy the properties, was financed by Paxson Communications, a fast-growing Florida company that owned television and radio stations and had no interest in the magazine business. Paxson's goal in the deal was obtaining a Minnesota television station in which Lang had an interest, so even that rescue looked shaky.

As Gloria sees it, "MacDonald, who had less experience with magazines than Dale Lang, soon began to lose much more than he anticipated on *Working Woman* and *Working Mother* and therefore to starve *Ms.*" Out of necessity MacDonald downsized all three magazines, and by mid-1997 Gloria reported, "The magazine's staff continued to publish, bravely and with impact; though its financial condition was again being held hostage, its editorial content was still in feminist hands."

34

Revolution From Within:
A Book of Self-Esteem

"Mort Janklow can get me a couple of hundred thousand dollars from Random House," Gloria told Letty Pogrebin in 1986. Gloria had ideas for two different books. "That's absurd. Ridiculous," Letty responded. "I'll act as your agent. I'll run an auction, and we'll get you much more than that."

Gloria wanted to write a book on the importance of self-esteem, and she even had a title: *The Bedside Book of Self-Esteem*. The other book would be an expansion of her *Ms.* article, "The Trouble With Rich Women," in which she had discussed the ways women in wealthy families were kept from controlling family money.

Soon after Letty began taking Gloria to visit publishers, Gloria's *Outrageous Acts and Everyday Rebellions* editor, Jennifer Josephy, called her. Josephy, who had moved to Boston to work for Little, Brown, had heard that Gloria was showing proposals. Gloria was apologetic. "I never thought of Little, Brown," she explained. Little, Brown, headquartered in Boston, was not as visible as many of the other publishers and also was considered a little stodgy. Gloria assured Jennifer that she and Letty were still in the process of meeting with publishers, so they would be happy to talk with her.

Accompanied by Little, Brown's editorial director, Roger Donald, and subsidiary rights director Susan Peterson, Jennifer went to *Ms.*'s shabby Times Square offices. There Gloria gave, Jennifer recalls, "an utterly charming presentation in which she talked about wanting to sell two books at once because she was concerned about her financial future and didn't want to worry about being an old lady walking around with shopping bags. It was just an oral presentation, though eventually they sent over a two-paragraph summary."

Letty selected the publishers to participate in the auction, and Bob Levine assisted. On March 24, 1987, the day before Gloria's fifty-third birthday, Letty and Bob began accepting bids. By the second day, Letty decided to sell the two books separately. Little, Brown bought the self-esteem book for $700,000, and Simon & Schuster's publisher, Joni Evans, bought the "book on rich women," as everyone called it, for $500,000, but she left Simon & Schuster soon afterward to become the publisher at Random House. In 1988 she hired Gloria as a Random House contributing editor, charged with bringing in new projects—even though Gloria was working on her self-esteem book. The appointment enabled Gloria to attend weekly editorial meetings, which she enjoyed as a relief from the solitude of writing.

Gloria was excited about the book contract. She and Pat Carbine had been negotiating since January to sell *Ms.* to Fairfax, and though the deal was not completed until October, relief seemed to be in sight. Finally, her assistant Kristen Golden recalls, "She had been handed a lifelong dream: to be funded to sit down and write a book. . . . It was the first time in her life to have money—she had lived on speaking fees of $40,000–$50,000."

Although Gloria had written in *Outrageous Acts,* "*What is so sacred about a long and continuous piece of writing?*" in fact she did want very much to produce a significant book. Gloria had not accomplished it during her year as a Woodrow Wilson fellow in 1978, but now she would.

Once she had time to settle down to make real her lifelong dream, however, Gloria engaged in the honored tradition of writers through the ages: she procrastinated. She did not just wash her hair or clean out her bureau drawers. Gloria took the first installment of her advance, bought the ground-floor apartment below hers, and began renovations.

She also helped her assistant, Kristen, financially. In December 1986, a few months after she had begun working for Gloria, Kristen had come out as a lesbian to her parents. The revelation so upset her father that he called in the debts she owed him. She had no way of paying them, so Gloria gave Kristen money from her book contract. "She said, 'If I didn't have it I wouldn't give it'—which was a lie," Kristen says, meaning Gloria would have found the money for her whether she had it or not.

Gloria's other assistant, Lee Chiaramonte, left in November 1987, and Kristen added Lee's duties to her secretarial duties and her work for *Ms.* She also helped research Gloria's book and tried to keep Gloria focused on her writing. Gloria would be several years late with both books, but her deadlines were completely unrealistic. She signed the contract for the self-esteem book on June 15, 1987, and it was due nine months later, on her fifty-fourth birthday. The "rich women book" was due a year after that.

Months passed. Deadlines came and went. Kristen decided to go back to school for a master's in business administration, but she stayed on with Gloria until August 1989 to help with the transition. In the meantime, Diana James arrived, courtesy of her chiropractor. A sister Ohioan, Diana had spent a year at Long Island University before she ran out of money. After that she had worked at a series of interesting jobs, including nine years at the research archives run by the C. G. Jung Foundation. The only job she had ever hated was her present one selling advertisements for *Self* magazine. She complained to everyone she saw, including her chiropractor, who asked around on her behalf. His daughter-in-law, who worked for Pat Carbine, told him about the opening.

Kristen interviewed Diana and sent her to Gloria's, where she was so nervous that she spilled her tea. After she had chatted with Gloria for a couple of hours, Gloria said, "Well, I guess the only thing we have to settle is when do you start?" Then she added, "And you know what the best part is? Now you can go back to Condé Nast, and say, 'Fuck you' to the world of advertising."

That was a preview. Since then, one service Diana has provided on her own initiative has been editing some of Gloria's responses to irritating questioners—in private. Glorias public statements are always conveyed uncensored, even in response to dumb questions (such as, What do you think about the style of women's bra straps showing?). "Whenever something happens involving women, every reporter in the United States wants to talk to Gloria," Diana explains. "Sometimes we prepare a statement when we know there will be too many requests for Gloria to handle—as in the Packwood case."

By the time Kristen left, she had been doing about three people's jobs. When Diana arrived, she reorganized Gloria's files, systematized her work life, and eventually hired an assistant, Pilar Settlemier. She also raised her speaking fees as high as Gloria would allow: $9,000 for nonprofit organizations and $12,000 for for-profits—when she took it, of course. As she told Diana, "The big rich organizations can get anyone they want. The rape counseling centers need me."

Besides scheduling Gloria, Diana's normal work includes constant telephone calls and piles of mail. Every week Gloria receives galleys of books with requests for blurbs; manuscripts with requests for intro-ductions; first drafts of books; movie treatments or film scripts for her advice or help; requests for speeches; letters from people she has met (and from those she hasn't), telling her their life stories; letters from crazy people, which Diana files in the Crazy People file and never shows Gloria, because Gloria would try to help them (and, she says, because Gloria has better things to do with her time).

By 1990 the self-esteem book was so far behind schedule that Diana and Pilar began working on it, too. Then Pilar left, and when the book was still not complete by the summer of 1991, everyone began pan-icking. The publication date was January 21, 1992, and a typical lead time from a completed manuscript to publication day is nine months. At that point Diana changed her routine. "It was wonderful . . . I'd get up in the morning at eleven and reach the office around noon. Take the phone messages. Ignore the mail. So many things were having to slide at that time. Then I would take the subway uptown and walk across Central Park to Gloria's. I used to look forward to the walk. I would arrive about four-thirty. We'd work and then stop for dinner—we would send out for Chinese food and work until three or four A.M."

The proposal for the self-esteem book had promised "a personal preface on my own life and times with self-esteem (and without it)" and "profiles of famous people you wouldn't think suffered from this problem." She also planned to include advice, anecdotes, ideas for organizing, a discussion of the psychological and political roots of the problem, especially among certain groups, and possibly cartoons or other illustrations.

However, as Gloria wrote in the book's introduction:

I spent months researching and interviewing, and more months writing 250 pages of psychological research, anecdotal examples, and philo-sophical prose. It was a peaceful time of sitting at my computer with my cat on my lap, traveling and *tummeling* less than I had at any time since I was in college, and finally having time to write something longer than an article.

Too peaceful. When Carmen Robinson, a friend from Montreal who is a family therapist, read that labored-over manuscript, she said, "I don't know how to tell you this—but I think you have a self-esteem problem. You forgot to put yourself in."

Gloria's editor, Jennifer Josephy, agreed with Carmen. Carmen had become Gloria's friend through her brother, Mort Zuckerman. "It took time for her to come to grips with what she was writing. Her tendency is to be more reportorial and I felt it had to have a big emotional component."

Then there was the problem of Gloria's tendency to make everything a communal project. Josephy recalls: "She was several years overdue. I met with her a few times at her apartment, but she talks to everyone about everything. So I'd hear about her talking to Robin Morgan. Or Suzanne Levine. I was already getting anxious about so many different opinions, but when she said, 'The cab driver said, "Do this," ' I thought, We're in trouble.

"I said, 'Gloria, I'm sure he's a charming guy, but you're going to have to get some help. You're getting too many opinions, and you're really only going to value what you pay for, just like psychotherapy.' I suggested Beth Rashbaum as an editor to sit down and spend hours and hours with Gloria. She worked with Gloria the way a good editor could, as I couldn't, because I didn't have the time to devote to one author."

Beth was a writer who, besides writing under her own name (including *The Courage to Raise Good Men*, with Olga Silverstein), freelances as both a ghostwriter and an editor. Ghostwriting was the last skill she needed for Gloria's project. Gloria's problem was not too little writing, it was too much. "That's very interesting," she often would say in response to Gloria's latest idea, "but just not in this book."

Beth believes she was useful in organizing, not writing—"if I'd rewrite a sentence, she'd rewrite it four times more herself." And by the time Beth began, Gloria "had done much of the book, but it was in about one hundred different pieces, none of which were cohering."

Through it all, Beth considered Gloria "tireless, indefatigable, and unbelievably upbeat." She notes, "I'd sit there in her office with the workmen, the houseguests, Diana, five faxes, the yoga teacher all around. Then the computer would go on the blink—and she'd be even and cheerful." While Beth was working with her, Gloria even had a nutritionist review her pantry and then began diligently to follow a new vegetarian regimen, part of an effort to prevent a recurrence of cancer.

Beth also thought Gloria wrote too much on some subjects and not enough on others. "The gist of our discussions was that I wanted more personal stuff in and more political stuff out and Gloria's attitude was, 'Why would anyone be interested in my experiences?' I had to keep reminding her that she was a celebrity, and that stuff mattered to people. She knows she is at some level, but it is not part of her view of herself."

Jennifer Josephy agreed with Beth. When she received Gloria's discussion of plastic surgery, Gloria had included nothing about her own eye-lift. Josephy recalls, "That was the only time Gloria got mad at me. I asked Beth to talk to Gloria. She had all this about plastic surgery and I knew about hers from doing the other book. She called me and said in a cold voice, 'If you have a problem with me, you talk to me. Don't ask someone else to do it.' I felt terrible, and she was right."

Meanwhile, it was becoming clear that even Diana and Beth could not provide enough help. Gloria was writing in longhand to curb her prolixity. Pilar suggested that they hire her friend Amy, a student at Barnard College. Amy was interested in the job, but because she took a full course load at school and usually had soccer practice or games afterward, she wouldn't be available until nighttime.

That would be perfect, Diana assured her. When could she start? "Saturday," Amy replied. That was how Amelia Richards came into Gloria's life. As Gloria describes Amy, who is tiny, athletic, vivacious, and very intelligent: "Take Tinkerbell, add the White Tornado, and give them good politics and a great heart, and you have Amy."

Amy's mother had left her father before Amy was born. Eight months pregnant, Amy's mother, Karen, moved in with her parents. Then she went on welfare, finished her undergraduate degree, earned a graduate degree, and worked her way up through a succession of jobs to become a consultant to AT&T. Amy eventually went to boarding school, financed by a combination of scholarships, financial aid, and her mother's contributions.

After a semester at Harvard, Amy dropped out to travel around Europe: "I hated Harvard. It was my reach school and it was the only school I got into that I wanted to go to. I really wanted to go to Smith or Dartmouth, but I think I would have hated them too—I hated the attitude. Everyone at Harvard acted so privileged. It is wonderful, but at the same time, those people are no better than anybody else. And there was definitely an attitude among the people I met that they were the crème de la crème. It really annoyed me, and I was in a different place in my life."

After traveling, Amy worked and went to school in Oregon, where she met Pilar. She transferred to Barnard to finish college. When she began working for Gloria in 1991, Amy was twenty-one years old.

Now there were often three of them—Gloria, Diana, and Amy—working at Gloria's, plus Beth Rashbaum coming over during the day or even at night after theater, and another fact checker, Mary Beth Guyther, who came in from Long island several nights a week. Gloria had finally stopped accepting speaking engagements, and Diana did not even answer the telephone. It was intense but fun, and at the end Gloria gave Diana a big bonus for all the extra work. Diana recalls: "We called ourselves elves—we'd end up dressing alike. We would be wearing black leggings with big old baggy sweatshirts. Big old baggy black sweatshirts. . . . I remember people asking me what I was doing for Labor Day: did we get a three-day weekend? I said we didn't get a three-minute weekend. Because we worked straight through weekends. It all went by in a complete blur."

Once a chapter was ready, Diana would call Moonlite Courier, an all-night messenger service staffed by Sikhs. At three or four in the morning, a maroon-turbaned Sikh would appear to deliver the copy to Boston so it would arrive at Little, Brown by the time it opened.

There was no outline. The book was set in type chapter by chapter. Josephy joked, "It's the first time I've done a book signature by signature." (Signatures are sixteen- or thirty-two-page sections of a book printed on a single large sheet of paper.) Sometimes Gloria sent a chapter to Carmen Robinson for her comments.

The result was *Revolution From Within: A Book of Self-Esteem*. Writing a self-help book seemed quite a departure for Gloria, who, perhaps more than anyone, had unfailingly interpreted personal problems in political terms. However, in spite of all those years of unexamined living (or perhaps because of them), once Gloria understood the power of the interior life, she was determined to tell the world about it.

Even so, as infatuated with internal journeys as Gloria became, it never occurred to her to forsake the external world. She always assumed that the book would combine an examination of the internal world with discussions of the very real social and political barriers women (the primary readers of such books) face. As in all her work,

Gloria filled *Revolution From Within* with pointed accounts of oppression and discrimination. The difference was that she used the stories to demonstrate the ways oppression or the lack of it could affect internal self-esteem, and she encouraged readers to look within themselves for part of the solution. *Revolution From Within* belonged to the genre taking over bookstores, shelf by shelf, section by section: recovery-movement books.

The recovery movement is part of a long tradition of self-help and personal development that reaches back to Benjamin Franklin and Ralph Waldo Emerson, includes Norman Vincent Peale and *The Power of Positive Thinking* from the 1950s, and extends beyond Werner Erhard and est of the 1960s. During the 1970s self-help began to be combined with self-actualization and personal fulfillment. Since the 1980s, the focus has become more spiritual, combining the language and practices of psychotherapy, New Age spirituality, and an unacknowledged debt to feminism.

With the addition of a healthy dose of capitalism, the recovery movement exploded in the 1980s and 1990s. It now offers a sort of populist, mass-produced therapy through self-help books, experts, gurus, therapists, and support groups. By 1997, a Recovery Network cable station was in the works. The movement's enormous popularity attests to a widespread hunger for answers.

Recovery-movement books address both behavior patterns and emotional problems. There are books for people suffering from bulimia, overeating, codependency, shopping too much, or loving the wrong kind of man. There is an entire subcategory dealing with the effects of childhood sexual abuse. The books typically provide lists of symptoms so that readers can determine whether they are suffering from the condition the book addresses. Then, for those who fit the profile, they prescribe multistep programs modeled on the twelve-step program made famous by Alcoholics Anonymous. The books often encourage readers to join a support group organized around their particular problem.

The recovery movement is controversial, and there are feminists among both its defenders and its detractors. Supporters believe that the movement empowers women by helping them to take control of their own lives. Roughly based on family-systems therapy, recovery-movement books encourage readers to examine their pasts and revisit their childhoods. The point is to understand that the source of their current problems lies in the dynamics of their families and in other childhood experiences that shaped them. Once they can recover the memories of those experiences and understand their effects, they can use that knowledge, along with support groups and multistep programs, to transcend their past, heal themselves, and move forward. At their best, the books and groups serve as inexpensive therapy, intended to help individuals more effectively help themselves.

Other feminists criticize the movement. They argue that the recovery movement infantilizes women by encouraging them to think of themselves as diseased or addicted or dependent or victims, when some of their behavior is normal. Wendy Kaminer, who critiqued the movement in *I'm Dysfunctional, You're Dysfunctional,* considers the recovery movement a reactionary force that encourages followers to stop thinking and to eschew skepticism, to embrace feeling over thinking, and to submit to higher powers (recovery experts or God).

Other feminist critics argue that the movement harms women not only as individuals, but as a group, by encouraging them to focus on their behavior patterns when they should be examining the underlying contexts of their lives. They contend that the behavior patterns women seek to change often are reactions to conditions in their present lives, rather than predetermined by their dysfunctional childhoods.

In *The Mismeasure of Woman,* social psychologist Carol Tavris suggested that the recovery movement has succeeded in redirecting women's legitimate anger and discontent into avenues that would not challenge the status quo, precisely because those avenues are more culturally acceptable for all parties. Noting that "our culture dislikes and fears angry women, but it is not threatened by sick women meeting together to get well," she quoted therapist Harriet Lerner:

> Society is more comfortable with women who feel inadequate, self-doubting, guilty, sick, and "diseased" than with women who are angry or confronting. . . . Women are, too, which is why they eat up these codependency books like popcorn. Women are *so* comfortable saying, "I am a recovering addict, the problem is in me." They are so uncomfortable saying that the problem is in society, in their relationships, in their financial standing. Women get much more sympathy and support when they define their problems in medical terms than in political terms.

Gloria herself acknowledges that women are rewarded for singing the blues, and in her preface she specifically differentiated her book from the self-help books that urged women to look within "with little mention of the external structures that undermine this [sense of self]-worth." In fact, she devoted much of her book to accounts of a wide variety of oppressive conditions in the external world and emphatically stated that both the internal and the external were important. "We make progress," she wrote, "by a constant spiraling back and forth between the inner world and the outer one, the personal and the political, the self and the circumstance."

However, employing the movement's language and conventions as well as much of its ideology, *Revolution From Within* offered standard recovery-movement advice and generally followed the recovery-movement format. It explained the way families or individuals affect one another, provided inspiring stories of people whose increased self-awareness helped them deal with various problems, and offered exercises, tests, and solutions. Gloria encouraged her readers to search for their "inner child" and reparent it in order to heal themselves; to seek their "true self"; to find a source of spirituality that suited them; and to join groups in order to recover their self-esteem.

Her stories, which she called parables, were woven together with a New Age universalism that embraced both the wholeness of the universe and a conscientious multiculturalism. In other words, the scope of *Revolution From Within* was nothing less than the entire universe—both the interior psychological and spiritual world, and the external physical and political world. The latter, in turn, embraced the natural world, all nations, all cultures, all religions, and all peoples. (Perhaps that is why Beth Rashbaum kept saying, "That's very interesting, but just not in this book.")

Gloria wanted her book to engage as wide an audience as possible. As she wrote in the preface, "Trying to approach self-esteem from many different vantage points on the spiral in the hope that this book will be useful to as many people as possible, I've included theory as well as practical exercises, scientific studies as well as a wide variety of stories and experiences that people have entrusted to me."

Furthermore, while she was demonstrating the value of self-esteem in a myriad of ways, she wanted to do it as accessibly as possible: "I've also tried to explain concepts as I go and keep scholarly references to a minimum, so that no reader is made to feel she or he should have read eighty-nine other things *first*. My sixteen-year-old self in Toledo certainly needed this book: I didn't want to write anything that would make her feel excluded."

In short, Gloria had two explicit goals: (1) she wanted *Revolution From Within* to prove the importance of self-esteem as a source of revolution, both personal and political to as wide and varied an audience as possible; and (2) she aimed at the reading and knowledge level of her sixteen-year-old self.

Like *Outrageous Acts and Everyday Rebellions* and *Marilyn, Revolution From Within* was an extension of Gloria's work as a feminist leader, offering variations on the themes of her speeches—consciousness-raising, a message of hope, and a call to action. As in her other books, *Revolution From Within* showcased her strengths. Gloria's ability to tell stories and move audiences translated well into the book's parables about herself and others, both famous and obscure. They were interesting and often moving. Her conscientious inclusivity meant no one was forgotten. Her aphorisms and stories ranged the globe, portraying Eastern, Western, advanced, primitive, ancient, and modern cultures, not to mention plants and animals.

However, as her most ambitious project, *Revolution From Within* displayed her best and worst proclivities. Some of Gloria's strengths were also her weaknesses, most notably her tendency toward excess. The fact that Gloria went to extremes made her the leader she became: If Gloria had not been extremely gifted, extremely dedicated, extremely committed, extremely needy, and extremely enduring, she could never have sustained the effort she made. A more measured Gloria Steinem would not have become the world's icon of feminism.

Sometimes, though, excess is just plain excessive, and so *Revolution From Within* was. Gloria made so many claims for a simple concept that it collapsed under their weight. When she speaks or appears on television, Gloria's aphorisms are powerful because they condense complicated concepts into a few words. In *Revolution From Within* she seemed to reverse the process. She took a simple idea that was true—that self-esteem is important—and used it to explain practically everything in the universe.

Taking as her thesis the unarguable fact that childhood experiences have psychological consequences in adulthood, she focused on it in a way that seemed to imply that nothing else mattered. Eliminating hierarchical families was crucial, she explained, "if we are to stop producing leaders whose unexamined early lives are then played out on a national and international stage." For example, after Saddam Hussein was beaten and tortured as a boy, he grew up to enjoy torturing others; the vicious Romanian dictator Nicolae Ceauşescu grew up in one room with nine siblings and an alcoholic father; George Bush had a controlling father who beat him with a belt; Ronald Reagan's father was an alcoholic.

In other words, she explained, there was an obvious solution:

> This is not to take free will away from them (or from us), or to excuse destructive behavior in them (or in us); for if anyone is willing or able to go back and confront those earliest years, feelings can be directed at their real sources instead of being expressed in bigger and bigger ways. But changing the way we raise children is the only long-term path to peace or arms control, and neither has ever been more crucial.

That formulation echoed the thesis of the self-esteem movement, which, as Elayne Rapping explained in *The Culture of Recovery,* was based on the teachings and methods of the recovery movement:

> [O]nce we learn to stop abusing ourselves and feel good about our ability to function and be productive citizens, we will automatically begin to treat others—no matter what their racial, sexual, cultural, and behavioral differences—as respectfully and lovingly as we treat ourselves. Thus, the ills of the world, all seen to result from self-hatred projected onto others, will gradually abate and disappear.

The idea is admirable, but hardly sufficient to explain all of human behavior. A whole world of people feeling good about themselves might or might not result in the disappearance of all destructive impulses. However, people seemed to read *Revolution From Within* for advice and illumination about their own lives, not the lives of nations. Gloria set out to write a book that would help people, and *Revolution From Within* did that.

Readers were particularly drawn to her personal stories. Just as interest in Gloria as a personality sometimes eclipsed her message, her autobiographical material attracted more media attention than her ideas, at least in the beginning. Readers were attracted, but not just because they were interested in Gloria as a celebrity. As Gloria's lawyer and agent Bob Levine observes, "What people related to in that book were not the conclusions or brilliant new insights. It was the process. They watched a cultural hero going through a process of self-exploration and coming out the way they came out. Here's one of the smartest, most accomplished, most politically active persons in the world, who ends up coming to the same conclusions they all did: that you've got to depend on yourself."

That assessment of the book's appeal is astute. People look to leaders as models. When Gloria began to focus on her internal life and exposed her vulnerabilities and fears, she enabled her readers to imagine that they, too, might transcend the same problems: love affairs that go wrong; a poor self-image; struggles with cultural standards of beauty. By writing of common problems and her own efforts to contend with them, she demonstrated that she receives the same cultural messages that other women do and that she has to grapple with them and sort them out just as other women do.

Sometimes the grappling went on in the very pages of the book. Gloria followed "Judging the Beauty Judges," an interesting and perceptive essay on the oppressive effects of socially imposed standards of beauty, with "The Body in Our Minds," an essay on her own struggles with body image. She wrote of herself, "I'm still trying to thread a path between outside images and inner self, and this is just a progress report. For instance: I'm still suspicious of the degree to which I make choices that society rewards."

However, that observation followed a discussion in which she managed to offer every possible reason for her struggle to be thin except the most obvious. In keeping with recovery ideology, part of the fault lay in her dysfunctional childhood: She had been "a chubby girl growing up in an isolated family whose food addictions and body image she absorbed." Another recovery movement favorite is genetic addiction: Her father had weighed more than three hundred pounds and "I am his daughter. Like a recovering alcoholic, I'm a foodaholic who can't keep food in the house. . . . I am not a thin woman, I'm a fat woman who's not fat at the moment." Then there was her mother: "Her soft maternal hips and breasts seemed connected in my child's mind to her fate of sadness. . . . I've longed for a more slender, boyish body to distance me from my mother's fate."

All these factors may well have contributed. But "the degree to which I make choices that society rewards" seems by far the more likely. Yet she wrote:

I'm still angry when people ask me accusingly: Why are you thin? Would they ask a recovering alcoholic why she isn't drinking? Nonetheless, I answer because I know this is a serious question for women: I'm thin mostly because of my family history, but also because I listened to my body and discovered the weight at which I feel best (which, interestingly, turned out to be the same weight prescribed by a medical fat-to-muscle test).

She protests too much. Gloria is not a recovering fat person. She's an extremely successful lifelong dieter who occasionally binges because of her abnormal eating patterns. (They are abnormal in a biological sense, in that her eating is not governed by hunger or satiation; in this culture, for her socioeconomic group, her eating habits are perfectly normal.) The unpleasant reality is that Gloria lives in a society in which one's self-image and one's self-esteem do not depend entirely on reparenting one's inner child; they are also affected by how one is perceived in the external world. As she herself discussed in the book and elsewhere, women are still judged by their looks. Women work at being thin because thinness is considered attractive in the society in which they live, and they want to be attractive.

In wanting both to be attractive and to be appreciated for her deeds rather than her appearance, Gloria is like most people, male and female. Those two desires are neither mutually exclusive nor reprehensible. Gloria always seems to think they are, though. She wrote of her disappointment that aging had not liberated her from that epithet, "the pretty one." "If that sounds odd, think about working as hard as you can, and then discovering that whatever you accomplish is attributed to your looks." Her self-esteem evidently had not increased enough to allow her to dismiss what others attributed her accomplishments to— or to realize that she had proven herself, even to those others, about twenty years ago.

For better or worse, Gloria's appearance is an integral part of who she is. However, apparently unable to make peace with that, she seems locked into a perpetual can't-live-with-'em, can't-live-without-'em struggle with her looks and their role in her life. The struggle is not unique to Gloria Steinem. It is one of the arenas in which she not only articulates the conflicts of women trying to find their way through times of enormous social and cultural change, she embodies them.

35

Rigor Mort

Among the parables Gloria told in *Revolution From Within* were the stories of two of her own love affairs, which she offered as a contrast between romance and love. Her second parable illustrated love; she wrote of her relationship with Frank Thomas in elegaic terms, disguising him as a doctor. In the first, "Romance," she dissected her relationship with Mort. He was unnamed and given no professional designation, but the relationship had been widely publicized. She did not paint a pretty picture. Furthermore, she explained that she was doing it for altruistic reasons: "If . . . we think about episodes from our own personal romantic histories, we can learn what we're missing, and then consider what we need to do to grow and change. I've contributed a memory of mine in the hope that it will lead you to meditate on one of your own."

The account of her affair with Mort made up only three and a half pages of the 350-page book, but it attracted immediate attention. Suzanne had seen it coming, but, as she says, "Gloria doesn't look to me on content. I'm helpful on organizing things."

Gloria did listen to Suzanne enough to remove an anecdote that Mort had told many times in public. Mort and Gloria had gone to dinner once about ten years before, but after spending an entire evening together, Gloria completely forgot the occasion and Mort recalled feeling as if he had been listening to the evening news. Gloria had included the story to demonstrate that they would not have been attracted to each other under normal circumstances—it was her tired and depleted state.

She did include a fictional anecdote about Mort's car to explain her lapse in choosing such an unsuitable object for her affections: "I was just so . . . *tired*," she wrote. "When I arrived at the airport late one night to find that he had sent a car, its sheltering presence loomed out of all proportion. . . . So I reverted to a primordial skills that I hadn't used since feminism had helped me to make my own life: getting a man to fall in love with me."

She depicted her lover as materialistic and self-absorbed: "Unlike other men in my life, who were as interested in my work as I was in theirs . . . this man answered questions about his own life and childhood, but didn't know how to ask them of someone else." His good qualities included "enormous energy and a kind of Little-Engine-That-Could attitude" and the fact that "he made every social decision [via his staff], so all I had to do was show up, look appropriate, listen, relax at dinners, dance, laugh at his wonderfully told jokes."

Although Gloria had lived among the wealthy for years, being in a relationship with someone that rich was different:

> I had to ignore the fact that the cost of a casually purchased painting on his wall was equal to what I had come up with for movement groups in years of desperate fund-raising—and was by a famously misogynist artist at that. I had to suppress the thought that his weekend house cost more than several years' worth of funds for the entire women's movement in this country—and maybe a couple of other countries besides.

Her friends felt marginalized by him and his friends. Eventually, so did she. His advice to her, "like a gourmet recipe for people with no groceries, . . . had no practical application." His sense of humor "centered around jokes he collected in a notebook and recited wonderfully, complete with ethnic accents; mine was improvised and had a you-had-to-be-there perishability."

Then there were his politics:

> When he supported the same policies and hierarchies that I was working to change, I thought: Nobody said we had to have the same views. When I told him about a trip I'd made to raise a few thousand dollars for a battered women's shelter that was about to close down, and he in the next breath celebrated an unexpected six-figure check that, he joked, would buy a good dinner, I said to myself: It's not his fault he can't empathize—and besides, everyone can change.

Finally, she explained, she "began to realize there might have been a reason why I was attracted to someone so obviously wrong for me." She concluded that she was searching in him for what she needed. She lacked her own agenda and was attracted to his strong sense of his own; she was too empathetic and was looking for someone she "*couldn't take care of*"; he wanted to change his life and she was "hooked on helping people change"; most of all, "if I had fallen in love with a powerful man, I had to realize that I was in mourning for the power women need and rarely have, myself included."

The official publication date of *Revolution From Within* was set for January 1992. However, quotations from what, at least in New York, would be the three-and-a-half most-talked-about pages of her book appeared in December. Leslie Bennetts, an experienced and respected former *New York Times* writer, profiled Gloria for the January 1992 issue of *Vanity Fair*, the celebrity-oriented glossy magazine. Although many of its articles are leavened with malicious gossip, Bennetts's article was sympathetic to Gloria and respectful of *Revolution From Within*.

"In many ways, this is Steinem's first book," Bennetts wrote, "the one she has been waiting all these years to write; despite a journalistic career that has spanned three decades, it is her first full-length statement of her philosophical take on the world." Following Gloria's lead, she characterized the book as "decidedly unconventional in its category-defying form," and derived from Gloria's awakened awareness of her own interior life.

Bennetts was particularly astute in describing the *Schadenfreude* Gloria arouses, noting that, for years, "Steinem was a lightning rod for an extraordinary degree of malice from friend and foe alike." She attributed the jealousy mostly to Gloria's apparent ability to have it all—

> whippet-thin and gorgeous, as glamorous as a movie star while maintaining impeccable credentials as a relentlessly earnest social activist, free of the burdens of domesticity but perpetually surrounded by brilliant, powerful men who doted on her—and she didn't have to wash their socks or clean up a nightly mountain of dinner dishes.

On the other hand, Bennetts conceded some of the resentment Gloria attracts might stem from the divergence between Gloria's words and her deeds. She quoted one detractor who complained that, though Gloria often repeated the classic aphorism, "A woman needs a man like a fish needs a bicycle," Gloria never "spent twenty minutes without a man."

Bennetts also described the rumors that Mort Zuckerman had promised to marry Gloria if she would get pregnant and that Gloria was going around to see fertility specialists. Both Gloria and Mort denied the rumor unequivocally to Bennetts, who offered it as yet another example of the virulent attacks Gloria had suffered. As Bennetts put it, "the ever-present Greek chorus keened its I-told-you-so's with obscene glee."

The *Vanity Fair* article may have put the pregnancy rumor to rest, but it stirred up more than it settled. Whatever Mort's sister Carmen Robinson had meant when she told Gloria, "You forgot to put yourself in," Gloria took her advice with a vengeance—literally. As Bennetts characterized Gloria's description of her affair with Mort:

> While the tone of her account is neither defensive nor self-justifying, she clearly felt the need to address why she had fallen in love with "someone so obviously wrong for me," a judgment she illustrates with a slyly telling series of contrasts between his values and her own.

Since Mort's money had been so prominent both in the gossip swirling around them and in Gloria's pejorative characterization of Mort in the book, Bennetts asked Gloria about its importance in their relationship:

> "It wasn't so much the money per se," she explains, "and it wasn't so much for myself as the idea that he could help the multitudes of causes that need that money—and possibly the magazine, although it was much harder for me to ask for something that was so closely associated with me." And did Zuckerman help *Ms.* magazine, which Steinem spent sixteen years trying desperately to keep alive before it was finally sold in 1987? "No," she says sourly. Nevertheless, the thought that "he could do a great deal of good with his power" remained tantalizing until the bitter end. . . . "In a way, I guess I was feeling as if, if I could change him, I could change the whole patriarchy," she says sadly.

That passage provoked a scream heard around the world of publishing. Liz Smith covered the article in her December 17, 1991, column:

> Not only did Zuckerman lend *Ms.* $700,000, but he has check stubs that show $406,151 in gifts to the magazine and its foundation. *Ms.* repaid the loan to Zuckerman with interest. The publisher also sent one

of his own top executives to spend two weeks trying to overhaul the magazine.

Insisting that "Zuckerman deserves credit and a correction," Smith added that during an interview with Bennetts she herself had said that, though she lacked proof, she felt "absolutely sure" that Mort had assisted *Ms.* magazine. If Mort received an apology, Smith suggested, "maybe he can drop his ill-advised threat to sue his old friend, *Vanity Fair* editor Tina Brown. After all, he is the godfather of one of her children and Tina certainly had no intention of harming him in her magazine."

That column evidently did not settle the matter, because the following day Smith devoted about two-thirds of her column to an effort to "rehang all this dirty linen like clean wash and help clear the air," explaining that though she, Liz Smith, had told Leslie Bennetts clearly that Mort had helped *Ms.*, when Bennetts had subsequently asked Gloria and Gloria replied "No," Bennetts had assumed that Gloria ought to know. Once the article appeared and Mort began complaining, Gloria insisted that she had thought Bennetts "was asking another question entirely—whether Mort Zuckerman had done anything to save the magazine at the end of its days."

Liz Smith even quoted the "actual transcript of Leslie's notes," which duplicated her *Vanity Fair* quotes:

I asked Gloria if his money was part of the appeal of the relationship. Gloria said, "It wasn't the money per se. It was the magazine. . . . It wasn't so much for myself as the idea he could help the magazine; that was part of it." Leslie: "And did he help the magazine?" Gloria: "No."

Liz Smith concluded that "the implication by Steinem to Bennetts stands—that Zuckerman hadn't done anything even though he could have." Not only that, but Mort also "guaranteed the *Ms.* paper supply in the end when the magazine was faltering. Some people feel this loan and the paper guarantees enabled the feminist founders of *Ms.* to sell the magazine . . ."

Smith also defended her honor as a journalist, stating for the record, "I had to ferret out all this information with no help from Mr. Z." Then she added another postrevelations chapter to the column, reporting that when they encountered each other at a party, "Mort and Gloria ended up sitting together on a sofa, and going at it hammer and tongs over their now public disagreements. At one point Steinem is reported to have said to Zuckerman: 'I was play-acting the whole time I was with you.' " (According to Gloria, she would not use the word *playacting*. All she recalls about the occasion is that she said to Mort that they should talk about the issue another time. Mort recalls her telling him she had been acting during their relationship and says he asked her how she could piss on her memories.)

With that, the rest of the New York City gossip columnist pack galloped into the fray. Called the following day, Gloria denied the account as it had run in Smith's column. Richard Johnson of the *Daily News*, in an item headed "Dating for dollars," concluded, "And here I was under the impression that feminists frown upon the age-old tactic of women using their feminine charms to extract money from men." That was the nub of it, of course, and Johnson later speculated in another column that observers were left wondering "what kind of feminist doctrine requires Steinem's dates to donate huge sums to her foundation."

Besides being hurt by Gloria's assertion in *Vanity Fair* that he hadn't helped the magazine, Mort recalls being stunned by her portrayal of their relationship. According to Mort, Gloria knew perfectly well that he cared about his work and his publications, but she chose instead to portray his life and values in monetary or material terms. Furthermore, he avers that Gloria never objected to the comfort provided by his money and, in fact, adjusted to it with relative ease. He had called the president of the hospital in Boston where she had gone for her cancer surgery, and when she did not want him to go with her to the radiation treatments, he arranged to have his car and driver take her. He also says he was stunned when she later said she resented it. Gloria notes that the hospital was only a few blocks away from her apartment, but she accepted because she knew he wanted to be helpful and she appreciated that. Koryne Horbal, who often accompanied her, says Gloria always looked up and down the street to be sure no one saw her before she got into Mort's limousine. (Although Koryne was among those friends who kept telling Gloria to end the relationship, she was amused by Gloria's embarrassment.)

Then the *New York Observer* got involved. A peach-colored weekly newspaper, the *Observer* is the Manhattan version of *Vanity Fair*— sophisticated, gossipy, and, like *Vanity Fair*, often malicious. In the December 30, 1991–January 6, 1992, issue, "Midas Watch" columnist Michael M. Thomas, a curmudgeonly author of financial thrillers who covers financial, political, and any other kind of affair for the paper, could not resist jumping in.

Using as an excuse his desire to defend his friend Liz Smith's honor, Thomas speculated about a

> body of romantic writing which also constitutes an entire new genre: I refer of course to the check stubs of Mortimer B. Zuckerman.
>
> I refer to the matter on which *le tout* New York presently hangs: namely, the pecuniary aspects of the lovers' triangle involving Mort Zuckerman, Gloria Steinem and *Ms.* magazine. Gloria says one thing, he says another, but he's got the check stubs to prove it. When Elizabeth Barrett penned "How do I love thee? Let me count the ways . . ." I doubt she had this sort of thing in mind, but there we are.
>
> In the event, a hundred years from now, students of pecuniary affection will be breathing Liz's name with the same reverence Johnson scholars reserve for Colonel Isham, who rescued the Boswell papers from Malahide Castle. As they ponder such knotty problems as: Was Gloria Steinem technically deductible, and if so, was she also depreciable?—or compose earnest dissertations on "The Role of the Form 1040 in American Romantic Writing of the Late 20th Century"—it is Liz Smith they will salute as patron saint of their new discipline.

The combination of Gloria's portrayal of Mort in the book and the press contretemps was irresistible, so the farce dragged on in the press for several weeks, to the amusement of all but the principals, whose propensity to worry so about their public image was what landed them there in the first place. In its January 13, 1992, issue, the *Observer* ran a piece by Clare McHugh, who discussed both the book and the press reaction:

> You're an admired feminist. You have an affair with a wealthy real estate developer. . . . When the three-year relationship ends, the reasons for the breakup and your feelings about him are known only to the two of you, as is true with most couples. Except that, in this case, strangers speculate about what ruined the romance. Then you write a book and, under the guise of providing other women with cautionary self-help information, appear to take revenge on your former lover by including a thinly veiled account of a hellish relationship with a contemptible man. Media hoopla ensues. You're surprised?

Noting the "scorched-earth candor" of the book's "Geraldoesque revelations," McHugh cited passages from Gloria's account, such as "I devoted most of my time trying to get him to drive a van instead of a limousine," and the fact that "he lived in a world where progress was measured in numbers and things" while in her milieu, "progress was measured by change in people."

Then McHugh dealt with the protagonists. Mort, she reported, was taking the high road publicly while "raging in private, urging friends to put out the word that although he realizes now how insensitive, perhaps even manipulative, his former lover is, he is nonetheless hurt and surprised by her pronouncements." Upon consideration, McHugh found both ex-lovers more similar than Gloria had depicted, concluding that "the current rush to lock up the legend of it has resulted in a clash of two self-obsessed personalities. Their friends point out that neither Mr. Zuckerman nor Ms. Steinem has a spouse or children, leaving them both plenty of time to fret about themselves and how they appear to the public."

Speculating further, she noted, "Ms. Steinem also has the task of addressing the many feminist fellow travelers who disapproved of her relationship with Mr. Zuckerman at the time." As for Mort, the *Vanity Fair* piece gave him the chance to "return fire." She quoted a mutual acquaintance of the pair's: "He's been humiliated by what she wrote, so of course he's leaping at the opportunity to show her up as a liar."

A few days later, again evidently feeling her honor as a gossip columnist impugned, Liz Smith commented in her column. " 'Why should I have to call an "effing" gossip columnist to straighten out my record?' So it was reported to me that Mort Zuckerman answered when advised to take his side of the Gloria Steinem controversy public and call me with his version of events."

Smith did not appreciate being called Mort's "spear-carrier" and wanted her readers to know that, in fact, Mort was not the one who provided her with the check stubs. She was a hard-working journalist herself, not "a kind of sap who just sits here in my office every day, waiting for the important, famous, rich, powerful people to call me up and *tell me* what to write in my column." Besides, she added, "My loyalties have always been with Steinem, who has been my friend for over 25 years." It was just that "in this happening, she apparently did not get her point across correctly to *Vanity Fair,* and Zuckerman deserved to have the matter straightened out."

The next week, Michael M. Thomas returned to the fray. Marveling at the "journalistic food chain," he explained,

> The particulars of this ziggurat of blahblahblah are as follows. My estimable friend Liz Smith took umbrage at an *Observer* piece by my estimable and glamourous colleague Clare McHugh. Ms. McHugh's story took as its gospel a *Vanity Fair* article by Leslie Bennetts. She is

estimable, too. The latter, in her turn, recited chunks of a book by the, yes, estimable Gloria Steinem about herself. Tinker to Evers to Chance to Tinker, etc.

Skewering each in turn, he described Liz Smith's evident pique. "What got Ms. Smith's goat, a normally somnolent animal of modest dimensions which, when aroused, resembles King Kong with horns, was Ms. McHugh's suggestion that Ms. Smith had been fed certain particulars of the story by outside agents."

As for Tina Brown, she was "a sort of 'Deep Stub,' " who published "what now seem to be half-truths of a pecuniary nature perpetrated by Ms. Steinem about Mr. Zuckerman, who recently stood as godfather to Ms. Brown's daughter."

Thomas's heart went out most to "Squire Zuckerman," because "Ms. Steinem has violated a key principle which those of us of a certain age—and she is older than I am—were brought up to love by. It is this: Love is a 'principals only need apply business.' . . . Visas for the most interior provinces of the heart are to be issued only to those directly involved."

However, in a "shamelessly exploitative era which subjected everything to the imperatives of profit and publicity . . . I'm not surprised at Gloria Steinem's emergence as the Ivan Boesky of Nookie. A taste for publicity was evident in the lass's demeanor from the outset." He could offer Mort but one consolation: "Ms. Steinem might have turned out to be a feminist version of Jeff Koons, with results too horrible to contemplate!" (Artist Jeff Koons immortalized his sexual activities with his wife, a Hungarian-born former pornography star who had also been elected to the Italian parliament, in a series of photographs, paintings, and sculptures, entitled "Made in Heaven.")

Needless to say, the humor was lost on Gloria—even Thomas's predilection for Steinemesque composites. As she wrote in "One Year Later," a postscript appearing in the paperback edition of *Revolution From Within*, "Okay, some of this is funny now. But at the time it was painful." She explained that Thomas had called her "the Ivan Boesky of Nookie" on the "theory that I must have been interested only in his money." Actually, Thomas probably recalled that not only was financier Ivan Boesky wealthy, but he had done the equivalent of kissing and telling himself. After admitting to insider trading, he made a deal with the Securities and Exchange Commission to tape record telephone conversations with business associates in exchange for leniency.

(According to Gloria, there was another association. Ivan Boesky had been "favorably disposed toward giving *Ms.* a large contribution until he learned that [I] was seeing Mort." However, once he knew of their relationship, "he became one of several well-to-do male contributors who pointed out that Mort was much richer than they and refused further discussions of a contribution.")

Meanwhile, Gloria had been trying since early December to get a letter of correction into the letters column of the February *Vanity Fair*. She had been in Mexico when advance copies of the issue had been sent out. Shortly after she returned, she had received a call from a *Vanity Fair* fact-checker asking if Mort had helped *Ms.* financially. After she responded that Mort had indeed helped, both by cosigning loans and through contributions, she learned for the first time what had happened.

She sent a letter of correction to *Vanity Fair*'s editor, Tina Brown, explaining that she had misunderstood Leslie Bennetts' question. "In the context of questions about the sale of *Ms.* magazine in 1987," she had answered what she believed was a question as to whether or not Mort had offered to help save *Ms.* from being sold. Mort had actually encouraged her to sell the magazine, so she had said no.

She also listed two other "unclarities" in the article. One was that Bennetts had quoted a journalist who had attributed *Ms.*'s problems to the fact that it was boring, whereas *Ms.*'s financial problems were due not to a lack of readers, but to inadequate advertising revenue. The third unclarity was that two lines—"I can't mate in captivity" and "A woman needs a man like a fish needs a bicycle"—had been attributed to her when she had not coined them.

Told that the February issue was closed, Gloria resubmitted her letter for inclusion in the magazine's March issue. She answered questions on the controversy but did not release her letter to the press because Tina Brown said she would not print it if it ran elsewhere. When she learned in January that *Vanity Fair* would publish only part of her letter in its March issue, she sent a letter to the *New York Observer*, which printed it in its entirety in the January 27, 1992, issue.

"I always thought women got in trouble by saying yes. Now I find saying no is also a problem," she wrote, explaining, as she had in the letter to Brown, that she had understood Leslie Bennetts to be asking whether Mort had offered to save *Ms.* from being sold. It was a misunderstanding—though Leslie had indeed checked Gloria's quotes afterward, she understandably had not checked her own questions.

Now Gloria had learned that a letter of correction would be printed in *Vanity Fair*'s March issue, but that it would be edited so that it would not include her reference to the fact-checking failure. The real mistake, as Gloria saw it, was that *Vanity Fair*'s research department had called neither her nor Mort. She noted that she had written to *Vanity Fair* explaining that Mort had been "among those friends who helped," and that she had "also corrected two smaller errors in the article that affected other people." However, she wrote, *Vanity Fair* had obviously had a problem with veracity, because not until she sent *Vanity Fair* a lawyer's letter did she receive word that her letter would be published, and even then, not in its entirety.

That did it for Leslie Bennetts. Up until then she had lain relatively low, no doubt recognizing the safest position in a cross fire. She had liked and admired Gloria for years, both personally and professionally, and McHugh's piece had quoted her conjecture about why Gloria had said what she had: "My best guess is that this was the emotional truth for Gloria. She feels that given what he could have done, he didn't do enough. It was small potatoes, since he didn't save the magazine."

Now Bennetts was seething, too. She wrote to the *Observer,*

Gloria Steinem's letter in the *Observer* [January 27] was so rife with falsehoods and misrepresentations that even under the circumstances—which are that Ms. Steinem told a lie, got caught, and is desperately trying to extricate herself from the consequences by scapegoating others—it is shocking to think she would so debase herself.

Before my article went to press, I read Ms. Steinem every single quote, giving her the context for each one—an exceptional personal courtesy that departs from both my own standard practice and that of *Vanity Fair*. Not only did Ms. Steinem approve them all, but in this particular case she even revised the quote slightly. . . . Ms. Steinem's subsequent assertion that she misunderstood the context of our discussion is ludicrous, and her attempt to hold *Vanity Fair*'s hard-working fact checkers responsible for not having caught her in her lie is truly obscene. Regrettably, neither I nor they thought it necessary to double-check Ms. Steinem's assertions about Mr. Zuckerman's support of *Ms.,* since Ms. Steinem herself, as founder and editor, seemed the ultimate source on the magazine; she is now blaming us for not having realized that her word on the subject was worse than worthless.

Bennetts was furious not only that the fact checker's job had been endangered—saved only by the completeness of Bennetts's interview notes—but that Gloria's letter referred to two other "errors." One had been that Gloria had not invented the woman-bicycle and mate-in-captivity lines, a fact that was "irrelevant" anyway, since Bennetts had never said that Gloria had invented them. The other reference to an "error" revealed Gloria's tendency to pronounce something wrong or erroneous when it merely is something with which she disagrees.

Bennetts explained,

> I reported that Ms. Steinem has always said that *Ms.* failed because advertisers didn't support it, but I added that not everyone agreed with this assessment, and I quoted a prominent journalist who said that *Ms.* failed because it was boring. That Ms. Steinem—herself a journalist—would characterize this report on a difference of opinion as an "error" is beneath contempt . . . Ms. Steinem is apparently trying to cast doubt on my reportorial reliability in order to deflect attention from her own blatant unreliability.

In conclusion, Bennetts responded to Gloria's parting shot, in which she accused *Vanity Fair* of being unwilling to admit its mistakes:

> Give me a break, Gloria: Whose mistake are we really talking about here? Any honorable person would long since have said, "O.K., I blew it and I'm sorry." The fact that Ms. Steinem is incapable of acknowledging her own dishonesty and bitterness is pathetic, but the fact that she will go to any lengths to blame her failings on other people is inexcusable.

To make matters worse—surprisingly, that was possible—during those same January weeks, Gloria was appearing on radio and television talk shows. Naturally, the interviewers asked her about both the love affair and the *Vanity Fair* quote, and she continued to repeat that she should have known better than to have given an interview to *Vanity Fair,* that she had done so only because she had respected Leslie Bennetts, that she had told the truth, and that it was the magazine's fault for making a fact-checking error.

Watching as the widely beloved, sweetly reasonable Gloria recited her side of the story and disparaged him on national television was Mort Zuckerman, and he continued to fume. Nor were his feelings assuaged when his butler appeared at the breakfast table with mysteriously hand-delivered letters from Gloria. Typewritten and single-spaced, the soothing, endearment-filled missives urged him to call her so that she could explain everything. He left them on the floor.

By the end of January, the *Vanity Fair* contretemps—mostly a New York affair anyway—had died a natural death. Looking back over a gulf of more than five years, the protagonists maintain their positions.

Gloria insists it was a simple misunderstanding—that whatever Leslie Bennetts said, what Gloria heard or understood her to mean, was to ask if Mort had helped to save *Ms.* from being sold. She asks why she would deny a fact known to dozens, perhaps hundreds of people, and was a matter of public record, since *Ms.* was owned by a foundation? Furthermore, she asks, why would she present herself as someone who couldn't get a friend to cosign loans or make charitable contributions? She also points to the fact that she answered no to Leslie Bennetts while she answered yes to the fact-checker, which seems to make it obvious that she was hearing a different question.

Leslie Bennetts holds her ground as well. While she cannot speak for Gloria's state of mind when she answered Bennetts's question, Bennetts is sure of what she asked and in what context she asked it. "We were discussing her treatment of Mort in the book," she recalls, "and because she had written that his money was such an issue, I asked her if the money was part of the appeal. Basically, I was asking her if she was a golddigger, which was a constant accusation at the time. She essentially said the money was part of the appeal, but not for herself; she cared about it because of what it could do for various causes, such as helping *Ms.* So I asked her, 'And did he help *Ms.*?' She made a face and said no. We were not discussing the financial status of *Ms.* We were not discussing cosigning loans or contributions. We were discussing Mort and his money and her desire to use it for her purposes. I don't believe there was any possibility she misunderstood that, particularly since I read back every goddam question, in every context, and she even rewrote that quote to her satisfaction."

Liz Smith is evidently the incurable romantic of the group. "Gloria was sort of weaselly about it," she recalls, "as if she didn't want to admit he had helped her. I didn't want to correct her publicly, but I expect in this case he did help a lot. . . . Gloria's always acted with me like it didn't happen.

"She and Mort were finished, and we all like to rewrite history, but I have a theory. I felt she and Mort really were in love with each other, but she just didn't approve of herself and gave herself a really hard time. I think he would have married her.

"They were star-crossed lovers, in that she couldn't let herself marry a millionaire. She always gave herself a hard time about that."

The reviews of *Revolution From Within* also began appearing in January, and the earliest ones were not enthusiastic. Even the normally neutral-to-positive *Publishers Weekly* had written in November, "Despite

eloquent passages and neat summaries of cross-cultural research, the
book is a derivative jumble." A number of feminist writers had refused
to review the book because they considered it intellectually weak and
too touchy-feely. In some cases they declined because they were loath to
hurt Gloria; others did not want to appear mean-spirited by insulting a
movement symbol; still others did not want to antagonize Gloria, who
has many contacts and loyalists in the publishing world.

Nevertheless, reviewers were found. Their reviews—at least the ones
written by critics who made the effort to be positive—probably could
be summed up as "love her, hated it."

Calling the book a "squishy exercise in feeling better," *Newsweek*'s
Laura Shapiro wrote on January 13, "Steinem's heart is in the right
place, but what on earth has happened to her mind?" Shapiro predicted that *Revolution From Within* would be a bestseller because
"self-help books sell like crazy, especially among women, and
Steinem's has everything: goddesses, guided meditation, directions on
how to find the child within, dream diaries, and droplets of wisdom
from a range of sources including the Gnostic Gospels and Koko, the
talking gorilla."

Nevertheless, Shapiro added, "Steinem's feminist politics" distinguished *Revolution From Within* from other self-help books. She closed
with a tribute to Gloria: "In a world run by men, Steinem towers by
virtue of her commitment, her ideals, and her tough thinking; with no
office and no pulpit, she is a genuine leader."

For *Time*'s Margaret Carlson, there was too little about Gloria herself, but she allowed that "one of the world's most interesting women
is incapable of writing an uninteresting book, even when she summa-
rizes most of the extant literature on the inner child."

Socialist-feminist Deirdre English reviewed the book for the *New
York Times*. When Gloria later responded to her critics, she referred to
English as one of the reviewers who had criticized her for exposing her
own self-esteem problems. In reality, English had praised Gloria:
"Those who like their icons to stay on pedestals will be discomfited
by Ms. Steinem's candid personal revelations. By letting us in on her
insecurities and how she is resolving them, Ms. Steinem gives us insight
into the costs, as well as the glories, of a public life."

English's major concern was an objection expressed by many feminists to the recovery movement in general. She feared that Gloria's
emphasis on self-help and personal recovery would push women back
to blaming themselves instead of society and would discourage activism

in favor of self-examination. English made a point of saying she never imagined Gloria would stop working for social change; she worried about the others Gloria would influence.

Spy magazine reported that *Revolution From Within* used "inner child" 24 times, "self-esteem" 172 times, "future self" 38 times, "true self" 20 times, and "self-absorbed" once.

Gloria was crushed. She was disappointed by the book's reception, but even more upset by the focus on her three-and-a-half-page account of her affair with Mort. She would never have used the story, she later assured reporters, had she thought the press would figure it out or be so obsessed with it. Anyway, why did no one ask about parable of the happy love affair? Why did they only concentrate on "romance"?

From the road, she asked her agent and lawyer, Bob Levine, to run interference for her. She wanted to do television and radio interviews, she told him, but not print. That way she would have a better chance of speaking for herself.

Although Gloria had defined her goals for *Revolution From Within* quite explicitly—to impress the value of self-esteem upon a wide variety of readers and to do so at a level accessible to her sixteen-year-old self—of course, she had wanted more. For all her praise of feeling and her disparagement of thinking, Gloria wanted respect as a writer and thinker, not just as a feeler.

Gloria eventually decided at least some of the fault lay in her critics, not in her book. She characterized some who responded negatively as "all head and no heart—including feminists." Complaining about reviewers who had trivialized the book by concentrating on its personal anecdotes, Gloria wrote, a year after its publication, in the Afterword for the paperback edition, that "they obscured the book's content, purpose, and politics." She described what she considered her book's overlooked strengths:

> I could find no major review that noted the book's criticism of traditional child rearing, educational testing, the content of education, gender and race roles, separation from nature, or even monotheism as thieves of self-esteem. There was none that supported, opposed, or even noticed its striving for inclusiveness across lines of sex and race, class, sexuality, and ability; none that mentioned its linking of the social justice and self-realization movements; and no examination, pro or con, of self-esteem as a practical source of revolution. . . . Certainly, no major publication analyzed this book's feminist world view, or took a look at self-esteem as a serious subject.

Among all the disappointments, there were bright spots. One was that *Time* ran a March 9 cover story about the antifeminist backlash, "The War Against Feminism" and featured a cover photograph of Gloria and Susan Faludi, whose *Backlash: The Undeclared War Against American Women* had been published the previous October. *Time* first described the criticism of Gloria's book and then noted its popularity: "With ordinary readers, Steinem's message has broken through . . . They want to know about the self and how to gain and trust their own." Gloria was quoted: "The point is for people to empower themselves, and this book is a form of consciousness-raising."

The other good news was that *Revolution From Within* began selling so quickly that it leaped almost immediately onto the bestseller lists and quickly became number one. It sold about 200,000 copies its first month in the stores. *Revolution From Within* eventually sold 400,000 hardcover copies before going into paperback. Like all of Gloria's books except *The Beach Book,* it remains in print.

At Gloria's book signings, lines formed around the block. Reviews from outside the Northeast, in a number of major cities as well as in more obscure publications and smaller communities, were positive. So while major publications were panning *Revolution From Within,* Gloria explained in the paperback's afterword, "I was doing book readings that had to be moved to movie theaters, churches, school gyms, town libraries, and shopping malls to accommodate those who were interested, and hearing people talk about the book as energizing, activating, a needed unity of the internal and the external. . . ."

As Gloria saw it, everyday people seemed to understand her message, whereas many overintellectualized, big-city media people were unable to connect with it. She wrote in the afterword that the very "chasm between what authorities believe and what people experience"—or "the distance . . . between intellectual women reviewers and everyday women readers"—illustrated one of the earliest lessons of the women's movement: don't trust the "experts" and their theories, trust the people and their experiences.

Then Gloria found what she considered an even more obvious explanation. In the midst of receiving disappointing reviews, Gloria began to read Susan Faludi's *Backlash.* Then, as she wrote in the afterword:

> I suddenly realized that, if I'd been watching another woman getting media treatment parallel to mine, I would have understood it in a minute and been angry on her behalf. . . . [but] I hadn't thought of bias

applied to this book's reception until I read [*Backlash*] again *after* my own media experience, and in the context of Faludi's many other examples. The message I'd been getting from mainstream media began to make sense: *If I or other women had self-esteem problems, they were a personal failing at best, and proof of feminism's failure at worst. It was feminism's fault for not solving them, not the fault of an unjust system for creating them.* [italics hers]

No wonder there was such a will to personalize everything. . . .

No wonder the media was obsessed with my brief romance story, yet had totally ignored the equally personal but happy love story a few pages later. . . . The first one supported the backlash belief that feminists can't have good relationships with men. The second did not.

No wonder there was such a will to believe that I had become weak, that examples from my own life would disillusion the readers, and that I would lead women away from activism. The backlash reason was simple: wishful thinking.

In other words, it was not the book, it was the backlash. The interest in what she had said about her relationship with Mort was not so much because she had kissed and told, but because it was the only story in the book that could be used to say "feminists can't have good relationships with men."

While Gloria did not receive the critical respect for *Revolution From Within* to the degree that she had hoped, she did receive an unending stream of affection and gratitude from readers who insisted she had helped them. Letters poured in from all over the country with heartwarming accounts of the ways *Revolution From Within* had inspired the correspondents and had given them the courage—or the self-esteem—to prevail over their difficulties. The letters were still arriving five years after the book appeared.

36

Freud, Incest, and Satanic Abuse

Gloria still was touring for *Revolution From Within* in the fall of 1992 when she realized she no longer wanted to write the book on rich women. She had proposed expanding "The Trouble With Rich Women" (*Ms.*, June 1986) five years before. Now it was three and a half years overdue, and the idea of expanding an existing essay into a book just did not seem as compelling. Furthermore, several of the wealthy women she had planned to interview had changed their minds about being named in the book. They were deterred, at least in part, by the negative media treatment of Louisville, Kentucky, heiress Sallie Bingham, whose efforts to gain more influence over her portion of the family money had led to the eventual sale of the family's newspaper holdings.

When her lawyer, Bob Levine, called Simon & Schuster and offered to return Gloria's advance in exchange for a release from the contract, the publisher refused. Simon & Schuster still wanted the book, especially after the enormous success of *Revolution From Within*. When Bob persisted, they threatened to invoke a clause in Gloria's contract giving them the right to the next book she wrote.

Gloria did not object to writing a book, she just no longer thought the "rich women" topic was viable for an entire book. She wanted to include it in a collection of essays. "You can have that if you want—on the same financial terms," Bob offered Simon & Schuster, and eventually this option was accepted. Since a collection rarely sells as well as a book of all new work, that deal was a testament to Bob's negotiating skills, the marketability of Gloria's name, the fact that *Outrageous Acts* still sold well after a decade in print, or all three.

Amy Richards graduated from Barnard in January 1993 and moved into Gloria's apartment, first as a housesitter, and later as a permanent housemate. Gloria had offered her a full-time job, and she eventually began helping with every phase of the new book. Amy is extremely efficient, but, as usual, Gloria only got up to speed when it was almost too late. The deadline for going to press was March 15, 1994; Gloria wrote most of the book between November 1993 and February 1994. About three weeks after Amy dropped the book's final essay, "Doing Sixty," at Simon & Schuster's offices, they had copies of *Moving Beyond Words*.

Of the book's six essays, three were original and three were revisions of articles published in *Ms.* In "The Masculinization of Wealth," Gloria elaborated on her rich-women concept. Another reworked essay, "The Strongest Woman in the World," profiled Bev Francis, a competitive bodybuilder, in an examination of "the politics of muscle."

The original version of "Sex, Lies, and Advertising" had appeared in *Ms.*'s first ad-free issue (July 1990). Gloria's declaration of independence from the demands and constraints of advertisers combined an angry exposé of advertisers' contemptuous treatment of women's publications with concrete suggestions for what might be done to change them. Often used in journalism and communications courses, the essay became another of Gloria's most-reprinted works.

Gloria had planned to write about the women's economic development movement, but once she began, she created a more ambitious piece. In "Revaluing Economics," she explained the adverse impact on women of both traditional economic concepts and commonly accepted methods and measures of economic development—in industrialized countries as well as in the third world. A first-rate piece of journalism, it showcased Gloria's ability to combine material from diverse sources and render it both interesting and relevant to her readers.

Original essays opened and closed the book. In "Doing Sixty," her closing essay, Gloria discussed her reactions to aging, describing the freedom she experienced when age allowed her to shed more of her "female impersonator" role. Proclaiming herself "a nothing-to-lose, take-no-shit older woman," she wrote exuberantly, "I'm looking forward to trading moderation for excess, defiance for openness, and planning for the unknown. . . . More and more, there is only the full, glorious, alive-in-the-moment, don't-give-a-damn yet caring-for-everything sense of the right now."

Gloria also celebrated her declining libido: "Why not take advantage of the hormonal changes age provides to clear our minds, sharpen our senses, and free whole areas of our brains? Even as I celebrate past pleasures, I wonder: Did I sometimes confuse sex with aerobics?" She did not mean to declare herself celibate for life. Her last public grand passion was her relationship with Mort, which ended completely in 1989 when she was fifty-five, but she still goes out with a number of men friends. They include a handsome, wealthy Israeli widower, Gil Shiva, and the writer William Goldman.

Although Gloria wrote in "Doing Sixty" that she looked forward to trading moderation for excess, she made that trade long ago (if she really ever was moderate), and most of her excesses have benefited humanity. In the 1980s and 1990s she did loosen up even further, and contemplating matters of the psyche seemed to be her favored venue.

The book's first and longest essay was a parody, "What If *Freud* Were *Phyllis;* or, The Watergate of the Western World." In a fifty-eight-page biography of "Dr. Phyllis Freud," Gloria used an extended role reversal to tear into the life and work of Sigmund Freud with such glee that what had seemed over-the-top in *Revolution From Within* began to look almost tame. As she explained in a prefatory note, she wrote the essay in a state of fury and, upon finishing it, "felt as spent and happy as Bev Francis after a workout."

Long before she became a feminist, Gloria had deplored Freud's antifeminist views and the disastrous effects of his theories on many women. "It was extremely difficult in the fifties or sixties to seek help in the psychiatric or psychological field, because they were—I mean, it was like sending a Jew to a Nazi, they were so hostile to women," she explains. "And I would see the wreckage. The wreckage of women who had been analyzed and were congratulated that they got married and were mature—when they were afraid to cross the street."

Further fueling Gloria's anger were her own experiences with the psychiatric profession. In addition to the encounters she had had with a psychiatrist when she was in her twenties, she had become involved with the American Psychiatric Association (APA) in the early 1980s. A group called Psychiatrists for Equal Rights asked her to help persuade the APA to support the Equal Rights Amendment more concretely by refusing to hold APA national conventions in states that had not ratified it. Then Gloria was asked to address the APA's convention in 1983 on the problem of psychiatrists sleeping with their patients, and some of the psychiatrists present exceeded her worst suspicions about the field.

As she wrote in the preface to the Freud essay, one member of her audience responded to her speech by protesting, "You don't understand. My patients behave very seductively with me." It took her a minute, she explained, "to realize that he was not only admitting something, but defending it." To make matters worse, he not only defended it, he did so by blaming his patients. To Gloria, that defense epitomized the ability of a powerful group not only to exploit the less powerful, but to define their exploitative acts so that the powerless, not the powerful, are blamed. (When she wrote the Freud essay in 1994, three-quarters of psychiatrists were male and three-fifths of the patients were female, and that represented considerable progress since 1981, when 89 percent of the psychiatrists were male.)

Freud's theories on women have always been controversial. In the 1920s analyst Karen Horney countered Freud's theory of female penis envy with one of her own on male womb envy. Even so, Freud's theories remain so influential that Gloria's description of the damage the theories inflicted is not an exaggeration. All the modern feminist classics, including Simone de Beauvoir's *Second Sex,* Betty Friedan's *Feminine Mystique,* and Kate Millett's *Sexual Politics,* dealt extensively with the damage wreaked by Freud's theories and the abusive ways in which they were applied. In the twentieth century the Bible no longer had been needed to put women in their place. Freud did it far more effectively by declaring that mentally healthy women desired a subordinate role in life and that those women desiring anything more were sick and needed to be cured of their penis envy.

As Millett described it,

> In convincing himself that the three traits of femininity [passivity, masochism, and narcissism] were in fact constitutional and biologically destined, Freud had made it possible to prescribe them and for his followers to attempt to enforce them, perpetuating a condition which originates in oppressive social circumstances. To observe a group rendered passive, stolid in their suffering, forced into trivial vanity to please their superordinates, and, after summarizing these effects of long subordination, choose to conclude they were inevitable, and then commence to prescribe them as health, realism, and maturity, is actually a fairly blatant kind of Social Darwinism. As a manner of dealing with deprived

groups, it is hardly new, but it has rarely been so successful as Freudi-anism has been in dealing with women.

In 1972 psychologist Phyllis Chesler published *Women and Madness,* an exposé specifically devoted to the mental-health profession's abusive treatment of women, including the very problem of therapists sleeping with their patients. Nevertheless, Chesler, Beauvoir, Friedan, and Millett never sought to deny Freud's genius or his positive contributions to psychology and twentieth-century Western culture.

Gloria made no such distinctions. As she saw it, Freud contributed nothing except encouraging people to talk, and the fact that Freud was still respected in the 1990s could only be due to historical momentum and to his usefulness in providing a rationale for patriarchy. As she explained in the essay's introduction, "Our problem isn't Freud but his existence as a code name for a set of cultural beliefs that serve too deep and convenient a purpose to be easily knocked off. Otherwise, his rep-utation would have been *bubkes* long ago."

Deciding she was up to the job of turning Sigmund Freud into *bubkes,* Gloria created an elaborate treatise on the life and work of Dr. Phyllis Freud, complete with footnotes equal in length to the text. She had originally planned a more limited role reversal, primarily directed toward what she calls "Freudian denial"—Freud's denial that many of his patients' stories of childhood sexual abuse actually occurred. However, once she got started researching and reading some of Freud's newly available letters and papers, Gloria decided she couldn't stop until she took on the "Freudian myth" and attempted to "exorcise its power with laughter once and for all."

Gloria's resentment of "Freudian denial" was exacerbated by her knowledge that Freud originally had believed his patients and then had changed his mind. Furthermore, she believes that he himself was prob-ably sexually abused and that those memories contributed to his change of mind. To make matters worse, Freud replaced his belief in his patients' stories with his theory of the Oedipus complex, which deemed the women's accounts to be fantasies based on their Oedipal longings.

In fact, Freud had pushed his patients so hard to remember molesta-tion that at least some of their stories probably *were* fantasies. Fur-thermore, Freud never said he did not believe real incest or molestation ever occurred.

However, these ameliorating facts counted for little. As Gloria rightly noted, Freud's theory that women's and children's reports of incest were fantasies served so "deep and convenient a purpose" that he might as well have said real incest never occurred. Soon after he conceived of the Oedipus complex, it so completely dominated psychological thinking that not only were women and children who told of actual molestation or incest often not believed, they were informed that their painful memories were wishful fantasies—and that their pain was due not to the trauma of their experience, but to their guilt about their own fantasies.

Since Gloria feels injustice keenly and powerlessness most of all, the cruelty of Freud's theory—essentially punishing incest victims a second time by disbelieving them and denying them comfort—enraged her. That particular denial of women's experiences by Freud epitomizes the myriad ways his theories denied women's reality and dictated to them instead what they were supposed to be feeling and thinking. Another favorite example of Gloria's is Freud's definition of clitoral orgasms as "immature" and his designation of women who enjoy them as "frigid"; she calls that theory Freud's "psychic clitoridectomy."

Dismissing not just those parts, but virtually all of Freud's work, as essentially valueless, Gloria describes it as merely one man's reaction to his own troubled past. As she told *Washington Post* reporter Marc Fisher in 1995, the curators for an exhibition of Freud's papers planned by the Library of Congress seemed to "have the attitude of 'he was a genius, *but*—' . . . instead of 'he's a very troubled man, *and*—' " Fisher had called her because she was the best known of fifty signatories to a petition protesting that the exhibit was an attempt to "force-feed [the general public] Freud by securing advertising space in a federal institution."

Gloria considers Freud's only positive contribution to be the concept that "talking helps." Yet, she notes indignantly, "He is still read. He is read in colleges, he is read by psychologists, there are thousands of papers being done, not as one would read, say, a craniologist, but as if his work had not been mostly disproved. Personally, I think the world would have been better off if he was never born. By far. Because every case was a lie. Every single case. They were interpretation, according to his preconceived formula."

What about Freud's theories of the unconscious? Gloria discounts Freud's conception as derivative: "The unconscious had long been known about. It had been written about for hundreds of years, and it was hardly his discovery. It was in Eastern thought. It was in Western thought. *The Philosophy of the Unconscious* was published when Freud was thirteen."

Asked if she doesn't think she is throwing out the baby with the bathwater, Gloria responds, "I don't think there was a baby in the bathwater. It was just very muddy water. . . . There is a lot of criticism of Freud now, but he's still read. . . . as if he has something to say, which is the problem. You could read him like you could read racists. . . . Freud is still more respected because misogyny is not yet taken as seriously as racism. I wouldn't say we shouldn't read anything. Just, in what context.

"A lot of people who read 'What If *Freud* Were *Phyllis*' said, 'You know, the exposé part is so interesting. Why don't you cut out the satire? The Phyllis part.' But I didn't want to give up the satire. Because I thought that all the bastard deserved was laughter. . . .

"And he knew about sexual abuse. He concealed it. I feel compassion for him. But I also feel compassion for Hitler and a lot of other people who were abused as children. Hitler in his bunker was still counting in his sleep the whiplashes that were part of his torture as a child: ein, zwei, drei—"

Does she think Freud is comparable to an evil genius like Hitler?

"Close. In terms of the damage that's been done. I would say it's the same genre. It's someone who . . . out of denial of his own sickness, destroys others and writes his own illness on the canvas of other people's lives."*

Marc Fisher, who called Gloria to get her comments about the Library of Congress exhibit, says talking to Gloria about Freud was like talking to a fanatic. He recalls, "She seemed to see this in such black-and-white terms. I was astounded that someone of that subtlety and intelligence would respond that way. It was like talking to someone in an extremist political group. She was so caught up in her ideology she was unwilling or unable to see shades of gray."

There was no gray in Gloria's essay on Freud. She attacked every aspect of his theories, life, personality, and character, describing the most egregiously offensive things Freud said or did (he provided plenty of ammunition) and interpreting them as simplistically and damningly as possible. Her clever 1978 satire, "If Men Could Menstruate," had inspired the essay's form as an extended sex-reversal. As in that article, Gloria's technique was exquisite. She is a gifted satirist. Like "If Men

---

*When Gloria read this quote in the manuscript, she changed it to read: "Obviously, you can't compare a man who murdered six million people with anyone. The degree of cruelty they absorbed in their childhoods was also different by light years. But there is a similarity in the fact that they both wrote their unhealed illnesses on the canvas of other people's lives."

Could Menstruate," the role reversal in "What If *Freud* Were *Phyllis?*" succeeded, demonstrating how undeniably sexist Freud and some of his theories really were.

However, the essay was labored (Suzanne Levine had suggested flip-flopping the footnotes with the text), and its ultimate effect was car-toonish and puerile. Gloria offered a convincing case that Freud was a big, bad bully and a mean, manipulative, pompous patriarch whose theories caused a great deal of harm. As an intellectually compelling argument for the proposition that Freud's reputation should be worth *bubkes,* though, it was not terribly persuasive.

Gloria's exploration of Freud's life and behavior certainly was a valid line of inquiry to better understand the genesis of his theories. The political content of his theories and their effects on others are equally worthy of consideration. However, in evaluating Freud's theories, or anyone's art or creative work, Gloria—along with some feminists and other ideologues from the right and left—does not merely examine the political content and political effects of a work, or the politics or behavior of their creators. They seem to use those elements as the cri-teria by which to judge the value of the work. Is it good for women or bad for women? Was its creator a feminist?

Regarding the failure of Marxism, Gloria once told an interviewer, "Marx is a great example of the means-and-ends argument. He lived off his wife's pawned jewelry, impregnated his maid, and let Engels take the blame. His daughter commited suicide. Marxism doesn't work, because you can't choose whatever means you want. He did it in a microcosmic way in his family."

For Gloria, ideological considerations seem to outweigh intrinsic intel-lectual or aesthetic merit in art as well. She quotes Alice Walker, "If art doesn't make you better, what's it for?" However, it is one thing to explain the politics of art, as Gloria does when she notes the power of naming: "Art is what white men do and hangs in museums. Crafts is what women and natives do." It is another to evaluate aesthetics politically.

Visiting the museum at the University of Wisconsin (Madison) for a 1992 exhibit of women's prints owned by Lang Communications, "Presswork: The Art of Women Printmakers," she assured an audience that the exhibit contained none of "Renoir's marzipan women" or Picasso's disconnected body parts with vacant heads. "You won't see emotionless abstractions. You won't see sexuality and sensuality depicted as a matter of dominance. What you will see is mutual sexu-ality." She also told the audience of more than a thousand at the

Elvehjem Museum that "what women bring to art is democracy, not only in the affordability of their work but also in the universality and sensitivity of the subject matter."

The political content of art and the implications of the Library of Congress's Freud exhibit were merely interesting academic exercises when compared to another controversy Gloria entered. The issue the press calls "the memory wars" includes a series of battles at the intersection of the recovery movement; psychological theory; sexual abuse—present, past, repressed, and recovered; the justice system; the mental-health profession; the child-welfare profession; religious fundamentalists; and gender politics. The memories in question are primarily recollections of childhood sexual abuse, and they are challenged because so many women (and some men) did not recall them until after they entered therapy, joined a support group, read one of the many recovery-movement books on the subject, or had them triggered by an event in their lives.

Feminists brought child sexual abuse to the public's attention in the first place. After discussing their own experiences in consciousness-raising sessions in the early 1970s, they began to suspect that childhood sexual abuse was widespread. Once follow-up studies confirmed its prevalence—in the present as well as in the past—feminists sought to publicize the issue. They pointed to its basis in the disparities in power among family members: men who felt entitled to molest their children; children, dependent and powerless to resist; women lacking the power, physical or financial, to protect their children. (There are female abusers, too, but they are much less common.)

That feminist context was lost almost immediately. Instead, the issue was medicalized. Rather than treat incest and child molestation as crimes for which the justice system punished perpetrators, they were transformed into a mental-health problem. Fathers (or other male relatives or acquaintances—the vast majority of molesters are heterosexual males) were diagnosed as sick; families were pronounced dysfunctional; in many cases, the mothers were blamed. An enormous child-protection specialty developed within the mental-health and social-service fields, and the remedies tended to concentrate on therapy for the victim and the rest of the family, as opposed to removing or punishing the perpetrator.*

---

*See Louise Armstrong's *Rocking the Cradle of Sexual Politics: What Happened When Women Said Incest,* Reading, Mass.: Addison-Wesley Publishing Co., 1994, for a book-length account of this sequence of events.

In the 1980s, the recovery movement's focus on adult women dealing with their past abuse also diverted popular attention from the issue
of current molestation. Incest survivor guides appeared and sold hundreds of thousands of copies. Many of them actively encouraged readers to believe they had been abused—even if they lacked memories of
such an experience. Gloria was a supporter. For example, in *Revolution
From Within* she recommended the most prominent, *The Courage to
Heal,* by Ellen Bass and Laura Davis, in which the authors explained,
"If you think you were abused and your life shows the symptoms, then
you were." (In the 1994 edition, the authors noted that after encoun-
tering some women who had been mistaken, they chose to modify their
statement. It now reads, "If you genuinely think you were abused and
your life shows the symptoms, there's a strong likelihood that you
were.")

Another popular guide, *Secret Survivors,* by E. Sue Blume, asserted
that incest is so prevalent it is an "epidemic" and that "many, if not
most incest survivors *do not know* that the abuse has even occurred!
[Blume's italics]." Inside the book's cover is "The Incest Survivors'
Aftereffects Checklist," which asks, "Do you find many characteristics
of yourself on this list? If so, you could be a survivor of incest." Of
thirty-four characteristics, the first is "fear of being alone in the dark;
of sleeping alone; nightmares, night terrors (especially of pursuit, threat,
entrapment)." The thirty-fourth is "multiple personality." On the cover
is an endorsement from Gloria Steinem: "Explores the constellation of
symptoms that result from a crime too cruel for mind and memory to
face. This book, like the truth it helps uncover, can set millions free."

The veracity of recovered memories did not become an issue until
women started to act on them. Adults began confronting their families,
breaking with them, and in a few cases, suing them. In response, many
parents blamed their daughters' therapists for implanting false memories through suggestion. The issue became even more controversial
when, in 1989, in Redwood City, California, twenty-eight-year-old
Eileen Franklin recalled previously repressed memories and accused her
father of killing her girlfriend twenty years before. He was convicted in
1990 solely on the basis of her repressed memories; he was released
on appeal five years later, when his attorneys demonstrated that all the
details of her allegations had been available in intervening years.

Although most of the accusers are women and most of the accused
are men, the debate does not divide neatly along gender lines. Some
women accuse their mothers of abusing them or colluding with their

abusers, so that a portion of the accused are women as well. There are mental-health professionals, feminists, and feminist mental-health professionals of both sexes on each side of the issue.

Skeptics contend that in many cases false memories are being implanted or suggested in a number of ways—through inept therapists, incest-survivor books, and even a recovery-oriented culture that suggests previous abuse as a relatively safe explanation for present problems. Among the skeptics are the accused (guilty and innocent), many therapists and mental-health professionals, critics of Freud (because they dispute Freud's theory of repressed memory), some memory researchers, and a number of feminists. They are concerned about justice and the rights of the accused, and some believe the focus on adult survivors and recovered memory distracts the public's attention and concern from the issue of present child victims.

On the side of the accusers are many members of the child-protection services, many therapists, recovery-movement adherents, some memory researchers, and many feminists, who believe the woman and child victims must be supported and believed. They point out that often there is no physical corroboration of sexual molestation, nor are there usually witnesses. If the children are not believed, the victims have no recourse. The watchwords of many in the recovered-memory group are: believe the children, children do not lie; believe the women, they are the experts. Some say it doesn't matter whether the abuse actually occurred; if the victim believes she was abused, she should be believed. *The Courage to Heal* notes that "some abuse is not even physical." The authors include as examples, suggestive remarks by one's father or the feeling that ones stepfather "was aware of your physical presence every minute of the day."

Gloria asserts that there is no recovery movement. Rather, it is only a term coined by the False Memory Syndrome Foundation, a controversial organization that supports people accused of sex abuse and promotes the idea that recovered memories are implanted or suggested. She says, "Of course there are suggestible people and inept therapists. What I would say personally—just me personally—is that thus far, I have seen an amazing number of people who remembered the truth, and I have never yet seen someone . . . who thought they were badly abused and was not. There's a constellation of symptoms. There's somatic symptoms. You remember with great pain and involuntary impact. It's not just one little picture that comes up. It's triggers in the environment. It's body memories. It's sleep patterns that are disturbed because of the hour in which abuse usually happened you wake up. It's very hard to implant that stuff. I am only speaking personally for the last twenty years, but I have never seen a case yet in which that has been implanted."

Furthermore, while Gloria is ideologically and emotionally predisposed to believe women and to ally herself with those she sees as less powerful (women versus men, children versus parents), her allegiance is reinforced by real-world experience. In numerous cases she has observed the consequences when members of the less powerful group are the accusers. Rather than accusing their parents of past molestation, many of the women Gloria has helped were accusing their husbands of molesting their children and fighting for custody in judicial and penal systems dominated by men. Men were the judges; fathers had the financial wherewithal to engage more and better lawyers and experts, and to drag out the cases; fathers seeking custody were considered, by definition, good fathers while mothers were held to impossible standards. (The double standard is so extreme that not only molesting and battering fathers get custody—one Florida man convicted of murdering his first wife obtained custody of the daughter from his second marriage because his wife was a lesbian.)

Divorced mothers generally have custody of the children, because few fathers seek custody in divorce proceedings. When custody is contested, fathers win more often than mothers do—sometimes even in cases where the abuse is not disputed. Some judges are so offended by women's accusations and solicitous of the men's reputations that they have denied access completely to mothers alleging abuse, or have enforced unsupervised visitation rights for the fathers. Consequently, some attorneys have begun to advise their women clients not to mention molestation, for fear they may lose custody entirely.

In the meantime, the number of women recovering memories of their own childhood abuse has grown exponentially, though, as Gloria sees it, "Revelations of any social ill increase, once they are possible to reveal." Furthermore, the nature of their memories has become increasingly bizarre. Simple incest is sickening enough, but many recovered memories now include sadistic abuse, ritual abuse, satanic ritual abuse, and multigenerational, interconnected satanic cults, all of which, Gloria notes, "have been reported before, from the Marquis de Sade to the British television documentary, 'Dispatches: Listen to the Children,' by Beatrix Campbell, a carefully researched report on ritual child sexual abuse in England from 1987 to 1990." These are the reason for

Blume's suggestion, in *Secret Survivors,* that "multiple personality" is an indicator of past abuse.

Multiple personality disorder (MPD) is the modern version of what used to be called split personality. The phenomenon of more than one personality or identity (or "alter," as they are now called), residing in the same individual has appeared throughout history, in various forms, including spirit possession and speaking in tongues. The manifestation was rarely diagnosed until the publication of the book *Sybil* in 1973. Before 1970, fewer than two hundred people all over the world had been reported as diagnosed with illnesses resembling MPD.

Following the publication of several books about multiple personalities and satanic abuse in the 1970s and 1980s, more than thirty thousand diagnosed cases of MPD have been reported. Multiple personality disorder has even been called "chic." Television's Roseanne Barr Arnold reports that her parents molested her from the time she was an infant and says she developed twenty or more alters as a result of the abuse. Phil Donahue, Oprah Winfrey, Sally Jesse Raphael, Geraldo Rivera, and Larry King have featured multiple personalities who switched alters on command from their television hosts.

Not everyone agrees that such a disorder exists. While they do not dispute the existence of people so disturbed they suffer bouts of amnesia, disorientation, and bizarre behavior, some skeptics believe the phenomenon of multiple personality disorder evolves from the interplay between therapists' expectations and their clients' responses. The disorder is so controversial, even within the therapeutic profession, that though it became official in 1980, by 1994 the *Diagnostic and Statistical Manual of Mental Disorder* renamed it Dissociative Identity Disorder, though the definition remained essentially unchanged.

Multiple personality disorder's official definition does not include a cause, but it is presumed to stem from abuse so terrible that the victim had to dissociate herself (most MPD sufferers are women) from the experience in order to survive. Gloria wrote in *Revolution From Within:*

> As is now known, MPD is almost always the result of frequent, sadistic, erratic, and uncontrollable abuse in childhood by someone on whom the child is dependent; abuse so intolerable that children learn to dissociate from it through a form of self-hypnosis and so escape into a "different" person who does not feel the pain. Having once split off from the core personality, this "alter" begins to acquire a separate life history,

complete with distinctive mannerisms, behavior, and social relationships, almost as if it were a person born at the moment of "splitting." Once this ability to dissociate has proven to be a valuable way of surviving and dealing with the world, alters continue to be born to meet different needs and demands.

That most MPD sufferers are women should not be surprising. Even feminists who are skeptical of the disorder—or of the prevalence of recovered memories of abuse in general—are sympathetic to women who believe they were abused. Some regard women's sense that they may have been abused as a reaction to metaphorical abuse and to reality-based feelings of powerlessness and vulnerability. In "Dividing to Conquer? Women, Men, and the Making of Multiple Personality Disorder" Debbie Nathan reviewed anthropological literature and quoted anthropologist I. M. Lewis, who called such states of spirit possession "thinly disguised protest movements directed against the dominant sex . . . in cultures where women lack more obvious and direct means for forwarding their aims."

Patients who are diagnosed with multiple personality disorder have typically been in the mental-health system for years before their MPD diagnosis. Some do not initially recall being abused. However, they are typically told what Gloria wrote—that MPD is so extraordinary a disorder that it is usually caused by extraordinarily severe abuse—and they are urged to work at recollecting the terrible events that must have prompted them to dissociate in the first place.

Since the 1980s an increasing number of patients have asserted that they were raised in families that belonged to satanic cults and that they were subjected to severe ritual abuse. According to Nathan, at a 1986 International Society for the Study of Multiple Personality and Dissociation (ISSMP&D) conference, the participants reported that a quarter of their patients alleged that they had been abused in cults. By the early 1990s, a leading therapist in the field believed that satanic-cult networks were cooperating with right-wing groups and the CIA to brainwash children, and specutated that 70 percent of people diagnosed as MPD sufferers had been abused in cults. In 1993 Ms. ran a cover story on the phenomenon, "Believe it! Cult Ritual Abuse Exists: One Woman's Story," written by a pseudonymous cult survivor (who was personally known to Robin Morgan, then Ms.'s editor in chief).

Gloria became interested in multiple personality disorder after reading a book by a feminist activist who had been diagnosed with it and

witnessing others in incest survivor programs. In the mid-1980s she
became sufficiently curious about the subject to attend exhibits of artwork by MPD sufferers—besides art exhibits, there are musical performance, magazines, books, and groups, both live and on-line—and
what she saw fascinated her. Because she and Carla Morgenstern were
producing reports for the *Today* show at the time (1986), they flew to
Chicago to meet with Bennett Braun, a psychiatrist and leader in the
multiple personality disorder field.

After talking with Braun, an associate, and some of his patients,
Gloria and Carla decided the subject was "too complicated to cover
in a six-minute segment without sensationalizing it," but Gloria continued her interest in the subject and in Braun's work. Braun, who was
affiliated with Rush Presbyterian–St. Luke's Hospital at Rush North
Shore Medical Center, was also one of those spokesmen who believed
many of his patients had been in cults. Gloria continues to support the
controversial Braun, and mentioned him in the acknowledgments of
Revolution From Within.

Tales of satanic-ritual abuse, complete with animal sacrifices, canni-
balism (especially baby-eating), rapes, orgies, and multigenerational
cults in families are hundreds of years old, but the addition of twentieth-century feminism to the mixture is new. Although Gloria is the
most prominent feminist attracted to the issue, she is not the only one.
In her article, Nathan speculated on the connection:

> Feminist attention to the satanic imprisonment and escape tales that often
> accompany MPD narratives generally focuses on three points: that cult
> abuse stories must be believed because women are telling them;
> that ritual abuse is shocking yet not surprising, given that we live in a
> gynophobic [woman fearing] culture; yet that by finding ways to live
> through the abuse—by developing MPD, for instance—victims show
> superlative feminine courage and resourcefulness. In fact, whether or not
> they consider it the result of cult abuse, for many feminists . . . to be mul-
> tiple is to be intelligent and highly creative, a "survivor" whose special
> talents allow her to weather the abuse yet emerge alive and productive.

In 1991 Sheila Nevins, a producer at Home Box Office who had
worked with Gloria years earlier on a *Ms.* television program, *She's
Nobody's Baby,* asked Gloria if she were interested in coproducing a
program on the subject of multiple personality disorder. Always open to
disseminating concepts through popular media, Gloria agreed.
Although about 90 percent of the cases are female, Gloria urged that

they include a male to show that both men and women were subject to MPD and that "the sexualization of power and violence victimized boys, too."

Her coproducer, Michael Mierendorf, spent two years creating the show, following three diagnosed MPD sufferers with a film crew to record them in a variety of situations with a number of different of alters. He and Gloria conarrated the program, *Multiple Personalities: The Search for Deadly Memories,* which aired in 1993 and won an Emmy Award in the news and documentary category.

Nathan became intrigued by the connection between feminism and multiple personality disorder through her interest in the subject of ritual abuse. In a rash of sensational cases in the 1980s, caretakers in day-care centers, nursery schools, and communities around the country were charged and convicted of satanic abuse and mass molestation of the children in their care. Eventually Nathan explored that phenomenon in *Satan's Silence: Ritual Abuse and the Making of a Modern American Witch Hunt* (1995).

Gloria, too, was drawn into the issue of ritual abuse in day-care centers, but she was drawn more to the side of the accusers. Initially skeptical, she saw the issue as a way to literally demonize childcare and perhaps to blame day-care centers for abuse that "was statistically more likely to have taken place in the home." However, she began to reexamine the possibility after reading physical evidence in a number of cases in the United States, Canada, and England. The McMartin Preschool, in Manhattan Beach, California, was the first major case, beginning in 1983. By the time it ended seven years later, it had become the longest and most expensive trial in U.S. history, costing about $15 million. Like the other cases, it rested entirely on the testimony of children and the child-protection workers who had elicited their stories. There was no physical corroborating evidence.

The school's teachers and owners were arrested—starting with the owner's grandson and eventually including the owner herself, seventy-six-year-old, wheelchair-bound Virginia McMartin. They were then imprisoned for durations ranging from months to five years to await trial. They were accused of forcing the children in their care into a variety of activities, including pornography rings; playing the naked-movie-star game; rape followed by a trip to the zoo; trips through underground tunnels; forced oral sex; being forced to ride a horse nude; being forced to watch pets or larger animals, including a horse, killed (other animals involved included turtles, rabbits, lions, a giraffe, and a sexually abusive elephant); hot-air-balloon trips; an airplane trip with the children packed tightly into crates; being abused while going through a car wash; participating in orgies in a local church; being forced to drink urine and to eat feces covered with chocolate sauce; being driven around in a van with a half-dead baby; being forced to touch dead people; fellating animals; participating in rituals where a baby's head was chopped off and its brains burned.

There were several trials, but when the juries viewed videotapes of the children's interviews, they concluded that the children's testimony was unbelievable and that unskilled or overzealous interviewers had coerced or led them into their fantastic allegations. In 1990, a group of parents, still unconvinced of the innocence of the accused, hired an archaeologist to conduct a search for the tunnels the children had described. Gloria contributed $1,000 to help finance the report, with the proviso that her gift be matched by Mothers Against Sexual Abuse.

Eventually, the archaeologist reported he had found evidence of a tunnel's existence, and Gloria found no reason not to believe his report. She is not alone. In the most recent edition of *The Courage to Heal*, the authors cited the McMartin case in a section on the attempts of the "backlash" to discredit authentic claims of sadistic ritual abuse.

Sometimes Gloria's choice of issues dismays some of her friends, who bemoan the ease with which "Gloria lets people use her." Occasionally one even talks to her about the potential for damage. Gloria seems unfazed. In addition to publicizing "the underground river of sexual abuse," she refers to the McMartin tunnels and the possibility of ritual abuse. As she says of the McMartin case, "I'm afraid it may have been just too terrible to believe."

37

The Kindness of Strangers

During her years in Toledo, Gloria had sought to find what was missing at home by entering the outside world, but she also was driven into the world by the need to escape. To Gloria, the entanglement of a family was "endangering . . . dangerous—I mean, you could come home and literally, the police would be there. Or the police would come and get me wherever I was. It was the source of danger and tragic events and upset and chaos and—difference."

Gloria needed her independence, but independence came with a price. "I used to walk around the streets of New York looking in lighted windows, thinking, Everybody has a family but me. Everybody has a home. I hadn't made my own home. You have to do that for yourself, but it was a lot of years before I did."

Gloria adds, "I always thought of myself as a survivor. But I was very frightened and depressed by the idea of ending up, in a sense, where I began. That's the price of changing a lot in your life, of going a great distance with your life. I don't anymore, actually. I feel more secure now. But for a long time, for most of my life, I certainly thought that if I could go this way, I could also go the other way.

"I must have worn out several records of Nilsson's song "Morning Glory." It's a song about a woman who wakes up sleeping in a doorway. It's a wonderful song and I listened to it compulsively because I was sure I was going to end up one day sleeping in a doorway. So I handled it by trying to embrace it. I said to myself ritually, if I'm a bag lady, I'll just organize the other bag ladies. It's a life like any other. But I both feared it and embraced it at the same time."

While Gloria did find both affection and achievement in the outside world, she continued to yearn for a family—or at least the sense of belonging a family provided. "For many years I was jealous of people with families. And so part of my attraction to friends, both men and women, was their families. I was, in a sense, joining their families."

Like many single adults, over the years Gloria created her own familial arrangements by accumulating a treasured collection of friends and ex-lovers she calls her "chosen family." One of its newest members has been living in her apartment since 1993. Amy Richards's room is the sleeping loft above Gloria's living room, but the two enjoy twice the space Gloria and Barbara Nessim occupied when Gloria first moved there.

After Gloria used her advance for *Revolution From Within* to buy the apartment below hers, she set about making a real home for herself. She converted the two large rooms on the ground floor into a study-den and a den-bedroom, and connected the ground floor with the parlor floor by adding what appears to be the world's narrowest circular staircase. Gloria and Amy fit; many others barely squeeze through. Since the prefabricated stairway was marked "medium" in the catalogue, Gloria jokes about what "small" must be.

With the ground-floor apartment came a garden and a large (for New York) kitchen—perhaps eight by ten feet. For years Gloria avoided domesticity so successfully that the tiny kitchen in her original apartment was regularly mentioned in profiles. Readers learned that Gloria had lived in the apartment four years before she discovered that the oven was broken; that her refrigerator was empty because Gloria feared she would eat anything she had in the house; and that the kitchen's most frequently used appliance was Gloria's doctor's scale.

Gloria's apartment and her clothes have been the subject of articles over the years, including some she has written herself. Those lifestyle pieces, more than any other coverage of Gloria, offer an ongoing chronicle of Gloria's struggle to reconcile the discrepancy between how she really lives and how she perceives her life. Apart from her looks, the subject about which she is most prickly is her socioeconomic status. Because she has imagination and an eye for a bargain, she has always lived well on less money than others would need. Her problem is that the way reporters interpret what they see is not always the way she thinks they should.

In 1973 she was profiled in the *New York Times Magazine*'s spring "New Fashions of the Times" supplement. Judy Klemesrud reported that "the country's No. 1 liberated woman" had "shed her Gernreich dresses for utilitarian sweaters and pants" and now referred to fashion as "a political statement." Klemesrud quoted Gloria on the subject of fashion: "When your inner identity begins to strengthen, you begin to care less about making a display case of your outside."

Unfortunately, Klemesrud also mentioned Gloria's "fashionable East 73rd Street brownstone apartment"; observed that a copy of *Harper's Bazaar* lay on her coffee table; noted that Gloria "declined to reveal how many pairs of aviator glasses she owned, but did say that she bought them at [expensive French purveyor] Lugene, Inc. ('They won't even give me a pair')"; and added that Gloria recalled "those mid-60's days—days when she wrote articles about textured stockings and was dressed to the nines—with about as much enthusiasm as a Rockefeller might exhibit for a mugger." Klemesrud also quoted, without comment, Gloria's observation that "blatant clothing excesses" reminded her of Suicide, a parlor game she and her friends had played in which they thought of "various ways that prominent people might do themselves in": "We had Leonard Bernstein leaping off his Adler elevator shoes. . . . and D. D. Ryan accessorized herself to death."

In response, Gloria wrote a letter to the editor that was almost as long as the article itself. After agreeing to be one of several people interviewed for what she had thought was going to be a "serious essay on the evolution of clothes as a reflection of political change," she protested, she found herself portrayed in an article about fashion that was only about her and that, furthermore, implied that the women's movement was about what women wore.

No detail was too inconsequential to mention. She objected to Klemesrud's depiction of her apartment as "fashionable"—"meaningless, except possibly to undermine any belief in the occupant's social conscience." She disapproved of the reference to *Harper's Bazaar*, since it was really part of some research: it contained a profile on a feminist lawyer and besides, the issue was a year old. Then, of course, there were the textured stockings. She had written only one article about textured stockings—and that was because the *New York Times Magazine* would only assign her such subjects, not because she owned them or had any interest in them.

Gloria also complained that by accompanying the piece with photographs, the magazine gave the impression she had posed, whereas she actually had declined to be photographed. Klemesrud noted in her rejoinder, "Ms. Steinem sent to the *Times*—at our request—several black-and-white glossies of herself for possible use with the article." When the editors decided to use a color photo instead, they had purchased one from photographer Jill Krementz.

In 1990, Gloria was still trying to have it both ways. In a six-page spread she wrote for *HG* (previously *House & Garden*), she explained, "I thought interior designers were for other people." Then, "through the accident of helping a rich friend interview designers" she had met the creative Filippa Naess, of New York and London, who agreed to take on Gloria's "small, low-budget project." Low-budget, that is, for Filippa. The photographs displayed Gloria's $75-a-yard draperies, her $110-a-yard upholstered chair, her $157.50-a-yard velvet-covered sofa, and her $2,700 custom-made coffee table. On the other hand, Filippa also passed along her professional discount to Gloria, bought some close-out fabrics, took her to inexpensive auction-house galleries, brought objects from England in her suitcases, dyed fabrics in her bathtub, and introduced Gloria to kilim rugs. Then Gloria became so addicted to these Middle Eastern rugs that Herb Sargent finally joked, "You've got a rug problem. Just say no."

In other words, as usual with Gloria, reality is not either-or, it's both-and. That is, there is perception and there is reality—except, with Gloria, even "both-and" is too simple. There is more than one perception and more than one reality.

First, there is the matter of how Gloria perceives herself. She cannot stand to be considered affluent. When told a *Wall Street Journal* article referred to her as a wealthy socialist, Gloria joked, "Well, they're half right." It is true that she is not wealthy. She has many wealthy friends, and some of them, like Marlo Thomas and Kristina Kiehl (who created the fund to pay Gloria's extra assistants), are there for her and watch over her, badgering lawyer Bob Levine to make sure Gloria sets up a pension plan and gets her will written. Nevertheless, access to wealthy circles is not the same as being wealthy oneself.

Furthermore, Gloria is a celebrity who has not cashed in on her celebrityhood. She uses her fame to promote things, but what she promotes are not products, they are Ms. Foundation projects or other people's work or her causes. Her apartment is valuable, but she works hard for her living, speaking, writing books, and producing whatever other ventures she can, such as television programs. Her books command six-figure advances, but they take several years to write and she works hard selling them.

All that said, it would appear that she is more affluent than she likes to consider herself. Six-figure advances are still six-figure advances. Also, having earning power one chooses not to exploit—or earning money and giving it away—are not the same as lacking the opportunity in the first place. In the same way that she is sensitive about her looks, Gloria feels misunderstood about her economic class and does not want to be considered one of *them* (the Toledo factory owners or their wives, perhaps). She periodically disparages wealthy people, still fearing, it seems, that being "fashionable" will be regarded as lacking a social conscience. However, no matter how she tries to identify with the poor and oppressed, she is not one of them, either. She is an upper-middle-class, Smith-educated white woman living in the most affluent section of Manhattan.

When she does acknowledge the circumstances of her present life, she often distances herself by framing them in social rather than personal terms. It is unfortunate that she is defensive, because she is correct. She likes to remind audiences that Emma Goldman herself insisted that "you can be a serious woman without dressing in sackcloth and ashes and giving up sex and dancing." She jokes, "The idea that social activists have to be joyless and suffering is just a way to reduce the number of social activists."

As for Gloria's individual situation, she notes that she tries to use her advantages "as subversively as possible." As she puts it, believing that "everyone has the right to 'bread and roses,'" she "strives for both moderation [in her own life] and spreading moderation around—which means taking from the rich *and* giving to the poor."

There is a third dimension, however, and that complexity is what makes her Gloria Steinem. Gloria is not as wealthy as some think she is. (She notes that somehow rich-and-famous is all one word to much of the public.) Neither is she unaffluent as she seems to conceive of herself to be, in a kind of antibourgeois romanticism.

Gloria's third perception and third reality are based, not on how she would like to be seen, but on what she would like to do. Gloria knows perfectly well that she is privileged. However, compared to her aspirations, her resources are minuscule. Gloria has lovely possessions, but she is completely unmaterialistic—if they were gone tomorrow, she would not be terribly upset. They are not what matter to her.

What matters to her are all that she sees wrong that she cannot fix, and all she would like to accomplish if she had the means: saving *Ms.*; starting institutions; saving women the world over, from battering and prostitution and forced pregnancies and custody battles and genital mutilation.

In light of all she wants to do, Gloria is always a beggar at the feast.

Gloria and Amy share Gloria's apartment with another contribution from Filippa Naess, an elegant Persian cat named Magritte, who patrols the rooms like a haughty queen—the image only breaks down when she sidles up to Gloria and flops on her back for a tummy rub. Gloria and Amy also house a steady stream of visitors, for sojourns ranging from one night to several weeks.

Amy described their friendship at the 1995 Veteran Feminists of America dinner in Gloria's honor: "Gloria is there when I say, 'So-and-so might call. Please don't tell my past lover I'm at the current lover's house.' And when I get back, she'll say, 'I did my job. I said I didn't know where you were.' . . . Or if I'm getting ready to go somewhere, she's always the one running around saying, 'Oh, I have the perfect scarf. Let me get it. It's much older than you are, but I know it's there somewhere.' . . . Gloria has also been a mother: 'Have you eaten enough? Are you warm enough?' . . . The other thing she does is she always lets me know how much I'm loved. . . .'

Besides Amy, Gloria's other surrogate daughter is her goddaughter, Rebecca Walker, whose mother is the writer Alice Walker. Rebecca, whom Gloria has known since she was five or six, stayed with Gloria during most of her college summers and later became a contributing editor of Ms. Whether Rebecca is involved in organizing or writing, Gloria helps where she can, with advice, introductions, and appearances for fund-raising.

Alice, who lives mostly in San Francisco, is one of Gloria's three or four closest friends, one of the women Gloria calls "sisters of my heart." The two met through the magazine, when Ms. published an early short story of Alice's, and for a few years Alice worked for the magazine a couple of days a week. Appreciating Alice both for her writing and for her instincts, Gloria describes her friend as her "moral compass," the person against whom she tests her own responses. When a group of girls interviewing Gloria on Take Our Daughters to Work Day asked who her best friends were, she told them, "Alice Walker is someone in my life who helps me know what's true to my inner voice. I think, could I tell this to Alice Walker? Because she's a very shit-free person."

Although Gloria thrives on the city and is usually surrounded by people, Alice craves the country, solitude, and privacy. In order to spend time together, they compromise on their preferences. Alice stays with Gloria in New York, and Gloria visits Alice in San Francisco. She also tries to spend a week or so around Christmas at Alice's house in Mexico. With Rebecca Adamson, a third friend, they bought a tiny house in the Badlands, a desolate area of South Dakota.

Born to a Cherokee mother and a Swedish-American father, Becky Adamson met Gloria through her work in economic development; they became friendlier when Becky joined the Ms. Foundation board. After working with Native-American tribes to help them start schools and control more of their own affairs, Becky founded the First Nations Development Institute in 1981, to develop and implement culturally appropriate development projects for Native-American communities.

Always interested in ideas for women's economic development, Gloria was drawn first to Becky's work and then to her spirituality. Apart from theosophy and her time in India, spirituality was not something Gloria had thought much about until her fifties. As a speaker she often called her audiences' attention to the many ways in which organized religion was used to oppress women, asking rhetorically why God always looked like a member of the ruling class. However, as she began turning inward, Gloria began to understand that spirituality was quite different from organized religion.

After spending time with Becky at a small development conference in South Dakota, Gloria turned to her and asked, "How old are you? You're so spiritually wise. You seem so much older than your spirit. . . . You are the most spiritual person I know." That comment, Becky observes, was made about the same time Gloria had breast cancer and was breaking up with Mort Zuckerman. Shortly afterward, Gloria went with Rebecca Walker to a weekend meditation class and began trying to incorporate meditating into her life.

In June 1995, Gloria joined a nine-woman safari Becky led into the Kalahari Desert in Botswana. Becky had been invited by the N/oakhwe people—the people derogatorily described as bushmen in the movie *The Gods Must Be Crazy*—to help them explore ways they might preserve their nomadic way of life. Until 1960, hunting down the N/oakhwe people and killing them like animals had been legal. By the 1990s they were being forced into settlements, because the government wanted the land for tourism.

Neither Becky nor Amy could believe Gloria was actually going camping. When she started to put on her backpack, Amy informed her that she was putting it on upside down. Gloria loved the experience, though. At the 1995 Veteran Feminists of America dinner, Becky recounted the story:

"I bet none of you have seen the outdoorswoman Gloria, the camper Gloria, the canoe Gloria. . . . Over lunch I mentioned that I had been invited to meet with the N/oakhwe people to talk about the human rights violations and would be camping out in the Kalahari Desert and she said, 'Well, I'd like to go.' I thought, never in my wildest did I think of Gloria in a backpack and a sleeping bag.

"On the way over I said, 'Gloria, I would have invited you all along. Have you ever slept outside?'

" 'Never.'

"And we're on our way for a three-week trip—which started by rowing across the Zimbabwe River. As we rowed—we each had our own canoe—the guide in the kayak is yelling, 'Stay to the left of the hippos. They're territorial, so don't row into the hippo herd.' And Gloria is rowing away and laughing and saying, 'Did you ever think you'd hear, stay to the left of the hippo herd?' " (When the guide later told them the alpha hippo defecates in the other hippos' faces, Gloria said, "Oh. Like the corporate structure.")

Because the Botswanan government had announced that any safari operator taking tourists to meet the N/oakhwe people would lose his license, the only way they were able to meet was to go into the open and wait for the N/oakhwe people to come to them. However, once the women arrived in the desert, their great-white-hunter guide, Alan, held the N/oakhwe in such contempt that he would not allow them near the camp. Then Gloria rode in the Jeep with Alan for a day. By the time they returned, Alan was talking indignantly about how "we've got to do something for these people."

After the trip, Gloria helped to raise funds for the N/oakhwe people, whom she described as "a human rainforest," and to publicize their plight. She explained that their noncompetitive, egalitarian culture has much to teach the industrialized world.

Another sister of Gloria's heart is an old friend of Becky—Wilma Mankiller, the first woman chief of the Cherokee Nation. Gloria and Wilma met when Wilma joined the Ms. Foundation board in 1985. Wilma had been a community organizer before she was elected tribal chief. Just as Gloria admired Alice Walker for her writing, she admired Wilma as a leader of people. She was also attracted to Wilma's Indian heritage.

Gloria's close friendships with African-American and Native-American women are not accidental. Gloria lives her life in a perpetual embrace of diversity, seeking to know, expose herself to, and befriend as wide a variety of people from as wide a variety of backgrounds—race, class, age, and sexual preference—as she can. If her pursuit of diversity seems somewhat self-conscious, Gloria's friends don't mind because they recognize and applaud the impulse behind it. As one of her friends, African-American television newswoman Carol Jenkins says, "Gloria is the most inclusive person I know. You never know who you're going to find at her house." Dorothy Pitman Hughes praises Gloria as "the least racist white woman I know." She notes, "Gloria often invites me to meetings, and I look around at all the white women and think, If every white woman would bring a black woman the way Gloria does, it would equalize things. . . . Someday, I'd like to work with Gloria organizing for sisterhood. Real sisterhood."

Gloria also acquires friends by drifting along as if she were in a stream, pulling up onto her raft anyone she sees floating by who seems interesting. She had gotten to know writer bell hooks through Rebecca Walker, who had studied with her at Yale. Then *Ms.* ran a 1993 cover story featuring a conversation among four writers who address feminism in their work—Gloria, bell hooks, Naomi Wolf, and Urvashi Vaid—and they so enjoyed talking to each other that they began going to dinner together.

One night Gloria mentioned that she was going to Bermuda to speak at a conference of black Bermudian women. When bell said she'd always wanted to go to Bermuda, Gloria urged bell, who is African American and writes about both feminism and race, to accompany her and to address the group as well. After they spoke in Bermuda, they entertained a steady stream of visitors in their hotel room. As Gloria recalls, "All during the day and into the night, women would be calling up and coming in. . . . I remember one young woman whose boyfriend was living with her in her mother's house was beating her. . . . We kept receiving in the room all night long, and under those circumstances, you get to know each other quite well. So we bonded, and we've been seeing each other fairly often since."

Another colleague who drifted into Gloria's life was Andrea Johnston, who interviewed her by telephone for the *Independent*, the Santa Rosa, California, newspaper. Gloria was coming to Northern California on her *Moving Beyond Words* tour. Inspired by a portable history of the Cherokee Nation that Wilma Mankiller had created—a series of flash cards that could be taken to school gyms and community centers—Gloria had been thinking about ways to make women's studies available in locations other than college campuses. She called the concept portable education. They began talking about the idea while Andrea was interviewing her, probably because Andrea was a junior-high-school teacher as well as a freelance writer.

Andrea pursued the idea and, after working with Gloria over the telephone for a few months, she stayed with Gloria on and off for a year to develop the project. Gloria calls it "inside out education, not outside in—so it's not like having a module or unit, it's a process." The process, as it evolved, was consciousness-raising for girls. They called the program Girls Speak Out and developed a two-session program in which a mixed group of about fifteen—women, as well as girls nine to fifteen years old—gather for activities and exercises. Gloria supplied some of the funding and raised the rest of it.

They created the exercises using literature like Alice Walker's children's book, *Finding the Green Stone,* and artifacts, stories of goddesses, and prepatriarchal history to describe societies in which women and girls had been honored and equal. Their goal was to find ways for the girls to "keep their power and keep their true selves." Gloria sees the process as "a potential national consciousness-raising movement for young girls. Because they can continue it in a different form. Not all will, but some will. It's like seeding." In connection with the project, she helped Andrea get a book contract and wrote the introduction. Early in 1997, Girls Speak Out joined a coalition of organizations including the YWCA and Girls Inc. to convene a national girls' conference in New York that was attended by 132 girls from thirty-six states. After discussing issues such as violence and girls' rights, one thirteen-year-old went to the microphone and said, "Thanks, Gloria and Andrea, for starting the girls' movement. Now we're going to finish it."

Gloria also sends offers of assistance to women in distress. After watching Phil Donahue interview Linda Lovelace, the actress who in 1972 starred in the notorious pornographic movie *Deep Throat,* Gloria contacted her to offer help. Linda Boreman Marchiano (her real name) had written *Ordeal,* a book exposing the fact that she had been coerced into starring in the movie by her then-husband, Chuck Traynor. Traynor had forced her into prostitution, beaten her frequently and severely, threatened her at gunpoint, and degraded her in every imaginable and unimaginable way, until finally she had escaped.

Marchiano had never heard of Gloria Steinem and wasn't sure what a feminist was, but she was grateful for any expression of concern. Up to that point most book reviewers had greeted her story with innuendo and sarcasm. Gloria invited her to the *Ms.* offices and introduced her to a number of feminists active against pornography, including Andrea Dworkin and Susan Brownmiller. As Marchiano wrote in her next book, *Out of Bondage,*

> No meaningful voice, no intellectual, had offered this kind of sympathy before. Gloria could have no firsthand knowledge of the world described in *Ordeal* but still, she was able to understand it. . . .
>
> Gloria wrote a lead article about me in *Ms.* magazine. ["Feminist Notes: Linda Lovelace's 'Ordeal,'" May 1980] Once Gloria's article appeared, an amazing phenomenon occurred. People started taking both my book and me seriously. Before then I had always been on the defensive, always explaining. As attitudes toward me changed, my own attitude changed. . . . I was getting a brand-new reaction from people: respect.

In 1997, Gloria became prominently involved with the issue of pornography again, when she wrote a January 7 op-ed article for the *New York Times* and spoke out against the movie *The People vs. Larry Flynt.* After noting that the movie whitewashed Flynt and glorified him as a First Amendment hero when he was only a First Amendment beneficiary, she asked if such a laudatory movie would have been made about a man who had depicted the torture of animals or Jews in the way Flynt's magazine *Hustler* portrayed women. When box-office sales diminished and the movie received fewer Academy Award nominations than expected, Gloria was accused of advocating censorship. Diana E. H. Russell, a well-known antipornography writer, sent her a T-shirt emblazoned, "I'm Against Pornography *and* Censorship," and she joked that she should wear it all the time.

Linda Marchiano's book sparked a reunion between Gloria and an old friend of hers, movie producer Rosilyn Heller. While considering basing a movie on *Out of Bondage,* Rosilyn noticed that Gloria had written its introduction. She contacted Gloria, and shortly afterward Gloria found herself in Los Angeles with an afternoon free. The two decided to visit some networks and see if they could sell the project. They made two visits, pitched two ideas, and sold them both.

The NBC executives rejected Linda Marchiano's story, but they were willing to consider a fictional version. On the spot, Gloria, who had speculated on the idea in her article "Linda Lovelace's Ordeal," suggested using the Persephone myth, in which a mother rescues a daughter who is being raped and held prisoner by Hades, King of the Underworld. Gloria recalls, "Only one-and-a-half reviewers would ever understand my version of this myth about Demeter and Persephone, but it was called *Season of Shame*, and I wanted to see a woman being rescued by her mother. That was the genesis to me—a strong, raging mother rescuing her daughter. So this was the story in which the daughter of a relatively powerful woman is seduced and ultimately forced into pornography. And the mother comes to rescue her. . . .

"Anyway, NBC was interested, but what's ironic is that they didn't want to do a movie against pornography because they had done too much *for* it. Very frustrating. Nevertheless, we sold it."

To CBS they sold *Mating in Captivity,* which was derived from Gloria's rejoinder that she wouldn't marry because "I can't mate in captivity." They envisioned a comedy about a group of women friends, "each of whom was in a different situation of the to-get-married, not-to-get-married, whatever combination," and their message would be "whatever your particular path is, is okay. The point was to disprove the Harvard study." (That is, a Harvard-Yale study that was misinterpreted to claim that a college-educated woman of thirty had only a 20-percent chance of marrying, and that by the time she was forty, she was, as *Newsweek* put it, "more likely to be killed by a terrorist" than to get married.)

Although scripts were commissioned for both, ultimately neither *Mating in Captivity* nor *Season of Shame* was produced. However, selling two movies in two appointments whetted their appetites, and they eventually sold an idea to Lifetime cable station that did get produced. Gloria wanted to dramatize the fact that many abortion opponents favor the death penalty, and about that time Rosilyn had received a story idea about a black woman on death row who is saved by a white woman. They put the two concepts together, reversed every cliché, and produced *Better Off Dead,* a television movie that aired in 1992.

First, they fought for the director they wanted. When they won, Neema Barnett became the first African-American woman director to direct a television movie. Then they made the prisoner, Kit, white and guilty instead of black and innocent. Their prosecutor, Cutter, was black, and they centered the story on the relationship between the two women. After successfully getting Kit the death penalty for shooting a policeman, Cutter learned more about Kit's life and began trying to save her. When Kit became pregnant by a prison guard with whom she had a real relationship, the antichoice, pro-capital-punishment governor denied her the abortion she requested. When Kit was eventually allowed to choose, she changed her mind and had the baby. Once it was born, Kit wanted to live. Then the governor proceeded with the execution.

Rosilyn, who was the first woman vice president of a major studio, brought her reputation and expertise to the partnership. Gloria says she brought the stories and the access, "because they're curious." Gloria brought a few other things. Although the two lead roles were equal, Lifetime wanted to grant only the white actress, Mare Winningham, top billing, Lifetime's reasoning was that Winningham was well known in television and had previously had above-the-title credit, while Tyra Ferrell, the black actress, had been in movies but not television (she played the mother in *Boyz N the Hood*).

"We argued and argued with these people," Rosilyn recalls. "It was so ridiculous. Finally Gloria called the head of Lifetime and said, 'Well, *we* know you people are not racist. It's the *appearance* of racism we're worried about.' That took care of the problem."

They also tried to sell a female *Roots*, about five or six generations of women in two families, one black and one white. Gloria recalls, "We did sell a female *Roo*." Gloria and Rosilyn wanted the series to be eight hours, and CBS gave them four. Although CBS bought it, Gloria and Rosilyn were dissatisfied with the script. Fortunately, when CBS was sold to Westinghouse in 1995, the network rejected the script, which meant they had their idea back.

Andrea Johnston and Rosilyn Heller are two of Gloria's myriad colleagues-who-are-also-friends, or vice versa. The ex-colleague and continuing friend whose name Gloria puts on forms as the person to be contacted in an emergency is Suzanne Levine, whom Amy describes as "Gloria's best girlfriend." More than a colleague, Bella Abzug is another of Gloria's most treasured friends. Gloria also considers Bella a role model. As she likes to say, Bella is "my spiritual mother—although she says she's not old enough."

Then there is Gloria's coven. Gloria does not reject traditions out of hand, but she is always checking them suspiciously for patriarchal, racist, or any other exclusionary tendencies. She also likes to invent new ones. In December 1987, around the time *Ms.* was sold, Gloria decided she could do more of what she wanted to do and less of what she had to do. To celebrate the solstice, she invited several women she knew slightly, and wanted to know better, to dinner. No one was well known to any other, but they sat down at the dinner table at eight, and when the talking stopped, it was three in the morning. They were television newswoman, Carol Jenkins, and writers Esther (E. M.) Broner and Marilyn French. Carol and Marilyn were Protestant, Esther was Jewish, and Gloria, whose roots and affiliations included Presbyterian, Jewish, theosophist, and Congregationalist, usually identified herself as a pagan.

Now they call themselves a coven and meet at least four times a year for the solstices and equinoxes, "more if someone needs it." The meetings include dinner at one another's apartments. According to Carol, evenings at Gloria's are particularly elegant, because everything is catered. They sometimes bring guests. Esther reports that some of Gloria's guests really annoy the others—desirable guests are those who embrace the spirit of the coven and do not monopolize the conversation. The last is important because each person present speaks uninterruptedly and coven gatherings tend to last into the small hours of the morning.

The right spirit is crucial, because coven gatherings are spiritual occasions (though when asked what they talk about, Carol says, "our mothers"). After starting with a blinking wand, they gradually gathered artifacts imbued with spirituality, and they make up ceremonies that enable them to support and nourish each other. On at least one occasion they met in a restaurant. According to Gloria, they held hands, lit candles, and cast spells by waving their wands and feathers, and no one even looked at them—"typical New Yorkers."

They joke about their coven, but they are serious about its spirituality and devoted to one another. They are also convinced that, as a group, they have such magical powers that they saved Marilyn's life. Marilyn had been diagnosed with cancer of the esophagus, and at one point she lapsed into a coma. Gloria, Carol, and Esther came regularly to the hospital where they talked to her, waved their wands, chanted, and performed what they hoped were miracle-inducing ceremonies.

Eventually Marilyn did enjoy a miraculous recovery. Once she was able to talk, she told her friends she had never felt so loved, though she had not been able to speak at the time of their visits. However, during one of the coven's visits, Bella Abzug visited, too. When Bella asked, in her booming voice, "Do you know who this is?" Marilyn roused herself enough to reply, "Bella."

"That miffed us a little," Carol confesses. However, Marilyn's inability to remember their visits—hardly surprising, since she was in a coma—has not stopped any of them, Marilyn included, from bragging. In 1997 Marilyn was writing about the experience.

The coven evolved because Gloria combined her organizer's ability to create interesting combinations of people with her dedication to friendship. There is no question that Gloria has a gift for friendship. Each friend volunteers a story about the special thing Gloria did for her, and each story is a variation on the same theme: Out of sensitivity or generosity or empathy, Gloria said or did or gave that friend exactly what she needed at that moment.

Gloria's generosity is legendary, though generosity implies sharing one's possessions, and Gloria seems to lack any sense of ownership in the first place. Both high school and college friends recall her giving them clothes practically off her back. Writer Jane O'Reilly says, "She not only asks if she can lend you money. She asks, 'Can I bring you money?' "

When Bella Abzug had to go to a number of appointments to determine the best treatment for her breast cancer, "It was Gloria who went with me to all of the doctors and made sure that I did the right thing. No hour was too late. No date was too important. She was there as a human being. As she has been for many."

She was there for Wilma Mankiller. The first time Wilma and Gloria met, Wilma told her, "You're a lot nicer and more sensitive than I expected," to which Gloria replied, "So are you." After that, Wilma stayed with Gloria a couple of times when she was in New York for Ms. Foundation board meetings. However, Gloria often has people coming through, and they did not become particularly close friends. Then Wilma became ill, and though she did not mention her condition, she did not look well. After a board meeting, she, Gloria, and Marlo Thomas shared a cab uptown. When they stopped to drop Wilma at her hotel, Gloria got out of the cab, too. "She stood right in front of my face and said, 'What's wrong with you and what can I do?' " Wilma recalls.

Wilma explained that her kidneys were failing, but that she was under a doctor's care. He wanted to remove both her kidneys, put her on dialysis, and wait for a kidney match for a transplant from a cadaver.

Gloria happened to know something about kidney transplants. A Yugoslavian journalist, Slavenka Drakulić, had stayed with her off and on over a five-year period when she visited the United States to obtain treatments and await a transplant. During that time, Gloria had gotten to know her Boston physician, Anthony Monaco, an internationally prominent transplant surgeon. Gloria called Dr. Monaco, and the surgeon agreed to see Wilma. However, Wilma stalled. She already had a doctor, and he was closer to her Oklahoma home.

Gloria refused to give up. She hardly knew Wilma, but she kept calling for about two months, badgering her until Wilma finally agreed to go to Boston. "The minute I talked to him I knew I wanted to use him," Wilma recalls. Dr. Monaco wanted to leave her kidneys intact and find her a live donor. Wilma's brother turned out to be a match, so they proceeded with the kidney transplant operation. Wilma credits Gloria quite simply with saving her life. "If she wasn't as persistent as she was, I wouldn't have called. She just kept bothering me until I called the doctor."

Gloria's chosen family treasures her friendship, and they love showing her they care, because they understand how much she appreciates their affection. As 1994 and Gloria's sixtieth birthday approached, Marlo Thomas and a few of Gloria's friends began talking about how to celebrate. Marlo, Nadine Hack, a prominent Democratic fund-raiser, Letty Pogrebin, and Marie Wilson wanted to honor Gloria in some way. "We always honor live conservatives and dead troublemakers," Letty said. So they thought about endowing a chair for troublemakers. Or a library. Or an old ladies' retirement home.

"Finally," Marlo recalls, "we decided to create something so that Gloria could continue doing what she always did—giving away every cent of every dollar she had." They planned to raise enough money to add a $6-million fund to the Ms. Foundation endowment so that Gloria could give the income away herself. They raised more than $1 million immediately. A couple of months before Gloria's birthday, they assembled a group of about twenty men and women such as Diane Sawyer, Home Box Office chief executive officer Michael Fuchs, Sophia Collier, and Katharine Graham to host a party at Marlo's and Phil Donahue's Fifth Avenue apartment. There, in front of the guests, who were, according to Marlo, "heavy hitters," some of the hosts pledged sums as high as $250,000 to encourage the others to do the same.

Then Marlo told Gloria that she and Phil wanted to take Gloria and about twenty friends to Jezebel's, a New Orleans-style restaurant that is one of Gloria's favorites. When they arrived, Gloria found about 135 guests at her surprise sixtieth-birthday party. Gloria's first comment was, "I had no idea. *No idea.* And not only is it the rarest of occasions in that sense, but also, you don't have to pay to come to my birthday." There was going to be a Voters for Choice benefit in her honor in Los Angeles the following week.

Her friends laughed, applauded, and quickly disabused her of the outlandish notion that her birthday dinner would not cost anyone anything. There was now a Gloria Fund, they explained, fully staffed, at the Ms. Foundation, and they had collected pledges of over $2 million in two months.

Gloria was "flabbergasted—she couldn't get over all the different plans," Marlo recalls happily.

Once again there were toasts and tributes. John Kenneth Galbraith recalled first meeting Gloria, thirty-two years earlier: "I was recovering from hepatitis and in low spirits, and I was revived by Gloria, who was strikingly beautiful and very young. . . . She is our most effective defender of women's equality, and she will continue to be loved and feared for the next many years."

Bella announced, "This is what seventy-three looks like." Then she added, "We have to think about what Gloria is and what she's done. She's crystallized the emotions and the yearnings of our entire gender. She's served as our most vivid expression of our hopes and demands. She's our pen and our tongue and our heart. She's Elizabeth Cady Stanton and Susan B. Anthony and Emma Goldman all rolled up into one—and she still doesn't gain any weight."

Pat Carbine recalled that when Gloria had been a *Look* contributor, she had fallen so behind in her assignments that her agent called to say that Gloria could no longer walk past the *Look* building on Madison Avenue because it made her feel so terrible. Taking pity on her, Pat recalled, *Look* released her from her contract.

Past and present *Ms.* leaders Pat Carbine, Suzanne Levine, and Marcia Gillespie also presented a mock cover of *Ms.* Marcia explained that since all *Ms.* publishers ever seemed to say to them was, "Can we put Gloria on the cover? Can we put Gloria on the cover full face? Can we put Gloria on the cover, three-quarters? Can we do a profile? Gloria Steinem from the rear?" the *Ms.* editors had prepared the ideal *Ms.* cover. A photograph of Gloria covered the page and teaser copy promised a plethora of treats: "Ten Surefire Tips for Meeting Deadlines," by Gloria Steinem; "Stories for Free Children: My Inner Child," by Gloria Steinem; "Gloria Steinem's Recipes From Within"; and a special pullout, "Steinem in the Year 2035: This Is What 101 Looks Like."

38

Gloria's Talents and Demons

In May 1996, seventy-two-year-old Angela LaFrieda learned that Gloria Steinem would be in Miami Beach to address the twenty-fifth-anniversary celebration of the Florida Women's Political Caucus. She knew it was time to seize her opportunity. For decades, Angela LaFrieda had been collecting everything Gloria Steinem had written.

On the day of the speech, LaFrieda arrived at the Eden Roc Hotel and secured a spot for herself in the lobby. She spread out a display of Gloria's books, the issues of *Ms.* with Gloria on the cover, and *Ms.*'s original Wonder Woman issue—all lovingly encased in plastic covers. Then she sat down to wait.

As soon as Gloria arrived, she was told about her visitor. She made her way over to the display and, after chatting, said she would be glad to sign all the books and magazines. "Oh, my prayers have been answered," LaFrieda said happily.

"Well, she tends to do that," Gloria replied, and spent the next half hour with her unusually devoted fan.

Later that month, I sat in Gloria's backyard, watching her cat dig up her flowers while we finished our final interview. I had just asked Gloria what else she hoped to accomplish before she died (write more books, organize a school for organizers "if I've got one more organization left in me," live among wild elephants, learn to skateboard) when suddenly she sighed. "That *New York Times Magazine* did it again. After they gave me these terrible assignments and were so outraged that you wouldn't be so honored to do anything for the *New York Times Magazine*—then, when they did their anniversary thing, they reprinted the worst one."

A few weeks earlier, the *New York Times Magazine* had celebrated its centennial by running excerpts from previous issues. A section of articles on women included Susan Brownmiller's "Sisterhood Is Powerful," Martha Weinman Lear's piece on the Equal Rights Amendment, Vivian Gornick's cover story "Who Says We Haven't Made a Revolution?" and a photograph of Bella Abzug and Betty Friedan leading a march. Only "Hosed. Big News About Nylons. By Gloria Steinem" was accompanied by an explanation: "In 1964 Ms. Steinem got an assignment from the Magazine—a report about the advent of textured stockings—an experience that surely helped refine her notions of gender stereotyping."

The centennial issue excerpted work by a glittering roster of 155 writers, including three-time winner of the Pulitzer prize Edward Albee, airplane inventor Wilbur Wright, John F. Kennedy, Winston Churchill, Nadine Gordimer, Norman Mailer, Simone de Beauvoir, David Halberstam, and Joyce Carol Oates. Most were described in a one-sentence biography. Gloria apparently needed none. There was merely a quotation from the author: "The *Times Magazine* gave me my most frivolous and seductive assignments. The irony was that women's magazines would let me write about Saul Bellow or James Baldwin."

Even after spending the last two years studying Gloria assiduously, I was astonished by her reaction. "Didn't you see what they said?" I asked.

"Well, I know. I said to the woman [at the *Times*], 'You know, I've written about how this was the low point of my entire journalistic life. Now you're going to reprint it again?' "

"They said that, though."

"You thought they did? Well, if you got it from what they said, then I feel better about it. I had said to them, 'Then quote from the introduction to *Outrageous Acts*, where I say this is the low point of my entire journalistic life.' They assured me that they would, but they didn't. They could at least have used Mary Lindsay." (In 1966, Gloria asked to profile New York Mayor John Lindsay and was assigned to write about his wife, Mary, instead.)

In other words, though the icon of feminism for the past quarter century can hardly avoid noticing that she is both a celebrity and an influential leader, she is so lacking in perspective—at least about the detested textured stockings—that she could not see that she was being esteemed rather than demeaned.

That combination of sublime and ridiculous is quintessentially Gloria. On the one hand, she so inhabits her role as a leader, both voicing and embodying the values she espouses, that she can be extraordinarily inspiring, even in private. Democratic Socialist leader Michael Harrington's biographer could have been describing Gloria when he wrote of his subject: "Like his predecessors, he believed that to awaken the conscience or change the consciousness of a nation, one had to build an organization, start a publication, speak on a thousand street corners to crowds of hundreds (or tens, if necessary), recruiting one's followers from those converted by the sound of one's voice and the strength of one's arguments."

On the other hand, Gloria can get carried away with her own craziness. As Suzanne Levine says, "Robin [Morgan] and I get hysterical. Gloria will come to dinner one night and say, 'Oh, I met this wonderful woman. She makes tampons out of lots of discarded packing crate material and she soaks it in herbs and then—' Or 'I saw the most wonderful movie about a woman who raises cattle and is gang raped and makes a sword out of a frying pan and kills all the people who raped her and then sets up a women's health center.'

"Sometimes she's a parody of herself. But I think if there's any one thing she's trying to get to the bottom of, it's what women are. . . . I think she's always thinking about what the common grounds are, and sometimes she's funniest when she's really stretching."

Gloria's contradictions are writ larger than life, created by her own unique combination of outsized abilities and enormous needs—or as she calls them, her "talents and demons." Those talents and demons shaped Gloria Steinem as a leader in ways both great and small. First designated by the media as the role model of a liberated woman, Gloria was not the leader many feminists would have chosen. As the years passed, though, they came to respect her abilities, appreciate her commitment, and recognize both the depth and breadth of her contributions.

Gloria's talents were obvious, but her demons played a role as well. Her aversion to marriage and lack of desire for children left her more available to the movement than she would have been with family commitments. As a woman alone, she probably seemed to the public to be more vulnerable and therefore less threatening. (Gloria may have regarded husbands as more threat than protector, but society did not.)

Also, because she was not a wife or a mother, she could not transgress in those roles—there was no husband to seem emasculated by her strength nor children to seem neglected because of her activities.

Gloria, in turn, was nourished by the public homage and affection. She became a public figure because she felt compelled to act, not because she was looking for adulation. As it turned out, becoming a public figure brought her more love than all her love affairs, more respect than any of her writing, a more authentic identity than any she had tried on over the years, and a more fulfilling life than any she could have imagined. As she once mused to an audience, "The world inside my house was very difficult and sad, so instead of looking for security and witnesses and support inside, I looked for it in the world. And the funny thing is that if you look for it in the world, you find it. Maybe it's a form of planning—what can I tell you?"

A combination of malleability and a laid-back, go-with-the-flow openness, Gloria's passivity is part of her personality, but it turned out to suit her ideologically as well. As a populist and social democrat, she believes in change and movement from the bottom up. So for her, much of the art of leadership has been the art of listening and responding. Her ideal form of power is the power to empower others. She likes to quote Pancho Villa on leadership, saying that a strong leader makes a weak people, and a strong people doesn't need a strong leader.

When groups gather to honor Gloria, the talk always seems to turn to the question of Gloria's saintliness. Not all feminists approve. Marie Wilson sees the insistence on Gloria's perfection in terms of the needs of those around her: "I think it's about projection. I think being protective about Gloria is really about 'I'm her friend and I get a lot out of whatever about my relationship, so I have to keep her perfect.'"

Furthermore, the implication that the best feminist is a saintly feminist distresses Marie. "To me, the idea that she's completely selfless, that she'll do anything, is a put-down. Gloria loves this. Gloria gets enormous rewards out of this. I find that offensive.

"I'm not interested in a selfless leader. I'm not interested in selfless women. I got into this movement because I wanted to have a self. And I wanted that self to be able to want things.

"If it's one thing people around her do continually, it's saying, 'She's so selfless. She never thinks of herself.' That isn't okay to say. It's bullshit. She likes this stuff.

"But it's interesting. Why does a woman who has as much self as Gloria have to be thought of as so selfless? I think the interesting thing is, Gloria has actually fulfilled more of herself than anybody I know. She doesn't have a family and children, but she really has a self."

Understanding the difference is the point. Gloria Steinem, the woman, and Gloria Steinem, the leader, are both products of their culture. As both woman and leader, Gloria responds to its messages, even as she strives to expose and change them. As she puts it, "A smart man wrote the Golden Rule, but women usually need to revise it to treat ourselves as well as we treat others. That would be a revolution."

To those interviewers who ask, Gloria usually says that she would like to be remembered as "a good person, in the Jewish sense," and she says she finds talk of sainthood embarrassing. To a certain extent, she obviously does. She is so determinedly egalitarian that when she gives a speech, she usually claps back when the audience applauds her and asks that the house lights be raised so there is less of a barrier between speaker and audience. Unwilling to be ungracious, she accedes to requests for autographs by giving them, but she asks for the requester's autograph in return.

At the same time, however, the high regard of the public nourishes her, and she responds to its valuing of selflessness, even while she dedicates herself to helping women overcome it. As Stan Pottinger says, "She could say, 'Don't touch my hem. I'm not Mother Teresa or Gandhi.' But she doesn't say it. Not," he adds, "because she's really promoting herself, but because she's part of the culture." In fact, Gloria abets her aura of self-abnegation, admitting ruefully that yes, it's true, she does put others ahead of herself—but she really is trying to overcome that tendency and learn to think more about her own needs. The problem with that characterization is that being a person who puts others first *has been* one of her own needs. She has needed to be that person—and to be seen as that kind of person—in order to approve of herself and to earn the approval of others.

Occasionally she expresses it that way herself. In "Doing Sixty" she wrote, "Even if we're no longer trying to surgically transplant our egos into the body of a husband or children, we still may be overly dependent on being needed—by coworkers and bosses, lovers and friends, even by the very movements that were intended to free us of all that." Although in that essay she attributed to her female conditioning her need to be "codependent with the world," as she puts it, at least she took a step closer to self-knowledge. What Gloria seems unable to believe is that she is good enough as a human being. She doesn't need to be a selfless saint.

Bella Abzug, who also disapproves of the Saint Gloria talk, protested at the Veteran Feminists of America dinner honoring Gloria, "I was having a big argument tonight as to whether or not Gloria is a saint. How can you emulate a saint? It's too hard. But I will say this about Gloria: She may not be a saint. But there's nobody gooder."

Because the qualities that rendered Gloria the leader she became are her personal qualities, she does not appreciate the uniqueness of her contribution or its magnitude. Writing is difficult for her and she wants to be appreciated as a writer. She is. However, because for her leading is doing what comes naturally, she does not seem to see the dimensions of her achievements. What she has accomplished—both in quality and in quantity—no one else could have done.

Bella and Stan Pottinger and Marie Wilson and so many others inside and outside the movement understand Gloria's place in history. Feminism's second wave had better theorists. There were more graceful writers. There were more eloquent speakers.

There was no better leader.

Author's Note

Biographers—particularly unauthorized biographers—face a variety of obstacles. If their subject is deceased, literary executors may deny them access to documents and papers. Living subjects may also deny their biographers access to documents. Living subjects may refuse to be interviewed and may ask their friends to refuse, as well.

I was fortunate. When I first approached Gloria Steinem, she agreed to talk with me once Carolyn Heilbrun's biography of her was published. Then, at our second interview, Gloria gave me a letter drafted by her lawyer, Bob Levine. It stipulated that in exchange for her agreement to be interviewed, she would receive a copy of the manuscript from which she could check facts and her own quotes. In the event of a disagreement about quotes, Gloria was to be the "absolute authority" unless I could prove to the contrary with a tape recording. If we disagreed about facts, my editor would be the arbiter.

Throughout the project, I had the same three goals: relate the narrative of Gloria's life, depict the person formed by those experiences, and, to the extent possible in a work about a contemporaneous actor in an ongoing revolution, examine the nature of Gloria Steinem's contribution as a historical figure. My editor, Hillel Black, and I decided that because control over the biography's contents would remain with its author and editor rather than with its subject, signing the agreement would not compromise the book's integrity.

Editorial control was the sine qua non. Living subjects often disagree with their biographers, and I assumed Gloria and I would have differences of opinion. Who among us sees ourselves or the circumstances of our lives exactly as others see us? In some respects, biographical subjects are the best source on their lives; in others, they are not. Furthermore, protecting and controlling their self-images often is important to public figures, not only for personal reasons, but because they fear their mission will be harmed if their image is damaged.

It is the biographer's job to act as a filter—to gather accounts and opinions, weigh them against one another, search for bias and hidden agendas, check verifiable facts, and then present what she believes to be the truth about her subject. I did that, but I have included some of Gloria's disagreements with my account of her life in the text, as well as in the notes, because I considered them part of the story. I include this summary of what happened as the result of our arrangement for the same reason.

In March 1997, I gave Gloria the manuscript for her comments and began my own fact-checking. After she read and returned it, I found that she had rewritten it in many places. Some of her changes were genuine corrections; because I had given her an uncorrected manuscript, I desired and expected them. Gloria also added quite a bit of material. Some of it was interesting or illuminating, and often touching or humorous, and I included it where I considered it appropriate.

However, many of her changes went beyond factual corrections or the offer of new material. Not only did she alter her own quotes, but she changed facts; she changed the quotes and opinions of other people; she rewrote some of my descriptions, characterizations, and opinions; she excised words, sentences, or even entire portions, including other people's quotes or her own quotes. Sometimes she provided a reason; sometimes she deleted without explanation. Some of what she added was inappropriate for a variety of reasons.

By the time she had completed her comments, her grandfather's estate was no longer "substantial," it was "small." Her grandmother's estate was no longer "comfortable"; it, too, was small. So were their Clarklake house, Sue's sailboat, and her mother's income from their lakefront property. Gloria wanted me or my publisher to hire an outside fact-checker to determine whether her mother had poisoned the Barnes's dog. She objected to being described—by me or by others whom I quoted—as ingratiating. She disputed my characterization of her as a celebrity in the 1960s.

As I indicate in the notes, Gloria rewrote much of the CIA-related material so that it conflicted with other sources' accounts and some of the verifiable facts. She wanted me to omit, on the grounds that I was wrong, my opinion that her feelings toward her father may have been more complicated than mere acceptance of his leaving and an understanding that he treated her better than he treated himself. She objected strenuously to my contention that she could have derived ego gratification from being a feminist leader rather than being a completely reluctant leader who wanted only to be a writer.

About five weeks after she had received the manuscript, Gloria spent a couple of weeks in Africa. While she was overseas, my publisher copied and bound the manuscript, labeled the cover on the front and back "ADVANCE UNCORRECTED MANUSCRIPT FOR REVIEW, PUBLICITY AND SUB-RIGHTS PURPOSES. PLEASE REFER TO FINISHED BOUND BOOKS WHEN REVIEWING THIS WORK," and sent it to book clubs, to some publications for possible excerption, to magazines requiring lengthy lead times for reviews, and to *Booklist, Kirkus Reviews, Library Journal,* and *Publishers Weekly,* periodicals that publish prepublication reviews.

When Gloria returned, she objected to the fact that the manuscripts had been sent out and that I had not sent her a copy of my manuscript showing her my changes. Calling them violations of our agreement, she refused to return any more of the manuscript with her comments. Eventually, my publisher agreed that I would send her a copy of the original manuscript with the changes I had made in response to her comments (I was still in the process of overall fact-checking), as well as any source notes I had written. This was a courtesy, not a submission for Gloria's approval.

Around the time Gloria saw what I was and was not changing, the scope of her response expanded. She had the manuscript—which she had been given for her personal comments—duplicated, and sent pages of these copies all over the country and even overseas. Neither my publisher nor I was told she was doing it, nor was I told to whom the pages were sent. Nor do I know what the recipients were told as to why the subject of a book would be sending out pages of the author's manuscript. I do know that I received a variety of responses, from helpful suggestions to critical comments telling me what I should and should not include in the book.

With regard to the experience, the two questions I have been asked most frequently have been, Are you sorry you signed the agreement? and, Has this changed your opinion of Gloria Steinem? My joking answer is, In biography, stick with the dead. My serious answer to both questions is, Unequivocally not.

The access was invaluable, and accuracy was always my goal. As for changing my opinion of Gloria Steinem, I was already quite familiar with Gloria's own views of herself and her life, as well as with the phenomenon of history according to Gloria. Both are well documented in the book, but it is important to keep them in perspective. The very tenacity with which Gloria attempted to make what she saw as "wrong" with this biography of herself "right" is the same tenacity with which, for so many years, she has attacked what she has seen as wrong with the world and tried to make it right. As I researched her life and her work, Gloria Steinem—both as a person and as a leader—continually rose in my estimation. We are all her beneficiaries.

Notes

In general, quotations from interviews are conveyed in the present tense. Exceptions and quotes from other sources are cited in the Notes. Thoughts, dreams, or feelings were related to the author by the person to whom they are attributed unless otherwise indicated. The following abbreviations will be used in the Notes:

GS   Gloria Steinem
SSP   Susanne Steinem Patch
GSP   Gloria Steinem Papers, Sophia Smith Collection, Smith College
CA   College Archives, Smith College
CDJ   C. D. Jackson Papers, Dwight D. Eisenhower Library
OAER   *Outrageous Acts and Everyday Rebellions*
RFW   *Revolution From Within: A Book of Self-Esteem*
MBW   *Moving Beyond Words*

Chapter 1: Ruth, Leo, and the Girls

Principal interviews contributing to this and to the following chapter were conducted with: GS, SSP, Louise Heskett, and Florence Steinem on the family and on life at Clarklake. Clarklake interviewees other than family members included: Alice Bunker, Neal and Mary Jane Austin Choate, Harry Cogan, Tom Collins, Dolores Field, Jackie Burton Hubbard, and Linda Tilden Kerr.

7 "Men must acquire": *Toledo News-Bee,* October 12, 1904. Quoted in Elaine S. Anderson, "Pauline Steinem, Dynamic Immigrant," Marta Whitlock, ed., *Women in Ohio History, A Conference to Commemorate the Bicentennial of the American Revolution* (1976), p. 16.

7 Biographical information on Pauline and Joseph Steinem is from interviews with family members and from written sources: Whitlock; Rosa B. Lewis, "Pauline Perlmutter Steinem," in *In Search of Our Past: Women of Northwest Ohio* (1987); Who's Who in America, 1910–1911 and 1924–1925; obituaries for Pauline, *Toledo Times,* January 7, 1940, and *Toledo Blade,* January 6, 1940; obituaries for Joseph, December 27, 1929, *Toledo Blade* and *Toledo Times.*

8 For background on the theosophical movement, see Cranston, 1993; Godwin; Head and Cranston, 1967; Meade; and Washington. Also see Edward Hower, "A spirited story of the psychic and the Colonel," *Smithsonian,* May 1995, pp. 111–27; and these pamphlets published by the Theosophy Company, Los

Angeles, Calif.: *Conversations on Theosophy; Reincarnation and Karma; Theosophy Simply Stated.*"

8 "the neurotic, the hysterical": Washington, p. 70.

9 "I believe in woman suffrage": Pauline Steinem, "Why I Am a Suffragist," *Toledo Blade,* October 28, 1914.

9 "the masculine point of view": Ida Husted Harper, *History of Woman Suffrage,* vol. 5 (reprint, New York, 1969), p. 263. Quoted by Sara Hunter Graham, "The Suffrage Renaissance: A New Image for a New Century, 1896–1910," in Marjorie Spruill Wheeler, ed., *One Woman, One Vote: Rediscovering the Woman Suffrage Movement* (1995), p. 166.

9 Pauline Steinem, "We want the man"; feminist, "You have no right . . .": *Toledo Blade,* October 13, 1910. Quoted in Whitlock, p. 18. The feminist was Harriet Taylor Upton of Warren, Ohio.

10 "an evil someone who had not evolved at all": SSP.

10 Description of newspaper's creation from Frank R. Hickerson, *The Tower Builders: The Centennial Story of the University of Toledo* (1972), p. 164.

10 Shipwreck story from Louise Heskett (a first cousin of Marie's) and accounts from the *New York Times,* November 14–17, 1854, quoted in GS, *The Beach Book* (1963), pp. 266–69.

10 Information on Ruth and Leo at the University of Toledo was provided by university archivist Barbara Floyd, Ward M. Canaday Center, William S. Carlson Library, University of Toledo, Toledo, Ohio.

11 Ruth Nuneviller, "The Tragedy Among the Waterpipes": *Toledo Universiteaser,* May 29, 1919.

11 "Do you think": Miss Ann Circe, "Answers," *Teaser,* September 25, 1920. "We understand": November 18, 1920. "Doesn't Leo": November 4, 1920.

12 "Mr. Steinem was most instrumental": "Students Form Literary Society," *Teaser,* December 2, 1920.

13 Ruth left her job: Frank Kane, "Mother Steinem Early Liberationist," *Toledo Blade,* May 10, 1972. The article reported that Ruth "worked on the *Blade* for five or six years and then quit to give birth to Susanne. After about 18 months, she decided that she couldn't stand straining baby food and those countless baby baths as a career, so she went back to work."

13 Information about Ocean Beach Pier is from interviews and Ted Ligabel, *Clark Lake: Images of a Michigan Tradition* (1991), pp. 100–108.

14 "more than half of the dance floor": *Toledo Blade,* April 30, 1928. Quoted in Ligabel, p. 103.

15 "Political freedom and the right": Lillian Symes, "Still a Man's Game: Reflections of a Slightly Tired Feminist," *Harper's Magazine* 158, May 1929, pp. 678–79. Quoted in Cott, *The Grounding of Modern Feminism* (1987), p. 152.

15 "companionate marriage," "a specialized site": Cott, p. 156.

16 Nothing came of the suit. According to the death records of Jackson County, Michigan, and reports in the *Brooklyn Exponent,* July 9 and July 18, seventeen-year-old Max Allen died on July 8, 1929, from a toboggan accident. The September 26 *Exponent* reported on the lawsuit. Dolores Field, who kindly researched the incident in both Brooklyn and Jackson, could find no further mention of the lawsuit, and Sue recalls being told that the toboggan had been pronounced safe.

17 Ruth Steinem's giving birth to a stillborn baby is recorded in a death certificate filed January 25, 1932, Lucas County (Toledo), Ohio.

18 Gloria's birth announcement was reproduced in Ligabel, p. 106.

Chapter 2: Life on the Lake

21 Christmas wishes are from GS, "The passionate giver," *Glamour,* December 1963, p. 97.

22 "He had the ring": Ann Landers, *Dallas Morning News,* July 28, 1996. A fifteen-year-old girl inquired, "What is Burma-Shave? It is not in the dictionary. All I could find is Burma—a country in Southeast Asia now called Myanmar." Her forty-three-year-old parents had never heard of it either. Ann Landers responded by printing some of her readers' favorite Burma-Shave verses. Ruth S. of Roselle, N.J., sent this one. Burma-Shave was last advertised in 1977, but its parent company, American Safety Razor Company, announced in July 1997 that an updated version of the 1925–64 roadside signs would be featured in a television commercial to run on national cable networks.

22 Gloria, eight, found their 1942–43 winter: The story of wartime rationing and German sailors in Florida is from GS. She did not know the year, but the date is my surmise, based on the fact that in 1942 the FBI captured some German saboteurs who had landed in Florida and New York and that the Steinems stayed home during the winter of 1941–42 for Sue's senior year in high school.

25 When she wrote a Thanksgiving poem: Written communication from GS.

27 "Love for Louisa": Martha Saxton, *Louisa May: A Modern Biography of Louisa May Alcott* (1977), pp. 277–78.

27 "a fear of the loss of independence": Madelon Bedell, *The Alcotts: The Biography of a Family* (1980), p. 243. See also MacDonald, pp. 78–81 and on *Work,* another Alcott novel Gloria read, pp. 83–88. Also see Louisa May Alcott's books.

27 "I don't believe I shall ever marry" Louisa May Alcott, *Little Women* (reprint, 1947), p. 406.

Chapter 3: Bad Times in Toledo

Principal interviews contributing to this and to the following chapter were conducted with: GS, SSP, Louise Heskett, Florence Steinem, Lillian Barnes Borton, Carole Roberts Berning, Ronald Duncan, Dixie Auxter Leeds, Blanche Miklosek DeBarr, Julia Robinson (formerly Rose Link), and Sue Bolander Zedecker.

35 "What I remember emotionally": GS.

37 In fact, Ruth had become so hallucinatory: The account of their visit to the doctor is from GS, "Ruth's Song (Because She Could Not Sing It)," OAER, p. 149. "How can I travel" is from p. 150.

38 "I did not blame him": Ibid., p. 150.

39 He talked proudly to others: Jackie Burton Hubbard. On his trips east, Leo visited the Burtons at Clarklake partly, Jackie suspected, because he was lonely and partly because her mother was such a good cook.

39 his cars always listed to the passenger side: Both Jackie Burton Hubbard and Harry Cogan of Clarklake recall the mystery of Leo's cars. Twice in later years, Leo hired Harry to drive him back from California: once to Washington where Sue lived, and once to New York, where Gloria lived. Harry hinted that he would like to meet them, but Leo ignored the hints. He left Harry at the airport in Washington and put him in a cab in New York. His daughters never knew that anyone else had driven him.

39 he had had a vasectomy: Readers may be surprised to learn that vasectomies have been performed for over three hundred years. According to Howard I. Shapiro, M.D., *The New Birth-Control Book: A Complete Guide for Women*

and Men (New York: Prentice Hall Press, 1988), they became routine as a method of sterilization in 1925.

40 "Call me if you need me": Louise Heskett.

41 "a dignified advertising man around 45": Kay Quealy, "Just Out of School, Local Girl Is Diamond Expert," *Toledo Blade,* 1946 (exact date unavailable), p. 30, GSP.

41 his mother had left his inheritance: Florence Steinem, Ed's daughter-in-law.

42 Ruth was the indirect cause: Details of the rat invasion are mostly from Lillian Barnes Borton and Carole Roberts Berning, though Gloria's account of the traps is from GS interview. Gloria has been accused of inventing or exaggerating the story of the rats, but from the others' accounts, I believe she understated the terror of the experience.

43 "I was just passing through": OAER, p. 152.

Chapter 4: Gloria Takes Control

46 Hostess and Interior Design: The merit certificates are in GSP.

48 Gloria talked to Prudy: Sue Bolander Zedecker, who was Prudy's closest friend. Prudy is deceased.

48 "Gloria has no one": Julia Robinson. Sue Bolander Zedecker says, "Everyone's mother sort of took her under their wing."

49 "We always knew when we had money": Ron Duncan.

49 Miss Capehart TV Contest: Written communication from GS.

50 never eat anything: "The Fast Track," *Chicago Tribune Magazine,* October 23, 1983. In a "Vital Statistics" column, this was Gloria's answer to a query on "the worst advice my mother ever gave me."

54 The family assembled in Toledo: Marcia Cohen, *The Sisterhood: The True Story of the Women Who Changed the World* (1988) pp. 51–52. Also, GS and SSP.

Chapter 5: Abloom in Georgetown

Principal interviews contributing to this chapter were conducted with: GS, SSP, Ellie Bush Chucker, Maxine Coleman Mills, Peggey Puglisi, Margaret Dorsey, Cyanne Hanson, Phil Leder, Lillian Menne Litz, Jacqueline McCartney Alvord, Ernest Ruffner, Cornelia Stewart Gill, Sharon Stokes Garrison.

56 she had been featured in *Glamour* magazine: "We name for *Glamour*": *Glamour,* no date. GSP.

60 "chirpy birds": Peggey Puglisi.

60 "It was no small thing": Sharon Stokes Garrison.

60 Gloria had been elected: Activities are from her high school yearbook, *The Westerner,* 1952.

61 Gloria was chosen to stand in: "Vivacious Gloria Steinem Proves Popularity in Senior Elections," *Western Breeze,* April 3, 1952.

61 "personality, popularity, and pulchritude": Charlotte Yates, "Menne Chosen 'Miss Western' in Breeze Popularity Contest," *Western Breeze,* June 10, 1952.

61 "an engaging grin": *Western Breeze,* April 3, 1952.

61 "I'm sure a lot of the boys": Sharon Stokes Garrison.

62 SAT scores shown on Gloria's Smith College transcript.

63 she planned to major in political science: From the April 3, 1952, *Breeze* article and interviews.

Chapter 6: Miss Steinem Goes to Smith

Principal interviews contributing to this and the following two chapters were conducted with GS, SSP, Sidney Abbott, Lucy Lindstrom Allard, Barbara Zevon Berlin, Rachel White Brown, Jane MacKenzie Davidson, Cornelia Stewart Gill, Dorothy O. Helly, Betsy McQuat Lameyer, Meredith Chase Morley, Phyllis Black Ozimek, Denise Rathbun, Phyllis Fewster Rosser, Anne Frederick Starbird, Jane Jones Reid, David Shaber, Patsy Goodwin Sladden, Betty Rose Tamallanca, and Judith Wheeler.

66 "two inches above the knee" and "skirts and sweaters": *Smith College Freshman Handbook,* [Class of] 1956, p. 36, CA.

66 "intended to tell you how to dress": "Wardrobe Includes Jeans": *Smith College Sophian,* August 1952, p. 3, CA.

66 For a detailed history of the "posture photos," see Ron Rosenbaum, "The Great Ivy League Nude Posture Photo Scandal," *New York Times Magazine,* January 15, 1995, p. 26.

66 Most of the thirty-five houses: Statistical information about Smith in 1952 is from *Smith College Bulletin, The Catalogue Number 1952–1953,* CA.

67 they were conflicted about their goals: Information on the individual colleges and the Seven Sisters grouping is from Helen Lefkowitz Horowitz, *Alma Mater: Design and Experience in the Women's Colleges From Their Nineteenth-Century Beginnings to the 1930s* (1984).

67 "Only our failures marry": The distortion of "Our failures only marry" is discussed in Liz Schneider, "Our Failures Only Marry: Bryn Mawr and the Failure of Feminism," Vivian Gornick and Barbara K. Moran, eds., *Woman In Sexist Society: Studies in Power and Powerlessness* (1971) pp. 579–600.

67 "We've heard too often": "We Do Not Agree" (editorial), *Smith College Sophian,* October 14, 1952, p. 2, CA.

67 "Don't students ask questions?": "Stage-Fright Or Stupidity?" (editorial), *Sophian,* October 13, 1955, p. 2. The writer suggesting organizations plant "stooges" noted, "Critical comments from boys indicate that this problem almost never arises at a men's college," CA.

68 "My college years were full": GS, "Why Young Women Are More Conservative," OAER, p. 239. Adapted from "The Good News Is: These Are Not the Best Years of Your Life," *Ms.,* September 1979, p. 64.

68 she hadn't learned a thing there: Barbara Zevon Berlin and Dorothy O. Helly heard Gloria comment in that way during speeches on college campuses.

68 she managed only D's: Gloria's Smith College transcript.

68 "I took geology": "Always ask the turtle" is one of Gloria's often repeated stories. Quoted here as reprinted from her 1995 commencement speech in the *Christian Science Monitor,* June 19, 1995, p. 17.

69 dean's list: Gloria's Smith College transcript.

72 more than 1,500 card-carrying Communists: Marcia Damon, "List For Communist Probe Cites Smith," *Sophian,* January 13, 1953, p. 1, CA.

72 "worse dragons than the evils": Marcia Damon, " 'Academic Freedom' Is Topic at NSA Meeting," *Sophian,* February 17, 1953, p. 1, CA.

72 Also that month: "Pres. Wright Answers Alumnae Who Attack Faculty Members," *Sophian,* March 4, 1954, p. 1, CA.

72 "Committee for Discrimination in Giving"; "young minds": Editorial: "Right to Defame," *Sophian,* March 4, 1954, p. 2. Coverage of the controversy continued in the *Sophian,* March 9, 16, and 18, 1954, CA.

73 A memorable figure: Information on Sylvia Plath is from Smith College
Bulletins and Anne Stevenson, *Bitter Fame: A Life of Sylvia Plath* (Boston:
Houghton Mifflin, 1989).

Chapter 7: Junior Year in Switzerland

78 "not two brain cells": Gloria Steinem to Ruth Steinem. Letter quoted in Carolyn
Heilbrun, *The Education of a Woman: The Life of Gloria Steinem* (1995), p. 56.

Chapter 8: The Terror of Marriage

Additional interviews contributing to this chapter were conducted with Blair
Chotzinoff, Anne (Cookie) Chotzinoff Grossman, and Herbert Grossman.

86 "sort of 'revirginized' myself": Joan Barthel, "The Glorious Triumph of Gloria
Steinem," *Cosmopolitan,* March 1984, p. 270.
86 She wrote several book reviews: In the *Sophian,* she reviewed Arthur Koestler's
Trail of the Dinosaur (February 16, 1956); two books by Bertrand Russell, *Satan
in the Suburbs* and *Nightmares of Eminent Persons* (March 1, 1956); Morey
Bernstein's *Search for Bridey Murphy* (March 15, 1956); and Edmund Wilson's
Red, Black, Blond and Olive (April 26, 1956), CA.
88 "We have decided to name": Gloria Steinem, "Senior Spring," *Smith Alumnae
Quarterly,* spring 1956, p. 155, CA.
88 "a unique opportunity": Adlai Stevenson, commencement speech, Smith
College, June 6, 1955, p. 4, CA.
88 "needs room to turn around in": Archibald MacLeish, commencement speech,
Smith College, June 3, 1956, p. 17, CA.

Chapter 9: An Abortion Alone

Principal interviews contributing to this chapter were conducted with GS, Anne
(Cookie) Chotzinoff Grossman, Blair Chotzinoff, Herbert Grossman, and Margaret Harrison Case.

89 "sort of Gershwiny": Frances Rowan, "Setting Compass for India," *Washington Post and Times Herald,* October 29, 1956, p. B4.
89 "Louisville Lou"; "a kind of semiparody": GS.
90 Chester Bowles was gratified: Chester Bowles to Barbara Jean Stokes, chairman
of the Asian Scholarship Fund, International Relations Organization (IRO), letter,
May 24, 1956, in response to Stokes's May 17, 1956, letter reporting on the
committee's progress since his spring 1954 lecture and requesting his permission
to name the scholarship after him, CA.
91 the committee was still discussing: October 9, 1956, agenda for October 10
meeting of the Chester Bowles Asian Scholarship Committee of the IRO. Item III
began, "The responsibilities of the girls going have never been clearly defined. . . .
Returning to Smith is the only thing that was ever definitely established." Item
V noted, "We have found that we possess very little information regarding living
accomodations [sic], traveling, university courses and the like," CA.
91 "not the stuff": GS to John Chapman, faculty committee member, letter, August
17, 1956, CA.
92 "Elizabeth Taylor coloring": GS.
92 "About Gloria, you know her": Kayla Achter to Lee Cottrell, president of the
IRO, letter, September 28, 1956. The next two quotes are from the same letter, CA.
93 "Gloria might contact these people": Kayla Achter to Lee Cottrell, letter,
October 6, 1956, CA.

93 After she finally secured airfare: GS to Barbara Jean Stokes, letter, October 22, 1956, CA.

93 About a month after she arrived: The account of her pregnancy and attempts to obtain an abortion is from Cohen, pp. 104–108 and GS.

95 "coarse and jejune": GS to Barbara Jean Stokes, letter, January 27, 1957, CA.

Chapter 10: Passage to India

Principal interviews contributing to this chapter were conducted with GS, Devaki and Lakshmi Jain, Jean Joyce, Martha and Tom Keehn, and A. M. Rosenthal. To avoid the distraction of scattered *sics,* I corrected the spelling in quotations from Gloria's reports and letters from India. Gloria ordinarily makes very few spelling errors.

98 "the Christians' conception of God": GS, *Chester Bowles Asian Fellowship Report No. 1* (from arrival in mid-February to end of March), p. 12. The next two quotes are from pp. 12 and 14, CA.

99 "the best lecturer and leader": GS, *Chester Bowles Asian Fellowship Report No. 2* (month of April, University of Delhi), p. 18, CA.

100 "needed only a babushka": GS, *Report No. 1,* p. 22. The next two quotes are also from *Report No. 1,* pp. 25 and 26.

101 "125-year old swami": GS, *Chester Bowles Asian Fellowship Report No. 3,* (month of May, New Delhi and the Radical Humanist Study Camp), p. 1. The next two quotes are from pp. 2 and 17–18, CA.

102 "I'm worried": Jean Joyce to Chester Bowles, copy of a letter enclosed with Chester Bowles to Barbara Jean Stokes, letter June 21, 1957. Bowles also sent a copy to Dr. Wright, Smith's president, CA.

103 "perhaps our hopes"; "animated suspension": Barbara Jean Stokes to Benjamin Wright, letter, July 12, 1957. The 1957 Bowles fellow and IRO vice president, Maggie Harrison, was still in the U.S. during the correspondence, and she wrote past president Lee Cottrell, "As for the whole problem of this scholarship. It's nuts; this much we have realized for a long time. It's also a very, very, good thing which mustn't be allowed to fail. Of this I think most of us are convinced, with the possible exception of Mr. Wright." She added later in the letter, "As for K. & G. Harumph," CA.

103 "ten Tibetan lamas": GS to Barbara Jean Stokes, letter, October 14, 1952. The next quote is from the same letter. CA.

103 "that divide our lives": MBW, p. 266. The next quote is from p. 265.

104 "someone told me": GS.

105 "the Burma Road": GS. Conventional histories of the Burma Road, which was built during World War II, do not mention Kwong. However, thousands of people were involved, so he may have been one of them.

106 Among them were Rear Admiral Quiggle: "Admiral Quiggle Missing From Ship Enroute to California From Japan," *Washington Post,* July 25, 1958. "Adm. Quiggle Feared Dead After Jumping From Ship," *Asahi Evening News,* July 25, 1958.

106 Gloria was interviewed: Betty Marsh, "American In India Tells of Assignment to Land of Contrasts," *Toledo Times,* September 12, 1958. The article reported: "More women in India work as doctors, lawyers and in government circles than do women here in the states, the visitor said."

Chapter 11: Fighting the Communists

Principal interviews contributing to this chapter were conducted with GS, George Abrams, Leonard Bebchick, Zbigniew Brzezinski, Wilson Dizard, Clive Gray, Morton

Horowitz, Robert Kiley, Cord Meyer, Karen Paget, Walter Pincus, Paul Sigmund, and one former officer of the NSA and the CIA who wishes to remain anonymous.

107 "If I brought up India": MBW, p. 266.

108 The NSA actually began: Background on the National Student Association and its relationship with the CIA is based both on interviews and on a number of published sources. See also Bird, 1992; Chafe, 1993; Cummings; Kessler; *Final Report of the Select Committee to Study Governmental Operations;* Marchetti and Marks; Meyer; Powers; Ranelagh; and Thomas.

110 "An individual in contact with you": Cord Meyer, *Facing Reality: From World Federalism to the CIA* (1980), p. 70.

116 "Mohini, an Indian girl, and Kofi, a Ghanaian": Philip Benjamin, "Youths Briefed on Red Festival," *New York Times,* July 4, 1959, p. 2.

116 C. D. Jackson was a leading figure: Background on C. D. Jackson is from Blanche Wiesen Cook, *The Declassified Eisenhower* (1981).

117 "unobtrusively quite active": C. D. Jackson to Frank Stanton, letter July 13, 1959. C. D. Jackson Papers, Dwight D. Eisenhower Library. The other quotes in the paragraph are from the same letter. All C. D. Jackson correspondence is from C. D. Jackson papers, Dwight D. Eisenhower Library.

117 "Gloria Steinem asked me to help": C. D. Jackson to Cord Meyer, letter July 15, 1959. Other relevant letters: GS to Jackson, July 10, 1959, asking for help. Jackson to Frank Stanton, July 13, 1959. Stanton to Jackson, July 14, 1959: "I was distressed to read Gloria Steinem's letter to you and called her immediately. She has just left my office." Jackson to Stanton, July 15, 1959: "[A]s usual when the boss man becomes aware, things turn out right," CDJ.

117 Gloria sent him a letter asking for help: GS to C. D. Jackson, letter June 1, 1959. The quotes in this paragraph are from this letter, CDJ.

117 "Was it permissible for a socialist": Michael Harrington, *Fragments of the Century: A Social Autobiography* (1972, 1973), pp. 138–39.

118 At one point Jackson wrote to ask Gloria: Jackson to GS, letter March 11, 1959, CDJ.

118 "The most tactful thing one can say": GS to Jackson, letter, March 19, 1959, CDJ.

118 Jackson was helping the CIA: Account of C. D. Jackson's activities is based on correspondence from CDJ.

118 The festival began during the last week: Account of the Vienna festival is based on interviews and Independent Service for Information on the Vienna Youth Festival, *Report on the Vienna Youth Festival,* 1960.

120 "Out of my way, Russian pig": Leonard Bebchick.

120 "Gloria is all you said she was": Sam Walker to Jackson, letter, July 24, 1959, CDJ.

121 "Gloria's group continues to do yeoman service": Walker to Jackson, letter, July 31, 1959, CDJ.

Chapter 12: Launched Into Social Orbit

Principal interviews contributing to this chapter were conducted with GS, George Abrams, Sam Antupit, Leonard Bebchick, Robert Benton, Clay Felker, Barney Frank, Milton Glaser, Patsy Sladden Goodwin, Tom Guinzburg, Robert Kaiser, Barbara Nessim, Henry Raymont, David Shaber, Dennis Shaul, Paul Sigmund, David Swanson, Sheila Tobias, Gus Tyler, Henry Wolf, and Susan Wood.

123 the New Journalism: For more on New Journalism, see Tom Wolfe, "Why They Aren't Writing the Great American Novel Anymore," *Esquire,* December

1972, in which he discussed the genre's development. He observed that "magazine writers—the very lumpenproles themselves!" had taken over from novelists by appropriating their tools: scene-by-scene construction, dialogue, using a character to tell the story, and recording "the everyday getures, habits, manners, customs, styles of furniture, clothing, decoration. . . ." See also Carol Polsgrove, *It Wasn't Pretty, Folks, But Didn't We Have Fun?: Esquire in the Sixties* (1995).

123 "If you're out with a very New York kind of girl": GS, "Big Weekend in New York," *Esquire,* September 1961.

127 "A gift for holding loosely": GS written communication to author.

130 Gloria disagreed with some of this account. My account of the Helsinki youth festival, the events leading up to it, and Gloria's role in both, is based on interviews with GS, Sam Antupit, Clay Felker, Barney Frank, Robert Kaiser, Henry Raymont, Paul Sigmund, David Swanson, Sheila Tobias, and Gus Tyler. Gloria disputes some of it.

For example, she contends that the newspapers were put out by Finnish students. Barney Frank, Paul Sigmund, and Gus Tyler were not involved with the newspapers. All the others contributed to my account. No one mentioned Finnish students. When I received Gloria's recollections, I asked Sheila Tobias about Finnish students. She replied, "I don't remember any Finnish students. They were all Americans." She did recall that production was subcontracted to local professionals.

Gloria also asserted that Ted Whittemore had not run the newspapers; that the newspapers were supervised by "a young Finnish socialist named Juhani Rinne"; and that Clay was the only one with final authority over the English edition. Sam Antupit and Bob Kaiser both told me Ted Whittemore was the managing editor. Sam said, "Ted was actually the managing editor of all the newspapers. I would say he did what Clay says he did. Ted really organized all of them." Sam also had told me, "There was this Finnish guy, Juhani Rinne—I'll never forget his name. He was our contact. We spoke with him daily about one thing or another—about logistics around Helsinki."

131 "Constant fear was hardly the condition": GS, "The Moral Disarmament of Betty Coed," *Esquire,* September, 1962, p. 155. The next quote is also from p. 155.

131 "Rent a very good painting": "The Student Prince, Or How to Seize Power Though an Undergraduate," *Esquire,* September, 1962, p. 83.

132 "If you . . . cannot tan at all": GS, *The Beach Book* (1963), p. 83. The other quotes are from pp. 5 and 6. *The Beach Book* was not overly successful in 1963, but it became a collector's item. In the *New York Observer,* July 21, 1997, booksellers Kinsey Marable & Co. advertised a copy for $225.

Chapter 13: "A Bunny's Tale"

Principal interviews for this chapter are GS, SSP, Sam Antupit, Bob Cuniff, Tom Guinzburg, Barbara Nessim, Ray Robinson, Ruth Whitney, and Susan Wood.

136 When pianist Marian McPartland: Bill Crow, *Jazz Anecdotes,* (New York: Oxford University Press, 1990), p. 189.

137 a WNS syndicate article: Betty Reef, "Pretty Girl Genius Helps Edit 'Help!' for Tired Minds," *Daily Oklahoman,* November 13, 1960, p. C11. The other quotes in the paragraph are from the same article.

138 During her month: GS, "A Bunny's Tale," *Show,* May 1963, p. 90. The account of her experience and the quotes are from this article and "A Bunny's Tale, Part II," which appeared in *Show,* June 1963, p. 66.

138 "the hidden qualities": Editors' note, "A Bunny's Tale," *Show,* May, 1963, p. 90.

139 a two-page account: GS, "Dateline: Helsinki. The Last Red Festival," *Show,* October, 1962, p. 123.

139 the American establishment: Jean vanden Heuvel and GS, "Richard Rovere's Ride," *Herald Tribune Books,* July 1, 1962, p. 3.

140 GS, "How to Put Up With/Put Down a Difficult Man": *Glamour,* November 1963, p. 116. The next four quotes are from the same article.

141 she panned it: GS, "Very basic training," *Book Week,* October 18, 1964, pp. 17–18. The review also covered *Nine to Five and After: The Feminine Art of Living and Working in the Big City,* by Irene Silverman.

141 GS, "Visiting Englishmen Are No Roses' ": *New York Times Magazine,* March 24, 1964, p. 63. In response to Malcolm Bradbury's complaint that the young American girl grew up into "the middle-aged American woman, with her shriek-ing voice and parchment skin, growing money trees, doing plant-prayer, gossip-ing about her neighbors . . . ," Gloria wrote, "My first impulse was to put on something frilly, retire to the kitchen and stop all mental processes, in order to avoid those acusations of rudeness and regain, in his eyes, my femininity. But, on second thought, I cannot believe that a man, even an Englishman, really enjoys being admired by women with no taste."

141 GS, "How to Find Your Type (And, If Necessary, Change It)": *Glamour,* February 1964, p. 11.

141 "Deception is neuter": "Secrets of Deception": *Glamour,* May 1965, p. 135.

141 "It's easy to see that a good spy": "So You Want to Be a Spy": *Glamour,* September 1964, p. 228.

141 "I had learned most of what I knew": GS, "College and What I learned There": *Glamour,* August 1964, p 167. The next quote is from p. 182.

142 profiles on celebrities and literary figures: "Mrs. Kennedy at the Moment," *Esquire,* October 1964. "Julie Andrews," *Vogue,* March 15, 1965. "Barbra Streisand Talks About Her 'Million-Dollar Baby,' " *Ladies' Home Journal,* August 1966. "A Woman for All Seasons" (Margot Fonteyn), *McCall's,* May 1967. "Maurice Joseph Micklewhite—What's 'E Got?" (Michael Caine), *New York Times Magazine,* December 4, 1966. "A Visit with Truman Capote," *Glamour,* April 1966, and "Go Right Ahead and Ask Me Anything," *McCall's,* November 1967. "James Baldwin, an Original," *Vogue,* July 1964. "A Day in Chicago with Saul Bellow," *Glamour,* July 1965.

142 "an infinitely elegant Beatle": GS, "Gernreich's Progress; Or, Eve Unbound," *New York Times Magazine,* January 31, 1965, p. 21.

142 "teenage marzipan Peter Lorre": GS, "A Visit with Truman Capote," *Glamour,* April 1966, p. 210.

142 "a kind of good-looking Eleanor Roosevelt": GS, "Mrs. Kennedy at the Moment," *Esquire,* October 1964, p. 126.

142 a piece on pop culture: GS, "The Ins and Outs of Pop Culture," *Life,* August 1965.

142 GS, " 'Crazy Legs'; Or, The Biography of a Fashion," *New York Times Mag-azine,* November 8, 1964, p. 58.

142 "I can call myself a writer": GS, "What's In It for Me," *Harper's,* November 1965, p. 169.

143 She was being written about by others as well: Mel Shestack to GS, letter January 13, 1965 refers to "the story I wrote for Writer's Digest . . . 'JOUR-NALISM'S GIRL OF THE YEAR'—that intrepid, glamorous free-lance writer: Gloria Steinem." Also, Richard Lee, managing editor, *Career Girl News,* letter,

December 12, 1965. He sent her three copies of the January *Career Girl News* and thanked her for the interview and loan of pictures, GSP.

143 "Strange things happen": GS to Mel Shestack, letter, dated only "Thursday," GSP.

Chapter 14: Some Enchanted Lovers: Ted Sorensen, Mike Nichols, and Herb Sargent

Principal interviews for this chapter were conducted with GS, Margaret Dorsey, Nora Ephron, Clay Felker, Tom Guinzburg, Ali MacGraw, Barbara Nessim, Jane O'Reilly, Phyllis Fewster Rosser, David Shaber, Dennis Shaul, Paul Sigmund, Eugene Theroux, and Susan Wood.

145 "frugality, abstemiousness, and Puritanism": *Current Biography Yearbook 1961*, p. 435.

146 Mike, who was born in Berlin: Biographical material on Mike Nichols is from *Who's Who in America 1997; Current Biography Yearbook 1961*, Barney Lefferts, "Now the Mike Nichols Touch," *New York Times Magazine*, November 22, 1964, p. VI–34; Vincent Canby, "The Cold Loneliness of It All," *New York Times*, January 23, 1966, p. II–7; "Sought-After Director: Mike Nichols," *New York Times*, January 25, 1967, p. 36; PMK Public Relations. See also Sean Mitchell, "Nichols on Nichols," *New York Newsday*, July 9, 1991, p. 52; and Peter Marks, "The Brief, Brilliant Run of Nichols and May," *New York Times*, May 19, 1996, p. 31.

147 "We are becoming the men": Gloria, an inveterate credit-sharer, notes that she did not coin the aphorism, though she repeated it. She also did not originate "A woman without a man is like a fish without a bicycle" or "If men could menstruate, abortion would be a sacrament" and some others with which she is associated. However, it was Gloria Steinem who made them famous. Thus, aphorisms mentioned in this book as "her" or "Gloria's aphorisms" may or may not have been said first by her.

148 If she married Mike Nichols: Phyllis Fewster Rosser.

149 "Who's Who of the World": Leroy Aarons, "Capote Is Cold Blooded to the Uninvited Masses," *Washington Post*, November 25, 1966. Quoted in Gerald Clarke, *Capote: A Biography*, (1988), p. 376. Account of the party is also based on Charlotte Curtis, "Capote's Black and White Ball: 'The Most Exquisite of Spectator Sports,' *New York Times*, November 29, 1966, p. 53. Enid Nemy, "Behind the Masks," *New York Times*, November 29, 1966, p. 53. Eugenia Sheppard, "The Capote Caper: Starring The Five Hundred," *World Journal Tribune*, November 29, 1966, p. 13. Suzy Knickerbocker, *World Journal Tribune*, November 29, 1966, p. 13. WRITER, "That's the Way the Ball Bounces," *Women's Wear Daily*, November 22, 1966, p. 1. GS, "The Party: Truman Capote Receives 500 "People I Like" (a first-person account), p. 50.

150 "the only really beautiful ballroom": Curtis, *New York Times*, November 29, 1966, p. 53.

150 "She had a very small part": Margaret Dorsey.

150 a January 1964 article in the *New York Post*: Nora Ephron, "Sun Bather," *New York Post*, January 10, 1964. The quotes in the next three paragraphs are from this article.

151 *Playboy* sued her for libel: Gloria was a surprise witness for the New York State Liquor Authority in New York State Supreme Court. The SLA was fighting the Playboy Club's right to a liquor license. Among the articles quoting Gloria were Edward Kirkman, "SLA Overrules the ABC, Okays the Piccolo

Club," *New York News,* May 25, 1963. Don Vandegrift, "A Bunny Turns Key on Playboy Club," *Journal American,* April 1963 (exact date not available).

152 Gloria appeared in a six-page spread: "A Girl—Signed Herself," *Glamour,* February 1964, p. 106. The quotes in the next paragraph are from the same article.

153 Gloria was written about: Examples are "Vogue's Notebook: The Joys of a New York Party for the International Rescue Committee," *Vogue,* November 15, 1964; "News Girl," *Newsweek,* May 10, 1965; Toni Kosover, "The Girl of Her Dreams," *Women's Wear Daily,* August 31, 1966; "Easy on the Eye," *Ladies' Home Journal,* January 1966. "Enter the Girl From Glamour," *London Daily Mail,* March 30, 1966. Lillian Roxon, "See-Through Discreetly," *Sydney Morning Herald Limited,* June 21, 1966; Nancy L. Ross, "Writer's Life Can Be Glorious and Beautiful," *Washington Post,* December 3, 1967; "Expressing the Trevira Era: Gloria Steinem in Oscar de La Renta's Bold New Knits," *Harper's Bazaar,* 1968; "Reporters: Thinking Man's Shrimpton," *Time,* January 3, 1969.

153 The longest feature: Harvey Aronson, "The World's Most Beautiful Byline," *Newsday,* September 25, 1965. The quotes in the next three paragraphs are from the same article.

154 "our foundress, Gloria Steinem": All quotes from Gene Theroux are E-mail communications. After agreeing to be interviewed, he left for India for a long assignment, but kindly allowed me to interview him by E-mail.

155 Gloria disputes the existence of this board, however informal. I based the statement on the following. Gene Theroux wrote by E-mail on October 9, 1996: "Suffice it to say, for now, that as Director of the IRS, I reported to a board of directors consisting, as I recall, of only three people: Gloria Steinem and Dennis Shaul and Paul Sigmund." On October 14, 1996, he wrote, "My contact with Gloria was infrequent while I was the Executive Director (and sole employee) of the Independent Research Service. She was living in New York, and I was living in Washington. She had already become a nationally known celebrity, and I was a law student. We did talk on the phone, and met less often, in connection with the IRS preparations for the Festivals (Algiers [Algeria] and Accra [Ghana], which were never held, and finally Sophia). The IRS office in Washington, by the way, was at 1101 Connecticut Avenue, N.W., a second-floor space over 'Ruth's Hat Shop.'"

When I received this portion of the manuscript back from Gloria with her comments, she noted that she had called Gene in India, and she changed the text to read that Gene "had been told that she would be on the board of the Service, along with Dennis Shaul, Paul Sigmund and others. He was disappointed that no such board ever met, and he never worked with Gloria." She also rewrote his quote.

On April 28, 1997, I sent Gene Theroux a long fax, enclosing copies of my manuscript pages, the pages from his E-mail letters upon which it was based, and a cover letter noting that in view of the telephone call he had received, I wanted to be "doubly sure I am good-and-accurate." I received confirmation the next day that he had received the fax and would respond to it soon. He never answered it.

Meanwhile, I contacted Paul Sigmund and Dennis Shaul. Paul originally had declined to be interviewed, but he had agreed to talk to me during fact-checking. About the time I had received Gloria's response to the Theroux portion, I had called Len Bebchick to ask if I could fax him chapter 11 for an over-all check on the NSA, CIA, and youth festivals material. When I learned that he was abroad and not expected back for three weeks, I asked Paul Sigmund to look at the chapter. He kindly agreed and meticulously went over the lengthy chapter, even correcting my spelling.

I first queried Paul by phone about the IRS board and then faxed him a copy of my manuscript pages, Gene's E-mail pages, and a cover note asking, "Does Gene Theroux's recollection of the after-Helsinki 'Bd of Directors' sound OK?" Paul confirmed the board and did not recall anyone being on it besides the three of them. He said that his role was mainly recruiting students.

I also reached Dennis Shaul, whom I had been pursuing without success throughout my research. His recollections are quoted in the text. After I wrote the portion that included his quotes, I called him back, explaining that because of the delicacy of the subject, I was concerned that I had been too casual. Therefore I wanted to read him his quotes. He approved them. I also faxed Dennis's quote to Paul, who thought it sounded fine except that he wasn't sure about "dinners." When I also mentioned to Paul the delicacy of the situation as my reason for wanting to be careful, he said something like "yes, the Redstockings." (See chapter 26, where this board—an extremely minor incident in Gloria Steinem's life—was used to attack her.)

About a month later, on June 4, I received a call from Dennis. Gene Theroux had called him from India, and as a result, Dennis was concerned that he had given me the wrong impression with his quote. I read it to him again and he approved it again. He said he would inform Gene that it was fine.

On June 27 I received a fax from Gloria, who wanted the material deleted. She enclosed a three-page fax from Gene Theroux, dated May 27, thanking Gloria for sending him pages from my manuscript, noting that he had never met me, and stating that what he had told me by telephone or E-mail had been in haste. Now that she had shown him what I had written, he wanted it edited to correct errors or misleading information for which he had been the source.

In the fax Gloria relayed to me, Gene Theroux wrote to Gloria that he could find no evidence that there was a board while he was involved with the organization. He cited the fact that though the Independence Research Service had stationery and a brochure, neither of them included Gloria's name or any listing of a board of directors. Nor, he wrote, had he seen anything like a corporate charter, by-laws, or board meeting minutes. Furthermore, he had never attended a board meeting, nor had he ever had dinner with Gloria.

He also expressed concern that his quote that Dennis and she were "two of the most remarkable, bright, witty and able people I have ever met" would imply that she, Gene, and Dennis had met together, though the three of them had not.

155 "We mean people": Marylin Bender, *The Beautiful People* (1967), p. 77. The following quote is from p. 141.
156 "a melodramatic love affair": Ali MacGraw.

Chapter 15: Becoming a Political Operative

Principal interviews for this chapter were conducted with GS, Ruth Bower, Clay Felker, John Kenneth Galbraith, Milton Glaser, George Hirsch, Peggy Kerry, Frank Mankiewicz, Laura Stevenson Maslon, George McGovern, and Alan Patricof.

157 "What the hell": Don Oberdorfer, *Tet!* (1971), p.158. Quoted in Todd Gitlin, *The Sixties: Years of Hope, Days of Rage* (1987), p. 299. Also quoted in William H. Chafe, *The Unfinished Journey: America Since World War II*, (1986), p. 346.
159 "hasn't yet been able to decide": "This Is New York?" *Newsweek*, April 8, 1968, p. 102.
159 a profile of Andy Warhol's superstar: Barbara L. Goldsmith, "La Dolce Viva," *New York*, April 29, 1968, p. 36.

160 the other reporters stepped back: Ann Costello (who worked as a researcher
     in the mayor's office).
161 "What are you doing": Robert J. Bliwise, "Master of New York," *Duke
     Magazine,* September–October 1996, p. 37.
162 "had been something between": GS, "Trying to Love Eugene," *New York,*
     August 5, 1968, p. 15.
162 Gloria had first met McGovern: The account of their friendship and political
     association is based on GS, "Campaigning," OAER; and "Coming of Age With
     McGovern: Notes From a Political Diary," *Ms.,* October 1972, part of which is
     included in "Campaigning." Also, George McGovern interview.
163 "McCarthy hates people": "The Cocktail Party," Books, Summer 1968. This
     anecdote also appears in "Campaigning."
164 "You said in that article," Nora Ephron, "Women," *Esquire,* November 1972,
     p. 18.
164 "endless 'lady' jokes": OAER, p. 100. The next two quotes are from the same
     page.
165 "those hippies should get out": George McGovern.
165 "The room was jammed": OAER, p. 102.
166 "a properly terrible sweater," GS, "Coming of Age," *Ms.* October 1972, p. 98.
166 "No broads": OAER, p. 116. The next quote is also from p. 116. Senator
     Ribicoff reportedly denies saying this.

Chapter 16: New Left Woman

Principal interviews for this chapter were conducted with GS, Ronnie Eldridge,
John Kenneth Galbraith, Dolores Huerta, Rafer Johnson, Florynce Kennedy,
Marion Moses, Mary Perot Nichols, and Arnaldo Segarra.

170 "had never before seen": Charlotte Curtis, "Southampton Meets 'La Causa,' "
     New York Times, June 30, 1969, p. 44.
170 "The only solution": GS, "The City Politic: More Hot-Weather Specials,"
     New York, August 24, 1970, p. 7.
172 "a firm and unequivocal commitment": R. W. Apple Jr., "Democratic Coun-
     cil Asks Pullout Within 18 Months," *New York Times,* February 10, 1970, p. 1.
     The next two quotes are from the same article, p. 11.
173 "a little truth-telling": GS, "The City Politic: The Making (and Unmaking) of a
     Controller," *New York,* May 5, 1969, p. 8. The Mailer-Breslin campaign was heav-
     ily populated with writers; in addition to interviews, this account is based on Joe
     Flaherty, *Managing Mailer;* Norman Mailer, *The Prisoner of Sex;* Peter Manso,
     ed., *Running Against the Machine,* 1969; Peter Manso, *Mailer: His Life and Times,*
     1985; and Carl E. Rollyson, *The Lives of Norman Mailer: A Biography.*
173 Hitler-Stalin pact; "a hip coalition": Flaherty, pp. 15, 19.
173 "We sat for a minute": Manso, 1969, p. 304.
173 "Mailer, the wild-eyed": Manso, 1969, p. 304.
174 "How much money do you have?": GS.
174 "Sitting at lunch one day": Mailer, p. 19.
174 "I get further off on the wrong foot": Manso, 1969, p. 305.
175 "It was an idea": Flaherty, pp. 39–40.
175 "compulsory free love"; "I am running to the left": "Mailer for Mayor,"
     Time, June 13, 1969, pp. 22 and 21.
175 "free Huey Newton": Flaherty, p. 37.
176 Norman Mailer wanted more: GS.

176 "Norman and I had dinner": Manso, 1985, pp. 502–03.
176 In 1968 she had written a feature story: GS, "The Black John Wayne," *New York*, November 11, 1968, p. 35.

Chapter 17: A Feminist Is Born

Principal interviews contributing to this chapter were conducted with GS, Dolores Alexander, Rosalyn Baxandall, Susan Brownmiller, Cindy Cisler, Anselma Dell'Olio, Jean Faust, Muriel Fox, Carol Hanisch, Irene Peslikis, and Colette Price.

183 "Blurring of sex lines": GS, "Notes on the New Marriage," *New York*, July 8, 1968, p. 29.
184 "*Born Female* is enough": GS, "'Anonymous' Was a Woman," *New York Times Book Review*, August 11, 1968, p. 8. The next quote is from the same page.
184 "those who want power": GS, "Women and Power," *New York*, December 23, 1968, p. 54.
184 "I was into the success": Liz Smith, "Coming of Age in America," *Vogue*, June 1971, p. 150.
185 "I used to seek out": Joan Barthel, "The Glorious Triumph of Gloria Steinem," *Cosmopolitan*, March 1984, p. 219.
185 "the sexual segregationist argument": GS, "Women and Power," p. 49. The next three quotes are from pp. 49, 55.
186 "This was a very interesting experience": Jean Faust, notes on "For Women Only: NBC TV, taped 12/18/68 for showing Jan. 6–10, 1969." Courtesy of Jean Faust.
186 Faust . . . was so impressed: The account and quotes are from Jean Faust to author, letter, April 23, 1996, and telephone interview.
186 Gloria had been humiliated: The anecdote about her experiences at the Plaza Hotel before and after the demonstration is based on the account in RFW, pp. 22–23. "It had been raised" is from p. 23.
187 The evening began with a playlet: Led by Anselma Dell'Olio, who wrote and acted in the playlet, the New Feminist Theatre toured and performed all over the country. To gain permission to hold an event at the church, members of the Red-stockings approached the writer Grace Paley, who was on the church board. Paley suggested they team up with the New Feminist Theatre, whose perfor-mance was already scheduled.
188 The first speaker described: Quotes and account of the Redstockings' speakout are based on audiotapes of the event. Copies of the audiotapes and information about other materials from the 1967–1973 period of the women's liberation movement are available from Redstockings Women's Liberation Archives, P.O. Box 744, Stuyvesant Station, New York, NY 10009. I am indebted to Rosalyn Baxandall, who was one of the speakers at the event, and Colette Price, another of the original Redstockings, for listening to the tapes with me, identifying the speakers, and describing the Redstockings and the speakout.
189 "the personal is political": Carol Hanisch, who worked closely with Red-stockings, was not an actual member because she lived in Gainesville, Florida. She used the phrase in a letter to a friend. In early 1969, she expanded that letter into a circulated essay, "The Personal Is Political," which was included in *Notes From the Second Year*, 1969, edited by Shulamith Firestone and Anne Koedt.
190 "Suddenly, I was no longer learning": GS, "Introduction: Between the Lines," OAER, p. 20.

Chapter 18: The Birth of NOW

Principal interviews for this chapter were conducted with Dolores Alexander, Rosalyn Baxandall, Rita Mae Brown, Caroline Bird, Anselma Dell'Olio, Jean Faust, Muriel Fox, Jo Freeman, Colette Price, Marlene Sanders, Mary Jean Tully, and Ellen Willis.

192 The most transformative movement: There are several excellent histories of feminism's second wave. This chapter draws mostly from Bird, 1968; Carabillo, Meuli, and Csida; Freeman; and Hole and Levine, as well as important histories of the radical feminists written by Echols and Sara Evans. A few of the most important anthologies of work from the period include Gornick and Moran; Koedt, Levine, and Rapone; Morgan; Schneir, *Feminism in Our Time;* and Tanner. For primary sources, a researcher of the period should see the radical journals from which the anthologies drew many of their short pieces. They include *Voice of the Women's Liberation Movement,* edited by Jo Freeman in Chicago; *No More Fun and Games,* published by Cell 16, a Boston radical feminist group; and New York Radical Women's *Notes From the First Year: Women's Liberation,* with subsequent editions of *Notes* for the second and third years.

193 "problem that has no name": Betty Friedan, "Twenty Years After," *The Feminine Mystique,* p. 22. The following quote is from p. xi.

195 "Commission meetings produced": Aileen Hernández, *The Women's Movement: 1965–1975,* paper for the Symposium on the Tenth Anniversary of the U.S. Equal Employment Opportunity Commission, sponsored by Rutgers University Law School, November 28–29, 1975, p. 6. Quoted in Toni Carabillo, Judith Meuli, June Bundy Csida, eds., *Feminist Chronicles, 1953–1993* (1993), p. 13.

198 "You put your body": Gitlin, *The Sixties: Years of Hope, Days of Rage,* p. 84.

199 The chairman turned them away: This account is taken from accounts in Freeman, pp. 59–60 and Hole and Levine, pp. 113–14. The anecdote was also told to the author by Ellen Willis in an interview.

199 "balling a chick together": Hole and Levine, p. 120.

199 "Take it off": Another transforming moment and favorite anecdote in the history of the women's liberation movement. It also appears both in Freeman, p. 61, and Hole and Levine, pp. 133–34, which quotes Ellen Willis, "Up From Radicalism: A Feminist Journal," *US* no. 2 (Bantam, October, 1969), p. 114. Ellen Willis also recounted it. Her quote is from the interview.

200 "Aside from her assumption": GS, written communication to the author.

201 "Being called 'unfeminine' ": GS, "After Black Power, Women's Liberation," *New York,* April 7, 1969, p. 10. The next three quotes are from the same page.

Chapter 19: On the Road With Glo-ball

Principal interviews for this chapter were conducted with GS, Dorothy Pitman Hughes, Jane Galvin-Lewis, Florynce Kennedy, Carol Merry-Shapiro, and Margaret Sloan-Hunter.

203 "a beautiful black female Saul Alinsky": GS, "The City Politic: Room at the Bottom, Boredom on Top," *New York,* June 30, 1969, p. 11.

205 "Women have been much too docile": Lawrence Meyer, "Steinem Talks at Academy," *Washington Post,* May 5, 1972. Quotes in this and the following two paragraphs are from the same article.

205 "I want to be so outrageous": Jane Galvin-Lewis.

205 "If God meant women": Ellen Frankfort, "Feminist Party convention: Urinary Politics," *Village Voice,* June 7, 1973. Article reproduced in Flo Kennedy, *Color Me Flo: My Hard Life and Good Times,* p. 81. The next quote is from the same article.

206 The second of five daughters: Biographical information on Flo Kennedy and her family is from Kennedy, *Color Me Flo.*
206 "Are you my alternative?": GS, "Introduction: Life Between the Lines," OAER, p. 10.
206 "To me it's a part": Kennedy, p. 7. The next three quotes are from the same source, pp. 39, 91, and 79.
208 Her assistant joked: Joanne Edgar.
209 " '_____ chic!' she snaps": Barbara Lewis, "Gloria Steinem, a golden girl for the 1970s," *Providence Sunday Journal,* November 29, 1970, p. W-7.
210 "history according to Gloria": Stan Pottinger. Marie Wilson called it "the truth according to Gloria."
210 in a catatonic state: Sally Quinn, "Salon for Gloria Steinem—'American Folk Hero,' " *Washington Post,* October 10, 1969, p. B1.
210 "Gloria is the best thing": Clay Felker.
210 Quinn teased him: Jerald F. terHorst and Col. Ralph D. Albertazzie, *The Flying White House: The Story of Air Force One,* (New York: Coward, McCann and Geoghegan, 1979), p. 281. Incident also described in Nora Ephron, "The Making of a Sex Symbol," *McCall's,* November 1972, p. 86.
211 "That's one of Henry's old girlfriends": The story was widely circulated, including "Notes on People: Women's Caucus Strikes Back," *New York Times,* July 15, 1971, p. 34; "Never underestimate . . ." *Newsweek,* July 26, 1971, p. 29.
211 "the attractive author": "Headliners: No Girl Friend, She," *New York Times,* July 18, 1971.
211 "quite hurt by Miss Steinem's attempts": Ephron, *McCall's* p. 130. The following Kissinger quote is also from p. 130.
211 she did so in her "City Politic" column: GS, "What Nixon Doesn't Know About Women," *New York,* July 26, 1971, p. 9. Regarding the joke about "Henry's old girlfriend," she wrote that the assumption had to be based on the photograph of her with Kissinger, from which McGovern had been cropped. As she saw it, people always identified women in a sexual way, instead of assuming that her conversation with Kissinger might have "the same information-getting purpose for me as it did for any other reporter." In fact, it "made no more sense than photographing Peter Hamill next to Martha Mitchell at a professional gathering and turning *them* into a 'personal' item."
211 "If elected I will not serve": Sally Quinn, "A Roast Pig at the Benefit," *Washington Post,* February 4 1972, p. B3.

Chapter 20: Marching for Women's Rights

Principal interviews for this chapter were conducted with GS, Dolores Alexander, Rita Mae Brown, Jacqui Ceballos, Muriel Fox, and Sandra Hochman.

214 "a modern female priesthood": Henry Luce, speech at a dinner on the occasion of *Time*'s twentieth anniversary. Quoted in Curtis Prendergast, *The World of Time Inc.; The Intimate History of a Changing Enterprise 1960–1980* (New York: Atheneum, 1986), p. 448.
214 "irrelevant, unstimulating and demeaning": "Woman-Power," *Time,* March 30, 1970, p. 59. *Newsweek* ran "Woman Power," March 30, 1970, p. 61.
214 In 1970 all the national magazines: Lucy Komisar, "The New Feminism," *Saturday Review,* February 21, 1970. "Rebelling Women—The Reason," *U.S. News & World Report,* April 13, 1970. Sally Kempton, "Cutting Loose," *Esquire,* July 1970. Helen Dudar, "Women's Lib: The War on 'Sexism,' " *Newsweek,* March 23, 1970. "Who's Come a Long Way, Baby?" *Time,* August

31, 1970. Woman's Place: A Special Issue, *Atlantic,* March, 1970. Susan Brown-miller, " 'Sisterhood Is Powerful,' " *New York Times Magazine,* March 15, 1970.

214 "Get the bra-burning": Edward Glynn, "How to Unnerve Male Chauvinists," *America,* September 12, 1970, p. 144.

214 "an instant revolution": Deirdre Carmody, "General Strike by U.S. Women Urged to Mark 19th Amendment," *New York Times,* March 21, 1970, p. 12. The next quote is from the same article.

215 reported in meticulous detail: Charlotte Curtis, "Women's Liberation Gets Into the Long Island Swim," *New York Times,* August 10, 1970, p. 32.

215 Jill Johnston jumped: Johnston wrote of the incident in *Lesbian Nation,* "A lot of people said and wrote that I went into the pool to protest the discrimination against lesbians by feminists, but I wasn't nearly so organized. I was hot and drunk and I like empty swimming pools and I'm a very good swimmer so I like to show off my skills. I wouldn't entirely deny my contempt for the event and the maxi decolletage or radical chic uptown depravity of its sponsorship and the pressing need to subvert such charities (the party cost $25 a head) and the temptation to upset a few silly prudish old culture people who have a new reason for their lives in feminism. . . . The reason I took off my shirt after the second lap was that it interfered with my stroke," pp. 16–17.

216 "limping octogenarians": Judy Klemesrud, "It Was a Great Day for Women on the March," *New York Times,* August 30, 1970, p. IV–4. The next quote is from the same article.

216 the overt barriers to employment: GS, "Why We Need a Woman President in 1976," *Look,* January 13, 1970, p. 58.

216 In remarks picked up in newspapers: George Lardner Jr., "Women Press Rights on Hill," *Washington Post,* May 7, 1970, p. B12. Another on her testimony was Vera Glaser, " 'Masculine Mystique' Is Called the Villain," *Detroit Free Press,* May 7, 1970, p. 1–C.

217 she spoke at Vassar's commencement: Marylin Bender, "Beards, Peace Symbols and Daisies at Vassar's Commencement," *New York Times,* June 1, 1970, p. 31. The speech was excerpted in GS, " 'Women's Liberation' Aims to Free Men, Too," *Washington Post,* June 7, 1970.

217 "the Mao Tse-tung of Women's Liberation": *Time,* August 31, 1970, p. 16. The next quote is from the same page.

217 "not only a critical observer": Introduction to "What It Would Be Like if Women Win," *Time,* August 31, 1970, p. 22.

217 "Well, as your local neighborhood lesbian": Dolores Alexander.

217 lesbians had been as closeted: For a history of the gay/straight split, see Sidney Abbott and Barbara Love, *Sappho Was a Right-On Woman: A Liberated View of Lesbianism,* (1972). See also Rita Mae Brown, "Reflections of a Lavender Menace: Remembering When Lesbians Challenged the Women's Movement," *Ms.,* July/August 1995.

218 "Kate Millett herself": "Women's Lib: A Second Look," *Time,* December 14, 1970, p. 50. The caricature had illustrated Helen Lawrenson, "The Feminine Mistake," *Esquire,* January 1971, which began, "You might have to go back to the Children's Crusade 1212 A.D. to find as unfortunate and fatuous an attempt at manipulated hysteria as the Women's Liberation Movement."

219 "a society free from defining": Judy Klemesrud, "The Lesbian Issue and Women's Lib," *New York Times,* December 18, 1970, p. 47. The next two quotes are from the same article.

219 "Gloria has beautiful political instincts": Kate Millett.

220 "I've never had a sexual relationship": Susan Mitchell, *Icons, Saints and Divas* (1997), p. 132.
220 "Not because her name appears": Eugenia Sheppard, "Gloria Hallelujah," *Harper's Bazaar,* February 1970, p. 143.
220 "a junkyard yielded fragments": GS, "After too much moving . . . cheerful rooms to live in, a private place to work," *House & Garden,* July 1970.
221 "seragliesque": Judith Levine, "The Personal Is Personal," *Village Voice,* March 17, 1992, p. 66.

Chapter 21: Esquire's Cruel Attack

Principal interviews contributing to this chapter were conducted with Deena Goldstone, Leonard Levitt, Jane O'Reilly, and Walter Pincus.

222 "a Barnard philosophy instructor": Marylin Bender, "Books to Liberate Women," *New York Times,* March 8, 1970, pp. VII–10. The quotes in this and the following paragraph are also from this article.
224 "long straight hair": "Parting Shots: Gloria in excelsis: It's the Steinem look," *Life,* August 11, 1972, p. 66.
224 *Vogue, Redbook,* and *Esquire:* Liz Smith, "Coming of Age in America," *Vogue,* June 1971. Liz Smith, "Gloria Steinem, Writer and Social Critic, Talks about Sex, Politics and Marriage," *Redbook,* January 1972. Leonard Levitt, "SHE," *Esquire,* October 1971. Marilyn Mercer, "Gloria: The Unhidden Persuader," *McCall's,* January 1972. "Gloria Steinem: The New Woman," *Newsweek,* August 16, 1971. *New Woman,* a new magazine, put her on its February 1972 cover with the banner, "MS. Steinem: Her Life Style as a New Woman."
224 "Depression's Child Yearns to Be Rockette": Smith, *Vogue,* June 1971, p. 92. The next five quotes are from pp. 91, 150, and 158.
225 "What gets nearly everyone": *Newsweek,* August 16, 1971, p. 51. The next five quotes are from pp. 51 and 55.
225 "Gloria is the kind of friend": Jane O'Reilly in a 1971 interview with Lisa Whitman, *Newsweek* researcher. Quotes in this and the following paragraph are from the interview. Notes in GSP.
226 "When she got out of Smith": Betty Friedan in a 1971 interview with *Newsweek* researcher. The quotes in the next paragraph are from the interview. GSP.
226 "most effective spokeswoman": The Editors, "Woman of the Year: Gloria Steinem," *McCall's,* p. 67. The next quote is from the same page.
227 sputtering at the unfairness of it all: One of the funniest exchanges occurred in the letters to the *Toledo Blade.* Objecting to Gloria's descriptions of the " 'slums of East Toledo,' " of "whites beating up blacks for Saturday night recreation," and of "the community and her home as infested by rats," Ohio State representative Barney Quilter, 641 Woodville Road (Gloria's former street), wrote indignantly, "I have lived in this area all my life and do not recall this situation ever existing—nor do any residents who have lived in the community as long or longer" (*Toledo Blade,* February 9, 1972). He conceded only the possibility that a rat occasionally might have infiltrated. Two women wrote in protest. Sherry M. Woeller asked if Quilter's experience meant "no child who lived there could possible have been so bitten" (February 26, 1972). The other was Lillian Barnes Borton, who assured readers there had indeed been rats and that she remembered when Gloria had been bitten (March 1, 1972).
227 "East Toledo is 'Joe' country": *Newsweek,* p. 53.

228 "I want to call attention": Howard Gardner, *Leading Minds: An Anatomy of Leadership* (1994), p. 14. Howard Gardner's concept and discussion of leadership illuminated for me the value and unique nature of Gloria's contributions through her personal life as well as through her work.

229 "as if I were holding a balloon": Carole Ashkinaze, "Gloria Steinem," *Atlanta Constitution,* August 31, 1976, p. 3B.

230 "enigmatic *femme fatale*": Levitt, *Esquire,* p. 87. The next quote is from the same page.

231 "Gloria chooses her men": Ibid., p. 200. The next quote is from the same page.

232 "[W]as Gloria ever conscious": Ibid., p. 200. The next two quotes are from pp. 210, 214, 90, and 92.

233 "seamless": Leonard Levitt used the word in an interview with the author. Deena Goldstone, a screenwriter who worked with Gloria when she wrote the television movie of "A Bunny's Tale," used the same word. See chapter 30, p. 346.

233 "I've never worn": Suzy Farbman, "Meet Gloria Steinem: A Feminine Feminist," *Detroit News,* November 22, 1970, p. 5F. She made the remark frequently. Liz Smith quoted her in the June 1971 *Vogue* article, "Any woman who spends more than fifteen minutes getting herself ready to face the world is just screwing herself."

234 Even today, female politicians: For an interesting analysis of this subject, see Linda Witt, Karen M. Paget, and Glenna Matthews, *Running as a Woman: Gender and Power in American Politics* (1994). See also Jill Ker Conway, *True North* (1994), pp. 148–52, for a description of a similar phenomenon among earlier women of accomplishment.

Chapter 22: Battle of the Titans

Principal interviews contributing to this chapter were conducted with GS, Bella Abzug, Nikki Beare, Porter Bibb, Janet Bode, Evelyn Cunningham, Joanne Edgar, Nora Ephron, Brenda Feigen, Ronnie Feit, Muriel Fox, Elinor Guggenheimer, Betty Harris, Sandra Hochman, Koryne Horbal, Frank Mankiewicz, George McGovern, Martha McKay, Carol Merry-Shapiro, Letty Cottin Pogrebin, Catherine Samuels, Marlene Sanders, and Marlo Thomas.

236 "more like a pinprick": " 'Women's Political Caucus'—What It Is, What It Wants," *U. S. News & World Report,* August 16, 1971, p. 67.

237 "Gloria Steinem, [Brooklyn Congresswoman] Shirley Chisholm": Bella Abzug, edited by Mel Ziegler, *Bella! Ms. Abzug Goes to Washington* (1972), pp. 160, 164. The next quote is from p. 204.

238 "union women": GS, "The City Politic: What Nixon Doesn't Know About Women," *New York,* July 26, 1971, p. 8.

238 "If I get called 'gal' " : "Never underestimate . . . ," *Newsweek,* July 26, 1971, p. 29.

238 "Some people have asked": Transcript of "The Hand That Rocks the Ballot Box," a documentary on the National Women's Political Caucus and the rise of women in politics, reported and produced by Marlene Sanders for ABC News, aired July 26, 1972. Courtesy of Marlene Sanders.

239 "every woman whose abilities have been wasted": National Women's Political Caucus Statement of Purpose.

239 "sexist": "Women at Caucus Heckle M'Carthy," *New York Times,* July 12, 1971, p. 24.

239 "silver-haired smoothie": *Newsweek,* July 26, 1971, p. 29.
239 "feel proud of, and fascinated by": Benjamin M. Spock, "Male Chauvinist Spoke Recants—Well Almost," *New York Times Magazine,* September 12, 1971, p. 100. The next quote is from p. 98.
240 "Spock bowed his head humbly": *Newsweek,* July 26, 1971, p. 29.
240 "stood up and thundered in the tones of Jehovah": Ann Hulbert, "Dr. Spock's Baby," *New Yorker,* May 20, 1996, p. 89.
242 "best white male candidate": Christopher Lydon, "Gloria Steinem Aids McGovern's Cause," *New York Times,* February 12, 1972, p. 15. The next two quotes are from the same article.
244 "Yes, Betty Friedan was coming to Harlem," Chuck Andrews, "Politics in Black," undated clipping from unidentified newspaper, GSP. The next quote is from same article.
245 "At the hotel I found Gloria lobbying": Shirley MacLaine, "Women, the Convention and Brown Paper Bags," *New York Times Magazine,* July 30, 1972, p. 19.
245 "Not having the gut instinct on this issue": GS, "Coming of Age with McGovern: Notes from a Political Diary," *Ms.,* October 1972, p. 103.
246 "It is probably too easy": Nora Ephron, "Women," *Esquire,* November 1972, p. 10.
246 "do her kneecapping for her": Harriet Lyons in interview with author. Others said the same thing, though less colorfully.
246 "Betty Friedan, overstating in her own frenetic style": GS, "Coming of Age," *Ms.,* October 1972, p. 103.
247 "One might be amused by the high-octave span": Theodore H. White, *The Making of the President* (1973), pp. 222–23.
247 "If you let Barnum & Bailey interpret": GS, "Coming of Age," p. 104.
247 "We've all been through this": Lynn Sherr, "Democratic Women," *Saturday Review,* August 5, 1972, p. 7.
248 "Honey, if you'll fuck for a dime": Germaine Greer, "McGovern, The Big Tease," *Harper's,* October 1972, p. 63.
248 "the ladies" were angry: Sherr, p. 8. The next quote is also from p. 8.
248 "There was some emergency": Debra S. Davis, "The World According to Gloria," *Media People,* December undated, p. 78, GSP. Other quotes in the paragraph are from same article.
249 "There was enormous pressure to withdraw": GS "Coming of Age," p. 104.
249 "Female members of the press lobbied": Ephron, p. 18. The next four quotes are from pp. 16 and 18.

Chapter 23: Ozma and the Wicked Witch

252 "Betty's lips tighten": Nora Ephron, "Women," *Esquire,* November 1972, p. 10.
254 "I was that girl with all A's": Paul Wilkes, "Mother Superior to Women's Lib," *New York Times Magazine,* November 29, 1970, p. 140.
256 "the albatross [the radical feminists] would like to shed": Ibid., p. 150. The following three quotes are from the same page.
257 "never been a part of the organized": "Lib Rip-Off?" *Washington Post,* February 9, 1972. The next two quotes are from the same article.
257 "The truth is that [working in the women's movement]": Lawrence Van Gelder, "Notes on People," *New York Times,* February 9, 1972, p. 28.
257 "no feud between Gloria and me": Lawrence Van Gelder, "Notes on People," *New York Times,* February 11, 1972, p. 19. The next quote is from the same item.

257 "I can't understand why you need": "League of Voters Keeps Ban on Men," *New York Times,* May 7, 1972, p. 27. The quotes in the next paragraph are from the same article.

258 "female chauvinist boors": "People: Bi-Chauvinism: Pigs vs. Boors," *Washington Post,* July 19, 1972, p. B3.

258 "no woman would ever want to go to bed": Betty Friedan, "Beyond Women's Liberation," *McCall's* August 1972, p. 83. The next four quotes are from pp. 82 and 83.

259 "In a tone of cold, measured outrage": Ibid., p. 82.

259 "For myself, I can now admit," GS, "Sisterhood," *Ms.,* Spring 1972, p. 46. This essay appeared as the introductory article in *Ms.'s New York* insert, December 20, 1971, p. 46, and is reprinted in OAER, p. 127.

259 "It's a little easier for me": Barbara Gehrke and Jeanne Cordova, eds., "Gloria Steinem: " 'I'm Tired of Hearing Myself,' " *Lesbian Tide,* January 1974, p. 8.

Chapter 24: *Ms.:* A Magazine for Female Human Beings

Principal interviews contributing to this and the following chapter were conducted with GS, Maria Astaire, Cathleen Black, Ruth Bower, Susan Braudy, Susan Brownmiller, Patricia Carbine, Joanne Edgar, Ronnie Eldridge, Nora Ephron, Brenda Feigen, Clay Felker, Nina Finkelstein, Jane Galvin-Lewis, Katharine Graham, Betty Harris, T. George Harris, Seena Harris-Parker, Dorothy Pitman Hughes, Marlene Krauss, Phyllis Langer, Bob Levine, Suzanne Braun Levine, Harriet Lyons, Carol Merry-Shapiro, Alan Patricof, Mary Peacock, Letty Cottin Pogrebin, Phyllis Rosser, Catherine Samuels, William Sarnoff, Margaret Sloan-Hunter, Judith Stillinger, Arthur Tarlow, Ruth Whitney, and Ellen Willis.

261 "*Ms.* is a magazine": *Ms., A Statement of Purpose,* brochure soliciting charter subscribers.

261 "Steinem promises to 'refuse ads . . .' " : "For the Liberated Female," *Time,* December 20, 1971, p. 52.

268 "If you understood it": Katharine Graham.

268 "I recall her encouraging me": Katharine Graham, *Personal History* (1997), p. 422.

269 "I remember we sat around": GS, speech at her surprise sixtieth birthday party. Videotape of party, courtesy of GS.

272 "I always assumed *Ms.*": "*Ms.* Politics and Editing: An Interview," *Feminist Revolution* (1975, 1978), pp. 167–68.

Chapter 25: "They Looked at Us Like We Were Martians"

281 "Is hair coloring dangerous": Sharon Krause, "The Dye is Cast," *Ms.,* October 1976, p. 19.

282 "openly hostile, defensive, male-dominated": James Warren, "Newspapers choose a savvy new leader," *Chicago Tribune,* May 26, 1991, *Womanews,* p. 1.

282 "They looked at us like": Cathleen Black.

285 "I confess—maybe I shouldn't": Susan Edmiston, "How to Say What You Mean—And Get What You Want," *Redbook,* March 1976, p. 178.

286 "*Ms.* would be rated 'X' " : Scott Winokur, "*Ms.:* off-color but not off limits," *San Francisco Examiner,* June 27, 1980, p. 1. Quotes in this and the following paragraph are from the same article.

Chapter 26: The Redstockings, Gloria, and the CIA

Principal interviews contributing to this chapter were conducted with GS, Rosalyn Baxandall, Rita Mae Brown, Phyllis Chesler, Cindy Cisler, Bob Clampitt, Jo Freeman, Aileen Hernández, Suzanne Braun Levine, Karen Paget, Colette Price, Eugene Theroux, and Ellen Willis.

291 In 1967 a New Left magazine called *Ramparts* revealed: Sol Stern, "NSA/CIA," *Ramparts,* March 1967, p. 29.

291 "I'm fine. I'll take the heat." George Abrams told me this anecdote twice. GS says "take the heat" is not a phrase she would use. She also notes that she answered whatever queries came her way as an individual.

292 "Far from being shocked": "C.I.A. Subsidized Festival Trips," *New York Times,* February 21, 1967, p. 33.

292 "Miss Steinem said yesterday that she had worked": Robert G. Kaiser, "Work of CIA With Youths at Festivals Is Defended," *Washington Post,* February 18, 1967. The next quote is from the same article.

292 "In my experience the Agency was completely different": Nancy L. Ross, "For Talented, Youthful Breed: Writer's Life Can Be Glorious and Beautiful," *Washington Post,* December 3, 1967, p. K7.

293 a sixteen-page tabloid-style press release: "Redstockings Discloses Gloria Steinem's CIA Cover-Up," May 9, 1975. Quotes in this and following paragraphs, through "because of its pressing importance" on p. 295, are also from the press release.

295 "It is necessary that people": Redstockings based this allegation on the foundation's report on the Vienna festival. Far from a secret report to the CIA, it was a publication intended for the public.

296 In fairness to Redstockings: For more information about governmental spying on U.S. citizens, see Donner; *Final Report of the Senate;* Kessler; Perkus; and Powers.

296 In addition to the genuine existence of outside agitators: For a discussion of the shift in radical feminist theory in the mid-1970s, see Echols, and Hester Eisenstein, *Contemporary Feminist Thought* (1983), upon which this account is based.

297 "With the Watergate revelations": "Betty Friedan Fears C.I.A. Movement Role," *New York Times,* June 23, 1975, p. 23.

298 Stone not only distributed the release: Account of Ingrid Stone's experience is based on Ingrid Hedley Stone, "I Wanted to Ask Gloria Steinem a Question," *Majority Report,* August 9, 1975, p. 3.

298 Arriving to save the feminist summer school: This account is based on "Sagaris: What Ever Happened and Why?" *Majority Report,* September 6, 1975, p. 7, and information from Aileen Hernández and GS. See also Janis Kelly and Fran Moira, "News Analysis: Sagaris: a case of mistaken identity (a school, not a community," *off our backs,* November 1975, p. 14.

300 "I had mixed feelings": Ellen Willis, *No More Nice Girls: Countercultural Essays* (1992), p. 150. Quote is from a footnote to her 1984 essay, "Radical Feminism and Feminist Radicalism," originally published in Sayres, et. al., eds., *The 60s Without Apology,* p. 118.

301 "They look on me as a traitor": William L. Kahrl, "Yet Time and change shall naught prevail . . . To Break the friendships formed at . . . ," *New Journal,* February 9, 1969.

302 "some of the American participation": GS, "Dear Sisters of the Feminist Press," *Women's Community Journal,* September 1975, p. 4. The quotes in the next paragraph are also from the letter.

302 "dropped all but advisory work": GS to Jean Kennedy, Talent Associates, May 29, 1964, GSP. The fact that Gloria disputes the prior existence of the board, in any form, has already been noted. In connection with this letter, Gloria points out that "she leaves her name on organizations she has helped to found," long after she has finished playing an active role in them.

302 "I was co-director through the 1959 Vienna Festival": Steinem, "Dear Sisters," p. 5. Quotes in the following three paragraphs are also from p. 5.

304 balanced but critical: Jo Freeman.

305 "innuendos": Redstockings, "Chronology of Some Events Surrounding the Random House Publication of *Feminist Revolution*." The chronology is one of the documents Redstockings sends to accompany the material excised from the Random House edition of *Feminist Revolution*.

305 "They're the Teamsters": Redstockings, "Fact Sheet." The fact sheet accompanies the chronology.

306 an article for the *Village Voice* recounting the history: Nancy Borman, "Random Action: Whatever Happened to 'Feminist Revolution'?", *Village Voice*, May 21, 1979, p. 107.

Chapter 27: The Ms. Foundation: The Cutting Edge

Principal interviews contributing to this chapter were conducted with GS, Sam Antupit, Brenda Brimmer, Julie Burton, Pat Carbine, Susan Dickler, Joanne Edgar, Aileen Hernández, Koryne Horbal, Diana James, Kristina Kiehl, Letty Cottin Pogrebin, Jeri Rasmussen, Amy Richards, Julia Scott, Marlo Thomas, and Marie Wilson.

314 "Executives with glass ceilings": Tamar Levin, "On Daughters-at-Work Day, Some Are Including Sons," *New York Times*, April 25, 1996, p. B11. Savitt's entire quote was, "It bothers me when companies where all the high officers are men say they're making it Take Our Children Day because they don't want to discriminate against boys. Executives with glass ceilings shouldn't throw stones. I think people are afraid to stand up for girls, or they think some affirmative-action bogyman's going to get them."

Chapter 28: Gloria's Little Marriages

Principal interviews contributing to this chapter were conducted with GS, Peter Braestrup, Blair Chotzinoff, Brenda Feigen, David MacIsaac, Letty Cottin Pogrebin, Stan Pottinger, and Frank Thomas.

319 "When we first met": RFW, p. 279. The next quote is from p. 280.

320 "We created a world": GS.

321 "we each began": RFW, p. 282. The next quote is from p. 281.

326 "Any male writer my age": " 'I'm Not Tough,' Says Gloria Steinem," *Oakland Tribune*, November 29, 1977, p. 14.

326 "a moving willow tree": Stanley Pottinger, *The Fourth Procedure* (1995), p. 37. The next two quotes are from pp. 38 and 39.

327 "If you want to understand": GS, speech "The Feminist Revolution," American Association of Advertising Agencies, Central Region annual meeting, Chicago, 1973.

Chapter 29: Ruth's Song

Principal interviews contributing to this chapter were conducted with GS, SSP, Jennifer Josephy, Suzanne Braun Levine, Letty Cottin Pogrebin, and Dick Seaver.

329 the Republican Party's strategy: See Tanya Melich, *The Republican War Against Women: An Insider's Report from Behind the Lines* (1996).

329 At the urging of National Women's Party: Background on the Equal Rights Amendment is based on Sharon Whitney, *The Equal Rights Amendment: The History and the Movement* (1984).

332 "Pity takes distance": OAER, p. 152.

332 "I'd been on the *Toledo Blade*": Winzola McLendon, "Gloria Steinem's Mother Wasn't All That Liberated," *New York Times,* May 2, 1972, p. 38.

332 "I do occasionally bask": Diana McLellan, "Liberated women . . . A Long Steinem Line," *Sunday Star,* Washington, D.C., February 13, 1972, p. F5. Accompanying this article was a photograph of Ruth surrounded by five of Sue's children. On the back of the clipping Ruth jokingly wrote that though she had not heard from Miss America host Bert Parks, she did have a part-time job in October, from ten to midnight, on a broom. GSP.

334 "many of us are still overcoming": OAER, p. 143. The next five quotes are from pp. 239, 240, 382, and 402–403.

336 "[I]t comes to the philosophy": Kathleen Hendrix, "Steinem, Nearing 50, at last Opens Book on Her Personal Life," *Los Angeles Times,* December 4, 1983, p. 33.

336 "This is a problematic statement": Angela Carter, "Gloria Steinem: From Miss to *Ms.*," *Washington Post Book World,* October 9, 1983, p. 2.

337 Gloria explicitly rejected suggestions: During an appearance on the *Phil Donahue Show,* for example, a man in the audience noted that she seemed to blame "chauvinistic society" for her mother's difficulties and asked how Gloria could be sure her mother would not have had problems anyway. He also asked if there might not have been some intrinsic cause for them and wondered if Gloria worried about that. Gloria responded that she did not think she had inherited any such thing, but rather drew strength from surviving, and she wondered what would happen to a man who had been asked to give up his name and his work and be completely isolated. In a subsequent interview she referred to "the man on the Donahue show who asked if I feared this illness was hereditary. He didn't mean if I thought patriarchy was hereditary, so that worried me because I haven't said what I meant to say." Ruth Mugalian, "Steinem Says," *Herald Suburban Living,* October 10, 1983, p. 2.

337 "I know I will spend": OAER, pp. 162, 164, 165.

338 "In my first days of activism": Ibid., p. 409.

Chapter 30: Of Bubble Baths and Birthdays

Principal interviews contributing to this chapter were conducted with GS, Phyllis Chesler, Deena Goldstone, Suzanne Braun Levine, Letty Cottin Pogrebin, and Marlo Thomas.

339 Although the October 21, 1983, article offered: GS, "An Unsinkable Feminist Sails into her 50th Year Jubilant About Her First Best Seller," *People,* October 21, 1983, p. 185.

340 "sometimes people confuse feminists with nuns": "Good Company," transcript, KSTP-TV ABC, Minneapolis, September 11, 1984. The next two quotes are from this interview.

340 "Has Gloria 'Bubbles' Steinem's mind turned to cheese?": Jane Myers, *Ann Arbor News,* December 18, 1983, p. C19.

343 "quite upset because she feels": Joyce Wadler, "The Feminist At 50," *Washington Post,* May 24, 1984, p. D9.

343 "I don't like New York very well": Chuck Offenburger, "Honoring Ms. Steinem," *Des Moines Register,* June 7, 1984.

343 Phil Donahue took a microphone: The account of the party is based on interviews, press coverage, and an unedited videotape, courtesy of GS.

344 "with her signature blond-streaked mane": Lynn Langway, with Nancy Cooper, Lucy Howard, and Gloria Borger, "Steinem at 50: Gloria in Excelsis," *Newsweek,* June 4, 1984, p. 27.

344 "Tan, bony, a trifle fragile-looking": Michelle Green, "Still a Feminist Fatale, Gloria Steinem Crashes Through the Big Five-Oh Barrier with a Star-Studded Tonic Boom," *People,* June 11, 1984, p. 48.

345 "It was a wonderful party": Dorothy Pitman Hughes to GS, letter May 28, 1984. GSP.

345 "You can perpetuate": Stephen Farber, " 'Bunny's Tale' Depicts Steinem's Playboy Days," *New York Times,* December 11, 1984, p. C25.

346 "Our concern was . . . commercial concern": Marilynn Preston, " 'A Bunny's Tale': Christie Hefner Thinks It's a Bust," *Chicago Tribune,* February 25, 1985, p. T–1.

Chapter 31: The Wrong Man

Principal interviews contributing to this chapter were conducted with GS, Koryne Horbal, Bob Levine, Suzanne Braun Levine, Letty Cottin Pogrebin, Caron Smith, Mort Zuckerman (who has not been quoted directly, at his request), and three sources who wished to remain anonymous.

348 By 1981, the median age: Figures are from a 1981 Simmons Survey, cited in Catherine Whitney, "Ms. At 10 Years: The Voice of Women in a Changing Decade," *Magazine & Bookseller,* May 1982, p. 59.

350 "a liar and a cheat": Robert Manning, *The Swamp Root Chronicle: Adventures in the Word Trade* (1979), p. 397. The next quote is from the same page.

351 "The doctor didn't say you *couldn't*": Betty Rollin, *First You Cry* (1976), p. 193.

352 "Being seen around together": Liz Smith, *New York Daily News,* June 27, 1984.

352 "That was some gemütlich party": Liz Smith, *New York Daily News,* April 23, 1985.

352 she was obsessed with him: Bella Abzug.

353 "Some say he": Jeanie Kasindorf, "Citizen Mort," New York, October 5, 1992, p. 46.

353 "It's sad because he *dreams* of it": Suzanna Andrews, "Mort's Retort," *Mirabella,* June 1992, p. 81.

353 "Through opinionated phrases": "Editors' Note," *New York Times,* August 7, 1985. The note was in response to Jane Perlez, "Mortimer Zuckerman—a Developer With a Zest for High-Stakes Dealing," *New York Times,* August 5, 1985.

358 "About the only thing Zuckerman": Nancy J. Perry, "Fortune People: Sic Transit Gloria Mundi," *Fortune,* August 31, 1987, p. 92.

Chapter 32: Marilyn Monroe: A Feminist Morality Tale

Principal interviews contributing to this chapter were conducted with GS, George Barris, Kristen Golden, Koryne Horbal, Kristina Kiehl, Suzanne Braun Levine, and Carla Morgenstern.

360 "I think women can learn from her": David Dale, "Gloria Steinem on Marilyn, Men, the Movement and *Ms.*," Unnamed, undated clipping from Sydney, Australia newspaper, GSP.
360 "help explain Marilyn as an individual": GS, *Marilyn: Norma Jeane* (1986), p. 8.
360 we "write what we need to know": RFW, p. 6.
360 "the child we used to be": GS, *Marilyn*, p. 76. The following six quotes are from pp. 75–76, 140, 141, 74, 64, and 86.
361 "The childhood of persons": W. Hugh Missildine, *Your Inner Child of the Past* (New York: Simon & Schuster, 1963). Quoted in GS, *Marilyn*, p. 77.
361 "I can't stand [Gloria]": Florence King, "Steinem Seeks the Real Marilyn Inside the Body," *San Jose Mercury News, Arts & Books*, p. 21. The next quote is from the same review.
363 "an experienced travel guide": RFW, pp. 157–58.
364 "Do we want to make the change": RFW, pp. 238–39. The next three quotes are from the same page.

Chapter 33: Ms. *Ms.*

Principal interviews contributing to this chapter were conducted with GS, Sam Antupit, Ruth Bower, Pat Carbine, Marcia Gillespie, Kristen Golden, A. M. Rosenthal, and Arthur Tarlow.

369 "had not passed sufficiently into the language": Dan Jacobson, UPI, June 19, 1986. The next quote is from the same dispatch. The following two quotes are from A. M. Rosenthal interview with the author.
371 "Ms. Steinem became a kind of brand-label": A. M. Rosenthal, "On My Mind: Ms. Steinem Carries On," *New York Times*, October 6, 1987.
373 "I wish I had six magazines like *Ms.*": Deirdre Carmody, "Power to the Readers: *Ms.* Thrives Without Ads," *New York Times*, July 22, 1991, p. D6.
373 "It's a nightmare from hell": Jay Stowe, "Off the Record," *New York Observer*, February 19, 1996.

Chapter 34: Revolution From Within: A Book of Self-Esteem

Principal interviews contributing to this chapter were conducted with GS, Kristen Golden, Diana James, Jennifer Josephy, Bob Levine, Suzanne Braun Levine, Letty Cottin Pogrebin, Beth Rashbaum, and Amy Richards.

376 *"What is so sacred about a long"*: OAER, p. 24.
377 "She said, 'If I didn't have it' ": Anecdote is from Kristen Golden. Shortly afterward, during an interview with Gloria, I mentioned her kindness in helping Kristen. Gloria, responded, "I did?" Reminded of the circumstances, she commented, "Oh yes. Her father was behaving very badly." Kristen and her father reconciled eight years later.
377 "Well, I guess the only thing": Diana James.
378 "I spent months researching and interviewing": RFW, p. 5.
382 The recovery movement is part: Background on the self-help movement and the development of the recovery movement is based on Wendy Kaminer, *I'm Dysfunctional, You're Dysfunctional*, pp. 45–67.
383 "our culture dislikes and fears angry women": Carol Tavris, *The Mismeasure of Woman* (1992), p. 203. Harriet Lerner quoted by Tavris on the same page. The Lerner quote is from an interview with Tavris and was originally quoted in Carol Tavris, "Do Codependency Theories Explain Women's Unhappiness—Or Exploit Their Insecurities?" *Vogue*, December 1989, pp. 220–26.

383 "with little mention of the external structures," RFW, p. 3–4. The following
   quote is from p. 8.
384 "Trying to approach self-esteem": Ibid., p. 8. The next three quotes are from
   pp. 9 and 16.
386 "[O]nce we learn to stop abusing ourselves": Elayne Rapping, *The Culture of
   Recovery: Making Sense of the Self-Help Movement in Women's Lives* (1996),
   p. 177.
387 "I'm still trying to thread a path": RFW, p. 241. The quotes in the next two
   paragraphs are from pp. 232–33, 241, and 247.

Chapter 35: Rigor Mort

Principal interviews contributing to this chapter were conducted with Leslie
Bennetts, Jennifer Josephy, Liz Smith, Mort Zuckerman, and two sources who
wished to remain anonymous. Additional information was provided by GS.

389 "If . . . we think about episodes": RFW, p. 262.
390 "I was just so . . . *tired*": Ibid., p. 264. Quotes in this and the following five
   paragraphs are from pp. 264–67.
391 "In many ways, this is Steinem's first book": Leslie Bennetts, "Deconstructing
   Gloria," *Vanity Fair,* January 1992, p. 90. The next six quotes are from this
   article.
392 "While the tone of her account": Ibid., p. 138. The next quote is from the
   same article.
392 "Not only did Zuckerman": Liz Smith, "A Contretemps Over Mort," *New
   York Newsday,* December 17, 1991. The quotes in the next paragraph are from
   the same column.
393 "rehang all this dirty linen": Liz Smith, *New York Newsday,* December 18,
   1991. Quotes in this and the next three paragraphs are from the same column.
394 "Dating for dollars": Richard Johnson, *New York Daily News,* December 19,
   1991.
394 "what kind of feminist doctrine": Richard Johnson with Kimberley Ryan,
   "Page Six," *New York Post,* February 8, 1994.
395 "body of romantic writing": Michael M. Thomas, "The Midas Watch: Year of
   Discontent Ends None too Soon," *New York Observer,* December 30, 1991–
   January 6, 1992, p. 16.
395 "You're an admired feminist": Clare McHugh, "Steinem, Zuckerman Duke It
   Out in Celebrity Dating Game Epilogue," *New York Observer,* p. 1. Quotes in
   the next three paragraphs are from the same article.
396 "Why should I have to call": Liz Smith, "The Truth About Mort," *New York
   Newsday,* January 12, 1992., p. 8. Quotes in following paragraph are from the
   same column.
396 "journalistic food chain": Michael M. Thomas, "The Midas Watch: Smith
   Re-enters War Between the Sexes," *New York Observer,* January 20, 1992,
   p. 1. Quotes in this and the following four paragraphs are from the same
   column.
397 "Okay, some of this is funny now": RFW, p. 329.
398 "In the context of questions": GS, "Ms. Understanding," letter to the editor,
   Vanity Fair, March 1992, p. 46. This quote is part of the portion *Vanity Fair* ran.
   A copy of the entire letter was provided to the author by GS.
398 "I always thought": GS, "No Facts, No Fair," letter to the editor of the *New
   York Observer,* January 27, 1992. Quotes in the following paragraph are from
   the same letter.

399 "My best guess is that this was the emotional truth": McHugh, p. 18.

399 "Gloria Steinem's letter in the *Observer*": Leslie Bennetts, "All's Fair," letter to the editor of the *New York Observer*, February 3, 1992. Quotes in this and the following four paragraphs are from the same letter.

400 Watching as the widely-beloved, sweetly reasonable Gloria: The source of this anecdote, who talked only on the condition of anonymity, was present.

402 "Despite eloquent passages": *Publishers Weekly*, November 29, 1991, p. 34.

402 "squishy exercise in feeling better": Laura Shapiro, "Little Gloria, Happy at Last," *Newsweek*, January 13, 192, p. 64. Quotes in this and the following paragraph are from the same review.

402 "one of the world's most interesting women,": Margaret Carlson, "Even Feminists Get the Blues," *Time*, January 20, 1992, p. 57.

402 "Those who like their icons to stay on pedestals": Deirdre English, "She's Her Weakness Now," *New York Times Book Review*, February 2, 1992, p. VII-13.

403 *Spy* magazine reported: Susan Mitchell, "Elizabeth Cady Stanton, We Hardly Knew Ye," *Spy*, July/August 1992, p. 26.

403 "all head and no heart": GS.

403 "they obscured the book's content": RFW, p. 329. The following quote is from pp. 329–30.

404 "with ordinary readers": Joelle Attinger, "Steinem: Tying Politics to the Personal," *Time*, March 9, 1992, p. 55. The next quote is from the same page.

404 "I was doing book readings": RFW, p. 332. The quotes in the rest of the chapter are from pp. 332–34.

Chapter 36: Freud, Incest, and Satanic Abuse

Principal interviews contributing to this chapter were conducted with GS, Phyllis Chesler, Marc Fisher, Denise Gooch, Diana James, Bob Levine, Suzanne Braun Levine, Sheila Nevins, and Amy Richards. I am also grateful to the psychologists participating in the roundtable discussion, "Delayed Memories of Childhood Sexual Abuse—Current Controversies," at the 1995 American Psychological Association's annual convention. By allowing me to sit in on the discussion, they afforded me a better understanding of the problems clinicians face in grappling with this complicated issue.

407 "nothing-to-lose, take-no-shit older woman": MBW, p. 280. The next four quotes are from pp. 283, 281, and 13.

409 "You don't understand": MBW, p. 24. The next quote is from the same page.

409 "In convincing himself that the three traits": Kate Millett, *Sexual Politics* (1969), p. 197.

410 "Our problem isn't Freud": MBW, pp. 30–31.

410 "the Freudian myth": MBW, p. 31. The next quote is from the same page.

410 Furthermore, she believes that he himself was probably sexually abused: See MBW, pp. 67–73. Discussing her essay in an interview with Charlie Rose, she said, "He accuses his father of sexual abuse and, you know, it's likely that it happened to him if it happened to his siblings. And he also accuses a nurse, who was his nurse until he was about three." May 11, 1994, transcript, "Charlie Rose."

411 "have the attitude of 'he was a genius, *but*' ": Marc Fisher, "Under Attack, Library Delays Freud Exhibit," *Washington Post*, December 5, 1995, p. A10. The next quote is from the same page.

413 "Marx is a great example of the means-and-ends argument": Michael Krasny, "The Good Life," *Mother Jones*, May/June 1995, p. 33.

413 "Renoir's marzipan women": Ina Pasch, "Steinem hails democracy in art with 'Presswork,' " *Wisconsin State Journal,* June 24, 1992. Quotes in this and the following paragraph are from the same article.

415 "If you think you were abused": Ellen Bass and Laura David, *The Courage to Heal,* p. 15.

415 "epidemic"; "many, if not most, incest survivors": E. Sue Blume, *Secret Survivorship,* p. xiii. The other quotes in the paragraph are from promotional copy in the book.

416 Skeptics contend that in many cases: See, for example, Carol Tavris, "Beware the Incest-Survivor Machine," *New York Times Book Review,* January 3, VII-1.

416 "some abuse is not even physical": Bass and Davis, p. 25. The next quote is from p. 26.

417 The double standard is so extreme: For examples and a discussion of this issue, see Armstrong; Chesler, 1986; Takas; and H. Joan Pennington, "The Hardest Case: Custody and Incest," The National Center for Protective Parents, Inc. (February, 1993).

418 Multiple personality disorder has even been called "chic": Joannie M. Schrof, "Questioning Sybil," *U.S. News & World Report,* January 27, 1997, p. 66.

418 "As is now known, MPD is almost always": RFW, p. 317.

419 "thinly disguised protest movements": I. M. Lewis, *Ecstatic Religions,* (New York: Routledge, 1989). Quoted in Debbie Nathan, "Dividing to Conquer? Women, Men, and the Making of Multiple Personality Disorder," *Social Text,* Fall 1994, p. 86. See also in the same issue, Janice Haaken, "Sexual Abuse, Recovered Memory, and Therapeutic Practice: A Feminist Psychoanalytic Perspective." My account of multiple personality disorder is based on Nathan's article and her book, with Michael Snedecker, *Satan's Silence* (1995).

420 "Feminist attention to the satanic imprisonment": Nathan, 1994, p. 103.

421 The McMartin Preschool, in Manhattan Beach: The account of the McMartin case is based on Armstrong; John Earl, "The Dark Truth About the 'Dark Tunnels of McMartin," *Issues in Child Abuse Accusations,* Spring 1995; Nat Hentoff, "Distorted Journalism," *Village Voice,* December 17, 1996; Debbie Nathan, "McMartin Preschool Tunnel Claims: Evidence of a Hoax," *FMS Newsletter,* as reproduced with author's permission from PsyLaw (Internet service), PsyLaw-L@utepa; Nathan and Snedecker, 1995; E. Gary Stickel, Ph.D., *Archaeological Investigations of the McMartin Preschool Site, Manhattan Beach, California, 1993;* Dr. E. G. Stickel and J. Gauley, "McMartin Tunnel Excavation" (videotape of presentation of tunnel findings, courtesy of GS); David Stout, "Virginia McMartin Dies at 88; Figure in Case on Child Abuse," *New York Times,* December 19, 1995, p. B14; and Roland C. Summit, "The Dark Tunnels of McMartin," *The Journal of Psychohistory* 21 (4) Spring 1994.

Chapter 37: The Kindness of Strangers

Interviews contributing to this chapter include those conducted with GS, Bella Abzug, Rebecca Adamson, Ruth Bower, Esther (E. M.) Broner, Marilyn French, Rosilyn Heller, Koryne Horbal, Diana James, Carol Jenkins, Andrea Johnston, Suzanne Braun Levine, Wilma Mankiller, Jane O'Reilly, Letty Cottin Pogrebin, Amy Richards, Marlo Thomas, and Marie Wilson.

425 "the country's No. 1 liberated woman": Judy Klemesrud, "And Now, a Word from Our Leader," *The New Fashions of The New York Times,* March 4, 1973, p. 84. Quotes in this and the following paragraph are from the same article.

425 "a serious essay": GS, "Ms. understanding," letter to the editor, *New York Times Magazine,* April 8, 1973, p. VI–11. Quotes in this and the following paragraph are from the same letter.

426 "Ms. Steinem sent to the *Times*": Judy Klemesrud, "Judy Klemesrud replies" response to the letter, *New York Times Magazine,* April 8, 1973.

426 "I thought interior designers": GS, "Ms. Steinem on the Home Front," *House & Garden,* October 1990, p. 180. Herb Sargent's quote is from p. 183.

426 wealthy socialist: Sarah Bryan Miller, "Why I Quit Now," *Wall Street Journal,* August 10, 1995, p. A8.

428 "Alice Walker is someone in my life": GS to group of girls interviewing her at Merrill Lynch during an appearance for Take Our Daughters to Work Day, April 27, 1995.

429 "How old are you?": Rebecca Adamson.

430 "Oh. Like the corporate structure": Rebecca Adamson. The account of the safari and the next quote are also from Rebecca Adamson.

430 "a human rainforest": GS, speech at a reception and briefing in honor of John Hardbattle, the spokesperson for the N/oakhwe people, December 7, 1995.

432 "Thanks, Gloria and Andrea": Andrea Johnston.

433 "No meaningful voice": Linda Lovelace with Mike McGrady, *Out of Bondage* (1986), p. 151.

433 a January 7 op-ed article: GS, "Hollywood Cleans Up *Hustler,"* *New York Times,* January 7, 1997, p. 17.

434 "I can't mate in captivity": Gloria credits the quip to stand-up comic Adrianne Tolsch.

434 "more likely to be killed": Eloise Salholtz, "Marriage Crunches: If You're a Single Woman, Here Are Your Chances of Getting Married," *Newsweek,* June 2, 1986, p. 55. Quoted in Susan Faludi, *Backlash: The Undeclared War Against American Women* (1991), p. 100.

437 "It was Gloria": Bella Abzug, speech, Veteran Feminists of America dinner, December 13, 1995. She also told the story at Gloria's surprise sixtieth birthday party in 1994.

437 The first time Wilma and Gloria met: Anecdote from Wilma Mankiller.

438 As 1994 and Gloria's sixtieth birthday: Account of the party is based on interviews with Letty Cottin Pogrebin and Marlo Thomas and a videotape of the party, courtesy of GS.

Chapter 38: Gloria's Talents and Demons

Principal interviews contributing to this chapter were conducted with GS, Bella Abzug, Patricia Carbine, Tom Fiedler, Suzanne Braun Levine, Stan Pottinger, and Marie Wilson.

440 seventy-two-year-old Angela LaFrieda: Anecdote is from Tom Fiedler, "Steinem rallies the troops at Dade caucus," *The Herald,* June 1, 1996, p. 2B, and from Tom Fiedler.

441 "Hosed. Big News About Nylons": *New York Times Magazine,* April 14, 1996, p. 135.

442 "Like his predecessors": Maurice Isserman, "Michael Harrington and the Debs-Thomas Tradition," Dissent, Fall 1996, p. 108.

443 "The world inside my house": GS, speech, Veteran Feminists of America dinner, December 13, 1995.

444 "Even if we're no longer trying": MBW, p. 259.

Select Bibliography

Abbott, Sidney, and Barbara Love. *Sappho Was a Right-On Woman: A Liberated View of Lesbianism*. New York: Stein & Day, 1972.

Abzug, Bella S. *Bella! Ms. Abzug Goes to Washington*. Edited by Mel Ziegler. New York: Saturday Review Press, 1972.

_____ with Mim Kelber. *Gender Gap: Bella Abzug's Guide to Political Power for American Women*. Boston: Houghton Mifflin, 1984.

Albert, Judith Clavir, and Stewart Edward Albert, eds. *The Sixties Papers: Documents of a Rebellious Decade*. New York: Praeger, 1984.

Alcott, Louisa May. *Works of Louisa May Alcott*. Edited by Claire Booss. New York: Avenel Books, 1982.

_____. *Little Women*. New York: Grosset & Dunlap, 1947.

Armstrong, Louise. *Rocking the Cradle of Sexual Politics: What Happened When Women Said Incest*. Reading, Pa.: Addison-Wesley, 1994.

Bass, Ellen, and Laura Davis. *The Courage to Heal: A Guide for Women Survivors of Child Sexual Abuse*. New York: HarperPerennial, 1994.

Beauvoir, Simone de. *The Second Sex*. Translated and edited by H. M. Parshley. Introduction by Deirdre Bair. New York: Vintage Books, 1989.

Bedell, Madelon. *The Alcotts: The Biography of a Family*. New York: Clarkson N. Potter, 1980.

Bender, Marylin. *The Beautiful People*. New York: Coward-McCann, 1967.

Bird, Caroline. *Born Female: The High Cost of Keeping Women Down*. New York: David McKay, 1968.

Bird, Kai. *The Chairman: John J. McCloy, The Making of the American Establishment*. New York: Simon & Schuster, 1992.

Blume, E. Sue. *Secret Survivors: Uncovering Incest and Its Aftereffects in Women*. New York: John Wiley & Sons, 1990.

Bolen, Jean Shinoda. *Goddesses in Everywoman: A New Psychology of Women*. Foreword by Gloria Steinem. New York: Harper Colophon, 1985.

Braudy, Leo. *The Frenzy of Renown: Fame and Its History*. New York: Oxford University Press, 1986.

Broner, E. M. *The Telling*. San Francisco: Harper San Francisco, 1993.

Brownmiller, Susan. *Against Our Will: Men, Women and Rape*. New York: Simon & Schuster, 1975.

Burns, James MacGregor. *Leadership*. New York: Harper & Row, 1978.

Carabillo, Toni; Judith Meuli; and June Bundy Csida. *Feminist Chronicles, 1953–1993*. Los Angeles: Women's Graphics, 1993.

Chafe, William H. *The Unfinished Journey: America Since World War II*. New York: Oxford University Press, 1986.

_____. *Never Stop Running: Allard Lowenstein and the Struggle to Save American Liberalism*. New York: Basic Books, 1993.

Chesler, Phyllis. *Women and Madness*. New York: Harcourt Brace Jovanovich, 1989.

_____. *Mothers on Trial: The Battle for Children and Custody*. New York: McGraw-Hill, 1986.

Clarke, Gerald. *Capote: A Biography*. New York: Simon & Schuster, 1988.

Cohen, Marcia. *The Sisterhood: The True Story of the Women Who Changed the World*. New York: Simon & Schuster, 1988.

Conway, Jill Ker. *True North: A Memoir*. New York: Alfred A. Knopf, 1994.

Cook, Blanche Wiesen. *The Declassified Eisenhower: A Divided Legacy*. Garden City, NY: Doubleday, 1981.

Cott, Nancy F. *The Grounding of Modern Feminism*. New Haven: Yale University Press, 1987.

Cranston, Sylvia. *HPB: The Extraordinary Life and Influence of Helena Blavatsky, Founder of the Modern Theosophical Movement*. New York: G. P. Putnam's Sons, 1993.

Cummings, Bernice, and Victoria Schuck. *Women Organizing: An Anthology*. Metuchen, N.J.: Scarecrow Press, 1979.

Cummings, Richard. *The Pied Piper: Allard Lowenstein and the Liberal Dream*. New York: Grove Press, 1985.

Donner, Frank J. *The Age of Surveillance: The Aims and Methods of the American Political Intelligence System*. New York: Alfred A. Knopf, 1980.

Dworkin, Andrea. *Letters From a War Zone*. Brooklyn: Lawrence Hill Books, 1993.

Echols, Alice. *Daring to Be Bad: Radical Feminism in America 1967–1975*. Foreword by Ellen Willis. Minneapolis: University of Minnesota Press, 1989.

Eisenstein, Hester. *Contemporary Feminist Thought*. Boston: G. K. Hall, 1983.

Evans, Sara. *Personal Politics: The Roots of Women's Liberation in the Civil Rights Movement and the New Left*. New York: Vintage Books, 1980.

Faludi, Susan. *Backlash: The Undeclared War Against American Women*. New York: Crown, 1991.

Firestone, Shulamith. *The Dialectic of Sex: The Case for Feminist Revolution*. New York: Bantam Books, 1970.

Flaherty, Joe. *Managing Mailer*. New York: Coward-McCann, 1970.

Freeman, Jo. *The Politics of Women's Liberation*. New York: Longman, 1975.

Friedan, Betty. *The Feminine Mystique*. New York: Laurel, 1983.

_____. *It Changed My Life*. New York: Laurel, 1991.

Gardner, Howard, with Emma Laskin. *Leading Minds: An Anatomy of Leadership*. New York: Basic Books, 1995.

Gilligan, Carol. *In a Different Voice: Psychological Theory and Women's Development*. Cambridge: Harvard University Press, 1982.

Gitlin, Todd. *The Sixties: Years of Hope, Days of Rage*. New York: Bantam Books, 1987.

Godwin, Jocelyn. *The Theosophical Enlightenment*. Albany: State University of New York Press, 1994.

Gornick, Vivian, and Barbara K. Moran, eds. *Women In Sexist Society: Studies in Power and Powerlessness*. New York: New American Library, 1972.

Graham, Katharine. *Personal History*. New York: Alfred A. Knopf, 1997.

Greer, Germaine. *The Female Eunuch*. New York: McGraw-Hill, 1970.

Harrington, Michael. *Fragments of the Century: A Social Autobiography*. New York: Saturday Review Press, 1972.

Head, Joseph, and S. L. Cranston, eds. *Reincarnation in World Thought: A Living Study of Reincarnation in All Ages*. New York: Julian Press, 1967.

Heilbrun, Carolyn. *The Education of a Woman: The Life of Gloria Steinem*. New York: Dial Press, 1995.

Herman, Judith Lewis. *Trauma and Recovery*. New York: Basic Books, 1992.

Hickerson, Frank R. *The Tower Builders: The Centennial Story of the University of Toledo*. Toledo: University of Toledo, 1972.

Hole, Judith, and Ellen Levine. *Rebirth of Feminism*. New York: Quadrangle Books, 1971.

Hollingsworth, Jan. *Unspeakable Acts*. New York: Congdon & Weed, 1986.

Horowitz, Helen Lefkowitz. *Alma Mater: Design and Experience in the Women's Colleges from Their Nineteenth Century Beginnings to the 1930s*. New York: Alfred A. Knopf, 1984.

Independent Service for Information on the Vienna Youth Festival. *The Background of the Vienna Youth Festival*. Cambridge, 1959.

_____. *Report on the Vienna Youth Festival: Held in Vienna, Austria July 26 through August 4, 1959*. Cambridge, 1960.

Jamieson, Kathleen Hall. *Beyond the Double Bind: Women and Leadership*. New York: Oxford University Press, 1995.

Johnston, Jill. *Lesbian Nation: The Feminist Solution*. New York: Simon & Schuster, 1973.

Jones-Terry, Ardenia M. *In Search of Our Past: Women of Northwest Ohio*. Toledo: The Roles and Achievements Committee of the Women Alive! Coalition, 1987.

Kaminer, Wendy. *I'm Dysfunctional, You're Dysfunctional: The Recovery Movement and Other Self-Help Fashions*. New York: Vintage Books, 1993.

Kennedy, Flo. *Color Me Flo: My Hard Life and Good Times*. Englewood Cliffs, N.J.: Prentice-Hall, 1976.

Kessler, Ronald. *Inside the CIA: Revealing the Secrets of the World's Most Powerful Spy Agency*. New York: Pocket Books, 1992.

King, Mary. *Freedom Song*. New York: William Morrow, 1987.

Koedt, Anne; Ellen Levine; and Anita Rapone, eds. *Radical Feminism*. New York: Quadrangle Books, 1973.

Lederer, Laura, ed. *Take Back the Night: Women on Pornography*. Afterword by Adrienne Rich. New York: Bantam Books, 1982.

Lerman, Hannah. *A Mote in Freud's Eye: From Psychoanalysis to the Psychology of Women*. New York: Springer Publishing, 1986.

Ligabel, Ted J. *Clark Lake: Images of a Michigan Tradition*. Clark Lake: The Clark Lake Historical Preservation Committee, 1991.

Lovelace, Linda, with Mike McGrady. *Out of Bondage*. Introduction by Gloria Steinem. Secaucus, N.J.: Lyle Stuart, 1986.

MacDonald, Ruth K. *Louisa May Alcott*. Boston: Twayne Publishers, 1983.

Mailer, Norman. *The Prisoner of Sex*. Boston: Little, Brown, 1971.

Manning, Robert. *The Swamp Root Chronicle: Adventures in the Word Trade*. New York: W. W. Norton, 1992.

Manso, Peter. *Mailer: His Life and Times*. New York: Simon & Schuster, 1985.

_____, ed. *Running Against the Machine: The Mailer-Breslin Campaign*. Garden City, N.Y.: Doubleday, 1979.

Marchetti, Victor, and John D. Marks. *The CIA and the Cult of Intelligence*. New York: Dell, 1974.

Matthiessen, Peter. *Sal Si Puedes: Cesar Chavez and the New American Revolution*. New York: Random House, 1969.

Mayer, Robert S. *Satan's Children: Case Studies in Multiple Personalities*. New York: G. P. Putnam's Sons, 1991.

Meade, Marion. *Madame Blavatsky: The Woman Behind the Myth*. New York: G. P. Putnam's Sons, 1980.

Melich, Tanya. *The Republican War Against Women: An Insider's Report From Behind the Lines*. New York: Bantam Books, 1996.

Meyer, Cord. *Facing Reality: From World Federalism to the CIA*. New York: Harper & Row, 1980.

Miller, Alice. *The Drama of the Gifted Child: How Narcissistic Parents Form and Deform the Emotional Lives of Their Talented Children*. Translated by Ruth Ward. New York: Basic Books, 1981.

Millett, Kate. *Sexual Politics*. New York: Avon Books, 1969, 1970.

Mills, Kay. *This Little Light of Mine: The Life of Fannie Lou Hamer*. New York: Penguin Group, 1993.

Mitchell, Susan. *Icons, Saints and Divas*. Sydney, Australia: Harper Collins, 1997.

Morgan, Robin, ed. *Sisterhood is Powerful: An Anthology of Writings from the Women's Liberation Movement*. New York: Vintage Books, 1970.

Nathan, Debbie, and Michael Snedecker. *Satan's Silence: Ritual Abuse and the Making of a Modern American Witch Hunt*. New York: Basic Books, 1995.

Perkus, Cathy, ed. *COINTELPRO: The FBI's Secret War on Political Freedom*. Introduction by Noam Chomsky. New York: Monad Press, 1975.

Pollitt, Katha. *Reasonable Creatures: Essays on Women and Feminism*. New York: Alfred A. Knopf, 1994.

Polsgrove, Carol. *It Wasn't Pretty, Folks, But Didn't We Have Fun?: Esquire in the Sixties*. New York: W. W. Norton, 1995.

Pottinger, Stanley. *The Fourth Procedure*. New York: Ballantine Books, 1995.

Powers, Thomas. *The Man Who Kept the Secrets, Richard Helms and the CIA*. New York: Alfred A. Knopf, 1979.

Ranelagh, John. *The Agency: The Rise and Decline of the CIA*. New York: Simon & Schuster, 1986.

Rapping, Elayne. *The Culture of Recovery: Making Sense of the Self-Help Movement in Women's Lives*. Boston: Beacon Press, 1996.

Redstockings. *Feminist Revolution: An Abridged Edition with Additional Writings*. New York: Random House, 1975, 1978.

Rollin, Betty. *First You Cry*. Philadelphia: Lippincott, 1976.

Rollyson, Carl. *The Lives of Norman Mailer: A Biography*. New York: Paragon House, 1991.

Rossi, Alice, ed. *The Feminist Papers: From Adams to de Beauvoir*. Introductory essays by Alice Rossi. New York: Bantam Books, 1974.

Saxton, Martha. *Louisa May: A Modern Biography of Louisa May Alcott*. Boston: Houghton Mifflin, 1977.

Sayres, Sohnya, Anders Stephanson, Stanley Aronowitz, and Fredric Jameson, eds. *The 60s Without Apology*. Minneapolis: University of Minnesota Press, 1984.

Schickel, Richard. *Intimate Strangers: The Culture of Celebrity*. Garden City, N.Y.: Doubleday, 1985.

Schneir, Miriam, ed. *Feminism: The Essential Historical Writings*. Introduction and commentaries by Miriam Schneir. New York: Vintage Books, 1994.

_____. *Feminism in Our Time: The Essential Writings, World War II to the Present*. Introduction and commentaries by Miriam Schneir. New York: Vintage Books, 1994.

Snitow, Ann; Christine Stansell; and Sharon Thompson, eds. *Powers of Desire: The Politics of Sexuality*. New York: Monthly Review Press, 1983.

Somers, Suzanne. *Wednesday's Children: Adult Survivors of Abuse Speak Out*. New York: Putnam/Healing Vision Publishing, 1992.

Stan, Adele M., ed. *Debating Sexual Correctness: Pornography, Sexual Harassment, Date Rape, and the Politics of Sexual Equality*. Introduction by Adele M. Stan. New York: Delta, 1995.

Steinem, Gloria. *The Beach Book*. New York: Viking Press, 1963.

_____. *Marilyn: Norma Jeane*. New York: Signet, 1986.

_____. *Moving Beyond Words*. New York: Simon & Schuster, 1994.

_____. *Outrageous Acts and Everyday Rebellions*. New York: Signet, 1983.

_____. *Revolution From Within: A Book of Self-Esteem*. New York: Little, Brown, 1992.

Stoltenberg, John. *Refusing to Be a Man: Essays on Sex and Justice*. Portland, Ore: Breitenbush Books, 1989.

Swerdlow, Amy. *Women Strike for Peace: Traditional Motherhood and Radical Politics in the 1960s*. Chicago: University of Chicago Press, 1993.

Takas, Marianne. *Child Custody: A Complete Guide for Concerned Mothers*. New York: Harper & Row, 1987.

Tanner, Leslie B., ed. *Voices From Women's Liberation*. New York: Signet, 1970.

Tavris, Carol. *The Mismeasure of Woman*. New York: Touchstone, 1993.

Tebbel, John, and Mary Ellen Zuckerman. *The Magazine in America, 1741–1990*. New York: Oxford University Press, 1991.

Thom, Mary, ed. *Letters to Ms.: 1972–1987*. Introduction by Gloria Steinem. New York: Henry Holt, 1987.

_____. *Inside Ms.: 25 Years of the Magazine and the Feminist Movement*. New York: Henry Holt, 1997.

Thomas, Evan. *The Very Best Men: The Early Years of the CIA*. New York: Simon & Schuster, 1995.

Tobias, Sheila. *Faces of Feminism: An Activist's Reflections on the Women's Movement*. Boulder, Col.: Westview Press, 1997.

United States President's Commission on the Status of Women. *American Women: The Report of the President's Commission on the Status of Women and Other Publications of the Commission*. Edited by Margaret Mead and Frances Balgley Kaplan. Introduction and epilogue by Margaret Mead. New York: Charles Scribner's Sons, 1965.

United States Senate. *Final Report of the Select Committee to Study Governmental Operations with Respect to Intelligence Activities, Together with Additional, Supplemental, and Separate Views*. Books I, II, III, and VI. Washington, U.S. Government Printing Office, 1976.

Vance, Carole S., ed. *Pleasure and Danger: Exploring Female Sexuality*. London: Pandora Press, 1989.

Wallace, Michele. *Black Macho and the Myth of the Superwoman*. New York: Dial Press, 1979.

Washington, Peter. *Madame Blavatsky's Baboon: A History of the Mystics, Mediums, and Misfits Who Brought Spiritualism to America*. New York: Schocken Books, 1995.

Wheeler, Marjorie Spruill, ed. *One Woman, One Vote: Rediscovering the Woman Suffrage Movement*. Troutdale: NewSage Press and Education Film, 1995.

White, Theodore H. *The Making of the President*. New York: Bantam Books, 1973.

Whitlock, Marta, ed. *Women in Ohio History, A Conference to Commemorate the Bicentennial of the American Revolution*, Ohio American Revolution Bicentennial Conference Series, no. 2. Columbus: The Ohio Historical Society, 1976.

Whitney, Sharon. *The Equal Rights Amendment: The History and the Movement*. New York: Franklin Watts, 1984.

Willis, Ellen. *No More Nice Girls: Countercultural Essays*. Hanover, N.H.: Wesleyan University Press, 1992.

Wills, Garry. *Certain Trumpets: The Call of Leaders*. New York: Simon & Schuster, 1994.

Witt, Linda; Karen M. Paget; and Glenna Matthews. *Running as a Woman: Gender and Power in American Politics*. New York: Free Press, 1994.

Wolfe, Tom. *Radical Chic and Mau-Mauing the Flak Catchers*. New York: Farrar, Straus & Giroux, 1970.

Young-Bruehl, Elisabeth. *The Anatomy of Prejudices*. Cambridge, Mass.: Harvard University Press, 1996.

The author is grateful for permission to quote extensively from the following works:

Nora Ephron, "Women," *Esquire,* November 1972. Courtesy Nora Ephron.

Eugenia Sheppard, "Gloria Hallelujah," *Harper's Bazaar,* February 1970. Courtesy of *Harper's Bazaar.*

Liz Smith, "Coming of Age in America," *Vogue,* June 1971. Courtesy *Vogue.* Copyright © 1971 by Condé Nast Publications, Inc.

"Gloria Steinem: New York's Newest Young Wit," *Glamour,* February 1964. Courtesy *Glamour.* Copyright © 1964 (renewed 1992) by Condé Nast Publications, Inc.

The copyrights on several photographs were unknown, and efforts to locate their holders were unsuccessful.

Index